Fulfilling a Dream

STONEHILL COLLEGE

1948 to 1998

Statue of Our Lady of Holy Cross, outside Donahue Hall.

Fulfilling a Dream

STONEHILL COLLEGE

1948 to 1998

RICHARD GRIBBLE, CSC

STONEHILL COLLEGE PRESS

Easton, Massachusetts

Library of Congress Catalog Card Number: 97–62189

ISBN 0-9660964-0-1

PRINTED IN THE UNITED STATES OF AMERICA.

Spes Unica is the motto of the Congregation of Holy Cross. The Congregation's founder, Father Basil Anthony Moreau, believed the cross is our only hope. Indeed, the cross is the preeminent symbol of Christianity, and in a paradoxical way it is the sign of hope for life eternal.

This book is dedicated to the priests and brothers of the Congregation of Holy Cross who have ministered at Stonehill College from 1948 to 1998. Their unselfish devotion to service has been a model of faithfulness and the rock upon which this institution was founded and from which it matured.

CONTENTS

※

CHAPTER 4

The Reason We Exist—Student Life: *1948–1964*

CHAPTER 5

A College Emerges—Accreditation and Academic Development: *1958–1964*

CHAPTER 6

Physical Expansion and Growth: *1958–1964*

CHAPTER 7

A Liberal Arts College Emerges: *1964–1971*

CHAPTER 8

Student Life and Unrest: *1964–1971*

Appendices

PREFACE

My association with Stonehill College began unassumingly in August 1988. For one week my ordination classmates and I were guests of the Holy Cross Community at North Dartmouth, as we gathered for our pre-final profession retreat. One evening we came to Stonehill and dined with the "Barn" community at the College; I remember very little of the evening save the hospitality and good food. I next found my way to Stonehill in April 1994 when I was welcomed by the president, Father Bartley MacPháidín, CSC, after attending the spring meeting of the American Catholic Historical Association held that year at the College of the Holy Cross in Worcester. Two weeks after my return to Washington, D.C., where I was completing doctoral studies at the Catholic University of America, I received a phone call from Father MacPháidín informing me of Stonehill's approaching golden anniversary and inviting me to write the College's history to mark the event. After the completion and acceptance of my dissertation, and with the approval of my Holy Cross superiors, I accepted the invitation to write the history, arriving in North Easton in June 1995.

The research and writing of Stonehill's fifty-year anniversary history has tested my skills as a historian and writer, but its completion would not have been possible without the assistance of many people. It was the confidence and trust of Bartley MacPháidín, CSC, in my ability and his initial invitation which made the project possible. The archival collections of Stonehill College and the Congregation of Holy Cross, Eastern Province, provided the principal primary sources for the history. Louise Kenneally, College archivist, and Father Augustine Peverada, CSC, Eastern Province archivist, allowed me total access to all materials, invaluable assistance in locating specific documents, and guidance when the paper trail did not seem to lead in any clear or coherent direction. Father William Blum, CSC, Holy Cross Indiana Province archivist at Notre Dame, and Father Robert Antonelli, CSC, archivist at the Holy Cross Generalate in Rome, also provided useful materials. Robert Johnson-Lally, archivist for the Archdiocese of Boston, was helpful in answering specific questions about Stonehill's early days. The staff of the Cushing-Martin Library, especially Jane Swiszcz in reference and Regina Egan in interlibrary loans, also assisted my efforts greatly. In an unfortunate note, this history was completed without being able to consult the archives of the Diocese of Fall River.

The expertise and critical eyes of many colleagues improved the text greatly through critical reviews and editing. Professors James Kenneally (Emeritus), Toni-Lee Capossela, Virginia Polanski, and Anne T. Carrigg read portions or the full text, providing many valuable suggestions. Fathers Robert Kruse, CSC, and Paul Duff, CSC, also provided assistance in their review of the text. Father David Arthur, CSC, provided invaluable service through a critical reading of the text, supplying many documents from his files and answering innumerable questions from his long and varied tenure at the College.

Additional people provided support and assistance in the completion of this history. Anne Pollick, director of alumni affairs, organized four "focus" groups of alumni who shared their experience of Stonehill through the decades. Joyce Barry, Stonehill College archival assistant, provided direction and always a positive word of support during the long days of research. Many others, including Elaine Melisi, Florence Tripp, and Professors Richard Finnegan, Rita Smith, Grace Donovan, SUSC, Frank Ryan, and Benjamin Mariante, provided documents and answered questions to fill in gaps in my research. Photographs in this book were obtained from the Stonehill College Archives, Holy Cross Fathers Eastern Province Archives, Stonehill's sports information director, and Stanley Bauman, a Brockton photographer.

The completion of a project as large and complex as the history of Stonehill College could not have been accomplished without an environment conducive to work and study and supportive of the writer's daily efforts. The men of Holy Cross with whom I lived, shared table, and prayed provided the sustenance needed to keep working when my enthusiasm waned or I became discouraged at my lack of progress. Father Frank Walsh, CSC, professor of psychology and religious superior for the Holy Cross Community in North Easton, and his assistant Father Paul Duff, CSC, gave me the opportunity to live with men whose inspiring lives and commitment to God and service to God's people brightened my daily existence. To the Congregation of Holy Cross and, especially, the Stonehill Community, I owe a great debt of thanks.

RICHARD GRIBBLE, CSC

INTRODUCTION

੪੬

In March 1935 Father Thomas Duffy, a member of the Congregation of Holy Cross and new superior of the Community's mission band in the east, came to North Easton, Massachusetts, to survey the estate of Frederick Lothrup Ames, which was being offered for sale by his widow, Edith Cutler. Duffy, along with the Superior General of Holy Cross, Father James Wesley Donahue, possessed a vision for the Congregation in the eastern United States, including the foundation of a college. Duffy's discovery of the Ames estate, which he described as "suitable for our purposes,"[1] initiated a dream that became Stonehill College, a Catholic institution of higher learning in the liberal arts tradition. Fulfillment of that dream took several years and was fraught with many difficulties, but Duffy's vision eventually was realized. Indeed, on October 12, 1998, Stonehill celebrates its golden anniversary.

The Ames estate was purchased in 1935 and a two-year pre-novitiate academic program, Our Lady of Holy Cross Seminary, was established. Candidates for the Community attended two years of school in North Easton, entered the novitiate in North Dartmouth, Massachusetts, and then completed their undergraduate training at the University of Notre Dame. Nothing of any significance transpired for the Congregation of Holy Cross for the next thirteen years in the region. The one possibility for growth, an offer in 1946 from Archbishop Richard Cushing to establish a new Catholic college in Boston, was investigated but rejected. The rather lethargic attitude of the Congregation during this period led Bishop James Cassidy of Fall River to encourage development "as [you, Holy Cross,] have simply encumbered the earth for fifteen years."[2]

Events of May 1948, however, ignited a fire that burned away previous inaction and led to the founding of Stonehill College. On May 3 the Eastern Vice Province of Holy Cross was established. This action, first attempted ten years earlier, had been the subject of much debate within the Congregation.[3] At this same time Thomas Duffy discovered, quite by accident, that the Franciscans had been invited by Archbishop Cushing to open a college on the border of Avon and Brockton to serve southeastern Massachusetts. This revelation led Duffy to make an impassioned appeal to Father Albert Cousineau, Superior General of Holy Cross, that the Community act immediately to develop the North Easton site into a college to avoid losing the opportunity forever. Duffy's strong stance and persistence led to the decision in mid-May to open a college on the Ames estate. The name Stonehill was derived from the mansion's original name—Stone House Hill House.

When Stonehill College opened its doors to students in September 1948, the dream seemed cloudy at best. Rather miraculously, the College had secured a charter and gained approbation from the Massachusetts Board of Collegiate Authority by the end of June, but recruitment of students and faculty, establishment of academic programs, and construction of necessary facilities took time. Notwithstanding the faithful efforts of Holy Cross religious, led by Father George Benaglia, Stonehill's first president, and dedicated laity, after 18 months the College had generated, through construction of a needed building and operations, a $200,000 debt with little prospect for repayment. It was the mission and supreme accomplishment of Francis Boland, CSC, president from 1949 to 1955, to liquidate that debt and stabilize the College financially, allowing it to become an accepted Catholic institution of higher learning in the liberal arts tradition.

Over the next two decades, substantial progress was made. James Sheehan, CSC, guided the construction of Stonehill's first new buildings since 1948. Richard Sullivan, CSC, the fourth president, led the College to its achievement of accreditation in 1959. Construction of a library and a dormitory met essential needs for the College, the latter making it possible for Stonehill to attract students beyond the immediate region. During the 1960s and 1970s the College became an accepted liberal arts institution through professionalization and wider recognition within the academic community. John Corr, president from 1964 to 1971, weathered the tumultuous sixties and championed canonical alienation (legal separation) of the College from Holy Cross, a process that was finalized in 1972. Canonical alienation gave Stonehill greater autonomy to move with the majority of American Catholic colleges and universities into a new era. Ernest Bartell, CSC, the sixth president, successfully spread the name and reputation of the College through expansion of academic programs, completion of a successful development drive, and liaison with education professionals throughout New England.

Bartley MacPháidín, who entered the president's office in February

1978, has moved the College from professional acceptance to national recognition. In addition to a massive building program including a new dining commons, the Pilgrim Heights residence complex, the Joseph Martin Institute, and a new library, MacPháidín has been the catalyst and driving force behind the College's rise in endowment, which in July 1997 stood at over $68.5 million. Today Stonehill College stands on the verge of the twenty-first century poised to make an even greater contribution to American society and the Church.

The story of Stonehill College is only one example of a genre of institutional histories of colleges and universities in the United States written in the past fifteen years. Many institutions of higher education in New England have produced their histories, including Harvard, Boston College, Tufts, Saint Anselm, and Brandeis. Various approaches have been used in the composition of these histories. Abram Sachar organized his history of Brandeis topically while positing it in the context of the tradition of private colleges in the United States. Valerie Ann McKeon, while describing the parallel development of Saint Anselm and other American Catholic institutions of higher education, emphasizes the uniqueness of the Benedictine influence on the college. Russell Miller's history of Tufts traces the first century of the university using a chronological and institutional approach.[4] Highly readable and informative histories of Wheaton and Radcliffe colleges and Suffolk University are examples of less scholarly approaches to local college histories.[5]

Numerous histories of Catholic colleges and universities have also been written. Three scholarly histories of recent vintage are those of Santa Clara, Villanova, and Georgetown. Gerald McKevitt, SJ, describes how Santa Clara was founded as a Catholic school to offset the Protestant influence that was "invading" the traditional Catholicism of mid-nineteenth-century California. McKevitt's account demonstrates the major shifts in Catholic higher education in the twentieth century, including the movement away from classical education, loss of *in loco parentis*, and the post-Vatican II shift toward greater secularization. David R. Contosta uses the words *American*, *Catholic*, and *Augustinian* to describe the history of Villanova University. Like McKeon's history of Saint Anselm, Contosta's emphasizes the influence of the Augustinian community in the development of the Philadelphia university. Georgetown University, the nation's oldest Catholic institution of higher learning, is described by R. Emmett Curran as a leader in Jesuit and American Catholic education.[6]

Histories of the institutions of higher learning sponsored by the men's and women's Congregations of Holy Cross have also been written. Father Arthur Hope's popular centennial history of Notre Dame, written for a

Catholic audience, makes no attempt to place the university in the wider context of American Catholic higher education or in the religious and/or educational history of the nation. Instead, the volume is anecdotal and provides colorful characterizations of people who have lived the history of Notre Dame. William Dunn, CSC, wrote a scholarly, well-researched, and highly readable account of Saint Edward's University. James Covert, professor of history at the University of Portland, effectively combined photographs with scholarly research to tell the story of that institution. Sister Louise Parent, CSC, produced a short chronicle of the first twenty-five years of Notre Dame College in Manchester, New Hampshire.[7]

This history of Stonehill is told within the context of United States and American religious history in the post–World War II period. The historian David Montgomery contends that the postwar period and, especially, the Cold War served as catalysts to the development of the academic community in the United States: "The Cold War reshaped university structures and the content of academic disciplines, just as it penetrated the whole fabric of political and intellectual life." Robert Wuthnow argues that religion in the United States after World War II was poised to be deeply influenced by changes in the social environment. Denominational and confessional identities, which had played such a prominent role immediately after the war, began to diminish in importance as time passed and with the rise of ecumenism, geographic mobility, and public emphasis on tolerance and diversity. The result was that by the seventies, people professed their religious preference in generic terms of conservative, moderate, or liberal.[8]

As a Catholic institution, Stonehill possesses the additional element of a longstanding tradition in American Catholic higher education. The great boom in college attendance after the war, fueled in large measure by the "GI Bill," could not be absorbed by public institutions alone; Catholic institutions also benefited from the flood of students, necessitating expansion of existing institutions and establishment of new colleges.[9] The augmentation of physical facilities in the fifties, however, was not matched by a similar explosion of intellectual pursuit. Jesuit Father William Leahy places the blame for this failure to progress, following the lead of Monsignor John Tracy Ellis' famous 1955 indictment of American Catholic intellectual life,[10] squarely on the shoulders of administrators and faculty who subordinated intellectual achievement to personal and institutional religious commitments. Additionally, Leahy suggests that expansion to meet immediate needs took precedence over academic excellence.[11] The achievement of greater parity on academic levels between Catholic and secular institutions would be realized only after the process of canonical alienation, first instituted at St.

Louis University, Notre Dame, and Webster College in 1967, freed Catholic institutions to pursue their futures with less fear of ecclesiastical intervention.

This history of Stonehill College was written in both traditional and innovative ways. A chronological format, with chapters organized around presidential administrations, is the more traditional pattern used in this volume. Although this technique tends to emphasize strongly top-level administrators, noteworthy faculty, and events that captured the attention of the student newspaper, the presentation has been balanced by dedicating chapters exclusively to student activities, where the flavor of day-to-day life for the typical Stonehill student can be better visualized. Unlike most writers of histories of colleges and institutions, the author of this volume is an outsider who researched and wrote the story without the burden of previous knowledge of people and events. As a member of the Congregation of Holy Cross, however, I was able to understand the relationship between the founding religious community and the College, an association that was highly significant during the College's first twenty-five years.

This history tells the story of Stonehill over its first fifty years in the context of Catholic higher education. I have made no attempt, however, to chronicle the history of the Holy Cross Community in North Easton, although events and people with historical relevance to Stonehill College are highlighted in the text. Additionally, I have not provided a complete record of the College's divisions and academic departments; rather, an integrative approach describes the historical significance of certain programs to the institution as a whole. Similarly, this history provides a flavor of student life, but has not attempted to chronicle all the events and people of student affairs. Historians are always faced with the question of what to highlight and what to leave out. It is hoped that readers understand my attempt to focus on the people and events that have been most historically significant in fulfilling the dream of Stonehill's founders.

This history of Stonehill College relates a success story that will serve various purposes for different groups. Historians and educators will find the volume useful as an example of Catholic higher education in the postwar period. Those interested in religious studies will discover in Stonehill's history an illustration of the relationship between the institutional Church, secular society, and the educational world. Alumni and friends of Stonehill can simply enjoy the opportunity to know more about their alma mater. Stonehill College today stands as a dream fulfilled. What it will be in the new millennium is ours to shape and realize.

ENDNOTES

1. "Chronicles of Our Lady of Holy Cross" (March 2, 1935), Archives of Stonehill College (hereafter ASC).

2. Quoted in James Connerton and Howard Kenna to Thomas Steiner (October 31, 1946), Stonehill College Papers, ASC.

3. The first formal major effort to establish an eastern province of Holy Cross was made in 1938. While various opinions were present, the strongest sentiment within the Congregation sought to keep the Community's organization in the United States centered on Notre Dame. Thus, any effort to decentralize and establish separate entities, especially institutions of higher learning, in other regions of the country encountered opposition.

4. Abram L. Sachar, *Brandeis University: A Host at Last*, Revised Edition (Hanover, New Hampshire: Brandeis University Press, 1995); Valerie Ann McKeon, "History of Saint Anselm College," Ph.D. diss. (Boston College, 1985); Russell E. Miller, *Light on the Hill: A History of Tufts College 1852–1952* (Boston: Beacon Press, 1966).

5. Paul C. Helmreich, *Wheaton College 1834–1912: The Seminary Years* (Norton, Massachusetts: Wheaton College, 1985); Dorothy Elia Howells, *A Century to Celebrate: Radcliffe College, 1879–1979* (Cambridge, Massachusetts: Radcliffe College, 1978); David L. Robbins, *A History of Suffolk University 1909–1996* (Boston: Suffolk University, 1996).

6. Gerald McKevitt, SJ, *The University of Santa Clara: A History, 1851–1977* (Stanford, California: Stanford University Press, 1979); David R. Contosta, *Villanova University: American—Catholic—Augustinian* (University Park, Pennsylvania: The Pennsylvania State University Press, 1995); R. Emmett Curran, *The Bicentennial History of Georgetown University* (Washington, D.C.: Georgetown University Press, 1993).

7. Arthur J. Hope, CSC, *Notre Dame: One Hundred Years*, Revised Edition (South Bend, Indiana: Icarus Press, Inc., 1978); William Dunn, CSC, *Saint Edward's University: A Centennial History* (Austin, Texas: St. Edward's University Press, 1986); James T. Covert, *A Point of Pride: The University of Portland Story* (Portland, Oregon: University of Portland Press, 1976); Louise Parent, CSC, *The First Twenty-Five Years of Notre Dame College Manchester, New Hampshire* (Manchester, New Hampshire: Notre Dame College, 1975).

8. David Montgomery, "Prosperity Under the Shadow of the Bomb," in Andre Schiffrin, ed., *The Cold War and the University: Toward an Intellectual History of the Postwar Years* (New York: The New Press, 1997): xi-xxxv; Robert Wuthnow, "Restructuring of American Religion: Further Evidence," *Sociological Inquiry* 66(3) (August 1996): 323–24. Wuthnow has a general study in his thesis: *The Restructuring of American Religion: Society and Faith Since World War II* (Princeton, New Jersey: Princeton University Press, 1988).

9. The rise in student enrollment was phenomenal. When the war ended there

were one million students in United States colleges and universities. By 1947 there were 2.3 million and in 1970 almost 8 million. Catholic colleges experienced a huge rise in enrollment as well, to a level of 430,000 in 1970, a 430 percent increase from 1945. Between 1945 and 1967 there were 41 senior colleges and 20 junior colleges for lay students founded in the Catholic tradition in the United States. See William P. Leahy, SJ, *Adapting to America: Catholics, Jesuits, and Higher Education in the Twentieth Century* (Washington, D.C.: Georgetown University Press, 1991): 125–27.

10. John Tracy Ellis, "American Catholics and the Intellectual Life," *Thought* 30 (Autumn 1955): 351–88. Ellis' essay was highly critical of the dearth of American Catholic intellectual life. This essay produced a renewed effort to make Catholic institutions of higher education better academically so that they could compete with secular schools.

11. Leahy, *Adapting to America*, 128–45.

New Awakenings in the East

In the late afternoon of September 13, 1841, the American schooner *Iowa* sailed into New York harbor after a five-week voyage from Le Havre on the French coast. Because of the late hour, the ship's passengers were not allowed to disembark, but Father Edward Sorin, leader of a band of seven religious of the Congregation of Holy Cross, prevailed upon the vessel's captain to allow him to set foot on American soil, a land that would become his home for the next fifty years. Sorin strolled about the dock on Manhattan's lower east side, gave thanks to God for a safe voyage, and asked for continued blessings in the adventure that lay ahead for the young French priest and the six brothers who accompanied him. The next day he said Mass for the first time in this new land—appropriately enough, the Triumph of the Cross, on the eve of the Community feast of Our Lady of Sorrows.

American Foundations

THE ARRIVAL OF EDWARD SORIN and his companions in New York ❦ initiated a new era in the history of this fledgling religious community. The Congregation of Holy Cross had been formed on March 1, 1837, when a Fundamental Pact was signed uniting the Brothers of St. Joseph, founded by Father Jacques Dujarié in 1820, and the auxiliary priests (band of diocesan clergy) from the Sainte Croix district of the city of LeMans, headed by Father Basil Anthony Mary Moreau. By 1839 the new religious community had 34 houses in France and 130 members: 12 priests, 115 brothers (24

I

professed, 78 novices, and 13 postulants), and 3 postulant sisters.[1] Moreau, the leader of the congregation, then placed the community under the guidance of the local bishop for service to the Church.

In the spring of 1839 Moreau had received a request from the United States for assistance: Bishop Simon Bruté of Vincennes (Indiana) sought religious to serve as teachers in his rural diocese. Before formal negotiations could proceed, Bruté died on June 26, 1839, but the plea for assistance was renewed by his successor, Celestin de la Hailandiere. A lawyer, Hailandiere had been ordained in 1836 after discovering his vocation coincidentally from the preaching of Bruté. He especially wanted teaching brothers so that Catholics would not be forced to attend public schools administered by Protestants, said schools being perceived as a threat to the faith of Catholic youth. But Moreau had made a promise to the bishop of Algiers to send religious there, so although sympathetic to the need, he was forced to turn down the bishop's request.[2]

In the summer of 1841, however, after the failure of the Algiers mission and attainment of some economic stability, Moreau was able to make arrangements to send religious to the United States. To lead the delegation, he chose Edward Sorin, born into a prosperous family of Ahuille near Laval. Six brothers were sent with Sorin: three who were teachers—Vincent, Anselm, and Gatian—and three who assisted with manual labor—Joachim, Francis Xavier, and Lawrence. The party boarded the *Iowa* on August 8 with hopes and dreams but with no certainty of the specifics of their mission.

Sorin, ordained in May 1838, had spent 15 months as curate in the town of Parce in the diocese of LeMans before he discovered Moreau and his auxiliary priests, who had become the talk of the region in their efforts to aid pastors in poor parishes. On August 15, 1840, Moreau, Sorin, and another priest, Pierre Chappé, took religious vows, the latter two promising to live under Moreau as the superior of the Congregation. Sorin's presence in the Community and his mission to America were fortuitous for the newly formed Holy Cross Congregation and for the American Church he would serve. The historian, James Connelly, CSC, wrote of Sorin, "He was the first Holy Cross religious to set foot in North America, and for the next fifty-two years he would shape the Congregation's life and work in the United States more than anyone else."[3]

The seven Holy Cross religious who arrived in New York on September 13, 1841, were met by Samuel Byerley, a friend of Bishop de la Hailandiere, who had made arrangements for the group's passage to Vincennes. After an arduous trip of 24 days by water and land, the party arrived at its destination on October 10 and was greeted briefly but cordially by the bishop.

Sorin and the brothers wasted no time in establishing themselves in the region. After an inspection trip of the area with the bishop, Sorin chose Black Oak Ridge, a predominately Catholic district in Daviess County 27 miles east of Vincennes, to settle the Community. The property included 160 acres of land, a little frame church (St. Peter's, dating from 1818), and two log cabins. One of these houses, built originally by the Sisters of Charity of Nazareth, Kentucky, functioned as a school under the direction of Charles Rother, who promptly joined the brothers and took the name of Joseph.

But the presence of Holy Cross religious outside Vincennes did not last long. During the next year Sorin and Bishop Hailandiere often disagreed over the handling of money and foundations. Sorin asked the bishop to assist with the payment of bills, since the Congregation had come only to assist the prelate's needs. Hailandiere, however, refused to help, claiming that his limited funds must be used to aid his own secular clergy. Another disagreement arose when the bishop would not endorse Sorin's idea to start a college in the area. Hailandiere did, however, offer Holy Cross a large piece of property as a school site 250 miles north in South Bend on the St. Joseph River. The Congregation reviewed its options and, after much thought and prayerful reflection, decided to move north.

On November 16, 1842, Sorin and seven brothers left St. Peter's and began the journey to South Bend.[4] Early winter weather made the trip difficult, but on November 26 all arrived without major incident. A small chapel and living quarters were built immediately. By the time the rest of the Community from Vincennes joined the group in South Bend in late February 1843, a small school was operating under the title, The University of Notre Dame du Lac, so named to honor the patroness of the Community and to describe the environment of lakes around which the school was built. In 1844 the Indiana legislature granted a charter for the university, only the third Catholic college in the United States to be legally incorporated.[5]

The establishment of Notre Dame was the first of several American educational foundings for the Congregation in the nineteenth century. Claude M. Dubuis, bishop of Galveston, Texas, asked Sorin (whom he had met when they traveled on the same vessel to the First Vatican Council in 1869) to start a college in south Texas. The 1870 Provincial Chapter of the American Province of Holy Cross decided "to accept the proposition of the Bishop of Galveston and establish a commercial college in the city of Galveston."[6] Holy Cross went to Galveston in 1870, but the foundation was short-lived (1870–1877), due principally to the departure of Brother Boniface Muher to be president of the newly established St. Joseph's College, in Cincinnati.

A permanent foundation did begin in Texas, however, when Mary Doyle, widow of a wealthy contractor who had built the capitol in Austin, offered the Church almost 400 acres three miles south of Austin to found a Catholic college. Bishop Dubuis made a proposal to Sorin, asking Holy Cross to start a school on Doyle's land, and upon receipt of proper permissions, Sorin accepted the offer. In 1874 the Congregation assumed administration of St. Mary's of the Immaculate Conception, the only Catholic parish in the city, completing the agreement. The first class in the new school, called St. Edward's College, entered in 1878. The arrival of Father John Lauth, CSC, as president in 1881 was capped on August 1, 1885, when the charter for St. Edward's University was obtained.[7]

The allure of the wilds of the Northwest also attracted the priests and brothers of Holy Cross. In July 1900 Archbishop Alexander Christie of Oregon City procured along the Willamette River in north Portland a run-down campus that had been abandoned by the Methodist Church five years earlier. Christie's purchase included a five-story building and 28 acres of land, with an option for an additional 43 acres; he opened Columbia University on the site in 1901. That academic year Christie visited Notre Dame twice, seeking the assistance of Holy Cross in the administration of the school. In the summer of 1902 Christie and Father John Zahm, CSC, provincial of Holy Cross in the United States, completed negotiations transferring ownership, administration, and operation of the school to the Congregation, which became the University of Portland in 1935.[8]

Foundation of Our Lady of Holy Cross in North Dartmouth

❦

FROM ITS EARLIEST DAYS the fortunes of the Congregation of Holy Cross had been blessed with educational and parochial foundations in the Midwest, the South, and the West, but the eastern section of the country did not attract the Community on any permanent basis until the period of the Great Depression.[9] James Wesley Donahue, superior general of the Congregation from 1926 to 1938, envisioned extending the Community into the east, in contrast to the views of others who believed that Holy Cross should limit itself to its cluster of apostolates at and around Notre Dame.[10] As a member of the mission band of the Congregation, Donahue had in 1912 visited southeast Massachusetts, preached in New Bedford, and come away from the experience favorably impressed with the area.[11]

Donahue's knowledge of the region, his position within the Congregation, and his vision for the future combined to bring Holy Cross to the East. In November 1931 James Cassidy, apostolic administrator and auxiliary bishop of Fall River, Massachusetts, invited Donahue to start a seminary in the diocese.[12] Because of the depressed national economy, land and real estate prices were low, giving religious communities excellent opportunities to

Rev. James Wesley Donahue, CSC,
Superior General of the Congregation of Holy Cross 1926–1938.

establish foundations. Cassidy encouraged Donahue to visit the area and investigate possible locations for a seminary. Donahue acknowledged the bishop's invitation and visited on two occasions, once in the company of the Canadian provincial, Alfred Charron, and a second time accompanied by James Burns, provincial in the United States.[13]

Favorably disposed to Cassidy's offer, Donahue proposed to the 1932 General Chapter of Holy Cross that the Community purchase property in southeast Massachusetts in order to open a minor seminary. The proposal was approved and negotiations to obtain a site were begun. Cassidy had suggested that Holy Cross purchase the former Crary Hospital on a 68-acre site in North Dartmouth. The main building, constructed about 1900 by Francis B. Greene, had been sold to Dr. William Kirby of New Bedford, who transformed it and a few small structures on the grounds into a hospital.

Our Lady of Holy Cross Seminary, North Dartmouth, Massachusetts.

Accusations of illegal surgical practices conducted on the premises prompted the government to close down the facility.[14] The Congregation offered to buy the property, but was rejected. However, when Kirby committed suicide[15] in August 1933, the property was transferred to the bank for sale. The Congregation sent Brothers Ephrem O'Dwyer and Lambert Barbier east to initiate negotiations on behalf of the General Administration of Holy Cross; the purchase of the property was consummated in late August 1933. Lambert exulted at the acquisition: "It is a wonderful place and nothing less than an answer to prayer. We should look at it as a gift from God." On December 8, 1933, the Superior General celebrated the first Mass at Our Lady of Holy Cross.[16]

Organization of people and programs characterized the first year for Holy Cross at North Dartmouth. In February 1934 Father Walter Marks came from the Foreign Mission Seminary in Washington, D.C., to serve as superior "pro tem." Until the arrival of William J. Doheny in May, Marks directed the efforts of several brothers in transforming the main building into one that could function as a seminary and headquarters for the Community's mission band operating in the east. Archibald McDowell, Robert Woodward, and George Fischer, the mission band team, came to North

Holy Cross Mission Band in the East.

Dartmouth in May, and by early summer they had begun their preaching ministry. The recruitment of students for the two-year pre-novitiate seminary was slow, but on September 10 nine students arrived and began the year with a retreat led by Father McDowell.

The North Dartmouth foundation was incorporated in August 1934. Donahue, members of the mission band, and the brothers comprised the corporation, which took the name "The Foundation of Our Lady of Holy Cross" and declared itself an institution "for benevolent, educational, religious and charitable purposes." Originally the Dartmouth foundation was legally owned by the University of Notre Dame, but it was decided to have the title vested in Massachusetts because the property was subject to laws of the commonwealth. This process was completed by December 21, 1934.[17]

Foundations in North Easton

ON MARCH 2, 1935, Thomas Duffy, CSC, arrived at Our Lady of Holy Cross to assume duties as superior of the eastern mission band. During the visit he and seminary superior William Doheny traveled to North Easton, about forty miles north, to tour the Frederick Ames estate, which was being

Frederick Lothrup Ames, 1876–1921.

Stonehouse House Hill House, Ames Mansion, North Easton, Massachusetts.

Chapel of Our Lady of Holy Cross Seminary, North Easton, Massachusetts.

offered for sale.[18] Both men "were more than impressed with its beauty and its suitableness for our purposes."[19] Duffy, like Donahue, possessed a vision for the Community in the East, including the foundation of a college. The Ames estate, built in 1905 at an estimated cost of $1.5 million, consisted of approximately 600 acres, a 50-room mansion, a glass-roofed clay tennis court, a marble swimming pool with fireplace, a squash court, a garage, a conservatory, and barns. Ames' death in June 1921 and that of his son Frederick, Jr., in a November 1932 plane crash provided the occasion for Edith Ames Cutler, Frederick Ames' widow, to sell the estate.[20] The facility was perceived by Duffy as the ideal location and environment for the realization of his dream of a Catholic college.[21]

In May 1935 Edith Cutler entered into negotiations with James Donahue for sale of her estate. Initially she asked $75,000 for the house, garage, tennis court, greenhouse, and about 350 acres of the property. Donahue, on advice from Cassidy, made a counteroffer of $40,000 in cash and $10,000 to be financed on time. Cassidy's approval of the sale and its negotiation was conditional: "I beg to repeat here, however, what I have previously said to you in person, to wit: that while I am approving of your congregation's attainment of this property I do not urge, I do not even advise such action."[22]

Ames estate indoor pool.

Negotiations were conducted through a series of letters for two months until on July 24, 1935, Cutler accepted Donahue's original offer.[23] The Community chronicle reported that the sale "assures the Congregation of an enviable and an ideal location for the expansion of its Eastern apostolate."[24]

Transfer of the seminary from North Dartmouth to North Easton was accomplished after the sale was finalized. Donahue had ordered an inspection of the mansion to determine additional costs to occupy the building. A detailed check revealed that there were some minor problems with the mansion's steam heating but that all repairs could be completed at an estimated cost of $1250.[25] With the financial details satisfied and episcopal approval obtained,[26] the move of the Community's operation to North Easton was completed when superior William Doheny began classes in the main house on October 31. Donahue was proud of the new foundation: "This *plant* is *tremendous* [Donahue's emphasis]. All eyes are on it."[27]

With a minor seminary in North Easton and a novitiate in North Dart-

Our Lady of Holy Cross Seminary Women's Guild.

mouth,[28] Holy Cross decided to solidify its foundation by expansion of its holdings. The 1935 purchase of the Ames estate included approximately 350 acres and two major buildings, but over 200 acres of the original estate remained in the custody of Edith Cutler. She offered to sell the remainder of the land to Holy Cross for $30,000, stating, "I would let you have it for a little less than I would some of these other buyers as I know that you would take a real interest in preserving it."[29] Donahue responded that the Community was interested and offered $5000 cash and $20,000 in a 5 percent mortgage. Although she claimed other buyers had offered more, Cutler eventually agreed to the Congregation's first offer. Brother Lambert, working with the attorney Daniel Buckley, completed the deal on March 4, 1937.[30] The *Brockton Enterprise* prophetically announced:[31]

> In all probability the expansion of the order [Holy Cross] in the locality means that in the near future the estate will house an eastern branch of Notre Dame University and officials of the Congregation of Holy Cross express their belief that a "prep" school or academy will be built on the estate in a year or two.

Our Lady of Holy Cross preparatory seminary, guided by William Doheny since his arrival at North Dartmouth in 1934, came under the direction of Gerald Fitzgerald in July 1937. Lay students (postulants) received two years of college training in the classical style of the period, were sent to the novitiate at North Dartmouth, and then completed their undergraduate training at Notre Dame. During the late 1930s the seminary stayed near its full capacity with an average enrollment of 20 students per year. In 1939 the Seminary Guild, a group of local women, was established to assist and foster the seminary program.[32] Fitzgerald served as superior of Our Lady of Holy Cross until 1943, when he took up duties with the military ordinariate as a "civilian chaplain." George Benaglia took the reins at the seminary and welcomed eleven seminarians that fall, a distinct drop due to the effect of World War II.[33]

The war years provided an opportunity for the seminary to aid the national cause. The Ames estate included a small airfield that the United States Navy asked to lease in order to train pilots. Fitzgerald was interested in the proposition more as a goodwill gesture than as revenue generation. The provincial, Thomas Steiner, was hesitant to grant permission, fearing that lands would be tied up for significant periods of time. However, he agreed to consider the lease if the government would roll back the $300 per year state tax that the community was paying on the site. The government responded with an offer of $300 per year in rent, effectively canceling the tax. The Navy leased Ames Field for two successive one-year periods, from October 1, 1942, to June 30, 1944.[34]

ENDNOTES

1. Joseph A. Kehoe, CSC, "Holy Cross in Oregon, 1902–1980" (Notre Dame, Indiana: Provinces Archives Center, 1982).

2. Arthur J. Hope, *Notre Dame: One Hundred Years*, Revised Edition (South Bend, Indiana: Icarus Press, Inc., 1978): 11–18. See also James Connelly, CSC, ed., *The Chronicles of Notre Dame Du Lac* (Notre Dame, Indiana: University of Notre Dame Press, 1992): xiii.

3. James Connelly, CSC, "Holy Cross in the United States: 150 Years," *C.S.C. Internazionale* VI(1) (Fall 1991): 2.

4. Hope, *Notre Dame*, 35–55. Of the seven brothers who accompanied Sorin in the November 1842 trek north to South Bend, only two were in the original six who had come from France. Although the Community's stay in Vincennes was brief, several men had joined Holy Cross and finished the novitiate, which had been established concurrently with the school and parish.

5. Connelly, *Chronicles of Notre Dame*, xxi. Notre Dame was the third Catholic college incorporated in the United States, but earlier foundations were: Georgetown in 1791, Mount St. Mary's (Emmitsburg, Maryland) in 1808, St. Joseph's College for Women (Emmitsburg) in 1809, St. Louis University in 1818, Xavier University

(Cincinnati) in 1831, and Fordham in 1841. Villanova, along with Notre Dame, was established in 1842.

6. Quoted in William Dunn, CSC, "The Finest Country in the World" (Notre Dame, Indiana: Provinces Archives Center, 1985): 2.

7. Ibid., 5–11. The complete history of St. Edward's University is found in: William Dunn, *Saint Edward's University: A Centennial History* (Austin, Texas: St. Edward's University Press, 1986); see pages 15–37 for information on early foundations.

8. Joseph A. Kehoe, CSC, "Holy Cross in Oregon, 1902–1980." The complete history of the University of Portland is found in: James T. Covert, *A Point of Pride: The University of Portland Story* (Portland, Oregon: University of Portland Press, 1976). During the nineteenth century Holy Cross religious entered numerous other educational apostolates. The foundation or direction of five additional colleges by the men was coupled with twenty-six secondary school academies by the Sisters of the Holy Cross and St. Mary's College at Notre Dame which awarded its first baccalaureate degree in 1898. See James Connelly, CSC, "Educators in the Faith: The Holy Cross Congregations and Their Schools in the United States, 1865–1900," paper delivered at the Conference of the History of the Congregations of Holy Cross in the United States (New Orleans, Louisiana: June 15, 1990): 5–19. The five additional colleges sponsored by Holy Cross priests and brothers were: University of Our Lady of the Sacred Heart in Watertown, Wisconsin, 1872–1912; Holy Cross in New Iberia, Louisiana, 1872–1874; St. Joseph's in Brownsville, Texas, 1873–1874; St. Joseph's in Cincinnati, Ohio, 1872–1921; and St. Isidore's (Holy Cross after 1890) in New Orleans, 1879 to the present. St. Mary's College, administered by the Sisters of the Holy Cross, was founded in 1844. The Brothers of Holy Cross founded numerous secondary schools in the latter half of the nineteenth century in the Midwest, the South, and the East.

9. In the mid- to late nineteenth century, Holy Cross religious were active in starting schools and orphanages throughout the Midwest and as far east as Baltimore, Camden, New Jersey, and Philadelphia. Many of the schools were short-lived, but these foundations demonstrate the zeal of the Community to answer the call of the Church.

10. The American provincials, James Burns (1927–1938) and Thomas Steiner (1938–1950), did not actively promote eastern foundations. Fear of expansion, due to lack of funds and personnel, and the desire to promote the fortunes of Notre Dame created a narrow view of the Community's future possibilities.

11. Maurus O'Malley, CSC, "The First Permanent Foundations of the Holy Cross Fathers and Brothers in the Eastern States," paper presented at the Conference on the History of the Congregations of Holy Cross (Wilkes-Barre, Pennsylvania: May 26, 1985). The mission band was a group of Holy Cross religious who traveled various sections of the country, preaching missions in parishes. This practice is what Jay Dolan calls "Catholic Revivalism." See Jay P. Dolan, *Catholic Revivalism: The American Experience, 1830–1900* (Notre Dame, Indiana: University of Notre Dame Press, 1978).

12. It should be noted that Cassidy invited Holy Cross to accept two other foundations in Fall River. In February 1933 Donahue was contacted about accepting a Polish-speaking parish, Our Lady of Perpetual Help, which was in financial straits. The bishop wrote, "I would be greatly relieved if your congregation would 'take a try' at this very, just now, difficult problem." At the same time the bishop suggested Donahue purchase an old Methodist church between Attleboro and Taunton for use as another parish or educational foundation. See Cassidy to Donahue, February 10, 1933, Archives of the Holy Cross Fathers Generalate (hereafter AHCFG), Rome, Italy. Most probably Cassidy wanted to make his offer to Holy Cross more attractive, thus the additional invitations.

13. James Cassidy to James Donahue, CSC, November 12, 1931; Donahue to Cassidy, November 20, 1931, AHCFG; "Chronicles of Our Lady of Holy Cross" (n.d. before June 5, 1934), ASC.

14. New Bedford *Standard-Times* (May 15, 1949); Richard Desharnais, CSC, "North Dartmouth, Massachusetts: 1934–1980," North Dartmouth File, Archives of the Holy Cross Fathers, Indiana Province (hereafter AHCFI), Notre Dame, Indiana. It should be noted that hard economic times caused by the Depression were another catalyst in Kirby's sale of the property.

15. Cassidy to Donahue, August 5, 1933, AHCFG.

16. "Chronicles of Holy Cross" (September 18, 1933, December 8, 1933), ASC.

17. Certificate of Incorporation, Commonwealth of Massachusetts, ASC; Incorporation for the Foundations of Our Lady of Holy Cross, August 9, 1934, Stonehill College Papers, Archives of the Holy Cross Fathers, Eastern Province (hereafter AHCFE), North Easton, Massachusetts; Thomas Steiner to James Burns, December 5, 1935, Burns Papers, AHCFI. James Wesley Donahue's vision for the Congregation's expansion in the East continued beyond North Dartmouth. Three foundations by the brothers were established within two years: Monsignor Coyle High School in Taunton in August 1934, the Vincentian Institute in Albany, New York, in 1935, and the juniorate near Valatie, New York, the same year. Connelly has summarized Donahue's purpose: "It appeared as if the superior general [Donahue] had intended from the beginning to establish a group of houses in the east which were more dependent on the general administration than on the province to which they belonged." James Connelly, CSC, "An Eastern Province in 1938," paper presented at the Conference on the History of the Congregations of Holy Cross (North Easton, Massachusetts: June 17, 1989).

18. Frederick Lothrup Ames had amassed a fortune from his family shovel business and his prize Guernsey cow herd. The history of the Ames family is colorful and multifaceted. For detailed information see: Winthrop Ames, *The Ames Family* (privately published, 1938) and William L. Chaffin, *History of the Town of Easton, Massachusetts* (Cambridge, Massachusetts: John Wilson and Son, 1886): 648–660.

19. "Chronicles of Holy Cross" (March 2, 1935), ASC.

20. Frederick Ames' widow married Roger Cutler in 1931.

21. Ames Family History Fact Sheet, Ames Family Papers; Brockton *Daily Enter-*

prise clipping (March 5, 1937), ASC; *Providence Visitor* (July 22, 1948), North Easton File, AHCFI.

22. Cassidy to Donahue, July 22, 1935, AHCFG. No reason for Cassidy's hesitation is extant, but it is possible that he possessed reservations on the usefulness of the property. There is no indication that Cassidy knew of Duffy's dreams or the larger vision of Donahue in the establishment of a college.

23. Edith Cutler to James Donahue, July 24, 1935, Superior General Papers, AHCFE. Donahue had to obtain permission from the Sacred Congregation of Religious to take out a $40,000 loan in order to purchase the property. See Donahue to George Sauvage, CSC, August 1, 1935, AHCFG. Sauvage was the Congregation's Procurator General, whose job was to interface with the Vatican on all matters requiring Roman approval.

24. "Chronicles of Holy Cross" (October 17, 1935), ASC.

25. Brother Claude to James Donahue, June 4, 1935, Stonehill College Papers, AHCFE.

26. Brother Lambert and a North Easton attorney retained by the Community, Daniel Buckley, worked out the legal details for payment and transfer of title. Some flaws in the original contract delayed the move from North Dartmouth. Cassidy gave permission for the move, despite his earlier hesitancy. See Donahue to James Burns, August 28, 1935, Ames Property Files, ASC; Cassidy to Donahue, October 11, 1935, AHCFG.

27. Donahue to James Burns, October 31, 1935, October 19, 1935, Ames Property Files, ASC.

28. Holy Cross foundations, with the addition of the North Easton property, were again poised for expansion. The decision was made to convert the North Dartmouth property into a novitiate to solidify the Congregation's new religious formation program in the East. In August 1936, after laying dormant for one year, North Dartmouth opened with Father Christopher O'Toole as master of six novices, all alumni of Our Lady of Holy Cross Seminary. Originally the novitiate was to be called Sacred Heart, to recognize the titular feast of the priests in the Congregation, but because the Holy Cross Community was not well known in the region, the provincial, James Burns, opted for the generic name Novitiate of the Congregation of Holy Cross, which was later shortened to Holy Cross Novitiate. O'Toole reported to the Superior General that "the new novitiate is running as smoothly as any house in the community I have lived in." "Chronicles of Holy Cross" (August 6, 1936); James Burns to Christopher O'Toole, September 1, 1936, O'Toole to Burns, August 28, 1926 [*sic*–1936], AHCFI.

29. Brother Lambert to Daniel Buckley, October 19, 1936; Edith Cutler to Brother Lambert, September 2, 1936, Superior General Papers, AHCFE. Cutler mentions no other specific buyers in her correspondence.

30. Donahue to Mrs. Roger Cutler, October 20, 1936, Superior General Papers, AHCFE; "Chronicles of Holy Cross" (March 4, 1937), ASC.

31. Brockton *Enterprise* clipping, n.d. [1937], Stonehill History Papers, ASC.

32. Thomas Steiner to Gerald Fitzgerald, May 22, 1939, Seminary Correspon-

dence, History of Stonehill, ASC. This guild, the first non-Holy Cross group formed to support what became Stonehill, became the Stonehill Guild in 1948. The guild provided economic and moral support to the Congregation's efforts in North Easton.

33. "Chronicles of Holy Cross" (January 1943 and September 13, 1943), ASC.

34. Gerald Fitzgerald to Thomas Steiner, September 28, 1940; Steiner to Fitzgerald, October 7, 1940; J.G. Willett to Fitzgerald, October 6, 1942; Lease between the United States Navy and Our Lady of Holy Cross Seminary, October 1, 1942, Stonehill History Papers, ASC. It should be noted that between 1936 and 1941, George Malovin of Brockton operated a flying school and chartered flights at Ames Field. After the Navy left in July 1944, the field was leased for $50 per month to Charles Del Sordo, who established the Ames School of Aviation. See *Brockton Enterprise* clipping (July 20, 1978). Rental Agreement between Our Lady of Holy Cross Seminary and Mr. Charles Del Sordo, November 30, 1944, Stonehill History Papers; "Chronicles of Holy Cross" (July 3, 1944), ASC.

CHAPTER I

1946–1949

A Dream Fulfilled

The end of World War II brought a rising tide of optimism to the American people. The nation had met the challenge handed it by the world, providing leadership, war materials, and combatants that defeated enemy forces on two fronts and, in the process, brought a sense of accomplishment and pride to its people. The United States emerged from the war as the leader of the free world, an enviable position in many ways but one that carried with it a heavy burden of responsibility. President Harry Truman responded to America's increased global presence and international responsibility by the establishment of a containment policy to stop the spread of international Communism.[1] While major strikes did accompany the return of America's work force to a peacetime economy,[2] the country economically, socially, and politically found itself at the beginning of a period of peace and domestic prosperity that would extend through the decade of the 1950s.

American Catholicism also rode the wave of optimism that existed in the country. Anti-Catholicism seemed to enter hibernation, and Catholics were more accepted than ever before. Catholic institutions, including schools and churches, mushroomed. Seventy percent of America's Catholics attended Mass regularly, and they felt a stronger sense of personal moralism, as evidenced by greater participation in the sacrament of penance. The Church in Boston experienced renewal with the arrival of Richard Cushing as archbishop in 1944, succeeding Cardinal William Henry O'Connell, who had held the episcopal reins of the archdiocese since 1907. Cushing brought a feeling of optimism and opportunity to the Boston Church through his energetic approach to institutional building and his willingness to help sponsor those who promoted and initiated development of the Church.

The Offer of a Boston Foundation in 1946

❦

THE FEELING OF OPTIMISM and desire for expansion that coursed through the veins of Archbishop Cushing was manifest to the Congregation of Holy Cross in 1946 with an invitation to open a college in the heart of Boston.[3] John Delaunay, CSC, professor of psychology and dean of students at the University of Portland, wrote to Thomas Steiner, provincial at Notre Dame, quoting the archbishop: "Whether Holy Cross can do anything or not, I want them to be on record as being authorized to start a college in Boston and that will stand whether I am alive or not." Delaunay, a friend of Cushing, who felt the archbishop was disappointed in the Congregation's earlier lackluster response to invitations to establish educational foundations in Boston, encouraged Steiner to act favorably on the invitation.[4]

Steiner, who was cautious and worried about the lack of personnel to staff the commitments presently held by the Congregation, responded to Delaunay's appeal with restraint. Possible foundations of Holy Cross abroad in Australia and domestically in Detroit and San Diego, plus the demands for people from the newly established King's College in Wilkes-Barre, Pennsylvania, would, it was perceived, severely strain the Community's personnel resources for some time, making other commitments not feasible. As a counterproposal, Steiner suggested development of the North Easton property, for a boarding school on the college level. Delaunay, however, expressing Cushing's displeasure with the Jesuits, whom he "doesn't want to open another school," continued to push for a Boston foundation. The archbishop pushed Delaunay for an immediate response in order to have a valid reason to exclude Benedictines and Augustinians, who had petitioned Cushing for entrance to the archdiocese.[5] Delaunay wrote, "The Archbishop would like to make it known publicly that the Congregation of Holy Cross will open a Catholic college in Boston." Delaunay suggested that Steiner send a team to "look over the field" and make a fair assessment of the offer.[6]

Steiner, on advice from the provincial council, wrote to Cushing that the Community was interested in the Boston foundation and that two priests, James Connerton and Howard Kenna, would be sent to Boston to investigate the opportunity fully. Cushing was pleased to receive Steiner's more encouraging response and spoke of the "tremendous possibilities for additional colleges for men" in the area. Steiner's instructions to Connerton raised a note of optimism and emphasized the pressure he felt to establish

(Left) Rev. Thomas Steiner, CSC, provincial of American (Indiana) Province 1938–1950. (Right) Rev. Thomas Duffy, CSC.

the Congregation in Boston: "It is a proposition that we do not want to turn down if we can possibly manage to take it, so we want to investigate it thoroughly."[7] Superior General Albert Cousineau, also optimistic on the project, increased the pressure on Steiner:[8]

> A day college in Boston would be a great opportunity for our apostolate and for vocations also. It is true that we have to be prudent. We are anxious here to know the outcome of the visit of Father Kenna and Father Connerton.

Steiner remained cautious despite the confidence of others. He believed, as did many at Notre Dame, that the Catholic colleges in the area (Boston College, Holy Cross, and Providence) provided adequately for the needs of the local Catholic population. He conceded, "Possibly another day college in Boston might work, but it does seem that there are plenty of them now." Steiner was also concerned about the attitude of Cushing, who was "telling everyone that Holy Cross is going to open a college in Boston."[9]

Connerton and Kenna, together with Thomas Duffy from North Easton, went to Boston and met with Cushing on October 9. The archbishop proposed that Holy Cross open an arts and letters day school in downtown Boston. The former Westminster Hotel, now used by the John Hancock Mutual Life Insurance Company, a nine-floor structure comprising almost half a city block, was the suggested site. The estimated purchase price for the building was $700,000, although much more would be needed to finance the foundation. Cushing, who "criticized the Jesuits for not doing more," felt that competition with Boston College would be good. He was convinced that there was ample student population to support a second Catholic college for men in the city, for no effort had been made to accommodate Catholics who attended Harvard, the Massachusetts Institute of Technology, and Tufts. Cushing, however, could make no definite pledge of financial support.[10]

Connerton's and Kenna's contradictory recommendations in their report to the provincial added confusion to an already complicated situation. The pair wrote that the Boston opportunity on the surface appeared to be good but required further investigation by one who could spend more time in the area. In an addendum to the original report, however, Connerton voiced a very different idea:[11]

> A College at North Easton would seem to be a better prospect in that we could go as far as the thing would justify itself and we would not be offending the Jesuits, whose long traditional training of Catholic Massachusetts deserves considerable regard.

The North Easton possibility drew support from Bishop James Cassidy in Fall River, who told Connerton and Kenna that he "would be pleased if we [Holy Cross] decided to do anything to develop the North Easton property as we have simply encumbered the earth for fifteen years." He saw it as "an ideal spot for a college or boarding school." Cassidy offered a gift of $25,000 to equip a house for faculty. Even Cushing saw some possibility for the Congregation in North Easton, "for Holy Cross has missed the ball there."[12]

Steiner took the advice of his investigation team and sent John Lane, CSC, to make a more thorough study of the possible Boston foundation. After one month, Lane reported that there was a definite need for a college in the area and that there should be no concern for availability of students. He concluded, "A college should be established provided [that] the financial considerations involved in the acquisition of a suitable site make the project appear feasible." With respect to North Easton he reported, "Because of the remoteness of the spot from Boston, I feel that any consideration of North

Easton as the location of a boarding school ought to be approached with the greatest caution."[13]

Financial demands, the uncertainty of support, and the timid approach of Thomas Steiner led to the Congregation's rejection of Archbishop Cushing's offer. Steiner told Albert Cousineau that Cushing's expectation of a foundation only within the next five years made the manpower problems solvable but that the financial risk was too high without a commitment of support from the archbishop. In February 1947 the Provincial Council, which estimated the total cost to establish a college in Boston to range from $1.0 to $1.5 million, stated that if Cushing would promise to fund half the project, the Congregation would borrow the other half and a college could be opened in two years. Although stating, "We are definitely interested and hope that we can see our way clear to handle the project financially," the Council voted to postpone action indefinitely.[14] Steiner thus wrote to Cushing, voicing concern over manpower and finances, which drew the following dejected response from the Boston prelate:[15]

> In view of the fact that times have not substantially changed during the past twelve months I think you should postpone indefinitely any consideration concerning the establishment of a college in the archdiocese of Boston. . . . Forget about the project for the time being. If and when conditions are more favorable I will contact you.

The timidness of Steiner and the resulting withdrawal of the invitation from Boston was a source of disappointment to the Superior General. He wrote to the American provincial:[16]

> It would be lacking in frankness with you if I did not tell you that your negative decision in all these proposals surprised me. I understand very well that you are now facing the most critical manpower shortage in years. We need not minimize that point. But it would be discouraging if we had to wait for new foundations till we had plenty of vocations.

The actions of Thomas Steiner that resulted in the loss of a Boston foundation certainly were influenced by recent events in the history of Holy Cross. Although not directly involved, Steiner most assuredly was aware of the Congregation's recent expulsion from administration of the College of St. Thomas in St. Paul, Minnesota. Fearing a repeat of history, Steiner may have been wary of the invitation.[17]

Financial considerations also played a significant role in Steiner's decision. While day-to-day operations of the Community and existing foundations taxed the Congregation's coffers, Steiner's major concern (although not specifically articulated) must have been the financial settlement the priests of Holy Cross owed to the brothers after the 1945 separation of the brothers into autonomous provinces.[18] In assets and cash, the priests awarded the brothers $5,330,522 as a result of the separation.[19] This extra financial burden weighed on Steiner and probably figured in his decision not to invest in such a speculative and uncertain venture as a new college.

Political decisions based on pride and territorialism also may have entered into the formula Steiner used to make his decision. Thomas Duffy and other Holy Cross religious in the East perceived the desire by many in the West to keep the Community centralized at Notre Dame and, thus, not to look favorably on foundations—especially educational ones—outside of Notre Dame. Thomas Duffy suggested that the opinion of Lane, who saw the Boston foundation as a safe proposition, should be heeded. He complained, "It seems too bad that there should be a general opinion as to the possibility of success in the East and a devastating opinion emanating from Notre Dame—just one man's opinion."[20] This impression, held by other members of Holy Cross,[21] was also expressed by Franciscans who heard of Holy Cross's rejection of Cushing's offer.[22]

The Founding of Stonehill College

CATHOLIC COLLEGES AND UNIVERSITIES in the United States have historically departed from the prevailing norms in three areas. In a social context, most teachers and students involved with Catholic higher education have come from groups who were in one way or another different from most American teachers and students. Institutionally the patterns of educational organization and administration were not those of other institutions of higher learning. Lastly, in ideology the beliefs and attitudes of Catholic educators were not the same as those of other Americans.[23] Beginning in 1940, in what the educational historian Edward Power refers to as "the period of awakening" for Catholic higher education,[24] a shift away from these historically traditional norms was initiated. Catholic colleges after World War II altered their philosophy and theology from dogmatics and apologetics to a more rigorist academic approach. Catholic higher education began to be concerned more about its image and, as a corollary, showed a new interest in the place its graduates occupied in American life and the extent of their intellectual influence. The quality of education gained greater emphasis. During this same period the doctrine of *in loco parentis* began to fade in significance. Catholic colleges and universities started to expand their offerings, initiate graduate programs, offer professional studies, and experiment with coeducation. As Power put it, "On the surface these were all excellent developments, but at the same time they complicated the lives of the colleges and made it extremely difficult for them to continue to operate as appendages of the Church, on the one hand, and as schools with aspirations for academic identity, on the other."[25]

Changes in society and the movement away from traditional understanding and norms in Catholic higher education forced institutions to rethink their purpose. The objective of undergraduate education in the past had been fundamentally ethical and spiritual, but the means to achieve this end was to be intellectual. Catholic higher education searched in the postwar period for a harmonious synthesis of the academic and the spiritual. One writer expressed the difficulty faced by Catholic institutions of higher learning as they tried to adapt to a changing world:[26]

> By its very nature Catholic education is a profoundly difficult synthesis. Certainly it is not merely a series of courses with philosophy and religion added to the curriculum. Certainly it is not merely pietism, chapels, sodalities, present on the same campus with the standard departments of instruction.

Postwar America saw a significant rise in the number of people attending institutions of higher learning. On June 22, 1944, President Franklin D. Roosevelt signed the Servicemen's Readjustment Act, which made college education and other forms of training available for returning veterans of the armed services who had served after September 16, 1940, been honorably discharged or released, and whose education had been interrupted by military service. Catholic colleges, which had suffered greatly during the war from a dearth of students, began to perceive the need for greater facilities and the need for expansion on all fronts. A survey conducted by *America* magazine in 1947 found enrollment in Catholic colleges at over 180,000, a rise of almost 17 percent from the previous year and a jump that was 5 percent above the national average.[27]

Faced with a challenge to their identity, changing educational patterns, and a rapid rise in enrollment necessitating new and expanded facilities, Catholic colleges and universities were forced to compete for fewer economic resources. The President's Commission on Higher Education in 1948 envisioned an average per-year student tuition of $300, a figure that represented only 53 percent of the amount needed for educational expenditures. Catholic colleges, the report noted, because of their lower endowments and fewer financial resources, would be hard pressed to find the other 47 percent of the needed monies save through a higher tuition fee. Smaller colleges were also forced to utilize the concept of a "living endowment," where the services of religious assigned to a college were donated, lowering school costs and keeping tuition increases to a minimum.[28]

The change and adaptation found in Catholic higher education after World War II was also present in the structures of the Congregation of Holy Cross. While debate in the East focused on the possibility of founding a college in downtown Boston, the Superior General and others were considering expansion of the Community through the establishment of a new province. Although the Community was present in many different locations, administration of the American elements of Holy Cross was securely fixed at Notre Dame. As early as 1938, however, James Wesley Donahue, whose vision had brought Holy Cross east, made overtures to establish an eastern province in the United States. At the July 1938 General Chapter of the Congregation held at Notre Dame, Donahue, citing the successful eastern foundations in 1933 and 1935, proposed the erection of an autonomous eastern province. Donahue was supported in his effort by James Burns, the American provincial, who believed that an eastern province would facilitate recruitment of vocations. The debate on the measure focused on finances, with Michael Mulcaire, CSC, vice president at Notre Dame, leading those who opposed the proposal. Donahue's bid fell short by one vote.[29]

The 1938 effort to found an eastern province failed, but the Chapter did elect Albert Cousineau, the first Canadian, as Superior General. Cousineau kept the concept of an eastern province alive through the war years, although the instability of the period was not conducive to new foundations. In January 1945, with vocations on the rise, Cousineau's thoughts again turned to "the question of dividing provinces." John Lucey, CSC, commented that it was Cousineau's support which in time brought the eastern province of Holy Cross into existence.[30]

In February 1948 Cousineau wrote to Steiner asking that financial data be gathered to examine the possibility for a new province. Steiner responded to the General, stating that the Provincial Council was not opposed to a new province but felt that the timing was not good. The provincial was still concerned about money. If an autonomous eastern province were established, Steiner wanted the new foundation to share the expenses, especially the education of seminarians and the debt incurred by the 1945 formation of autonomous provinces of priests and brothers.[31]

On April 21, 1948, after Steiner was satisfied with the financial agreement, a vice province in the "Northeastern States" was formed, with the decree to become effective on May 3. James Connerton was appointed vice provincial, with Thomas Duffy[32] and John Lane as councilors.[33] The foundation was made with little fanfare and as little publicity as possible so as not to foment the ire of those in the West who continued to argue against eastern foundations.[34] Cousineau wrote to Connerton:[35]

> We may seem to be very much conciliatory with the Indiana Province. We had to be so. The success was not possible without that. And, according to my experience, we will gain more, in the long run, by our kindness and friendly relations, even if we have to make certain sacrifices.

An eastern vice province was now in existence, but some catalyst was necessary to push Holy Cross off its seat of complacency in North Easton. The needed thrust came suddenly, unexpectedly, and coincidentally with the vice province's foundation. Unknown to Holy Cross, Archbishop Cushing in February 1948 began negotiations with Franciscans of the Holy Name Province, headquartered in New York, about establishing a college adjacent to North Easton in the Brockton-Avon area. On April 21, 1948, Father Mark Kennedy, OFM, president of Siena College in Loudinville, New York, met with Cushing, who outlined his plans for a college and recounted Holy Cross's earlier refusal of the Boston foundation. Five days later Kennedy toured two potential sites in Brockton and was satisfied that a college could be built in the area.[36]

In late April[37] John Blunt, a Brockton lawyer and nephew of Monsignor Hugh Blunt, superintendent of Boston's archdiocesan school system, hosted a luncheon for Kennedy. George Benaglia, superior at Our Lady of Holy Cross, was also invited. During the meal Benaglia learned of Cushing's invitation to the Franciscans.[38] Benaglia immediately relayed this startling news to Thomas Duffy, who hastily wrote an impassioned plea to the Superior General, requesting action and lamenting the Congregation's lethargic efforts in the east:[39]

> If it is true [the offer to the Franciscans], and it appears to be, then I think our development at North Easton is finished. We will have all we can do to survive. . . . We have done little here in the way of growth, during the past fifteen years. . . . We have tried, as you know, even from your first visit to North Easton, to develop our property here. We have constantly and consistently met with the opposition of the authorities at Notre Dame. This work of the East has been looked upon as Donahue's Folley [*sic*] and has never been encouraged.
>
> Let us admit that we have all suffered a dire loss, in money, foundations, vocations and everything else, and build up the great University of Notre Dame. Perhaps Donahue and the rest of us here were all wrong, and have been mistaken down through the past fourteen years.
>
> When in the name of God shall we ever rise from our lethargy and get going

in a country where so many others have succeeded? . . . If this [no action] is to be the case, then why bother about anything else for Holy Cross.

Duffy's strong call for action was in line with his personality and conviction that Holy Cross must develop in the East. From the time he discovered the Ames estate in 1935 he never lost his dream that the site afforded the Congregation a great opportunity for future development. Brother Maurus O'Malley, CSC, commented that Duffy did not possess charisma, but that he never stopped when he believed his cause right, a quality that made him invaluable when immediate action was imperative to safeguard Holy Cross' interests in the area.[40]

Duffy's letter initiated a flurry of activity. Connerton, after consulting with Duffy and Benaglia, decided that Holy Cross must move immediately in North Easton or lose the opportunity to make it the site of a Catholic college. Discussions were held with the general staff of the Congregation, which was headquartered in New York. On May 16, two weeks after Duffy learned of the offer to the Franciscans, Connerton requested permission from the Superior General "for the erection of a college on the community property at North Easton, Massachusetts." The reasons given in support for the request were:[41]

1. A partial college already existed there; only science facilities at an estimated cost of $25,000 needed to be constructed.
2. The local ordinaries, Cushing and Cassidy, had approved the project.
3. The Franciscans were tentatively offered a school in Brockton, but Cushing said he would withdraw the invitation if Holy Cross wanted to open a college.

As approval was readily granted,[42] Connerton instructed Duffy and Benaglia to proceed with all preparations to open the college in September. "Stonehill," derived from the original name of the Ames mansion, "Stone House Hill House," was the appellation given the College by Connerton as a way to "please many of the heirs still living and all the surrounding vicinity."[43]

The rapid decision of Holy Cross to begin a college in North Easton requires some examination. Knowledge that Archbishop Cushing had extended an invitation to the Franciscans was undoubtedly the event which precipitated the decision to found a college, but other factors were also present. The pragmatism which seems to have dominated Thomas Steiner's previous thinking in declining Cushing's invitation to Boston became moot when the realization struck that if Holy Cross did not act immediately, the time, personnel, and economic investment at North Easton would be virtually wasted. In other words, Holy Cross would have to take the chance immediately or lose the possibility for all time. It is the opinion of Philip Kelly, CSC, a member of the mission band in residence at North Easton at the time, that Connerton acted to start Stonehill as a way "to anchor the community in the area."[44] One cannot discount, as well, the embarrassment the Congregation must have felt when the Franciscans readily assented to the archbishop's request, with no previous history of favor from him or any local foundations. Cushing was clearly partial to Holy Cross; the Community merely needed to respond favorably in order to receive his approval.

Community approbation having been received, it was necessary to secure episcopal and state permission before formal plans to open the College could proceed. Although only a small portion of the North Easton site lay in the archdiocese of Boston, Cushing was immediately informed of the Congregation's decision and approval was requested for the foundation. Cushing responded with congratulations but stated that since the site was located almost entirely in the diocese of Fall River, it would be inappropriate for him to make a public statement. Most importantly, however, Cushing withdrew his invitation to the Franciscans:[45, 46]

> I am afraid that our plans for Brockton have collapsed. The Holy Cross Fathers have formed a Vice-Province in the East and the Vice-Provincial called recently to tell me that they are planning on a college in Northeaston [*sic*]. That is the end of our plans, for that area could not support two colleges.

Bishop James Cassidy in Fall River gave his assent readily to the project, praising Holy Cross for the higher order of its collegiate and university endeavors.[47]

Before seeking approbation from the Commonwealth of Massachusetts, Stonehill needed a charter to operate as a college. The charter granted to the Foundation of Our Lady of Holy Cross had to be revised to allow Stonehill to grant degrees and operate as a college. Connerton placed George Benaglia, his choice as president, in charge of the effort to secure a charter. Benaglia, in turn, assigned Fathers Victor Dean and James Moran to the task.[48] Time was of the essence because the Board of Collegiate Authority was scheduled to meet on May 29 for the final time in academic year 1947–1948. Through the assistance of Father Timothy O'Leary, assistant superintendent of parochial schools in the Archdiocese of Boston, Stonehill obtained and then used as its template the charter of Merrimack College, which was founded in 1947.[49] The more difficult and time-dependent task was accumulating and organizing the data needed to accompany the charter request. Moran and Dean obtained financial data and records of the Congregation's previous educational foundations in the United States from Louis Kelley at the Generalate in New York. The material was organized and the application completed in less than ten days. Benaglia found a printer in Boston who could produce the 50 required copies and have them ready at 8:30 A.M. on May 29.[50]

Brother Oswald Rumrill, CSC, and Benaglia picked up the application and supporting documentation and presented it on May 29 at 8:50 A.M., only ten minutes before the start of the Collegiate Board meeting. The board members read the petition with interest but decided that a special meeting would be necessary on June 29 at Deerfield Academy to review the application more completely and to hear testimony from the petitioners.

Stonehill's application to the Collegiate Board described the College's primitive organizational structure. Officers of administration (Board of Trustees), with Benaglia as president, Moran as vice president, and Robert Woodward, CSC, as dean, were to "bear the full and complete responsibility for the College."[51] A board of advisors for the College, composed of leaders in business, government, and the Church, was formed at this time. The board was headed by Bishop Cassidy and his coadjutor James Connolly, and it included the attorneys Joseph Duggan of New Bedford and Daniel Buckley of North Easton as legal advisors and Judge Harry K. Stone of Brockton. The autonomy of the Eastern Vice Province necessitated that the corporation be managed by local personnel. Thus, Connerton asked Steiner to reorganize the members of the Foundation of Our Lady of Holy Cross to show Connerton as president, Dean as secretary, and Duffy as treasurer. The purpose of the College was "to direct the moral, religious and academic training of young persons and adults; to establish, maintain and conduct curricula generally maintained, established and conducted in institutions of higher learning; . . . ."[52]

In June Archbishop Cushing, who had been publicly silent about the North Easton foundation because of his need to settle the situation with the Franciscans, wrote in support of the Holy Cross effort. Cushing described the community's "academic qualifications" and "record of achievement in the field of higher learning":[53]

> For a considerable period of time, I have been convinced of the need for such
> an institution in the southeastern portion of Massachusetts. It is obvious that
> the North Easton location in the Diocese of Fall River will serve a region pres-
> ently lacking in collegiate facilities, and at the same time, a college site in a
> town immediately contiguous to the archdiocesan boundary line will also be
> advantageous to students removed from the center of the metropolitan area.

Officially Stonehill College did not exist and thus was not legally able to recruit students or advertise, but the time between the May 29 and June 29 meetings had to be utilized so that the College could open in September as planned. Connerton delegated to Thomas Duffy "all matters which he thinks need not be brought to me" concerning the foundation of the College. The Brockton *Enterprise* provided free advertising when it described Holy Cross's plan to establish a college at North Easton. Connerton, wary of possible fines for unauthorized advertising, believed there was no harm in providing information, especially to prospective students. Prospective students who inquired were told of the College's planned opening. The General and Vice Provincial Councils, in anticipation of a favorable decision from the state, authorized the expenditure of $25,000 on the new Stonehill enterprise.[54]

On June 29, 1948, the Board of Collegiate Authority reviewed the application and heard from members of the proposed corporation. Approval was granted for the new college to grant degrees in all fields except medicine.[55] The decision was hailed by the media as the beginning of the "Notre Dame of the East."[56]

Approval by the Collegiate Board set in motion the monumental challenge of organizing a college in less than two months. The many tasks to be completed before students could be welcomed in September necessitated the cooperation of all. A spirit of service existed; religious were satisfied to do what was necessary to meet the needs as they arose. Leo Gorman, CSC, acted as dean and registrar. James Martin, CSC, acted as secretary, since there was no money to hire a professional. Informality was the rule of the day that summer. Student applications, which flowed in mainly from the surrounding communities of Brockton, Taunton, Fall River, and New Bedford, as well as a few from Boston, were evaluated by Gorman. Selectivity was not stringent; 250 applicants were accepted.[57] Daniel Redgate of Brockton was the first applicant; the first registered student was Owen Carroll of Boston.[58] Admission requirements included three courses in English, one each in history, algebra, geometry, and laboratory science, and two courses in ancient or modern language.[59]

Development efforts were necessary to assist the foundation, especially considering the fledgling status of the Vice Province and its less than harmonious relationship with the mother province at Notre Dame.[60] Benaglia requested permission from both Cushing and Cassidy to canvas local parishes for contributions, with the hope that the bishops' approval would translate into economic support. Both ordinaries, however, refused to approve any development drive in parishes, a decision that contrasted sharply with practice in other dioceses.[61]

The construction of a new building to house both classrooms and laboratories was the principal new facilities requirement for the College. Plans were made to hold all classes in the mansion and on the adjacent indoor clay tennis court, but the need for more space was recognized immediately. Emery LaLiberte, a Brockton architect who became closely identified with Stonehill College, designed the new building. His initial plan for a six-room one-story building was estimated to cost $52,000. The design, with a per-room cost of $13,000, far exceeded the $25,000 allotted by the Congregation to start the College.[62] Connerton asked Brother Josephus Schaub, CSC, who had come to North Easton in August 1945 and was serving as head of maintenance, to look over the plans and see if the structure could be built more cheaply.[63] Connerton's idea was to construct a temporary building in order to cut costs,[64] but the harsh local climate and promising enrollment figures demanded a more permanent structure from the outset. James Mullen, a North Easton contractor on the rebound from the Depression and alcoholism, was given the job of chief contractor.[65]

The founding of Stonehill in the fall of 1948 was only one of several important college foundations in southern New England during this period. In June 1946 the "Haverhill Group," a committee of people interested in securing education opportunities for returning veterans, began to meet with Archbishop Cushing about founding a Catholic college in North Andover, Massachusetts. The initial suggestion of the group was a two-year training center to serve as a feeder for Boston College, but after consultation with William Kelleher, SJ, president of Boston College, a four-year school became the plan. Therefore, in the fall of 1946, while Holy Cross wavered about a Boston foundation, Cushing invited the Augustinians to open a college at a rural site in North Andover. The call was accepted and plans were immediately put into action in order to open in the fall of 1947. Through the guidance of Father Vincent A. McQuade, OSA, the doors to Merrimack College opened on September 29, 1947.[66]

The Jesuits, traditional leaders in Catholic higher education, were busy in Connecticut with a new foundation of their own. In December 1941 the Society purchased land near Bridgeport for the purpose of starting a high school or college. An adjacent parcel of land, which included a 40-room house, was acquired at the same time. While a prep school was started almost immediately (1942), the college foundation would not take shape for a few years. In May 1945 the charter for Fairfield University of St. Robert Bellarmine (later shortened to Fairfield University) was approved; the institution welcomed its first class of 303 freshmen in the fall of 1947. James H. Dolan, SJ, served as the first president.[67]

A third major foundation of higher education in the region was Brandeis University in Waltham, Massachusetts, just west of Boston. Israel Goldstein, acting on his long-held belief in the need for a Jewish university in the United States, spearheaded the effort to take over the administration of Middlesex University, a financially strapped medical school. In January 1946 Goldstein received a letter from a representative of Middlesex stating that a group of the school's trustees would be interested in establishing a new university of liberal arts and professional schools. One month later, control was transferred to Goldstein by electing him president of the board of trustees. Goldstein proceeded to establish a foundation, sponsored by the legendary scientist Albert Einstein, to raise money for the school. The university was named in honor of Louis Brandeis, the supreme court justice who was viewed as liberal in his Americanism and self-affirming in his Jewishness. Disputes between Goldstein and Einstein forced a one-year delay in the school's opening and the former's withdrawal from influence as the project's guiding light. Brandeis University opened in the fall of 1948 with Abram Leon Sachar as president.[68]

Growing Pains: 1948–1949

ON SEPTEMBER 20, 1948, 134[69] men started classes at Stonehill. The College bulletin informed the students:[70] ❧

> The system of studies [at Stonehill] has been designed to produce a twofold result: to prepare the young man to meet the demands which are being made upon him by the increasing complexities of modern social and economic life, and to train him to live in conformity to the will of God.

The bulletin also quoted Cardinal Newman's description of Catholic education as the reunion of the spiritual and intellectual aspects of human existence. Benaglia underscored this philosophy with his own ideas for education at Stonehill: "We seek not the development of mental giants—we desire to train young, healthy, intelligent men who have a genius in the desire and the defense of Truth, of Decency and of Justice."[71] Stonehill's first president believed that the College's role was to provide knowledge, but that proper moral guidance was equally important because parents and guardians had entrusted these young men to the school. Benaglia viewed students as charges who were to be encouraged to develop their talents and sense of moral responsibility.[72]

By any reasonable standard, facilities were primitive, administrative methods and standards unsettled, and faculty numbers and diversity of expertise inadequate when Stonehill opened its doors. Classes were held in the

Founder's Day, October 12, 1948:
Rev. James Connerton, CSC, Bishop James Cassidy, Rev. George Benaglia, CSC.

"green" room, lounge, and library of the main building, as well as on the old indoor tennis court which doubled as the gymnasium. Benaglia, who besides being president retained his role as director of the seminary and superior of the religious community, headed the College's administration, including James Moran as dean, Robert Woodward as registrar, and Brother Oswald Rumrill as treasurer. The religious faculty the first year consisted of three Holy Cross priests: Francis O'Hara, chemistry and biology; Edward Shea, Latin and romance languages; and Victor Dean, religion and English. In addition, there were five laymen to complete the faculty: John Collon, English and French; Vincent Gagliarducci, English and history; Samuel Hanna, math and German; George Sullivan, physical education; and Richard Sweeney, chemistry. Students paid $210 per semester in tuition, plus a $10 registration fee.[73]

The College's official opening, known today as Founder's Day, was celebrated on October 12, 1948. A Pontifical Mass was offered on campus,

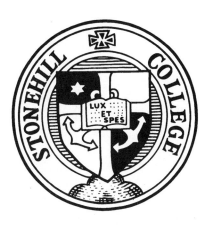

COLLEGE SEALS.
The original seal (left) was designed in 1951 by Br. Barnabas O'Toole, CSC, secretary and sacristan in the College's early days. The present seal (right) was designed in 1997. Both depict a book and star to symbolize the light of truth and crossed anchors to signify hope. The oak and laurel leaves in the new seal represent strength and achievement.

with Bishop Cassidy as the celebrant; James Connerton preached the sermon. Many dignitaries were present for the event, including Bishops James Connolly, auxiliary in Fall River, and Russell McVinney, ordinary in Providence; Merrimack president Vincent McQuade, OSA; and delegations from Boston, Assumption, St. Anselm, and Providence Colleges. Speaker of the House Joseph Martin, State Commissioner of Education John Desmond, Judge Harry K. Stone, and Dr. John Kelly, president of Bridgewater State Teacher's College, were also in attendance.[74] In his comments, Cassidy voiced a prophetic message about Stonehill's future:[75]

> Just as the oak tree, rising from a mere acorn, grows tall and powerful; so also will the influence of Stonehill reach out, from these humble beginnings, to enrich an area far greater than Southeastern Massachusetts.

Guests were treated to a hot lunch of beef tenderloin, potatoes, peas, macaroons, and coffee after the Mass.

When the light and glitter of the opening celebration were extinguished, the darkness of the College's immediate reality was easily recognizable. The new classroom building became a major financial liability that was not completely liquidated for more than five years. Originally scheduled to be ready for the start of classes in the fall, the project encountered delays and over-

*Rev. James Moran, CSC,
academic dean 1948–1950.*

spending due to changes of design and grossly underestimated costs. When the footing for the building was laid on July 8, a one-story six-room structure was envisioned. Shortly after construction began, however, it was decided that a second floor of classrooms and laboratories was necessary for the College to achieve accreditation. Steel for the frame of the building was obtained only when Stonehill arranged to exchange 35 tons of war surplus steel for I-beams.[76] Revision of the original design created delays and raised costs.

Financial difficulties, centering around the classroom building, dominated the activity of Benaglia. By mid-September over $50,000 had been spent on the structure, and the president reported that at least two more months of work were needed at a weekly payroll of two to three thousand dollars.[77] Vice provincial steward John Lane reminded Benaglia that only $50,000[78] had been authorized for the building and demanded an itemized account of all expenditures on the project. Shoddy accounting practices raised Lane's ire when Benaglia accidentally failed to report more than $24,000 owed for building materials.[79]

The financial situation at Stonehill placed the College and the Vice Province in adversarial roles. Bills accumulated by the College for operational expenses as well as the classroom building construction forced the Vice Province to lend Stonehill over $124,000 between July 19 and November 30, 1948. The money came from King's College, which had been en-

Stonehill College Library from 1948 to 1962.

dowed by William Hafey, Bishop of Scranton.[80] In sending Benaglia $30,000 in November, Lane wrote, "We are just about at the end of our means for giving assistance, so I hope this will carry you through until some income becomes available."[81]

Stonehill did try to raise revenue but found itself stymied at every turn. Many of the 134 men who started at Stonehill on September 20 were veterans,[82] but the College's new birth and unaccredited status proved problematic in securing government payment for these men under the GI bill. Benaglia had earlier made proper application for Stonehill to be eligible to train veterans under the provisions of public law 346 (in arts and sciences leading to the A.B. and B.S. degrees), but payment, despite written requests for action, was painfully slow.[83] The College also attempted to cut costs by applying for military surplus materials.[84] Connerton suggested that a new class be admitted in the spring semester in order to gain added tuition payments and defray costs. This proposal, however, was not feasible because physical facilities were already strained.[85] Benaglia, unable to understand

Classroom building and science labs in 1949.

the hostility of the Vice Province and its threats to cut support to the College, could only lament:[86]

> What are we to do? Close down the place? We are hampered on all sides in our development and the outlook is that we will be just another small time school. It seems to me that we should be given a fair chance to get started properly.

The opening of the classroom building on February 4, 1949 raised a glimmer of hope in an otherwise dismal state of affairs. During the second semester Benaglia borrowed another $30,000 from the Vice Province, a move which drew more criticism upon the president's head. Although Connerton approved the loan, he wrote to Benaglia in a tone that indicated a lack of trust in his judgment and financial acumen. He asked for an accounting of monies borrowed. John Lane continued the barrage against Benaglia and threatened him with the wrath of the Superior General if, in order to meet Stonehill's debts, the Vice Province was forced to borrow money from the outside.[87] Stonehill's operational deficit for the year was $32,028.56.[88]

The financial predicament in which Stonehill College found itself after one year of operation was caused by a combination of circumstance and lack of financial expertise. Records indicate that Benaglia was asked to run a college that possessed virtually no means to raise funds. For example, tuition receipts, even if collected in a timely and complete manner, would not have covered expenditures. While Benaglia investigated ways to cut costs, it is the opinion of Thomas Campbell, CSC, who spent the summer of 1948 at North Easton assisting in preparations for the College, that Benaglia possessed "a total lack of business sense."[89] Campbell's comment appears accurate upon examination of subsequent financial statements of the College that showed an annual surplus with the debt remaining constant or being reduced.[90] Benaglia can also be faulted for not seeking government and private grants for education.

Connerton's responsibility for Stonehill's financial problems must also be acknowledged. As founder and president of King's,[91] he was in the best position to be informed and had the greatest opportunity to offer suggestions and seek relief, yet he offered no advice. Connerton placed Benaglia in an unenviable situation, yet provided no assistance. The failure in leadership exacerbated a problematic situation that clouded Stonehill's history for the next five years.

Stonehill's founding thus came at a high price. The accumulated debt placed a burden on the College that would not soon be lifted, but the human toll was just as great. Benaglia reflected, "It was a rough year, probably the roughest I have known." Despite disappointments, Connerton was able to write to Benaglia, "You are certainly to be congratulated for everything about Stonehill and the Seminary. Doubtless the many trials you had to face this year have borne abundant fruit."[92]

ENDNOTES

1. In 1947 the Truman Administration introduced a twofold containment policy to keep Communist influence in Europe at a minimum. On March 12 the so-called "Truman Doctrine" was initiated when the United States agreed to take up payment of assistance to Greece and Turkey to ward off Communists when England removed its support. On June 5 in a Harvard speech, Secretary of State George Marshall introduced the "Marshall Plan" as an economic bailout of Europe, again to "contain" the spread of Communism. An excellent study of this period is: Wilson Miscamble, CSC, *George F. Kennan and the Making of American Foreign Policy, 1947–1950* (Princeton, New Jersey: Princeton University Press, 1992).

2. In the fall of 1945 and spring of 1946 major strikes among auto workers, under Walter Reuther, and miners, under John L. Lewis, placed almost 750,000 workers on the picket line. In 1946 alone 116 million man-days of work were lost due to strikes. These strikes, a threatened walkout by railroad workers and, most especially, the shift in control of the Congress to Republicans in 1946 produced the

Taft-Hartley Act of June 1947, which sharply curtailed the provisions of the National Labor Relations (Wagner) Act of 1935, labeled the Magna Carta of organized labor rights in the United States. Taft-Hartley placed restrictions on unions, strengthened management, and provided for a sixty-day "cooling off" period when ordered by the president, before strikes could be initiated. A good summary of the details of this period in American labor history is given in: Robert H. Zieger, *American Workers, American Unions, 1920–1985* (Baltimore: The Johns Hopkins Press, 1986).

3. Cushing's 1946 offer was actually the third time the archbishop had requested Holy Cross' presence in the archdiocese. In January 1945 George Benaglia, superior of Our Lady of Holy Cross at North Easton, informed Steiner that Cushing wanted Holy Cross to staff a high school in Brockton. The initial idea was to renovate the old city infirmary, a 180-acre site, that contained several buildings. Benaglia suggested that someone should come east and consult with Cushing, who "is a fast worker and wastes no time." Steiner wrote the archbishop and told him the Congregation would investigate the feasibility of the Brockton site for a high school. The trip east, however, was never made, which caused confusion in the mind of Holy Cross as to precisely what Cushing wanted, although a day school appeared to be the proposed foundation. Nothing was settled during the year, although it seems that Steiner was not positive on the invitation. When the plans for Brockton never materialized, a second invitation, more specific in nature, was extended by Cushing to obtain Holy Cross brothers to teach in a high school in Quincy. The General Council of the Congregation authorized that $60,000 be spent to purchase property in Quincy for the proposed foundation, but Steiner, citing new foundations in New Haven and Cleveland for the brothers, refused to commit to a Boston area high school, although internal plans to support a Quincy foundation were initiated. Cushing, most probably out of frustration and lack of patience, withdrew his invitation, deeming it "not to be acceptable . . . at this time." See Benaglia to Steiner, January 5, 1945; Steiner to Cushing, January 19, 1946; John Wright to Brother William, CSC, January 25, 1946, Steiner Papers, AHCFI; Steiner to Benaglia, January 11, 1945, Stonehill History Papers, ASC.

4. John Delaunay to Thomas Steiner, September 11, 1946, Connerton Papers, AHCFE. Delaunay to Steiner, August 21, 1946, Steiner Papers, AHCFI.

5. Cushing held reservations about the teaching methods and course offerings at Boston College. Perceiving a need for another Catholic institution of higher education in the Boston region, the archbishop sought the services of the Congregation of Holy Cross with whom he felt comfortable. Cushing realized that Holy Cross would not be able to start an institution for five years, but without some commitment from the Congregation now he had no valid reason to say no to others who sought to enter the archdiocese. There is no extant source that describes why Cushing lacked confidence in the Jesuits. One outstanding essay that outlines Jesuit higher education in the 1950s is: William C. McInnes, SJ. "The Current State of the Jesuit Philosophy of Education," in Roland E. Bonachea, ed., *Jesuit Higher Education: Essays on an American Tradition of Excellence* (Pittsburgh: Duquesne University Press, 1989),

26–45. When Holy Cross eventually turned down his offer, the Augustinians were invited to start Merrimack College in 1947.

6. Steiner to Albert Cousineau, CSC, June 8, 1946, Superior General Papers; Steiner to Delaunay, August 26, 1946, Steiner Papers, AHCFI; Delaunay to Steiner, September 11, 1946, Provincial Papers–Connerton, AHCFE.

7. Steiner to Cushing, September 19, 1946; Cushing to Steiner, September 23, 1946; Steiner to Connerton, September 19, 1946, Provincial Papers–Connerton, AHCFE.

8. Albert Cousineau to Steiner, October 7, 1946, Superior General Papers, ACHFI.

9. Steiner to Cousineau, October 17, 1946, Superior General Papers, AHCFI. Speaking of the invitation to Boston, Steiner told the General, "We in the west have never warmed up to the proposition."

10. Connerton and Kenna to Steiner, October 31, 1946, Provincial Papers–Connerton, AHCFE.

11. Connerton to Steiner, October 31, 1946, Provincial Papers–Connerton, AHCFE. Connerton and Kenna had met with Father William Kelleher, SJ, President of Boston College, during their trip. Kelleher told them that "the Archbishop did not understand or properly appreciate college administration and policies." Although Connerton seemed to side with the North Easton foundation, he did not want the Boston option precluded: "I have only one suggestion to make, namely, that the archbishop's offer not be rejected because of the freedom he has given us in regard to time in which to make a decision. Even though it is decided to start something at North Easton, I do not feel that the possibilities of Boston should be precluded, especially if there is any thought of establishing an eastern province in the near future." See Connerton to Steiner, November 18, 1946, Provincial Papers–Connerton, AHCFE.

12. James Connerton and Howard Kenna to Thomas Steiner, October 31, 1946, Stonehill History Papers, ASC.

13. John Lane, CSC, to Thomas Steiner, January 8, 1947, Provincial Papers–Steiner, AHCFI; Jerome Lawyer, CSC, "James Connerton," unpublished essay. Lawyer says that Lane also investigated a site near Boston Common for a Community establishment of higher education.

14. Meeting Minutes of Provincial Council, February 14, 1947, AHCFI.

15. Steiner to Cushing, March 6, 1947; Cushing to Steiner, March 8, 1947, Provincial Papers–Steiner, AHCFI.

16. Albert Cousineau to Steiner, July 10, 1947, Superior General Papers, AHCFI.

17. Joseph B. Connors, *Journey Toward Fulfillment: A History of The College of St. Thomas* (St. Paul: The College of St. Thomas Press, 1986): 228. Pages 227–65 cover the period of Holy Cross at the College. After serving St. Thomas for five years, the Community was summarily dismissed in 1933. The details of the story are beyond the scope of this effort, but a basic outline can help us determine the mindset of Steiner. In July 1928 Archbishop Austin Dowling asked Holy Cross "to take over and assume possession, management control, operation and administration" of St.

Thomas, whose prep school had recently lost accreditation and whose four-year college program was in financial and academic trouble. The agreement was for five years, but could become permanent. Holy Cross sent experienced people to the College, including Matthew Schumacher as president and William Cunningham, whom Edward Power has called, "The dean of American Catholic educational philosophers." While Holy Cross entered into the agreement with the idea that it would be a permanent commitment, events would lead to the Community's dismissal. The death of Archbishop Dowling on November 29, 1930 brought John Murray to the see of St. Paul. Murray was pressured by the College's board of consultors to return the institution to diocesan control once Holy Cross' contract expired. Murray needed little outside incentive, however, as he believed in the philosophy of St. Paul's first archbishop, John Ireland, that St. Thomas should never be administered by a religious community. Thus, in June 1933, without justifiable cause, Holy Cross' contract with St. Thomas was not renewed. Under the Congregation the prep school regained accreditation in one year, a major building was constructed, and the prestige of the College grew. The Congregation was removed, not because of some inadequacy in its administration, but because Archbishop Murray and the College's board of consultors wanted responsibility to return to the archdiocese. Holy Cross felt betrayed, abandoned, and cheated.

18. From the 1837 "fundamental pact," which had joined the Brothers of St. Joseph with the auxiliary priests and created the Congregation of Holy Cross, the Community was one society of priests and brothers. In 1945 autonomous provinces of clerics and brothers were created.

19. Philip Armstrong, CSC, *A More Perfect Legacy: A Portrait of Brother Ephrem O'Dwyer, CSC 1888–1978* (Notre Dame: University of Notre Dame Press, 1995): 97.

20. Thomas Duffy to Albert Cousineau, April 26, 1948, Superior General Papers–Cousineau, AHCFE.

21. Philip Kelly, CSC, tape recording, "The Foundations of Stonehill," expresses this idea, as have many others in conversations.

22. Memorandum, February 7, 1948, Mark Kennedy Papers, Archives of the Franciscan Friars, Holy Name Province (hereafter AFFHN), New York, New York. Kennedy wrote, "It came out that this college had been offered to the Holy Cross Fathers, who turned it down for the reason that they are building no other Notre Dames outside South Bend. They intend to concentrate at South Bend."

23. Philip Gleason, "American Catholic Higher Education," in *The Shape of Catholic Higher Education*, Robert Hassenger, ed. (Chicago: University of Chicago Press, 1967): 15. The best history and analysis of American Catholic higher education in the twentieth century is: Philip Gleason, *Contending With Modernity: Catholic Higher Education in the Twentieth Century* (New York: Oxford University Press, 1995).

24. Edward J. Power, *Catholic Higher Education in America: A History* (New York: Appleton-Century Crofts, 1972): 381–472.

25. Ibid., 381, 382, 439.

26. John Pick, "Education and the Postwar World," *America* 72 (February 3, 1945): 347–48.

27. Allan P. Farrell, "National Enrollment Statistics from 1947–48," *America* 78 (December 13, 1947): 285; Farrell, "Enrollment in Catholic Universities and Men's Colleges, 1947–1948," *America* 78 (January 31, 1948): 485–86. Some schools with more dramatic rises in enrollment between 1946 and 1947 were: Boston College, from 4618 to 6430, 28 percent and Regis College in Denver, from 497 to 825, 40 percent.

28. Cyril F. Meyer, "Financing Catholic Higher Education," *America* 78 Supplement (April 3, 1948), xv.

29. James T. Connelly, CSC, "An Eastern Province in 1938," paper delivered at the Conference of the History of the Congregations of Holy Cross (North Easton, Massachusetts: June 17, 1989).

30. Albert Cousineau, CSC, "Circular Letter," January 7, 1945, AHCFE; John Lucey, CSC, interview with the author (August 31, 1995).

31. Steiner to Cousineau, February 16, 1948, Provincial Papers–Steiner; Meeting Minutes of Provincial Council, March 3, 1948, AHCFI; Steiner to Cousineau, March 13, 1948, Provincial Papers–Connerton, AHCFE.

32. Duffy was unaware of the April 21 letter. He wrote to Cousineau, frustrated at the inability of Holy Cross to grow in the East: "We should have a Provincial, or at least a Vice-Provincial, who could live here, or at least close by, and deal directly with our local problems as they arise. . . . We cannot, we will not, advance in the work of Holy Cross, while our Provincial continues to live at Notre Dame. Understand me right—Notre Dame will continue to grow as we all want it to and as it has done in the past; the rest of the community will stagnate, as we have done here for fourteen years." Duffy to Cousineau, April 26, 1948, Superior General Papers–Cousineau, AHCFE.

33. Cousineau to James Connerton, April 22, 1948, Provincial Papers–Connerton, AHCFE.

34. Christopher O'Toole to Connerton, May 21, 1948, Provincial Papers–Connerton, AHCFE. Whether it was planned or coincidence, the announcement and erection of the vice province was accomplished while Thomas Steiner and Howard Kenna were in South America visiting Holy Cross foundations in Chile. Maurus O'Malley, CSC, who says that Steiner and Kenna were never favorable to eastern foundations, calls the South American visit "the most expensive trip they ever took." Conversely, Christopher O'Toole, who was assistant provincial to Steiner, referred to the foundation as "the finest pioneering move since the time of Father Sorin." See Maurus O'Malley, CSC, "The First Permanent Foundations." Bad blood between the Indiana and new Eastern vice province developed nonetheless. In October 1948 O'Toole wrote to Assistant General Louis Kelley with complaints about the Eastern Vice Province's request for economic assistance from the "mother province." "You can imagine what 'good' feeling toward the Vice Province this untimely request has

stirred up in the Provincial Council. That is precisely the objection that those who objected to the Vice Province brought up—namely, that it would mean that the Mother Province would have to lay out a considerable sum of money. It is too bad that the administration of the Vice Province cannot go along modestly and slowly with the resources that are at its command [*sic*] and develop in the way that any other new Province or Vice Province develops in other communities."

35. Albert Cousineau to James Connerton, April 22, 1948, Connerton Papers, AHCFE.

36. "Preliminary Summary on Proposed Brockton, Massachusetts, College," May 3, 1948, AFFHN. Kennedy reported, "It would seem an opportunity to accept the offer of the Archbishop; [*sic*] especially in view of the fact that the Archbishop, once the offer is accepted, would leave it to the Order when to begin operations as long as it were [*sic*] begun within five years."

37. Extant sources differ on the date. One says April 27, another early May. Based on subsequent correspondence, a date prior to April 27, possibly only by a day, is most probable. Both the *Boston Globe* and *Brockton Enterprise* on April 27, 1948, reported, "Prospects for the establishment of a new college in Brockton to be run by the Franciscan fathers were very favorable." This gives further evidence of an April 26 date or before.

38. George Benaglia, CSC, "Recollections of Founding of Stonehill College," Stonehill College Papers, AHCFE; "Preliminary Summary on Proposed Brockton, Massachusetts College," May 3, 1948, AFFHN.

39. Duffy to Cousineau, April 26, 1948, Superior General Papers–Cousineau, AHCFE.

40. Maurus O'Malley, CSC, "First Permanent Foundations of the Holy Cross Fathers and Brothers in the Eastern States," paper delivered at the Conference on the History of the Congregations of Holy Cross (Wilkes-Barre, Pennsylvania: May 26, 1985).

41. Connerton to Cousineau, May 16, 1948, Provincial Papers–Connerton, AHCFE. This letter was backdated at the request of Assistant General Louis Kelley, who wrote to Connerton on May 17 asking him to "confirm our conversation and state your reasons." Kelley to Connerton, May 17, 1948, Stonehill College Papers, AHCFE.

42. Connerton to John Lane, CSC, May 19, 1948, Founding File, ASC.

43. Connerton to Christopher O'Toole, CSC, May 18, 1948, Provincial Papers––Connerton, AHCFE.

44. Philip Kelly, CSC, "Foundations of Stonehill College," audio tape (January 3, 1994).

45. Richard Cushing to Connerton, May 21, 1948, Stonehill College Papers, AHCFE. Cushing at the same time wrote to John Delaunay, CSC, at the University of Portland, "In view of the plans of your community, I will tell the Franciscans that there is no room for two colleges in that area." See Delaunay to Connerton, May 21, 1948, Stonehill History Papers, ASC.

46. Cushing to Mark Kennedy, OFM, May 29, 1948, AFFHN.

47. James Cassidy to Connerton, May 24, 1948, Stonehill College Papers, AHCFE; Cassidy to Joseph Duggan, May 29, 1948, Stonehill History Papers, ASC.

48. George Benaglia, "Recollections of Founding of Stonehill College," n.d., Stonehill College Papers, AHCFE.

49. John Lucey, CSC, to David Arthur, CSC, October 4, 1970, Stonehill History Papers, ASC. Father Philip Kelly, CSC, claims that the Stonehill Charter was obtained from Regis College through the assistance of Frank Morrisey (who became a judge) and Fred Sullivan, Deputy Commissioner of Education of Massachusetts. Kelly's account, however, cannot be corroborated.

50. Benaglia, "Recollections of Founding of Stonehill College," n.d., Stonehill College Papers, AHCFE.

51. It should be noted that when the college opened, Moran was the dean and Woodward the registrar.

52. "Ordinances of the Foundation of Our Lady of Holy Cross, Incorporated Relating to the Governance of Stonehill College," n.d., Stonehill College Papers, AHCFE.

53. Cushing to Joseph Duggan, June 3, 1948, Stonehill History Papers, ASC.

54. Connerton to Benaglia, May 29, 1948, Stonehill History Papers, ASC; Connerton to Duffy, May 29, 1948, Provincial Papers–Connerton; Vice Provincial Council Meeting Minutes, June 21, 1948, AHCFE.

55. Certificate of Change of Purpose, June 30, 1948, Stonehill History Papers, ASC.

56. George Benaglia, "Recollections of Founding of Stonehill College," n.d. Stonehill College Papers, AHCFE.

57. Extant records do not exist as to the number of applicants, but those present at North Easton in the summer of 1948 claim that close to 50 percent of those who applied were accepted. It should be noted, however, that this lack of selectivity in no way indicates poor quality of students. Many early graduates distinguished themselves in public and private sector careers.

58. George Benaglia, "Recollections of Founding of Stonehill College," n.d. Stonehill College Papers, AHCFE; Owen Carroll to author, September 9, 1995, Stonehill History Project Papers, ASC.

59. Bulletin of Stonehill College, 1948–1949, ASC.

60. The Eastern Vice Province had few economic resources, and the Indiana Province believed that the financial status of the eastern foundation was not their problem. This became more clear in the fall, when Connerton requested $150,000 from the Indiana Province. Assistant Provincial Christopher O'Toole responded, "Of Course this is out of the question. First of all we haven't got it and secondly, the entire picture has changed since the chapter. Now the Vice Province is on its own." Christopher O'Toole to Louis Kelley, October 1, 1948, Provincial Papers–Steiner, AHCFI.

61. George Benaglia, "Recollections of Founding of Stonehill College," n.d.,

Stonehill College Papers, AHCFE; Meyer, "Financing Catholic Higher Education," xvi. Meyer concluded, "To survive they [Catholic colleges run by religious orders] will need a well organized appeal launched on a diocese-wide basis, backed by diocesan officials." In February 1946 a collection was taken in the Diocese of Syracuse for support of Jesuit-operated LeMoyne College and in 1950 St. John Fisher in Rochester, administered by the Basilians, was the benefactor of $1 million raised in a diocesan development drive.

62. Duffy to Connerton, May 23, 1948; Connerton to Duffy, May 26, 1948, Provincial Papers–Connerton, AHCFE.

63. Josephus Schaub, interview with author (November 9, 1995), Stonehill History Project Papers, ASC. Later, when it became obvious that Benaglia could not adequately supervise the College's physical plant, Connerton appointed Brother Josephus as head of buildings and grounds at the College.

64. Connerton told Steiner, in an apparent effort to conceal what an adequate facility would cost, that a temporary building to meet the need for science labs was all that was envisioned. See Connerton to Steiner, June 4, 1948, Provincial Papers–Steiner, AHCFI.

65. Mullen had a successful contracting business in Boston in the 1920s, when effects of the Depression destroyed him financially. Suffering from alcoholism, he moved to North Easton and there met George Benaglia, who introduced him to Alcoholics Anonymous. Benaglia wanted Mullen to have the classroom building job to restore his confidence and return him to productive work. James Mullen, interview with the author (August 11, 1995), Stonehill History Project, ASC.

66. E.G. Roddy, Jr., *Merrimack College: Genesis and Growth, 1947–1972* (North Andover, Massachusetts: Merrimack College Press, 1972): 9–11, 14, 17–18, 24.

67. Charles F. Duffy, SJ, *Chronicles of Fairfield University 1942–1992, Book One: The Founding Years* (Fairfield, Connecticut: Fairfield University Press, 1992): 3–6, 13.

68. Israel Goldstein, *Brandeis University: Chapter of Its Founding* (New York: Block Publishing Company, 1951): 16, 21–27, 37–38, 79, 97–107.

69. Figures differ in extant sources as to the precise number who started classes in September 1948. The 134 figure comes from the records of the director of institutional research at Stonehill College and is the most accurate and official. The "Chronicles of Our Lady of Holy Cross" states that 140 entered that fall.

70. Bulletin of Stonehill College, 1948–1949, ASC.

71. George Benaglia, "Middleboro Speech Notes," n.d., Benaglia Papers, ASC.

72. Countering Catholic higher education's prevailing trend against *in loco parentis*, Benaglia strongly maintained his traditional view.

73. Faculty Survey, Benaglia Papers; Bulletin of Stonehill College, 1948–1949, ASC. As one comparison for tuition rates, Merrimack, when it opened in 1947 with 165 students, charged $300 per academic year.

74. "Chronicles of Our Lady of Holy Cross" (October 12, 1948), ASC.

75. "Dedication of College," n.d., clipping, Benaglia Papers, ASC.

76. James Mullen, interview with author, August 11, 1995; Joseph Schaub, interview with author, November 11, 1995, Stonehill History Project Papers, ASC. I-beams for the building were manufactured by Brayton, Wilson, and Cale.

77. Benaglia to John Lane, September 23, 1948, Stonehill History Papers, ASC.

78. The original $25,000 authorization was doubled in the summer by the General Council in New York.

79. Lane to Benaglia, September 30, 1948 and October 14, 1948, Stonehill History Papers, ASC; Benaglia to Lane, October 18, 1948, Stonehill College Papers, AHCFE.

80. James Connerton to Thomas Steiner, May 3, 1946, King's College Papers, AHCFE. Hafey gave King's $250,000 in 1946 to purchase buildings and get a college established. Another $250,000 was promised for 1947. See also Donald J. Grimes, CSC, "Vision and Fulfillment: Bishop William J. Hafey, the Congregation of Holy Cross, and the Founding of King's College, 1943–1946," paper presented at the Fifteenth Annual Conference on the History of the Congregations of Holy Cross, King's College (Wilkes-Barre, Pennsylvania: June 15, 1996).

81. Lane to Benaglia, November 15, 1948, Stonehill History Papers, ASC.

82. The exact number of veterans is not known; extant records do not indicate veteran status. Conversations with those who started in 1948 indicate that a significant number (possibly as much as 33 percent) of the students were veterans. Nationwide 4.3 million of the 12 million World War II veterans applied for GI bill benefits. The percentage of veterans in some colleges was striking. Some examples for the 1947–48 academic year were: Boston College, 55 percent, College of the Holy Cross, 51 percent, Merrimack, 60 percent, and King's College, 84 percent. See Farrell, "Enrollment in Catholic Universities," 486.

83. Benaglia to John Desmond, August 13, 1948, August 20, 1948, Benaglia Papers, ASC.

84. Public law 889 authorized the military services to donate obsolete equipment, books, and other materials to colleges and universities. Father Philip Kelly was designated a purchasing agent for military surplus materials for Stonehill.

85. Connerton to Benaglia, October 20, 1948, Benaglia Papers, ASC.

86. Benaglia to Lane, November 27, 1948, Benaglia, ASC.

87. Connerton to Benaglia, May 19, 1949, Stonehill College Papers, AHCFE; Lane to Benaglia, June 10, 1949, Benaglia Papers, ASC.

88. Stonehill College Financial Report, 1948–1949, Stonehill College Papers, AHCFE.

89. Thomas Campbell, CSC, interview with the author, September 15, 1995; Joseph Schaub, interview with the author, November 9, 1995, Stonehill History Project Papers, ASC. Benaglia economized whenever and wherever possible; nothing not required was considered.

90. Stonehill College Financial Records, AHCFE. Chapter 2 fully describes the amortization of the Stonehill debt to King's College. The operational profit between

July 1, 1950, and June 30, 1953, was $91,520.80. See also, Richard Gribble, CSC, "The Infamous Debt: Stonehill College, 1948–1954," paper presented at the Conference on the History of the Congregations of Holy Cross (Wilkes-Barre, Pennsylvania: June 15, 1996).

91. Connerton was founding president of King's in 1946 and held the office until 1949. Brothers and priests in the Eastern Vice Province felt it was impossible for him to continue as president and attend to the affairs of the entire Community as vice provincial. He was replaced by John Lane, CSC.

92. George Benaglia, "Recollections on Founding of Stonehill College," n.d., AHCFE; Connerton to Benaglia, May 2, 1949, Benaglia Papers, ASC.

CHAPTER 2

A Question of Survival

Battered and bruised as a result of the battles fought in its first year, Stonehill College nevertheless survived its initial test and began to set its course for future development. Hopes had been high that the College would soon be recognized as an institution of learning and scholarship, but many years, several presidents, and much hard work and pain would be required before this dream would be considered even a possibility. The College's huge financial debt and gloomy prospects for development complicated its forward progress and created obstacles that only those with great vision and faith in the institution and its people considered surmountable.

Stonehill was, at the time of its founding, a small player in the large and complicated game of Catholic higher education then in transition in postwar America. Educational methods adapted in ways consistent with four basic principles of the American ideal. First, democratization was emphasized in the relationship between educational institutions and the clientele they served. Second, a reigning spirit of voluntarism led to the initiation of many new endeavors in education. Several new Catholic colleges were founded to provide for veterans and others who sought higher education in the postwar period. Next, the Catholic ghetto collapsed as the process of assimilation in education gained energy. Catholics held their own educational position, but they did not want to separate widely from larger society. Lastly, secularity or religious neutrality in the administration and academic aspects of Catholic colleges became more pronounced. This shift in emphasis, foreshadowing a new direction in the history of Catholic higher education, did not, however, change the primary institutional objective, which was to be "a synthesis, both in educational theory and in practice, between knowledge and sanctity."[1] The formation of Christian character continued to hold its place as the purpose of Catholic education.

The transition that Catholic colleges experienced in the 1950s, drawing them away from certain traditional aspects of ecclesiastical control, did not change the fact that most schools continued firmly in the grasp of clerics. Philip Gleason described the phenomenon in this way: "Throughout American Catholic history, the accepted view was that if an activity was religious, a priest, or at least a religious, should be in charge of it; and education was viewed as such an activity."[2] Thus, while Catholic colleges and universities made strides toward a new more American-oriented concept of educational instruction, rooted in democracy, freedom, and religious neutrality, these institutions doggedly held to certain traditional practices. Catholic identity was maintained through the development of Christian character, education for the spirit and the intellect, and the physical presence of recognized Church authority (priests and religious) on campus. Roy Deferrari of The Catholic University of America warned Catholics to maintain their identity, echoing an earlier Catholic separatist belief: "If a group of Catholics . . . finds itself in surroundings definitely inimical to Catholic faith and morals and utterly unsympathetic with the opinions of the minority, it must necessarily withdraw."[3]

A New President and a Different Course

❧   IN THE SPRING of 1949, James Connerton and his councilors discussed the future direction of the College and the possibility of a new administration. Canon law stipulated that one could hold the office of superior for only six years, a provision which, because George Benaglia had been appointed in 1943, necessitated a change. The Vice Provincial Council debated whether "an indult to effect this [Benaglia's] continuance of office" or a new person as president was best for Stonehill.[4] Adherence to canon law gave Connerton and those who wanted a new direction for the College a convenient excuse to seek a new president. Brother Harold Rogan, CSC, who served as the College treasurer, and Father John Lucey, CSC, who arrived at the College in the summer of 1949, believe that Benaglia was replaced as president because of the precarious financial situation of the College.[5]

Connerton had certainly made his decision to replace Bengalia as early as March 1949, for he began at that time to speak with Father Francis Boland, a professor of political science at Notre Dame, about the position of president at Stonehill. Earlier that month Boland had opted to join the Eastern Vice Province, a decision which delighted Connerton and prompted him to travel to Indiana to consult with the Notre Dame professor. Boland had earlier written, "North Easton is, of course, my hope for the future and I feel that I can do some good work there in whatever way you [Connerton] suggest."[6] On March 17 the two men discussed the Stonehill presidency and Boland assented to the assignment.[7]

Francis Boland was a well-known and highly traveled academician. A native of Everett, Massachusetts, he had taught at Notre Dame from 1924 to 1930, served as vice president at St. Edward's in Austin, Texas, from 1930 to 1934, and returned to South Bend as prefect of discipline and organizer and chair of the political science department. He served as dean of the College of Arts and Letters there from 1940 to 1943. From 1943 to 1947 he served as a Navy chaplain and was present at the battles of Iwo Jima and Okinawa near the end of the Pacific campaign. Boland was known also as the coauthor of *Catholic Principles of Politics* (originally published as *The State and the Church*), with Reverend John A. Ryan, the Catholic social reformer and longtime head of the social action department of the National Catholic Welfare Conference (NCWC).

The deal to bring Boland to Stonehill, negotiated by Connerton and Boland and apparently satisfactory to them, was not immediately communicated to Thomas Steiner, Provincial of the Indiana Province, who assumed that Boland would continue "to teach and prefect at [the] University of Notre Dame." Connerton's request that Boland report to Stonehill as soon as possible irritated Steiner greatly, since Boland had been assigned summer school classes and thus a replacement would have to be secured "at some expense" to the university. Steiner complained to the General Council, "We would never think of ordering one of our own men out of the Vice Province without getting a release from the Vice Provincial, but this does not seem to be the method employed by the Vice Province."[8]

Boland's arrival at Stonehill was greeted with optimism, despite the dismal reality of the situation. Connerton painted a rosy portrait, speaking of Stonehill's first year as "a wonderful, promising experience," and he portrayed the future as "a sure-fire undertaking." He also praised Boland: "Everyone feels that we have given to Stonehill a leadership that is bound to put the new college on the map and keep it there."[9]

The new president also expressed optimism, qualified by his realization that the College's financial situation was critical. Boland congratulated Benaglia, who now served as the College vice president, for "an especially good job in getting things organized and underway," but at the same moment told Connerton that the vice provincial's suggestion that the College borrow an additional $30,000 was too conservative. Rather, he said, $50,000 would

Rev. Francis Boland, CSC, president 1949–1955.

be necessary "to meet our obligations and to provide for the expense necessary for our operation on a minimum standard of efficiency." He concluded:[10]

> While things look rather dismal at the moment, still I am sufficiently optimistic to feel that if we can get things organized a little better this year, then we will be in a position to establish a budget and know where we are going. Of course, each year with an increase in students we will require a further outlay for operation. But I am hopeful that with the help of the Lord we will make steady progress.

On September 18 Boland greeted 231 students (including seminarians) as classes began for Stonehill's second year. In his opening address to the students, he spoke of faith as "the distinguishing mark of the Catholic college" and, along the lines of the prevailing ideology of Catholic higher education, professed the belief that Stonehill's mission "is to teach the doctrine of Christ as applicable in the various fields of knowledge and to prepare students for the full and complete way of Christian life."[11]

From the outset Francis Boland exercised a military style of leadership as the tone of his presidency. He immediately centralized the administrative functions of the College under his personal control, a move that appeared consistent with his personality and method of operation. Those who served in the administration as dean and vice president considered their duties "insignificant" and their positions "honorary." Boland made all decisions pertinent to the College's use of money as well as faculty hirings, dismissals, and assignments. This autocratic style was recognized by one contemporary as necessary for the situation: "Everything had to come under one man and we were lucky we had a man who was able to handle things."[12] On a counter note, the impression Boland made on the College community earned him the nickname "The Commander," in reference to his days as a Navy chaplain. One early Stonehill student reflected, "He [Boland] was uptight most of the time and was very job oriented. . . . He was very much a loner and as a result he became the enemy of the faculty and the student body."[13]

Boland's relationship with members of the Congregation was difficult and, many times, adversarial. In his role as religious superior of the Foundation of Our Lady of Holy Cross, he dictated all local community obediences and published the community's daily routine. Many members of the community found him to be "unapproachable," "sour" on young priests, and overbearing in the extreme. Some also believed Boland possessed a paranoid complex. His temper was legendary and episodes of his explosive personality were numerous.[14] Yet, despite these alleged flaws, he was respected by most members of the Community, who realized after reflection that "he did what he had to do." The autocratic style of leadership, coupled with an introverted and suspicion-filled personality, not only colored his relationship with the Holy Cross Community but characterized his whole administration as president.[15]

The internal conflicts at Stonehill did not, however, dampen recognition of Boland's performance by others. Connerton, in his fall 1949 provincial visit, expressed joy and confidence, reporting that Boland "has met the problem of disorganization squarely and already has the situation well in hand."[16] The community outside Stonehill recognized him as a leader in education, and in July 1950 he was appointed by Paul Dever, Governor of Massachusetts, as a member of the Board of Collegiate Authority. This honor was sustained with his reappointment to the board four years later by Governor Christian A. Herter. Further recognition of Boland's leadership came when Stonehill was admitted as an associate member of the National Catholic Education Association (NCEA) in the summer of 1950.[17]

Nevertheless, Boland's initial optimism about Stonehill soon faded and his relationship with James Connerton quickly began to deteriorate. Boland could not share the youthful enthusiasm of the students, predicting that nothing "sensational will happen [here] within the next few years."[18] His first encounter with frustration occurred when he asked permission of the vice provincial for funds to repair college facilities; repeated requests led to a bitter conflict between the two men. Canon law and the statutes of the

Rev. John Lucey, CSC, academic dean 1950–1954.

Congregation dictated this procedure, but the process as a whole created a negative attitude in Boland's mind.[19] More frustrating to Boland was Connerton's often-used policy of attaching conditions to his approval of projects—for example, that the College make some effort to pay its huge debt to King's College, which in November 1949 stood at just over $200,000. Boland perceived this as economic blackmail that held hostage the advancement of the College. Connerton, in an effort to ameliorate Boland's frustration, wrote to the president expressing "sincere congratulations upon the splendid work which you are accomplishing."[20] Boland, who sought greater independence and authority, was sadly disappointed.[21]

Stonehill's limited expansion and development in its first year under the rein of Francis Boland still allowed the addition of 10 new faculty members to meet the needs of a student enrollment that nearly doubled. Besides Boland, the Congregation's members increased by three: Leo Flood, who acted as vice president, Thomas Lane, and Joseph Wiseman. When Flood was reassigned after only a few months, his work was continued by the appointment of Benaglia to the vice presidency. At this early date, dedicated lay faculty members continued to join Holy Cross in its mission of higher education. Brassil Fitzgerald, in English, Gilman H. Campbell in education, and

C. James Cleary in history came to Stonehill in its infant second year.[22] Fitzgerald's lectures were legendary. Students often commented that if you sneezed, you missed a century in Cleary's rapid-fire history presentations, which were always conducted without the aid of notes. The faculty's voice in the administration of the College was barely audible; teachers met once at the outset and again at the close of each year. Clerical and lay faculty were close; lay professors often spoke with the religious faculty about their lives and problems. Stonehill in some respects promoted a family atmosphere in which the faculty took responsibility for the work of the College, sharing both its successes and its failures.[23]

Professors' lives were not easy, as teaching requirements were heavy. Most taught four or five classes, often four different courses, with class lists of 40 to 50 students each. Most professors taught 18 hours per week. The religious faculty found their lot even more difficult. Many religious were pulled from doctoral programs to fill gaps in teaching assignments. Many felt completely inadequate teaching subjects about which they knew little.[24] Besides this, religious worked in local parishes on weekends, a duty that took significant time away from class preparation and other aspects of their teaching ministry. These problems of overdemanding schedules and inadequate academic preparation were not, of course, exclusive to Stonehill, but were found in many Catholic colleges and universities as enrollments soared and facilities expanded.[25]

Academic programs at Stonehill allowed students to pursue baccalaureates: A.B., B.S., and B.S. in Business Administration. Majors in economics, education, English, history, philosophy, biology, chemistry, mathematics, and business administration were offered. Father James Moran, dean of the college, had recommended in April 1949 an accounting program along the lines of the business major program at Notre Dame. The proposal was shelved at the time, but it was resurrected in the fall when the problem of staffing was solved by seeking qualified business accounting specialists in the North Easton area to teach on an adjunct basis.[26] In the spring of 1950, after obtaining the permission of Connerton and Bishop Cassidy, Boland decided to initiate a coeducational summer school program. The president did not expect great success at the outset, but he felt that an experienced and well-qualified faculty would ensure good prospects for a sizeable summer school program in the future.[27]

The troubled financial status of Stonehill College dominated Boland's activity and continued to color his relationship with the vice provincial. From the outset, Boland was aware of the institution's financial troubles and Connerton's dissatisfaction with the College's financial records. He was also informed that repayment of the debt was a high priority. Connerton optimis-

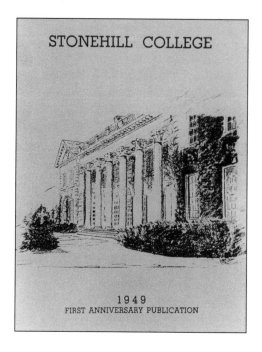

Stonehill College first anniversary publication, 1949.

tically projected that "within a couple of years" Stonehill would generate funds to maintain itself and return $10,000 to King's.[28] The reality of the situation, however, was that the College possessed no viable means to generate revenue other than tuition payments and a small farm at the south end of the property where chickens and steers were raised.[29]

The downward spiral of the financial condition was not easily stopped. In the fall of 1949 Boland was forced to borrow $45,000 more from the Vice Province (actually King's) at the old rate of 2 percent per annum. Boland hoped that this sum would allow the College to clear all local debts and free it to operate on a sound and unencumbered basis.[30]

The call in February 1950 for Stonehill to make a $3800 interest payment on the loan from King's ignited Boland's short-fuse temper. He not only questioned the accuracy of the amount, stating that it was actually $2058.45, but actually took the offensive in the dispute, claiming that the Vice Province owed Stonehill $15,000 for maintenance of the seminary. He countered the request for payment by suggesting that the Vice Province pay King's the interest on the loan and credit the balance of the $15,000 on the principal.[31] Boland went further and boldly asked the Vice Province to assume responsibility for the debt so that the College could provide for necessary and normal expansion.[32] The vice provincial steward, John Lane, responded by citing errors in the College's December 1949 financial statement and challenging its accuracy with regard to the listed property assets of the College. The whole affair led Boland to call for a complete review of the financial relationship between the Vice Province and The Foundation of Our Lady of Holy Cross.[33]

Embers of the fire created in the call for payment of interest were still smoldering when the Vice Provincial Council called for a $10,000 principal payment on the debt.[34] Boland again sprang to the defense of the College, hinting at his resignation:[35]

> For us to pay $10,000 at the present time, in view of the essential repairs that are imperative to the buildings, would leave us in a financial position practically the same as last summer. I would not care to accept responsibility for administering the affairs of the institution under those conditions.

Citing a recent audit indicating that the average annual operating deficit for Our Lady of Holy Cross Seminary was almost $12,500, Boland pressed his earlier suggestion that the Vice Province pay Stonehill, but now demanded $24,000 as payment for two years' support of the seminary. If this could not be done, then he asked for a reprieve on payment until the fall tuition was received.[36] Boland's demands did not hide the fact that Stonehill managed an operational profit its second year of $26,591.33.[37]

The Journey Toward Commencement

DESPITE HIS PREOCCUPATION with finances, Boland still had to administer all aspects of a College and supervise a religious community. Because he was never able successfully to separate these two responsibilities, the policy of micromanagement he applied as a college administrator carried over to his role as religious superior, leading to the alienation of many members of the Community. Boland was scrupulous to a fault, a quality that, as has been noted, was helpful to a college struggling to survive financially but devastating in relationships with fellow religious.

A liberal arts curriculum was established by Boland as he expanded and strengthened the College's academic offerings. Well-planned programs were developed to give genuinely deep knowledge in one field, with more limited experience in a number of related fields. Such programs were intended as additions to what Roy Deferrari of The Catholic University of America would later term "the sacred three disciplines" of liberal arts education— theology, philosophy, and history.[38] Boland added programs in general science, modern languages, accounting, and general business to the majors options. All degree programs required 48 courses, including 8 in theology,[39] 6 in philosophy, 10 in social science, and 2 in math or science; only 3 elective courses were allowed.

The year 1951 was a landmark for Stonehill's academic programs. Adult education, a new program of instruction that came to maturity in the postwar era and was popular throughout the country, was started on February 12. Stonehill, following the lead of Merrimack,[40] organized its program at night offering noncredit classes "to stimulate cultural interests and to afford an opportunity to adults . . . for greater intellectual advancement."[41] The program, coeducational from the beginning,[42] was highly successful, with 352 enrolled in spring courses of seven or fifteen weeks in duration. Professors from the day college, including Brassil Fitzgerald, Gilman Campbell, and C. James Cleary, taught such courses as "Selected Plays of Shakespeare," "Problems of High School Administration," and "Studies in American Constitutional History." Boland was confident that the initial success of the program reflected its future potential for sustenance and growth.[43]

A second important development in 1951 was the establishment of St. Pius X Seminary. In January 1951 the Vice Provincial Council outlined a plan to educate seminarians on the college level. Traditionally, lay seminarians received two years of school at Stonehill, were sent to the novitiate at North Dartmouth, then completed their undergraduate education at Notre Dame. The opportunity now existed, however, for seminarians to complete their education at Stonehill, since freshmen through seniors were now on campus. The Council thus agreed in April to petition the Superior General to spend $30,000 to renovate the old cow barn on the Ames estate for use as a seminary. To convince the General of its determination, the Council's petition said that no money would be borrowed; it would be taken from bank holdings, raised in development, and saved through the use of seminarian labor in the renovation.[44]

Permission was received to proceed, and Father Denis Sughrue was placed in charge of the building program. Approximately $25,000 was spent on materials for the renovation. The seminarians did the majority of the rough work, including roofing, painting, cement mixing, and electrical wiring. On August 27, 1951, the facility, dedicated to St. Pius X, who was canonized that same summer, opened with 15 newly professed Holy Cross seminarians in residence, along with Father Richard Sullivan as superior (and professor of philosophy at the College), Sughrue as confessor pro-tem, and Brother Herman Zaccarelli as the Community cook.[45]

The fall of 1951 was memorable for the arrival of women on campus in the day school. Of the 293 students who started classes in September,

ATTEND MAY DEVOTIONS
HELD DAILY AT ONE

ON PAGE TWO, READ
'TO SUMMIT UP'

Vol II   STONEHILL COLLEGE, NORTH EASTON, MASS, FRIDAY, MAY 4, 1951   No. 7

NFCCS AWARDS NEW RADIO COMMISSION TO STONEHILL

McCORMACK EMCEES FIFTH ANNUAL CONGRESS

On April 13, 14 and 15, the Fifth Regional Congress of the NFCCS was held in Boston. Highlight of the affair for the Stonehill delegation was the unanimous awarding of the newly created Radio Commission to Stonehill College. The voting took place at a Saturday night executive session, which lasted well into the early hours of Sunday morning. The Stonehill delegation had petitioned for a Radio Commission in New England and the establishment of its chair at this campus.

Evidence of the success of the Congress is seen in the attendance figure of over 2000 Newman Club and NFCCS members. The opening meeting on Friday was emceed by Dick McCormack of Stonehill who

Newman Key Awarded Here

At the recent combined Newman Club-NFCCS Congress in Boston, a Stonehill Associate Professor was presented an award by Archbishop Richard J. Cushing. Mr. Frank W. Kerwin, of the Stonehill Business Department was presented the Newman Club Gold Honor Key and a Certificate of Merit for "... furthering the work of the Newman Club Federation, thus bringing greater honor to the name of our patron, John Henry Cardinal Newman and . . . participating in the Apostolic work of the Catholic Church."

The award recognized the achievements of more than twenty years of active and alumni service to the Newman Club Federation. Beginning in his undergraduate days at Boston University, Mr.

"VIDEO VARIETIES" RECEIVES PLAUDITS

by Paul Doody

The Speech Arts Club of Stonehill College under the moderation of Rev. Henry E. Malone, C.S.C. presented Video Varities, a compilation of several variety acts, on April 20, 21. The regular members of the club were assisted by talent from the Stonehill night classes and by outside local talent. The show was directed by Jay Doyle, lights were by Al Petruccelli and stage was by John Simas, Henry Perra and Joe Moran. Guiding the show through its entirety was the experienced hand of Dick McCormack, singing star of station WPEP in Taunton, who rendered a few songs in addition to acting as M. C.

"Songs My Mother Used to Sing" were presented by Bill Burke of Bridgewater, a members of the night classes, A "Quartet" composed of Bob McGinniss, Jay Doyle, Phil Ward and Terry Byrne rendered their arrangements of "Old Favorites". Don Senna and Bob Maura presented "Two Sophomores

Announcement of Coeducational Program Inaugurates New Era

Draft Quiz on May 26th

Colonel Chester A. Furbish, Director of Selective Service for Massachusetts, said today that application blanks for the ETS tests to be given college students in May and June are available at Local Boards. The test scores, OR scholastic standing in college or university, will be used by local boards in determining the eligibility of registrants to be considered for occupational deferment as students.

Colonel Furbish said that State Headquarters and local board offices were already being deluged with inquiries and that an information bulletin soon to be issued would leave unanswered no questions a registrant contemplating taking the test might ask. He suggested that until the information bulletin is issued specific queries

TEACHER TRAINING ALSO CONTEMPLATED

On Saint Patrick's Day, March 17, 1951, Father Francis Boland, C.S.C., President of Stonehill, released to the press a momentous decision that will rank high in the history of the college.

The decision made after considerable deliberation is, "to open the college to women students to provide an opportunity to all Catholic boys and girls, and to students of other denominations, in this area, to receive a Catholic education". From the inquiries that have come to the college concerning the program, it is hoped that a sizeable number will enroll in September. Father Boland answered many questions when he said that "transfer students will be accepted up to the junior year."

Stonehill goes coed in the fall of 1951.

nineteen were women. The presence of coeds at Stonehill was directed not by a spirit of justice but by world events, when the reality of need and survival triumphed over the staid traditionalism of all-male Catholic colleges.

The United States' entry into the Korean conflict in the summer of 1950 and the consequent increase in draft calls created a situation in which America's colleges would, as in World War II, again strain to compete for lower numbers of available male students. At this time, however, the situation for some colleges and universities was desperate, for they had only recently expanded their facilities to meet the increased student need of the immediate post-World War II years. Stonehill had not expanded its facilities, but its tuition-dependent, precarious finances could not sustain a significant drop in enrollment. Thus, out of practical necessity, the Vice Provincial Council, at the suggestion of Boland, began to discuss the possibility of coeducation at Stonehill. The council agreed that coeducation "may be necessary for survival," but made no decision until it could consult with the Superior General and his council.[46]

The Stonehill College Council, predicting "a great curtailment of enrollment of college students next September because of the Draft and possible military training," requested that the vice provincial seek approval for the admission of women to the College. Connerton thus wrote to the Superior General, Christopher O'Toole, about the possibility of coeducation. Not convinced of the need himself, Connerton suggested that seminarians attend Stonehill instead of Notre Dame in order to maintain sufficient numbers of male students at the College.[47] O'Toole, a traditionalist in the promotion of all-male educational institutions, agreed with Connerton's plan to educate seminarians "until the draftees have completed their service in the Army or Navy and are able to take up once again their education." The General argued that Stonehill's facilities did not lend themselves well to coeducation and that if women were admitted, the practice would have to be continued for several years. The ever-present financial issue at the College was also invoked as a deterrent to coeducation. The General suggested that "regular payment on the debt to King's College could be postponed, as long as the interest were kept up, until you are again in a position to begin reducing the debt."[48]

O'Toole's February 1951 rejection of the coeducation plan did not stop Boland from continuing his campaign for the proposal. Using an economic argument that attracted the attention of the ever money-conscious vice provincial, Boland prevailed upon Connerton to revisit the issue with the General Council. Additional data, including projections for college student enrollments, was presented to support the request. A recent meeting of the presidents of Catholic colleges and universities in Chicago had produced the consensus that small colleges would be obliged to go coeducational in order to survive the critical years in the immediate future. Boland informed the General that no Catholic college for women existed in Massachusetts south of Boston and that many women had made inquiries at Stonehill. Both Archbishop Cushing and Bishop Cassidy approved of the idea. Lastly, Boland allayed fears by promising that all reasonable safeguards would be made to keep women and seminarians apart.[49]

Boland's plea, voiced by Connerton to the General, produced the desired result. On March 7 approval was given for the coeducation plan at Stonehill. Writing about the success of Stonehill's coed adult education program, O'Toole sounds as if he is trying to convince himself in his letter that his decision is reasonable. After tenaciously holding to his traditional philosophy of education, O'Toole bows to reality and a more logical approach to the situation: "It may be that, aside from the intrinsic value of the education itself for women, coeducation at Stonehill is the solution for your present problems in getting off to a good start, academically and financially. The General's approval came with the cautions that an atmosphere supportive of religious life be maintained and that seminarians were to take classes alone or with other males.[50] Approval from the General gave Boland the permission he needed to proceed. He quickly sought and received approbation from Bishop Cassidy for the venture, and on March 18 he announced publicly that Stonehill would go coeducational in the fall.[51]

There was general optimism at Stonehill that the coeducation plan would be beneficial to the College and its students. Aside from Merrimack, which had admitted women in 1950, Catholic colleges were not generally convinced of the wisdom of such a move. By 1955 only 15 founded as all-male institutions had admitted women on an equal basis. Coeducation was instituted at the College of the Holy Cross in Worcester and Boston College only in 1969 and 1970, respectively.[52] Boland believed that the presence of women "may prove to be helpful in [the] future development of the college." When 19 women (17 freshmen, 1 sophomore, and 1 junior) arrived on campus in the fall, they "were accepted . . . by the male students."[53]

The events of 1951, which generated a program of adult education, a new seminary, and coeducation, stood as moments of reprieve from the storms of financial peril that continued to encircle the College. Although it is clear from personal interviews and a review of extant records that Francis Boland, through his obstinate, temperamental, and over-bearing personality, did not endear himself to many (especially his fellow Holy Cross religious), he was always a staunch defender of Stonehill College. He perceived the institution to be in his charge and requiring his vigilance and protection.

The College's public achievement did not dampen, however, the feud between Connerton and Boland. A disagreement over the division of property and money between the Vice Province and Stonehill became a raging battle, with Boland and Connerton matched in a private and public duel. One contemporary saw their feud as the result of an "inability to communicate" coupled with an "inflexibility of opinion" needed to achieve agreement.[54] Furthermore, the issue of the repayment of the debt owed to King's was complicated by disagreements over cash support for seminarians and ownership of properties on the Stonehill campus.[55]

Resuming an earlier discussion, James Sheehan, the new vice provincial steward, informed Boland that the Council stood ready to credit Stonehill $24,000 for two years of support for the seminary, with the amount being charged "against your ownership of the property." The president fired back in an angry tone that he had previously been told that the College owned no property save the classroom building constructed after Stonehill opened its doors.[56] The exchange became so heated that Connerton was forced to step in and referee the disagreement. He rebuked Boland: "I am sorry to be obliged to say that your reply to Father Sheehan's kind letter to you on October 3, in fulfillment of his duty and at the request of his higher superior, is not acceptable either as to tone or content."[57] Connerton pursued the issue further and, after a review of Stonehill's latest financial statement, where "interest on loans," "services of religious," and "interest to the Vice Province," amounting to a total of $11,000, were listed as "operating expenses," wrote to Boland: "I herewith instruct you to write out a check payable to the Vice Province of Our Lady of Holy Cross in the exact amount litsed [sic] on your statement [$11,000] for the items mentioned above and send it to Father Sheehan, the Vice Provincial Steward at Wilkes-Barre at once."[58]

Boland wrote back that if Stonehill made the suggested payments, on the basis of projected income and expenses the College would have a January 1951 balance of only $337.74. He concluded, "If it is still your wish that the above amount be forwarded, your instructions will be carried out immediately."[59] In a familiar move of amelioration, the vice provincial softened his approach: "May I take the occasion to compliment you on your expert conduct of the college and to assure you that my eagerness to obtain as soon as possible a payment on the loan from us, stems from our desire to take care of our own financial obligations."[60] No payment was made at this time.

Connerton continued to seek payment in a forceful manner, while rendering Boland sufficient "backhand" support to win the president to his side. During his spring 1951 official provincial visit to the religious community at Stonehill,[61] Connerton heard many criticisms leveled against Boland. The vice provincial, in turn, informed the president, who accepted the news in a favorable manner. Connerton concluded, "In his understanding of the college world and his business administration of his college, Father Boland seems to me to be an expert in a tough position."[62]

Connerton's words of encouragement were apparently not enough for Boland, who was weary of battling uphill in what he perceived as a war that would produce no victors. Thus, in September 1951, "after mature and very serious deliberation," he tendered his resignation as president "in the interests of all concerned and for personal reasons." Connerton simply answered, "I cannot accept your resignation." In a repeat of the earlier-established pattern, Boland was praised, this time by the Superior General: "You are doing a great job at Stonehill, and the work is bound to succeed."[63]

The heated and seemingly adversarial nature of the relationship between Connerton and Boland raises the natural question as to why the president was maintained in office. The way the vice provincial repeatedly pushed the president to the limits and then backed off in an irenic manner indicates that Connerton believed that Boland was the only one qualified for the job. If he felt another Community member could have better handled the situation, there would have been no reason to appease Boland in any way. If the president quit, then an easy opportunity to appoint another religious, requiring no explanation, would be presented. Connerton's actions suggest that this was not his plan. Boland's scrupulosity in fiscal matters and autocratic method in business dealings were advantageous to the College, which had few resources and a monstrous debt to repay. Connerton must have decided, therefore, to continue with the man whom he had originally selected to make Stonehill a healthy and vibrant establishment in Holy Cross.

Resolution of at least one aspect of Stonehill's complicated financial picture was achieved in late 1951. The dispute over land and fiscal holdings was to Boland a problem that jeopardized the College's immediate status and its future. He reminded Connerton that when approval to operate as an institution of higher education was granted, the Board of Collegiate Authority assumed that Stonehill was the sole possessor of "some 565 acres of land and a number of buildings, all free of debt and unencumbered in any way." Furthermore, it was presumed by the Board that the College's income would be used for its development. If the Board knew that Stonehill owned nothing, "drastic action would be taken."[64]

With Connerton and Boland unable to reach agreement, the dispute was placed before the Superior General for adjudication. Boland pressed the General to cede all useable grounds and buildings to the College, which, in turn, would return one hundred acres to the Congregation for its use. O'Toole was further advised that if Stonehill was to develop, it would need legal title to all lands and buildings.[65]

In November 1951 the Superior General, Christopher O'Toole, published a settlement. The loan of $175,000 received by Stonehill College was to be repaid in 10 years. The loan of $24,102.16 received by Stonehill from the mission band (part of the original loan to construct the science building) was to be assumed by the Vice Province. This, together with the unpaid assessments (June 1948 to June 1951) that Stonehill owed the Vice Province for services of religious on campus would be regarded as payment in full for seminary maintenance and tuition during the same period. Beginning in January 1952, the cost of operation for the pre-novitiate seminary, plus tuition for professed seminarians at St. Pius X and other Eastern Vice Province members studying at Stonehill, was to be regarded as the return for services of Community members assigned to teach at the College. All present College

Cap and Gown Day celebration.

buildings and the land they occupied was to be given to Stonehill, along with an adjoining one hundred acres for future development.[66] Although it took a few months for all parties to accept the specifics of the decision, O'Toole declared in late January 1952 that the issue was settled.[67]

With some resolution to the financial picture achieved, Stonehill College could shift its focus to a great milestone: its first commencement. Graduation festivities began in February 1952 with the inauguration of the "Cap and Gown Day" celebration. This originally patriotic gesture, scheduled to coincide with the national celebration of George Washington's birthday, became an annual event to mark the academic achievement of Stonehill's seniors. Graduates paraded in cap and gown across campus to the gymnasium to attend a presentation by an invited speaker.[68]

On June 1, 1952, 65 men received degrees as Stonehill's first graduating class. The celebration, originally planned for outdoors, had to be moved into the gymnasium because of rain. The weather and the large number of people rapidly transformed the gym into a steam bath. Nothing, however,

Stonehill College's first commencement, 1952.

could stifle the spirit and pride of the graduates, their families, and especially those staff and faculty of the College who had eagerly awaited this day. Representatives of many local colleges, including Boston College, Boston University, Bridgewater State Teachers' College, Emmanuel College, Fairfield University, Holy Cross, Merrimack College, and Providence College attended the ceremony and witnessed William Sullivan collect the majority of the academic prizes for the class of 1952.[69]

Ecclesiastical and civil dignitaries were also present for the event. Bishop James Connolly, now ordinary of Fall River, presided at the ceremony. His comments that day were filled with hope:[70]

> Small in number, it [Stonehill] is large in scope and possibility. Not too conspicuous for buildings or physical facilities, it is rich in the caliber of those that man it. It is richer still in the presence of the Catholic ideal that inspires it.

Massachusetts Governor Paul Dever, the principal commencement speaker, said in reference to Holy Cross' tradition of higher education, "Gentlemen, you are the first graduating class of a new college, but you are the heirs of an ancient tradition." Connolly, Dever, and Monsignor Cornelius T.H. Sherlock, superintendent for Boston's archdiocesan schools, received Stonehill College's first honorary degree.[71]

The Path to Economic Solvency

❧   STONEHILL'S FIRST COMMENCEMENT paved the way for expansion and progress in all aspects of the College's life. The immediate struggle to obtain students, however, initially obscured future prospects. From 1952 to 1955 enrollment at Stonehill actually decreased by 10, but the number of women increased by 29. Boland appeared optimistic about the prospects of enrollment, but his hopes did not initially become a reality.[72]

The reasons for Stonehill's inability to attract more students are conjectural, but the struggle to obtain government funds for veterans was one significant problem. In September 1950 Boland made application for Stonehill to be listed in the *Education Directory Part 3: Higher Education*, a necessary step for the College to receive veterans' benefits under the GI bill. Since Stonehill was not accredited, it could not be listed unless three accredited colleges or universities would accept credits achieved by Stonehill students. Thus, Boland submitted the names of three colleges, Notre Dame, Holy Cross, and Emmanuel, which led to Stonehill's placement in the 1951–1952 *Education Directory*.[73] The listing removed the difficulty that Stonehill had experienced in the collection of veterans' benefits, but it did not stimulate enrollment at the College.

Progress in academic programs and the hiring of faculty were measured but steady. The College continued to offer its three basic degrees—A.B., B.S., and B.S. in Business Administration. An accounting major, started in the fall of 1952, was the only new program. The most significant additions in this period were professors and administrators who would later play a large role in the history of Stonehill College. Henry Cruickshank in accounting, Herbert Wessling in speech and economics, David Arthur, CSC in philosophy, James Burns in sociology, and John Reedy in biology all came to Stonehill in its first seven years. As the faculty expanded, it was possible to organize the academic division with the appointment of department heads by the president.[74]

Francis Boland initiated a rudimentary campus ministry program which fostered religious activities on campus. Catholic periodicals of the day—both professional journals and popular magazines—wrestled with the question of Catholic identity and how it should be demonstrated in institutions of higher education. Upon his appointment as president, Boland assigned

First Acres *publication, 1952.*

Victor Dean as "religious counselor," a position that in 1950 became known as "director of religious activity." From 1951 to 1953 J. Marc Hebert, CSC, served in this role, with Joseph Lorusso, CSC, taking the reins in the fall of 1953. Boland continued the practice and expanded the content of an annual three-day student retreat. Begun in 1949, this event became a mainstay in the religious life of the campus. Attendance was mandatory for Catholic students, with non-Catholic students, faculty, and administrators encouraged to attend.[75] To promote participation, classes were canceled during the retreat.

Financial debt precluded any significant expansion of Stonehill's facilities during the Boland years, but following a master plan developed by the architecture firm of Maginnis and Walsh,[76] a grotto, very similar in style and design to the Lourdes Grotto at the University of Notre Dame, was built in 1953. Contributions were collected for the grotto's construction beginning in March 1949 under the guidance and sponsorship of Henry Howley. Construction began in May and the site was blessed and dedicated on December 6, 1953, with Bishop Connolly presiding and the Superior General of Holy Cross, Christopher O'Toole, in attendance.[77]

The first commencement in June 1952 was a milestone event for Stone-

May Day celebration at the Grotto.

hill, but the Boland years saw other memorable graduations. In 1953 the first woman, Luice Moncey,[78] graduated from Stonehill, a triumph for those who had promoted coeducation in the fall of 1951. Archbishop Cushing addressed the graduates that year. In subsequent years C. Gerald Lucey, Mayor of Brockton, and the Honorable John McCormack, Speaker of the House of Representatives, gave commencement addresses. Among those receiving honorary degrees were Archbishop Cushing, Bishop Russell McVinney of Providence, and Representatives John McCormack and Joseph Martin. Boland boasted of the College's progress and hopes for future development.[79]

Indeed, Stonehill now enjoyed a dedicated group of professors, a slowly expanding majors program, and a growing number of alumni. But the College was still burdened with a debt of almost $175,000 to King's College that, by virtue of the November 1951 decision by the Superior General, it was responsible for liquidating. In June 1952 and February 1953 Boland grudgingly paid the first two installments of $10,000. He suggested to Connerton that the College would be most grateful if the payment was returned in whole or part and grumbled openly that the College would make no progress under this "very crippling burden."[80] Boland continually complained that he was badgered to make payments on the debt, implying that such expenditures were a hardship and would prevent the College from expanding. Financial records, however, show that between July 1, 1950, and June 30, 1953, the College's operational profit was $91,520.80.[81] Since the opening year deficit had been erased by the surplus of 1949 to 1950, this three-year profit appears unencumbered and could, therefore, have been used to make payments on the debt. Surprisingly, Connerton never challenged Boland with these figures or used them as evidence that Stonehill had the ability to make future payments.

Despite the tough exterior that Francis Boland demonstrated to others in his defiant stand against the vice provincial, the fatigue of battle began to overtake him. He was disgusted with the relationship between the College, which he represented, and the Vice Province. Still he rose once again to challenge a new policy initiated in December 1953 by the Vice Provincial Council that required all income-producing houses of the province to pay an annual assessment of $6000. Boland rejected the idea, saying the new payment should be removed from the science building debt.[82]

The last chapter in the long saga of Stonehill's loan from King's College began to unfold in May 1954. Connerton wrote to Boland that the Superior General, Christopher O'Toole, strongly urged Stonehill to borrow the amount owed to the Province ($166,400) from a private source so that the effort of King's College to gain accreditation would not be jeopardized by its outstanding loan. Connerton informed Boland, "It seems that the accreditation committee is demanding recall on the loan."[83]

Boland, as in the past, responded quickly and defensively, but on this occasion he flatly rejected the idea that a loan be secured to repay the Province immediately. He claimed it was no concern to Stonehill if the origin of the loan was King's or another source. The College's responsibility lay solely in meeting the terms of the loan as previously established. He concluded, "It is neither my obligation nor my intention to negotiate a substitute loan for the prevailing Provincial loan." Boland went on to claim that the essential reason for King's failure to gain accreditation was the College's disproportionate emphasis on athletics rather than the loan to Stonehill.[84]

Connerton informed the General of Boland's refusal to act and asked for punitive measures against the Stonehill president. The provincial suggested that O'Toole approve Boland's expansion plans[85] only on the condition that Stonehill repay King's. Boland, informed of Connerton's request, took it as a personal affront and again submitted his resignation, after consulting a physician about his health. Connerton again rejected the request and asked for proof of Boland's "failing health."[86] The president was outraged:[87]

> I would like to inform you that I have been ordained thirty-one years, minus a few days, and during every one of these years I believe that I have rendered reasonably valuable service to the Holy Cross Congregation. In fact I would be glad to match my record of service with anyone now in the community. During these past five years I have been here at Stonehill College and despite many obstacles placed in my way, I believe that I have made, through very hard work, a substantial contribution to the advancement of this college. Now I ask to be relieved of my duties because of rapidly failing health. You reply by demanding a doctor's certificate to prove it. The implications of your order are quite obvious and, perhaps, I should have anticipated this sort of thing, after my thirty-one years of service to the community.

Connerton informed O'Toole of Boland's desire to step down as president but said he believed that "we can make arrangements satisfactory to him." The provincial, in his general pattern of offense followed by retreat, wrote, "I am glad to attest to your magnificent performance at Stonehill. This I have considered a real blessing, as I did your decision to join us here in the East."[88]

Connerton now found himself in the middle in his attempt to mediate the dispute between King's and Stonehill. In response to King's officials who demanded action, the provincial asked for patience. But in August the Provincial Council voted "to request immediate recall of the loan that the Province made to Stonehill College." In case of an unfavorable reply from Boland, the Council asked the General "to mortgage Stonehill College property to the extent of its debt to the Province," considering this "the only means under the circumstances whereby the Province can pay the debt it owes King's College, at once."[89]

Boland, informed of the Council decision, did not respond, which prompted Connerton to again ask the General to intercede "with whatever insistence you feel should accompany your support of the Provincial Council." O'Toole, after a review of accreditation reports from King's that convinced him the primary problem was the loan, wrote to Boland:[90]

I urge you to cooperate in every way possible with Father Connerton in arrangements for the return of the loan mentioned. . . .

   I realize fully how you may feel about this question, especially in view of the
interest that, as president, you are bound to take in your own institution. However, I beg of you, for the sake of the common good, to do everything possible
in cooperation with Father Connerton so that King's will not have to submit
to another evaluation two or three years from now.

The General's plea for action achieved immediate but temporary results. Boland started negotiations with banks in North Easton to obtain a
loan to liquidate the debt. Meanwhile, unknown to the Stonehill president,
the Provincial Council voted to raise the interest rate on the loan from 2
percent to 3.5 percent per annum in an effort to make the transaction appear
to accreditators to be a better investment. When Boland discovered the interest hike he quickly ceased discussions with bankers, angry that the Council
would plot behind his back.[91]
   The accreditation team scheduled to visit King's was mistakenly informed that the loan had been repaid. If the truth were discovered, the Superior General feared that King's College and the Congregation would be
embarrassed. Boland's refusal to proceed prompted O'Toole to push Connerton to force the issue:[92]

   I beg of you to insist that Father Boland close negotiations for the loan, even
   though the terms are not favorable. There is no other course of action for us to
   take now. Stonehill has simply to get the money and return it to King's. Please
   tell Father Boland that this must be done and done immediately. . . . If Father
   Boland cannot make the loan immediately, then have him draw on his cash
   reserves to return as much as possible to King's while awaiting closing of the
   loan.

Whether it was the plea of the General or an order of obedience given
by Connerton, Boland repaid the outstanding loan to King's College in November 1954. Together with James Sheehan, the president negotiated a
$100,000 loan from The First National Bank of Easton at 3⅞ percent for
five years. This sum, together with $61,000 drawn from cash reserves, was
paid to King's, and the infamous debt was liquidated. O'Toole reported to
Connerton, "The loan has finally been returned."[93]
   Although the battle over the debt was Boland's primary concern, this
struggle did not stifle his vision for the College or preclude steps to initiate
physical expansion. Save for maintenance to existing structures, clearing an
athletic field, and construction of the Lourdes Grotto, no expansion had

been made at Stonehill since the construction of the classroom and science laboratory building in 1948. Boland wrote to Connerton in March 1954, with more specifics in April, about plans for expansion of the campus. He requested permission to negotiate a $1 million loan to construct new buildings for a library, a cafeteria, offices, and class and conference rooms. He realized the risk in securing such a loan, but in claiming assets of $500,000 and a debt of $171,000, he believed the College could make the payments. Connerton recommended that an architect be retained to draw up plans and encouraged Boland to start a capital campaign. Tentative approval was given by the Provincial Council, which was "most eager to cooperate as soon as we see the picture as clearly as possible."[94]

Connerton, convinced of the merits of expansion at this time, recommended that the General grant permission for the loan. Approval was granted contingent on obtaining a rescript from the Vatican.[95] However, the immediacy of the fight over liquidation of the King's debt forced plans for expansion to be shelved until the fall. In November the Stonehill Building Fund was established by Boland in response to Connerton's request to initiate a fund-raising effort to support physical expansion of the College. George Benaglia, who had served as professor of classical languages and vice president for the past four years, was assigned as director of the campaign. The immediate goal was $1.5 million for classrooms, an auditorium, a cafeteria, a gymnasium, and office space. Future needs for a chapel, a library, and a dormitory would necessitate an additional $3.5 million.[96] Realization of these dreams would take several years.

After six years of battling religious superiors, acting as guardian for the local Holy Cross Community, and defending Stonehill, Francis Boland's health was broken. O'Toole admitted that the nervous strain of his position probably caused Boland's enlarged heart condition, which had precipitated his second request to resign. Connerton contemplated seeking an indult from the Vatican for Boland to remain superior and, thus, president beyond the fixed limit of six years, but he decided against it in view of the president's poor health. Bittersweet acclaim was given the president by Connerton in a letter to the General discussing Boland's request to accept a position as chaplain in a New York City veteran's hospital: "As you perhaps know also he [Boland] has fulfilled his obedience splendidly and has given Stonehill College a standing of distinction."[97] On July 27, 1955 a farewell dinner was held for Boland and George Benaglia, who had been assigned as president of King's College, while welcome was extended to James Sheehan, CSC, whom Connerton appointed as the next president of Stonehill College.[98]

Francis Boland saved Stonehill College from economic ruin, but at a great cost to himself and his relationship with the Holy Cross community. It

Initiation of Stonehill building fund in November 1954.

was obvious that exacting supervision of the finances of Stonehill was necessary; the huge debt and lack of economic resources necessitated such a disposition. Richard Sullivan, CSC, who served under Boland and would himself become president in 1958, commented, "For six years he [Boland] guided the destiny of this young college during the difficult years of the Korean War. Stonehill will always remain most indebted to him for his devotion and his efficient care."[99]

The requirement that Boland serve in the dual roles of president and religious superior was problematic. He did not possess the personality to shift roles easily, to present a tough exterior and discipline in matters pertaining to the College and a more pastoral approach in his relationships with members of the Congregation. Boland was successful in his role as president;

he loyally defended the College in all matters against all perceived foes, regardless of their role. Proud of this accomplishment, he could state with confidence, "I am handing over to my successor a college that will survive."[100]

ENDNOTES

1. Philip Gleason, "Changing and Remaining the Same: A Look at Higher Education," in Stephen J. Vicchio and Virginia Geiger, SSND, eds., *Perspectives on the American Catholic Church, 1789–1989* (Westminster, Maryland: Christian Classics, Inc., 1989): 229–30; Gleason, *Contending With Modernity: Catholic Higher Education in the Twentieth Century* (New York: Oxford University Press, 1995), 236–60. J.A. Magner, "Concept of a Catholic University," *Catholic University of America Bulletin* 20 (October 1952): 1; Paul E. Campbell, "What Makes a Catholic College Catholic?" *Catholic World* 179 (September 1954): 426–30.

2. Philip Gleason, "American Catholic Higher Education: A Historical Perspective," in *The Shape of Catholic Higher Education,* Robert Hassenger, ed. (Chicago: University of Chicago Press, 1967): 31.

3. Roy J. Deferrari, "Challenge to Catholic College and Their Graduates," *Journal of Religious Instruction* 17 (October 1946): 168.

4. Vice-Provincial Meeting Minutes, April 5, 1949, AHCFE. Canon law also mandated that the position of college president and religious superior be held by the same individual. Thus one's removal as superior meant removal as president.

5. Harold Rogan, CSC, interview with author, August 6, 1995; John Lucey, CSC, interview with author, August 31, 1995. Rogan was informed by Frank Kerwin, who did the bookkeeping and conducted the audit for the College's operational budget, that Benaglia's lack of financial administrative ability was the reason for his ouster as president.

6. Francis Boland to James Connerton, March 2, 1949; Connerton to Boland, March 5, 1949, Boland to Connerton, March 12, 1949, Stonehill College Papers, AHCFE. When the Eastern Vice Province was founded in May 1948, religious were divided by the location of their service. However, any religious who was from the east and serving in the west or from the west and serving in the east was granted the privilege of choosing, within one year, the province in which he desired to serve. Boland, a native of Massachusetts but serving at Notre Dame, chose the east.

7. Augustine Peverada, CSC, interview with the author, August 20, 1995. Father Peverada was a teacher in the minor seminary and was scheduled to speak with the vice provincial when a messenger interrupted, stating to Connerton, "Father Boland can see you now." Connerton immediately went to discuss his plans with Boland, indicating his sense of urgency about the matter and his strong desire for Boland to be president.

8. Steiner to Connerton, July 5, 1949; Connerton to Steiner, July 9, 1949; Steiner

to Louis Kelley, July 18, 1949; Steiner to Kelley, July 20, 1949, Provincial Papers–Connerton, AHCFE.

9. Connerton to Boland, August 14, 1949, Provincial Papers–Connerton, AHCFE.

10. Boland to Connerton, August 17, 1949, Provincial Papers–Connerton, AHCFE. Boland analyzed his new position in a letter to a friend: "Sometimes I wonder if congratulations or commiserations are in order [over my appointment as president] since, as you know, the problems of a small college are many and varied. However, we seem to be making some little progress and I am sure that eventually things will get squared away." See Boland to Joe Barr, September 27, 1949, Boland Papers, ASC.

11. Francis Boland, "Address to Students," September 1949, Boland Papers, ASC.

12. John Lucey, CSC, interview with the author, August 31, 1995, Stonehill History Project Papers; Richard Sullivan, CSC, interview with David Arthur, CSC, June 16, 1993, ASC.

13. Owen Carroll to author, September 9, 1995, Stonehill History Project Papers, ASC.

14. Many anecdotal stories of Boland's control of the College and Holy Cross religious circulate. One example illustrates the situation: Due to financial constraints, Boland ordered ice cream to be placed under lock and key. One day when the president was out, four Holy Cross faculty members "raided" the ice cream. Unexpectedly Boland arrived home early, forcing the priests to hide for fear of being discovered.

15. Thomas Campbell, CSC, interview with author, September 15, 1995; J. Marc Hebert, CSC, interview with the author, September 15, 1995; Harold Rogan, CSC, interview with David Arthur, CSC, June 3, 1993, ASC; John Lucey, CSC, interview with author, August 31, 1995. One illustrative story demonstrates both the authoritarian and seemingly paranoid nature of Boland's personality. Fathers Hebert, Campbell, Joe Keena, and Roger Quilty banded together due to "the insufferable conditions under which he [Boland] placed religious." The ill feeling of this group was recognized, and fear existed that it would "poison" the attitude of others. Thus the four were reassigned to various locations to arrest the spread of their influence. Hebert claims that the transfers were engineered by George Benaglia (who was vice president) at the request of Boland.

16. "Report of Provincial Visit to Stonehill College," November 29, 1949, Connerton Papers, AHCFE.

17. Paul Dever to Boland, July 19, 1950, Boland Papers; *The Summit*, February 1955; James Whelan to Boland, July 31, 1950, Boland Papers, ASC.

18. Boland to Paul Bartholomew, November 4, 1949, Boland Papers, ASC.

19. John Lane to Boland, May 29, 1950, Provincial Papers–Connerton, AHCFE. Lane explained to Boland that Canon law and the Congregation's constitutions and statutes dictated procedures that needed to be followed with respect to obtaining proper permissions before spending money on a project. On January 29, 1953, the

Sacred Congregation of Religious set the limit value for alienations and debts by Catholic colleges and universities in the United States at $5000. This limit was raised progressively to $15,000 in June 1962 and to $1 million in July 1981. Today the limit is $3 million. See T. Lincoln Bouscaren and James I. O'Connor, eds., *Canon Law Digest* IV (1958): 203.

20. Connerton to Boland, February 2, 1950, Boland Papers, ASC.

21. Boland to Connerton, September 22, 1949, Connerton to Boland, September 30, 1949, Boland to Connerton, January 16, 1950, Connerton to Boland, March 16, 1950, Provincial Papers–Connerton, AHCFE.

22. *The Summit* (November 3, 1949), ASC.

23. Thomas Campbell, CSC, interview with author, September 15, 1995.

24. Ibid., David Arthur, CSC, interview with James Kenneally, May 23, 1993. All Holy Cross professors were assigned to Stonehill (and any other apostolate of the Community) by the vice provincial. John Lucey, CSC, has said that the prevailing attitude of the day considered religious "in a sense qualified [to teach]." The state of the Vice Province and Stonehill itself often did not allow religious to be properly trained for the ministry of teaching at this time.

25. Deferrari, "Challenge to Catholic Colleges," 164–165.

26. James Moran, CSC, to Thomas Murphy, April 25 1949; Thomas Murphy to Moran, September 21, 1949, Academic Dean Papers, ASC.

27. Boland to Connerton, March 14, 1950; Connerton to Boland, March 16, 1950, Provincial Papers–Connerton, AHCFE; Boland to Paul Byrne, March 23, 1950, Boland Papers, ASC.

28. Connerton to Boland, August 14, 1949, Provincial Papers–Connerton, AHCFE.

29. Thomas Campbell, CSC, interview with author, September 15, 1995. The farm, managed by Brother Laetus (Larry) Triolo, sold eggs and cattle and generated some revenue. This contribution was small in numeric value but large in personal sacrifice.

30. Boland to John Lane, November 28, 1949, Academic Program File, ASC.

31. The estimated cost to maintain the seminary was $10,000 per year. The figure of $15,000 represented Stonehill's support of the seminary since April 1948, which was the date of the last payment received from the province (before the formation of the Eastern Vice Province) in support of the seminary.

32. Boland to Connerton, February 8, 1950, Provincial Papers–Connerton, AHCFE. Boland said that if the Vice Province could assume responsibility for the debt temporarily, it would allow Stonehill to seek a loan from the federal government or another source. Under the burden of a $200,000 debt, Stonehill had no chance to secure outside financing.

33. Boland to John Lane, March 13, 1950, Provincial Papers–Connerton, AHCFE. This question of the division of property and monetary assets between the College and the Vice Province would not be settled for another year.

34. Vice Provincial Council Meeting Minutes, March 3, 1950, AHCFE.

35. Boland to Connerton, May 2, 1950, Provincial Papers–Connerton, AHCFE.

36. Boland to Connerton, April 20, 1950; Boland to Connerton, May 2, 1950, Provincial Papers–Connerton, AHCFE. Frank Kerwin of the Accounting Department conducted the audit of the seminary and calculated the average annual deficit between June 1946 and June 1948 as $12,477.24.

37. Financial Statement Stonehill College, July 1, 1949, to June 30, 1950, Financial Papers, AHCFE.

38. Roy J. Deferrari, *Some Problems of Catholic Higher Education in the United States* (Boston: St. Paul's Editions, 1963): 45–47.

39. All Catholic students were required to take one two-credit theology course each semester.

40. Merrimack had started an evening division in the fall of 1948, only one year after it opened. See Roddy, *Merrimack College*, 31–32.

41. Stonehill Yearbook 1951, ASC.

42. John Lucey, CSC, claims that one primary motivation to start the program was to give women an opportunity to attend classes.

43. Stonehill Yearbook, 1951; Boland to George C. Shields, May 11, 1951, Boland Papers, ASC. Boland's prediction was fulfilled as the program, called the Institute for Adult Education, opened on October 8, 1951, with 300 students.

44. Vice Provincial Council Meeting Minutes, January 27, 1951, and April 30, 1951, AHCFE.

45. Ibid., June 13, 1951, August 13, 1951; *Acres* 1952, ASC.

46. Vice Provincial Council Meeting Minutes, October 20, 1950, December 19, 1950.

47. Connerton to Christopher O'Toole, December 12, 1950, Superior General Papers–O'Toole, AHCFE. The desire to maintain Stonehill as an all-male college became a prime mover for the establishment of what became St. Pius X Seminary.

48. O'Toole to Connerton, February 1, 1951, Superior General Papers–O'Toole, AHCFE.

49. Connerton to O'Toole, March 1, 1951, Superior General Papers–O'Toole, AHCFE.

50. O'Toole to Connerton, March 7, 1951, Superior General Papers–O'Toole, AHCFE.

51. Boland to James Cassidy, March 8, 1951; Cassidy to Boland, March 9, 1951; Boland to Cassidy, March 16, 1951, Boland Papers; Stonehill Yearbook, 1951, ASC.

52. Edward J. Power, *Catholic Higher Education in America, A History* (New York: Appleton-Century-Crofts, 1972), 446.

53. Boland to George S. Shields, May 11, 1951, Boland Papers; "Chronicles of Our Lady of Holy Cross" (September–October 1951), ASC.

54. Anonymous to Christopher O'Toole, November 1951, AHCFG.

55. The question of ownership of property between the Congregation of Holy Cross and Stonehill College was not settled until 1968. Chapter 9 relates the full story.

56. James Sheehan, CSC, to Boland, October 3, 1950; Boland to Sheehan, October 6, 1950, Provincial Papers–Connerton, AHCFE.

57. Connerton to Boland, October 13, 1950, Provincial Papers–Connerton, AHCFE.

58. Ibid.

59. Boland to Connerton, October 16, 1950, Provincial Papers–Connerton, AHCFE.

60. Connerton to Boland, October 18, 1950, Provincial Papers–Connerton, AHCFE.

61. The constitutions and statutes of Holy Cross required the provincial or his representative to visit each house of the Community on an annual basis.

62. Summary of Vice Provincial Visit to Stonehill College, March 20, 1951, Provincial Papers–Connerton, AHCFE.

63. Boland to Connerton, September 4, 1951; Connerton to Boland, September 10, 1951, Stonehill College Papers, AHCFE; Christopher O'Toole to Boland, October 15, 1951, Boland Papers, ASC.

64. Boland to Connerton, June 20, 1951, Stonehill College Papers, AHCFE.

65. Anonymous to O'Toole, November 1951; O'Toole to Connerton, November 20, 1951, AHCFG.

66. Settlement of Financial and Property Relations Between the Vice Province and Stonehill College, Decision of the Superior General, November 20, 1951, Boland Papers, ASC; O'Toole to Connerton, November 20, 1951, AHCFG.

67. John Lucey, who was dean at Stonehill but also wore the hat in 1952 as assistant vice provincial, argued that the figures on the mission band loan were inaccurate and that the province could not be responsible for the full tuition of all scholastics. In the summer of 1952 the Vice Province was raised to the level of a Province and held its first chapter. The financial arrangement between the Province and Stonehill was discussed, with some capitulants unconvinced of the wisdom of the General's decision. Thus, after reviewing the decisions of that chapter, the General wrote to Connerton (who continued in the role of provincial) to make sure that all misunderstandings and friction were cleared up before the fall term began. See Lucey to O'Toole, January 9, 1952, AHCFG; O'Toole to Connerton, June 25, 1952, Superior General Papers–O'Toole, AHCFE.

68. Cap and Gown Day was held through 1962 but was discontinued by request of the senior class on November 13, 1962, Student Affairs Papers, ASC.

69. Commencement Program, Stonehill College 1952, ASC.

70. James Connolly, Commencement Address, 1952, Deans' Papers, Commencement, ASC.

71. Paul Dever, Commencement Address 1952, Deans' Papers, Commencement File; Commencement Program, Stonehill College, 1952, ASC.

72. Boland to Marie [unknown], March 5, 1953, Boland Papers, ASC.

73. Boland to John Dale Russell, July 17, 1950, September 8, 1950; Fred J. Kelly to Boland, October 16, 1950, Boland Papers, ASC. Some schools accepted Stonehill's credits only on a provisional basis, which troubled the government. Another delay for Stonehill was the discovery that MIT, one of the three schools originally submitted as those that accepted Stonehill credits, would not accept certain science courses, necessitating the submission of Emmanuel as a backup.

74. Boland to Richard Sullivan, CSC, February 23, 1954. Chairs assigned were: Richard Sullivan, CSC, philosophy and theology; Brassil Fitzgerald, English; John Reedy, science; Edward Shea, CSC, modern languages; George Benaglia, CSC, classical languages; Henry Cruickshank, business; James Sheehan, CSC, mathematics.

75. As late as 1961 the retreat was still mandatory for Catholic students. See *The Summit* (February 10, 1961), ASC.

76. Josephus Schaub, interview with the author, November 9, 1995. Boland hired Maginnis and Walsh to create a master plan for the expansion of the campus. This plan called for development of the College toward Route 138. The Grotto is situated away from the principal development of the campus because the plan Boland commissioned was not implemented. Rather it was the decision of Father James Sheehan, Boland's successor as president, to develop the College from the main building directly south toward Route 123. This is the state of the campus today.

77. Henry Howley to George Benaglia, March 13, 1949; Boland to Howley, May 18, 1953, Presidents' Papers, Grotto File; "Chronicles of Our Lady of Holy Cross" (December 6, 1953), ASC.

78. Moncey came to Stonehill as a junior transfer student. She was very active on campus in the speech-arts society, *The Summit* (student newspaper), and student government.

79. Boland to Theodore Heshburg [*sic*], March 18, 1953; Boland to Joseph Martin, March 9, 1954, Boland Papers, ASC.

80. Boland to Connerton, June 4, 1952, Boland Papers, ASC; Boland to Connerton, February 6, 1953, January 9, 1953, Provincial Papers–Connerton, AHCFE.

81. Financial Statements of Stonehill College, 1951, 1952, 1953, Financial Papers, AHCFE. The per-year breakdown on the profit was: July 1, 1950, to June 30, 1951—$37,466.02; July 1, 1951, to June 30, 1952—$43,804.51; July 1, 1952, to June 30, 1953—$10,250.27.

82. Vice Provincial Council Meeting Minutes, December 19, 1953, AHCFE.

83. Connerton to Boland, May 29, 1954, Provincial Papers–Connerton, AHCFE. In the spring of 1954 King's was visited by representatives of the Middle States Accrediting Association, which denied the school accreditation. One of the reasons given for the rejection was the large loan to Stonehill. Surprisingly, the local council at King's was apparently never asked or consulted about the six payments of $175,000 made to Stonehill between August 1948 and November 1949. Since Connerton was president of King's at the time of his appointment as vice provincial, it is probable that the loan was made secretly, although it is difficult to see how the King's community could have remained ignorant of the transaction for so long. See "A Brief on the Loan to the Province of Our Lady of Holy Cross" (August 1954), Archives of King's College (hereafter AKC).

84. Boland to Connerton, June 1, 1954, Provincial Papers–Connerton; Connerton to O'Toole, June 19, 1954, Superior General Papers–O'Toole, AHCFE. Connerton admitted to O'Toole that Boland had inside information from the accreditation team that he received even before Kings.

85. Boland at this same time had initiated a development campaign to construct

new facilities at Stonehill, which were badly needed due to the increase in enrollment.

86. Connerton to O'Toole, June 8, 1954, Superior General Papers–O'Toole, AHCFE.

87. Boland to Connerton, June 14, 1954, Provincial Papers–Connerton, AHCFE.

88. Connerton to O'Toole, June 19, 1954, Superior General Papers–O'Toole; Connerton to Boland, n.d. (Feast of Corpus Christi, 1954), Provincial Papers–Connerton, AHCFE.

89. Connerton to William Beston, CSC, August 28, 1954, AKC; Provincial Council Meeting Minutes, August 27, 1954, AHCFE.

90. O'Toole to Boland, October 2, 1954, Boland Papers, ASC.

91. Hilary Paszek, CSC, to William Beston, CSC, August 8, 1954, AKC; Provincial Council Meeting Minutes, June 28, 1954; O'Toole to Connerton, November 18, 1954, Superior General Papers–O'Toole, AHCHE.

92. O'Toole to Connerton, November 18, 1954, Superior General Papers–O'Toole, AHCFE.

93. Application for Loan, November 22, 1954, Financial Records Statement, n.d. History of Stonehill Papers, ASC; O'Toole to Connerton, December 7, 1954, Superior General Papers–O'Toole, AHCFE. On March 25, 1955, a check for $6777.31, to cover interest, was submitted by Stonehill as final payment of the debt.

94. Connerton to Boland, April 1, 1954, Boland Papers, ASC; Boland to Connerton, April 5, 1954, April 8, 1954, Provincial Papers–Connerton, AHCFE.

95. Canon Law required that loans above $5000 required special permission from the Vatican. O'Toole was cautious, however, and requested a rescript for $500,000 stating, "When further authorization is needed for a greater amount we can get it." O'Toole to Connerton, July 7, 1954, Superior General Papers, AHCFE.

96. *The Summit* (November 1954), ASC.

97. O'Toole to Connerton, February 16, 1955; Connerton to O'Toole, May 23, 1955; Connerton to O'Toole, June 10, 1955, Superior General Papers–O'Toole, AHCFE.

98. "Chronicles of Our Lady of Holy Cross" (July 27, 1955), ASC.

99. Richard Sullivan, "Eulogy for Francis Boland" (January 3, 1961), Sullivan Papers, ASC.

100. David Arthur, CSC, interview with the author, November 7, 1995. Boland's loyalty to Stonehill was, however, not complete. He served the majority of his ministry at Notre Dame, a fact that did not escape him in executing his will. Personally wealthy, Boland left $10,000 to the "Holy Cross Fathers' Seminary at North Easton" but $50,000 to Notre Dame to endow two scholarships for law students. Additionally, the remainder of his estate not specifically designated was given to Notre Dame "for construction costs of the contemplated new library"—today Hesburgh Memorial Library. See Francis Boland, "Last Will and Testament" n.d., Archives of the University of Notre Dame (hereafter AUND).

CHAPTER 3

Stability and Growth

The period after World War II found Catholic colleges engaged in efforts to better achieve their purpose, fulfill their character, and make a unique contribution to higher education in America. The critical and necessary question Catholic colleges were forced to answer was how to bring unity to the twin objectives of academic achievement and scholarship, on the one hand, and the moral formation of youth, on the other. Theologian Gustave Weigel wrote that any institution of higher learning is a useful training center only insofar as it is an aid to the scholar. A college or university can only be helpful, he suggested, if the institution is what it claims to be—an impartial establishment of academic excellence:[1]

> In the realm of information the college must be comprehensive and objective. It must not approach the data with a previous emotional commitment. A party-line college is no real college. Suppression of validly acquired data or their presentation only to be refuted are not tactics proper to a center of contemplation.

There were two basic schools of thought regarding the question of whether Catholic colleges were compromising their religious values while attempting to satisfy academic standards. The more traditional view promoted the belief that Catholic schools should be affiliated with the Church and its mission for the salvation of souls. One writer noted that many Catholic colleges appeared to be secular to outsiders, as they merely added religion courses to their curriculum to justify the appellation of "Catholic." Such tokenism, it was perceived, created no depth of thought or integration in knowledge, because in general Catholic institutions cannot match secular colleges in resources. This critic concluded, "If our colleges do not produce this [Catholic] brand of spirituality, they will have failed—no matter how 'intellectual' their alumni may be."[2]

A more progressive contemporary understanding promoted the idea that while Catholic colleges need to maintain visible Catholic signs, they also need to be able to duplicate the work of secular institutions. This view held that if Catholic colleges and universities could not offer an academic program on a par with secular schools, there was no reason to exist. A Catholic institution that did not compete with its neighbors in quality of teachers, majors programs and course offerings, and general advancement of the intellectual life was not providing sufficient service. One writer concluded:[3]

> If we actually produce colleges which have a high intellectual standard and in which the student at the same time is enabled to develop himself spiritually and in social responsibility, we will have created the most perfect educational system possible. . . . This is the good for which we may well strive.

Catholic higher education in America and intellectual life in general were forced into a position of defense with the publication in 1955 of Monsignor John Tracy Ellis's essay, "American Catholics and the Intellectual Life." Originally presented at St. Louis in a May meeting of the Catholic Commission on Intellectual and Cultural Affairs, the essay strongly assailed American Catholics for their dearth of intellectual activity and achievement. Ellis, the dean of American Catholic historians in the twentieth century, addressed five areas that he perceived as requiring attention. First, he said, Catholic colleges need to concentrate their endeavors in areas and fields of knowledge where the possibility of their contribution is greatest and leave other areas to secular institutions. Next, Ellis perceived that excessive competition between Catholic schools had resulted in mediocrity for all involved. Third, he boldly proclaimed that some Catholic colleges should be eliminated to prevent senseless duplication. Fourth, Ellis believed that American Catholics—possibly through the ghetto mentality so prevalent in the early and mid-twentieth century—did not possess any great love for scholarship. Lastly, Ellis stood firmly in the progressive camp when he suggested that Catholic colleges were overemphasizing moral development at the expense of intellectual excellence.[4]

Two basic responses to Ellis's essay predominated: (1) argue against its validity or (2) accept the thesis and try to improve things. The historian

Joseph Blaney was one of the very few who challenged Ellis's thesis. He did not disagree that the contributions of Catholics to intellectualism were sparse, but countered that too much emphasis had been placed on the academic side of education. He continued to push for a greater sense of Catholic spirituality in education and concluded, "Until this question [spiritual life on campus] is resolved, all other discussion is dangerously distracting." One woman religious, Sr. Annette Walters, CSJ, blamed American Catholic intellectual failures on the fact that earlier Catholics had produced no historical pattern of intellectualism to follow.[5] Without making excuses, Gustave Weigel offered an explanation of the conditions Ellis described, suggesting that American Catholicism's long obsession with an apologetic defense of its position had placed it in a backwards situation. He also argued that many with the capacity for intellectual achievement were directed toward the priesthood and/or religious life, vocations that often did not allow the opportunity for academic achievement.[6]

Most American Catholics involved in higher education took their reprimand from Ellis and sought ways to rectify the problems he outlined. Many Catholic schools abandoned neo-scholasticism as the centerpiece of their core teaching and began to opt instead for a general "pursuit of excellence," with excellence understood as the way the intellectual life was pursued at Harvard or Berkeley. Professors on Catholic college campuses began to perceive Catholic sociology or a Catholic approach to education as outmoded and embarrassingly parochial.[7] Archbishop Richard Cushing of Boston, a staunch supporter of Catholic education, realized that Ellis's challenge necessitated a progressive response:[8]

> It is no longer possible to argue the objection that standards of scholarship are maintained elsewhere which we [Catholic colleges] are not able to meet, or even that opportunities for advancement are greater elsewhere than we are able to provide. The time has come when we should make a concerted effort to present Catholic education to our people as an advantage and an enviable privilege rather than as a duty to the Church which comes into conflict with the ambitions of worldly success.

The Third President

AS PREVIOUSLY NOTED, in June 1955 Holy Cross Father James Sheehan was nominated by the Provincial Council to be the third president of Stonehill College and was officially appointed by James Connerton with a letter of obedience in July.[9] Sheehan, a native of Brockton, Massachusetts, who held a doctorate from Notre Dame, had originally come to Stonehill in the

Rev. James Sheehan, CSC, in conversation with students.

fall of 1951 to teach chemistry. In 1954 he assumed the collateral duty of director of student affairs. From 1950 to 1956 he also served as provincial steward. Sheehan was a quiet and unassuming man who certainly felt more comfortable in the laboratory then at a desk, let alone in a position that required daily interaction with the public. Indeed, at his wake in September 1977, the eulogist said of him, "In 1955 he was appointed President of Stonehill, a job he felt most uneasy with and unqualified for. . . ." Despite his lack of self-confidence and personal comfort, however, Sheehan took the reins as president, continued leadership, and "got the College moving."[10]

Sheehan inherited an institution with potential awaiting the opportunity to develop. An enrollment rise of 45 percent was matched by an equally impressive 54 percent rise in full-time faculty.[11] Several important scholars, who during their tenures made significant contributions to the College, joined the Stonehill faculty at this time. Holy Cross priests Thomas Lockary, William Hogan, E. Peter Royal, Francis Grogan, and William Gartland arrived during these years. Maryalice Moore, John Sullivan, and Marguerite Antoine made contributions through their teaching and scholarship.[12] Still, growth continued to be slow at the outset of the new administration. This sluggishness was due in large measure to Sheehan's introverted personality which, at times, caused near paralysis when he had to address groups or meet with individuals or organizations needed to promote expansion of the College.

The 1950s was a "period of awakening" when Catholic colleges throughout the nation began to experience new patterns of faculty organization. Faculty committees were founded to provide professors greater input in policy decisions, and deans discovered the benefit of department heads. Contemporary studies revealed that professors received "adequate to good compensation, but working conditions and professional status were lower than [those of] secular institutions."[13]

In addition to the topic of intellectualism, two other issues evoked wide discussion and heated debate in academic circles: academic freedom and the role of Catholicism in American higher education. Conservatives, professing that teachers had the responsibility to defend traditional wisdom and transmit only established truths and theories, marched behind William F. Buckley, whose 1951 book, *God and Man at Yale: The Superstitions of "Academic Freedom,"* assailed the university's failure to review material presented in the classroom. Progressives, however, found their champions, among others, in the editors of *America*, who challenged many of Buckley's precepts.[14]

Stonehill in the 1950s possessed no forum for debating issues pertinent to the faculty or the College at large, including academic freedom and the role of the Church in American higher education. One faculty member of the period suggested that the two meetings of all professors, at the outset and end of each academic year, "served the purposes of the catalog and the President."[15] Professors were, however, encouraged by the College to participate actively in professional organizations and attend annual conventions in their disciplines. Faculty committees active in the 1950s were the board of admissions, board of athletics, and committee on scholarship. In 1957 committees for publications and discipline were established. The most important College governance body involved with the day-to-day operations of the College was the Academic Council. This group was composed of the various academic department heads and the dean, who served as *ex officio* chairman. The council described itself as "a standing committee [which] serves in academic matters of the college."[16]

The debate on Catholic intellectual life ignited by Monsignor Ellis's 1955 essay appeared to spark little discussion at Stonehill. The absence of any organized faculty forum for discussion was one problem, but there is, additionally, no extant record of the administration being concerned about Ellis's indictment and what it might mean for the College. With the heavy load of classes and the emphasis on teaching, professors at Stonehill did not have the opportunity or time to actively engage in scholarship. While individuals may have followed the debate that raged at other schools through scholarly journals, Stonehill's faculty as a whole did not perceive the issue as pressing.

The governance of the College continued to be controlled by the Congregation of Holy Cross. The House Council, appointed by the provincial and composed of Holy Cross religious assigned to the College, advised the president on routine decisions on a daily basis, in addition to making recommendations on such matters as physical plant expansion and new academic programs. The Board of Trustees was also a Holy Cross body consisting of the provincial and his councilors. The Board of Advisors, which was appointed by the president and was composed of business people and other professionals, gave financial advice and participated in development planning from the outset of the College. Superior General Christopher O'Toole recognized that the expansion of Stonehill would require the assistance of the advisors because of the extra Holy Cross perspective they could provide.[17]

Expansion of College Facilities

❦

IMMEDIATELY AFTER ASSUMING the office of president, Sheehan began to investigate ways to expand the College physically. In 1955 the College, which served a student population three times that of 1948, had no additional physical space save the classroom building.[18] Facilities were overextended, and expansion was a necessity if the College was to continue to grow. Sheehan asked the Provincial Council to consider several options. One idea was to purchase an old hangar from military surplus to meet present and future needs.[19] Another was to convert the gymnasium into classrooms or a library. Prefabricated buildings were also suggested us a way to meet expanding needs inexpensively.[20]

Accordingly, financing a proposed classroom building and a cafeteria was the first step in Sheehan's plans for expansion. The president made inquiries of the Federal Housing Administration on the possibility of borrowing funds to build the proposed cafeteria under the provisions of a new law that provided financing for "other educational facilities."[21] Sheehan's initial plan was to secure a $300,000 federal government loan for the cafeteria and to borrow $150,000 from a local bank for the classroom building. The building fund, started by Boland the previous year, would supply the addi-

Rev. Thomas Duffy, CSC (standing), and Rev. James Sheehan, president 1955–1958, discuss plans for Holy Cross Hall.

tional funds to complete the classroom project. The Provincial Council authorized Sheehan to borrow up to $500,000 for the proposed expansion.[22]

In December 1955 Sheehan began to negotiate with the Institution for Savings in New Bedford about a loan for the classroom project. The initial request of the Provincial Council to secure a $150,000 loan was increased to $225,000 so the College could consolidate all major debts into one payment.[23] The General Council, however, authorized borrowing only an additional $25,000.[24] The president pleaded with the provincial, James Connerton, to help:[25]

> If this is the limit of the amount we are authorized to borrow, then I do not see how we can proceed with our building plans. . . . I believe this is a crucial point since we must have this building next year or take immediate steps to limit our enrollment now. The rate at which we are receiving applications makes it appear that we will not be able to handle all these students with our present facilities.

Sheehan's plea was answered on February 7, 1956, when a $275,000 loan was approved and secured from the Institution for Savings in New Bedford.[26]

The first Mamma Mia Night fundraiser:
A. Edward Lalli, Don Ameche, James Sheehan, CSC, Rocky Marciano, and Thomas
Duffy, CSC.

Francis Boland had established the Stonehill Building Fund in 1954 when he unveiled a master plan for future expansion. The exodus of both Boland and the building fund director, George Benaglia, forced Sheehan to begin the process anew. Thomas Duffy, whose visit to North Easton and the Ames estate in 1935 and whose frantic letter in the summer of 1948 had played integral roles in the founding of the College, was appointed director of the building fund. Duffy, a Stonehill professor of theology since 1953 (and later director of off-campus activities), asked A. Edward Lalli of the Board of Advisors to be his assistant in the development campaign. At this time the "Society of the Men of Stonehill College," under the guidance of New Bedford businessman Vincent T. Hemingway, was formed. It joined the Stonehill Guild in assisting College officials in the development effort. Duffy, in a gesture of solidarity, became a founding member.[27]

Duffy organized many fundraisers, some of which became annual events. In March 1956 the first "Irish Night," with special guests Notre Dame football coach, Terry Brennan, and Irish consul to the United States, Joseph Shields, was held at West Junior High School in Brockton. The event

Mamma Mia Night program.

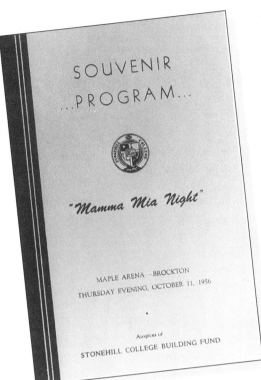

attracted over 1000 people. In September the first "Mamma Mia" night, an evening of food and entertainment, was held. Father Patrick Peyton, the famous rosary priest, founder of family theater, and member of the Eastern Province of Holy Cross, assisted Duffy by placing him in contact with numerous Hollywood personalities who attended the various fundraisers. Jack Haley, who acted as master of ceremonies for Irish nights, was joined by actor Frank Fontaine. "Mamma Mia" dinners attracted comedians Jerry Colonna and Lou Costello, actor Don Ameche, boxer Rocky Marciano, and musical celebrities Vic Damone and members of the Lawrence Welk band.[28] In December 1956 Duffy started the Century Club, an organization of friends of the College who promised to contribute $100 annually to the building fund. The goal was to enlist one thousand members.[29]

In October 1957 the development drive was expanded to include a "Family Division." Sheehan announced the program's one-year goal of raising $325,000 for the construction as well as equipment and furnishings for the proposed cafeteria, which would double as a student union. This particular fund would be used to pay off the anticipated government loan being negotiated for the construction of the building. John S. Ames, Jr., Daniel F. Buckley, and Dr. Jacob Brenner served as honorary cochairmen for the drive. The program was advertised as part of the overall $5-million fundraising campaign that Boland had originally announced in 1954. The Family Division was organized into four categories—alumni, students and friends, faculty, and volunteers—each of which was assigned a monetary goal. Four additional divisions—parents, house mothers, clergy, and staff—were also assigned goals. By May 1958 the effort had netted $163,000 from 600 donors—a substantial amount, but only half the original goal.[30]

Fundraising efforts were concurrent with the development of the president's new master plan for expansion of the College. Sheehan shifted the orientation of Boland's dream campus away from Route 138 (Washington Street) and toward Route 123 (Belmont Street), making a north-south line from the old Ames mansion the visual center of the new plan. Connerton explained the change to the Superior General as a way "to shorten the access of students coming over the new super highway [State Route 24] from points North and South as well as East."[31] Sheehan's plan called for the construction of new buildings on land cleared in the flat area south of the main building. A road from Belmont Street along the centerline of the campus would connect the structures with outside traffic. The new design was presented at the March 1956 Irish Night fundraiser and was well received.[32]

The desperate need for classroom space became the top priority in the expansion effort. Emery LaLiberte, architect for the science building, was again engaged by the College in the winter of 1956 to design a building with ten large classrooms and three offices. Sheehan underscored the urgency of the project: "I believe this is a crucial point since we must have this building next year or take immediate steps to limit our enrollment now."[33] Plans were rapidly drawn and approved by the Provincial and General Councils in February, and bids were extended in April to several contractors of southeast Massachusetts and Rhode Island. The contract was awarded to Crowell Constructors of Brockton in 1956.

Holy Cross Hall was constructed expeditiously "to cope with its [the College's] rapidly growing enrollment."[34] On May 24, 1956, an informal ground-breaking ceremony was held, with Sheehan, Connerton, and about 100 students present. The cornerstone of the building was blessed and laid on November 30, with Sheehan presiding. The building was blessed and dedicated by Bishop James Connolly of Fall River on January 27, 1957, and there was an open house and reception for about 800 guests. The new classroom building welcomed its first students four days later.[35]

Cornerstone laying ceremony for Holy Cross Hall:
James Doyle, CSC, George DePrizio, CSC, James Sheehan, CSC, Richard Sullivan, CSC,
Bruce Crowell (contractor), and Emery LaLiberte (architect).

James Sheehan's initial 1955 inquiry into financing for the proposed cafeteria led to a full campaign to secure a government loan. From the beginning, Sheehan enlisted Stonehill's friends to aid the effort. Congressional Representatives John McCormack and Joseph Martin were both asked to help expedite Stonehill's $300,000 loan application with the Housing and Home Finance Agency (HHFA). Although McCormack wrote on Stonehill's behalf,[36] the HHFA informed Sheehan that the amount of the loan could not be justified by the College's present and projected enrollment. The request was reduced to $200,000, an amount acceptable to the acting regional administrator for the HHFA.[37]

Holy Cross Hall in 1957.

Although the College and government appeared to agree upon the amount of the loan and its use, the process of approval was agonizingly slow. Preliminary approval of Stonehill's application was granted in March 1956, with final approval contingent upon the College's eligibility, the necessity of the planned facility, and a satisfactory review of the College's full application.[38] As Stonehill submitted its final application in July, Sheehan again wrote to Martin and McCormack for their assistance.[39] The loan's delay, coupled with the requirement that government funds could be released only when the proposed building was substantially completed,[40] forced Sheehan to seek private sources of money to avoid further delay of the cafeteria's construction. In February 1957 a loan was negotiated with the First Safe Deposit National Bank in New Bedford for $200,000; provincial approval was given in April. Meanwhile, in March the College's student newspaper, *The Summit*, reported that the Housing and Home Finance Agency had approved Stonehill's loan request.[41]

Ground-breaking ceremony for cafeteria and student union:
Emery LaLiberte (architect), Richard Sullivan, CSC, James Sheehan, CSC, and
Ted Gadoury (contractor).

With financing finally secured, the design and construction of the new cafeteria could proceed. The Provincial Council approved Emery LaLiberte's plan for the structure in July 1957, allowing a formal contract to be signed between Stonehill, LaLiberte, and the Housing and Home Finance Agency.[42] When the plans were submitted "for courtesy approval" to the Superior General, however, he unexpectedly suggested several revisions. He considered the facility too small for future needs and challenged the location of stairwells, the kitchen, and restrooms. Superior General Christopher O'Toole asked that the architect make the changes suggested, concluding, "The [General] Council is not disposed to approve the plans as they now stand."[43]

O'Toole's request placed the project on hold until agreement could be reached on the building's design. Sheehan wrote to him of the urgency of the project: "We shall not be able to take in more students unless we have it [the cafeteria]." DePrizio, concerned about the possible loss of the govern-ment loan, told the General that technicalities with the government loan might preclude changes at that point, since the three-party agreement had been signed on August 13. The provincial admitted that the General Council should have reviewed the plans before government approval was sought. He told O'Toole that he would seek permission from the government for the suggested changes but alerted the General, "We may have to request your permission to go ahead with the building plans as they now stand."[44] On August 30 the government approved (without O'Toole's recommended changes) the final plans and specifications for the cafeteria. In order not to delay construction, the General approved the project, but with the proviso that the facility be built to allow future expansion.[45]

Construction of the cafeteria, Sheehan's second major expansion proj-ect, was riddled with problems almost from the outset. The Ted J. Gadoury construction firm of Manville, Rhode Island, was awarded the contract for a bid of $290,335.[46] Ground-breaking for the new cafeteria and student union was held on October 22, 1957, with completion projected at 300 days. In February 1958 *The Summit* reported all was on schedule and that, according to the contract, the building would be ready for the fall semester. The cornerstone was laid on May 20 by Sheehan, but only two days later he was informed by Gadoury that construction had been impeded by financial problems. During the summer the project closed down completely, only to be restarted in the fall with a new administration at the helm of Stonehill College.

A New Seminary at Stonehill

❧

As PART OF a national postwar religious revival, Catholicism reached its apex in visibility, unity, and strength. Catholics were united in their loyalty to both nation and Church. "American religion's Indian summer"[47] was marked by many manifestations of Catholic revival. Bishop Fulton Sheen's books, such as *Peace of Soul* (1949) and his five-volume *Life Is Worth Living* (1953–1957), and his television evangelization placed the Catholic name and ideal in the living rooms of many American homes. Thomas Merton's autobiography, *The Seven Storey Mountain* (1948), and his message of con-templative spirituality were introduced to American Catholics. Attendance at Catholic schools between 1949 and 1959 more than doubled from 2.6 to 5.6 million students, and the number of Catholic colleges and hospitals increased dramatically during the decade. Candidates for the priesthood and religious life swelled seminaries and convents to record levels; church attendance by Catholics was reported at 82 percent, more than 14 points higher than the national average.[48] Church historian Hugh Nolan described the spirit of the times: "The Catholics of that era were a joyous group positive of their identity, proud of their Church and of their priests and of their schools."[49]

American Catholicism's revival in the 1950s was experienced by the Congregation of Holy Cross through increased vocations. During the Sheehan administration, Holy Cross decided that a new seminary was necessary to meet the burgeoning seminarian population that was part of the Catholic renaissance of the period. In January 1956 James Connerton informed the Superior General that a new headquarters for Our Lady of Holy Cross Seminary was needed. Facilities in the wing of the main building, which provided living space for lay seminarians and staff, were no longer adequate. In December, while on a visit to the College, the Superior General gave permission to secure an architect and appoint a procurator for the project. The Provincial Council swiftly named a committee under Father John Murphy to fund a new seminary and to begin long-range planning for the financial needs of seminarians.[50]

The prospect of transferring financial responsibility for lay seminarians from the College to the Province prompted DePrizio to seek a revision of the 1951 financial agreement between Stonehill and the Congregation. The provincial suggested that Stonehill be placed under the same financial arrangement as other income-producing houses in the Province. This arrangement would require Stonehill to pay an assessment for the services of each religious assigned to and residing at the College. In turn DePrizio offered to pay 50 percent of the tuition plus lab fees for lay seminarians attending the College. O'Toole had no objection to the plan but left the arrangements to be worked out between the Province and the College.[51] DePrizio used his provincial authority to inform Sheehan in August 1957 of the new financial arrangement, but the president argued for reconsideration, claiming that the College's financial burden was too great to provide full tuition for all professed members of the Congregation and half for lay seminarians. DePrizio, however, was only partially sympathetic. He agreed that the College should not be responsible for the tuition of nonprovince professed members, but concluded, "The Provincial Council is unanimous in asking Stonehill College to assume the assessment. . . ."[52]

The Congregation first explored the possibility of securing land in West Haven, Connecticut, for the new seminary. The site was attractive for many reasons. Its central location within the Eastern Province and immediate proximity to Notre Dame High School, a Community apostolate, made the

Ground-breaking ceremony for Holy Cross Seminary.

site ideal. Additionally, Archbishop Henry J. O'Brien of Hartford favored the project. Affiliation of the seminary with The Catholic University was another possible benefit that could be explored. DePrizio was excited about the project and energetically wrote to the Superior General, outlining the many benefits provided by the proposed site, and asking permission to proceed with negotiations to acquire the property.[53] O'Toole, who agreed that a seminary was needed, was also enthusiastic, but he gave his approval cautiously: "I heartily approve of the idea. The only thing that concerns me is how you are going to finance it."[54]

DePrizio's plans continued to develop once approval had been granted by the General and his council. A tentative faculty of Holy Cross religious were recruited for the seminary,[55] and John Murphy, provincial steward, began negotiations for the purchase of the West Haven site. In July 1957 he offered $425,000 for the building and grounds, but the county commissioner countered with a demand for $500,000.[56] The unexpected rejection of Murphy's offer forced DePrizio to consider possible alternatives. Renovation of Pius X, including conversion of the refectory into bedrooms, was the best immediate answer to the shortage of space. In the end, the county commissioner's refusal to lower the price, coupled with the Congregation's

Holy Cross Fathers retreat house, formerly Pius X Seminary.

inability to secure financing, forced a retreat from West Haven and return to North Easton.[57]

The immediate need for space for seminarians forced the Provincial Council to act swiftly. The Council decided that the best plan would be to build a new seminary at North Easton, simple and not large but designed so that expansion was possible. In October plans drawn by William B. Cramm were approved by the Council and forwarded to the General. Cost estimates varied widely, from $500,000 to over $1.1 million. Not until April 1958 was a satisfactory design consisting of one dormitory wing, a recreation room, a refectory, and a kitchen accepted by the Provincial Council at an estimated cost of $590,000. Endorsement of the plan and approval from the General to negotiate a $400,000 loan from the Institution of Savings of New Bedford paved the way for the ground-breaking on May 30, 1958.[58]

ENDNOTES

1. Gustave Weigel, "Enriching the Intellectual Life of the Catholic College," *NCEA Bulletin* 52 (May 1956): 13.

2. Joseph J. Blaney, "How Christian Is the Catholic College?" *Catholic World* 184 (January 1957): 279, 282.

3. R.W. Roloff, "Are Our Catholic Colleges So Bad?" *Catholic World* 185 (June 1957): 209.

4. John Tracy Ellis, "America Catholics and the Intellectual Life," *Thought* XXX (Autumn 1955): 351–88. Ellis' critique was not the first time American Catholicism had been called to task over its failures in intellectual achievement. In 1922 Carlton J.H. Hayes, in a *Catholic Mind* essay, bemoaned the fact that Catholic youth had received all too little intellectual stimulus during their academic training. In his 1927 book, *The Catholic Spirit in America*, George Shuster, *Commonweal* editor and later president of Hunter College, wrote, "Catholics have not done what might reasonably have been expected of them to foster letters, speculation, and the arts." John O'Brien from Notre Dame in 1938 stated that Catholics were too little visible in proportion to their numbers and that provisions for producing scholars were extremely limited.

5. Blaney, "How Christian Is the Catholic College?" 276–77; Sr. Annette Walters, CSJ, "Why Is the American Catholic College Failing to Develop Catholic Intellectualism?" *NCEA Bulletin* 53 (August 1956): 172–78.

6. Gustave Weigel, SJ, "American Catholic Intellectualism—A Theologian's Reflection," *Review of Politics* 19 (July 1957): 304.

7. Philip Gleason, "What Made Catholic Identity a Problem?" in *The Challenge and Promise of a Catholic University*, Theodore Hesburgh, CSC, ed. (Notre Dame: University of Notre Dame Press, 1994): 94–96.

8. Quoted in Thurston N. Davis, "Should Catholic Lambs Eat Ivy?" *America* 93 (May 21, 1955): 206.

9. Provincial Council Meeting Minutes, June 22, 1955, AHCFE; James Connerton to James Sheehan, Letter of Obedience, July 5, 1955, Sheehan Papers, ASC.

10. Eulogy at the wake for Father James Sheehan, n.d. [September 1977], Sheehan Papers, ASC; Richard Sullivan, CSC, interview with David Arthur, CSC, June 16, 1993, ASC.

11. Statistics, Director of Institutional Research, Stonehill College. Enrollment went from 350 to 509, with a rise in the women from 22 to 28 percent. Faculty numbers rose from 25 to 39 during the same period.

12. In a pattern which would continue, the percentage of Holy Cross religious in the classroom dropped during the Sheehan years, from 40 percent in 1955 to almost 31 percent in 1958. Similar trends were seen in Catholic colleges throughout the country. Merrimack, for example, between 1947 to 1957 went from 69 to 30 percent. F. G. Roddy, Jr., Merrimack College: Genesis and Growth, 1947–1972 (North Andover, Massachusetts: Merrimack College Press, 1972): 57–58.

13. Edward J. Power, *Catholic Higher Education in America, A History* (New York: Appleton-Century-Crofts, 1992), 426; Edward J. Power, "Is the Catholic College Academically Respectable?" *Homiletic and Pastoral Review* 56 (June 1956): 737.

14. "Fr. Gillis on America," *America* 87 (May 24, 1952): 219–20. The editors attacked some of Buckley's precepts. Yet, *America* was balanced with an assault by Robert Hartnett, SJ, "Commies and Academic Freedom," *America* 89 (April 18, 1953): 77–79 and 89 (May 16, 1953): 187–90, which saw Communists involved with the call for total academic freedom.

15. David Arthur, CSC, interview with James Kenneally, May 23, 1993, ASC.

16. Meeting Minutes of the Academic Council, November 30, 1956, Academic Council Papers, ASC.

17. Christopher O'Toole to James Sheehan, September 17, 1957, Sheehan Papers, ASC. The trustees met irregularly but approximately six times per year. The Board of Advisors generally met twice annually.

18. Between the fall of 1954 and the fall of 1955 alone, enrollment rose 25 percent, with projections for similar increases in the future. The problem for the College was not obtaining students but limiting growth to manageable levels. See Sheehan to William D. Jones, November 9, 1955, Sheehan Papers, ASC.

19. Joseph Martin to James Sheehan, November 8, 1955, Sheehan Papers, ASC. Representative Martin informed Sheehan estimated costs to dismantle, move, and reassemble a large hangar from Squantum Naval Air Station in Quincy, Massachusetts to be $800,000. The projection was considered "a terribly steep price."

20. James Sheehan, CSC, "Memo to [Provincial] Council Members" (September 28, 1955), Executive Council Papers, ASC.

21. The law had previously granted loans for the construction of dormitories and similar housing only.

22. James Sheehan to Federal Housing Administration, August 15, 1955; William D. Jones [Federal Housing Regional Administrator] to Sheehan, August 30, 1955, Sheehan Papers, ASC; Provincial Council Meeting Minutes, November 4, 1955, AHCFE.

23. Boland's 1954 loan of $100,000, secured from the First National Bank of North Easton to pay off the King's debt, required repayment. Only $25,000 had been paid, thus Sheehan sought an additional $75,000 in his present request to settle the first debt and consolidate payments. The interest rate of 3.75 percent offered by the New Bedford bank was the same as that from North Easton. See James Sheehan to James Connerton, December 12, 1955, Sheehan Papers, ASC.

24. Bernard Ransing, CSC, to James Connerton, January 4, 1956, Sheehan Papers, ASC. The General Council also authorized securing a $300,000 government loan for the cafeteria project.

25. James Sheehan to James Connerton, January 15, 1956, Sheehan Papers, ASC.

26. Extant data does not indicate why the loan was $50,000 more than that requested by Sheehan in December 1955. The $75,000 owed to the First National Bank of North Easton was swiftly repaid on February 21, 1956. See James Sheehan to James J. Carpenter, November 8, 1956, Sheehan Papers, ASC.

27. *The Summit* (October 1955), ASC. Recall that the Stonehill Guild was originally formed in 1939 as the Seminary Guild.

28. Ibid., March 1956 and *The Summit* (September 1956); "Chronicles of Our Lady of Holy Cross" (March 1, 1956), ASC.

29. *The Summit* (December 1956), ASC. The Century Club grew slowly, with a membership of 165 reported at the close of the year.

30. *The Summit* (October 22, 1957, November 12, 1957, March 31, 1958, May 5, 1958), ASC.

31. James Connerton to Christopher O'Toole, February 24, 1956, Superior General Papers–O'Toole, AHCFE.

32. *The Summit* (March 1956); "Chronicles of Our Lady of Holy Cross" (March 3, 1956), ASC.

33. LaLiberte, who received an honorary doctorate in 1963, was a great benefactor of Stonehill College. His work was charged at rates below those of other architects and on several occasions he donated his services to the College. His contribution to the overall design of Stonehill College was significant. See James Sheehan to George DePrizio, n.d.; Sheehan to Connerton, January 15, 1956, Sheehan Papers, ASC.

34. *The Summit* (March 1956), ASC.

35. "Chronicles of Our Lady of Holy Cross" (May 24, 1956, November 30, 1956, January 27, 1957, January 31, 1957); *The Summit* (November 1956, January 1957), ASC.

36. James Sheehan to John McCormack, October 31, 1955; Sheehan to Joseph Martin, October 31, 1955; McCormack to Albert M. Cole, November 7, 1955; McCormack to William D. Jones, November 7, 1955, Sheehan Papers, ASC. McCormack stated in his letter to Albert Cole that he and Martin were alumni of Stonehill.

37. William D. Jones to James Sheehan, November 17, 1955; Sheehan to Jones, December 21, 1955, Sheehan Papers, ASC.

38. William Jones to James Sheehan, March 9, 1956; Jones to Sheehan, July 11, 1956, Sheehan Papers, ASC.

39. Sheehan wrote to McCormack on at least three different occasions and Martin on four occasions (extant correspondence) enlisting their assistance in Stonehill's loan application with the Housing and Home Finance Agency.

40. The stipulations of these government loans stated that the money approved would only be released after the project was underway and construction seemed satisfactory. In order to begin, it was thus necessary to secure other sources of funding, which would be repaid upon release of the government loan.

41. James Sheehan to George DePrizio, February 28, 1957; DePrizio to Sheehan, April 13, 1957, Provincial Papers–DePrizio, ACHFE; *The Summit* (March 1957), ASC.

42. Ralph B. Cornell to James Sheehan, August 13, 1957, Sheehan Papers, ASC.

43. Christopher O'Toole to George DePrizio, August 24, 1957, Superior General Papers–O'Toole, AHCFE.

44. James Sheehan to Christopher O'Toole, August 26, 1957, Sheehan Papers, ASC; George DePrizio to O'Toole, August 27, 1957, Superior General Papers–O'Toole, AHCFE.

45. George DePrizio to Christopher O'Toole, August 31, 1957, Superior General Papers–O'Toole, AHCFE; O'Toole to James Sheehan, September 17, 1957, Sheehan Papers, ASC.

46. Leo Stein to James Sheehan, October 16, 1957; Sheehan to Ted J. Gadoury, Inc., October 22, 1957, Sheehan Papers; Gadoury to Sheehan, May 22, 1958, Cafeteria–Physical Plant Papers; *The Summit* (May 20, 1958), ASC.

47. James J. Hennesey, SJ, *American Catholics—A History of the Roman Catholic Community in the United States* (New York: Oxford University Press, 1981): 284.

48. Ibid., 296; Will Herberg, *Protestant—Catholic—Jew,* Revised Edition (Garden City, New York: Doubleday & Company, Inc., 1960): 48.

49. Quoted in Hennesey, *American Catholics,* 287.

50. James Connerton to Christopher O'Toole, January 16, 1956, Superior General Papers–O'Toole; Provincial Council Meeting Minutes, December 19, 1956, January 6, 1957, AHCFE.

51. George DePrizio to Christopher O'Toole, August 6, 1957; O'Toole to DePrizio, August 12, 1957, Superior General Papers–O'Toole, AHCFE.

52. George DePrizio to James Sheehan, August 27, 1957; Sheehan to DePrizio, October 25, 1957; DePrizio to Sheehan, November 4, 1957, Sheehan Papers, ASC. DePrizio's letter of August 27 reads as if the General had authorized his original plan, yet O'Toole had stated clearly that the decision was a local one.

53. George DePrizio to Christopher O'Toole, April 30, 1957, May 9, 1957, Superior General Papers–O'Toole, AHCFE. DePrizio listed many benefits to the West Haven site. Besides its ideal location within the Eastern Province of Holy Cross, he claimed that a charter from the State of Connecticut would be easily obtained, that the site would bring prestige to the Congregation as he planned to establish the Province headquarters there, and that the proposed building was suitable for the purposes of classrooms, auditoriums, dormitory space, and a chapel. DePrizio also wanted to avoid North Easton as a site, claiming that it was off the "main line," Stonehill was coeducational, and the Province wanted to avoid associating the seminary with any one college, to avoid creating a mentality that forms a "Stonehill Priest" versus a Holy Cross Father.

54. Christopher O'Toole to George DePrizio, May 4, 1957, Superior General Papers–O'Toole, AHCFE.

55. Those suggested as faculty members were: Richard Sullivan (philosophy), John Lucey (classics), Robert Griffin (English), Thomas Campbell (dogmatic theology), plus a brother from Notre Dame High school to teach science and a diocesan priest for Canon Law.

56. George DePrizio to Christopher O'Toole, July 17, 1957, Superior General Papers, AHCFE.

57. Provincial Council Meeting Minutes, July 18, 1957, AHCFE.

58. Ibid., October 28–29, 1957, December 12, 1957, February 14, 1958, April 7–8, 1958, May 12–14, 1958; Bernard Ransing to George DePrizio, May 19, 1958, Superior General Papers–O'Toole, AHCFE.

CHAPTER 4

The Reason We Exist—Student Life

Stonehill College, as an apostolate of the Congregation of Holy Cross, continues the Community's long-standing mission as educators in the faith. Started with little forethought and planning in the summer of 1948 in response to threatened competition from Franciscans, the College was, by any reasonable standard, not very impressive in its early years. The campus contained only one building designed as a classroom, a converted tennis court used as a gymnasium, and a former mansion that housed all other facilities, including a library, a cafeteria, administrative offices, and living quarters for the Holy Cross religious assigned to the College. Students, however, are the heart and soul of any school; they are the reason educational institutions exist. The lack of facilities did not deter energetic students from matriculating at Stonehill, organizing and participating in a lively student life, and in the process gaining a good education, academically and experientially. The story of Stonehill College is, therefore, necessarily the story of the activities and contributions of its students.

Student Life, Organizations, and Clubs

AFTER A SLOW START, student enrollment at Stonehill rose significantly throughout the 1950s, stretching the College's limited facilities. When 134 men started classes in September 1948, it was projected that—unless it was curbed—student population would quickly overtax the College's physical space and overburden teachers, who were already teaching courses of 40 or more students per class. However, the United States' entry into the Korean conflict in the summer of 1950 and the reinstitution of the draft led to plum-meting college attendance throughout the country. Stonehill was especially vulnerable, because its precarious financial picture depended upon student tuition to provide money to operate the College. Between 1951 and 1953 enrollment, even with the addition of women in 1951, dwindled from 293 to 264.[1] The lean years, however, gave way in the administration of James Sheehan to rapid growth, from 350 students in 1955 to 509 in 1958. This rise in enrollment also concerned the Provincial Council, which in 1961 recommended that Stonehill's enrollment be capped at 900, a figure thought to be properly serviceable by the College facilities. The 900 ceiling, however, was exceeded the next year, and in 1963 attendance topped 1000 for the first time. At this point, two-thirds of the students were male and 90 percent came from Massachusetts.[2]

Tuition was another source of concern for students at the College. The passage of time, rising costs, and greater numbers of students led to higher operating costs. When Stonehill opened its doors in September 1948, full-time tuition was $210 per semester or $10 per credit hour for part-time students. The sum was slightly higher than at some neighboring schools, but as one Stonehill student of the period commented, "It was possible to earn your tuition in the summer."[3] Tuition was raised, however, out of necessity to meet operational costs. The first increase came in the fall of 1954, to $220 per semester. In 1959 a 27 percent rise from the previous year was implemented; by 1964 tuition was $450 per semester or $27 per unit for part-time students.[4]

Progress in establishing scholarships and other forms of financial aid came with the rise in enrollment. Before the first students started classes, Harry K. Stone, judge of the Brockton probate court, an original member of the Board of Advisors and a lifelong friend and benefactor of Stonehill, established the first two student scholarships. One, the Idletta E. Stone Scholarship, was named for Stone's mother; the second, The Reverend Alexander Hamilton Scholarship, was named after a member of the first graduating class of The College of the Holy Cross in Worcester. Each was a full-year grant in tuition ($420).[5] Judge Stone also established the Dewey D. Stone loan fund at Stonehill for financially needy students.

Scholarship programs grew consistently with the development of the College. Beginning in 1956, Stonehill conducted an annual competitive examination for local high school seniors to award over $38,000 to 20 incoming freshmen. A policy established in 1959 granted four-year full-tuition scholarships to all children of full-time faculty members. An important benefactor in these early years was Cardinal Francis Spellman of New York, who by 1961 had given the College $20,000 to establish scholarships for

> Violation of any of these regulations is punishable by fines or by revocation of all parking privileges.
>
> **DRESS**
>
> All students must conform to the basic standards of good taste in the matter of dress.
>
> For the Men Students: suit coats, blazers or sport coats, collared shirts, ties and neat trousers are required for attendance at class.
>
> For the Women Students: They must be neatly and modestly dressed at all times. Sneakers of all types are prohibited. Bermudas and slacks are not to be worn on campus except for participation in athletic activities.

Student handbook 1961: dress code.

graduates of Brockton's Cardinal Spellman High School. Between 1962 and 1965, four awards of $100 annually, granted in the names of Bishop Cassidy, Pope John XXIII, Bishop Connolly, and Pope Pius XII, were established. By the fall of 1963 the College provided over $279,000 in annual aid to students.[6]

Student life at Stonehill was governed by rules and regulations which, although consistent with the progressive attitude of 1950s America, deviated from Catholic higher education's recent divorce from the conservative tradition of *in loco parentis.*[7] Before dormitories were constructed, students who lived too far to commute resided in "certified" private homes in Easton and Brockton.[8] A member of the College administration, normally a priest, was responsible for ensuring that the owners enforced rules including a curfew, prohibition against entertaining members of the opposite sex in living quarters, possessing or using alcohol, and leaving the house on weekends without parental consent. On school nights a curfew room check was conducted at 11 P.M., with lights out at midnight. Parents were informed of violations of rules and disciplinary action was taken.

Rules for student dress became increasingly formal with the passage of time. When the College opened with men only, students were expected to dress in coat and tie for class and meals. When women were admitted in the fall of 1951, dresses or skirts were normative; slacks were allowed only in extremely inclement weather. In 1961 coat, tie, and dress slacks were mandated as standard apparel for men.[9]

An unusual aspect of student life at Stonehill was the presence of seminarians and lay students on the same campus, taking many of the same classes. Traditional seminary life placed priest candidates and religious in an isolated environment. At Stonehill priests, brothers, and seminary students had their own living quarters. Since many courses were open to all students, however, there was interaction between the religious and secular student bodies. Seminarians by edict sat in the back few rows of any classroom. While seminarians were not prohibited from talking with their nonreligious classmates, friendships were not fostered. Relationships with women were the most worrisome and problematic. Seminarians were instructed to be cordial and to answer greetings and questions from female students, but they were not to initiate a conversation. Women, in turn, were asked not to look in the direction of seminarians, for "it would be unseemly and might cause them to lose their vocation."[10]

Student government was established at the outset of the College, but almost two years elapsed before it gained any significant voice on campus. A student council was formed in the fall of 1948 "to promote religious, academic, and social welfare of students." The council's first-year objective was to draft a student charter. By 1949 the task was enlarged to writing a constitution, which was completed and accepted in April 1950. Jim Kehoe was elected the first council chairman. The council met weekly (with rare exceptions) throughout the academic year, making recommendations about the status and activities of clubs, campus events, and student accountability. The College dean and president held veto power over the decisions of the council, but this was rarely exercised.[11]

The governance structure changed with the needs of a growing student body. A new student constitution was introduced in October 1956 and ratified in February 1957. The document provided for a three-branch government: legislative, executive, and judicial. The heart of the new constitution was the establishment of a student senate to replace the council; it consisted of 17 members, 4 from each class, plus a senior nonvoting member to serve as president and chief executive officer of the government.[12] In October 1960 the legislative branch expanded again with the addition of a "congress of representatives," which consisted of one representative from each of Stonehill's 22 approved clubs and one from each class.[13]

Student government often acted to police the student body as a means to develop personal responsibility. In March 1954 a demerit system was introduced to curb inappropriate behavior, on or off campus, which reflected poorly on the College. Misdemeanor offenses included drunkenness, vandalism, and failure to observe traffic ordinances or follow school regulations. Demerits were assigned commensurate with the severity of the offense. Any student who received demerits was granted a hearing before the Student Senate; any who accumulated five demerits was interviewed by the College president. Demerits were recorded from the beginning to the end of one academic year.[14]

First issue of The Summit, *November 3, 1949.*

In 1964 cheating was addressed by student government. The senate recommended that the administration publicize penalties for cheating, that professors enforce the policy, and that the dean prosecute violators.[15] Development of personal responsibility among all students, however, remained the goal.

The relationship between student government and the administration was generally harmonious, as both parties expressed similar goals and methods to attain them. One major disagreement, however, presented itself in December 1959. Led by its president, Paul Reed, the Student Senate voted to recess indefinitely because its members were "no longer able to carry out [their] oath to represent the student body which elected them." The senators were upset that Stonehill's administration had changed student regulations without consulting them.[16] Reed wrote to Stonehill's president, Father Richard Sullivan, with his objections. Sullivan responded sensitively but made it clear that the senate and the administration each have a place and function.

He explained that the College Board of Discipline, under the supervision of the president, made regulations for the good of the majority of students. Sullivan's explanation paved the way for the Senate to return to session after the semester break.[17]

The student newspaper, *The Summit*, published its first edition on November 3, 1949, under the editorship of William Sullivan and the watchful eye of its faculty advisor, Brassil Fitzgerald. The purpose of the paper was "to bring to the students news items, articles of interest, and student humor and to provide for the outside world an insight into the many aspects of life at Stonehill." The paper's name was derived from the concept that the Catholic educator teaches from the summit of a hill where one can examine human works but look unhindered to God. The masthead—a hill surrounded by a cross, present from the premier issue—was designed by Leonel Neron.[18]

The Summit quickly became a favorite with students in its presentation of College news and student opinion. The paper reported club news, sports stories, and other campus activities. Regular features in the paper were: "Our Lady on the Hill," a seasonal or religious poem or prose article by a student, usually accompanied by a photo of the Blessed Mother Mary; "Cruising the Campus" and "Stonehill Pebbles," which reported close-ups on campus personalities; "Did You Know," a column that disclosed interesting and little-known facts about the College; "Vets on Campus," which provided useful information for veterans and introduced them to the College; and "What's What in Books," which gave information on contemporary literary endeavors. The paper published on an irregular monthly basis for its first four years, but academic year 1953–1954 experienced "the temporary absence" of the paper. It was replaced by a flyer, "This Week at Stonehill," written by a team of five students headed by Terence Byrne.[19]

Student efforts in journalism and writing were present in two additional annual publications. The first student yearbook, edited by William Sullivan, with James Moran as business manager, was published in the spring of 1949. In 1952 the book was given the name *Acres*, a title that continues today. In the spring of 1960 the magazine *Cairn*, an annual journal of literature and arts, was first published "to provide a creative forum for Stonehill students, staff, and alumni."[20]

Student clubs were active on campus from the outset at the College. Almost from the beginning Stonehill participated in the National Federation of Catholic College Students. The glee club gave periodic concerts during the year and provided music at many liturgical functions. Most academic disciplines had their own organizations, such as the math, business, science, and political science clubs. By the mid-1950s more groups, such as the

Professor Herbert Wessling.

Monogram Club (open to varsity lettermen), the Residents Club (organized to assist those who boarded in the area), the Veterans Club, the Lafayette Society (to promote French culture), and the Young Republicans and Young Democrats were prominent on campus.[21]

The debate team, originally organized under the direction of John Collan in December 1949, was brought to high stature on campus through the work and support of Professor Herbert Wessling, who came to the College in 1952. Stonehill was small and without prestige, but it challenged the giants such as Harvard and MIT, and in a replay of David and Goliath was often victorious.[22]

Service organizations were also popular on campus. The Crosiers, organized for women in 1954, developed greater spirit on campus through its promotion of voluntarism. In 1959 the men's service club, the Ethosiles, was formed; the name was changed to Purple Key in 1962, when it advertised itself as "a society of men which endeavors as a whole to serve the college administration in its attempts to build the name and fame of our Alma Mater." One annual service project for Purple Key was its participation in the freshmen orientation program.

Crosiers service club pin.

Members of Purple Key service club.

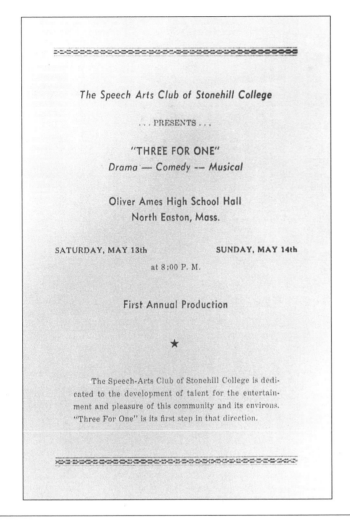

The Speech Arts Club of Stonehill College

... PRESENTS ...

"THREE FOR ONE"
Drama — Comedy — Musical

Oliver Ames High School Hall
North Easton, Mass.

SATURDAY, MAY 13th   SUNDAY, MAY 14th
at 8:00 P. M.

First Annual Production

★

The Speech-Arts Club of Stonehill College is dedicated to the development of talent for the entertainment and pleasure of this community and its environs.
"Three For One" is its first step in that direction.

Playbill for speech-arts first production, "Three for One."

The Speech-Arts Society was, in these early years, the most active and highest-profile club on campus. It was originally organized in March 1950 under the direction of Henry Malone, CSC. After James Doyle, CSC, supervised the group for one year, Herbert Wessling was given the club reins in the fall of 1952. The Speech-Arts Society annually produced two plays. Its first production, given at Oliver Ames High School in May 1950, was "Three for One," a synthesis of three one-act plays: a drama, *The Man with His Heart in the Highlands*, a comedy, *These Doggone Elections*, and a musical, *Dancing Acres*.[23] Stonehill College witnessed many fine produc-

Saxon Society banquet.

tions from the Speech-Arts Society in its early years, including *George Washington Slept Here, The Student Prince, You Can't Take It With You, Jayne Eyre, The Curious Savage* and the Greek classic *Oedipus Rex*. In the early 1960s *Craig's Wife, Pygmalion, The Pleasure of His Company*, and *Harvey*, were produced at the high school, Ames Memorial Hall, and North Junior High in Brockton. Shakespeare was first presented in the spring of 1961, with excerpts from *Hamlet, Romeo and Juliet, Macbeth, Henry V*, and the *Taming of the Shrew*. In 1964 a Shakespeare Festival was held, with *As You Like It* the featured production. Plays were selected by a committee headed by Wessling. Many of the productions were directed by students.[24]

The radio division of the Speech-Arts Society provided a second dimension to this popular and well-respected club. Shortly after the society was organized, a radio production, *The Life of St. Patrick*, was broadcast over WBKA in Brockton. In the spring of 1951 the club began a harmonious relationship with WPEP in Taunton. Plays, such as *God and a Red Scooter*, a radio version of Charles Dickens' *A Tale of Two Cities* and *The Monkey's Paw*, were read at Taunton's Park Theater and later rebroadcast over WPEP. Brockton station WBET also aired many radio plays. Some of the most popular were *My Double and How He Undid Me, The Million Pound Bank Note*, and *Curly*, a story about a caterpillar who disappeared and touched off a national search. Herbert Wessling's friendships with officials at WPEP and WBET paved the way for these Stonehill productions.[25]

The Saxon Society, established in 1955, was Stonehill's academic honors fraternity. The group was founded to give "the highest possible recognition to students of outstanding scholarship and character." Members were juniors and seniors selected for scholastic accomplishment, character, and leadership. Students' names were placed in nomination by the academic council, forwarded to subcommittee for discussion, and then returned to the full council for final approval. New members were announced by the president and inducted on March 7, the Feast of St. Thomas Aquinas. Saxon Society members enjoyed the privilege of unrestricted cuts in class and had the option as seniors of submitting a thesis in lieu of a comprehensive examination. In October 1960 the Saxon Society was incorporated into the Delta Epsilon Sigma Honor Society.[26]

Sports on Campus

SHORTLY AFTER TAKING OFFICE as president, George Benaglia hired George Sullivan, an all-American tackle from Notre Dame's 1946 national championship football team, as Stonehill's first athletic director. Sullivan had served in the Navy's V-12 program at Notre Dame after graduation, but sought a position as a coach. Benaglia's original plan was for Sullivan to develop a football team, but when Francis Boland assumed the reins as president in the summer of 1949, the idea was quickly scuttled.[27] Sullivan was assisted in his duties by the Athletic Board of Authority, which was formed in October 1950.

Stonehill College launched its sports program in the late fall of 1948, when a basketball team was formed with Sullivan as coach. Because no facilities were available on campus (the "gymnasium" at this time was still a clay tennis court), the team practiced at Oliver Ames High School and played home games at the Brockton Armory. Money for uniforms was raised through a raffle; players and coach traveled to away games in private vehicles. Predictably the first year's record was 4–10, but the yearbook reported that Sullivan and the basketball team "can be truly called the originators of the Stonehill Spirit."[28]

Basketball rapidly became king at Stonehill, initiating a tradition that continues today. *The Summit* and yearbook covered the games extensively. Students gathered for the games as a community event; attendance for many was as important as class. Before home games, the Student Council scheduled pep rallies with bands. The tradition of beating a drum in the campus quadrangle before the first home game began in these first years. In the

Beating the drum in the campus quad before the first home basketball game.

team's second season, Stonehill entered the Southern New England Coastal Conference (SNECC), which included Bridgewater State Teachers' College, Bradford Durfee Technical Institute, Curry College, Bryant College, New Bedford Textile, and Assumption College. Sweet success followed the team as they captured the conference championship and finished the season 15–1. Bill Herlihy and all-conference selectees Dapper McDonald and Paul Sincero were the team leaders. In short order, with only freshmen and sophomore players, Stonehill had established itself as a basketball force in southern New England.[29]

Stonehill's basketball program matured and gained great success throughout the 1950s and into the new decade. In 1952, 1955, 1956, and 1963 Stonehill captured the SNECC championship. In 1960 and 1961 the team played in the post-season National Association of Intercollegiate Athletics (NAIA) tournament. The first freshmen team was fielded in 1962.[30] Standouts on these teams included Ed Kavanaugh, Paul McDonnell, Don Edmonston (who made the National Catholic All-American squad), George Peterson (small college division Catholic College All-American), Leo Denault, Joseph Walsh, and Dick Munson. Fran O'Brien in 1962 became the

The 1949–1950 men's basketball team, Southern New England Coastal Conference (SNECC) champions.

first Stonehill coach to be nominated by the Greater Boston Sportswriters for the small college New England coach of the year.[31] The 1952 team, which claimed a 19–7 record (18–4 in college competition), was feted with a special banquet at which Arnold "Red" Auerbach, coach of the Boston Celtics, was the principal speaker. Stonehill's success on the court led frustrated coaches from other schools in the SNECC in 1953 to write to Boland asking that the College withdraw from the league,[32] but no action was taken on either side.

Basketball placed Stonehill on the sports map of the region, but other sports had their genesis in this same period. On March 30, 1950, boxing came to Stonehill. In an imitation of the "Bengal Bouts"[33] popular at Notre Dame, the Brockton Music Hall was host to eight matches held as a benefit for the college yearbook. Brockton favorite son Rocky Marciano attended the event, which drew a good crowd. An annual boxing exhibition was held for the next several years. In the spring of 1950 Stonehill fielded its first baseball team under Coach Sullivan. With the assistance of Brother Josepheus, a field was cleared in the flat area below the main building.[34] Without any uniforms other than caps for identification, the team posted a 3–3 record in its maiden season. In its second season the team played a full 16-game schedule. The spring of 1951 witnessed the start of tennis as a club sport on campus; Dave Gates led the team to an undefeated season.[35]

Sullivan left his position as the athletic director and coach at Stonehill in June 1951. Ostensibly he resigned in order to attend law school, but it is clear that Boland was pleased with his exodus. In the fall of 1950 the president had sent a series of letters to Sullivan voicing his displeasure with the coach's lack of supervision of athletes who received scholarship assistance. Boland regularly inspected the locker room, located under the kitchen in the main building, and often found it dirty. He once threatened to fine both Sullivan and the athletes $10 per day if the gym was not satisfactorily cleaned. When Sullivan tendered his resignation, Boland wrote, "The condition [in which] you left affairs here at [the] College was unsatisfactory. . . . I had not presumed you would leave the job in this bad condition."[36] Sullivan returned to Notre Dame, entered law school, and eventually returned to Massachusetts, where he served as a judge in the district court of Stoughton.

In August 1951 Joseph Cheney, also a Notre Dame graduate, took the helm of Stonehill College's athletic program. Cheney had to survive an early attempt by students to have him ousted for "incompetent, ungentlemanly conduct as coach." The complaint, initiated by the Student Council, was endorsed and forwarded in February 1953 by the Athletic Council, but Boland took no action on the petition.[37] Cheney was not a gifted coach, but he was willing to hold many jobs and seemed satisfied with little compensation—an attitude that fit Boland's needs.

From the outset, Stonehill had fielded athletic teams, but the College's loyal fans had no team name to invoke or Alma Mater to sing. After a campus-wide competition was held in 1952, Edward Shea, CSC, chairman of the Athletic Board, suggested the name "Chieftains" for Stonehill's athletic teams. The name was derived from the fact that the athletes played on the same fields where the legendary King Philip once had his headquarters, a historical site located on the Stonehill College campus. The student Alma Mater took much longer to generate than the team name. Virginia Yosgandes, dean of Women, wrote lyrics to a tune by Alexander Peloquin. Published in September 1962 as the Stonehill Alma Mater, the song was never utilized.[38]

During the latter half of the 1950s and early 1960s, the Stonehill athletic program expanded greatly. Robert Daly, who became athletic director in 1956, was followed by William Gartland, CSC, in 1959 and Paul Duff,

Mary Virginia Yosgandes, first dean of women.

CSC, in 1963. Boxing continued as an annual tournament until the spring of 1956, when the Athletic Board dropped it due to "inadequate facilities." Baseball, led by its captain Lou Gorman, lost the conference championship in a playoff in 1952 but captured the crown the next year. Tennis on campus received a major boost in the fall of 1952 when the Stonehill College Women's Guild financed the construction of four new courts. It became a varsity sport in 1959, coached by William Keegan, CSC, finishing 2–8 in its maiden season of competition. Golf and soccer joined the varsity ranks in 1960 and 1961, respectively.[39]

Women's sports at Stonehill, like men's, began with basketball. *The Summit* in December 1952 reported that Coach Joseph Cheney had scheduled three games for a coeducational basketball team, but formal women's basketball was not launched until October 1959, under the guidance of Virginia Yosgandes. The team achieved a 5–5 record in its second season. In 1962 Nancy Carroll was appointed the first director of women's athletics, and the College joined The Greater Boston Women's Basketball League.

Intercollegiate athletics was the most visible sport forum, but an active

Rev. William Gartland, CSC.

intramural program was present on campus, beginning with football in the fall of 1950. The league included eight teams; two games per week were scheduled. The first-year champions were the Briarcliff Bombers, who defeated the Math Club 13–12. When St. Pius X Seminary opened the next fall, the seminarians fielded a team that won the championship. Led in its early years by Tom Tobin, Michael Novak, and Vince Spinelli, who had played tackle for the University of Miami, the Pius X squad was always competitive. In the winter, basketball was offered; softball was the spring intramural sport.[40] Beginning in the fall of 1951, an annual tennis tournament was held for students. Intramurals were quite popular—especially basketball, in which close to half the male student body participated.[41]

Holy Cross Father David Arthur, who was appointed the first intramural director upon his arrival at Stonehill in the fall of 1954, organized the program more formally. Working without an assistant, he scheduled all games, prepared the facilities, wrote up game summaries, and often acted as timer and scorekeeper.[42] Arthur, who served as director from 1954 to 1956 and again from 1957 to 1962, was succeeded in the interim by Father William Keegan, CSC, and Brother Leo Newton, CSC.

Traditions and Celebrations

CATHOLIC EDUCATION in the United States has always had the task of integrating the intellectual and moral formation of students. At Stonehill College, especially in the early years, a Christian atmosphere was fostered in both formal and informal ways. In the fall of 1949 Father Victor Dean, who had worked with James Moran to organize and submit Stonehill's application to the Massachusetts Board of Collegiate Authority in the summer of 1948, was appointed the first director of religious activities. He and his successors—especially, J. Marc Hebert, CSC—published a weekly bulletin of religious activities on campus. Students were invited to attend daily Mass in the chapel of the main building; confession was also offered. No formal program of campus ministry was present, but students and religious faculty mingled freely in an atmosphere conducive to conversation and the fostering of relationships.[43]

In the spring of 1949 the tradition of an annual three-day student retreat was begun. On February 27 through 29 Edward Hartnett, CSC, a member of the Holy Cross mission band, led the first retreat. Classes were canceled on these days; attendance was mandatory for Catholics and encouraged for all others. The retreat tradition continued—some years in the fall and others in the spring—throughout the 1950s, with directors including Holy Cross Fathers George Fischer, Philip Kelly, James Lowery, Charles Wallen, Frank Gartland, and Tom Tobin.[44]

The appointment of Joseph Lorusso, CSC, as director of religious activities in the fall of 1953 led to an expanded religious presence on campus. The dedication of the Lourdes Grotto in December 1953 was the catalyst for rosary devotions and processions, which were offered in October and for many years during Lent. Lorusso organized the Crusaders Club in 1955 "to re-emphasize the role of the Catholic layman in the mission field." Members of the Confraternity of Christian Doctrine (CCD) Club, organized at this same time, sponsored workshops on Catholic education of children and served as teachers to the mentally handicapped at Myles Standish State School in Taunton.[45]

Stonehill sponsored other religious activities not directly related to the College. Between 1959 and 1964 a series of five liturgical workshops were held on campus. Organized by James Doyle, CSC, and William Hogan, CSC, experts were invited to campus to discuss new Roman directives on lay participation in the Mass. In the early 1960s summer lay retreats, held in O'Hara Hall, were offered under the direction of Fathers Philip Kelly and Charles Mahoney.

Mardi Gras celebration.

Junior prom, 1957.

1955 commencement:
Francis Boland, CSC, Raymond P. Perra (valedictorian), Dr. Robert Porter, Msgr.
Timothy F. O'Leary, Representative John McCormack, Bishop Matthew Brady,
Representative Joseph Martin (honorary degree recipients), and an unknown observer.

The growth of the College through the 1950s provided the catalyst for the initiation of various annual campus events and celebrations. In the fall of 1949 the Stonehill Club of Brockton sponsored the first "Harvest Festival," a dance where a queen, chosen from nominations by Stonehill students, was crowned. Over the years the festival found different occasions to celebrate, such as welcoming the soccer season in 1963. Junior week, another annual tradition, was started in 1955. Activities included a community Mass, Communion breakfast, and attendance at a basketball game and/or a play. They culminated in the gala junior prom.[46] In February 1958 the first Mardi Gras celebration was held. Stonehill's first winter carnival, sponsored by student government and campus organizations, was held February 23–25, 1962 and featured tobogganing, snow sculpture, cross country skiing, and a dance.[47]

Richard Sullivan, CSC, Senator John F. Kennedy, and George DePrizio, CSC, October 6, 1958.

    Stonehill was fortunate in its early years to attract many notable people to its campus as speakers. Commencement exercises were graced by the presence of Bishop Lawrence Shehan of Bridgeport (who later became Cardinal Archbishop of Baltimore), Massachusetts Governors Foster Furcolo and John Volpe, Supreme Knight of Knights of Columbus, Luke Hart, Senate majority leader Mike Mansfield, Church historian Monsignor John Tracy Ellis, and Senator Edward Kennedy. These men, along with Cardinal Francis Spellman, Monsignor Humberto Medeiros (later Cardinal Archbishop of Boston), and the "rosary priest," Patrick Peyton, were some who received honorary degrees from the College. Leaders in the worlds of academia, religion, and politics came to campus, sponsored by the Saxon Society, Young Republicans and Democrats, and the Stonehill College Women's Guild. The political scientist Waldemar Gurian, noted essayist Erik von Kuehnelt-Leddihn, the Pulitzer Prize winning poet Stanley Kunitz, and political figures Senator John F. Kennedy, Representative John McCormack, and Boston Mayor Joseph Hynes engaged students and faculty with addresses on campus.

1. Statistics from the Office of the Director of Institutional Research, Stonehill College. Male enrollment lowered by 70 and female enrollment rose by 41 during this period.

2. "Stonehill College 1963," Report of the Institutional Research Center. Other programs of learning were also growing at Stonehill. In 1962 there were 342 enrolled in adult education and 250 students in summer school. In 1963 tuition was $900 per year; room and board at O'Hara Hall, the first College dormitory, was $850 per year.

3. As a comparison, tuition rates in 1952 for local Catholic colleges were: Merrimack $350/year and Boston College $470/year. Group interview of Stonehill graduates of the 1950s with the author (November 14, 1995), Stonehill History Project Papers.

4. Statistics from the Office of the Director of Institutional Research, Stonehill College.

5. Thomas Duffy to James Connerton, July 29, 1948, Stonehill College Papers, AHCFE; Harry Stone to George Benaglia, October 18, 1948, Deans' Papers, ASC.

6. News Release, December 3, 1956, Public Affairs Papers; Stonehill Catalog, 1959–1960; Richard Sullivan to Cardinal Francis Spellman, November 22, 1961; Grace Donahue to Aloysius Cussen, December 12, 1961; Student Aid Report 1963–1964, Sullivan Papers, ASC. The 1963–1964 report gave the following statistics: Non-College sources of aid, $98,097, and Stonehill direct support source of aid $181,239, for a total of $279,336. As a means of comparison in academic year 1996–1997, the College dispersed $7.3 million for student financial aid, a figure that represents 25 percent of the total education and general budget.

7. Education had traditionally been considered a parental right. When students left home for school, the institution assumed the role of parent. In the 1950s this tradition of *in loco parentis* began to collapse; colleges no longer perceived their role as overseers of students.

8. Room and board costs were low. One woman reported paying six dollars per week for room and ten meals, breakfast and dinner Monday through Friday. Helen Derby was one of the best known and most beloved of the "House Mothers" who boarded female students in Easton. Group Interview "1950s," November 14, 1995.

9. Stonehill Student Handbooks, 1955–1961, ASC.

10. Group interview "1950s," November 14, 1995; Joan Camber to Anne Pollick, November 10, 1995, Stonehill History Project Papers, ASC.

11. *The Summit* (November 3, 1949, April 5, 1950); Student Council Meeting Minutes, n.d. [1950], Student Council Papers, ASC.

12. "Constitution for Stonehill Student Government" (October 1956), Student Government Papers; *The Summit* (March 1957), ASC. The judicial branch of the

new constitution called for a five-member general court to judge student disciplinary cases.

13. *The Summit* (March 16, 1960); "Constitution of Stonehill Student Government" (October 7, 1960), Student Government Papers, ASC.

14. Student Council Meeting Minutes, March 25, 1954, Student Government Papers, ASC.

15. Thomas Byron to Aloysius Cussen, CSC, November 13, 1964, Cussen Papers, ASC.

16. Changes in curfew hours and rules regarding the type of establishments where College-sponsored off-campus social functions could not be held were questioned.

17. *The Summit* (January 6, 1960, February 24, 1960); Richard Sullivan to Paul Reed, January 25, 1960, Student Government Papers, ASC. In the first annual Student Government day, held on April 8, 1961, Sullivan presented his understanding of student government: "Your [student government] goal should be to determine what you can do to improve the College in all intellectual, moral, and spiritual areas."

18. *The Summit* (November 3, 1949), January 23, 1953, ASC.

19. *Acres* (Student Yearbook), 1954, ASC. No extant data has been found that states why the paper was not published, but the College's precarious financial situation is the probable answer.

20. "*Cairn* Constitution," n.d., *Cairn* Files, ASC.

21. Stonehill College Catalogs, 1948–1963, ASC.

22. *The Summit* (March 2, 1951, March 31, 1953); Herbert Wessling, interview with James Kenneally (January 29, 1993), ASC.

23. *The Summit* (May 11, 1950).

24. Ibid., May 23, 1951, February 2, 1952, December 1954; English Department Meeting Minutes, March 1956, English Department Papers, ASC.

25. *The Summit* (April 5, 1950, November 17, 1950, March 2, 1951, March 16, 1951); Stonehill College Yearbook, 1951, ASC.

26. "The Saxon Society," short descriptive paper, Saxon Society File; "Saxon Society Summary," Delta Epsilon File, Deans' Papers; *The Summit* (February 1956); James Doyle to "Members of the Academic Council," November 16, 1959; "Memo," Office of the Dean [Aloysius Cussen], February 8, 1961, Academic Council Papers, ASC.

27. When Boland first arrived, he saw football practice gear (probably surplus from Notre Dame) on an open field on campus. He summarily stated, "There'll be no football here." John Lucey, CSC, interview with David Arthur, CSC, (September 21, 1993), ASC.

28. *The Summit* (December 15, 1949); Stonehill Yearbook 1949, ASC.

29. *The Summit* (November 23, 1949, November 2, 1951); Stonehill Yearbook, 1949, ASC.

30. From the outset of men's basketball, the College fielded varsity and junior varsity squads. Debate between the NCAA and NAIA officials on the eligibility of

freshmen for varsity competition led to the establishment of a freshmen team, with the junior varsity dropped.

31. *The Summit* (April 18, 1962).

32. "Chronicles of Our Lady of Holy Cross" (March 20, 1952); Meeting Minutes of the Southern New England Coastal Conference, March 19, 1953, Athletic Department Papers, ASC.

33. In the late nineteenth century the University of Notre Dame initiated an annual boxing tournament as a benefit for the Bengal missions (today the nation of Bangladesh) in which Holy Cross religious have continuously served since 1857.

34. Stonehill had a definite home field advantage for baseball. Despite the efforts of many, the field remained strewn with rocks, "bad hops" on ground balls were normative. Although a disadvantage to both teams, Stonehill players were at least aware of the situation.

35. *The Summit* (May 5, 1950, March 16, 1951, May 25, 1951), ASC.

36. Francis Boland to George Sullivan, September 21, 1950, November 28, 1950, June 21, 1951, Boland Papers, ASC.

37. "Memo" n.d., Joseph Cheney File, Athletic Department Papers, ASC. Athletes who played under Cheney have commented that his coaching knowledge was limited, especially in baseball. Group interview "1950s," November 14, 1995.

38. "Memo" n.d., Athletic Department Papers; *The Summit* (September 27, 1961), ASC. The words of Stonehill's Alma Mater are:

All Stonehill rise and sing today
Our Alma Mater's praise,
Dear home where happy work and play
Fill all our student days.

For quiet grotto's patient stones
And columns white and tall,
For scholars' strong resounding tones
That herald learning's call.

We raise our voices proud and clear
To sing our loyalty!
And echoes of our song we hear
From every rock and tree!

O purple hills all frosted white
With summer clouds or snow,
In Stonehill hearts be ever bright
Though far from you we go.

39. *The Summit* (December 1956, October 10, 1952, May 22, 1953, October 31, 1952, March 11, 1959), ASC.

40. Francis Boland suggested that archery be offered as a spring intramural sport for women but the program was never organized. David Arthur, CSC, interview with author (November 7, 1995).

41. Students of the period often engaged in "pick-up" basketball games in the gymnasium between classes. The lack of shower facilities earned those who participated the title "gym rats." Group interview, "1950s," November 14, 1995.

42. Preparation of the gym for basketball was a time-consuming and difficult task. The tile floor required court boundary lines, painted in water colors, to be drawn almost every week. The building was not heated, which made for many cold winter mornings of labor. This was merely a collateral duty for Arthur, as he was a full-time instructor in the Department of Philosophy. David Arthur, CSC, interview with author (November 14, 1995).

43. Group interview, "1950s," November 14, 1995; *The Summit* (October 31, 1952), ASC.

44. "Summary History of Stonehill College," n.d., Files of the Assistant Academic Dean, Stonehill College; *The Summit* (March 17, 1950, October 22, 1957, April 6, 1960, January 11, 1961, February 21, 1962), ASC.

45. *The Summit* (November 25, 1958, October 7, 1957, November 5, 1958); *Acres* (1956), ASC.

46. The first junior prom was actually celebrated at Boston's Hotel Statler Bay State Room on May 4, 1951. See *The Summit* (May 25, 1951), ASC.

47. Ibid., January 10, 1962, February 21, 1962, ASC.

CHAPTER 5

A College Emerges — Accreditation and Academic Development

Stonehill College, under the watchful eye of James Sheehan, began the necessary but uncertain process of expansion in order to meet the needs of its growing enrollment. With the burden of debt to the Eastern Province of Holy Cross removed and the fear of loss of students from the draft dispelled, and in an environment where American Catholicism was approaching its zenith, the time was right to move the College forward from its humble beginnings in search of greater acceptance. Sheehan's efforts included the construction of Holy Cross Hall, which provided badly needed classroom space, and the initiation of construction of a cafeteria and student union. Stonehill had begun its climb to a secure position in the academic community.

Nevertheless, the importance of the physical plant expansion could not mask the fact that Stonehill's academic program, the heart of any institution of higher learning, had not reached the point where the College could be accepted as a full-fledged liberal arts institution. Dedicated teachers had come to share in the mission started in 1948 and academic offerings were greater, but the stigma attached to a school without recognition from its peer institutions continued to plague the College and, most profoundly, its students. Guided by Father Richard Sullivan over the ensuing six years, however, Stonehill became the college—physically and academically—that had been the dream of its founders during the harried summer of 1948.

Richard Sullivan, CSC, was appointed by the provincial, George De-Prizio, as the fourth president of Stonehill College on June 24, 1958. Sullivan had served at the College since 1951 as a professor of philosophy and direc-

Rev. Richard Sullivan, CSC, president 1958–1964.

tor of Pius X Seminary, and since 1955 he had been vice president of the school. A native of Indiana, Sullivan had studied at Notre Dame, the Gregorian University in Rome, and the University of Laval in Quebec City, where he earned a doctorate in 1951. He was well equipped for the presidency, particularly by virtue of his broad experience as professor of philosophy at both Notre Dame and Stonehill, as director of novices, and as formation director for seminarians. Superior General Christopher O'Toole had every confidence, stating in his letter of confirmation of the appointment, "Father Richard Sullivan will make an excellent President."[1]

Sullivan was the most gifted and capable man to serve as Stonehill's president during the College's formative years. His combination of academic expertise, administrative ability, and an extroverted and positive personality allowed him to successfully complete the tasks of his office and endeared him to many people. He was more effective in his work as president than any of his predecessors because of his unique combination of talents and the fact that he refused to alienate anyone. He utilized his gifts, the office of president, and Stonehill's human and physical facilities to secure for the College a level of recognition that has only grown with time.

Sullivan also brought his philosophy of education to the presidential office. He was convinced that "the important element of the College is the person and not the thing." He insisted that faculty and administrators remain "most interested in the person of the student, his development and growth." The classroom was his emphasis: "There is no substitute for a class well taught." He believed that Stonehill's "reputation and image must be built upon the academic work of the College."[2] As the leader of an institution established to train both leaders and followers, Sullivan held the traditional view of the purpose of Catholic education:[3]

> There are two types of ignorance which must be expelled by two types of knowledge. The first is natural, belongs to the intellect alone and is the purpose of the Catholic College as college. The second is supernatural [,] belongs to the intellect and the will, is a combination of knowledge, love and moral virtues and is the purpose of a Catholic College as Catholic.

Sullivan believed that the greatest obstacle to the achievement of the goals of Catholic education was financial. Catholic colleges constantly wrestled with the tension of furnishing facilities and providing just salaries without raising tuition to a level that would prohibit Catholic students from attending. The solution to the dilemma was slow, cautious, but continuous growth. Sullivan envisioned Stonehill at this time to be a teaching institution where professors could follow the work of researchers and present it, together with their own discoveries, to students.[4]

From the outset Sullivan was accepted by the College and the greater academy in his position as president. The Superior General congratulated him for his ability to draw the faculty together and encourage teamwork at the College. He received high marks from Stonehill's Board of Advisors for his ability to financially manage the College; by the end of his administration, it had achieved a one-year operational profit of almost $162,000.[5]

Recognition from the outside was immediate when, less than one month after his appointment, he was appointed by Governor Foster Furcolo to the Massachusetts Board of Collegiate Authority.[6] In order to publicize the College and keep current on the affairs of Catholic higher education, Sullivan immediately joined the National Catholic Education Association (NCEA), and by October 1959 he was appointed to its executive committee. The next year he was elected chairman of the New England regional unit of the college and university department of the NCEA. Sullivan's leadership was also responsible for Stonehill's acceptance in 1961 as a member of the College Entrance Examination Board and in 1964 as a member of the New England Colleges Fund, a voluntary organization whose purpose was "to provide a fair and effective way for businessmen to strengthen the best in independent liberal arts colleges in New England."[7]

The Battle to Achieve Accreditation

❦ ACCREDITATION, THE *sine qua non* for higher education in the United States, first became a significant issue in Catholic colleges and universities in the 1930s. The NCEA and the North Central Association (NCA) felt that as the number of doctoral programs rose, Catholic higher education needed some means to measure the quality and effectiveness of institutions. Soundness of academic programs—especially, graduate schemas—plus the viability of living endowments and financial concerns were all scrutinized. In 1937 the NCEA asked all member institutions to file a report on faculty competence, library holdings, and administrative structure with respect to accreditation. This show of power angered schools and led to the association's removal from the accreditation process. Local civil agencies henceforth handled accreditation matters at Catholic colleges and universities.[8]

Francis Boland made the first overture toward accreditation in July 1950 when he inquired about the criteria for membership in the Association of American Colleges. He was told that colleges could not be recommended for membership in the national body until accredited by a regional association, and that accreditation procedures could be initiated only two years after a school had its first commencement. Boland informed Vice Provincial James Connerton of the requirements, and the investigation was halted.[9]

In the spring of 1954, in anticipation of Stonehill's third graduating class, the college dean, John Lucey, CSC, restarted the accreditation process. He wrote to the New England Association of Colleges and Secondary Schools, requesting the proper forms and inquiring about the latest date for an application to be submitted. He was informed that the deadline was October 1, but that an earlier submission would allow more time for the assignment of an inspection team to visit the College. Lucey was hopeful that a team could come in the early part of the fall semester.[10] Francis Boland, for reasons that are not clear, did not support Stonehill's application for accreditation. Connerton complained to the Superior General:[11]

> Father Boland does not seem to be interested or gives us any indication of aggressive interest in the accreditation of Stonehill College which surely should be sought this year. He seems to have put the whole responsibility of that upon Father Lucey, but offers Father Lucey no encouragement.

Most probably Boland, understanding the financial straits of the College, believed that any effort expended toward accreditation at this time would be wasted.

In the summer of 1954 Father James Doyle, CSC, who had first come

Rev. James Doyle, CSC, academic dean 1954–1960.

to Stonehill in 1952 as an instructor in theology, was appointed dean of the College, replacing John Lucey, who had served from 1950 to 1954. Doyle was amazed to learn that an accreditation team from the New England Association of Colleges and Secondary Schools had been invited to Stonehill. He quickly canceled the visit "so that [he] could become more acquainted with the College and at least take a few steps in preparation for the visitation."[12] Although Doyle's initial reaction may have been motivated by his unfamiliarity with the job, it is clear, as future events would prove, that his decision was prudent.

After establishing himself as dean, Doyle promptly reinitiated the accreditation application process. In January 1955 he requested "the minimum requirements for accreditation" from the New England Association.[13] A review of the material sent revealed that Stonehill did not meet certain recommended standards, especially in library facilities.[14] Additionally, Doyle was informed of the criteria upon which applications are judged, including the adequacy of the physical plant and the financial ability of a college to carry out its purposes. He was hesitant to pursue the effort further at this time, believing that Stonehill would not meet the criteria. However, he felt "pressure on . . . every side to get this thing started and live with the results."[15]

The personal initiative and drive of James Sheehan, coupled with pressure from the Provincial Council and former students[16] pushed Stonehill to seek accreditation as soon as possible. In order to prepare the College for a visitation team, two preliminary evaluations of Stonehill were conducted in February 1957. Dominican Father Vincent Dore, academic vice president at Providence College, evaluated Stonehill for constituent membership in the NCEA. Dore reported the College's strengths: administration, faculty, classrooms, admission and graduation requirements, and student-faculty relationships. Weaknesses were noted in the library and science laboratory facilities. He concluded that Stonehill "more than adequately meets the needs for Constituent Membership in the N.C.E.A." and concluded, "I personally believe they are in a strong position to receive favorable action from the New England Association on accreditation."[17] Augustinian Father Joseph J. Gildea, Dean of Merrimack College, which had gained accreditation in December 1953,[18] visited Stonehill specifically to evaluate the College before the association's visitation. He recommended that the duties of the College vice president be defined and that the library should have an appropriation in the budget and not merely report what was spent.[19]

In May 1957 Doyle, after informing the faculty,[20] made formal application for accreditation to the New England Association. The association suggested that the team originally assigned to visit Stonehill in the fall of 1954 be sent now; this was acceptable to Doyle.[21]

The visitation team, Wilfrid Lake (chair) of Northeastern University, Katharine R. Jeffers of Jackson College, and Vincent Dore, O.P. of Providence College, came to Stonehill on November 7 and 8. The team walked the campus, met with faculty and administration, evaluated records, and critically toured the physical plant. Lake and his associates were impressed with the College's academic programs, with the exception of the A.B. in education, "believing it would be more appropriate to major in the subject matter field since the whole objective of the program is preparation for secondary school teaching." The gymnasium was labeled "inadequate" and the library "barely adequate." Despite these comments the team, citing Stonehill's progress, the need it met for the area, and its adherence to the association's minimum standards, concluded, "We unanimously recommend that the application of Stonehill College for membership in the New England Association of Colleges and Secondary Schools be approved."[22]

The visitation team's recommendation, although unanimous, did not convince the standing committee of the association of Stonehill's worthiness. Doyle informed the faculty that Stonehill's application had been "postponed." The dean was notified that the standing committee entertained several reservations against the College's application: a weak library, need for more facilities, questions about admission standards and admission of students "on condition," inflated student grades, and the need for more lay faculty members.[23] Sheehan, who found the association's rejection "incredible," was informed that the standing committee found no great weaknesses and believed Stonehill to be headed in the right direction. Bewildered and confused, Sheehan wrote to the provincial:[24]

> All of the above [information] is very vague, nebulous and confusing to Father Doyle and myself. It leaves us very much up in the air with a very definite feeling that we have been given rather summary and unjust treatment.

Richard Sullivan's appointment as president was the catalyst needed to redouble the College's efforts to secure accreditation. The dean, James Doyle, recounted, "He [Sullivan] surely had accreditation uppermost in his mind. . . . If credit is to be given in the final accreditation, Father Sullivan deserves it. He gave the impetus to get this thing done once and for all."[25] Consultants, contacted by Doyle to recommend improvements, noted that the Holy Cross religious at the College were overly burdened with duties at the College and weekend parochial assignments. Sullivan immediately wrote to local pastors to request relief from some parish duties, especially Saturday confessions. In response, one fiery local pastor accused Sullivan of "ducking service," calling Stonehill's priest professors "lazy."[26]

In December 1958 Stonehill formally reapplied to the New England Association for accreditation. The visitation committee, chaired by David R. Dunigan, S.J., director of student personnel at The College of the Holy Cross, and including Eleanor Clifton, dean at Simmons College, and Wilfrid Lake, dean at Northeastern University, visited the campus on October 7 and 8, 1959.[27] The team noted many improvements at the College since the 1957 visitation. The library was larger, now seating 175 and with holdings over 19,000 volumes. Admission standards had been clarified and "conditional" acceptances eliminated. Grading standards had been improved, the education major eliminated, and faculty numbers and salaries increased. The team also noted the physical plant improvement, particularly the new student union and plans for a dormitory. The committee believed that the library was still too small, that faculty offices needed improvement, and that science offerings and faculty required augmentation. As with the visit two years earlier, the visitation committee unanimously recommended Stonehill for admission to the association.[28]

The president was unofficially informed in November that the College had been "conditionally accredited" and would be revisited in three years. The meeting of the standing committee to decide Stonehill's application had been slated for 75 minutes, but it ran three hours. The visitation committee chair, Father Dunigan, who championed Stonehill's bid, was challenged by John Usher Monro, Harvard's dean of freshmen studies, who balked at even conditional accreditation. The final vote was 4–3, with Frederick Copeland of Amherst College, chair of the standing committee, casting the deciding vote.[29] In January Sullivan received the association's congratulations from Copeland, who concluded, "Clearly, the vote of the Committee was not unanimous and as a consequence we recommend that Stonehill College be revisited in three years. We shall be particularly concerned with curricular improvements."[30] Official notification of Stonehill's election to membership in the New England Association was received on December 8.

Accreditation had been achieved and the College celebrated the event,[31] but Sullivan, motivated by the conditional nature of the acceptance and in response to the visitation and standing committee reports, immediately initiated a self-study to find deficiencies and propose solutions.[32] Preliminary to this self-evaluation, in the fall of 1960 Father Edward V. Stanford, OSA, former president of Villanova, was engaged to examine the College and produce a report. Stanford's review produced four recommendations:[33]

1. That Stonehill College and Our Lady of Holy Cross be legally separated.
2. That trustees become more involved in the affairs of the College by changing the composition of the body to include lay people.[34]
3. That the Board of Advisors consist of lay people who are approved by the trustees and serve terms of office.
4. That courses be consolidated rather than expanded to bring greater strength and direction.

The purpose of the 1960 self-study was twofold: first, to re-examine the aims and purposes of the College and to re-evaluate course offerings in light of these aims and purposes, and second, to study the curriculum, guided by the comments of the accreditation committees.[35] Academic departments met with a special committee established by the Academic Council, headed by C. James Cleary, to study the College's curriculum and make recommendations for improvements.[36]

The study produced a few major changes to Stonehill's academic programs. The College first defined its aim: " . . . to impart a broad liberal culture permeated with Christian ideals and a Christian sense of values."

Each department reviewed its course offerings in light of Stanford's recommendation for consolidation. The structure of the teacher training program was inverted. In the past, students desirous of a career in teaching majored in education and minored in a field of expertise. Now students would major in one discipline and take sufficient education courses to satisfy state certification requirements. General education requirements for bachelor of arts students were increased to include one year of mathematics and one year of laboratory science. Lastly, the general business major was changed to a management major, with students required to take courses in philosophy and social science.[37]

Sullivan was confident that the College's physical growth[38] and its introspective evaluation would bring Stonehill unconditional accreditation at the 1962 revisitation. In January 1962 he requested a fall date for the inspection. A visitation team including James E. Fitzgerald, SJ, president of Fairfield University (chair), Albert Imlah, professor of history at Tufts, and Oliver Brown, professor of chemistry at Connecticut College for Women was assigned to visit Stonehill on October 25 and 26, 1962. On October 9 Sullivan submitted a formal application for continued membership in the New England Association, which described the improved quantity and quality of the faculty, use of more selective admissions (300 admitted of 1100 applicants), and the expansion of the College's physical plant.[39]

The visitation team was pleased with the progress that the College had made in a relatively short time. Dean Aloysius Cussen, CSC, who replaced James Doyle in 1960, had helped to placate the committee with a report that outlined for the team the discrepancies noted in the 1959 visitation and the measures taken to correct them.[40] Sullivan and his fellow administrative officers were praised for "providing strong, competent and realistic leadership." Shortcomings and limitations noted by the committee were "not serious." The report of the visitation committee concluded, "Stonehill is meeting a definite need in the area in which it is located and its future is assured."[41]

On December 7 Stonehill College received unconditional accreditation. Reporting the news, Sullivan wrote in his datebook, "The shadows of many years have been removed." In January Sullivan was informed that the standing committee had voted to continue the 1959 accreditation, rather than granting a whole new evaluation.[42] The visitation committee's recommendation was wholly positive, noting "significant progress since the 1959 evaluation." George DePrizio, provincial of the Eastern Province, congratulated Sullivan for his accomplishments and concluded, "Stonehill is really on its way."[43]

Curriculum and Faculty Expansion

❦ THE BATTLE TO ACHIEVE accreditation, as has been noted, required careful scrutiny of the College's academic programs and led to several changes and an expansion of the majors options. In the fall of 1958 bachelor of arts programs were offered in economics, history, history of government, English, philosophy, education, and pre-theology. The bachelor of science listings were in general science, biology, business administration, accounting, general business, and economics. One year later majors in chemistry, mathematics, and French were added. As described in the discussion on accreditation, the education major was changed as a result of the 1959 visitation to emphasize expertise in a discipline rather than courses in education themselves.[44] In the fall of 1960 a program in medical technology, consisting of at least three years of the biology program and one year of medical technology training at an accredited hospital, was introduced at the College. Thus, in 1963 Stonehill offered 14 majors in its bachelor of arts and science programs. Students were required to complete 47 semester courses, with a cumulative average of 70 to achieve their degrees. Course listings numbered 240, but students had only 6 electives.[45]

Academic expansion beyond the day school was also explored in this period. A masters program in education was preliminarily discussed in the spring of 1963. The opportunity and timing for such a move were thought to be right. Other Massachusetts colleges and universities were offering similar programs, and Stonehill had the authority (from its charter), to offer such a degree. At this time, however, plans never went beyond the discussion stage.[46] The Sullivan years witnessed the first debate over the institution of courses for credit in the evening college. The president had been "strongly urged" to inaugurate programs in office management and business "to meet the local need." After discussion with officials from local colleges that offered similar programs, Sullivan decided that adding to the already existing evening adult education program was the most prudent move.[47] Other short-term additions to the College's academic offerings were evening courses in English and sociology for nursing students and the introduction of the Stonehill College Sisters' Institute, authorized by Bishop Connolly, which offered credit courses to women religious on Saturdays.[48]

The Sullivan era at Stonehill was a time when many Holy Cross religious who had played formative roles in the history of the College came to campus or were assigned to new significant positions. In the summer of 1960 James Doyle, who had served as dean since 1954, was reassigned to King's College. In February Sullivan had recommended David Arthur, who had just been assigned as director of the library, for the position. In late April the

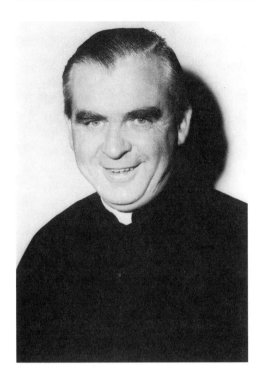

Rev. Aloysius Cussen, CSC, academic dean 1960–1964.

provincial, George DePrizio, indicated that Arthur would be appointed, but in June Aloysius Cussen, CSC, was assigned. Cussen, a Boston native, was completely surprised with the decision.[49]

Several additional changes in Holy Cross personnel on campus were made at this time. In 1961 Francis Grogan, who had served as registrar since 1955, was replaced by John Corr, who in three years would be Sullivan's successor as president. Several faculty appointments were also made, including Robert Kruse, CSC, Stonehill's first freshman academic award winner, who was assigned to theology, Thomas Feeley, CSC, to philosophy, and Paul Duff, CSC, as religious counselor and later prefect of discipline. Sullivan at times battled with DePrizio over appointments in an effort to appease his fellow religious and to maintain the highest standards for the College.[50] In April 1962 Brother Herman Zaccarelli, CSC, was assigned by the provincial as director of food services, a new position created because of "the growth in boarding enrollment" and the "complex problems created by the expansion of the cafeteria facilities."[51]

Efforts toward fundraising, publicity, and service to the region were combined in the development of the Stonehill Community Plan. Initiated by the Board of Advisors at the request of Sullivan, the "plan constitute[d] a

Br. Herman Zaccarelli, CSC, explains culinary principles to friends at food institutes.

sound approach to obtaining much needed help in college development and expansion." The plan was advertised as "a partnership with higher education from which corporations, businesses, and Stonehill College all will profit."[52] It was hoped that local businesses, which received benefits from Stonehill's graduates, would contribute in some way to promote the work of the College. Committees, organized and led by businessmen in five local regions in southeast Massachusetts, were arranged to reach the largest possible audience with Stonehill's message of educational and industrial cooperation.

The faculty at Stonehill College continued its steady growth in all areas. By 1963 there were 45 full-time and 11 part-time faculty members who served in 11 different academic departments. Professors were still hired by the president, and teaching loads remained heavy. Still, students and outsiders alike commented about the family nature of the College: "Close and warm faculty support has become so much of a tradition at Stonehill it is easily taken for granted, but please be assured we are grateful for it."[53]

Accreditation brought with it pride and the desire to enhance the professionalism of the College's teachers. In the past, necessity had forced professors to teach outside their areas of expertise, but at this point faculty insisted that they teach only in their own fields and that they no longer be required to supervise extracurricular activities, as they had been doing since the 1950s.[54] Faculty members began to organize symposia on contemporary issues. Two topics of the day were "The West: Grand Design or Redesign" and "*Mater et Magistra*," a discussion of Pope John XXIII's 1961 social encyclical letter.[55]

In the 1960s faculty salaries and methods of evaluation for promotion and tenure began to be critically reviewed. Salaries continued below the medians published by the National Education Association. Sullivan, realizing this discrepancy, made the move to pay faculty for teaching summer school, a practice that had not been common earlier. Stonehill was advised by Roy Deferrari, professor emeritus at The Catholic University of America, that faculty salary increments should be made contingent on teaching performance and publications.[56] In 1960 Aloysius Cussen, CSC, published "Policies on Promotion" for all faculty. Satisfactory teaching was the primary criterion, followed by professional growth, acceptable research and publications, and, for promotion to professor, attainment of the Ph.D. or an equivalent terminal degree. In January 1963 Sullivan initiated, through the Academic Council, a rank and tenure committee to consist of the dean, two priests, and two members of the lay faculty.[57]

The growth of the faculty in numbers led to its more formal organization. In 1958 faculty committees were organized by departments, with the Academic Council—which served "to determine general academic regulations and policies at Stonehill"—as an overseer. In December 1959 Doyle announced that the Council membership would be augmented by four professors, one each in science and business and two in liberal arts. By the end of Sullivan's tenure as president, seven faculty committees were functioning: scholarship, athletics, publications, communication-arts, discipline, financial, and rank and tenure.[58]

The first campaign of non-religious faculty to organize as a body was initiated in the fall of 1960. Originally founded by Professor Maryalice Moore and Professor Herbert Wessling to provide social and intellectual activities, the association eventually created a "Constitution of the Lay Faculty Council." The document gave three objectives for the proposed body: "to improve our communications and our relationships with the administration and students at Stonehill College, to establish contacts with other college faculties and organizations, and to enlarge the concepts of the lay faculty functions used to further stimulate our intellectual life."[59] Aloysius Cussen, CSC, the academic dean, was not keen on the proposal:[60]

Prominent faculty and administrators:
Professor John Reedy, Professor Henry Cruickshank, Professor Brassil Fitzgerald,
Richard Sullivan, CSC, James Lowery, CSC, and James Doyle, CSC.

I am sure you will agree that this is not a healthy situation. While we do not want to suppress legislative complaints or stifle honest debate, this can get out of hand. We want to preserve and build upon the communal spirit that has existed heretofore. Any serious division among us will only defeat that aim. And in the long run the ones who really suffer are the students.

Although Cussen wrote to the dean at Boston College to request a copy of the constitution for the lay faculty group there, he was not in favor of the organization and squelched the effort.[61]

Academic freedom continued to be debated by Catholic intellectuals of the period. A conservative strain, championed in the late 1950s by Paulist Father James Gillis, claimed education must lead students to sure knowledge of permanent truths. Gillis often referred to what others called academic freedom as "intellectual and moral anarchy." He wrote:[62]

> In the name of learning, the professors are destroying learning. They are providing a race of agnostics or even universal skeptics. They teach that there is no such thing as truth, pure and simple. There is your truth and my truth and the other fellow's truth. No truth is permanent. . . . There is no norm of truth, no standard.

Columbia sociologist Robert MacIver, in contrast, supported free intellectual pursuit: "When a scholar says something is true, he means true so far as our knowledge goes and no further. His truth has no finality; it is never absolute.[63]

Academic freedom throughout this period was upheld with discretion at Stonehill. Richard Sullivan was granted permission by Bishop James Connolly of Fall River to provide faculty access to books on the Roman Index of Forbidden Books.[64] Sullivan readily delegated permission to professors to read these sources, provided that the material be prudently utilized. Cussen was more traditional than Sullivan in his belief that teaching at a Catholic college imposed certain limits:[65]

> The old question of academic freedom is a difficult one at best. However, I feel that when a man accepts a contract to teach in a Catholic college he accepts the responsibility of teaching within the framework of Catholic principles. I don't mean to say that everything can be reduced to black and white, but at the same time, there must be a spirit of cooperation on both sides. I frankly feel, in general, instructors have much more freedom in a Catholic college than they do in any so-called non-sectarian college.

ENDNOTES

1. George DePrizio to Richard Sullivan, June 25, 1958, Sullivan Papers, ASC; Christopher O'Toole to George DePrizio, June 3, 1958, Superior General Papers– O'Toole, AHCFE. Sullivan was installed as president on June 27. See *The Summit* (September 24, 1958), ASC.

2. Richard Sullivan, "Talk to Faculty, May 26, 1959; Address, "Education for Responsible Leadership," August 27, 1958; "Address to Faculty Dinner," June 2, 1961, Sullivan Papers, ASC.

3. Richard Sullivan, "Address to Students," September 19, 1960, Sullivan Papers, ASC.

4. Richard Sullivan to Anne C. Flood, February 20, 1961; *The Catholic Transcript* clipping (October 15, 1964), Sullivan Papers; Richard Sullivan, interview with the author, October 31, 1995, ASC.

5. Christopher O'Toole to Richard Sullivan, May 28, 1959, Sullivan Papers; Financial Statements for Stonehill College, 1958–1964. Beginning with a deficit of $6,418.61 in his first year, the College's average annual operational profit for the next five years was $78,230.

6. Owen B. Kiernan to Richard Sullivan, July 25, 1958; Harry J. Elam to Sullivan, July 26, 1962, Sullivan Papers, ASC. Sullivan was reappointed in July 1962 by Governor John Volpe.

7. Richard Sullivan, personal datebook, October 25, 1961, Sullivan Papers; *Summit* (April 16, 1964), ASC.

8. Philip Gleason, *Contending With Modernity: Catholic Higher Education in the Twentieth Century* (New York: Oxford University Press, 1995): 184–206.

9. Francis Boland to Guy Snavely, July 6, 1950; Snavely to Boland, July 10, 1950, Boland Papers, ASC; Boland to James Connerton, June 20, 1961, Stonehill College Papers, AHCFE. Boland stated, "In view of the present property status of the College and its financial operation, it would be foolhardy to ask for an investigation preliminary to application for accreditation."

10. John P. Lucey to Edward Y. Blewett, February 17, 1954; Blewett to Lucey, February 19, 1954; Lucey to Blewett, March 24, 1954, Accreditation File, ASC.

11. James Connerton to Christopher O'Toole, May 19, 1954, Superior General Papers–O'Toole, AHCFE.

12. James Doyle to Edward Blewett, September 24, 1954, Deans' Papers; James Doyle, interview with David Arthur (June 2, 1993), ASC.

13. James Doyle, CSC, to Dana M. Cotton, January 5, 1955, Accreditation Papers, ASC. The minimum requirements for accreditation published by the New England Association of Colleges and Secondary Schools in December 1951 included: (1) an institution will generally not be considered for accreditation until two years after the first graduating class, (2) ratio of students to faculty should not exceed 15:1, (3) teaching load in no case should exceed 18 classroom hours per week, (4) a senior college should offer instruction in at least 8 major fields where at least one teacher should be full time, (5) graduation for the baccalaureate should require the equivalent of 120 semester hours, and (6) library should contain at least 8000 volumes, exclusive of documents.

14. The inadequacy of the library had been noted by several people. A review of the library holdings by the Academic Council in December 1956 noted, "The library was not meeting minimum requirements for accreditation." The provincial, George DePrizio, wrote to James Sheehan, "The library is the item in the academic set-up that needs attention most." See Academic Council Meeting Minutes, December 12, 1956, Academic Council Papers; George DePrizio to James Sheehan, February 17, 1957, Sheehan Papers, ASC.

15. New England Association of Colleges and Secondary Schools, Application Criteria, n.d., Accreditation Papers; James Doyle, CSC, interview with David Arthur, CSC, June 2, 1993, ASC.

16. The Provincial Council in November 1956 stated that the accreditation process should begin immediately in the new year. The council called for a renovation of the library in order to prepare for this visit. Additionally, the council believed that it would be advantageous for accreditation if the lay seminarians were removed from the main building to provide additional space for the College's administrative needs. The decision went all the way to the Superior General, who agreed that the move should be made. Thus, in the fall of 1957 the lay seminarians were moved to Pius X Seminary and boarded in the refectory, which had been renovated during the summer for their use. Several Stonehill graduates experienced difficulty in gaining entry into graduate school because of the College's status as a nonaccredited institution. Some schools would not take courses from nonaccredited schools as a rule; others asked student applicants to interview before courses would be credited. Still, it is the opinion of James Doyle that Stonehill's nonaccredited status did not impede students from matriculating.

17. Vincent Dore, O.P., "Report of Visit to Stonehill College," February 1957, Accreditation Papers, ASC.

18. E. G. Roddy, Jr., *Merrimack College: Genesis and Growth 1947–1972* (North Andover, Massachusetts: Merrimack College Press, 1972): 25.

19. "Summary of Recommendations of Father Gildea, OSA," February 22, 1957, Accreditation File, ASC.

20. James Doyle to "Members of the Faculty," September 10, 1957, Dean's Papers, ASC.

21. James Doyle, to Nathaniel Kendrick, May 21, 1957; Richard G. King to Doyle, September 8, 1957; Wilfrid Lake to Doyle, October 29, 1957, Accreditation File, ASC.

22. New England Association of Colleges and Secondary Schools, "Evaluation Report for Stonehill College" (November 7–8, 1957), Accreditation Papers, ASC.

23. Nathaniel C. Kendrick to James Doyle, December 10, 1957, Accreditation Papers, ASC.

24. James Sheehan to George DePrizio, December 10, 1957, Sheehan Papers, ASC. Father James Fitzgerald, SJ, dean at the College of the Holy Cross and a member of the standing committee, informed Sheehan that he should not be worried, as 90 percent of small colleges are rejected or postponed on their first application. The consolation did not soothe the sting of rejection felt by Sheehan and Doyle.

25. James Doyle, interview with David Arthur, CSC, June 2, 1993, ASC.

26. Richard Sullivan to William Gunn, October 28, 1958; Gunn to Sullivan, November 20, 1958, Sullivan Papers, ASC. Gunn sarcastically wrote: "You in ducking service in this parish, a natural springboard to Stonehill College, are making a mistake. You will find that your teachers, excused from parish duty, will go to bed, lazy like, rather than correct class papers. You are teaching secular laymen whom you will never know except by hearing confessions and preaching in parish churches. As

soon as you become monks only, your congregation will die the death; the Catholic Church will to a certain extent shrivel and die as it nearly did when only monks were preaching Christian doctrine. The backbone of the Catholic Church is hearing confessions which your congregation wishes to avoid. O.K. Die."

27. James Doyle to "Members of the Faculty," May 22, 1959, Deans' Papers, ASC.

28. "Evaluation Report for Stonehill College," October 7–8, 1959, New England Association of Colleges and Secondary Schools, Accreditation File, ASC.

29. Dana M. Cotton to Richard Sullivan, December 8, 1959, Accreditation Papers, ASC; Richard Sullivan personal datebooks, November 13, 1959, November 18, 1959, Sullivan Papers, ASC.

30. Frederick Copeland to Richard Sullivan, January 7, 1960, Accreditation Papers, ASC. Copeland specified areas that needed improvement: (1) There were weak offerings in science, especially physics, weak staffs in chemistry and math; (2) social service offerings were questioned—"Is it possible for three teachers to handle 26 offerings in history, government, and economics?; (3) more emphasis should be placed on curricula over physical development; and (4) questions continued on selectivity in admissions and apparent "inflated" grading system.

31. Sullivan called a school holiday on December 17 to celebrate the event.

32. J.J. Burns to Richard Sullivan, February 22, 1959, History Department Papers, ASC. The idea of a self-study originally had been proposed by the president in early 1959 as a tool to aid the accreditation bid. At that time faculty members had suggested that such a self-evaluation could best be initiated by a critical review by an outside person.

33. Memorandum for Richard Sullivan of the Visit of Rev. Edward Stanford, October 13, 1960, Provincial Papers–DePrizio, AHCFE.

34. This recommendation had been made as early as 1951, when Francis Boland and Christopher O'Toole agreed upon a financial settlement between the Congregation of Holy Cross and Stonehill College. The long process of separation involved the creation of new corporations and alienation of the College from the Holy Cross Community. These important topics are fully described in Chapter 9.

35. Richard Sullivan to Robert Strider, October 9, 1962, Sullivan Papers; "General Report from September 1956 to December 1961," Cussen Papers, ASC.

36. English Department Meeting Minutes, October 13, 1960, English Department Papers, ASC.

37. "News Release," November 1960, History of Stonehill Papers; "General Report from September 1956 to December 1961," Cussen Papers, ASC.

38. The College had completed the student union, built a new dormitory and a new library. These events are the subject of Chapter 6.

39. Richard Sullivan to "Faculty Members," July 11, 1962; Richard Sullivan to Robert E.L. Strider, October 9, 1962, Sullivan Papers, ASC.

40. "Chronicles of Our Lady of Holy Cross" (October 25, 1962).

41. "Re-Evaluation Report," October 25–26, 1962, New England Association of Colleges and Secondary Schools, Accreditation File, ASC.

42. Practically speaking, this meant that the College would need to renew its accreditation in 1969 (10 years after its original confirmation) rather than 1972.

43. Richard Sullivan, personal datebook, December 7, 1962; Robert Strider to Sullivan, February 11, 1963, Sullivan Papers, ASC; George DePrizio to Sullivan, December 27, 1962, Provincial Papers–DePrizio, AHCFE.

44. Gilman Campbell to Richard Sullivan, August 10, 1962, Education Department Papers, ASC. Campbell supported the College's decision to focus on the discipline of expertise over teaching skills. He wrote, "The student must acquire a solid understanding of [the] subject matter before he attempts to teach."

45. Stonehill Catalogs, 1958–1963, ASC; "Stonehill College 1963," n.d., Director of Institutional Research, Stonehill College.

46. Gilman Campbell to David Arthur, n.d. [March 1963]; Campbell to Aloysius Cussen (Memo), January 16, 1963, Education Department Papers, ASC.

47. Meeting Minutes of Executive Council, January 17, 1960, and January 24, 1960, Executive Council Papers; Richard Sullivan to Frederick C. Copeland, January 28, 1960; Copeland to Sullivan, February 16, 1960; Sullivan to Herman La-Mark, March 17, 1960, Sullivan Papers, ASC.

48. Memorandum, Office of Dean, n.d. [1962], Cussen Papers; Richard Sullivan to "Reverend Mother," September 8, 1961, Sullivan Papers, ASC. The Sisters's Institute began in 1961 and ended in 1967; the special nursing program ran from 1962 to 1965. The nursing program was canceled due to decreasing interest.

49. Richard Sullivan to George DePrizio, February 14, 1960, Provincial Papers–DePrizio; Provincial Council Meeting Minutes, April 29, 1960, AHCFE; "Chronicles of Our Lady of Holy Cross" (January 21, 1960); DePrizio to Sullivan, February 16, 1960; Aloysius Cussen to Richard Sullivan, June 4, 1960, Sullivan Papers, ASC. In a twist of fate, Arthur succeeded Cussen as dean in 1966.

50. Sullivan had the ability as president to integrate and satisfy the needs of the College and the individual. Duff's initial response to his Stonehill appointment was disappointment. His letter of obedience to Stonehill was sent in the mail although at the time he was living at the provincial house in Bridgeport. Additionally Duff wanted to complete development projects that were in progress. Sullivan spoke with the provincial, which resulted in Duff's gradual transition to the College, allowing him to complete former projects. In 1960 Sullivan defended William Gartland, who had been removed by the provincial as director of student activities, which allowed him to stay at the College in another capacity. Sullivan also fought for William Hogan, asking that he not be transferred to Holy Cross College in Washington (the Congregation's American house of theology).

51. George DePrizio to Richard Sullivan, April 30, 1962, Provincial Papers–DePrizio, AHCFE.

52. Meeting Minutes, Board of Advisors, January 20, 1962; "The Stonehill Community Plan," n.d., Board of Advisors Papers, ASC.

53. "Stonehill College 1963," n.d., Director of Institutional Research, Stonehill College; Faculty Memo, n.d. [1964], History Department Papers, ASC. For academic year 1964–1965, four full-time history professors taught 705 students, an

average of 176 per instructor. In philosophy, the average was 154 students per professor.

54. Meeting Minutes, English Department, January 6, 1959, English Department Papers, ASC.

55. *Mater et Magistra* was the source of much debate in Catholic circles. Liberal Catholics saw in the letter support for their "New Deal" liberalism, while conservatives rallied around the quip in William F. Buckley's *National Review* editorial, "*Mater, si, Magistra no.*"

56. Richard Sullivan, CSC, interview with David Arthur, CSC, June 16, 1993; Roy J. Deferrari to Aloysius Cussen, December 30, 1960, Cussen Papers; Executive Council Meeting Minutes, December 12, 1959, ASC. In 1959 Stonehill faculty salary ranges compared with NEA medians were: instructor: $4700–5000, $4562; assistant professor: $4500–5100, $5595; associate professor: $5100–5600, $6563; professor: $5900–6100, $8072.

57. "Policies on Promotion," n.d., Cussen Papers; Meeting Minutes of Academic Council, January 8, 1963, ASC.

58. Faculty Handbook, 1958, *The Summit* (December 9, 1959); Richard Sullivan, personal datebook, July 10, 1963, Sullivan Papers; Stonehill College Catalog, 1963–1964, ASC.

59. Chronicles of Our Lady of Holy Cross, (October 25, 1960); Faculty Meeting Minutes, November 22, 1960, Cussen Papers, ASC.

60. Aloysius Cussen to C. James Cleary, November 10, 1960, Cussen Papers, ASC.

61. Aloysius Cussen to John McCarthy, November 15, 1960, Cussen Papers, ASC. Cussen never favored individual faculty initiatives to organize. He once wrote, "I think it is essential that all faculty members adhere to all general college regulations. Once you allow individual faculty members to set up their own rules and regulations you will have chaos." Cussen preferred that faculty members with complaints and/or issues speak to him personally.

62. James Gillis, CSP, "Catholics and Intellectuals," *Catholic World* 183 (June 1956): 171.

63. Quoted in Patrick Allitt, *Catholic Intellectuals and Conservative Politics in America, 1950-1985* (Ithaca, New York: Cornell University Press, 1993), 46.

64. Richard Sullivan to Faculty (memorandum), March 2, 1964, Sullivan Papers, ASC.

65. Aloysius Cussen to Donald L. Nicknair, March 28, 1962, Cussen Papers, ASC.

CHAPTER 6

Physical Expansion and Growth

The battle for accreditation and the development of Stonehill as an accepted academic institution was paralleled by significant expansion of the College's physical facilities. James Sheehan started this expansion drive with the construction of Holy Cross Hall, which provided badly needed classroom space for the burgeoning student enrollment. With the aid of a government loan, construction of the cafeteria and student union began in the fall of 1957. Plans were also initiated to build a new seminary for the Holy Cross Community on the Stonehill campus. During the presidency of Richard Sullivan, the campus would be transformed with the construction of a library, a men's dormitory, a scholasticate for Holy Cross Brothers, and additions to buildings recently constructed.

Renovations and Additions

WITH EXPANSION of the College's facilities as the goal, new fundraising efforts were started by Sullivan. Thomas Duffy, who had served as the director of Stonehill's development efforts during the Sheehan administration, was replaced by James Lowery, CSC. Although Duffy loved Stonehill, the fund-raising methods he used were often overzealous and pursued with little subtlety. When, for example, he sponsored an auto show in 1958 to celebrate the College's tenth anniversary, the Provincial complained to the Superior General about the situation:[1]

His technique of constant dunning of people has reached the point where it has become obnoxious, and we have been subjected to criticism and embarrassment. Father Duffy has absolutely no delicacy about the matter of fund-raising.

Duffy, after having been associated with Holy Cross in North Easton for 18 years, received a new assignment, becoming chaplain to a group of medical mission sisters in Philadelphia. To those at the College who understood Duffy's good will and love for Stonehill, the transfer was a great shock, and Duffy himself was devastated by his change of apostolate.

The more affable approach of Father Lowery to his new work did not, however, guarantee him any more success than his predecessor. In the fall of 1958 Lowery announced a new drive directed toward residents in Easton. As in the family division campaign of the 1957 drive, John S. Ames, Daniel F. Buckley, and Jacob Brenner acted as honorary cochairmen. The campaign, which began on November 3 and was scheduled to end on January 9, 1959, set its goal at $100,000, but only minimal contributions were received—about $9100 gathered by December 2.[2] Another campaign, directed by Abraham Brooks and Louis Lyne, and initiated at the same time and with a similar goal, raised only $16,000.[3] The Holy Cross Community itself was a constant benefactor of the College. Through the Sorin Fund, established in 1953, the Congregation annually contributed a percentage of the salaries granted to religious to the College as a donation for its operation, maintenance, and expansion. In 1964 the Congregation's cumulative contribution to Stonehill was $1,167,523.[4]

The generally weak financial picture of the College demanded caution in expansion, but the Superior General realized that Stonehill would never fulfill its potential without some risks. He therefore advised Sullivan:[5]

As you plan for the future of Stonehill, think in terms of big ideas. It is true that you won't be able to realize all of these at once, but they will be realized sometime later on. You have the space, the location and the attraction that should make Stonehill, one day, a great college and university, and now is the time to begin planning for it.

Stonehill's gymnasium, originally the Ames family's indoor pool and tennis court, was the first project for Sullivan's improvements and expansion. A new tile floor had been added to the building in November 1951, but a complete renovation of the building was necessary, especially in light of the ongoing efforts to secure accreditation. In April 1958 the Provincial Council authorized $60,000 for the renovation. Permission was secured

Cafeteria and student union.

from the General Council in July for a new floor, showers and dressing rooms, a coach's office, and heating for the building.[6]

The project was scheduled for the fall of 1958. Emery LaLiberte's design was placed on bid to local contractors, but all proposals exceeded the allotted funds. The Fallon Company was eventually awarded the contract and the project was completed quickly, but Sullivan was forced to draw from the cafeteria building fund to complete the work.[7]

The cafeteria/student union project had been started on October 24, 1957, with a contractual completion date set in 300 days so that the facility would be ready for the start of the 1958–1959 academic year. As noted previously, however, the project slowed in the spring of 1958 and halted altogether shortly after Sullivan became president of the College. The Ted Gadoury Company, contractor for the project, became financially strapped and was unable to pay its subcontractors. Sullivan, working with LaLiberte and Gadoury's bonding company, Phoenix Fire Insurance Company of Hartford, Connecticut, tried to get the project back on course.[8] Phoenix Fire suggested that the terminal date for completion be set as December 31, with Stonehill to receive $50 for each day after September 7 (the 300th day of the project) that construction continued. Sullivan pondered the offer, but on August 14 he exercised his option and terminated the contact with Gadoury "because of persistent failure of satisfactory performance and because of continued violations of the terms and provisions of the contract."[9]

The project lay dormant until Phoenix Fire hired Norman Foster, a local contractor, to complete the work.[10] Construction resumed in the late fall and the building was dedicated by Bishop James Connolly on May 25, 1959, one full academic year later than scheduled.[11] The delay was costly to Stonehill on two fronts. First, students continued for another year to be crowded into an inadequate "cafeteria" facility in the main building. Second, the delay forced Stonehill to renegotiate the loan with the Housing and Home Finance Agency, which by law could not release funds until the project was near completion. Eventually the College lost almost $12,000 in the form of interest on loans, architect fees, and salaries for clerical personnel from the debacle. In restitution, however, a settlement of $13,056 was paid to the College by the bonding company.[12]

The completion of the cafeteria project was welcomed by all and was certainly advantageous in view of the fall accreditation visitation just ahead. However, the facility was built for Stonehill's enrollment in 1959, and it was too small—as had been predicted by the Superior General in his initial review of the plans—for the burgeoning student body, which by 1962 had grown to 900. In February 1962 Sullivan requested permission to expand the facility to almost double its original size. The president was hopeful that the cost of the addition could be consolidated into the original $200,000 loan. First estimates of $125,000 for the addition quickly doubled, but approval was granted nonetheless by the General Council in less than two months.[13]

Sullivan wasted no time in getting the project underway. Emery LaLiberte was asked to design the addition to his own building.[14] Bids were let and the contract awarded to the John and Leo Marshall Company of Pawtucket, Rhode Island, for $254,726. Meanwhile, Sullivan was working to add the cost of the addition to the original loan from the government. He was told in late May that it would be six weeks before any decision on the loan would be made, and that if Stonehill proceeded it was at its own risk. In an unusual demonstration of confidence from the usually cautious provincial, George DePrizio gave Sullivan permission to sign a contract for the addition when an official of the Housing and Home Finance Agency (HHFA) informed Stonehill, "[they] would be perfectly safe." The contract for the work was signed on June 1.[15] Construction started in the early summer, and the addition to the government loan was granted on July 27. In October 1962 the cafeteria/student union reopened with expanded facilities, including a bookstore and "college spa" that offered snacks and coffee at nonmeal hours.[16]

The growth that necessitated this almost immediate addition to the cafeteria strained Stonehill's meager academic facilities as well. Rising enrollment created an immediate need for more classrooms and faculty offices, and an imminent need for science labs. The question became how to meet all these needs in the most efficient and cost-effective manner. Sullivan originally suggested a new building, but by January 1962 he shifted his thought to an additional wing for Holy Cross Hall. The concept of building additions became a pattern at Stonehill as the most effective means to expand economically and meet the needs of the College.[17]

The College's needs and the options to meet them raised the first dispute between the usually placid president and his provincial, George DePrizio. DePrizio suggested that a new building with science labs, classrooms, and office space was the best solution and would solve Stonehill's penchant for underbuilding. More importantly, however, was the provincial's strong belief that the Congregation's Community life at Stonehill suffered because of the environment in which religious were forced to live.[18] For DePrizio the first priority for any addition to the College was the construction of a residence for priest and brother faculty members so that Community life could be preserved away from the administrative functions of the College. He wrote to Sullivan, "I shall not recommend or approve a new building project until the question of the faculty residence is settled honestly and decisively."[19] It was perceived by the provincial that limited Community funds and the exposure created by large loans mandated that priorities be set. DePrizio appeared to place Community life above the needs of the College, but religious at the College were willing to stay in the cramped quarters of the mansion if it would aid the College's progress, and they backed Sullivan against the provincial.

Although the lay faculty of the College began to pressure Sullivan for action on the "*immediate* [Sullivan's emphasis] need for classrooms,"[20] the issue remained unresolved for several months. In April 1962 Sullivan wrote to DePrizio and told him that he and the Stonehill Council did not experience a major intrusion in their religious life from others who worked in the main building. He claimed that only during the day work hours did the building not function as a "religious" house. During these hours the priests, brothers, and postulant seminarians were working themselves and thus had no need for the environment Community life demanded. Sullivan stated further that all the discussion on buildings, faculty office space, and a home for the religious faculty did not answer the need for more classrooms in the fall of 1963. He concluded by asking approval to proceed with plans for a 10-classroom addition to Holy Cross Hall. DePrizio only responded, "I must confess my continual reluctance to postpone the matter of faculty housing. I think we are making a great mistake."[21]

While the cafeteria addition was taking shape in the summer of 1962, discussion of the need for classrooms remained on hold. In the fall Sullivan renewed his request to proceed with the classroom addition, "as this is most urgent."[22] The October Provincial Council meeting discussed the subject. In an about face, DePrizio agreed to an additional wing to Holy Cross Hall, consisting of 13 classrooms and a 180-seat auditorium. Still, nothing was finalized for three more months, wasting precious time needed for the construction project. Furthermore, Sullivan proposed to the Council, in addition to the Holy Cross project, renovation of the science building. The combined cost of $600,000 would be financed through the New Bedford Institution for Savings.[23] Although worried about Stonehill's ability to handle the loan payments, DePrizio forwarded his recommendation to the General, who approved the project in January 1963.[24]

Architectural plans for the Holy Cross addition, which would be larger than the original building, were quickly drawn by the ever-present Emery LaLiberte. Bids for the project, which included 12 classrooms, language and business labs, a lecture hall for 250, plus faculty offices and lounge, were let, and the contract was awarded to F.L. Collins & Sons, Inc. of Fall River. Sullivan informed the Board of Advisors of the plans, the contractor chosen, and the projected cost of $600,000.[25] The contract was signed in March, with a scheduled completion date in September in order to be ready for the fall semester.

During the summer, while the addition to Holy Cross Hall was in progress, the science building was also renovated. New classrooms in Holy Cross made it possible to convert classrooms in the science building to biology, chemistry, and physics laboratories. The addition to Holy Cross and the renovation of the science building were completed on schedule to meet Stonehill's returning and new students in the fall.

Since Stonehill's establishment in 1948, College activity had been centered in its main building, which at various times housed every aspect of the College, including a weight room and showers for athletics. Although central to the College's life, the Ames mansion had never received a name. In 1960, however, members of the Holy Cross Community began to talk about naming the building after James Wesley Donahue, whose vision had brought the Community to the region in 1933 and who had negotiated the purchase of the Ames estate in 1935. In December 1963, during the Congregation's annual Christmas party, the main building was renamed and dedicated in the name of Father Donahue. Richard Sullivan spoke at the dedication, which included the unveiling of a new portrait of Donahue by local artist Charles Kerins:[26]

> It is in accordance with the natural and supernatural virtues of piety that we at Stonehill honor the memory of Father Donahue to whom we owe the existence of the College. Without his apostolic courage and desire to spread the work of

Holy Cross, we tonight would not have this college which serves over a thousand students and is the center of training for our scholastics, seminarians, and brothers.

A Library for the College

THE BATTLE FOR accreditation revealed one fact that most people familiar with the College already knew: The library facilities and its holdings of books, periodicals, and documents were marginal. The College's failed accreditation attempt in 1957 led the Academic Council to call for a review of the library collection by each department. Improvements were made so that by the time of the 1959 visitation, books and monographs totaled over 14,000 and bound periodicals over 800. Space was limited, however, because the library was still located in the main building.[27]

Sullivan, fully aware of the College's need for a new library, went to Bishop Connolly in the spring of 1960 for assistance. The president envisioned a small "basic" structure and asked the bishop to finance the $75,000 estimated cost. Connolly responded negatively: "Regretfully, I must say that it will be impossible for me to do anything at this moment to help with your Library Fund." Sullivan was disappointed, especially when he learned from a cleric in the Fall River diocese that $175,000 could be provided for the project.[28]

Summer came with no progress being made in securing funds for a library, something the president felt was necessary for the College to receive unconditional accreditation. In July Cardinal Cushing[29] wrote Sullivan and asked him to come for a visit, stating, "It is nothing important, it is simply a matter of information."[30] In his meeting with Stonehill's president, Cushing squelched a rumor that he wanted the College to sell him land on campus for the construction of a new hospital. Before departing, Sullivan, when asked about the College's needs, told the cardinal of the need for a library. Cushing responded with an offer to assist financially. Initially he offered Sullivan $175,000, saying, "Keep it under $200,000 for my part."[31] Elated with the offer, Sullivan quickly informed the Provincial of Cushing's gift and requested permission to proceed with building plans. DePrizio forwarded the request to the General Council, which approved the project in less than two weeks.[32]

Working in conjunction with the architect Emery LaLiberte, Sullivan sought advice on library designs from various sources. He requested copies of the library plans at the University of Portland in Oregon and King's College. Father David Arthur, director of the library, was sent to local colleges, including King's, to study existing designs and to speak with library officials in order to avoid problems they had experienced. He also wrote to the American Library Association seeking advice. Stonehill's immediate need was for a building to house 80,000 books and to seat 250, but future prospects would require a library able to house 300,000 volumes and seat 400. Sullivan was sent information on the designs of libraries at Furman University in South Carolina, Greenville College in Illinois, and Concordia College in Massachusetts.[33]

LaLiberte quickly produced a design for an expandable library at a projected cost of just under $300,000.[34] Informed of the estimate, Cushing raised his contribution to $300,000, but insisted that his involvement not be revealed to the public at the time.[35] Modifications to LaLiberte's initial design, necessitated by Arthur's findings, raised the price tag to $335,000 and forced Sullivan to again seek permission. Superior General Christopher O'Toole readily granted the request, although he realized that the College would need to raise $35,000 for the project.[36]

On April 5, 1961, at the inaugural Stonehill College President's dinner held at Bruno's restaurant in North Easton, the library project and Cardinal Cushing's gift were publicly announced. The event attracted 275 people, including Cushing, Connolly, and Congressman Joseph Martin. Sullivan called the celebration Stonehill's "coming out party," an indication "that the College is being accepted as a grown-up citizen of the community." Cushing announced at the dinner that he would give $350,000 to $400,000 for the project, and Martin named Stonehill to be the repository for his papers. Sullivan thus requested that the facility be named The Cushing-Martin Library.[37]

Public announcement of the library allowed the College to secure bids for the project. The low bid, by the Fallon Company, was $439,889. Architect's fees and the cost of furnishings raised the final cost to just over $500,000.[38] The unexpectedly high price tag led Sullivan to drive to Boston immediately, accompanied by David Arthur, to inform the cardinal about the situation and seek his advice. Upon arrival they were told by the housekeeper that Cushing was out, but they could wait. Although the cardinal was initially annoyed that the two men had come unannounced, he soon calmed down, listened to the news, and responded, "Richard, take the lowest bid. I will make the absolute ceiling on my gift of $500,000. You take care of everything over that. Send the bills in monthly and I will pay within 30 days." Cushing followed up his verbal offer in writing the next day.[39]

Ground-breaking for the library was held on July 17. Sullivan had earlier announced the project and the gift of Cardinal Cushing to the faculty, who received the welcome news with joy. Construction proceeded well, with only minimal delays. When the project was not finished in June 1962, the

Laying of the cornerstone of Cushing–Martin Library:
Richard Sullivan, CSC, Aloysius Cussen, CSC, Cardinal Richard Cushing, Governor
John Volpe of Massachusetts, and Congressman Joseph Martin.

president was worried that there would not be sufficient time to transfer books and materials to the new building before school started.[40] The library was, however, dedicated on September 20, with Cushing, Martin, Governor John Volpe, and representatives from 40 colleges present. In his comments for the occasion, the cardinal predicted Stonehill's future: "This College is going to go."[41]

A Dormitory and a Seminary

THE AMERICAN CATHOLIC renaissance of the 1950s produced a multitude of vocations to the priesthood and religious life. Holy Cross's benefit

Holy Cross Seminary.

from this upsurge, plus the desire to move postulant seminarians from the main building at Stonehill, led the Community to build a new seminary. Construction began in 1958, at the end of James Sheehan's administration, and continued during the Sullivan years. (Stonehill's president was involved only in a supportive function.) The initial wing of the seminary was dedicated on September 27 by Bishop Albert Cousineau, the former Superior General of Holy Cross. In April 1959 the seminarians from St. Pius X moved to their new home a quarter of a mile south. Father Roger Quilty became the first religious superior at the new seminary.[42]

The seminary grew over the years, as wings were added in expectation of more vocations. A gift from Philip Hemingway allowed the construction of St. Joseph's Chapel and a new library wing, which was started in March 1961. Bishop Connolly blessed the chapel on May 12, 1962. The first Mass was celebrated by Superior General Christopher O'Toole and the sermon preached by Richard Sullivan.[43] In January 1963 discussion began on the construction of another wing to house four classrooms, a recreation room, and additional dormitory facilities. The Provincial Council waited over a year before giving its approval to the expansion, which was begun in April 1964 and completed in December 1965.[44]

The new seminary enhanced the College's physical appearance and provided needed living space for seminarians, but dormitories for lay students were still absent. From the beginning Stonehill's status as a day school with no residence halls severely limited its ability to serve students who came from any great distance. "Approved houses" were arranged in Easton and Brockton for the few who did not commute, but Sullivan realized that the College could never attract a wide range of quality students without a dormitory. Thus, his administration placed a high priority on the construction of on-campus housing from the very outset. The Provincial Chapter held in the summer of 1958 recommended "that a men's dormitory should be constructed at Stonehill College as soon as it is financially possible."[45] Proceeding as he had with the library project, Sullivan obtained plans for dorms at Notre Dame and the University of Portland and consulted with LaLiberte about the design for Stonehill's first student residence. Sullivan wrote the Superior General about the College's plans, hoping for quick approval.[46]

Approval of the dormitory project was needed on two different fronts. The design required the approbation of the Superior General. Although the Provincial and General Councils of Holy Cross approved the project in principle, they were hesitant to give official sanction until a satisfactory financing arrangement was presented. Additionally, the local Council suggested caution on further publicity about the project until approval was obtained.[47] Meanwhile Sullivan applied to the Housing and Home Finance Association (HHFA) for a loan to finance the dormitory. He and LaLiberte presented their case to the government and requested a loan of $875,000 based on preliminary cost estimates for the project. In September 1959 Sullivan was informed that the requested amount had been reserved for the College.[48]

While the debate over approval of the project continued, a name for the future dormitory was needed. At Stonehill's 1959 commencement, Cardinal Francis Spellman was given an honorary degree. He returned the favor, announcing that he would give $5000 to the dormitory project if it would be named after John O'Hara, Cardinal Archbishop of Philadelphia and former president of Notre Dame. By July Spellman had given a total of $15,000 to the project. O'Hara preferred that the building not be named for him, but he answered Sullivan's query on the matter, "I cannot refuse him [Spellman] anything he asks."[49]

Sullivan was able to convince the provincial that the dorm was badly needed and that the College could meet the financial burden it would entail. DePrizio thereafter supported the project and made a strong appeal to the Superior General for permission to accept the government loan. He told O'Toole that turning down the loan now would preclude Stonehill from being approved for any future loans. Additionally, DePrizio argued that building the dorm would facilitate accreditation, allow needed expansion, and remove Stonehill from its status as merely a local college.[50]

On November 28 DePrizio informed Sullivan that the General Council, "after long and careful consideration of the plan submitted, . . . is not favoring the loan at this time."[51] Sullivan responded to the provincial in an impassioned letter:[52]

> I feel very certain that if we do not build the Dorm, Stonehill will stop where it is. The Dorm will continue our impetus; its refusal would certainly create the natural attitude that there is no use trying to make progress; there would be little enthusiasm in asking for help when we have refused such a favorable deal as the loan.

Sullivan claimed that the Holy Cross Community would be embarrassed and asked if he could communicate directly with the General on this issue. DePrizio gave his full approval.

Sullivan promptly wrote to Rome and countered the reasons given to DePrizio for the General Council's negative decision. The thought that a future transaction was possible was rejected by Sullivan as false hope, and he pointed out that the government loan rate was more than 2 percent lower than a comparable deal negotiated with a commercial lender. Sullivan also argued that refusing the loan now would create an impression of ingratitude and probably preclude future government assistance, thus handicapping ongoing development efforts. Sullivan was also highly concerned that the three-year tentative accreditation, which had just been received,[53] might be withdrawn if the standing committee of the New England Association heard of Stonehill's refusal of the loan.[54]

Sullivan wrote to the General and the Council twice more in the succeeding days, arguing for reconsideration of their earlier decision. Speaking of the vital nature of the dorm, the ongoing accreditation fight, and the real and immediate need for the dorm he concluded, "I sincerely think in the light of reason and not knowing what Divine Providence holds in store, that our development would stop right where it is at the present time."[55] Somehow O'Toole, who was in India at the time, received news of the crisis and cabled Sullivan, "Have cabled Rome to grant permission for loan, meanwhile do not refuse." On December 12 a telegram from the General Council arrived, "Dormitory approved—inform provincial."[56] Sullivan had won his battle.

With the major hurdle of approval negotiated, Sullivan proceeded to secure private financing and accept bids for the project. In accordance with HHFA regulations that alternative financing be attempted for projects, with government money supplied when construction reached 80 percent completion, Sullivan wrote to three local banks requesting a loan of $875,000. Rejections by these lending agencies, all of which gave the amount of the loan request and the presently tight financial conditions as reasons for their disapproval, paved the way for Stonehill to receive the government money almost immediately.[57] Bids were let on the project and the contract awarded on August 11, 1960, to the John Fallon Company of Quincy for $760,369.[58] Ground-breaking for the dorm was held four days later.[59]

As Sullivan's dream for a dormitory progressed, he continued to work for additional features in the facility. In comparison with the approved HHFA loan, the projected cost of the project would leave approximately $50,000 in extra funds. Sullivan requested permission from the government to use the excess funds to construct a road from highway 123 to the dorm and to run electrical conduits from the central part of campus to the residence hall. This request was initially rejected, but intercession by Congressman John McCormack resulted in the government's paying for 50 percent of the additional work.[60] Sullivan also sought funds for the construction of a dormitory chapel. The president reported that a total of $10,000 had been donated at an April 25 fundraising dinner in New York to enable the construction of a small chapel that could accommodate 35 people.[61]

O'Hara Hall, under the direction of its first rector, Paul Duff, CSC, received its first students in the fall of 1961. The building was dedicated on November 11 in an elaborate ceremony with Cardinal Spellman, Archbishop John Krol of Philadelphia, Bishop Connolly, Bishop Jeremiah Minihan auxiliary in Boston, and over 300 others in attendance. Father Chet Soleta, vice president for academic affairs at Notre Dame, gave the main speech, after which a buffet dinner was enjoyed by all invited guests.[62]

Richard Sullivan was the driving force behind the construction of the

Dedication of Cardinal O'Hara Hall, Cardinal Francis Spellman presiding.

library, the dormitory, and the additions to Holy Cross Hall and the cafeteria. Perhaps his most passionate campaign, however, was the construction of a women's dormitory, which he championed in opposition to most of his peers and religious superiors. When the Provincial Council authorized the men's dormitory in the summer of 1958, it had called for, "coeducation . . . on the day school basis only." Sullivan disagreed with this policy and placed the priority of a women's dorm above that of housing for the religious community. He saw it as an issue of practicality over idealism. Stonehill's need for women students, which was the catalyst to effective implementation of coeducation in 1951, continued to exist. Sullivan supported Virginia Yosgandes, dean of women, who called the lack of housing for women "the most pressing problem at Stonehill College."[63]

The provincial, George DePrizio, staunchly rejected the prospect of a women's dormitory as "out of the question." His argument was twofold. First, he believed that the College could not at the time undertake any further financial obligation. He also argued that the construction of a women's dorm would naturally attract more women students, which would swell the already large enrollment. He summarized his thought:[64]

Cardinal O'Hara Hall.

We have to face the hard fact that our province cannot provide personnel to meet the challenge of a heavy enrollment increase. I feel that it is far better to keep our colleges small, thereby retaining the control largely through our C.S.C. personnel. The increase in enrollment at Stonehill for the next few years should come normally through the admission of additional men students.

Sullivan realized that a dorm could not be built immediately, but he wanted the question left open, especially with the accreditation visitation team to return in the fall of 1962.[65]

DePrizio, who wondered if his opinion on the subject was too narrow, raised the issue with the Superior General. In his response, the General resurrected DePrizio's favorite issue of a residence for the religious faculty of the College:[66]

In my opinion it is quite clear that a faculty house where the religious life and community life can be properly observed is far more important than a women's dormitory. I suppose that the dormitory could be more easily financed than the faculty house but we should put first things first and provide suitable and respectable housing for our Religious. There is a tendency in the community to think last of accommodations for our Religious and, as a result, we have suffered spiritually and academically. If Stonehill College can, through a loan from F.H.A. [Federal Housing Authority], finance a faculty house then this project will have my complete support.

Sullivan investigated the possibility of a women's dormitory on his own initiative, working with LaLiberte on a design and discussing construction through private financing with Tom Gilbane of Providence. Gilbane said that he was interested and would assist in securing a loan. In the summer of 1961 Sullivan received unexpected support when the Provincial Chapter recommended that a women's dormitory be included in the building program at Stonehill.[67]

The issue then became a debate over priorities, between the needs of the Holy Cross Community and those of the College. Sullivan did not disagree with his religious superiors on the need for a religious faculty residence, but he reasoned that the $36,000 annual payment needed to fund the building would never yield a financial return, whereas the dormitory, which would involve the same annual payment, would generate income.[68] DePrizio nevertheless held fast to his conviction that the Holy Cross Community must come first in future decisions on housing: "It is ridiculous to take upon ourselves the burden of a women's dormitory when our own religious need housing so badly."[69]

In 1963 Sullivan raised a new issue, hoping it might break the stalemate. He argued that it was impossible to maintain discipline among students who lived off campus, even in "approved" houses, whereas rules could be strictly enforced in a dormitory.[70] DePrizio countered with a new argument himself, stating that a moratorium should be called on all building at Stonehill so the College could regroup academically, financially, and spiritually. However, he strengthened his previous hard line stance against the promotion of women students:[71]

> May I respectfully recommend to you and your [House] Council that until such time as a women's dormitory is erected a new policy be established—namely that preference be given to girl students within the commuting distance only, and that the number of out-of-area girl students be controlled and eventually reduced to a minimum.

Sullivan responded that the discipline problems were real and that a public perception was growing that Stonehill was unconcerned with the welfare of women students. He chided the provincial with a plea for justice:[72]

There is no doubt that we owe treatment to girls which would not make them feel like "second-class citizens." We asked them to come when we needed students and they have added to the College by their academic accomplishments, devotion, and loyalty.

The practicality of the admission of women in 1951 had become for Sullivan an issue of equity and justice.

After a protracted battle, both sides found victory. The Provincial Chapter of 1964 mandated that both a women's dormitory and a faculty residence be built by September 1965. Loans from the HHFA for the projects could be paid by the income from the dorm, the Sorin Fund, and profits from the cafeteria.[73] The faculty residence was, in fact, never built, but the support of Richard Sullivan, who became provincial (and thereby chairman of the Board of Trustees) led eventually to the construction of the first women's dorm, Boland Hall, in 1967. Without Sullivan's advocacy, many good women students would have been forced to choose other colleges.

Construction of the new seminary on campus was a catalyst to Holy Cross' renewed efforts at religious formation. Priest candidates lived together as a seminary community and attended classes at the College. In February 1961 George DePrizio met with Brothers Ephrem O'Dwyer, CSC, provincial of the Eastern Brothers, and Elmo Bransby, CSC, assistant provincial, about the possibility of erecting a scholasticate for brother candidates at Stonehill. Before this time brother candidates in the East were sent to Dujarie House at Notre Dame or St. Vincent's Hall at St. Edward's University in Austin for their academic training.[74] DePrizio weighed the options but felt that the disadvantages of a scholasticate outweighed its advantages. One of the provincial's concerns was that the College would be obligated to provide partial scholarships for the approximately 50 brothers who would attend classes at Stonehill. Additionally, he believed that the College's struggle for recognition would be impaired by the presence of additional religious students.[75] He advised the Superior General, "We have come to the conclusion that it would be very unwise to enter into this project."[76]

For reasons that are unclear, the provincial reversed himself one week later, writing to Sullivan that the details could be worked out. A committee consisting of John Murphy, the rector of the seminary, Aloysius Cussen, Sullivan, and three brothers chosen by Brother Ephrem, were appointed to work out plans for the scholasticate. DePrizio even claimed that the project should pose "no great or insurmountable difficulties."[77] Brother Ephrem and Father Sullivan met to discuss the specifics of the foundation. Brothers were to meet all the requirements for admission and graduation; brother professors were to meet the College's standards for teachers. Most impor-

Moreau Hall.

tantly, a site on Route 138, convenient to the College and to the city of Easton, was chosen for the scholasticate. To facilitate securing a construction loan, the Eastern priests' province donated the land and gave the brothers legal title.[78]

The new scholasticate, called Moreau Hall after the Congregation's founder, Basil Moreau, was built in 1962 under the supervision of project architect Charles A. Maguire and Associates. The house opened in the fall with 23 candidates and a faculty of six. Brother Pacificus (Patrick) Halpin, CSC, was the first director.[79]

* * *

In his governance of all Holy Cross fortunes in the East, Sullivan gained the respect of all as noted by his Provincial, "Your zeal and devotion are well known to all. Your spirit of kindness and understanding has opened a new chapter at Stonehill."[80] His tasks as president were not easy, but he accomplished them with grace and professionalism. The College's growth in students, expansion, and acceptance by the wider academic community was largely due to his endeavors. His successor, John Corr, inherited an institution free from economic burden and academically and foundationally ready for the considerable challenges of the late 1960s.

1. George DePrizio to Christopher O'Toole, June 10, 1958, Superior General Papers–O'Toole, AHCFE.

2. Resumé of Development Projects, n.d. [March 1962], College Relations Papers, ASC. This summary states that the Easton drive eventually raised $119,576. Confirming extant records are not available.

3. *The Summit* (October 8, 1958); "Chronicles of Our Lady of Holy Cross (September 17, 1958); "President's Report, 1958–1959," Sullivan Papers, ASC.

4. Richard Sullivan, CSC, interview with the author, October 31, 1995, Stonehill History Project Papers, ASC; Statistics, Office of the Treasurer, Stonehill College. The Sorin Fund was the common Community fund to which all salaries of religious were given. After the provincial assessment for the operation of the province was the paid and money and living expenses for the priests and brothers removed, the Congregation gave the rest of the money back to the College as a donation. The money was to be used for new projects unless the Community decided it was best used for current operational needs.

5. Christopher O'Toole to Richard Sullivan, March 13, 1959, Sullivan Papers, ASC.

6. Provincial Council Meeting Minutes, April 23, 1958; George DePrizio to Christopher O'Toole, June 11, 1958; O'Toole to DePrizio, July 4, 1958, Superior General Papers–O'Toole, AHCFE. Bernard Ransing to DePrizio, July 4, 1958, Sullivan Papers, ASC.

7. Richard Sullivan to George DePrizio, July 11, 1958; Sullivan personal datebooks, October 16, 1958, Sullivan Papers, ASC; Christopher O'Toole to George DePrizio, July 4, 1958, AHCFG. Fallon bid $63,000, but the Superior General allowed only $60,000 to be borrowed for the project.

8. Richard Sullivan to George DePrizio, July 22, 1958, Sullivan Papers, ASC.

9. Richard Sullivan to George DePrizio, August 7, 1958, Sullivan Papers; Sullivan to Ted J. Gadoury, August 14, 1958, Cafeteria—Physical Plant Papers, ASC.

10. "President's Report, 1958–1959," Sullivan Papers, ASC.

11. Richard Sullivan, personal datebook, May 25, 1959, Sullivan Papers, ASC.

12. Richard Sullivan to George DePrizio, August 8, 1959, Provincial Papers–DePrizio, AHCFE; Sullivan, personal datebook, September 9, 1959, Sullivan Papers; Sullivan to Joseph Duggan, Cafeteria Legal Matter, Physical Plant Papers; "Chronicles of Our Lady of Holy Cross" (September 17, 1959); Sullivan to John T. Balfe, November 18, 1959, Sullivan Papers, ASC. Gadoury's bankruptcy cost Phoenix Fire Insurance Company about $100,000 in construction costs and restitution.

13. Richard Sullivan to George DePrizio, February 19, 1962; Sullivan to DePrizio, March 14, 1962, Sullivan Papers, ASC; Bernard Ransing to DePrizio, March 31, 1962, AHCFG.

14. Richard Sullivan to George DePrizio, March 23, 1962, Sullivan Papers, ASC.

15. Richard Sullivan, personal datebooks, May 25, 1962, May 30, 1962, May 31, 1962, Sullivan Papers; "Chronicles of Our Lady of Holy Cross" (June 1, 1962), ASC.

16. *The Summit* (October 17, 1962), ASC.

17. Richard Sullivan to George DePrizio, December 20, 1961; Sullivan to DePrizio, January 5, 1962, Sullivan Papers, ASC.

18. George DePrizio to Richard Sullivan, January 8, 1962, Sullivan Papers, ASC. From the time of Stonehill's birth in 1948, most religious assigned to the College lived in the main building, the old Ames mansion. Postulant seminarians were also housed here. This building was also the center for the College's administrative offices and, in the earliest days, classrooms, the library, cafeteria, and bookstore. Religious occupied the servants' quarters, which were large enough for only a bed and one other piece of furniture. Recreation space was limited and was often shared by non-Community members present in the house.

19. George DePrizio to Richard Sullivan, January 18, 1962, Sullivan Papers, ASC.

20. Richard Sullivan, personal datebooks, January 20, 1962, Sullivan Papers, ASC.

21. Richard Sullivan to George DePrizio, April 7, 1962, Provincial Papers–DePrizio, AHCFE; DePrizio to Sullivan, May 2, 1962, Sullivan Papers, ASC.

22. Richard Sullivan to George DePrizio, September 24, 1962, Provincial Papers–DePrizio, AHCFE.

23. Provincial Council Meeting Minutes, October 14, 1962, AHCFE; Richard Sullivan to George DePrizio, December 19, 1962, AHCFG.

24. George DePrizio to Richard Sullivan, December 26, 1962, Sullivan Papers, ASC; DePrizio to Germain M. Lalande, December 27, 1962, Superior General Papers–Lalande, AHCFE; Richard Vincelette to DePrizio, January 8, 1963, AHCFG.

25. Richard Sullivan to Faculty (memo), February 12, 1963, Sullivan Papers; Sullivan to Board of Advisors, March 6, 1963, Board of Advisors Papers, ASC. The actual cost of the addition was $459,129. See Richard Sullivan, personal datebooks, January 9, 1964, Sullivan Papers, ASC.

26. "Chronicles of Our Lady of Holy Cross" (December 22, 1963), ASC.

27. Meeting Minutes of Academic Council, January 13, 1958; "General Report from September 1956 to December 1961," Cussen Papers, ASC.

28. Richard Sullivan, interview with the author, October 31, 1995; Sullivan to James Connolly, April 12, 1960; Connolly to Sullivan, April 13, 1960; Sullivan, personal datebooks, April 5, 1960, Sullivan Papers, ASC. Sullivan's datebooks speak of a priest in Fall River who knew money, to be distributed over a 15-year period, could be allotted by the diocese for the library. The name of the cleric is not mentioned.

29. Archbishop Cushing had received the red hat as a cardinal in 1958.

30. Richard Cushing to Richard Sullivan, July 19, 1960, Sullivan Papers, ASC.

31. Richard Sullivan, personal datebook, July 23, 1960; Sullivan to George DePrizio, July 23, 1960, Sullivan Papers, ASC.

32. Bernard Ransing to George DePrizio, August 9, 1960, Sullivan Papers, ASC. Cushing asked Sullivan not to start construction until the spring of 1961 so that a good design could be obtained and other donors sought for the project.

33. Richard Sullivan to Paul Waldschmidt, August 16, 1960; Sullivan to American Library Association, Administrative Division, September 23, 1960; Alphonse F. Trezza to Sullivan, October 4, 1960, Sullivan Papers, ASC.

34. Meeting Minutes, Executive Council, August 30, 1960, Executive Council Papers, ASC.

35. Richard Sullivan, personal datebook, December 3, 1960, Sullivan Papers, ASC. Extant documentation does not reveal why Cushing desired to keep his assistance a secret at this time.

36. Christopher O'Toole to George DePrizio, January 20, 1961, AHCFG.

37. Richard Sullivan, personal datebook, April 5, 1961; Sullivan "President's Address," April 5, 1961, Sullivan Papers; "Chronicles of Our Lady of Holy Cross" (April 5, 1961), ASC. Martin's connection was a contribution of $1000 plus a promise to deposit his papers at the College. See Richard Cushing to Sullivan, May 29, 1961, Sullivan Papers, ASC.

38. Richard Sullivan to Richard Cushing, July 7, 1961, Sullivan Papers, ASC.

39. Richard Sullivan, personal datebook, July 7, 1961; Richard Cushing to Sullivan, July 8, 1961, Sullivan Papers, ASC.

40. Richard Sullivan to John Fallon, June 8, 1962, Sullivan Papers, ASC.

41. Richard Sullivan, personal datebook, September 20, 1962; Sullivan to George DePrizio, September 24, 1962, Sullivan Papers, ASC. In January 1963 the Cushing-Martin Library was designated a depository for United States government documents through the efforts of Congressman Joseph W. Martin; in the spring of 1964 the first set of documents arrived at the library.

42. George DePrizio to Richard Sullivan, September 18, 1959, Sullivan Papers; *The Summit* (October 1, 1959), ASC.

43. *The Summit* (March 22, 1961), ASC; George DePrizio to Richard Sullivan, April 19, 1962, DePrizio Papers; "Dedication Festivities—St. Joseph's Chapel and Library Wing," May 12–13, 1962, Provincial Council Papers, AHCFE.

44. Provincial Council Meeting Minutes, January 25, 1963, November 30, 1963; "Province Office Bulletin," April 20, 1964, AHCFE. The cost for the addition was $340,000.

45. George DePrizio, "Circular Letter," September 1958, Provincial Chapter Papers, AHCFE.

46. Richard Sullivan to Edmund P. Joyce, September 2, 1958; Sullivan to Christopher O'Toole, December 9, 1958, Sullivan Papers, ASC.

47. Provincial Council Meeting Minutes, December 19–20, 1958, AHCFE; George DePrizio to Richard Sullivan, January 10, 1959, Sullivan Papers, ASC.

48. Richard Sullivan, personal datebook, January 16, 1959, Sullivan Papers; "Chronicles of Our Lady of Holy Cross" (February 18, 1959); Ralph B. Cornell to Richard Sullivan, September 28, 1959, O'Hara Hall Papers. ASC.

49. Francis Spellman to Richard Sullivan, June 9, 1959; Spellman to Sullivan,

June 16, 1959, Sullivan Papers, ASC; Sullivan to George DePrizio, July 22, 1959, Provincial Papers–DePrizio, AHCFE; John O'Hara to Sullivan, August 3, 1959, Sullivan Papers, ASC. Apparently the Superior General had been informed that Spellman was to give $60,000 to the dormitory project, providing it was called O'Hara Hall. See Christopher O'Toole to DePrizio, June 9, 1959, Superior General Papers–O'Toole, AHCFE.

50. Richard Sullivan to George DePrizio, October 21, 1959, Provincial Papers–DePrizio; DePrizio to Christopher O'Toole, October 27, 1959, Superior General Papers–O'Toole, ACHFE.

51. George DePrizio to Richard Sullivan, November 28, 1959, Sullivan Papers, ASC.

52. Richard Sullivan to George DePrizio, November 29, 1959, DePrizio Papers, AHCFE.

53. Remember that Sullivan had been informed by phone of the committee's decision before official word was received by mail. Accreditation was publicly announced on December 4.

54. Richard Sullivan to Bernard Ransing, November 29, 1959, Sullivan Papers, ASC.

55. Richard Sullivan to Bernard Ransing, December 1, 1959; Sullivan to Christopher O'Toole, December 2, 1959, Sullivan Papers, ASC.

56. Christopher O'Toole to Richard Sullivan, telegram, December 11, 1959; Richard Vincelette to Sullivan, telegram, December 12, 1959, Sullivan Papers, ASC.

57. Government regulations stated that if three private lenders refused to loan money, the government money could be secured at the outset of a building project.

58. Richard Sullivan, personal datebook, July 26, 1960; Sullivan to James Connolly, July 27, 1960; Sullivan to DePrizio, July 29, 1960, Sullivan Papers, ASC. The low bid on the project was submitted by the Volpe Company of Boston, but because their bid did not list all subcontractors as required for government loan projects, the offer was passed over.

59. The opening of the new seminary in 1959 and the need for student housing allowed St. Pius X to function as a men's dorm for one year. DePrizio gave approval of the project, and in the fall of 1960 thirty-five male students took up residence in the temporary facility.

60. Board of Advisors, Agenda, November 19, 1960, Board of Advisors Papers, ASC.

61. Richard Sullivan to Daniel J. O'Neil, November 23, 1960; Sullivan to George DePrizio, January 28, 1961, Sullivan Papers, ASC. The New York fundraiser was held at Massoletti's Restaurant. O'Hara, the guest of honor, could not attend due to ill health. Sadly, O'Hara died on August 28, 1960, before the dormitory was opened. The chapel, fashioned from space already present in the original plans, required Stonehill to accept an amendatory loan of $865,000, since the government cannot sponsor Church-related projects.

62. Richard Sullivan to Jack Haley, October 30, 1961; Sullivan to Frank Gartland, CSC, November 15, 1961, Sullivan Papers, ASC.

63. Provincial Council Meeting Minutes, October 17, 1958, AHCFE; Richard Sullivan, interview with David Arthur, June 16, 1993; Sullivan interview with the author, October 31, 1995, Stonehill History Project Papers, ASC; "Report of the Dean of Women," August 19, 1960, Provincial Papers–DePrizio, AHCFE. Yosgandes reported, "I am convinced, however, that the present situation [lack of a women's dormitory] as I have outlined it, cannot be permitted to continue indefinitely. Its least serious result, the loss of fine students from out of state, would be most regretable [*sic*]."

64. George DePrizio to Richard Sullivan, August 17, 1960, Sullivan Papers, ASC.

65. Richard Sullivan to George DePrizio, August 25, 1960, Sullivan Papers, ASC.

66. George DePrizio to Christopher O'Toole, August 30, 1960 (typed but not sent), Provincial Papers–DePrizio, AHCFE; O'Toole to DePrizio, May 5, 1961, AHCFG.

67. Richard Sullivan, interview with the author, October 31, 1995, Stonehill History Project Papers; "Chronicles of Our Lady of Holy Cross" (March 29, 1961), ASC; George DePrizio, "Circular Letter" (May 13, 1961), Provincial Chapter Papers, AHCFE. The Chapter recommendation was ignored, save Sullivan's personal promotion of the women's dorm project.

68. Richard Sullivan to Christopher O'Toole, November 21, 1961, Sullivan Papers; Sullivan, interview with the author (October 31, 1995), Stonehill History Project Papers, ASC.

69. George DePrizio to Christopher O'Toole, n.d. [1962], Superior General Papers–O'Toole, AHCFE.

70. Richard Sullivan to George DePrizio, March 21, 1963, Provincial Papers–DePrizio, AHCFE.

71. George DePrizio to Richard Sullivan, March 26, 1963, Sullivan Papers, ASC.

72. Richard Sullivan to George DePrizio, March 3, 1964, Provincial Papers–DePrizio, AHCFE.

73. "Decrees and Recommendations of Fifth Provincial Chapter, March 30–April 4, 1964, Provincial Council Papers, AHCFE; "Chronicles of Our Lady of Holy Cross" (April 9, 1964), ASC; Richard Sullivan to Germain M. Lalande, April 20, 1964, AHCFG.

74. Laurian LaForest, CSC, "Moreau Hall, North Easton, Massachusetts: A Brief History" (Archives Holy Cross Brothers, Eastern Province 1990), (hereafter AHCBE).

75. DePrizio believed that the College would never achieve greatness if it was perceived by outsiders to be an institution that emphasized education for religious.

76. George DePrizio to Christopher O'Toole, March 27, 1961, Sullivan Papers, ASC.

77. George DePrizio to Richard Sullivan, April 8, 1961, Sullivan Papers, ASC.

78. Ephrem O'Dwyer to "Brothers in Christ," June 14, 1961, Sullivan Papers, ASC.

79. Moreau Hall served the Brothers of Holy Cross until 1980. In 1981 the building was sold to the town of Easton and opened as a public school to relieve overcrowding in other locations.

80. George DePrizio to Richard Sullivan, February 16, 1960, Sullivan Papers, ASC.

CHAPTER 7

A Liberal Arts College Emerges

Stonehill College's open-ended charter from the Commonwealth of Massachusetts allowed the institution to confer all degrees except medical. This wide spectrum of academic possibilities was voluntarily narrowed, however, as the College initiated programs to create a liberal arts college; no plans for professional schools were seriously considered. Stonehill offered programs in the humanities, science, and business, but the College's hasty and poorly planned genesis created problems that limited the development of new academic programs that the school's burgeoning enrollment and the needs of contemporary higher education mandated. Through the hard work of many dedicated people, Stonehill managed to survive its early years, despite a huge debt and dearth of income, ineffective development efforts, and lack of facilities. Accreditation in 1962 and the construction of O'Hara Hall provided the catalyst that set the College on the course for greatness, fulfilling the dream Holy Cross held since the Ames estate was purchased in 1935. The stage was now set for Stonehill to expand its academic programs and become a true liberal arts college.

Catholic Higher Education in the 1960s

THE AMERICAN CATHOLIC RENAISSANCE of the 1950s raised hopes and created an atmosphere of optimism in all areas of Church life, including higher education. The rapid and extensive expansion of facilities to meet the need of the postwar rise in enrollment masked the critical question: What was the purpose of Catholic higher education in contemporary America?

Catholic educators began to challenge the traditional reasons for the existence of their colleges and universities. The historian Philip Gleason described this time as a period of crisis in Catholic education that necessitated new ideas: "The most critical problem today is in the area of ideological adjustment—it is a crisis of purpose, a question of the fundamental *raison d'être* of Catholic higher education."[1]

The question of purpose in Catholic higher education was the central issue of debate at a fall 1963 symposium held at Notre Dame titled, "Prevailing Winds on the Catholic Campus." College and university administrators and several bishops gathered to look at new ideas in liturgy and lay participation and to renew intellectual curiosity in higher education. One participant summarized the belief of those in attendance: "It is imperative that those of us who direct activities on Catholic campuses listen to the wind that is blowing, for whether we sail with it or against it, its direction will determine our course."[2]

Leading Catholic educators articulated various opinions on the new purposes of Catholic higher education. Jesuit Fathers Michael Walsh, president of Boston College, and theologian Michael Buckley, professed that Catholic educational institutions in the future must be "the place where the Church does its thinking." In order for this to be a reality, they said, colleges and universities must truly be what they advertise themselves to be, with programs that comprise every form and movement of human knowledge. While maintaining its concern for faith and morals, Catholic colleges and universities must serve the good of society as a whole, a responsibility that was perceived by some to have been abdicated by the Church.[3] Theodore Hesburgh, CSC, president of Notre Dame, expressed the idea that Catholic higher education could not effectively operate by strictly adhering to external authority. He offered a counterview: "The best and only traditional authority in the university is intellectual competence: this is the coin of the realm."[4] John Courtney Murray, SJ, whose writings on the relationship between Church and state led to the adoption of the Declaration on Religious Liberty at Vatican II,[5] expressed best the challenge before the Church:[6]

> [The purpose of the Catholic university is] to live on the borderline where the Church meets the world and the world meets the Church . . . , to interpret the Church to the world and the world to the Church. The borderline is ever shifting. Our task is to find it.

The majority of administrators of Catholic institutions of higher education believed, moreover, that the religious and moral development of students must be an integral part of the Catholic college's new pursuit of truth.

Educators inside and outside the Catholic community encouraged innovative ideas and challenged the Church to change and update its institutions of higher education to become fully competitive with other schools. John Brosnan, chancellor of The State University of New York, wrote:[7]

> Catholic educators should see that their buildings and equipment fully measure up to every required standard and, when resources permit, that they rank with the very best. Catholic educators should see that their students measure up in intellectual maturity and intellectual discipline to every demand of the most exacting times. To that end, academic standards must be the highest and must be rigidly enforced, without fear of favor.

Catholics themselves sounded a warning that it was necessary to meet the challenge of competition from secular universities. Neil McCluskey, SJ, at Notre Dame asked why Catholic colleges were not enjoying the fruits of the nationwide rise in student enrollment. He postulated that high tuition rates and academic budgets, starved by heavy interest rates on postwar physical expansion projects, detracted from the ability of Catholic institutions to compete.[8]

The more expanded purposes of Catholic higher education forced college and university leaders to rethink the unique contribution that their institutions presented to the faithful and the general public. Theodore Hesburgh, CSC, expressed the belief that a great Catholic university must be a great university that is Catholic. He clearly placed his emphasis on intellectual development, describing the institution as a "community of scholars," but he did not fail to express the other half of Catholic higher education's dual role:[9]

> Here is the total spectrum, the Catholic university does have something to offer. Call it faith, call it belief, call it a simple parallel course depending on other sources of strength, other sources of knowledge, a belief in an ultimate good surpassing all natural endeavor. The Catholic university must be all that a university requires and something more.

The Stonehill College Self-Study

THE APPOINTMENT OF Richard Sullivan as provincial of the Eastern Province of Holy Cross in the spring 1964 Chapter left a vacancy at the helm of Stonehill College. In May John Corr, CSC, who had served at Stonehill from 1961 to 1964 as registrar and director of admissions, was appointed by the Provincial Council as the fifth president of the College. A

*Rev. John Corr, CSC, president
1964–1971.*

native of Roslindale, Massachusetts, Corr had served as associate director of Family Rosary and Theater under Father Patrick Peyton and taught economics at King's College. Corr was inaugurated with great fanfare on October 9, with representatives of 142 colleges and universities in attendance. George Shuster, president emeritus at Hunter College of New York and assistant to the president at Notre Dame, delivered the inaugural address.[10]

Corr's inauguration initiated a new openness in the office of president to faculty and students, which led to more productive dialogue and a spirit of communal responsibility for the operation of the College. In his inaugural address, Corr set the tone for his presidency:[11]

> If he [the President] is wise, he will listen patiently to what is said and seek to carry the implications of the soundest of these judgments into the forum of the college so that in partnership with his own faculty and administration and with the assistance of the students the necessary searching self-criticism may take place. This kind of criticism is needed not so much because without it a college cannot exist, but because without it a college does not deserve to exist.

Corr placed himself in the mainstream of administrators in promoting an educational philosophy that advocated the prevailing twofold purpose of Catholic higher education. He spoke to the faculty of its duty to provide students with "not just the cold unappetizing facts" but "an appreciation of

the love of Truth." He encouraged professors to promote independent thinking, intellectual growth, and the exact expression of ideas admonishing
them, saying, "If Stonehill doesn't do this then the fresh air of today's world
will choke our students into a stillness from which it will be difficult to
recover." Corr also challenged students to approach the intellectual life free
of fear,[12] and to seek "a knowledge of Truth . . . and a love of God and the
things of God." He concluded, "If you have not seen the place of God and
His creation in all the activities of man and society, then either you or Stonehill *or* [Corr's emphasis] you and Stonehill should have a re-examination."
He encouraged the students to become "intellectual apostles."[13]

Corr came to the presidency of Stonehill with a philosophy of administration quite different from that of any of his predecessors. The College's
early years were characterized by the presidents' significant personal
involvement in day-to-day decisions and operations, due in large measure to
lack of facilities and funds and facilitated by the relative smallness of the
College. Although handed an impossible task, George Benaglia in any case
lacked fiscal acumen, a situation that led to the appointment of Francis Boland, who saved the College financially but with disastrous results in his
relationship with members of the Holy Cross Community. James Sheehan
and Richard Sullivan, using different styles, were integrally involved with all
College operations. John Corr, on the other hand, directed the fortunes of
Stonehill by acting as a catalyst for others and delegating much of his authority to subordinates. Corr was the first president of Stonehill who allowed administrators to fulfill their duties without constant supervision. He
did not accept the status quo but, rather, challenged faculty members to
reach for higher goals in their efforts to maintain academic excellence. Educational professionalism, especially in the office of dean, came to Stonehill
with Corr's assumption of the office of president.

Corr was a natural leader in his ability to delegate authority without
relinquishing responsibility. From the outset, he actively harnessed his available resources to make Stonehill a true liberal arts college that could serve
all New England. Exercising his new, less-directive form of leadership, he
addressed alumni in October 1964 and asked them to get involved in monetary support and recruitment. Even before his inauguration, Corr had informed the Board of Advisors that he would need their assistance in finding
ways to raise funds for faculty salary increases and, especially, student scholarships. John Corr was a Catholic educator who believed in greater utiliza-
tion of the laity, as canonized by the ongoing Second Vatican Council.[14]

Corr's leadership style allowed his full participation in outside activities
associated with the office of president. Like his predecessors, Corr was appointed by Governor Endicott Peabody to the Massachusetts Board of Colle-

giate Authority. Like Sullivan, he was active with the NCEA, serving two terms as the chairman of the organization's New England Colleges and Universities Department. Corr regularly spoke to outside groups and at baccalaureate and commencement ceremonies at local high schools, academies, and colleges. In an unprecedented move, which demonstrated his progressive and ecumenical spirit, Corr in April 1967 presided at services and preached at Easton's Unity [Unitarian Universalist] Church during the absence of its pastor.[15]

Corr's first major administrative task in December 1963 was to complete the College self-study initiated by Richard Sullivan in response to the recommendations of the 1962 accreditation visitation team.[16] Dean Aloysius Cussen, CSC, announced to the Academic Council that curriculum, majors programs, the academic calendar, honors programs, and the size and composition of the student body would be some of the topics examined. With the approval of the Academic Council, Sullivan held a kickoff meeting on January 24, 1964, at which the basic elements of the study were explained to the faculty.[17]

The study was organized around five committees, three to investigate and obtain data and two to coordinate, assimilate findings, and give advice. The three investigative committees dealt with curriculum, intellectual climate, and student affairs. An executive committee, chaired by Cussen, was appointed by the president and directed to hold an election for an advisory committee and to appoint members to the three principal committees. The five-member advisory committee was elected by the faculty.[18] The three investigative committees reported to the executive committee, which in turn discussed its feelings and conclusions with the advisory committee. Final decisions were forwarded to the Academic Council for approval, with the president having the final approbation.

Beginning in the spring of 1964, the investigative committees met regularly (generally weekly) to discuss areas assigned to them. The curriculum committee, chaired by Roger Quilty, CSC, investigated graduation requirements, the academic calendar, fields of study and concentration, distribution of courses, and independent study. The committee on intellectual climate, headed by Francis L. Clinton, researched the opportunities for outstanding and advanced students, construction, purpose, and use of comprehensive examinations, scope and duration of orientation programs for the student body, role of faculty advisors, admissions procedures and goals, power and function of administrative offices, and library procedures. The committee on student affairs, led by Peter Lucchesi, looked at student activities, development of student responsibility, student government, relationship of students with the administration, disciplinary matters, religious activities, and athletic programs.[19]

The self-study continued through the transition of presidents. Corr fully committed himself to the investigation with the knowledge that he was the first president of Stonehill who could "give his blessing and encouragement to the first unhurried and extended exercise in total self-criticism that the College has been yet able to undertake." He believed that self-criticism was good and concluded that "without it, a college does not deserve to exist." Corr challenged the self-study committees to see how they could best prepare "apostolic intellectuals."[20]

Many suggestions and recommendations were proposed to the executive and advisory committees during the self-study's two-year duration. The discussions were often facilitated by advisors and consultants hired by the College, such as Charles Donovan, SJ, of Boston College and Francis Rogers of Harvard, both of whom came to speak to the faculty about self-evaluation in 1964. Two years of investigation, countless meetings, and numerous iterations of committee reports produced, in the fall of 1966, several concrete proposals for change. A restructuring of the requirements for the AB degree and lowering the number of classes taken per semester from six to five (as a first step toward demanding more from students in fewer courses) were two major recommendations. Faculty were also encouraged to experiment with new ways of presenting material.[21]

A Liberal Arts College

IN MAY 1966, after six years as dean, Aloysius Cussen was assigned by Corr as a special assistant to the president to administer federal and other associated programs for higher education.[22] The provincial, Richard Sullivan, commented on his decision, "I do feel this is a good time for the break in the Dean's office since Father Cussen has successfully seen the conclusion of the self-study through to accomplishment." Known as a person who could "light up a room" with his mere presence, Cussen returned to the classroom as a professor of economics as well. Corr thanked Cussen "for six years of difficult and exacting labor."[23]

Cussen's exodus created a vacancy that was quickly filled with the appointment of David Arthur as Stonehill's fifth academic dean. Arthur had come to Stonehill in 1954 and served in several capacities at the College, including the roles of professor of philosophy, intramural athletic director, and most recently director of the library.[24]

Arthur's arrival in the dean's office led to significant improvements and

Rev. David Arthur, CSC, academic dean 1966–1970.

progress in Stonehill's academic programs. Three principal factors created a situation where, for the first time at Stonehill, the role of academic dean exercised authority and responsibility in meeting current curricular needs and planning for the future. First, Arthur's initiation of doctoral studies in education at the University of Michigan in 1965 introduced him to many new ideas circulating in higher education. Next, the self-study had generated an agenda of recommendations that fell under the dean's purview for implementation. Lastly, the leadership style of John Corr allowed Arthur, as well as other members of the administration and faculty, to conduct their work with full authority.[25] Arthur broke from the mold forced upon previous academic deans at Stonehill and contradicted the view of the author-educator John Corson, who described the responsibilities of a dean in a small liberal arts college "to be small."[26] He was, furthermore, a good communicator, initiating in the summer of 1966 periodic (generally every month) information memos addressed to faculty to keep them abreast of the activities of his office.

In his efforts to implement the self-study recommendations, the new dean emphasized the principles of individual human worth and student responsibility. He stressed the need for flexibility and the development of individuality in meeting the needs of students, while at the same time assuring adequate preparation for future educational possibilities. Arthur wrote, "The basic concept of the Stonehill program is to make each student as responsible as possible for his own education consistent with requirements and his maturing status." Consonant with prevailing winds in Catholic higher learning, Arthur developed an academic program at Stonehill that imparted values primarily, and knowledge and educational techniques secondarily.[27]

Arthur immediately set to work to implement the recommendations of the Executive Committee resulting from the two-year self-evaluation. In the fall of 1966 he organized three committees to complete the self-study by investigating the College's business, science, and upper biennium programs. The science committee report offered a few suggestions for the biology and physics programs, but judged the present facilities so inadequate that without improvement, accreditation would be lost in science. The report concluded, "The committee feels it would be wise to phase out the present science majors over the next four or five years or prepare to make a substantial outlay in this area."[28]

Implementation of a five-course semester, recommended by the self-study and advocated earlier by Cussen,[29] was a top priority for the new dean. Stressing student responsibility, Arthur praised the new system for the time it gave "to BECOME students, to become more aware of the fact that it is THEIR [Arthur's emphasis] education." The new system also allowed professors to probe more deeply into issues, with the expectation that more available time per course would facilitate livelier discussions, allow more time to read, and give students a better understanding of topics covered in class. The five-course semester and revamping of baccalaureate requirements provided more electives, thus allowing students greater freedom in their choice of programs of study. The vestiges of program study were present but in retreat. Design of a curriculum that strengthened Stonehill's liberal arts program was the objective of the architects of the new plan.

Arthur also designed a new freshman grading policy. The dean studied grade patterns for freshmen and discovered "a substantial lack of correlation between freshmen grades as a whole and the rest of the school, and between an individual's freshman grades and his later work." This revelation and the psychological lift that he perceived would be attained from a "fresh start" led Arthur to initiate plans for a complete revision of the freshmen grading policy. Freshmen grades would not be used in the cumulative graduation average, but freshmen were required to achieve a 1.75 grade point average to be unconditionally eligible for advancement to sophomore status.[30] After the first year all marks, including failures, would be retained, with a 2.0 average required for graduation. The program was hailed for its innovation and fairness to students.[31]

The 1967 fall semester brought a new form of grading to the whole College: a shift to letter marks. One year earlier, upon assumption of his new position, Arthur asked the faculty to contemplate the shift, suggesting four reasons:

1. To bring Stonehill's grading policy in line with the majority of colleges.
2. To avoid the perception of a grade as a numerical percentage of something.
3. To avoid the false impression of precision in a matter that defies exactness.
4. To simplify administrative procedures in the dean's office.

Less than one month after the plan was introduced by Arthur, the Academic Council voted to accept the change. An *ad hoc* committee was then formed to determine how best to implement the new policy and, most importantly, how to translate previously achieved number marks into the new letter system.[32]

Arthur next turned his attention to the practice of comprehensive and final examinations. In consultation with the Academic Council, an investigation was conducted on the usefulness and benefit of senior exams. Council members felt that a comprehensive examination in a particular discipline helped a student synthesize material, but that the present format of testing knowledge in all areas was too broad to be of assistance to the individual student. Thus, the council voted to eliminate the requirement but gave departments the option to require some examination prior to graduation. Arthur voiced opposition to the latter move, believing that the new five-course semester and the introduction of independent study obviated any need for exams.[33] While comprehensive exams were eliminated, finals in courses were mandated, with exceptions to be made at the department level. The previous regulation that the final examination count between 25 percent to 50 percent of the total grade was dropped, and values of all tests were left to the discretion of the teacher.[34]

Arthur's initial efforts to update and further Stonehill's academic programs were manifest in the institution of a pass/fail option, independent study, and student evaluations of faculty. A pass/fail option, to be exercised by juniors and seniors for one elective course per semester outside the major program, was introduced in the fall of 1967. The rationale was to encourage students to broaden their intellectual interests by taking subjects outside their major area without fear of a low grade.[35] Next, Arthur engaged James Kenneally, chairman of the History Department, to experiment with students in the area of independent study. An initial test with three students was "considered . . . a great success."[36] In line with his promotion of student responsibility, Arthur suggested the need for a more quantitative evaluation of teachers by students. The proposal was made in May 1967 and approved by the Faculty Assembly in November. A volunteer committee was organized to generate an evaluation form to be used for the semester in progress.[37]

The self-study provided much of the impetus for changes in the academic face of Stonehill College, but it was not the only source of progress. Financial stability, increased enrollment, and an expanded faculty created an atmosphere in which new academic majors and programs could thrive. Majors in sociology, religious studies, and child development were added to the academic offerings. The college studies major was inaugurated to allow the creation of a self-designed program giving credit for traditional course work, service projects, and special research. Besides new majors, a program in psychology plus numerous course offerings, including fine arts and ecumenical religious studies, were added to the curriculum.[38]

Stonehill investigated programs of cooperation with other colleges and universities. The College entertained but rejected a planned joint venture with the University of Southern California (USC), wherein a student would attend three years of liberal arts training at Stonehill and then transfer to a two-year engineering program at USC. The student would have been awarded both the AB and BS degrees in the five-year program.[39] Locally Corr and Arthur began to negotiate with Wheaton College on a free exchange of facilities, joint appointments of faculty, course exchange for students, and interlibrary loan privileges, the latter two being established in February 1968.[40]

The 1962 accreditation report on Stonehill granted the College a seven-year extension beyond its conditional three-year accreditation in 1959. In 1969 the College, seeking renewal of its academic status, again hosted a visitation team from the New England Association of Colleges and Secondary Schools. On March 16 through 18, the team of Vincent Dore, O.P., chancellor of Providence College, Oliver L.J. Brown, professor of chemistry at Yale, and Gordon B. Cross, president of Nichols College, visited the campus. They commented favorably upon the administration, school spirit, willingness to experiment with independent studies and declared the library "outstanding for a college of this size." The team also pointed out several problems, including weak business programs, the lack of a student infirmary, inadequate indoor athletic facilities, and the underutilization of the language lab. In their report, which unanimously recommended the College's accreditation be renewed, the team remarked "that definite progress has been made both in quality and quantity [of academic offerings] since the 1962 evaluation of Stonehill College."[41] In December the Commission on Institutions of Higher Education voted to continue Stonehill's membership in the New England Association. David Arthur reported to the faculty, "The College has been carefully evaluated and found to meet standards agreed upon by qualified educators."[42]

In February 1951 Stonehill College had established a coeducational continuing education program in the evening that offered noncredit courses in many academic areas, most taught by the day school faculty. The postwar need to provide academic services for working men and women enabled the program to grow successfully from the outset and serve the Easton community and surrounding regions. In the fall of 1969 Stonehill began to consider the establishment of a full-credit evening college. Brother John Weihrer, who had been the director of continuing education since 1964, wrote a formal proposal for the new venture to meet the need of the local community and to generate revenue for Stonehill. He outlined the advantages of such a program, noting particularly the economic boon for the College and faculty, its probable aid to development drives, and the attractive face it provided the College when seeking loans from government and private sources. In order to cut costs and financially aid professors already affiliated with the College, Weihrer proposed that at least 50 percent of the faculty for the evening college be drawn from the day faculty.[43]

Although Weihrer hoped the evening college might open that fall, the proposal's submission to the Academic Council was delayed when David Arthur voiced reservations about the project. Arthur was concerned that the image of the day college, whose academic programs he directed, might be damaged by a full-credit evening division. He suggested, therefore, that "a wall of separation" be constructed between the two programs.[44] Arthur also feared that the recent reaccreditation might be jeopardized because, at the time of the visitation, the evening division had offered only noncredit

Br. John Weihrer, CSC.

courses. Lastly, the dean, who was working hard to keep a lid on student protests—which had reached their height at Stonehill in the spring of 1970[45]—thought the present unstable environment not conducive to initiating new ventures.[46] Weihrer wrote to Arthur in an attempt to ameliorate his feelings and asked him to serve as chairman of an advisory board for the proposed college.[47]

Arthur's reservations did not stop the proposal from being forwarded to the Academic Council for discussion. Different opinions and fears circulated at a February 25 meeting. In support of the proposal, research conducted on other schools revealed no adverse effect upon accreditation. Additionally, Weihrer reported that 68 percent of the College faculty who responded to a survey indicated a desire to participate in an evening college program. In opposition, some members of the Council feared that the small-college atmosphere of Stonehill would be threatened and that evening seminars offered to day college students would be hampered. Although no definite decision on the proposal was made at this time, Weihrer was authorized to develop a formal plan and establish an advisory board.[48]

Weihrer's plan, a "Statement of Policy, Regulations, and Programs," was published concurrently with the formation of the advisory board. On April 15 the board presented Weihrer's plan to the Academic Council, asking for its approval. The program was outlined and specifics on day-to-day operations were discussed. It was "to be responsive to the current needs of the urban community in its varied aspects."[49] The evening college would be structured on a 15-week semester, with classes offered four nights per week with two 75-minute sessions each evening. An advisory board, selected by the academic dean, was to oversee the evening college, outline policy, programs, and regulations, and be directly responsible to the Academic Council for its operation. Although strong opinions were presented on each side, both the Academic Council and Board of Trustees approved the plan, and Weihrer was appointed as the director.[50]

Approval of Evening College led to a flurry of activity in the summer of 1970 to prepare for the start of fall classes. Father Peter Donahue, CSC, who was appointed dean of Evening College, worked with Weihrer to accomplish the many necessary tasks. Major programs were established in three areas: a BA in liberal arts, a BS in Business Administration, and a BS in Urban Studies.[51] At the outset the program depended heavily on government funds obtained for the Law Enforcement Education Program (LEEP). Weihrer enlisted Senator Edward Kennedy's assistance in obtaining LEEP funds necessary to attract students and finance the law enforcement major.[52]

Evening College opened its doors on September 14 and welcomed 181 students.[53] Although 53 courses were offered, only 17 were actually taught. The first year was successful, but some obstacles and disagreements arose. Conflict between Weihrer and Donahue precipitated the former to submit his resignation to Corr: "The present Dean of the Evening College . . . resents my being the Director. . . . Under such circumstances I do not believe that I can accomplish the duties required of me." Corr ably settled the situation by giving Donahue control of credit evening college and making Weihrer director of continuing education.[54]

The completion of Evening College's first year was welcomed with a sense of accomplishment, but the advisory board made several recommendations for change based on its observations of the initial year. Majors programs were streamlined and adjusted to approximate those of the day program, including the elimination of requirements for theology and philosophy save a single course in each discipline. The advisory board promoted the belief that Evening College should not be seen as a poor relative to the day school, but should stand on its own merit.[55]

The philosophy of American Catholic higher education in the wake of Vatican II and its endorsement of historical criticism was debated at Stonehill in the latter half of the 1960s in a struggle between the departments of philosophy and theology. Until the fall of 1966, all Catholic students were required to take two two-credit courses in theology each year. That fall, however, the requirement was changed to one three-credit course per year, in an effort to make theology a more accepted rigorous academic discipline.

Evening Division students register for classes.

At the same time members of the department, led by Robert Kruse, CSC, began to challenge the staid methods of theological discussion, adopting both a more ecumenical approach and the historical-critical method. College catalogs of the period reflected these changes. References to Catholic theology were changed to "systematic reflection upon Christian faith" (1967–1968) and "understanding an appreciation both of the Catholic religious tradition and the religious foundations of other Christian and non-Christian bodies."[56] Movement away from the traditional theological approach was supported by Corr's progressive patronage of canonical alienation of the College from Holy Cross.[57]

While theology moved in a progressive manner, the Department of Philosophy continued to champion neo-Thomism and its more traditional approach to the intellectual life. The department chairman, James Dillon, and certain colleagues, including Peter Royal, CSC, and Thomas Feeley, CSC, believed that excessive change was moving the College away from its roots and was problematic to its Catholic identity.[58]

The controversy came to a head in late 1969. Fewer theological require-ments and sweeping changes in department course offerings brought a chal-lenge from the Department of Philosophy. The academic council investigated the matter through a subcommittee chaired by David Arthur. Arthur ruled that it was inappropriate for representatives in one department to challenge course offerings in a second. Thus, the complaint brought by the Depart-ment of Philosophy against the Academic Committee was dropped. The more progressive spirit was triumphant in the symbolic gesture of changing the department name to "Religious Studies" in the fall of 1971. The contro-versy may have had as much effect on the Holy Cross Community as on the College, with forces marshaled on both sides of the issue.[59] As a result of this dispute, a series of faculty seminars on the Catholic identity of Stonehill were held in the spring of 1970.[60]

Academic Freedom and Faculty Organization

❦

THE UNSETTLED PERIOD of the 1960s in America raised many concerns in the academic community. Student rights and freedoms and the period of unrest experienced in this decade colored life on college campuses across the nation. Under the general cry of "academic freedom," professors called for more rights and renewed their efforts to organize and create solidarity in academic ranks. The events of the decade propelled the drive for student and faculty freedom beyond that in any previous period.

Academic freedom in its classic sense proposes that, as a result of their citizenship in a free society, professors and students have similar rights of free expression and the freedoms of inquiry, association, and publication.[61] During the 1960s this theory and its principles of implementation were per-ceived by many in academic circles to be in jeopardy. The historian Philip Gleason referred to academic freedom as "the most crucial problem facing Catholic higher education" during the period. Historically, an incompatibil-ity between traditional supernatural religion and academic freedom kept the issue of faculty rights out of the minds of educators at Catholic colleges, but when teachers in secular schools began to question their freedom, the shroud was lifted and Catholic scholars began to assert themselves and voice their opinions.[62]

Catholics entered the battle over academic freedom late. As Church institutions began to close the gap with secular schools in facilities, degree programs, and general scholarly acceptance, an environment was created on Catholic campuses in which professors and students began to seriously question their perceived lack of freedom. In response, Catholic institutions placed more emphasis on freedom, personal commitment, and responsible deliberation by all members. The combination of opposing camps within Catholic life, student unrest, and instability in society generated a crisis in Catholic higher education.

Pressure placed upon Catholic colleges and universities to conform to secular rules and standards exacerbated an already troublesome situation for administrators and faculty. Educators perceived danger for the future of Catholic higher education if colleges and universities did not rapidly become what their titles and charters claimed them to be. In their view, competition from secular schools in salaries, academic opportunities, and available facilities would drive all but a cadre of loyal students and teachers from Catholic institutions.[63] In order to meet this challenge Catholic schools needed to be liberated from their historical roots. Speaking at Notre Dame's 125th anniversary convocation in 1967, Theodore Hesburgh stated that higher education must not succumb to the present crisis: "Freedom and autonomy are still central to the university's life and spirit. . . ."[64] The theologian Michael Buckley, SJ, expressed the sentiments of many Catholic educators who pondered the need for Catholic education in a rapidly changing and highly competitive world:[65]

> The Church must have theology. If the Church is to have theology, she must have universities or a university presence; and if these institutions are to be universities, their discussion must not be ecclesially limited.

While many Catholic[66] and secular colleges and universities suffered through disagreements and other problems related to academic freedom in the 1960s, the experience at Stonehill was quite different. Stonehill professors continued to struggle with the more mundane issues of class size and salary. In the fall of 1969 the average number of students per faculty member ranged from 44 for those in the department of classical languages to over 121 for the psychology program.[67] Faculty salaries, which had perennially been low, remained so but with the promise for improvement. Budget discussions in the summer of 1968 recommended that all faculty salaries be raised to the American Association of University Professors (AAUP) "B" average within four years. This goal was to be reached through fundraising (investments and tuition) and the administrative decisions to hire no new faculty until student enrollment reached 1400 and to initiate no new programs or expand existing ones until the goal was reached.[68]

Formal faculty organization began at Stonehill with the establishment of a local chapter of the AAUP. The parent body, founded in 1915 by John Dewey and A.O. Lovejoy, was established to create a "more comprehensive" professional organization than what was afforded by groups organized around a single academic discipline.[69] Upon assumption of the office of dean, David Arthur suggested to the faculty that an AAUP chapter be started at Stonehill. In February 1967 the Faculty Assembly took up the issue, but not until September did a group of professors meet formally, under the leadership of James Kenneally and John Carty, to form a local chapter. In late November the chapter was inaugurated. C. James Cleary was elected president and three committees—student affairs, faculty affairs, and administration affairs—were created.[70]

Faculty influence outside the classroom expanded in the more open environment that was a trademark of the leadership styles of Corr and Arthur. One discovery by the intellectual climate committee of the 1964 self-study was a dearth of opportunity for faculty to exchange ideas and opinions in academic areas. In response, Arthur suggested faculty members be organized into divisions of broad subject areas (such as humanities, natural science, social science, and business) rather than departments to facilitate a meaningful exchange of ideas. The recommendation, however, was never formalized.[71]

Faculty committees were expanded and served as the vehicle for professors to participate in governance and decision making.[72] One example of power exercised by the faculty came in late 1969, when the Academic Council voted, at the recommendation of the Rank and Tenure Committee, that the latter group's composition, presently appointed by the president, be replaced by faculty members of the rank of professor elected by their peers.[73]

Organized faculty meetings had been held from the earliest days of Stonehill, but only in the mid-1960s did the faculty as a body exert significant influence on College affairs. Consisting of all faculty, administrators, and research personnel whose appointment carried with it faculty rank, the body had historically been presided over by the academic dean. In 1967 a discussion arose about electing a faculty member to preside. Although Arthur was ready to relinquish his position, a "faculty moderator" was not chosen until 1969.[74] The Faculty Assembly became the principal forum for members to discuss issues, hear opinions, and make decisions. Its improved status was recognized by one of its members:[75]

> The position of the Faculty Assembly represents a high point in the Faculty's search to have its collective voice heard on the important issues facing the College at this time. It would be irresponsible for the faculty to abdicate this challenge to make it[s] feelings known to the entire College community on any pressing issues."

Better organization greeted many new faculty members and new positions during the 1960s. C. James Cleary, who came to Stonehill in 1949, was appointed to the new position of associate academic dean in March 1968. David Arthur hoped that an assistant would allow the occupant of the dean's office to teach one class and thus achieve closer student contact.[76] Many new faces who would play important roles in the lives of Stonehill students arrived on campus in this period, including John McCarthy, CSC, Judith Sughrue, William Braun, CSC, Chet Raymo, John Carty, Richard Finnegan, Robert Goulet, Peter Beisheim, John Broderick, Anne T. Carrigg, Thomas Clarke, CSC, Joyce Collins, Charles Curran, Paul Foucré, Fred Petti, Paul Gastonguay, and Bartley MacPháidín, CSC.

In the spring of 1970 David Arthur announced his resignation as academic dean in order to complete his doctoral program at University of Michigan. Arthur's many accomplishments as dean were recognized in an announcement of his move: "He has been a particular advocate of increased participation by the faculty in academic-making processes as well as promulgation of closer relations between faculty and students."[77] He had overseen the implementation of the self-study recommendations, initiated a highly praised freshmen grading system, and promoted student rights and responsibilities through a reorganized academic plan that offered greater elective options and independent study. The Brockton *Enterprise* described Arthur as being "noted for his innovative approach to contemporary education."[78] Arthur himself rightly described how Stonehill came of age in his tenure as dean: "In former years it seemed that Stonehill's problems were about three years behind the concerns of the 'mainstream' institutions. Now, it seems, we are only about one year behind and catching up rapidly."[79]

A search committee under the guidance of Professor Robert Reordan and consisting of department chairs began to meet almost immediately to seek a replacement for Arthur. The committee recommended in May that an interim dean be appointed, since it would be impossible to fill the position permanently by the start of the fall semester.[80] Thus, in July Edmund Haughey, CSC, director of admissions, was appointed interim dean. The committee ultimately recommended Haughey, who was permanently appointed by Corr in January 1971.[81]

Campus Housing and Classroom Expansion

A MASTER PLAN for Stonehill College had been designed at the request of Francis Boland by the Boston architects Maginnis and Walsh in 1951. When Holy Cross Hall and the student union/cafeteria were constructed during the administration of James Sheehan, however, the plan, which directed expansion toward Route 138, was disregarded and a north-south orientation toward state highway 123 was implemented. Needs for classrooms, dormitories, and recreational facilities were growing, so John Corr sought professional expertise to develop a new master plan. After consultation with the Administrative Council, Corr engaged the firm of Taylor, Lieberfeld, and Heldman, Inc. in March 1965 "for a survey of the College facilities and future plans."[82] The consultants were asked to project activity levels associated with anticipated instructional programs, to determine corresponding space requirements, and to make proposals for necessary additional construction. The report recommended a new science building, conversion of the student union/cafeteria to an activities center (with the consequent need for a new cafeteria), expansion of the gymnasium, erection of a chapel, and provision of library facilities dependent on increased enrollments.[83] Architect W. Chester Browne produced a new master plan for the College based on the report.[84]

Generally people evaluate the progress of physical expansion in terms of new buildings that dot the landscape, but a well-built infrastructure is equally necessary to support what is more observable. For example, from its inception Stonehill used a series of leaching fields to deal with sewage. By the mid-1960s, however, this unpleasant and outdated system required correction. In December 1965 the Stonehill Administrative Council voted to install a modern sewage system on campus and connect it to the Brockton city lines.[85] The project was completed in July 1966 at a cost of $60,000, including $30,000 paid to the city of Brockton. This decision, although invisible to most, paved the way for future expansion restricted only by money and campus space.

The proposal to construct a home for religious on campus, which had complicated the latter portion of Richard Sullivan's presidency, was again raised immediately upon Corr's assumption of office. Despite the decree of the Provincial Chapter of 1964, completion of a design, and determination of a location, the religious faculty house had not been constructed. In early 1965 the local house council met to re-evaluate the need for such a building. Four different locations for the house were offered.[86] Thomas Lockary, CSC, professor of mathematics, promoted the belief that the building should not isolate the faculty: "And a necessary part of the framework within which we can teach effectively, especially in the 'small' liberal arts college, is regular communication and contact between faculty and students, in and out of the classroom."[87]

The Provincial Council decided that the structure should be built between the Grotto and the campus road leading to Route 123, a central location but sufficiently far from student scrutiny. Emery LaLiberte completed an initial design for a three-floor structure with private rooms for all religious at an estimated cost of $700,000.[88] Rising costs and the forthcoming review of campus needs by Taylor, Lieberfeld, and Heldman, Inc. led the local council to place the project on hold while seeking a less expensive alternative. By October 1966 Corr recommended to the house council that he write to the provincial to suggest that plans be dropped at this time.[89]

Richard Sullivan's earlier battle with the then provincial, George De-Prizio, over a home for religious faculty had been integrally connected with construction of a women's dormitory. In April 1964, following the Eastern Chapter of Holy Cross that appointed him provincial and mandated construction of a women's dormitory, Sullivan sought and received permission to proceed with design of the new residence. The dorm, to be located north of Holy Cross Hall, was designed by the College architect, Emery LaLiberte, at an estimated cost of $1.2 million.[90] As previously mentioned, the project was to be financed by a loan from the HHFA, the Sorin Fund, and excess profits from the operation of the cafeteria.

Construction of the women's dormitory was delayed, however, by La-Liberte's sudden death from a heart attack in March 1965. Because detailed design of the structure had not been completed,[91] Corr was forced to hire another architect to finish the project. The W. Chester Browne Company of Boston was engaged and immediately set to work to review LaLiberte's design.[92] Browne's reservations about completing LaLiberte's work, coupled with Corr's personal dislike for the design, led him to recommend that the original drawings be scrapped and a new building be designed by Browne. Whereas LaLiberte had envisioned a two-winged L-shaped building, Browne opted for a multilevel structure that provided more student beds and less wasted space, at an estimated cost of $1,535,458. The HHFA granted a loan of $1,150,000; the remaining $385,458 would be taken from cash reserves. The C.A. Batson Company of Brockton was awarded the role of primary contractor for the project.[93]

Ground-breaking for the first women's dormitory on campus, named after Father Francis Boland, who pioneered coeducation at Stonehill in 1951, was held on August 2, 1966. The project was widely advertised to generate interest in the construction of additional dorms dedicated to women.[94] Although there were some delays in the initial stages,[95] the building was ready to accept residents in September 1967.[96] Corr proudly reported, "The new women's dorm is working out very well; the girls all seem pleased with the accommodations."[97]

A burgeoning enrollment, which had reached 1243 by the fall of 1967, required that additional student housing be built as soon as possible. The need to lower costs and decrease construction time led to a revolutionary concept in college student housing at Stonehill. Inspired by the design of Louisburg Square on Boston's fabled Beacon Hill, the idea of "Towne-

Boland Hall.

houses" was introduced by Corr and supported by the planning committee of the Board of Advisors. Each building would house 12 students in an environment that, it was hoped, would more closely approximate a living situation outside the institutional environment of the College. Units could be built in six months at greatly reduced costs.[98]

Construction of Commonwealth Court, an arrangement of 14 townehouses, began on March 1, 1968. It was designed by Robert A. Green of Rhode Island and constructed by Paul G. Cleary and Company of New Bedford. The total cost of $526,912 came well under the budget of $700,000. This new concept in student living was heralded for its innovation by the Boston *Pilot*: "With the stress on personal development among the young people of today, Stonehill has sought to create the distinctive environment which will foster responsibility and maturity."[99] As with Boland Hall, Corr could proclaim, "A full semester of use has proven the Town Houses to be successful in every way, both for students and the administration."[100]

Commonwealth Court's success and the continuing need for more student housing led to the construction of a second village of townehouses, Colonial Court, immediately north of Holy Cross Hall and just west of Boland. Similar in design and orientation to Commonwealth Court, the new residences provided accommodations for 168 students in 14 units. This new housing captured the attention of the media, including television, and feature articles about it in New England journals and the *New York Times*.[101]

Despite some concern with the isolation created by students living

(Right) Ames Gates at Colonial Court.
(Below) Colonial Court townehouses.

within a "cocoon" of 12 peers,[102] Corr believed the townehouses to be the best solution to the need for rapid construction of student residences at a reasonable cost. He therefore requested permission from the new provincial, William Hogan, to construct three more townehouses in the area of Commonwealth Court. These were built and opened in the fall of 1970.

Colonial Court was expanded, but with one major change: the introduction of coed living. The Student Affairs Committee in March 1971 began to discuss housing of men and women in three new "experimental" houses scheduled for construction in Colonial Court. The committee viewed the trial, prompted by a growing trend of the day on college campuses, as a possible means to ease social isolationism at Stonehill. The newly formed College Council[103] spent the better part of three weekly meetings discussing the issue before voting on May 11 "to accept in principle the concept of co-ed living as a limited experiment."[104] Corr, for his part, criticized the experiment as ill-conceived and without sufficient basis. He believed it was necessary to work out problems with the parietal policy on campus before coeducation was attempted.[105] Despite his reservations, however, three coed townehouses began to operate in the fall of 1971.

Rising enrollment and the need for faculty office space created the necessity for a second addition to Holy Cross Hall. Faculty offices did not exist save in a common area on the second floor of the cafeteria. In order to foster greater student-teacher exchange, individual faculty offices were considered necessary.[106] In a rather bold move, Corr engaged W. Chester Browne to design an addition before the process to seek approval for the project was even initiated,[107] although assent from both the Administrative and Provincial Councils was required and eventually obtained. The February 1967 approval of the addition by the General Council of Holy Cross set the project in motion.[108] Financing for the estimated $1.7 million project was secured by government loans and grants, a private loan from the New Bedford Institution of Savings, and cash reserves.[109]

The contract for the three-story, 36,000-square-feet-addition, including 57 private faculty offices, 15 classrooms, administrative offices, and seminar rooms, was awarded to the J.T. Scully Company. Construction began in June 1968, and the building was ready for use in September 1969. In a ceremony on October 17, 1970, at which actor Jack Haley, representing the Board of Advisors spoke, Holy Cross Hall was rededicated in the name of Thomas Duffy, CSC, who, along with James Wesley Donahue, first discovered the Ames estate in 1935 and whose efforts in 1948 prompted Holy Cross to found the College.[110]

Transition and College Development

❧   FROM THE OUTSET, fundraising at Stonehill had been less than successful. The efforts of Thomas Duffy and James Lowery were sincere but were never sufficiently broad or professionally implemented to achieve the desired results. In January 1967 Leo Wesner, fresh from seven years at Boston College, was appointed director of the Office of Development and given the title assistant to the president for development, but he resigned after only two years. In March 1969 Corr retained the services of the Martin J. Moran Company of New York to professionalize development efforts. Moran's local agent, Walter Mullen, immediately organized a six-month campaign with a goal of $1.1 million, which he declared to be "readily available."[111] Like all previous efforts, however, the drive failed to achieve its goal, precipitating an angry response from the usually placid Corr:[112]

> In short Walt, I'm really not satisfied with what has happened in reference with what I had hoped would happen. We are trusting you completely to lead us in this area of fund raising. . . . I certainly do expect a lot more activity for the money we are paying and activity other that [*sic*] what we are already engaged in.

The "Development for the Seventies," a major fundraising campaign, was initiated by Corr to raise capital for future expansion projects, faculty enhancement, and student scholarships. This major undertaking continued throughout the decade but ended in the administration of Ernest Bartell, CSC. In January 1970 Corr and Edward T. Martin, chairman of the Board of Advisors, announced a campaign with a goal of $15 million. A kickoff dinner was held on March 11 at Holy Cross Seminary, with many dignitaries in attendance.[113] At the banquet Corr spoke of the need for Stonehill to accept the challenge created by a dynamic and rapidly changing world and to respond to the demands of education in the 1970s. John F. Collins, former mayor of Boston, assumed the chairmanship of the campaign.

The new development campaign was structured in two phases with separate goals. Phase I—1970 to 1972—had a goal of $5 million for library resources, faculty endowment, academic and curriculum development, scholarship endowment, and construction of a college center ($2.5 million). Phase II—1972 to 1980—had a goal of $10.25 million for academic and curriculum endowment, faculty compensation ($3 million), new science facilities ($2.5 million), library expansion, student residences, and refurbishment of existing facilities.[114]

John Corr's efforts to professionalize the College's development program was one example of a different but successful leadership style. Corr was less visible than his predecessors in the day-to-day management of affairs at Stonehill College, but his leadership was highly effective. His ability to delegate authority and his philosophy of education, which permeated his administration and transformed Stonehill into a true liberal arts college, were pillars of his leadership style. Corr championed the individuality of the student and tailored academic programs with the like-minded dean, David Arthur, to achieve this end. He was a progressive thinker who understood

Bulletin for "Development for the Seventies" program.

the need for the education process to evolve constantly in order to meet the needs of students and faculty. One year before he left the office of president he stated:[115]

> The College of the 70's must be a base of action—a source of intellectual and professional energy that will respond to and interact with the realities of life. It must reflect the critical needs of the day. It must be energized by the creative tensions around us. It must create a learning environment that will motivate its students to a responsible participation in life.
>
> The College that functions under this mandate will render exceptional service to society. The college that accepts this as a challenge is a college that strives for greatness.

Corr believed that higher education must be open to transformation, and he held the conviction that Catholic education had to offer something in addition to "a fuller knowledge of the human being." He concluded, "If it's [Catholic higher education] no different than public education, it has no reason to exist."[116]

In April 1971 John Corr offered his resignation as president of Stonehill College. In a letter to the provincial he stated that he had come to the office with certain goals and that those objectives had been met or ". . . are within the grasp of my successor without undue stress on him. I, therefore, feel it is time for new ideas and ideals as Stonehill approaches her second quarter century." Corr's success as president did not mask the fact that he suffered greatly in his position. The upheaval of the sixties caused him great pain. His naturally quiet demeanor found little rest in his seven years as president. Corr stayed at Stonehill and worked full time on the newly initiated "Development for the Seventies" campaign.[117]

*   *   *

The administration of John Corr—coming on the heels of Richard Sullivan, who had achieved recognition for the College within the academic community—was a time when Stonehill College came of age and took its place alongside established institutions in the long tradition of Catholic liberal arts education. During his tenure, enrollment rose by 400 students, faculty numbers almost doubled, and the operating budget increased by 63 percent.[118] William Hogan spoke for many: "Under Father Corr's guidance, Stonehill College has made truly monumental progress—academically, in community services and in physical growth."[119]

Through the efforts of many dedicated men and women, and under the leadership of four Holy Cross priests, Stonehill College had grown from a dream in 1948 to a fully accredited college in 1962. This milestone was rightly celebrated, but it served as only the starting point for the evolution of the school during the 1960s into a true institution of higher learning in the liberal arts tradition. Under the watchful but less visible leadership of John Corr, Stonehill, through the institution of greater professionalism in academic administration (especially in the office of dean), enhancement of academic programs, and the construction of badly needed student housing, classrooms, and faculty offices, began to take its place in every aspect as a respected representative of Catholic higher education in America. Stonehill also began to fall in line with the pattern established by other liberal arts institutions nationwide. Development in all areas was far from complete, but the critical first steps beyond mere membership in the academy and advancement on the road to educational greatness among peer institutions had been taken.

ENDNOTES

1. Philip Gleason, "American Catholic Higher Education: A Historical Perspective," in *The Shape of Catholic Higher Education*, Robert Hassenger, ed. (Chicago: University of Chicago Press, 1967): 51.

2. Sister M. Emmanuel, "Prevailing Winds on the Catholic Campus," *Critic* 22 (December 1963–January 1964): 61. Other participants at the conference included Sister Bertrande, president of Marillac College, John J. Ryan, professor of English at St. Anselm College, Theodore Hesburgh, CSC, president of Notre Dame, John J. Wright, bishop of Pittsburgh, and Joseph E. Cunneen, managing editor of *Cross Currents*.

3. P.H. Ratterman, SJ, *The Emerging Catholic University* (New York: Fordham University Press, 1968): 33; Michael Buckley, SJ, "The Function of a Catholic University," *U.S. Catholic* 34 (September 1969): 47; Michael Walsh, SJ, "Nature and Role Today," in *The Catholic University: A Modern Appraisal*, Neil McCluskey, SJ, ed. (Notre Dame: University of Notre Dame Press, 1970): 52–54.

4. Theodore Hesburgh, CSC, "The Vision of a Great Catholic University," *Catholic Mind* 66 (February 1968): 48.

5. Murray was seen as the principal architect of the document that proved to be the most significant contribution of the American Church to Vatican II. In the 1940s and 1950s, Murray's writings on Church-state issues were scorned by Vatican officials, who ordered Jesuit leaders to curb his activities. Murray was effectively silenced by his superiors, as he was required to submit all he wrote for evaluation and censoring before publication. He was, however, selected to be Cardinal Francis Spellman's *peritus* for the Council. Adoption of the Declaration on Religious Liberty vindicated Murray and canonized many of his ideas.

6. John Courtney Murray, SJ, "The Vatican Declaration on Religious Freedom: An Aspect of Its Significance," in Leo McLaughlin, SJ, John Courtney Murray, SJ, and Pedro Arrupe, SJ, *The University in the American Experience* (New York: Fordham University Press, 1966): 10.

7. John F. Brosnan, "Catholic Higher Education: A View From Outside the Institution," *NCEA Bulletin* 56 (August 1959): 120.

8. Neil McCluskey, SJ, *Catholic Education Faces Its Future* (Garden City, New York: Doubleday & Company, Inc., 1968), 217–17, 220. McCloskey stated that while the overall enrollment in colleges and universities rose 10 percent, Catholic schools in the 1960s lost students. For the 1968–1969 academic year, only one-half of the 170 four-year Catholic colleges and universities surveyed met their predicted freshmen enrollment. As a note of comparison, Stonehill's enrollment during this same year rose 5 percent.

9. Hesburgh, "The Vision of a Great Catholic University," 54.

10. *The Summit* (May 21, 1964); John Corr "Inauguration Program," Corr Papers, ASC; Corr to Richard Sullivan, July 24, 1964, Provincial Papers–Sullivan, AHCFE.

11. John Corr, "Inaugural Address," October 9, 1964, Corr Papers, ASC.

12. John Corr, "Speech to Faculty," September 9, 1964; Corr, "Address to Students," September 21, 1964, Corr Papers, ASC. Corr believed in the freedom of academic pursuit: "If the intellectual life is to flower, the atmosphere must be free of fear. Fear that only the certain is acceptable, that the probable is perilous, and that the possible is impossible. Fear that the new will be suspected, insight ridiculed,

experience exorcized. An intelligent man, a man with ideas, will always have a hearing and should have a hearing so that error may be corrected, truth might be disseminated, and new ideas may be brought into being."

13. John Corr, "Address to Students," September 21, 1964, Corr Papers, ASC.

14. *Stonehill* 3(1) (December 1964); John Corr, "Address to Alumni," October 11, 1964, Corr Papers; Board of Advisor Meeting Minutes, May 16, 1964, Board of Advisor Papers; Corr to "Administration, Faculty and Staff of Stonehill College," November 10, 1964, Corr Papers, ASC.

15. Endicott Peabody to John Corr, January 6, 1965; Brother Gregory Nugent, FSC to Corr, February 23, 1968; Richard Matre to Corr, May 5, 1968; Corr to Richard Cushing, September 18, 1967, Corr Papers; *Easton Bulletin* (April 27, 1967); *Stonehill College News* (April 24, 1967), Public Affairs Papers, ASC. The *Stonehill College News* reported that Corr's assistance at Unity Church was the first time in the Diocese of Fall River a Catholic priest had been a guest minister at a Protestant church.

16. Richard Sullivan to George DePrizio, December 14, 1963, Provincial Papers–DePrizio, AHCFE. Apparently Sullivan first heard of the idea of a self-study while attending a seminar at The College of the Holy Cross in Worcester.

17. Richard Sullivan to Faculty, January 9, 1964, Sullivan Papers, ASC.

18. Memorandum, Office of the Dean (Cussen), December 16, 1963, Academic Council Papers; Aloysius Cussen to Faculty, April 22, 1964, Cussen Papers; Richard Sullivan to Faculty (memorandum), March 2, 1964, Sullivan Papers; Roger Quilty, CSC, to "Colleagues," April 13, 1964, Cussen Papers, ASC.

19. *Stonehill* 4(1) (April 1966), Corr Papers; Roger Quilty to "Colleagues," April 13, 1964, Cussen Papers; "Summary of Executive Committee Meetings 1964," uncatalogued material, ASC.

20. *Stonehill* 3(1) (December 1964); John Corr, "Speech to Faculty," September 9, 1964, Corr Papers, ASC.

21. "Executive Committee Self-Study," March 25, 1966; Aloysius Cussen to Members of the Academic Council, March 25, 1966, uncatalogued material; John Corr, "Stonehill College Acts to Meet Today's True Education," n.d., Corr Papers, ASC.

22. Before he was appointed president, Corr had served as registrar, with Cussen as his superior. Possible friction from this earlier relationship was a catalyst to Cussen's reassignment to a position of lesser influence.

23. Richard Sullivan to John Corr, May 13, 1966; Corr to Faculty (memorandum), August 26, 1966, Corr Papers, ASC.

24. See chapters 2, 3, 4, and 6 for a description of Arthur's earlier assignments at Stonehill.

25. Duties of the academic dean, as published in 1968, included faculty recruitment, evaluation, assignment, and welfare and student enrollment, status, and programs of study.

26. John Corson, *Governance of Colleges and Universities* (New York: McGraw-Hill Book Company, Inc., 1960): 76. Corson concluded, "Because the educational

program consumes a major part of the college's budget, the president controls most curricular and faculty decisions and markedly limits the role played by the dean." This analysis accurately described Stonehill College before Arthur's assumption of the office of academic dean.

27. David Arthur, "Reflections on the Academic Program at Stonehill College" (May 3, 1968), Arthur Papers, ASC.

28. Academic Council Meeting Minutes, October 6, 1966, Academic Council Papers; "Report of Science Curriculum Committee," April 1967, Arthur Papers, ASC.

29. Faculty Assembly Meeting Minutes, October 5, 1965, Faculty Assembly Papers, ASC. Cussen spoke in favor of a shift to five courses per semester to allow students to achieve greater depth in their classes. *The Summit* reported the proposed change in its April 29, 1966 issue.

30. David Arthur to King Broderick, January 26, 1968; Arthur to Johnny L. Arrette, May 10, 1968, Arthur Papers, ASC.

31. "Technics, Tools for Education Innovation," *College and University Business Magazine*, 44 (3) (March 1968):61. Many college deans and other administrators wrote to Arthur about Stonehill's plan and its effectiveness. Arthur responded to one such letter, "We have been quite satisfied with this system." David Arthur to Charles Grigsby, January 5, 1970, Arthur Papers, ASC.

32. David Arthur to Mark Wong, October 7, 1966; Arthur to Faculty, October 19, 1966; "Report of Ad Hoc Committee on the Grading System," n.d. [1967], Arthur Papers, ASC. Possible grades in the new system were: A, B+, B, C+, C, D+, D, and F.

33. Academic Council Meeting Minutes, January 12, 1967, and February 23, 1967, Academic Council Meeting Minutes, ASC.

34. David Arthur to Faculty, December 1, 1966, January 3, 1968, Arthur Papers; Academic Council Meeting Minutes, December 15, 1966, Academic Council Papers, ASC.

35. The professor was not informed that the student had chosen pass/fail for a course. Initial data showed that student performance did not falter when the option was chosen.

36. Faculty Assembly Meeting Minutes, September 13, 1966, Faculty Assembly Papers; James Kenneally, "Report on Independent Study," n.d., Arthur Papers, ASC. Kenneally also experienced problems with independent study. He found that students would often not assume the added responsibility for such independence. Kenneally's discovery was verified by Paul Dressel who claimed that independent study had two major flaws: (1) It was assumed to relieve the burden on faculty and be cost effective; the reality was that it was more expensive. (2) Faculty discovered that students were often not ready to assume responsibility for independent study. See Paul L. Dressel, *College and University Curriculum* (Berkeley: McCutchen Publishing Corporation, 1971): 63.

37. David Arthur to Faculty Members, May 2, 1967, Arthur Papers; Faculty Assembly Meeting Minutes, November 16, 1967, Faculty Assembly Papers, ASC.

38. *Stonehill* (Spring 1971), Public Affairs Papers, ASC. David Arthur was no

longer dean at the time College Studies was started, but its genesis came from the spirit he gave to the office.

39. A.C. Ingersoll to John Corr, November 4, 1968; Corr to Ingersoll, November 15, 1968, Corr Papers, ASC.

40. W.C.H. Prentice to John Corr, June 17, 1967; David Arthur to Walter Kenworthy, December 5, 1967; Arthur to Kenworthy, February 27, 1968, Arthur Papers, ASC. Corr also investigated programs of cooperation with Curry College and the Holy Cross Sisters at Cardinal Cushing College in Boston, but no formal agreements were reached.

41. "Re-Evaluation Report," 1969, Accreditation Papers, ASC.

42. Rosemary Pierrel to John Corr, January 14, 1970, Accreditation Papers; David Arthur to Faculty, December 6, 1969, Arthur Papers, ASC.

43. Edward M. Kelly to Ralph D. Dean, October 10, 1969; John Weihrer, CSC, "A Proposal for an Evening College," n.d., Evening College Papers, ASC. Weihrer had investigated similar evening college programs at Bryant, Merrimack, Suffolk University, Providence, and Boston College and discovered that all experienced economic benefit from them. Additionally, he believed that such a program would appear favorable for the College in its service to the local community and result in the reward of loans for future expansion programs.

44. Arthur had concerns about the evening division proposal. First, the uncertainty of the late 1960s, with its student protests, made the launching of a new program a risk. Secondly, reaccreditation in 1969 was based upon a day program only. He did not want any new venture to jeopardize the status of the day college.

45. Chapter 8 gives full details on student unrest at Stonehill in the later 1960s and 1970.

46. John Weihrer to Vincent P. Wright, January 7, 1970, Evening College Papers; David Arthur to Robert R. Ramsey, Jr., February 5, 1970, Arthur Papers, ASC.

47. John Weihrer to David Arthur, March 9, 1970, Arthur Papers, ASC. Arthur took no action on the invitation.

48. Academic Council Meeting Minutes, February 25, 1970, Academic Council Papers, ASC.

49. Board of Advisors, Evening College to Academic Council, April 15, 1970, Evening College Papers, ASC.

50. Academic Council Meeting Minutes, April 30, 1970, Academic Council Papers; Board of Trustees Meeting Minutes, April 20, 1970, Board of Trustees Papers, ASC. The Academic Council voted 6–5 and the Board of Trustees 3–2 for approval. John Corr, a member of the board, voted against the measure, probably for the same reasons articulated by Arthur—its possible damage to the day school and the uncertainty and instability present due to student unrest. The original Board of Advisors was John Weihrer, CSC, chair, Peter Donahue, CSC, Francis G. Lee, Maryalice Moore, and Robert Reordan. Augustine Peverada, CSC, history professor and original member of the committee, was reassigned to Maine in the summer of 1970.

51. *Stonehill College News*, n.d. [Summer 1970], Public Affairs Papers; Evening College Catalog, 1970–71; Peter Donahue, CSC, interview with the author, June

19, 1996, Stonehill College History Project Papers, ASC. Major fields were: BA in economics, English, history, humanistic studies, political science, sociology; BS in Business Administration in accounting, management, and marketing; and a BS in Urban Studies in municipal management and law enforcement.

52. John Weihrer to Edward Kennedy, May 6, 1970, and August 7, 1970, Evening College Papers, ASC. Stonehill received a $24,000 LEEP grant in the Evening College's first year. The LEEP program was initially a source of concern for many because it brought law enforcement officers to campus with holstered weapons. Students whose actions had helped to generate the Communiversity the previous spring were distrustful of guns on campus. See John Weihrer, "Twenty-Fifth Anniversary Presentation for Stonehill Evening College," n.d. [1995], Evening College Papers, ASC.

53. This number comes from Evening College statistics. Peter Donahue published a "Newsletter" on October 27, 1970, which claimed that there were 203 registered students, 58 of whom were seeking degrees. Evening College attracted many students, with enrollment exceeding 500 by the fall of 1973.

54. John Weihrer to John Corr, November 6, 1970, Presidents' Papers; Peter Donahue, interview with the author (June 19, 1996), Stonehill College History Project Papers, ASC.

55. Advisory Board, Evening College Meeting Minutes, April 23, 1971, Evening College Papers, ASC.

56. Stonehill College Student Handbooks, 1966–1971; Stonehill College Catalogs, 1965–1970, ASC.

57. Chapter 9 fully describes Stonehill's move toward canonical alienation—the legal separation of the College from the Congregation of Holy Cross. One reason for this move was to enhance the College's ability to gain federal loans, which necessitated that theological offerings in Catholic and non-Catholic traditions be available to students.

58. Robert Kruse, CSC, interview with the author, July 11, 1996; David Arthur, interview with the author, July 18, 1996; C. James Cleary, interview with the author, July 16, 1996, Stonehill College History Project Papers, ASC.

59. The Holy Cross Community, which at the time was splintered into at least three subgroups, became even more fractured over this issue, with strong opinions held on each side.

60. *The Summit*, numerous issues (January–May 1970).

61. An excellent summary of the history of academic freedom in American Catholic higher education is found in: Charles E. Curran, *Catholic Higher Education, Theology and Academic Freedom* (Notre Dame: University of Notre Dame Press, 1990): 1–25.

62. Philip Gleason, "The Crisis in Catholic Universities: An Historical Perspective," *Catholic Mind* 64 (September 1966): 44–55.

63. One author perceived the problem for Catholic higher education as a need to move beyond the provincialism of the 1950s: "In keeping with the youth of the American Catholic College went a sense of immaturity and a need for security. Both

have led to the adoption of a ghetto mentality on the part of students and professors. This, in turn, has led to an inferiority complex, which leads to further insecurity. The vicious circle goes on." See Gerald F. Kreyche, "American Catholic Higher Learning and Academic Freedom," *NCEA Bulletin* 62 (1965): 214.

64. Hesburgh, "The Vision of a Great Catholic University," 44.

65. Michael Buckley, SJ, "The Catholic University as Pluralistic Forum," *Thought* 46 (Summer 1971): 207–08.

66. The most notorious and celebrated case of infringement of academic freedom in a Catholic institution was at St. John's University in New York. In March 1965 two hundred professors walked out of a faculty meeting to protest the absence of their voice in the decision-making processes of the institution. For nine months the administration made attempts to correct the problems raised. However, on December 15, thirty-three members of the faculty, some with tenure, were summarily terminated from their posts. The whole faculty on January 4, 1966 went on strike, charging the administration with violation of the 1940 "Statement of Principles on Academic Freedom and Tenure." See John T. Noonan, "Academic Freedom and Tenure: St. John's University (N.Y.)," *American Association of University Professors Bulletin* 52 (1966): 12–19 for a complete analysis of this incident. Noonan concluded that the rights of the tenured professors had been violated.

67. Faculty Statistics, Fall 1969, Arthur Papers, ASC.

68. McCluskey, *Catholic Educations Faces Its Future*, 225; Budget Committee to College Council (*sic* Academic Council), August 22, 1968, Academic Council Papers; John Corr to Faculty (memorandum), February 28, 1967, Corr Papers, ASC. Faculty salary ranges in February 1967 were: instructors—$5500–8000 ($6890 average); assistant professor—$6500–9000 ($7902 average); associate professor—$7500–10,000 ($9235 average); professor—$9500 and up ($10,688 average). Stonehill's enrollment in the fall of 1968 was 1350. It should be noted that in academic year 1967–68, none of the 115 Catholic institutions of higher education responding to a survey made the AAUP's category "A" for salaries. Boston College, Notre Dame, Marquette, Santa Clara, and St. Mary's (Moraga, California) were in the high "B" range. Level B average AAUP salaries were: instructor—$7300; assistant professor—$9180; associate professor—$11,530; professor—$16,310.

69. Willis Rudy and John S. Brubacher, *A History of American College and Universities* (New York: Harper & Row, 1968): 307–08. At its initial meeting the AAUP attracted 867 professors from 60 different institutions. The association met active opposition from the outset. The *New York Times* blasted the group as "organized dons." The Committee on Academic Freedom of the Association of American Colleges, composed of college presidents, believed it could speak more effectively for the professors than the professors themselves through the AAUP.

70. David Arthur to Faculty, August 31, 1966, Arthur Papers; Faculty Assembly Meeting Minutes, February 16, 1967, Faculty Assembly Papers; AAUP Chapter Report, September 21, 1967; AAUP Chapter Meeting Minutes, November 9, 1967 and November 30, 1967, Faculty Papers, ASC.

71. David Arthur to Faculty Members, May 18, 1967, Dean's Papers, ASC.

72. In 1967 the faculty rejected the idea of a College senate and made the decision to work through elected committees. See David Arthur to Philip Sharkey, December 23, 1968, Arthur Papers, ASC.

73. Academic Council Meeting Minutes, October 29, 1969, Academic Council Papers; John Corr to David Arthur, January 19, 1970, Corr Papers, ASC; C. James Cleary to John Corr, November 13, 1969, Provincial Papers–Sullivan, AHCFE. In May 1971 the College faculty committees were: library, graduate studies opportunities, faculty affairs, intercollegiate athletics, development, admissions, academic standing, student affairs, counseling, intramural athletics, alumni, public relations, publications, and rank and tenure.

74. James Dillon to Faculty, November 3, 1969; Faculty Assembly Meeting Minutes, December 14, 1967; Dillon to "All Faculty," n.d. [March 1969], Faculty Assembly Papers, ASC.

75. Edward MacLeod to Faculty, November 6, 1970, Faculty Assembly Papers, ASC.

76. Arthur had taught one course per semester his first two years as dean. The only other dean who taught after Arthur was Sr. Jo-Ann Flora, who taught writing.

77. Stonehill College News, n.d. [1970], Arthur Papers, ASC.

78. Brockton *Enterprise* clipping (April 30, 1970), Arthur Papers, ASC.

79. David Arthur to Faculty, March 17, 1970, Arthur Papers, ASC.

80. Meeting Minutes, "All Department Chairs," May 18, 1970, Dean's Papers, ASC.

81. Grace Donahue to Edward Klein, July 6, 1970; Robert Reordan to John Corr, January 20, 1971; Corr to Edmund Haughey, February 9, 1971, Dean's Papers, ASC.

82. Administrative Council Meeting Minutes, January 6, 1965, Administrative Council Papers, ASC.

83. "Report to Stonehill College: A Program for Physical Plant Development," October 1965, Stonehill College Papers, AHCFE. In September 1967 another report, "Physical Plant Needs and Priorities," Stonehill College Papers, AHCFE, was written. It made different recommendations, including a new house for religious faculty, conversion of the student union to a science building, and construction of a combined dining hall and athletic facility.

84. *The Summit* (March 25, 1966). Browne's plan included a new religious faculty house, auditorium, gymnasium and pool, dining hall, new classrooms, a chapel, and four men's dormitories.

85. Administrative Council Meeting Minutes, December 20, 1965, Stonehill College Papers, AHCFE; John Corr to Richard Sullivan, July 14, 1966; Sullivan to Germain Lalande, August 8, 1966, AHCFG.

86. Provincial Council Meeting Minutes, October 10, 1964, Provincial Council Papers, AHCFE. The four sites were: (1) center of the quadrangle near the lake, (2) east of Holy Cross Hall, (3) between the Grotto and the road leading to Route 123, and (4) near Donahue Hall.

87. Thomas Lockary, CSC, to John Corr, July 17, 1964, AHCFE.

88. Richard Sullivan to Germain Lalande, November 15, 1964, Provincial Council Papers–Sullivan, AHCFE.

89. Richard Sullivan to Germain Lalande, January 23, 1965, Provincial Papers–Sullivan, AHCFE; Executive Council (House Council) Meeting Minutes, October 20, 1966, Executive Council Papers, ASC. The first residence built by the Holy Cross Community for its members was erected in 1977, when the hay and horse barn from the Ames estate were renovated.

90. Richard Sullivan to Germain Lalande, April 20, 1964, May 8, 1964, and November 15, 1964, Provincial Papers–Sullivan; Provincial Council Meeting Minutes, October 17, 1964, Provincial Council Papers, AHCFE.

91. Richard Sullivan to Germain Lalande, October 21, 1965. Sullivan reported the working drawings were 80 percent completed at the time of LaLiberte's death.

92. John Corr to W. Chester Browne, April 15, 1965, Corr Papers, ASC.

93. John Corr to Richard Sullivan, July 14, 1966, Provincial Papers–Sullivan, AHCFE; John Corr to Faculty, August 26, 1966, Corr Papers; *Summit* (March 22, 1967), ASC.

94. *Stonehill College News* (August 25, 1966), Public Affairs Papers, ASC. This news release claimed, "It [Boland Hall] is the first of a planned five-dormitory complex for women. . . ."

95. Corr was encouraged by Browne to use a more autocratic style in his relationship with the Batson Company to keep the project on schedule.

96. The opening of the dormitory allowed women who had been occupying an apartment complex on Elm Street in Brockton, rented by the College, to move on campus. Extant data does not demonstrate that Corr was as great a champion of women as Sullivan, but in January 1965 he did form a committee, chaired by the dean of women, Virginia Yosgandes, to give him advice on women's issues. Other members were Louise Hegarty, Elizabeth Mahoney, Maryalice Moore, Judith Sughrue, and Frances Burlingame, consultant and former faculty member.

97. John Corr to James O. Dunn, November 15, 1967, Corr Papers, ASC.

98. *Stonehill* 5(1) (December 1967), n.d. (Summer 1968), Public Affairs Papers, ASC.

99. Boston *Pilot* (November 2, 1968).

100. John Corr to Richard Sullivan, February 21, 1969, Provincial Papers–Sullivan, AHCFE.

101. *Stonehill* (Winter 1969), Public Affairs Papers, ASC.

102. Karen Haskell to John Heslin, January 7, 1970, Assistant Dean of Student Affairs Papers, ASC. Haskell, dean of women, voiced the opinion that no more townhouses should be constructed until a detailed study was conducted on their effect on student life. She was concerned that the townhouse environment isolated students in cliques of twelve.

103. Establishment of the College Council is described in Chapter 9.

104. Student Affairs Committee Meeting Minutes, March 3, 1971, Dean of Student Affairs Papers; College Council Meeting Minutes, April 22, 1971 and May 11, 1971, College Council Papers, ASC.

105. John Corr to Vincent P. Wright, June 10, 1971, Corr Papers, ASC. Corr's reservations were in three areas: (1) Social—proponents said that a coed situation is like "outside" conditions, but Corr disagreed and asked what social advantages were achieved by coed living. (2) Moral—he advocates a review of the parietal program. (3) Psychological—he stated that a problem already existed at Stonehill with cliques, and that coed living would only exacerbate this undesirable condition.

106. One anecdote of the period illustrates the need for faculty offices. Brassil Fitzgerald, one of the leading members of the faculty since the opening of the College, would counsel students in his car.

107. John Corr to Richard F. Barrett, October 31, 1966, Corr Papers, ASC.

108. Richard Vincelette to Jerome Lawyer, February 25, 1967, Provincial Papers–Sullivan, AHCFE.

109. Provincial Council Meeting Minutes, January 23, 1967, Provincial Council Papers; Jerome Lawyer to Germain Lalande, February 11, 1967, Provincial Papers–Sullivan, AHCFE.

110. John Corr to J.T. Scully Construction Company, May 31, 1968, Corr Papers; Stonehill College News n.d., Public Affairs Papers; *The Summit* (October 14, 1970), ASC.

111. Walter Mullen to John Corr, March 31, 1969, College Relations Papers, ASC.

112. John Corr to Walter Mullen, August 6, 1969, College Relations Papers, ASC.

113. Some of those in attendance were Secretary of Transportation John Volpe, Speaker of the House John McCormack, Senators Edward Kennedy and Edward Brooke, Representative Margaret Heckler, Governor Francis Sargent, and Bishop James Connolly.

114. Brochure, "Development for the Seventies," College Relations Papers, ASC.

115. *Stonehill College News* (March 11, 1970), Public Affairs Papers, ASC.

116. *The Port* clipping (Massachusetts Port Authority), April 24, 1971, Corr Papers, ASC.

117. John Corr to William Hogan, April 21, 1971, Provincial Papers–Hogan, AHCFE. Corr outlined the goals he had set: (1) make Stonehill a quality college, (2) increase enrollment, (3) revamp curriculum in line with the self-study, (4) provide necessary physical facilities, (5) bring about a separation of Stonehill and the Congregation of Holy Cross (this is the subject of Chapter 9), (6) maintain a high quality of education, and (7) initiate a major development program for future growth. Corr stayed in his new position less than one year before accepting an assignment to St. Francis Xavier Parish in Burbank, California in February, 1972.

118. State Report to "The New England Colleges Fund," n.d., Corr Papers, ASC.

119. Quoted in the Brockton *Enterprise* clipping, n.d. [spring 1971], Corr Papers, ASC.

CHAPTER 8

Student Life and Unrest

The decade of the 1960s was a significant one for Stonehill College in its academic and physical development as a Catholic institution of higher learning. Through the leadership of John Corr and David Arthur, it emerged as a recognized representative of the Catholic liberal arts tradition in the United States. The era of the 1960s in America was, however, a time of turmoil leading to problems for society and the Church. Swift and drastic changes in society, controversial political decisions that polarized opinions, and instability of the world order caused by the ongoing "Cold War" generated a period of great upheaval from which certain sectors of the national community still suffer. Stonehill College experienced the challenges of this era and participated, along with its peer institutions, in the new ideas and actions generated to respond to the problems of the day. Student life at Stonehill in the 1960s was colored by the era, but experiences there were tame in comparison with those at many other colleges. The College's innovative solution to unrest demonstrated its unique contribution to Catholic higher education in America.

American Catholicism in the 1960s

THE UNITED STATES in the 1960s moved from an euphoric state created by the newfound optimism of the postwar period to a tinderbox of dissent, disappointment, and tension that, when sparks were provided, generated firestorms across the nation. The Cold War, which began after World War II and was fed by the Korean conflict, McCarthyism, and a massive arms race, reached its apex in the Cuban Missile Crisis in October 1962. With the world on the brink of nuclear destruction, Americans felt helpless to control their fate—a feeling contrary to their past experience. The Civil Rights Movement, initiated in December 1955 with the Montgomery bus strike, reached its climax with the August 1963 March on Washington and the work of Martin Luther King, Jr. This movement, together with the rise of Black Power, race riots in urban centers, and a tragic backlash by white racists, revealed deep divisions within America's cultural pluralism.

Dissent against authority was a hallmark of this decade. As the historian Allen J. Matusow describes it,[1] the 1960s saw American society begin to unravel on many fronts. The rise of the counterculture made drugs, flower-children, and the desire to "drop out" of society common features of the decade. Television news and other media were filled with the elements that brought about the demise of American liberalism. In this regard, the war in Vietnam was one of the most divisive conflicts experienced in American history. Generating an ever-increasing level of protest, it gave new life to the country's long history of peace movements and pacifism, and produced a whole series of folk heroes, whose overt acts of defiance of authority led to the creation of numerous fringe groups—all seeking change from the status quo. Vietnam was Lyndon Johnson's Waterloo, and it created divisions that are still alive today. Finally, the decade's tensions and problems were exacerbated by the assassinations of John F. Kennedy, Martin Luther King, Jr., and Robert F. Kennedy, for the deaths of these leaders concretized the feelings of alienation, dissent, and helplessness felt by many during the period.

American Catholicism experienced many of these same feelings as they arose from sources internal and external to the Faith. The decade opened with Catholicism at its historical apex: The optimism of the 1950s, the election of the first Catholic president, and the visit to America by the reigning Pontiff, Paul VI, gave American Catholics a sense of purpose and pride that had never been greater. Shortly after the Pope's visit, however, events and changing attitudes brought dissent and division. The historian James Hennesey, SJ, described the 1960s in American Catholicism as a "revolutionary moment" when three streams converged to create conflict and destroy unity. The end of the immigrant Church and the completion of its Americanization process created a sense of lost purpose for many Catholics. The Vatican II Council and its policy of *aggiornamento* changed staid tradition so radically and swiftly that many were unable or unwilling to adjust. The death in November 1963 of John F. Kennedy sent a shock wave through American Catholicism that may well have been greater than that experienced by the nation as a whole.[2]

In other words, the 1960s quickly and summarily snuffed out the promising process of renewal that had been generated only a few years earlier. Philip Gleason refers to this period as one of "disintegration" when he describes his experience as "the strongest sense of a church, a religious tradition, that was coming undone, breaking apart, losing its coherence."[3] The dislocation felt by many American Catholics in the wake of Vatican II and the perceived mandate to update religious practice and tradition led to confusion when the 1968 publication of the encyclical letter *Humanae Vitae* reconfirmed the traditional view against artificial means of contraception. Catholics, it seemed, were being told to accept modernity and, at the same time, reject the prevailing sociological and psychological understanding of human sexuality.

Growth in Student Responsibility

MOVEMENT TOWARD greater student participation and responsibility was generally encouraged in Catholic colleges and universities in the sixties. Robert Hassenger suggested that students work as co-equals with faculty and administration in fixing policy within the institution. He stated that college years must be a time where the natural growth and maturing process is fostered and not stunted:[4]

> While seeking to develop high-quality graduate and professional programs, Catholic higher education should provide sufficiently maximal personal development by students. This means students must have freedom to make mistakes and the opportunities to learn from them.

Stonehill College in the sixties shifted away from the traditional view of *in loco parentis* in a transition consistent with the generic trend toward greater freedom and responsibility for students. Students were given more autonomy over their lives in ways that were easily recognizable. Greater freedom was also experienced through the aforementioned curriculum advances the period brought, especially the introduction of more majors and electives. Beginning with David Arthur, academic deans corresponded directly with students (vice parents, as before) on matters of grades, deficiencies, and disciplinary problems. More independence was also apparent in the relaxation of the dress code for students. The formal rules for women's attire (in place since 1951) mandating dresses or skirts for class attendance and meals were gradually eliminated. The dress code for men, which required jackets, ties, and slacks on campus, was also relaxed. By 1970 the Student Handbook did not even mention student attire.[5]

Other student rules inconsistent with the changing times were also re-

Brother Mike's.

laxed. Curfew restrictions for women living off campus were liberalized. The College policy on student marriages, like the dress code, gave way from a 1963 rule that mandated automatic dismissal for failure to inform College officials a full semester prior to a planned marriage to no mention of a policy in the 1970–1971 Student Handbook.[6] The College policy on alcohol received a major overhaul as well. In 1973 Massachusetts law lowered the legal drinking age from 21 to 18. Five years earlier the Administrative Council had produced a plan that recognized student responsibility, yet met the letter of the law.[7] This policy shift to greater student freedom and the desire by the administration to keep students from driving and drinking led in April 1970 to the establishment of Brother Mike's, which served beer in a little-used recreation room in O'Hara Hall.[8]

Despite these and other advances in autonomy, many students perceived a great sense of apathy on campus. As early as 1960 "The Committee for the Abolishment of Stonehill's High School Atmosphere" published a short-lived newsletter that criticized the indifference of students and their organizations and the rote method of learning encouraged by some professors. In October 1967 another "underground" publication of short dura-

Rev. Paul Duff, CSC.

tion, *Super Sheet*, circulated on campus. It stated its purpose in its premier issue: "The inception, development, and distribution of the *Super Sheet* was carefully planned to penetrate the apathy barrier and elicit a reaction—a responsible response."[9] Indeed, a 1968 student survey revealed a lack of pride among Stonehill students, dissatisfaction with social life on campus, and a feeling of cultural isolation.[10]

Stonehill moved decisively to update its policies in order to grant greater freedom, but College officials realized that some longstanding stereotypes needed to change first. One report in 1964 stated that students had been taken for granted and that faculty often knew nothing about individual students beyond observation in class. It suggested that empowering students to more responsible action was "most basic to our work."[11]

Dean of Students, Paul Duff, CSC, argued that a realistic approach toward the concepts of new freedom and thought was necessary and that a happy medium must be attained between old-style paternalism and total freedom. In a report to the Board of Advisors, he observed:

> Since change is an absolute fact with which all educators today must deal, Stonehill has elected to move positively with the concept of change rather than hold on to old concepts to the point where circumstances force change and all too often force them upon institutions with embarrassment and difficulty.

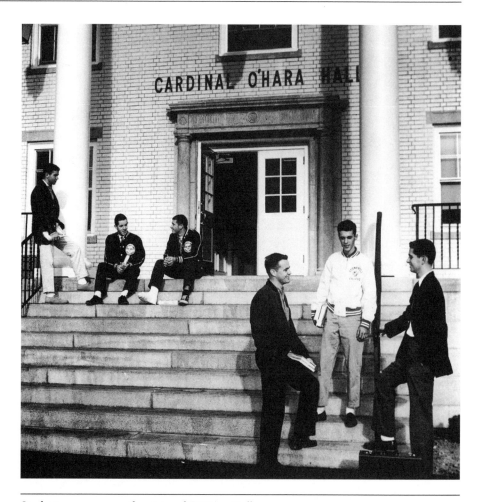

Students converse on the steps of O'Hara Hall.

In line with this philosophy, Duff enumerated efforts to increase student responsibility, such as allowing the Student Senate to allocate the $30,000 student activity fund and setting up student committees to "parallel" faculty committees and to address student concerns.[12]

Student participation in the College's governance was clearly a priority in the rapidly changing environment of the 1960s. David Arthur promoted this belief in speaking at a seminar sponsored by Christians for Student Action when he challenged students to form the aforementioned parallel committees. Additionally, Arthur promoted student membership on College committees. In December 1968 John Corr announced that 26 students, elected by their peers, had been placed on most College committees.[13]

Stonehill students most visibly demonstrated their ability to govern in the establishment of dorm councils. At both Boland and O'Hara Halls, students governed and policed themselves, a major shift from the "approved houses"[14] of previous years. House councils, a home court, an honor board, and student proctors comprised the governance structure. The townehouses were governed by a court that monitored a group of houses, with a student proctor for each unit. Dean of Women Karen Haskell accurately summarized the College's intent in granting greater student freedom:[15]

> While the decision-making processes of running a dormitory provide the women with important learning through the proper assumption of responsibility, the activities are designed to enrich and expand their interests. The combination provides the richest kind of learning—learning through doing in a realistic living situation.

Dormitory and townehouse life required the investigation and implementation of a parietal policy at the College. In their efforts to establish such a policy, the Student Affairs Committee sought assistance from other institutions of higher learning by means of a questionnaire.[16] Responses to the questionnaire, together with local input, helped shape a parietal policy for the dorms and a less restrictive one for the townehouses.[17] Each townehouse was given the option of reducing visitation hours as deemed appropriate by the residents. Successes with the parietal policy and coeducational townehouse experiment of 1971–1972 led to coeducational living as one of several approved living situations for Stonehill students.[18]

Student Activism on Campus

BEGINNING WITH the free speech movement at the University of California at Berkeley in 1964, college campuses in the 1960s exploded in a flurry of activity, including demands for student rights and freedom, protests against the war in Vietnam, and support for the Civil Rights Movement.[19] Several reasons have been postulated to explain why such massive dissent occurred at this time. One historian of this period, Seymour Lipset, suggested that the student activism of the 1960s was different from dissent in earlier periods. He argued that students attacked all existing structures and used tactics that alienated the majority in order to criticize a world they perceived to be intolerable. Activism was greater because of students' availability for political movements, fewer commitments and responsibilities on the part of students, and a university environment that made mobilization relatively simple.[20]

Educators John Searle and P.H. Ratterman, SJ, postulated other reasons for the student protest phenomenon of the 1960s. Searle looked beyond the standard reasons of protest—reaction to Vietnam, feelings of social insignificance, and rebellion against parents—in his analysis. He suggested that affluence, style of upbringing, crisis of authority, sheer numbers of students, unresponsiveness of institutions, and obsolete structures of contemporary universities created an environment where dissent could thrive.[21] Ratterman argued in a more conventional manner that student unrest was generated by the existence of the radical left, a drive for civil liberties, and the influence of secular humanism observed in the drive for academic freedom.[22]

In the spring of 1966 a special committee established by the Council of the American Association of University Professors (AAUP) in 1960 began to meet with representatives of several other student and faculty organizations. The output of this coalition effort was the "Joint Statement on Rights and Freedom of Students," a major document addressing students, the issues, and the attitude of the day. Generated by the call for academic freedom and increasing student protests, this document endorsed a concept of community responsibility, wherein students, faculty, and administration were encouraged to work together in the formulation of institutional policy. The statement sought to guarantee freedom in the pursuit of truth through open dialogue and argument. In early 1968 the National Catholic Education Association (NCEA) endorsed the statement.[23]

Student dissent on Catholic college and university campuses created what Philip Gleason described as a "crisis."[24] One celebrated response to this crisis was the hard-line stance of Theodore Hesburgh, CSC, at Notre Dame concerning student protests. In 1969 the Notre Dame president issued an ultimatum to protesters, stating that the type of student dissent that substitutes force for rational persuasion would be punished first by suspension and then, if necessary, by notification of police officials. He concluded in a letter addressed to students and parents, "We rule ourselves or others rule us, in a way that destroys the University as we have known it and loved it."[25]

Hesburgh's confrontational approach was criticized by several educators. Robert Hassenger suggested that students would not stand for such a tactic and probably would transfer to another school. The weekly *Commonweal*, in an editorial on education, referred to the policy as "delusioning." The historian Joseph Walsh called for "a delicate balance" in response to demonstrations, which if handled correctly could be a great moral teacher for all concerned.[26]

The need to assist black students was recognized nationally. At the an-

Student food "riot," April 1967.

nual National Conference on Higher Education, Lewis B. Mayhew called for action but was not optimistic about the future:[27]

> The Negro community must be helped into the mainstream of the national intellectual life. Further national leadership from the Negro community at least proportionate to Negroes in the total population must be identified and cultivated. Similar claims could be made for other minority groups but the Negro community is so qualitatively significant [as] to deserve special attention. At this point one cannot be sanguine that higher education will respond.

Integrating the campus and providing opportunities for African-American students was discussed by the Stonehill administration in the late 1960s. The catalyst for action may have been an article in the student-generated alternative publication *Super Sheet*:[28]

> Our school must actively seek integration. Such integration should not just be confined to combining black with white, but should embrace a cross section of student America.
>
> Only when Stonehill ceases to evade true integration can we, as college students, begin to participate in social reality.

In March 1968 the College Council recommended that 10 "Presidential Scholarships" for African-Americans be awarded, beginning in September.

Stonehill officials stipulated that the fulfillment of normal admission requirements must accompany the scholarships, but agreed to consider a reduced academic load and a tutoring program for students. Additionally, students would have to be recruited for the program. David Arthur worked with the Academic Council to gain approval; the scholarship program was not initiated, however, until the fall of 1972.[29]

The Civil Rights Movement thus became the first source of student activism at Stonehill College. Probably because of the almost complete absence of African-Americans on campus, however, reaction to the Civil Rights Movement was muted and made no apparent impact until the outbreak of violence in Selma, Alabama in March 1965. Thomas Lockary, CSC, professor of mathematics, traveled to Selma with a group of concerned Boston-area citizens to march with thousands of others from all regions of the country. That same spring, Rev. Virgil Wood, a black minister, addressed students in a lecture titled, "Problem of the American Negro." In September 1963 *The Summit* ran an opinion survey that asked questions about the issue of civil rights as experienced on and off campus.[30]

The assassination of Martin Luther King, Jr., in Memphis, Tennessee, elicited a response by the Stonehill community. Led by Robert Kruse, CSC, chairman of the theology department, a peaceful march from the College to the Chapel of Our Savior in Brockton's Westgate Mall was organized on April 9, 1968. Late morning and early afternoon classes were canceled to allow students to participate. The next day's issue of *The Summit* carried a full-page cover photo of Dr. King.[31]

The war in Vietnam, which generated dissent, protest, and division throughout the nation and its institutions of higher education, was a source of unrest at Stonehill as well, but not immediately. In October 1965, as evidenced by editorials, letters to the editor, and a survey in *The Summit*, the prevailing attitude on campus was one of support for the United States' effort in Vietnam. One essay titled "Why Not Victory?" asked, "What's wrong with America winning for a change? Why not a victory in Vietnam?" The author chided students on other campuses for their attempt to deny America the "right to seek victory over freedom's common enemy in Vietnam." Another writer analogized any possible thought of United States' withdrawal from Vietnam to Neville Chamberlain's ill-fated 1938 meeting with Adolf Hitler, after which he proclaimed "peace in our time." A survey at the time gave 85 percent approval for United States policy, with only 2 percent in opposition.[32]

Cracks in the predominate support for Lyndon Johnson's policy, however, began to emerge. One *Summit* photograph captured what many perceived to be apathy about the war on campus. Displaying garbage strewn on

Stonehill students march for civil rights, April 1968.

the quadrangle lawn, it was accompanied by the caption, "While Harvard students contemplate and Berkeley students demonstrate, Stonehill students precipitate." By the middle of 1967 *The Summit* was openly opposed to the war. One essay began, "I, as an American citizen, condemn our government's role in Vietnam."[33] In November the editor, Julia MacDonnell, wrote a two-page insert for *The Summit*, titled "The Stonehill Happening," which recognized a new energy on campus:[34]

> Stonehill has finally begun to stir. The complacent acceptance of "things as they are" is suddenly gone and students are less satisfied with last year's answers. Discontent is ruffling the smooth edges of campus life.
>
> We students have become jarringly aware that our slumber was dangerously long and deep. We wake to see a world of knowledge and involvement just beyond our grasp.

Faculty protest against America's Vietnam policy united with student efforts in January 1968. Led by chairman Robert Kruse, CSC, and Rev. Robert Hardina, Stonehill's entire theology faculty signed a letter that was sent to President Johnson and numerous other national political leaders, urging that the Selective Service Act be amended to provide alternatives to armed service for those, who on grounds of conscience, could not participate in a particular war—in this case, Vietnam. The signatories believed that conscientious objection under the present act was too general and made no provision for objection on philosophical grounds.[35] The letter became the catalyst for a faculty forum held on January 4, 1968, in Hemingway Auditorium, openly debating the issue of Vietnam. A second opinion survey run by *The Summit* now showed over 70 percent opposed to America's military policy and over 85 percent opposed to selective service. The tide of opinion had turned.[36]

Student activism at Stonehill gained more adherents and became more vocal in the fall of 1969. Julia MacDonnell, representing *The Summit*, and Frank Driscoll, president of the Student Senate, issued a joint manifesto calling for College administrators to join in the National Vietnam Moratorium Day to be held on October 15:[37]

> We request in short, that as an administrator, as a man of influence in the community, you come with us on Oct[ober] 15 to discuss and contemplate Viet Nam [*sic*] and its related problems. We intensely urge you to put down your daily work against the backdrop of the thousands of anonymous graves that have been the fruit of this war.

A similar plea was addressed to the faculty: "Leave your classroom one day in memory of the American and Viet Namese [*sic*] dead in hopes that their slaughter might not continue."[38] John Corr responded with a policy that allowed free choice: College offices and classrooms remained open, but students could absent themselves without penalty and faculty could cancel a class, keeping in mind the need to assure that course material was properly covered.[39]

Student publications increasingly served as channels of expression for the burgeoning dissent on campus. The October 16, 1969, issue of *The Summit* typified this trend. The front cover, without copy, pictured a dove, sketched in black, centered on a white background. The two center pages of the paper were a collage of war-weary soldiers, starving children, and antiwar statements highlighted by the headline, "War is not healthy for children and other living things." A photograph of a young Vietnamese girl covered the back page, accompanied by a poem, "Armageddon For A Soldier," describing the evils of war.

Alternative publications, using polemic in their presentations, echoed *The Summit's* sentiments. As mentioned previously, *Super Sheet* was published for a short period in 1967. In November 1969 *Atman*, a publication

On the cover of The Summit *peace issue, October 16, 1969.*

of the Social Community Action Bloc (S.C.A.B.), first appeared. Advertised as an alternative to *The Summit,* its stated purpose was "to report the truth as it reveals itself to the inquiry of those who look beneath the smiling veil of Maya that covers the Stonehill malaise. . . ." *Atman* forcefully attacked traditional institutions and organizations stating, "Because our basic premise is to radically change the existing structures of our country, we must support all movements that point to that end."[40] Complaints voiced against *Summit* leaders for the liberal direction of the paper led to MacDonnell's resignation as editor. She immediately joined the *Atman* staff.[41]

The arrival of a new decade did not in any way dampen the feelings and activities of student unrest. Fears of possible loss of control prompted Stonehill officials to make contingency plans. The Board of Trustees published a set of rules for the academic community and outsiders in dealing with protests, demonstrations, and marches. Punishments for acts of noncompliance with the directive were listed. Additionally, Corr asked the College attorney to devise a policy of action in the event of unauthorized disruptive acts by the student body.[42]

Incidents inside and outside the College brought student unrest to its apex in the spring of 1970. The case of sociology professor Martin Barroll became a rallying point for student distrust of the administration. Barroll was informed that his contract at Stonehill would not be renewed for the next academic year due to "departmental incompatibility." Barroll appealed to the Faculty Affairs Committee, stating that his academic freedom had

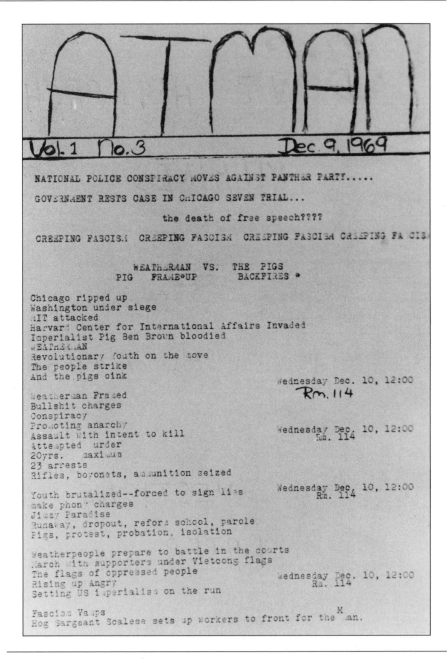

December 9, 1969, issue of Atman.

been violated. The committee's investigation led to rejection of the appeal, however, effectively defusing faculty concerns over academic freedom. The Student Senate, which did view the dismissal as a breech of academic freedom, initially voted to call a student strike, but after a meeting with all concerned parties rescinded its order.[43]

A successful "free day," held on April 29 to foster intellectual discussion on the topic of student rights and academic freedom,[44] raised hopes that tensions from the Barroll case would be eased. Five days later on May 4, 1970, however, the revelation of America's bombing of Cambodia, combined with the killing of four students by Ohio national guardsmen at Kent State University, brought student dissent to its climax. Corr wisely recognized the severity of the problem and responded immediately. While student representatives from colleges and universities across the country met at Yale on May 5 to ponder their actions in the wake of these two events,[45] Corr declared May 6 a day of mourning at Stonehill, stating:

> All of us today share a deep sense of sorrow and anguish at the violence which has resulted in the death of four students at Kent State University. We understand and sympathize with the concern of students and Americans everywhere who are shocked and appalled at events which are dividing our people.

Masses for the slain students and for the dead in Indochina were offered throughout the day.[46]

The day of mourning was used to organize a march and demonstration in front of the draft lottery office in Brockton. Participants gathered in Hemingway Auditorium, where several Stonehill professors spoke on various aspects of the expanding war, Kent State, and rising student activism. About 200 marchers then began to walk from campus to the draft office, where they were met by a similar-size group from Bridgewater State and Massasoit Community Colleges.[47]

Students, however, were not content with the College's response of a one-day period of mourning and declared that it should be extended "until the end of the academic year":[48]

> We are appalled at the tragedy of Kent State, but we are further appalled at those forces which are the cause of this. We demand to *know* [student emphasis]. For this is our right as students. Nonetheless, we believe that the present classroom structure is entirely inconducive to the type of dialogue and free expression in which we will engage. So we want to study and understand in a free and creative atmosphere those forces that gave us Vietnam, Cambodia, Laos, and the racial and political repression that exists now in the United

States. Through this action we hope to display our solidarity with the national student association and the national strike it has called.

At the same time, one group of students called for a complete shutdown of the College in order "to bring pressure to bear on the U.S. Government to force it to alter its disastrous and destructive course."[49]

On May 7 John Corr called a special meeting of the faculty to discuss a response to the tense situation. At the meeting, students (who were always welcome at public faculty forums) and faculty filled Hemingway Auditorium. Initially Corr offered to release a statement of the College's concern over recent events and its sympathy for the victims at Kent State. He was about to dismiss the meeting, but, at the suggestion of David Arthur,[50] he brought the issue to the floor for discussion by the assembled faculty members. Corr and Arthur were determined that the College would not close and that students would have the opportunity to finish the semester in a normal manner. The meeting produced the concept of a "Communiversity" that would use College facilities for extracurricular seminars, discussions, meetings, and forums. All opinions could be shared with participants from the Stonehill community and representatives from organizations in the surrounding area.[51] While this alternative program would be offered, the school would remain open, the schedule followed, and classes conducted. "Anything else," Corr declared, "is an abdication of responsibility."[52]

At a long and tension-filled faculty meeting the next day, the Communiversity proposal was discussed, as well as faculty rights and objectives and the rights of students. After the discussion concluded, the faculty voted 61 to 6 to "support for the remainder of this academic year the movement for a free university [while] at the same time guaranteeing the right, without intimidation, of a teacher to meet his class and a student to have a class taught."[53]

Stonehill's "free" university operated for the final two weeks of the academic year in May 1970. The Communiversity advertised its purpose "to further an awareness of the nature and gravity of the present national crisis." Regularly scheduled classes[54] met, but the majority of activity on campus centered about the numerous seminars offered by faculty and concerned outside groups. Open to students and the public, seminar topics included "Social Stratification," "Theology of Revolution," "Contemporary Social Issues," "Biological Warfare," "Draft Resistance," and "The United States in Latin America." A bookstore filled with antiwar and social responsibility titles was operated in the faculty lounge of Duffy Academic Center.

In the wake of the Communiversity, student activism at Stonehill began to wane, but the alternative program had left its mark. The 1970–1971

Student Handbook for the first time provided rules for demonstrators and counterdemonstrators on campus. In September the Student Academic Committee invited students, faculty, and administration to discuss a revival of the Communiversity in order to provide an alternative learning experience. Limited response doomed any resurrection of the free university concept. In the spring of 1971 the Stonehill chapter of the Student Mobilization Committee to End the War in Southeast Asia sponsored films and lectures in Hemingway Auditorium.[55]

Reaction to the Communiversity was mixed but generally supportive. The reaction of some irate parents was echoed by Associate Academic Dean C. James Cleary, who labeled the program "outrageous, totally ridiculous, a disaster." Conversely, Robert Kruse, CSC, called the Communiversity "immensely stimulating intellectually" and "a positive way to channel the discontent and threats of the most radical student leaders." The Brockton *Enterprise* concluded, "It was a responsible manner for expression of concern."[56] Student reaction to the Communiversity was mixed. One member of the class of 1971 commented, "Closing the campus temporarily transformed a major disruption into an open classroom to the benefit of students and faculty who shared the experience." Others, however, expressed less commitment: "People took their grades and ran."[57]

In retrospect, Stonehill's response to student dissent following the Kent State tragedy was professional, innovative, and balanced. Limits were set by refusing to close, but the College remained open to alternatives that would satisfy demands, quell dissent, and, at the same time, provide an environment in which concerned students could gain from the knowledge of others. The plan allowed learning in a nontraditional but nonetheless efficacious manner. Stonehill was fortunate that it was not forced to deal with a full-fledged student strike, unauthorized occupation of buildings, or criminal activity. Still the ability of John Corr and David Arthur to keep order and provide a productive learning environment was noteworthy.

Dissent and activism at Stonehill were colorful and played a dominant role in student activities in the 1960s, but compared with other institutions of higher learning, Stonehill's response to the events of the day was barely noteworthy. Many reasons may explain this muted response to a pressing national issue. As has been noted earlier, Stonehill had never found itself on the front lines of any major issue confronting higher education. Academic freedom and intellectual life were hotly debated on many campuses, but not at Stonehill, which at the time dealt with economic survival and issues of faculty compensation and class size. The efforts of Corr and Arthur to give students more responsibility most certainly made them feel less alienated from faculty and administration and led to less tension.[58] The presence of a cadre of young professors, who were willing to listen and join students in their drive, also brought a dampening effect. Students of this period, in agreement with David Arthur, have suggested that "Stonehill was in a time warp. We were five years behind everyone else." Students, who were generally conservative and sheltered, waited for faculty to act and then followed. Stonehill made great strides in this period to contemporize its academic and curricular programs, but the passion of the sixties experienced on many college and university campuses was absent.[59]

Student Sports and Activities

❧   CONSISTENT WITH the general expansion of facilities, academic programs, and student responsibility, the Stonehill sports program enjoyed growth during the mid- and late 1960s. Greater complexity in the College's structure led in 1967 to the appointment of a full-time director of athletics, a position that had previously been a collateral duty. George Blaney was hired as men's basketball coach and athletic director, a combination that became a tradition.[60]

The decade of the 1960s did not change the status of basketball as king on campus. To enhance school spirit, a new tradition, the "Mayor of Spirit," began in the fall of 1965. The Mayor, elected by the student body, promoted enthusiasm and spirit among those in attendance at basketball games. A second new tradition, Homecoming Weekend, began in December 1967. Stonehill women were nominated by campus clubs for the role of queen; selection was by the social committee, which comprised students, the deans of men and women, and the basketball coach.

Basketball teams during this period posted the best and worst records in Stonehill history, as the team joined the ranks of the NCAA. The 1964–1965 campaign was one of constant frustration, as the team gained only a single victory in 20 games. In the 1970–1971 season, however, Stonehill's team achieved a 21–4 record and gained a NCAA tournament invitation. Some of the standout players in these years were Ron Richard, Art Horan, Gerry Mooney, and, especially, Mike Allocco, who earned the distinction of All-American.[61]

Soccer rapidly came into its own during this period. In its third season (1963), the soccer team, under coach John Heslin, won the league championship and gained a bid to the National Association of Intercollegiate Athletics (NAIA) tournament. The squad repeated as league champions the next season and again was selected for the postseason tournament, but College officials decided both years to decline the invitation for financial reasons. *The Summit* challenged the decision: "It is the opinion of this reported [*sic*]

Stonehill radio, WSTO.

that soccer can no longer be held back. The team must be allowed to accept the challenges offered them [*sic*]. The crossroads must be passed and the right road chosen."[62] On a more positive note, soccer proudly claimed the College's first All-American athlete, Angelo Caranfa, who earned this honor in 1965.

New sports were added to the intercollegiate program. Sailing, which began as a club sport in October 1959, joined the varsity ranks in the fall of 1964. Cross country, coached by John McCarthy, CSC, director of religious activities, started in 1968 with four competitive meets. Hockey, which organized in 1967, became a varsity sport in the fall of 1978.

Football, the dream of George Benaglia that had been quickly dashed by Francis Boland on his arrival, finally came to Stonehill in 1970. *The Summit* reported in February 1967 that club football was organizing on campus, but the program did not come to fruition until the spring of 1970, when volunteer coach David Knight took the reins of the program. Stonehill's maiden season on the gridiron started at Worcester State on October 4, 1970. The team, nicknamed the Knights after the coach, dropped its initial contest, and posted a 1–4 record its first year, but spirit and optimism were high and a new tradition had been born.[63]

Nonathletic student activities were also popular in the sixties. Under the

Stonehill debate team receives congratulations.

capable direction of Professor Ronald J. Fraser, the theater club continued to produce first-rate plays in the 1960s, including such classics as *The Crucible, Medea, A Man for All Seasons, Major Barbara,* and *Antigone.* In the fall of 1968 the Greasepaint Players of Stonehill College made their debut with a production of *The Roar of the Greasepaint, The Smell of the Crowd.* The new group, formed as an alternative to the Stonehill Theater Company, aimed to introduce College audiences to more musicals and less traditional theater.[64]

Campus radio came to Stonehill in February 1965, broadcasting from the basement of Donahue Hall. WSTO, 640 AM, broadcast news and campus information for an hour each weekday morning and music, news, and other programming on Monday through Thursday in the afternoon and early evening. In the fall of 1966 the station moved its operation to the lower campus and occupied the space formerly used by the "Sportsman's Club" behind the student union.[65]

The debate team continued to shine, playing David to some predomi-

Donataire Society.

nant collegiate Goliaths. Under the direction of its moderator, Roger Quilty, CSC, the team achieved impressive records each year. In February 1966 Stonehill debaters were rated better than 100 of 122 schools in an intercollegiate tournament at Harvard, and in April 1967 they attended the National Debate Tournament in Chicago, which was limited to the top 38 teams in the country.[66]

New clubs arose to meet the needs of students and to respond to the concerns of the period. Christians for Student Action and Young Christian Students addressed issues of social justice raised by events of the 1960s in the United States. The Dorm Club was formed for resident students, whose numbers swelled with the construction of Boland Hall and Commonwealth and Colonial Courts. A new women's service club, the Donataire Society, which paralleled the men's Purple Key Club, aided the administration and organizations on campus. In March 1970 the Stonehill Ecology Action Society (SEA) was formed with the intention of "working against pollution and the destruction of the environment by man's careless habits." The group, under the direction of Thomas Feeley, CSC, sponsored Earth Day (April 22, 1970), campus cleanup projects, and a "Dirty Picture Contest," which aimed to best depict humanity's self-destruction through damage to the ecosystem.[67] The RFK Society, which was established in the spring of 1969 and supplied big brothers and big sisters to many youths in Brockton and Easton, was one of the most popular service groups on campus.

Religious activities on campus became more formalized with the appointment in the summer of 1964 of John McCarthy, CSC, "to take care of the spiritual needs of the students exclusively."[68] A chapel seating 100 was fashioned in the basement of the south wing addition to Holy Cross Hall and doubled as McCarthy's office. Confessions were heard daily and Mass was celebrated three times daily, with Exposition of the Blessed Sacrament each afternoon between the noon and 4 P.M. Masses. Sunday liturgies were celebrated in the chapel of O'Hara Hall. The annual student retreat continued to be offered through the fall of 1966, when lack of participation led to its replacement by evenings of Christian renewal, generally offered on special Church feast days and featuring discussions and films on issues in the Christian life.[69]

The Stonehill campus played host to several special activities. In the spring of 1966 a new event, sponsored by the Student Senate, "The Week of Economic Recovery for Men (W.E.R.M.) was inaugurated. One weekend was celebrated in the tradition of Sadie Hawkins, where women were expected to ask for dates and pay for them. In February 1967 Stonehill's first Winter Carnival was held, with skiing at Blue Hills in Canton and tobogganing and barbecues on campus.[70]

Stonehill continued to attract many famous, provocative, and interesting speakers to campus, such as the essayist Erik von Kuehnelt-Leddihn, Pulitzer Prize-winning poet Stanley Kunitz, science fiction writer Isaac Asimov, civil rights leader James Farmer, and Commander John L. From, Jr., commanding officer of the *USS George Washington*, the first nuclear ballistic missile submarine. Commencement speakers Senator Leverett Saltonstall, Representative Margaret Mary Heckler, former astronaut Michael Collins, and Berkeley professor Eric Hoffer offered challenges and encouragement to Stonehill's graduating classes.

ENDNOTES

1. Allen J. Matusow, *The Unraveling of America: A History of Liberalism in the 1960s* (New York: Harper & Row, 1984).

2. James Hennesey, SJ, *American Catholics: A History of the Roman Catholic Community in the United States* (New York: Oxford University Press, 1981), 307–31. The historian Jay P. Dolan, in *The American Catholic Experience*, demonstrates

that by 1960 Catholicism in America had lost the ghetto mentality it possessed previously. Catholic immigrants and their descendants had become fully assimilated. With no need to defend their presence in the United States, Catholics had to find other issues for their concern.

3. Quoted in David O'Brien, *Public Catholicism* (New York: Macmillan, 1989): 234.

4. Robert Hassenger, "Student Freedom on the Catholic College Campus," *Ave Maria* 109 (February 8, 1969): 7–12.

5. Students were fined $5.00 for each violation of the dress code. Formal rules for women's attire were instituted in 1951. Formal dress for men, however, was not mandated until 1961. Student handbooks in the 1960s described the transition, from business attire for all students, to slacks and sneakers for women, to elimination of a dress policy.

6. Karen Haskell, dean of women, Paul Duff, CSC, dean of students, and Roger Quilty, CSC, worked together to gradually update staid policies with their roots derived from *in loco parentis*. The transition in the policy on marriage is a good example of how the College removed itself from the personal lives of its students.

7. Stonehill College [Administrative] Council Memorandum, April 1, 1968, College Council Papers, ASC. The alcohol policy developed by an *ad hoc* committee of the Administrative Council was: (1) Juniors and seniors were personally responsible for Massachusetts' law on alcohol. (2) Alcohol was permitted in the townehouses by juniors and seniors only, but no other place on campus. (3) Freshmen and sophomores were forbidden to possess or use alcohol on campus.

8. The idea for Brother Mike's was first conceived in academic year 1968–1969. When the alcohol policy was liberalized, some student abuse occurred. A little-used recreation room in O'Hara Hall was converted by Brother Mike Massaro, CSC. A loan of $10,000 from the Stonehill College Student Senate Fund was used to complete the conversion. The loan was repaid by 1972.

9. Memorandum, n.d.; *Super Sheet* (October 1967), Miscellaneous Publications Papers, ASC. A three-page letter of sarcasm titled "Plummit" was also published in the late 1960s.

10. "Student Attitude and Evaluation Study, 1968," Student Government Papers, ASC. It should be noted that a greater sense of harmony and community was generally expressed about student life in the 1960s in many interviews with Stonehill alumni and in group discussions than was portrayed by these "underground" publications.

11. "Progress Report of the Student Affairs Committee," n.d. [October 1964], Faculty Assembly Papers, ASC.

12. Paul Duff, "Student Activities Policies at Stonehill," May 3, 1968, Arthur Papers, ASC. In 1973 Duff, now special assistant to the president, remarked, "We're [Stonehill] basically a conservative institution. Where we've expanded considerably is in student participation. Students have a very large role here, ..." See Pamela Ballard, "Stonehill College: A Success Story," "Pictorial Living" Section, *Sunday Herald Advertiser* (May 13, 1973): 31.

13. *The Summit* (December 12, 1968), ASC. In most cases, students were seated as voting members of committees, but with some cases, such as Academic Council, students were nonvoting members. This policy, however, changed with time, so that by January 1970 the Academic Council itself voted to raise student participation from one nonvoting to two voting members.

14. Recall that prior to the construction of Boland Hall, women students who did not commute were required to live in homes approved by the College. These residences were administered by "house mothers" who made their residents follow a strict set of rules. A similar arrangement existed for male students before construction of O'Hara Hall.

15. Karen R. Haskell, memorandum, December 1, 1967, Arthur Papers, ASC.

16. Richard Grant to "Dear Sir," January 12, 1970, Corr Papers, ASC.

17. Townehouse parietals were: Sunday–Thursday, 1 P.M. to 11 P.M.; Friday and Saturday, 1 P.M. to 1:30 A.M. Boland and O'Hara Hall's hours were: Friday and Saturday, 8 P.M. to 1 A.M.; Sunday 1 P.M. to 5 P.M.

18. Victor Caliri, CSC, memorandum, n.d., Student Residence Papers, ASC.

19. A good general summary of student protest in the 1960s is presented in: Alexander Astin, Helen Astin, Alan Berger, and Ann Bisconti, *The Power of Protest* (Washington, D.C.: Jossey-Bass Publishers, 1975).

20. Seymour Lipset, "American Student Activism," in *The University and Revolution*, Gary R. Weaver and James H. Weaver, eds. (Englewood Cliffs, New Jersey: Prentice-Hall, Inc., 1969): 19, 20–28, 32.

21. John R. Searle, *The Campus War* (New York: The World Publishing Company, 1971): 157–60.

22. P. H. Ratterman, SJ, *The Emerging Catholic University* (New York: Fordham University Press, 1968): 13–32.

23. Ibid., 123, 131. One section of the statement reads: "Freedom to teach and freedom to learn are inseparable facets of academic freedom. The freedom to learn depends upon appropriate opportunities and conditions in the classroom on the campus, and in the larger community. Students should exercise their freedom with responsibility." Interestingly, this statement is very close to the 1948 United States National Student Association's Basic Policy Declaration, which spoke of "the right and responsibility of the student to participate fully in independent inquiry and criticism. It is his right to question, criticize, and dissent from ideas with which he comes in contact, and to hold and advocate his personal beliefs free from all pressures which tend to restrict the student in his pursuit of knowledge."

24. Philip Gleason, "The Crisis in Catholic Universities: An Historical Perspective," *Catholic Mind* 64 (September 1966): 52.

25. Theodore Hesburgh, CSC, "Action in the Face of Student Violence," *Catholic Mind* 67 (April 1969): 14–15, 17. The John LaFarge Institute in New York City in the summer of 1969 issued a similar plan of twelve guidelines, one of which stated there should be no negotiation under duress. See *New York Times* (July 1, 1969), Section I, 34.

26. Hassenger, "Student Freedom on College Campuses," 7–8; "Hesburgh's Law: Notre Dame University," *Commonweal* 89 (March 14, 1969): 719–20; Joseph L. Walsh, "Law and Order on the Catholic Campus," *Commonweal* 90 (September 19, 1969): 562.

27. Lewis B. Mayhew, paper presented at the Twenty-Third National Conference on Higher Education, March 3, 1968, Stonehill College [Administrative] Council Papers, ASC.

28. *Super Sheet*, No. 6, 1967, Miscellaneous Publications File, ASC.

29. Stonehill College [Administrative] Council Meeting Minutes, March 23, 1968, March 30, 1968, and September 9, 1968, College Council Papers, ASC. While this program was delayed, financial assistance for African-American students from Makin High School in Washington, D.C., operated by the Brothers of Holy Cross, was provided in 1968.

30. *The Summit* (April 22, 1965), ASC. The survey revealed the nature of the student body: 63 percent favored total integration, 58 percent supported the August 1963 March on Washington led by Martin Luther King, Jr., and 88 percent believed that racial problems existed in the North. However, only 28 percent said they would do something to promote integration, 75 percent disagreed with the methods of the NAACP, and 64 percent said integration should proceed more gradually.

31. John Corr to Faculty, memorandum, April 8, 1968, Corr Papers, ASC.

32. *The Summit* (October 29, 1965), ASC.

33. *The Summit* (November 12, 1965), April 26, 1967, ASC.

34. Ibid., November 29, 1967.

35. Ibid., January 4, 1968.

36. Ibid., January 11, 1968, February 28, 1968.

37. Frank Driscoll and Julia MacDonnell to "The Administration," n.d. [October 1969], Corr Papers, ASC.

38. Frank Driscoll and Julia MacDonnell to "Faculty," n.d. [October 1969], Corr Papers, ASC.

39. *Stonehill College News* (October 6, 1969), Public Affairs Papers, ASC. Speaking of the Communiversity, one student of the period commented, "[It was the] first time Stonehill got involved in the outside world. We were doing what everyone else was doing. We felt we had a voice." Group interview, 1970s, November 19, 1996, Stonehill History Project Papers, ASC.

40. *Atman* 1(2), November 12, 1969, Miscellaneous Publications File, ASC.

41. Many letters to the editor complained of *The Summit's* bias and its overemphasis on the Vietnam issue. Other world, national, and local events, as well as campus news, were often ignored, leading to letters asking for a change in direction for the paper. *Atman* claimed that MacDonnell was "forced" to resign from *The Summit* staff.

42. Board of Trustees, "Rules and Regulations for the Maintenance of Public Order," December 22, 1969; Calvin H. Bowker to John Corr, March 4, 1970, Corr Papers, ASC. The policy devised by Bowker for the College was: (1) Obtain names

and residence addresses of instigators, (2) report facts of disturbance and details to attorneys, (3) obtain a temporary restraining order as necessary.

43. *The Summit* (April 30, 1970); Memorandum of Students, n.d. [May 1970], Corr Papers, ASC The two specific reasons given for Barroll's dismissal were: (1) that he had not achieved a doctorate or made efforts toward that end, (2) he was not sympathetic to the goals of the Sociology Department. After the Student Senate removed its call for a strike, a referendum vote by the student body suggested that one be called. No such action materialized. Two senior history projects cover the whole period of student unrest at Stonehill and give detailed coverage of the Barroll incident. See Elizabeth Dolan, "Student Activism: Stonehill College 1967–1970" (December 17, 1981) and Simon Mooney, "Better Late Than Never: Student Activism at Stonehill From 1967–73" (Spring 1992), History Department Papers, ASC.

44. Student Senate to Faculty, April 29, 1970, Student Government Papers; Vincent Wright to Faculty, memorandum, April 29, 1970, Corr Papers, ASC.

45. The participants called for a strike to begin on May 5 and to continue until three demands were met: (1) The United States must end its oppression of political dissidents and release all political prisoners, (2) the United States must cease its expansion of the war into Cambodia and Laos and then unilaterally and immediately withdraw from Southeast Asia, (3) universities must end their complicity with the United States war machine by ending defense research and ROTC. See Petition, "National Student Strike Organized," May 1970, Corr Papers, ASC.

46. John Corr, memorandum, May 6, 1970, Corr Papers, ASC.

47. *The Summit* (May 14, 1970), ASC.

48. Student memorandum, n.d. [May 1970], ASC.

49. Campus Note, n.d. [May 1970], Corr Paper, ASC.

50. David Arthur, CSC, interview with the author, July 18, 1996, Stonehill College History Project Papers, ASC. Arthur was out of town when the meeting was called and was not aware of Corr's desire to squelch discussion. He believed the issue warranted faculty discussion.

51. While Corr's response appears reasonable and balanced, many angry letters arrived in his office about the decision. One such response read, "Your decision to allow the students the option of attending classes or attending discussions on the Viet Nam [*sic*] situation is deplorable." Telegram from Mr. and Mrs. Manuel Silva to John Corr, May 8, 1970, Corr Papers, ASC.

52. John Corr, Statement to Faculty, May 7, 1970, Corr Papers, ASC.

53. Faculty Meeting Minutes, May 7, 1970, Faculty Assembly Papers, ASC.

54. The question of how semester grades would be determined was outlined by the Faculty Assembly and approved by Corr. In consultation with the professor, a student was allowed to substitute participation in the Communiversity for the remainder of the course. Grades in this case would be what the student had earned to date with an explanation from the instructor what continuing in the course or participation in the Communiversity would do for the grade's enhancement. Those students not opting for the Communiversity would take all exams and complete all

requirements deemed necessary by the instructor for the successful completion of the course.

55. Stonehill Student Handbook, 1970–1971; James Vaughan to "Faculty and Staff Members," March 22, 1971, Corr Papers, ASC.

56. C. James Cleary interview with the author, July 16, 1996; Robert Kruse, CSC, interview with the author, July 11, 1996, Stonehill College History Project Papers; Brockton *Enterprise*, editorial, n.d. clipping, Corr Papers, ASC. James Kenneally, who gave seminars at the Communiversity, summarized the program's effectiveness: "The first week was successful, the second was not. A lots of students had serious problems with conscience as far as attending classes after Kent State. A lot of students took advantage of the Communiversity." See Simon Mooney, "Better Late Than Never: Student Activism at Stonehill From 1967–73," Spring 1992, History Department Papers, ASC.

57. Jeanne Maynard Darling to author, October 21, 1996; group interview 1970s, November 19, 1996, Stonehill College History Project Papers, ASC.

58. One member of the class of 1973, a freshman at the time of the Communiversity, expressed well the changing environment: "We all changed and went through so much growing up and such life experiences that you never forgot how you felt. . . . I loved the freedom on campus." Kathy Finn Ditrapano to author, November 12, 1996, Stonehill History Project Papers, ASC.

59. Group interview, 1960s, March 26, 1996, Stonehill History Project Papers, ASC.

60. *The Summit* (April 12, 1967).

61. Stonehill Basketball Records, Athletic Department Papers; *The Summit*, numerous issues, ASC.

62. John Corr to John McGee, CSC, November 5, 1964, Corr Papers; *The Summit* (November 19, 1964), ASC.

63. *The Summit* (February 15, 1967, April 23, 1970, October 7, 1970, October 14, 1970, October 21, 1970).

64. Ibid., November 6, 1969. A short history of theater arts at Stonehill is given in: Kevin Spicer, "The History of the Theater at Stonehill College" (April 21, 1986), Stonehill College Papers, ASC.

65. *The Summit* (April 8, 1965, February 15, 1967); group interview, 1960s, March 26, 1996, Stonehill History Project Papers, ASC. A short history of Stonehill's radio station is presented in: Chris Saunders and Tom Mulvey, "From Off-White to Orange and Blue: WSHL-FM" (May 18, 1977), Student Organizations Papers, ASC.

66. *The Summit* (April 5, 1967). In the national tournament Diane Detellis and Bob Watter teamed to place Stonehill 18 of 38, barely missing the final 16 qualifying round.

67. Ibid., April 30, 1970, ASC.

68. John Corr to Faculty, August 21, 1964; Richard Sullivan to James Connolly, January 5, 1965, Corr Papers; John McCarthy, CSC, interview with the author, July 22, 1996, Stonehill History Project Papers, ASC.

69. *The Summit* (February 14, 1969); Group interview, 1960s, March 26, 1996; John McCarthy, CSC, interview with the author, July 22, 1996, Stonehill College History Project Papers, ASC. McCarthy viewed the retreat as "an extension of high school" and thus was favorable to a more contemporary approach to better serve students.

70. *The Summit* (March 4, 1966, February 8, 1967), ASC.

CHAPTER 9

Separation and Alienation

From its inception Stonehill College and the Congregation of Holy Cross had been integrally linked. The Community purchased the Ames estate, operated a minor seminary, obtained the charter and approval for the College's foundation, and supplied the necessary leadership during the critical early years. In 1962 Stonehill achieved full accreditation and began to evolve into a true liberal arts college consistent with the tradition of Catholic higher education in the post-World War II period. Upheaval experienced by American society and the Church during the 1960s necessitated changes in many institutions, including those of higher education. Greater attention to academic freedom for both students and faculty, promotion of student responsibility and the end of *in loco parentis*, and expanded curriculum offerings as a result of electivism changed the face of Catholic higher education in America. The greatest change, however, would be experienced when colleges and universities began to separate legally from their parent religious communities. This almost revolutionary decision, prompted by forces internal and external to the Church, would allow Catholic colleges and universities to compete with secular schools in every way, without ecclesial restriction. The move, however, created confusion for religious founders and raised fears of secularization within the Catholic community. Keeping pace with its peer institutions, Stonehill College faced the challenge of legal separation from Holy Cross and canonical alienation of the founding religious congregation and the institution.

Catholic Higher Education: Post-Vatican II

ӨӨ IN ITS PROMOTION OF *aggiornamento,* the Second Vatican Council revolutionized Catholicism and sent the Church into new uncharted and, at times, shoal-ridden waters.[1] The Council spoke on all major issues, including education. During its fourth and final session, the assembled bishops passed *Gravissimum educationis,* the Declaration on Christian Education. The document speaks of the inalienable right of education and outlines parental and state rights and responsibilities along traditional lines. The bishops stated that institutions of higher learning must shoulder the double responsibility of preparing students to fulfill their duty to society and to witness their faith in the world. Another critical concept articulated throughout the Council's 16 documents, but most fundamentally in *Apostilicam actuositatem,* Decree on the Apostolate of Lay People, was the need for greater lay participation in all aspects of the life of the Church.[2]

In the wake of the Council, the direction and purpose of Catholic higher education in America was challenged by forces inside and external to the Church. Harvey Cox, in his popular book *Secular City,* indicted the Church for its participation in higher education, suggesting that it abdicate its contemporary role:[3]

> The anachronistic posture of the Church is nowhere more obvious than in the context of the university community. . . . The whole idea of a "Christian" college or university after the breaking apart of the medieval synthesis has little meaning. The term *Christian* [Cox's emphasis] is not one that can be used to refer to universities any more than to observatories or laboratories. . . . The idea of developing "Christian universities" in America was bankrupt before it began. . . . The organizational Church has no role. It should stay out.

The columnist Richard Horchler referred to Catholic education as a "time bomb" ready to explode as it sought how to implement Vatican II's mandate of *aggiornamento* with respect to participation by the laity.[4]

Catholic insiders, of course, expressed concerns of a different nature. Educational observers and leaders feared that Catholic colleges and universities would, if radical changes were not immediately addressed, fall fatally behind peer secular institutions, which were rapidly adjusting to meet the challenge of modernity. A close connection between institutions of higher learning and the Church had been presumed for centuries, but during the post-Vatican II period Catholic colleges and universities felt pressured to distance themselves from control of dioceses or religious orders. Contemporary cultural patterns indicated no firm support for the formerly assumed integration of Catholicism and higher education. Educators began to believe it impossible for Catholic schools to accomplish satisfactorily the traditional dual roles of educational and moral training.[5] The priest-sociologist Andrew Greeley argued that Catholic colleges and universities would keep pace academically with secular schools only to the extent that administrators were free from the traditional controls and restrictions of religious communities.[6]

Solutions to contemporary problems faced by Catholic higher education in America were proposed. Educators first stated that Catholic schools needed to stop worrying that change was a threat to religious commitment. In the spirit of Vatican II, one educator suggested, "Catholic colleges must then be catholic, not in the triumphal, defensive ways of the past, but with the spirit of *aggiornamento* and dialogue."[7] Catholic educators began to realize that the challenge of modernity could be met only if institutions of higher learning accorded proper stature to the laity as faculty colleagues and administrators. In order to compete, Catholic schools would need to draw on all resources, rather than looking only to the gifts and talents of members of religious orders, as they had traditionally done. On a more pragmatic level, the realization that many smaller colleges would not be able to survive without federal and state financial assistance forced these institutions to distance themselves from Church influence, thus making them more attractive for government loans and grants.[8] Vatican II had faced the new world; it was now time for American Catholic higher education to do likewise.[9]

In the midst of this period of confusion and change, Catholic colleges and universities began to ask themselves what it meant to be a Catholic institution of higher education. Traditionally the answer had been to develop moral virtues, through worship and devotion, and intellectual competence through the curriculum. Probably because two decades of growth and vitality had produced a mood of unquestioning self-confidence, the Catholicity of institutions was assumed; no one asked questions or regarded it as a problem. (The so-called Catholic renaissance continued well into the 1960s.) This working consensus began to break down when people asked in intellectual terms how Catholic faith should influence the work one does as a scholar and teacher.[10]

Theodore Hesburgh, CSC, in 1967 offered a fourfold description of the contemporary Catholic university. It must first be a beacon of the light of intelligence to all people. Secondly, it must serve as a bridge across the chasm of misunderstanding that often exists between the Church and society. Next, it must be a pontifex, or bridge builder, in its role of mediator between the Church and the world. Lastly, the Catholic university must be the crossroads where intellectual trends meet for dialogue and where the Church confronts the modern world. He suggested further that these lofty goals could be achieved through the traditional teaching of philosophy and theology, an updated and changeable academic program, pastoral influence, and administrative efforts. For Hesburgh, a Catholic university must be a great university, "a community of scholars, learning and teaching and at the service of mankind's total development in our day."[11]

The question of Catholic identity, which was debated worldwide, became the basis for high-level discussions by educators from many of the nation's best-known Catholic institutions. In March 1967 a planning committee of 16 representatives from major Catholic universities met at Notre Dame to discuss a North American response to an August 1965 meeting of the International Federation of Catholic Universities. This meeting produced the decision to convene an invitational seminar in July 1968 at Notre Dame's ecological center at Land O'Lakes, Wisconsin. The document generated at this latter meeting, known as the Land O'Lakes Statement, maintained that a Catholic university must be fully modern, with a strong commitment to and concern for academic excellence, autonomy, and academic freedom, and a place "in which Catholicism is perceptibly present and effectively operative."[12]

Separation of Properties

❦   THE NEED TO DEFINE OWNERSHIP of lands and properties at Stonehill was recognized by Francis Boland as early as 1950. Recall that Boland was in a heated battle with the provincial, James Connerton, about payment of the $175,000 debt accumulated in the College's first 18 months of operation. Pressed to make interest payments on the loan, Boland suggested that reimbursing the Vice Province was impossible because it was Holy Cross and not Stonehill that owned the institution's lands and facilities. With the disagreement unresolved by 1951, Boland wrote to the provincial, noting the urgency of a solution: "I wrote you urging a settlement of the properties to be assigned to the College. In my opinion an immediate settlement is imperative."[13]

Although the Superior General ruled in 1952 on assets and monies owned by Holy Cross and the College, there had been no move to define ownership of the land, which remained as an asset of "The Foundation of Our Lady of Holy Cross, Incorporated." In 1961 the issue was resurrected when the College attorney, Joseph Duggan, recommended that the Eastern Province incorporate so that properties could be legally separated between the Congregation and the College.[14] Stonehill President Richard Sullivan advised George DePrizio of Duggan's idea and suggested that the issue be determined at the next Provincial Chapter, slated for May. DePrizio wisely

President's medal, awarded by Stonehill's presidents for service to the College or the Community.

perceived that the issue was too complex to solve during the limited time of a Chapter and thus appointed Sullivan chairman of a committee to study the advisability of separating Stonehill from the Foundation of Our Lady of Holy Cross.[15]

Sullivan's committee[16] convened and began to investigate the issue of separation. The Stonehill president stated initially that separation could clarify the assets and liabilities of the College and the Congregation. Others suggested that separation might foster development efforts for the College in that separating the College and Holy Cross would clear up contributors' confusion about where their money would go and how it would be used. Additionally, separation would aid efforts to gain government grants and loans when the College gained its autonomy. Sullivan concluded that the Eastern Province should incorporate and leave Stonehill as The Foundation of Our Lady of Holy Cross.[17]

The committee took the view of its chairman and recommended separation. Joseph Duggan, however, became uncharacteristically wary of the move and how it might negatively affect the liberal charter that Stonehill had received in 1948. These fears were allayed, however, when it was suggested (as Sullivan had earlier advised) that the Province separate from Our Lady of Holy Cross and, thus, keep the College's favorable charter intact. All properties and assets of the Foundation, save those in North Easton, would be conveyed to the new corporation. The Board of Trustees followed this plan and voted "to make a distinct separation of the cash accounts and the accounting records of the College and the Community so there will exist two separate organizations."[18]

Two years passed before any formal action was taken on the recommendations of Sullivan's committee and the board. During the interim, Sullivan was appointed provincial of the Eastern Province. He wrote to his successor at Stonehill, John Corr, with recommendations on how the North Easton property should be divided between the College and the Congregation upon the formation of the new corporation. He thought the land should be separated into three parcels, with the College taking the large middle piece (approximately 400 acres) and the Community holding claim to two sections of approximately 90 acres each on the east and west sides.[19]

On November 2, 1964, the Provincial Council voted to create the Holy Cross Fathers, Incorporated. Sullivan notified the Superior General, who confirmed the decision, stating, "It is best that the Province form a new corporation separate from that of Stonehill College." Sullivan gave no details on his proposed division of the land, mistakenly concluding, "I do not think that there will be any difficulty on the part of the College with the division. . . ."[20] The new Community title, made official on March 23, 1965, paved the way to separation.[21]

Physical division of the North Easton property did, however, raise disagreements within the Congregation. Corr complained to Sullivan that the proposed property division would hem in the College and prevent future expansion. The Superior General, Germain Lalande, held the opposite view, believing that under the proposed settlement the Congregation was too generous: "We feel it would be imprudent to transfer to Stonehill College a piece of property larger [than] that which the Provincial Council has decided to transfer to the College." Ultimately, however, he agreed to a division giving Stonehill a total of 350 acres.[22]

While the physical separation of lands was debated in the Massachusetts land court, a second discussion on a financial settlement between the College and the new Holy Cross Fathers, Inc. was taking place. Questions concerning seminarian scholarships and religious faculty compensation had been with Stonehill since its inception, but now studies were done to "accurately" state the financial responsibility of each party. Results varied greatly, with two reports in 1968 illustrative of the inability of those involved to pinpoint financial liability. For example, that year one study stated that Stonehill owed the Community $18,578, while a second claimed the amount was $650,000.[23]

Related to the physical and financial division of the College and the Community was the separation of the roles of superior and president. From the beginning these two positions had been held by one man, a situation which proved highly problematic for Francis Boland and which was a hindrance to the ongoing separation process. As early as 1961 Provincial George DePrizio, at the behest of Richard Sullivan, suggested to the Superior General that the roles of president and superior be separated. In 1965, with Sullivan as provincial, an indult from the Vatican was obtained that allowed division of the positions. The House Council, which had advised the president/superior, became the advisory board for the superior and an administrative council consisting of the academic dean, dean of students, treasurer, director of development, and college chaplain was formed to assist the president.[24]

Final settlement of the property issue took more than three years, as legal complications kept the matter in the land courts.[25] In March 1968, however, problems were resolved and the court settlement was near. John Murphy and Jerome Lawyer, members of the Provincial Council, were assigned by Sullivan to represent the Community in the final negotiations.[26] Under the agreement, the Foundation, which was still controlled by the Provincial Council in its role as the Board of Trustees, ceded to the Holy Cross Fathers all its assets in land and buildings. The Community then returned to Stonehill 350 acres of land and all buildings thereon. The official transfer was completed on April 23, 1968.[27] Because the financial studies varied so greatly, the division was finalized without the transfer of money. In lieu of a settlement, the Provincial Council published a financial agreement that would govern future relations between the College and the Congregation.[28]

Changes in College Governance

THE CONCEPT OF GOVERNANCE[29] at Stonehill College from its inception was, as with lands and finances, dominated by Holy Cross. The Board of Trustees, consisting of the provincial and his councilors, ran operations in conjunction with the president, who was appointed (along with all other Holy Cross personnel at the College) by the provincial. The lay Board of Advisors met bimonthly, but played no significant role in governance decisions. The Academic Council served to advise the dean, but its members were department chairs only. Faculty committees provided a wider view of issues, but it is only with the advent of David Arthur as dean that committees truly served their appointed purpose.[30]

From the outset of his administration, John Corr worked for changes in College governance that would increase lay representation in the decision-making process by tapping the expertise of all in the Stonehill community. As one of his first acts, he changed the organizational structure of the College, placing the offices of vice president, academic dean, dean of students, and treasurer under the office of president. Next, he expanded the role of the Board of Advisors, suggesting that its membership be increased and divided into eight committees that would meet as necessary to complete their assigned tasks. In October 1965 Edward Stanford, OSA, past president of Villanova University, came to Stonehill to meet with Corr and other administrators about the organization and operation of the College.[31]

The Intellectual Climate Committee of the 1964 self-study suggested reorganizing the Academic Council to make it more representative. In September 1967 David Arthur circulated a proposal to separate the College into divisions, with each division entitled to elect a representative to the Council. With the approbation of the faculty, the change was instituted; the new composition was the academic dean and 10 elected members having faculty status. The directors of admissions, library, and counseling services were granted *ex officio* status.[32] The reconstituted body stated its function: "Primary responsibility for the determination of academic policy shall be with the Academic Council, which represents and is responsible to the faculty."[33]

Student unrest and the introduction of the Communiversity were the most visible activities at Stonehill in the spring of 1970, but significant changes in College governance had their genesis at this same time. Corr, who was open to any and all approaches to governance that would enhance the operation of the College and who fully believed in delegation of authority,[34] assigned Faculty Moderator James Dillon to work with College Executive Vice President Vincent Wright in the appointment of a committee to investigate possible changes in Stonehill's governance structure.[35] A committee of three faculty members, two administrators, and three students was formed in March. This body, chaired by Francis Hurley, CSC, chairman of the Biology Department, met with an invited group of faculty members and administrators in a two-day session (May 7–8) at Holy Cross Seminary to discuss all aspects of college governance. Issues dealing with the rights and responsibilities of trustees, administrators, faculty, and students were discussed in an open forum where self-perceptions and the opinions of others were outlined.[36]

Hurley's Governance Committee conducted an exhaustive investigation of all aspects of College governance through a series of extensive interviews, review of documents, and discussions. After the initial May session, the committee met daily from late June to mid-August. September meetings were used to draft the final report. Interviews were conducted with 61 individuals, including the College president, members of the Board of Trustees, faculty, students, and alumni. The committee noted a lack of communication on all levels and recommended an informational, nonpolicymaking weekly meeting attended by the executive vice president, dean of students, academic dean, treasurer, faculty moderator, director of public affairs, editor of *The Summit*, a representative of WSTO, and the president of Stonehill's student government. The meeting's aim was to allow the free and frank exchange of information concerning issues before faculty committees.[37]

The need for planning was another observation of the committee. The formation of a new planning committee was suggested, along with the reorganization and/or elimination of many other committees. The principal aim was to remove governance structures that were no longer useful and create them where new needs had arisen.[38]

Formation of a college council was the farthest-reaching and most significant recommendation made by the Governance Committee. Organizationally the council was to be placed under the president, with "policy-making authority over all important issues within the College." The council members would be the executive vice president (chair), academic dean, dean of students, and treasurer, plus five elected faculty members and three students. The council was to serve as a funnel through which all decisions and recommendations of the academic, student affairs, budget, and planning committees would flow.[39] In November the faculty overwhelmingly approved the report of the Governance Committee recommending organization of the Council, which first met in March 1971.[40]

Alienation of the College from Holy Cross

MOST CATHOLIC colleges and universities in the United States were ❦ founded and sponsored by religious communities. Like Stonehill and its relationship with the Congregation of Holy Cross, these institutions of higher education were governed by boards of trustees, composed of members of the sponsoring religious order, which made all decisions pertinent to college operations. As has been outlined earlier, however, the decade of the 1960s was a crisis period for Catholic higher education because of outside competition from secular schools, rising needs with declining available funds and fewer religious personnel to meet them, and a major shift in Church understanding of the role of the laity. Solutions to this crisis were sought in a radical restructuring of governance that would remove control from religious communities, passing it to lay-dominated boards of trustees.[41]

Many factors contributed to this significant shift in governance, which determined the future direction of Catholic higher education in America. Educators noted that because institutions received their charter from the state, their service should be oriented to the good of the community at large. A seminar in 1968 announced: "Religious orders must come to realize that the institution is a public responsibility, and not just a congregational matter."[42] These increased aspirations for Catholic institutions caused some to believe that they could not compete with secular schools under their present close connections to founding religious orders. Neil McCluskey, SJ, claimed that, under the existing form of governance, Catholic colleges and universities could not update rapidly enough to keep pace with the new expectation that Catholic colleges must have the same standards of academic excellence as any other school.[43] Financial considerations constituted a third factor. It was believed that removal of Church control from colleges would result in greater availability of government money in the form of grants or loans.[44]

President Paul Reinert, SJ, of St. Louis University suggested four reasons for shared control in Catholic higher education. First, such a move would improve the administrative and managerial structure and organization of the institution. Second, shared control was more representative of the institution as a whole. Third, this concept would provide the institution's board with experience, influence, and access to financial support. Lastly, greater lay participation was in keeping with prevailing thought in the wake of Vatican II.[45]

The predominant opinion that favored lay control was countered by traditional arguments for the status quo. One argument held that the changes needed to bring Catholic colleges in line with their secular peers could be best implemented by clerics, since the laity traditionally held no authority to change longstanding Catholic doctrine.[46] The chief rebuttal to those who endorsed change, however, was centered in the fear that a lay board would lead to secularization of the institution. This perception, held most strongly by those in position to lose power through a shift to lay control, was rejected by Michael P. Walsh, SJ, among others, as counterproductive to "the inexorable trend" toward laicization:[47]

> The point remains that the Church will maintain its influence in the Catholic university not through construct, but through commitment; not through laws and edicts, but through convictions and professional dedication of her members and friends.

Another writer suggested that "laicization may be the surest way to develop future generations of Catholics notable for the strength of their faith and for their ability to understand it."[48]

Alienation, the canonical authorization granted by the Holy See to remove Church control from college governance, was first granted in the United States in 1967. St. Louis University and Webster College, which restructured their boards of trustees, perceived alienation as the means to achieve long-range goals, in line with the precepts of Vatican II.

The Congregation of Holy Cross instituted alienation at Notre Dame and the University of Portland in this same pivotal year of 1967. The Indiana provincial, Howard Kenna, presented his reasons for the change in a report published by *The Ave Maria*. He agreed with the Danforth Report's conclusion that the close relationship between universities and sponsoring religious communities was an obstacle to improvement. Kenna wrote, "If we can settle what is the major obstacle to progress in Catholic education, we will be advancing our own apostolate in our educational institutions."[49] In a letter to members of the Community, he spoke forcefully of how the change would benefit the Congregation and attempted to allay the fears of those who perceived the past labor of hundreds of religious as going to waste.[50]

Implementation of alienation at Notre Dame created a new attitude on campus. The process helped in the discovery of solutions to complex issues by drawing on the best available minds to tackle the problems presented. Increased involvement by the laity boosted the public image of the university. Theodore Hesburgh reported, "Professionalism is the new emphasis, not blind and often uncomprehending or mechanical or unmotivational obedience. In a word, we are vastly better off in every way."[51]

While George DePrizio had ordered the appointment of a committee in 1962 to investigate physical separation of Stonehill College from the Holy Cross Community, it was John Corr who publicly and privately championed the need for alienation. In a letter to Richard Sullivan, Corr voiced the opinion that "the corporate college should be a separate entity that must fight its way in the world and must compete with other existing institutions and must be able to have at its disposal the best possible personnel for carrying out the aims and objectives of the school." He further told the provincial that Stonehill had a right to compete with other institutions and should not be hampered by the Church in any way.[52] In December 1966 Corr expressed a similar progressive tone in a speech to the NCEA:[53]

> The hue and cry has been of late to open up the Boards of Directors to the laymen. May I ask why? If we, as institutions are to survive then I think we should open our Boards to the most qualified, be they laymen or religious.

Early the next year Corr pointed out to the faculty that, despite the College's historic link to the Congregation of Holy Cross, the school was a public trust and, therefore, should have lay participation on the Board of Trustees.[54]

David Arthur joined Corr in a call for alienation. He suggested that the present composition of the Board of Trustees did not contain the breadth needed to serve as a public trust. He believed that the base of Holy Cross religious, from whom the College's future leaders would be drawn, was too narrow. In keeping with prevailing trends, he called for more participation by the laity in all aspects of decision making, including membership on the Board of Trustees. Financial concerns were also considered by the dean in his promotion of alienation.[55]

The alienation question reached the provincial level in 1967 at the summer Chapter. A position paper, "The Stonehill College Problem," presented at the Chapter asked that the concept of alienation be approved. A plan for implementation similar to that used at Notre Dame and Portland earlier in the year was offered. Joining others, the paper suggested the role of the laity and the concept of Stonehill as a public trust as two reasons for alienation. Alienation would free the College from canonical obstacles to its development, release Holy Cross from the commitment to "fill slots" in College positions, and be a positive step toward institutional poverty, which demands that religious communities divest themselves from their holdings.[56] The Chapter decree stated that Stonehill (and sister school King's College) should:[57]

> . . . proceed to investigate and accomplish the process of transferring ownership to an independent Board of Trustees or Directors, preserving for the Congregation of Holy Cross in return the right of exercise of the apostolate of Christian education in each institution.

The Provincial Chapter decree led to the formation of a committee to investigate the issue fully, but the early eagerness for change seemed to dissipate. In April 1969 the committee voiced reservations in many areas over alienation. Some said there was no guarantee that a lay board of trustees would operate better than a group of religious or be of benefit to the College. Others perceived, as well, that finding qualified and dedicated people to serve without salary would be difficult. Questions concerning assignment of properties, financial settlements, the current system of contributed services by religious, and possible loss of the Sorin Fund were raised.[58]

The 1970 Chapter that elected William Hogan as the fourth provincial of the Eastern Province passed resolutions reaffirming the 1967 decree and calling for investigation of alienation at King's and Stonehill. Although Hogan wrote privately of his concern,[59] he enumerated many reasons for the move,[60] and he initiated dialogue with Edward Heston, CSC, Secretary of the Sacred Congregation of Religious, asking what was necessary for alienation.[61] At the same time, the Governance Committee added ammunition to the alienation drive by recommending the laicization and diversification of the Board of Trustees.[62] Still, the College attorney, Calvin Bowker, advised

Rev. William Hogan, CSC, provincial of the Holy Cross Eastern Province 1970–1973.

caution: "We feel that as a policy matter, a very careful examination should be made before control of the Board is relinquished to a majority of laymen."[63]

Corr, in an attempt to get the process back on track, wrote to Hogan, stressing the urgency of the alienation question:[64]

> The role and composition of the Board of Trustees and the possibility of lay participation on the Board of Trustees are significant topics which should be given attention as soon as possible in order for college governance at this level to keep pace with developments at other levels.

The Holy Cross Community at Stonehill supported Corr and met to discuss the composition of the proposed board. While the plans differed in terms of number of trustees and the ratio of lay to religious members, all included a significant Holy Cross presence—none less than one-third membership.[65]

In the summer of 1971 arguments about the need for alienation—which was now a given—gave way to discussion of the bylaws that would dictate College governance. Working with the present Board of Trustees, Hogan insisted that Holy Cross be removed from ownership in order to eliminate liability, that some guarantee be made to assure that trustees could not

Bishop Daniel Cronin of Fall River.

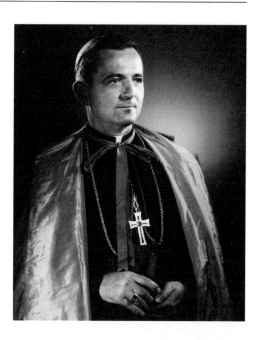

change the system of electing trustees, that the Catholicity of the College be maintained, and that a Holy Cross priest always be president unless, in the mind of the provincial, an acceptable candidate was not available.[66]

Stonehill's formal appeal to achieve alienation began in June. Hogan wrote to Daniel Cronin, Bishop of Fall River, requesting a *nihil obstat* letter to be presented to the Congregation of Religious in a formal request for alienation. Hogan assured Cronin that the Catholic nature of the College would be maintained and that a Holy Cross presence on the Board of Trustees would remain. Cronin had "no objection to the alienation as proposed" and sent the letter.[67]

Hogan next contacted the Superior General, Germain Lalande, to ask his help in acquiring the necessary indult from canon law to initiate alienation. Lalande was concerned with financial issues and feared that the Province might find itself legally responsible for loans should the College default. His solution was to have the College temporarily cede to the Province a portion of land as collateral until any outstanding College loans upon which the Congregation was a cosigner were paid. He further suggested that Stonehill be legally bound to pay each year a "substantial part" on debts before using funds for capital expenditures.[68] Ernest Bartell, CSC, who took the reins as president of Stonehill in the fall of 1971, informed Hogan that the General's request was legally impossible. Hogan relayed this message to Rome along with the additional information that the New Bedford Institu-

Gaudate Medal, awarded for twenty years of service to the College.

tion for Savings, which held the loan titles, would not release the Congregation as cosigner on College loans. The only option was a second mortgage, which would jeopardize the College's ability to borrow in the future. Although it is not clear that Lalande was convinced, he agreed to the alienation effort on October 12 and within one week the indult was received. At the same time, the name "The Foundation of Our Lady of Holy Cross, Incorporated" was changed to "Stonehill College, Incorporated," thus granting the College its own identity.[69]

The construction of a new set of bylaws was necessary now that the indult had been received and the corporation name changed. A "Church-State Check List," used to generate the bylaws, emphasized the need to place academic freedom over religious indoctrination in the College's daily operations. In strong language the list suggested, "To establish that the test [alienation of Stonehill from Holy Cross] will be successfully met, all feasible and acceptable action to reduce a church atmosphere should be taken." The document went so far as to recommend the elimination of the cross, statues, and other religious symbols from campus.[70] John McCarthy, religious superior of Holy Cross at Stonehill, in an effort to maintain balance, requested that the Community's voice be heard in the composition of the new bylaws.[71] A balanced approach that sought input from lay and religious and aimed to safeguard the College's traditional Catholic identity was adopted.

Composition of the bylaws went through several iterations, with a final version signed in the Boston office of Richard Barrett, of Powers and Hall, on February 14, 1972.[72] Under the College's new governance plan, the Board of Trustees would consist of between 15 and 24 people, with a minimum of 5 members of Holy Cross. Incorporators, members of the Congregation under contract at Stonehill, elected 7 of their peers to the Board of Fellows, who, in union with lay fellows, would elect the trustees. The position of president was to be held by a Holy Cross priest if a qualified candidate was available.[73] Ernest Bartell believed that the alienation process would better define Stonehill as a Catholic institution, give greater opportunities to all aspects of the College, and make it a more viable alternative for higher education in the greater Boston area.[74] The new day that had come to Stonehill was well summarized by the editor and essayist, John Cogley:[75]

> An era has ended; an historic period has passed. Like all historical periods, it was on balance a mixture of magnificence and mistake, of benevolence and mischief, of accomplishment and stupidity. We can praise it or denounce it, but we cannot prolong it. It is over. A new day has dawned for the Church and with it a new day for Catholic education.

Stonehill's shift in governance to lay participation was consistent with prevailing trends in American Catholic higher education and, at the same time, maintained the College's Catholic identity. The bylaws opened the College to greater possibilities through the inclusion of the laity, but their mandate for a Holy Cross priest as president and the power vested in the Holy Cross religious working at the College (Incorporators) assured the founding religious community that its voice and influence in Stonehill's direction would remain strong.

ENDNOTES

1. The revolutionary nature of the Council was recognized by Karl Rahner, SJ, probably the best-known Catholic theologian in the twentieth century, when he divided Church history into three periods: the apostolic age, the period 100–1965, and the post-Vatican II era.

2. The Declaration on Christian Education, October 28, 1965, and the Decree on the Apostolate of Lay People, November 18, 1965, were two of eleven documents accepted in the fourth and final session of the Council.

3. Harvey Cox, *Secular City: Secularization and Urbanization in Theological Perspective*, Revised Edition (Toronto: The Macmillan Company, 1966): 193–94.

4. Richard Horchler, "Time Bomb in Catholic Education," *Look* 30 (April 5, 1966): 25.

5. Paul Reiss, "The Catholic College: Some Built-In Tensions," in Robert Hassenger, ed., *The Shape of Catholic Higher Education* (Chicago: University of Chicago Press, 1967): 254–57, 266, 272.

6. Andrew Greeley, *The Changing Catholic College* (Chicago: Aldine Publishing, Company, 1967): 206.

7. Robert Hassenger, "The Future Shape of Catholic Higher Education," in Hassenger, *Shape of Catholic Higher Education*: 330.

8. Government support for Catholic colleges and universities was extremely important in the overall issue of canonical alienation. The 1966 *Horace Mann League vs. Board of Public Works* dispute in Maryland was a test case. The Maryland State Court, citing separation of church and state, upheld complaints registered against the issuance of government grants to Catholic colleges. Eventually the United States Supreme Court overturned the decision. However, fear that Catholic colleges would be unable to compete for government economic assistance changed the thinking of many administrators of Catholic colleges and universities. Joseph Preville of the Harvard Divinity School commented, "Clearly, the 'Horace Mann' decision paved the way for the emergence of the lay trustee at American Catholic colleges and universities." Theodore Hesburgh, CSC, president of Notre Dame, predicted in the wake of the Mann decision: "Legal control of boards with a majority of lay trustees is definitely the pattern of the future." See Joseph R. Preville, "Catholic Colleges, the Courts and the Constitution: A Tale of Two Cases," *Church History* 58 (June 1989): 202.

9. John F. Brosnan, "Catholic Higher Education: A View from Outside the Institution," *NCEA Bulletin* 56 (August 1959): 118–19; Neil G. McCluskey, SJ, *Catholic Education Faces Its Future* (Garden City, New York: Doubleday & Company, Inc., 1968): 227.

10. Philip Gleason, "What Makes Catholic Identity a Problem," in Theodore Hesburgh, CSC, ed., *The Challenge and Promise of a Catholic University* (Notre Dame, Indiana: University of Notre Dame Press, 1994): 91–93; Gleason, "Changing and Remaining the Same: A Look at Higher Education," in *Perspectives on the American Catholic Church, 1789–1989*, Stephen J. Vicchio and Virginia Geiser, SSND, eds. (Westminster, Maryland: Christian Classics, Inc., 1989): 228.

11. Theodore Hesburgh, CSC, memorandum (January 10, 1967), Corr Papers, ASC.

12. Neil G. McCluskey, SJ, "This Is How It Happened," in Neil G. McCluskey, SJ, ed., *The Catholic University: A Modern Appraisal* (Notre Dame, Indiana: University of Notre Dame Press, 1970): 3; "Land O'Lakes Statement: The Nature of the Contemporary Catholic University," in *American Catholic Higher Education: Essential Documents, 1967–1990*, ed. Alice Gallin, OSU (Notre Dame, Indiana: University of Notre Dame Press, 1992), 7–12.

13. Francis Boland to James Connerton, June 20, 1951, Stonehill College Papers, AHCFE. Boland wanted to show that, since the College owned virtually nothing, it had no collateral to use in payment of the debt principal.

14. "Chronicles of Our Lady of Holy Cross" (March 19, 1961), ASC.

15. Richard Sullivan to George DePrizio, March 21, 1961; DePrizio to Sullivan, Provincial Papers–DePrizio; Circular Letter of the Provincial, May 13, 1961, Provincial Chapter Papers, AHCFE; DePrizio to Sullivan, January 31, 1962, Sullivan Papers, ASC. The 1961 Provincial Chapter recommended that a committee be formed to study the advisability of separation, the formation of a distinct corporation for the Province, and a redefinition of property lines.

16. Committee members were all Holy Cross priests: Richard Sullivan (chair), John Corr, Aloysius Cussen, John Lucey, John Murphy, and Roger Quilty.

17. Richard Sullivan to members of the Corporation of Land Committee, February 2, 1962; "Summary of North Easton Property," n.d., Presidential Papers; Richard Sullivan, personal datebooks, March 19, 1962, ASC. College officials believed, as did most in Catholic higher education, that under America's system of the separation of church and state, schools with religious affiliation were less likely to be awarded government monies. The ever-increasing need for federal and state loans and grants began to force separation in the minds of many educators.

18. Board of Trustees Meeting Minutes, June 21, 1962, Board of Trustees Papers, ASC.

19. Richard Sullivan to John Corr, October 21, 1964, Provincial Papers–Sullivan, AHCFE.

20. "Agreement of Association," November 2, 1964; Richard Sullivan to Germain Lalande, November 8, 1964; Lalande to Sullivan, December 10, 1964, AHCFG.

21. Germain Lalande to Richard Sullivan, March 17, 1965, AHCFG.

22. John Corr to Richard Sullivan, January 8, 1965, Stonehill College Papers; Germain Lalande to Richard Sullivan, March 17, 1965, Provincial Papers–Sullivan, AHCFE. From extant data it is unclear what amount of land Lalande believed was to be ceded to the College. It appears that he was confused with the 400-acre section, believing it to be 400 acres in addition to the 100 given in the 1952 resolution ordered by Christopher O'Toole. If this is true, then Lalande thought Stonehill would have virtually the entire property, leaving the Congregation with little upon which to build in the future.

23. "Summary Statement on Separation of Stonehill and the Congregation of Holy Cross," n.d., Stonehill College Papers, AHCFE; Jerome Lawyer to John Corr, May 7, 1968, Presidents Papers, ASC.

24. George DePrizio to Christopher O'Toole, n.d. [1961], Superior General Papers–O'Toole, AHCFE; John Corr to David Arthur, October 7, 1969, Corr Papers; Corr to Richard Sullivan, August 30, 1966, Presidential Papers, ASC. Corr commented on being both superior and president, "This, I believe, is not applicable in the present day. . . ."

25. Extant data does not reveal what complications caused the lengthy delay in the court's actions. The need to redraw the physical plans to show all the buildings on the land caused some delay. Additionally, complications arose because the road from the College to Route 138 cut through Holy Cross property.

26. Richard Sullivan to John Corr, September 8, 1969, Provincial Papers–Sullivan, AHCFE. Sullivan here reveals his philosophy on the land separation: "The thought about the division of land, as we have both agreed, is based on the fact that Stonehill should have all the land necessary for its development, and that the remainder of the land should be a source of security for the Province."

27. Richard Sullivan to John Lucey, May 3, 1968, Stonehill College Papers, AHCFE.

28. Provincial Council Meeting Minutes, October 25–27, 1968, Provincial Council Papers, AHCFE. The agreement stated: (1) All seminarian tuition would be discounted 20 percent; (2) seminary faculty members teaching at the College would be given salaries to be distributed as follows: $3000 as assessment, $2000 for living expenses, and the remainder to the Sorin Fund.

29. A good working definition of governance is: "The process or art with which scholars, students, teachers, administrators, and trustees, associated together in a college or university, establish and carry out the rules and regulations that minimize conflict, facilitate their collaboration, and preserve essential individual freedom." See John Corson, *Governance of Colleges and Universities* (New York: McGraw-Hill Book Company, Inc., 1960): 12–13.

30. David Arthur to "Committee Member," November 18, 1968, Arthur Papers, ASC. In this letter Arthur gives two goals for faculty committees: (1) To give faculty members an opportunity to become part of the decision-making process of the College and (2) to provide the College with expert professional information upon which to base its decisions.

31. John Corr to "Administration, Faculty and Staff of Stonehill College," November 10, 1964; Corr to Board of Advisors, January 8, 1965, Corr Papers; "Reconstitution of the Board of Advisors," February 3, 1965, Board of Advisors Papers; Edward Stanford, OSA to John Corr, November 22, 1965, Presidents Papers, ASC.

32. David Arthur to Faculty Member, May 18, 1967, September 25, 1967, October 13, 1967, Arthur Papers; Faculty Meeting Minutes, October 5, 1967, Faculty Assembly Papers, ASC.

33. "The Academic Council," December 14, 1967, Academic Council Papers, ASC.

34. In keeping with his general pattern, which granted autonomy and freedom to all responsible people, he wrote, "The consensus opinion seems to be that we have a good thing in Stonehill College, and our efforts should be to build on and improve what we now have. In order to do this, we need the involvement of the entire Stonehill College Community, that is the students, faculty and administration." See John Corr, Memorandum to Faculty and Students, January 22, 1970, Corr Papers, ASC.

35. John Corr to Faculty, January 12, 1970, Corr Papers, ASC. Corr stated, "At the outset, let me say that I favor any responsible approach to a better governance of the College. And more, I welcome greater involvement by all sectors of the College." Corr asked that a report from the committee be submitted by October 1, 1970.

36. Vincent P. Wright to Administration and Faculty, March 10, 1970, Faculty Assembly Papers; Wright to "Seminary Participants," Memorandum, May 4, 1970, Corr Papers, ASC.

37. *Stonehill* (Fall 1970), Public Affairs Papers; "Report of Committee on Governance," October 1, 1970, Corr Papers, ASC.

38. "Report of the Committee on Governance," October 1, 1970, Corr Papers, ASC.

39. Ibid.; Faculty Handbook, Article VII, March 27, 1971, Faculty Assembly Papers, ASC.

40. Vincent P. Wright, "Governance 1971–72," August 21, 1972, Wright Papers; "Report of the Committee on Governance," October 1, 1970, ASC. The report intentionally did not define "important" with respect to issues it would review. This lack of specificity would cause significant problems between the president and the council in the 1970s.

41. Two important works which give excellent general summaries about canonical alienation are: Alice Gallin, OSU, *Independence and a New Partnership* (Notre Dame: University of Notre Dame Press, 1996) and Martin J. Stamm, "The Laicization of Corporate Governance of Twentieth Century American Catholic Higher Education," *Records of the American Catholic Historical Society of Philadelphia* 94 (1–4) (1983): 81–99.

42. "Why Have Lay Trustees?" Seminar in Governance in American Catholic Higher Education, February 9–10, 1968, Loretto Heights College, Denver, Colorado.

43. Neil McCluskey, SJ, "The Governance," in McCluskey, *The Catholic University: A Modern Appraisal* (South Bend, Indiana: University of Notre Dame Press, 1970): 148.

44. Daniel A. Degnan, SJ, "Secularizing Catholic Colleges," *America* 118 (May 25, 1968): 696. Degnan claimed that in the 1963–64 academic year, only 30.4 percent of the operational fund for private schools came from tuition. Government assistance, from state or federal levels, plus private financing was necessary for operation.

45. "Shared Control in Catholic Higher Education," Seminar in Governance in American Catholic Higher Education, February 9–10, 1968.

46. Christopher Jencks and David Riesman, *The Academic Revolution* (New York: Doubleday & Company, 1968): 351.

47. Michael P. Walsh, SJ, "Nature and Role Today," in McCluskey, *The Catholic University:* 51.

48. Gerald J. Dalcourt, "Lay Control of Catholic Colleges," *America* 117 (October 14, 1967): 412.

49. John Reedy, CSC, and James E. Andrews, "Control of Catholic Universities: Holy Cross Rethinks Its Relationship to Notre Dame and Portland Universities," *The Ave Maria* 105 (January 28, 1967): 17.

50. Howard Kenna, CSC, to Fellow Religious, December 13, 1966, Provincial Papers–Kenna, AHCFI.

51. Theodore Hesburgh, CSC, "The Changing Face of Catholic Higher Education," *NCEA Bulletin* 65 (August 1969): 56.

52. John Corr to Richard Sullivan, August 30, 1966, Presidents Papers, ASC.

53. John Corr, Speech to the NCEA, December 3, 1966, Corr Papers, ASC.

54. John Corr, Speech to Faculty, February 16, 1967, Faculty Assembly Papers, ASC. Corr was in contact with Paul Reinert, SJ, at St. Louis University about its alienation process.

55. David Arthur, "Need for a Change," n.d. [1967], Presidents Papers, ASC.

56. "The Stonehill College Problem," n.d. [1967], Presidents Papers, ASC.

57. "Decrees and Recommendations," Provincial Chapter, 1967, AHCFE. C. James Cleary, Professor of History, and later acting dean, executive vice president, and interim president, stated concerning Holy Cross' overall involvement with alienation: "There was an eagerness [on the part of the Holy Cross Community] to engage the secular world." C. James Cleary, interview with the author, July 16, 1996, Stonehill College History Project Papers, ASC.

58. Agenda for Committee on Corporate Revision of Stonehill College, April 11, 1969, Presidential Papers, ASC.

59. William Hogan to John McCarthy, September 30, 1970, Presidents Papers, ASC. Hogan wrote, "I am deeply concerned about proceeding to the accomplishment of the separation of college and community."

60. Meeting Minutes, Holy Cross Community at Stonehill College, October 27, 1970, Presidents Papers, ASC. His list of reasons for alienation included: (1) To "DeRomanize" the College, (2) to give greater witness to poverty, (3) to guard against legal repercussions concerning Church and State, (4) to permit religious greater apostolic opportunities, and (5) to give the laity a greater role.

61. Edward Heston to William Hogan, November 8, 1970, Presidents Papers, ASC.

62. "Report of Committee on Governance," October 1, 1970, Corr Papers; Vincent P. Wright, "Governance 1971–1972," August 8, 1972, Wright Papers, ASC.

63. Calvin H. Bowker to John Corr, February 5, 1971, Presidents Papers, ASC. Bowker was also wary of the composition of the newly formed College Council and its ability to appeal to the Board of Trustees over the president if disagreement existed. This fear would be manifest in a confrontation between the president and the council between 1973 and 1975.

64. John Corr to William Hogan, February 24, 1971, Provincial Papers–Hogan, AHCFE.

65. Meeting Minutes of Holy Cross Religious at Stonehill College, April 21, 1971, Presidents Papers, ASC.

66. William Hogan to Board of Trustees, June 9, 1971; Hogan to Richard Barrett, July 22, 1971, Presidents Papers, ASC.

67. William Hogan to Daniel Cronin, June 9, 1971; Cronin to Ildebrando Cardinal Antoniutti, June 18, 1971, Stonehill College Papers, AHCFE.

68. Germain Lalande to William Hogan, August 6, 1971, Presidents Papers, ASC. The loans taken for the various building projects had been signed by representatives

of The Foundation of Our Lady of Holy Cross. Physical separation of lands did not remove financial responsibility as there was no transfer of funds and no arrangements for changes in loan signers. Thus, the General was concerned that a financial failure by the College would fall back upon the Congregation.

69. Ernest Bartell to William Hogan, September 14, 1971, Stonehill College Papers; Hogan to Germain Lalande, September 30, 1971; Lalande to Hogan, October 12, 1971; Hogan to Lalande, October 26, 1971, Provincial Papers–Hogan, AHCFE. Lalande was still concerned about the relationship between the Community and the College and told Hogan that mutual collaboration be "specifically spelled out." Although there was much talk during the period of some definitive agreement, it was not until March 1984 that a "Statement of Principles" outlining the relationship between the two corporations was actually formalized. Currently the College operates under an updated 1989 agreement.

70. Stonehill College, "Church-State Check List," December 9, 1971, Presidential Papers, ASC. The list recommended that theology requirements and religious services be downplayed and that any statement indicating objectives of a religious nature be struck from the bylaws. The source of this checklist is not extant.

71. John McCarthy to William Hogan, January 18, 1972, Presidents Papers, ASC.

72. Ernest Bartell to William Hogan, January 31, 1972, Presidential Papers, ASC.

73. Stonehill College By-Laws, 1972, Presidential Papers, ASC.

74. Ernest Bartell, interview with the author, July 25, 1996, Stonehill College History Project Papers, ASC.

75. Quoted in Robert Hassenger, "The Future Shape of Catholic Higher Education," in Hassenger, ed., *The Shape of Catholic Higher Education*: 334.

CHAPTER 10

1971–1978
❧

Paradoxical Viewpoints

American tribulations in the 1960s left in their wake a disheveled society searching for direction. The new decade commencing in 1970 began with lingering uncertainties about civil rights, political assassinations, the counterculture, and Vietnam. The nation explored new ideas, pursued solutions to its problems, and looked to heal the wounds that had fractured American unity. In short, after a period characterized by radical change, Americans sought stability in all aspects of daily life.

American Catholic higher education also sought a new direction. How the process of canonical alienation would change the direction and characteristics of Catholic education was still to be determined. Sailing into uncharted waters, where laity, clerics, and religious shared equally in all facets of the educational process, American Catholic colleges and universities struggled in their continuing efforts to provide quality education.

The experience of Stonehill College in the 1960s, although not as radical as that of many other liberal arts schools, nevertheless markedly changed the institution and forced it to chart a new course. The demise of *in loco parentis*, professional development in administration, student protests, and, most especially, the ongoing process of separation from its parent religious body challenged Stonehill to meet the new decade with a sense of openness. The challenge was accepted by a new president who, while experiencing conflict from within the institution, set Stonehill on a progressive course from which it has not since diverged.

American Catholic Higher Education in the 1970s

❧   AMERICAN CATHOLIC higher education was greatly influenced by the Second Vatican Council and its philosophy of *aggiornamento*. In its 16 documents, the Council endorsed two nuclear ideas that promoted the maturation of Catholic colleges and universities in the United States. First, Vatican II verified the intrinsic value and autonomy of the secular. Secondly, the Council documents, especially *Gaudium et Spes* and *Apostolicam actuositatem*, validated the importance of the laity's role and responsibility. Thus, the spirit of Vatican II was directly responsible for the advent of canonical alienation, first implemented in 1967 at St. Louis University and Webster College.

Catholicism, in general, and Catholic higher education, in particular, were forced to rethink their purpose and direction.[1] The National Catholic Education Association (NCEA) listed the major changes common to most institutions after Vatican II: (1) canonical alienation brought to colleges and universities an independent board of trustees and increased involvement of the institution with the outside community; (2) changes in society led to the abandonment of *in loco parentis*; and (3) the spirit of openness promoted by *aggiornamento* encouraged development of campus ministry programs, greater diversity in course offerings, and a more ecumenical emphasis in the department of religious studies.[2] The introduction of these changes created a new environment for the Catholic institution of higher learning. Observers outlined certain characteristics common to Catholic colleges and universities: They were chartered by the state and enjoyed tax-free status, were privately supported, and promoted the ultimate goal of forming people able to assume responsibility in the Church and in the world. Catholic identity was preserved by the institution's association with and commitment to the Church and its maintenance of departments of philosophy and theology.[3]

Catholic higher education continued to receive input from many sources that generated differing opinions on the correct direction to be followed. Educators maintained the traditional dual purpose—education of the mind and development of the individual—as the expressed goals. In an attempt to articulate the nature, governance, activity, and responsibility of Catholic higher education, a conference of educators met in Rome in 1972. The assembly generated "The Catholic University in the Modern World," a document that stated the need for commitment to academic excellence, university autonomy,[4] and academic freedom but concluded, "In a Catholic university, . . . , Catholic ideals, attitudes and principles penetrate and inform university activities in accordance with the proper nature and autonomy of these activities."[5] The National Conference of Catholic Bishops' report, "To Teach as Jesus Did," spoke in a similar vein: "Everything possible must be done to preserve the critically important contribution made by Catholic institutions through their commitment to the spiritual, intellectual, and moral values of Christian tradition."[6] The International Federation of Catholic Universities (IFCU) also reinforced the traditional understanding but suggested, as well, that Catholic higher education had the further mission of fostering dialogue between the Church and the world.[7]

Catholic educators of the period expressed both the traditional understanding and innovation of Vatican II in describing the purposes and goals of higher education. Jesuit Father Raymond Schoder of Loyola University in Chicago suggested that Catholic education must be truly Catholic in its development of the whole person—intellectually, morally, and spiritually. The method used to achieve this end must be unitive, with all aspects of the process fitting into "a smoothly working whole." He concluded, "Catholic education really means teaching all the truths that other schools teach, but in the illuminating *context of supernatural truths* [Schoder's emphasis] also." Along similar lines, George Kelly, professor of contemporary Catholic problems at St. John's University in New York, concluded that Catholic education can only achieve academic quality equal to that of its secular counterparts when it works from principles and objectives that have stood the test of time. In the spirit of Vatican II, he called for Catholic universities to rediscover internal autonomy and academic freedom which were endemic to the medieval university from which modern education was born.[8]

The central question discussed by Catholic educators and debated in monographs and periodicals concerned the ramifications of canonical alienation on program offerings and general direction of institutions of higher learning. Jesuit educator Michael Buckley's observation of problematic situations caused by alienation led him to suggest that such a condition was to be expected and was only symptomatic of the growing pains institutions must endure in order to discover their role as universities. He claimed that change is fostered by crises produced by confrontation and uncertainty, while growth makes colleges and universities precisely what they claim to be—Catholic.[9] The historical development of Catholic education was used by another writer to suggest that change is natural to any organization that seeks growth along progressive lines. As a timeless entity, the Catholic university must seek to engage modernity, not be hostile to it.[10] Theodore Hesburgh, CSC, who guided the implementation of alienation at Notre Dame, continued to emphasize the academic role of the university:[11]

> One may add descriptive adjectives to this or that university calling it public or
> private, Catholic or Protestant, British or American, but the university must

first and foremost be a university, or the qualifiers qualify something, but not a university.

The NCEA supported the autonomy and freedom that alienation brought to institutions of higher education. A 1976 statement, "Relations of American Catholic Colleges and Universities with the Church," voiced concern over perceived attempts by the American bishops to demand more influence in the philosophy and operation of Catholic institutions of higher learning. The NCEA feared that interference by the bishops would deprive church-related schools of equal treatment with peer institutions before the law and serve only to weaken the service these colleges and universities could bring to the American Church:[12]

> An authentic Catholic institution of higher learning must be free to be Catholic. If the integrity and freedom of the academy is attacked, undermined by "academic laws of the Church," the Church will be the first to suffer. Its enemies will contend derisively that truth cannot be upheld and defended without resort to penalties and outside sanctions, confirming for some the suspicion that Catholic institutions cannot be true universities.

Canonical alienation and the freedom it brought from control by the institutional Church was viewed by its supporters as a bulwark against intransigence and the fear of secularization that sought to thwart the progress of Catholic education.[13]

The voices of Catholic educators who promoted the benefits of canonical alienation did not silence those who believed education and the Church were moving in the wrong direction. Some writers echoed the opinion of Harvey Cox, that the Church should get out of the business of education entirely if colleges and universities could not free themselves from outside influences.[14] However, the bulk of opponents to Catholic higher education's progressive swing took a more pragmatic approach. Some, citing a report by the prestigious education magazine *Change* that 61 percent of Catholic colleges and universities were "relatively unhealthy" economically and less than 2 percent "healthy," suggested that a financial plan to save schools was needed, not a move to compete academically with secular institutions. Monsignor John F. Murphy, executive secretary of the College and University Department of the NCEA, claimed that Catholic institutions would survive only if they understood their purpose, clearly and consistently communicated it to the faculty and students, and fully implemented it in programs and activities.[15] Others suggested that Catholic institutions would have the best chance of surviving if they emphasized their uniqueness rather than imitating the public university. Changes in the Church and the resignations of many priests and religious prompted some educators to argue that Catholic colleges and universities could restore confidence and maintain stability in the Church, but only if they maintained their tradition as educators of the intellect and formators of the heart.[16]

Additional voices opposed the progressive direction of Catholic education that canonical alienation fostered. Echoing the sentiments of Pope Paul VI[17] on the need to strengthen the intellect with the Word of God, opponents of alienation charged that Catholic higher education had moved away from the source of strength provided by the magisterium and that philosophy departments had lost their focus by offering many options with fewer standards. One writer, Germain Grisez, lamented: "The theology in Catholic higher education consequently has followed the general theological movement outside the Church, setting aside the ultimate authority of the magisterium in favor of personal opinion or popular opinion, otherwise named 'conscience' and '*sensus fidelium*.' "[18] The trend toward elimination of differences between Catholic institutions and their nonsectarian counterparts was forcefully challenged by traditional and conservative voices.

The conservative Catholic voice was best represented by the writings of James Hitchcock, professor of history at St. Louis University. He argued that the effort to transform Church-affiliated institutions into the "Catholic Ivy League" resulted in a "failure to transmit any lively sense of the Catholic tradition, a transmission which often enough is not even attempted." Hitchcock challenged recent reductions in theology and philosophy requirements, arguing that a religious vision must be the base of all Catholic education and a unifying element of Catholic college life: "Thus a college which legitimately calls itself Catholic cannot . . . recognize the 'right' of a student to ignore religion, for example, or to approach religion in so idiosyncratic a way as to miss many of its essential features." He claimed that it would not be popular to place religion at the core of the curriculum in higher education, but that it would be a courageous act. Hitchcock concluded his argument by suggesting that Catholic colleges and universities should conduct a self-examination to see if they have compromised their identity for the sake of public recognition.[19]

The loss of Catholic identity, in the classroom and in the practice of the Faith, was the principal concern of most conservative Church educators. Evidence of this apparent deterioration was exhibited by the smaller number of students attending Mass on campus and by reductions in requirements for philosophy and theology. The Church's failure, however, was perceived not only in the classroom but in the dormitory and the world at large. One writer described how the pendulum had swung from one extreme to another in Catholic higher education: "In the past we [Catholic institutions of higher education] were often guilty of being 'more Catholic than the Pope'; we now sometimes strive to become more Ivy League than the Ivy League schools themselves."[20]

A New President

🍀   IN THE SPRING OF 1971, while Catholic higher education searched for identity and Stonehill moved toward canonical alienation, John Corr announced his resignation as president. In April William Hogan, CSC, provincial of the Eastern Province and chairman of the Board of Trustees, formed a presidential search committee[21] to review the records of ten Holy Cross priests who agreed to be considered for the post. Ernest Bartell, a member of the Indiana Province and native of River Forest, Illinois, was selected. Bartell came to Stonehill from Notre Dame, where he had been chair of the Department of Economics and was currently director of the Center for the Study of Man in Contemporary Society. The new president, while only 39, possessed impressive credentials, including a Ph.D. from Princeton and numerous publications in the fields of education and economics. Noted by one local newspaper for his "intense activity even in repose," Bartell was the first president of Stonehill College who entered his post with a proven administrative record in higher education and familiarity with educational activity in the greater Boston region.[22] One congratulatory letter anticipated a bright future: "Your superb qualifications, and the demonstrated genuinity of your commitment to Excellence in American Education is indeed reassuring, and I have every confidence that your administration will prove truly outstanding."[23]

Bartell's impression of Stonehill upon his arrival was very positive,[24] yet he knew the College faced many challenges and needed direction to continue its recent history of steady progress. The task facing Bartell was outlined by David Arthur:[25]

> These, I believe, are the chief problems that the new president will face: keeping the institution financially solvent, developing a distinctive program, and attracting students. The latter two can be delegated to other administrators and to the faculty, but the first can be handled only by the president.

Bartell believed that Stonehill must look beyond its immediate confines, seeking recognition and acceptance on both regional and national levels. Confident that the College possessed all the potential necessary to achieve its proper place within the academy,[26] he encouraged the Stonehill community

Rev. Ernest Bartell, CSC, president 1971–1977.

members to work together to identify and proclaim the College's goal for Catholic education in the future, however demanding the objective might be, and to make every effort to achieve it.[27]

From his previous research on higher education in Boston, Bartell possessed an understanding of the present direction of higher education and the role of the Church in it. He staunchly rejected the idea that Catholic institutions could safely hide behind the economic and academic qualifications of higher education held prior to Vatican II. Rather, he insisted that Catholic colleges and universities must justify their existence by bridging the gap between immutable Christian principles and contemporary life. He believed that the successful school would be one able to make choices that respect the need for organic change and growth but also maintain harmony and open communication among all interests and persons who comprise the educational community.[28] With a view to the future, he wrote,[29]

> Since very many institutions of Catholic origin are rooted in the tradition of the liberal arts, the future of Catholic higher education as a whole may depend upon our collective ability to advance and adapt the liberal tradition to the realities of economic life and social status in the latter years of this century.

Although a proponent of the progressive direction of Catholic education and its emphasis on higher standards of academic excellence, Bartell also believed that private institutions must demonstrate clearly and persuasively the special character of educational services they offer. Decentralization, diversity, and the loss of ecclesiastical traditions had created tensions and conflicts with traditional authorities that could best be calmed by the maintenance of some unique character. Bartell believed that the greatest potential for the demonstration of uniqueness was to be found in smaller institutions that offered specialized programs not easily duplicated by the more politically vulnerable public sector. He suggested the need to review the moral vision that had traditionally characterized Catholic higher education and to make it the distinctive element by which Church institutions of higher learning should be recognized.[30]

Bartell's overall grasp of trends in American Catholic higher education and his vision for Stonehill placed the College in a position to successfully navigate the highway to the future. As one of his first acts, in the fall of 1971 he called the "President's Quarter Century Conference." Representatives from all facets of the campus community—faculty, students, administration, staff, and alumni—were asked to prepare papers to "establish an inventory of this total academic community that will be a worthy record of Stonehill and will become the base upon which we shall build its future."[31] The conference, held November 5–7, presented status and progress reports on governance, finances and development, curriculum, faculty, library operations, maintenance, continuing education and the evening division, athletics, residence life, counseling, campus ministry, and pastoral care. Although the conference sessions were at times stormy, when sensitive issues were raised and volatile personalities collided, overall the three-day meeting accurately presented the present state and future possibilities of the College. William Hogan, CSC, in his role as chair of the Board of Trustees, reported where the College presently stood: "Stonehill has been growing in the realization of its developing aims; however, there is need for a growing awareness of deeper life-values for all, along with furtherance of the intellectual climate."[32] The conference energized and enlightened Bartell and provided him with a foundation on which to build his administration.

The new president's vision for Stonehill was rooted in the belief that the College must become involved with the outside community. Bartell personalized this policy with many undertakings that demonstrated his interest in students, higher education, and the general activities of southeastern Massachusetts. He was actively engaged with the NCEA in financial planning and served as vice chairman of the Colleges and Universities Department of the association. His appointment to the Commission on Governmental Relations for the American Council on Education continued his national involvement. More locally, Bartell was a member of the executive committee of the Association of Independent Colleges and Universities in Massachusetts (AICUM) and served as president of the Southeastern Association for Cooperation in Higher Education in Massachusetts (SACHEM).[33] This latter connection led to increased cooperation between Stonehill and area schools, especially Wheaton College, where cross-registration for courses began in the fall of 1972.[34]

Bartell's leadership with SACHEM and AICUM was instrumental in the promoting Stonehill's name in southeastern Massachusetts. Through his introduction of an internship program, Richard Sullivan had introduced local businesses to Stonehill's students in an attempt to initiate a relationship between the College and the local community. Bartell took Sullivan's preliminary efforts and expanded them, establishing a community research office that was to apply the College's academic talents and professional research skills to the study of selected area economic problems. Professor J. Laurence Phelan was named by Bartell as community research director.[35]

One of Stonehill's most significant contributions to the outside community in this period was its outreach programs to local high schools. In the fall of 1971 Stonehill and Brockton High School began an experimental interchange program, permitting select secondary school students to attend classes for college credit. Initially courses in biology, sociology, and mathematics were offered. In a reciprocal agreement, Stonehill students and faculty were eligible to use athletic and classroom facilities at Brockton High. The program aimed to spur interest in Stonehill and to enable energetic high school students to graduate from college in three years. Over the next few years the program was expanded to include Cardinal Spellman, Taunton, Oliver Ames, Bridgewater-Raynham, and Coyle-Cassidy high schools.[36]

The most extensive academic outreach program to the local community, and the one that won Stonehill recognition in the Boston area, began in the spring of 1975. In response to Judge W. Arthur Garrity's ordered desegregation of Boston's public schools, Stonehill was paired with Hyde Park High School in a program designed to provide additional opportunities for inner-city school children.[37] That summer, a workshop for 52 Hyde Park High students was held at Stonehill, with the twofold purpose of leadership training and design of remedial and enrichment academic programs for the high school students. This program generated ideas that were used in academic year programs beginning in the fall.

The Hyde Park cooperative program began its first formal programs in the fall of 1975 under the direction of program coordinator Sr. Suzanne Kelly. Kelly used the information and experience gained during the summer on such items as course offerings, criteria for the selection of student participants, admission policies to Stonehill, and funding for the project. Enrich-

Walter Mullen, director of development 1970–1984.

ment programs in the study of ethnic heritage, drama, and journalism were started. Remedial reading and tutorial programs, along with an extensive intramural sports program, were also offered. Funding for the Hyde Park project was provided in a collaborative effort by the state and local businesses, such as the First National Bank of Boston. The Stonehill and Hyde Park High cooperative produced valuable results for numerous students, teachers, and other participants, although the program's potential to recruit minority students was not tapped. Before Stonehill's participation in the program ended in the spring of 1986, the effort had yielded a bonanza in public relations for the College.[38]

The College's development efforts, which previously had been less than successful in achieving their goals, became more prosperous under Bartell. The president worked closely with Walter Mullen, director of development, to erase the long history of failure in fundraising through an energetic annual campaign, special-purpose drives, an ongoing special gifts appeal, and a program of deferred giving.[39] The first milestone of the renewed development endeavor came in 1975, when the $5 million goal for Phase I of the Development for the Seventies campaign was achieved.

Bartell's greatest contribution to Stonehill's development efforts came in his knowledge of finances and his ability to increase the College's endowment. Building an endowment for the College had not been possible in the early years and was of no apparent priority during the 1960s. However, the College treasurer, Edward Casieri, noted, "This lack of an endowment represents a pressing financial need, which must receive some attention soon."[40] As an economist versed in the trends of Catholic higher education,

Edward Casieri, college treasurer.

Bartell realized that raising an endowment was of vital importance if the College was to gain national status as a Catholic liberal arts institution. His initial efforts raised Stonehill's endowment fund from virtually nothing in 1971 to $2 million in 1977.[41]

Faculty Development and the Tenure Debate

FROM ITS BEGINNING Stonehill College filled its faculty ranks with many dedicated religious and laity who were often asked to make numerous sacrifices to benefit the College. Development of the College financially, the professionalization of academic life under David Arthur, and the process of canonical alienation removed many of the hardships faced by faculty in Stonehill's first quarter century. Faculty status in 1971 was described in two reports. Dean Edmund Haughey enumerated some of the issues facing faculty members, including the question of unionization, the surplus of Ph.D.s in the job market, leveling of growth at Stonehill, changing values of students, and the general economic malaise of the nation. A second report by Thomas Feeley, CSC, professor of philosophy, noted the poor self-image held by many faculty members and proposed ways to create a positive image.[42]

While the number of faculty had increased and the College had made great strides along the road to full acceptance as a liberal arts institution, there had never been a formal program of faculty development at the College. In 1974, however, Stonehill received a grant from the Fund for the Improvement of Post-Secondary Education (FIPSE) to initiate a faculty development program. Conferences conducted by educational specialists for representatives of Stonehill and three other colleges[43] listed in the grant led to the development of a pilot program for long-range faculty development.

During academic year 1975 through 1976, Professors Chet Raymo and Anne T. Carrigg drafted a master faculty development plan for Stonehill. The program was developed "to create an exciting atmosphere in which to teach, to examine and [to] talk about teaching, and to grow in individual and collective effectiveness."[44] The scheme, discussed at several sessions of the Academic Committee in the fall of 1975, outlined the traditional faculty standards of effective teaching, noncurricular contributions to the College, and scholarly and/or creative activity and called for "a *full personal commitment* [report emphasis] to the College and its students." The report suggested five specific areas where faculty development was necessary: reasonable job security, financial incentives, reduced teaching loads and paid sabbaticals, promotion, and special awards. The academic dean was to appoint a faculty development coordinator annually.[45] Tom Clarke, CSC, the first coordinator, was appointed in the fall of 1976.

One significant recommendation in the overall plan was the institution of a system of post-tenure review. All tenured faculty would be reviewed by an *ad hoc* faculty review committee at seven-year intervals. Criteria for review would be the same as those applied at the time of a faculty member's initial tenure application. The committee could recommend promotion or merit increment or, if repeated deficiencies were present, suggest dismissal along approved AAUP guidelines. Lack of action on this proposal by the administration led to the plan being shelved.[46]

Faculty salaries continued to be an issue, but in the 1970s the concept of merit pay first arose. In March 1972 the Faculty Assembly discussed merit pay as an increment above the annual cost-of-living allowance (COLA) to insure that teachers were moving up in their respective faculty categories. Bartell maintained that he was "committed to the goal of raising [the] general level of salaries of [the] faculty," but he perceived no special case for merit incentive.[47] No plan for merit incentive pay was adopted at this time.

Battle lines were drawn over the issue of faculty tenure quotas. Tenure, the contingent right of a faculty member appointed to a tenure position to retain that status until retirement, was first described in the AAUP's "General Declaration of Principles" in 1915. Tenure provided faculty members the freedom to think and speak without politically inspired interference. In

(Left) Rev. Edmund Haughey, CSC, academic dean 1971–1973.
(Right) Paul Gastonguay, associate academic dean 1978 to 1998.

February 1972 the College Council reviewed three different options pertinent to tenure: make no change to the current no-quota College policy, set some form of quota, or do away with tenure all together.[48]

A confrontation between the faculty and the president began in October 1972, when the Faculty Assembly reported that Bartell favored tenure quotas at Stonehill. The purported reasons were that tenure puts an economic strain on the College and severely curtails the ability to bring new faculty to the College. The faculty responded immediately: "The faculty of Stonehill College, both non-tenured and tenured, feel that it is in their best interests and the best interests of the College not to adopt a tenure quota." The College Council spent several sessions discussing the tenure question. Council members recognized the problem of complacency in some tenured faculty and acknowledged the academic and budgetary constraints brought by tenure, but they concluded "that a policy of quotas would be destructive."[49]

The Board of Trustees took up the tenure quota issue in the spring of 1973. The board ruled that "no more than 65 percent of the faculty of Stonehill College be on tenure concomitant with a 60 percent limitation on senior ranks." The board also suggested the need for renewable contracts or other means for faculty who qualified for tenure but for whom there was no opening. The faculty, citing AAUP guidelines, opposed the ruling.[50] The trustees reviewed their decision in December 1974 and stipulated that the quota would be based on the number of full-time faculty only. In October 1976 the board recognized a temporary extraordinary situation that would compromise the 65 percent quota for the next few years.[51] The board thus ruled that tenure decisions presented by the Rank and Tenure Committee would be reviewed under the quota when the special situation had passed.[52]

The Battle Over Governance

❦ THE FAVORABLE RECEPTION of Ernest Bartell upon his selection as president of Stonehill soon became a memory as personal and professional challenges quickly arose. Because he was not a member of the Eastern Province of Holy Cross, Bartell's appointment, in the eyes of certain Community members, introduced an outsider to the inner circles of the College. Bartell's long association with Notre Dame was problematic for others, including many students, who feared he would attempt to transform Stonehill into a "Notre Dame of the East."[53] Although Bartell expressed excitement and claimed his first year a success, he had to admit, "The honeymoon is over, ..."[54]

A situation ripe for conflict began to develop when the College community, accustomed to a less directive style of administrative leadership, encountered a new president who used a more directive and personally involved approach to governance. Bartell came to the presidency less than one year after the "Report on the Committee on Governance" suggested the formation of the College Council. The council was supposed "to provide a system of government that will allow the administration, the faculty, and the students complementing voices in the decision-making process," but its specific role and jurisdiction in governance were poorly defined.[55] The Governance Committee felt that the College Council's input on major policy questions would strengthen the president's role. Bartell, however, disagreed with the peripheral role assigned to the president by the council and most members of the Stonehill College community; he believed the president belonged in direct control. The president did hold veto power over council decisions, but by a two-thirds vote the council could override the veto and send a measure to the Board of Trustees for a final decision, thus effectively bypassing the president. To complicate things further, this governance structure had not been well understood by Bartell when he assumed office.[56]

The spring of 1973 found Bartell and the College Council at odds on issues of authority and power of decision. In February Bartell, citing discrepancies between the "By-Laws" and the "Ordinances and Organization" of the College, called "for [a] reevaluation of the governance structure in its present form." The council president, Paul Gastonguay, however, reasserted the council's role of protecting the decision-making powers of all College groups by maintenance of the governance structure in place.[57] *The Summit* described the disagreement as a "lack of communication" between opposing forces, each seeking control. The council accused the president of usurping its power and failing to inform the members of pertinent decisions. Bartell countered that the council's present configuration and its power of veto gave the office of president no voice. In the summer the Board of Trustees appeared to end the conflict by ratifying the authority of the council.[58]

The confrontation between the president and the Stonehill community did not end, however, with the trustees' vote of confidence in the council. At an emotional September 1973 Academic Committee meeting, faculty members took issue with Bartell and the Board of Trustees over the philosophy of governance. They perceived their power ebbing away due to the president's management efficiency model of governance.[59] Finally, on February 1, 1975, the Board of Trustees appointed a special committee to examine the governance structure "related [to] problems of communication in order to further discuss the purposes of the institution." This committee met on February 3 and recommended that Dr. Joseph Kauffman, professor of higher education at the University of Wisconsin, be retained as a consultant in an attempt to bring final resolution to the governance question. The trustees approved the selection.[60]

Kauffman evaluated Stonehill's governance structure on two separate visits. On February 28, 1975, he attended a meeting of the College Council to better understand its operation. His official visit was conducted April 1 through April 3. Bartell and the administrative division heads wrote separate letters to Kauffman to express their objections to the operation and composition of the council. The division heads called for the council's suppression, arguing that it provided "no constructive role . . . in helping Stonehill fulfill its mission." Bartell also believed the council superfluous, but concluded that if a top-level internal body must exist, "it must have a clearly defined mandate and jurisdiction, well-differentiated from my own and for which the members can be held both responsible and accountable if they are to exercise effective authority."[61]

Kauffman's report aimed to resolve the confrontation between the president and the council. The consultant recommended that while some form of all-college body was a good idea, it should be an "*advisory*" [Kauffman's emphasis] body, with the academic dean or president as chair. Such a shift in understanding would require a change in the communication pattern between the council and the Board of Trustees. He further recommended that in the ordinances the president be named "the chief executive and administrative officer of the College with authority, delegated by the Board, for the operation and development of the institution within the framework of approved Board policy." Finally, Kauffman suggested that the trustees become more active in the governance of the College.[62] The special committee forwarded Kauffman's recommendations in total to the trustees, who implemented them in the fall of 1975.

A Crisis in Foreign Languages

IN JANUARY 1975, when the confrontation between the president and the College Council was still unresolved, an even more impassioned battle pitted Bartell against the faculty. In the fall of 1971 foreign language requirements at Stonehill were eliminated, precipitating a steady drop in the number of students taking language courses. David Arthur, director of institutional research, described the economic ramifications of the situation in a 1974 special report, calling it "a serious cause for concern."[63]

In the fall of 1974 acting Academic Dean C. James Cleary and President Bartell began to explore options for improving the situation. Cleary had earlier received complaints "concerning problems which seem to have developed" with course offerings in French. He suggested to the president that the College's two French teachers be told that unless there was a marked renewal of interest in the French program, it would be terminated at the end of the next academic year. He further suggested only elementary and intermediate German be offered beginning in the fall 1975 semester. Bartell assessed the situation and formed a plan of action. He negotiated a cooperative deal with Wheaton College, which was also experiencing student losses, to establish a common language program. This would maintain course offerings for both institutions and reduce economic losses.[64] Bartell then decided to eliminate the German department and French program at Stonehill; students wanting these subjects could take them at Wheaton.

Bartell's decision was first communicated by Cleary in early January to Edward MacLeod, Paul Foucré, and Mario Giangrande, professors whose appointments would be lost in the move. The dean, who informed Bartell that the three affected teachers had challenged the decision, recommended that division heads meet to discuss the situation before a College Council meeting scheduled for January 16.[65] The stage was set for the most divisive confrontation experienced at Stonehill College.

Foucré, MacLeod, and Giangrande wrote to the council to express their objections to the decision. They claimed that such action would end Stonehill's claim to be a true liberal arts college. Specifically the professors claimed that it was infeasible (due to transportation difficulties) to have SACHEM[66] responsible for offering languages, that primary responsibility for determining academic policy lay with the Academic Committee (with its decisions subject to the College Council), and that AAUP guidelines on the termination of tenured faculty had not been followed.[67]

The January 16 College Council meeting drew an overflow crowd of faculty and spectators hostile to the decision and the process used in its generation. The council asked Cleary to attend its session and answer questions pertinent to the growing language controversy. The dean stated in the meeting that the decision was based on the inviability of the programs due to small numbers and numerous complaints from students on the quality of courses offered. For the council members, the principal complaint was that neither the Academic Committee nor College Council were consulted on the move, despite its impact on the College and the careers of three faculty colleagues. Cleary responded that the decision did not represent a major policy change and thus was not under the purview of the council. The council closed its session by voting 6–3, with one abstention, that the decision to eliminate French and German offerings (and the jobs of three tenured professors) "constitutes a major policy change" and asked that any action be held in abeyance until the Academic Committee and College Council could review the situation.[68]

The confrontation between the administration and the faculty divided the College, with each side staunchly defending its position. An Academic Committee meeting on January 20 issued a statement that discontinuance of the French and German programs would seriously damage Stonehill's reputation as a liberal arts college, and that the outside community would receive a bad impression and negative publicity would be the result. The administration restated its three principal arguments for the inviability of the programs: insufficient students, financial losses, and student complaints.[69] Another round of letters sent to Foucré, MacLeod, and Giangrande expressed disappointment that the professors had done nothing to stimulate interest or improve their programs when they observed declining student numbers, even though asked to do so by the dean's office.[70]

A ray of hope for resolution of the conflict came on January 21 when the Faculty Affairs Committee was informed that the president and dean had agreed to follow AAUP guidelines and Stonehill's governance procedures in seeking a solution; this news was communicated to the College Council the next day.[71] Possibilities for peaceful resolution were dashed, however, when the opposing sides interpreted the guidelines and procedures in different ways. Bartell argued that AAUP guidelines for the discontinuance of a department had been followed, thus allowing professors in the affected disciplines to be discharged. For their part, faculty members stated that the language programs had not been eliminated but only transferred to Wheaton. The result was that a nontenured (from Stonehill's point of view) faculty member would replace a tenured professor in violation of AAUP guidelines.[72]

The conflict reached its climax at the end of January. The Academic Committee met and made concrete proposals to improve the German and French programs, including the formation of an *ad hoc* subcommittee to work closely with the language department over a two-year period in an effort to revitalize itself. Cleary, however, continued to defend the administration's decision before the College Council, despite the Academic Committee's offer and growing opposition throughout the Stonehill community.[73] The council chairman, Paul Gastonguay, made a personal plea to the administration to accept the Academic Committee's proposal as a compromise that would improve the College and allow all parties concerned to believe their needs were being addressed. He concluded:[74]

> I assure you, you have made your point. And it will not be forgotten. The impact of your action on faculty improvement (and alleviation of the "tenure syndrome") has already been made. . . . I really fear, and am convinced, that if you push for dismissal, even after everything that has been achieved so far, the effect will not be an improvement of education here, but the creation of so much turmoil that the quality of performance of all will be dotted with preoccupations, ...

But Gastonguay's plea went unheeded, and the Faculty Assembly gathered to express its opinion. The overflow meeting heard two reports from the Faculty Affairs Committee, one of which recommended that a vote of no-confidence be taken against the president. The assembly discussed the issue at length and adopted the motion "that the Faculty Assembly cast a vote of no-confidence in Ernest Bartell, CSC, President of Stonehill College." The meeting ended with a request that the Board of Trustees meet immediately with the assembly "to discuss the vote of no-confidence and other issues."[75]

The Board of Trustees complied with this request and met on January 31 in Hemingway Theater. They reviewed the events of January and formed a special committee, chaired by William Ribando, CSC, to fully investigate the language controversy. The special committee adopted the suggestion offered by the Academic Committee meeting of January 20 and formed an *ad hoc* committee to review and make recommendations for improvement of the language department.

Professors Robert Goulet and Richard Finnegan were assigned to the *ad hoc* committee and given one year (versus two years recommended by the Academic Committee) to make a full report.[76] A preliminary report, submitted in less than a month, recommended that Constance Schick, a former professor of languages at Stonehill, return to help organize the language department. Dr. Schick was retained and asked to submit a master plan on the revitalization of the language program. She reported that to attract more students, the base and role of foreign language instruction must be broadened to include interdisciplinary classes and double majors. She recommended that "viable programs" in German, French, and Spanish be maintained.[77]

The use of Joseph Kauffman to referee the confrontation between Bartell and the College Council prompted the *ad hoc* committee's call for consultants to evaluate and make recommendations pertinent to Stonehill's language programs. Professors Paolo Cucchi of Princeton and Sol Gittleman of Tufts were engaged to review the French and German programs, respectively, in October 1975. They recommended that instruction be more practical, with more emphasis on culture and less on literature, and that overseas programs be developed for qualified juniors and seniors. Teachers were urged to seek all opportunities for added training, especially through the National Endowment for the Humanities summer program.[78]

The *ad hoc* committee recommendations submitted in January 1976 were similar to those contained in the consultants' report. A rigorous and concretely defined program of professional self-improvement for French and German instructors was suggested, as was a master plan with rationale and supporting data for the reorganization of the language department to serve the needs and interests of Stonehill's students. The consultants also suggested that cooperation with local colleges be explored, thus indirectly supporting Bartell's proposed plan with Wheaton. The suggestions of the committee and the consultants became the basis of a new three-part language department plan promulgated in March 1976, featuring language instruction and humanistic and cultural education.

ENDNOTES

1. John W. Donohue, "Catholic Universities Define Themselves: A Progress Report," *America* 128 (April 21, 1973): 354–55.

2. "Catholic Higher Education in the 1970s," *America* 130 (January 26, 1973): 45.

3. "Relations of American Catholic Colleges and Universities with the Church," *Catholic Mind* 74 (October 1976): 51–64.

4. This reference to autonomy meant internal autonomy, nothing outside the civil or ecclesiastical laws.

5. "The Catholic University in the Modern World," in Alice Gallin, ed. American Catholic Higher Education: Essential Documents, 1967–1990 (Notre Dame, Indiana: University of Notre Dame Press, 1992), 37.

6. Quoted in "Relations of American Catholic Colleges and Universities with the Church," 54.

7. "The Contemporary Catholic University: A Report," Stonehill College Papers, AHCFE.

8. Raymond Schoder, "What Catholic Colleges Are For," *American Ecclesiastical Review* 163 (September 1970): 154–55, 158; George A. Kelly, *Why Should the Catholic University Survive?* (New York: St. John's University Press, 1973): xv, xviii.

9. Michael J. Buckley, SJ, "The Catholic University as Pluralistic Forum," *Thought* 46 (Summer 1971): 200, 207, 212.

10. Walter P. Krolikowski, "The Protean Catholic University," *Thought* 48 (Winter 1973): 467, 473.

11. Theodore Hesburgh, CSC, "The Vision of a Great Catholic University in the World of Today," *Notre Dame Journal of Education* 4 (Fall 1973): 230.

12. Quoted in John Maher, "Catholic Colleges Say They Don't Want Vatican to Increase Control, Supervision Over Them," *Our Sunday Visitor* 64 (April 25, 1976): 3.

13. M.A. Fitzsimmons, "The Catholic University: Problems and Prospects," *Notre Dame Journal of Education* 4(3) (Fall 1973): 253.

14. One example of this opinion was: "The phrase 'Catholic University' is a strict contradiction in terms. A man may be ever so devout and still be a genuine member of the community of learning, so long as he makes himself the final authority of what he believes and confesses. But any man who binds himself to the doctrines enunciated by others, whatever these doctrines may be and whether those doctrines may be or whether he perceives their truth for himself or not—such a man is not an appropriate candidate for membership in the community of a university. Such obedience to dogma may be right, but nothing is gained by pretending that it is compatible with the moral obligation of the community of learning." See Robert Paul Wolff, *The Ideal of the University* (Boston: Beacon Press, 1970): 129–30.

15. Edward Wakin, "Can Catholic Colleges and Universities Afford to Stay Catholic," *U.S. Catholic* 43 (September 1978): 29–33.

16. J. Patrick Gaffney, "Contemporary Perspectives on the Church and Catholic Higher Education," *Horizons* 3 (September 1976): 88; Gerhart Niemeyer, "The Need for the Catholic University," *Review of Politics* 37 (October 1975): 486–87. Monsignor Murphy wrote that a Catholic institution will survive only if it "clearly understands its Catholic purpose, clearly and consistently communicates it to faculty and prospective students, and fully implements it in programs and activities."

17. In an address to delegates attending a conference in Rome on Catholic universities on November 27, 1972, Pope Paul VI stated, "It is incumbent on the Catholic universities, . . . to allow knowledge and intellectual effort to be seen in their true light. To show that, in practice, the intellect is never diminished but is on the contrary stimulated and strengthened by the Word of God—that interior source of profound understanding—by the scale of values which springs from it, in short by the coherence of thought and action which results from it: . . . ." See George Kelly ed. *Why Should the Catholic University Survive?, A Study of the Character and Commitments of Catholic Higher Education* (New York: St. John's University Press, 1973), 107.

18. Germain Grisez, "American Catholic Higher Education Evaluated," in Kelly, *Why Should the Catholic University Survive?*, 46–47.

19. James Hitchcock, "How Is a College or University Catholic in Practice?" *Catholic Mind* 74 (January 1976): 9, 11, 14, 19.

20. Robert H. Vasoli, "Catholicism on the Catholic Campus," *Thought* 47 (Fall 1972): 345, 348.

21. Vincent P. Wright to Faculty, April 23, 1971, Wright Papers, ASC. The presidential search committee was composed of representatives from the Board of Trustees, the Board of Advisors, the College administration, the faculty, and students.

22. Bartell was one of a team of educators who conducted two studies on higher education in the Boston area in 1969 and 1971. See Arthur J. Corazzini, *et al.*, *Higher Education in the Boston Metropolitan Area* (Boston: Board of Higher Education, 1969) and Corazzini, *et al.*, *Higher Education in the Boston Metropolitan Area Follow Up Study* (Boston: Board of Higher Education, 1971).

23. Margaret Heckler, MC, to Ernest Bartell, October 31, 1971, Bartell Papers, ASC.

24. Bartell believed that Stonehill was small enough to "capitalize on [its] personalism." He held the conviction that the personal touch would aid the development of the whole human person. See Pamela Bullard, "Stonehill College: A Success Story," *Sunday Harold Advertiser*, May 13, 1973, "Pictorial Living" Section, 31.

25. David Arthur to Vincent P. Wright, May 24, 1971, Presidents Papers, ASC.

26. Ernest Bartell to Joseph F. Murphy, July 20, 1971, Bartell Papers, ASC. Bartell wrote, "The excellent location, magnificent setting and enthusiastic academic community do combine to form a great potential for the future. The nation still needs an outstanding Catholic college, and it is my belief and hope that Stonehill can earn that position."

27. Ernest Bartell to Faculty, August 31, 1971, Bartell Papers, ASC.

28. Ernest Bartell to Parents, March 10, 1975, Bartell Papers, ASC; Ernest Bartell, "On Trying to Define a College," NCEA *College Newsletter* 35(2) (December 1972): 3.

29. Ernest Bartell, "The Climate of An Academic Institution," NCEA *College Newsletter* 36(1) (September 1973): 2. He wrote further, "There is a special urgency today to seek the identity of our institutions of Catholic higher education . . . in

an honest confrontation with the contemporary academic climate in which we find ourselves. Vision, perspective and ultimate direction are needed today as never before in Catholic higher education."

30. Ibid; Brockton *Enterprise* clipping, (October 9, 1973), Bartell Papers, ASC.

31. Ernest Bartell, Speech to Faculty, August 31, 1971, Bartell Papers, ASC.

32. William F. Hogan, "Report to President's Quarter Century Conference," November 5, 1971, Bartell Papers, ASC.

33. *The Summit* (February 24, 1972, April 27, 1972); "The Stonehill Letter," n.d., Public Affairs Papers, ASC.

34. Ernest Bartell to W.C.H. Prentice, June 9, 1972, Presidents Papers; *Stonehill*, "The President's Report" (Fall 1972), Public Affairs Papers; Edmund Haughey "Report of Academic Dean," Summer 1973, Haughey Papers, ASC. In the fall of 1972, 22 Stonehill students and 27 from Wheaton participated in the cross-registration program. Similar privileges were also extended to faculty.

35. "Summary History of Community Research," n.d., Community Research Analyst Papers; Ernest Bartell, interview with the author, July 25, 1996, Stonehill History Project Papers, ASC. In its two-year effort, the Research Office generated (1) a report on local primary health care, that noted deficiencies and led to the expansion of Cardinal Cushing Hospital, (2) a two-volume study demonstrating population patterns in Brockton, and (3) a detailed economic survey that illustrated Stonehill's significant role in generating millions of dollars of revenue for the region.

36. *Stonehill College News*, n.d. [1972], January 1973, Public Affairs Papers; Ernest Bartell, interview with the author, July 25, 1996, Stonehill History Project Papers, ASC.

37. Stonehill was not originally one of the 22 Boston area schools picked for the project. At the last minute, however, the loss of one volunteer sponsor left an opening that was filled by Stonehill when the invitation was extended.

38. Suzanne Kelly to James C. [*sic*] Cleary, Brian Murphy, and Ronald Scarbrough, July 21, 1975; "Stonehill-Hyde Park Collaborative Program," n.d., Presidents' Papers, ASC.

39. Walter A. Mullen, "Report to the President's Quarter Century Conference," November 5, 1971, Bartell Papers, ASC.

40. Edward Casieri, "Report to President's Quarter Century Conference, " November 5, 1971, Bartell Papers, ASC.

41. News Release, July 16, 1977, Public Affairs Papers, ASC.

42. Edmund Haughey, CSC, "Report to the President's Quarter Century Conference," November 5, 1971; Thomas Feeley, CSC, "Report to the President's Quarter Century Conference," November 5, 1971, ASC.

43. Ernest Bartell to Parents, March 10, 1975, Bartell Papers, ASC. The other three schools covered by the FIPSE grant were University of California at Santa Cruz, North Carolina School of Art, and Mercer University in Georgia. The amount of the grant for the first year was $22,528. See Geno Ballotti to Edward Casieri, January 23, 1975, Deans' Papers, ASC.

44. "A Funded Program for Faculty Development," n.d., Deans' Papers, ASC.

Raymo and Carrigg exhorted the faculty to excel: "There can be no stronger faculty than one which is unified, confident, and proud of its ability to set and maintain high standards for itself. If the faculty turns away from this responsibility, it will have increased the necessity for the non-teaching part of the community to do this work on its own."

45. Faculty Development Program," November 1975, Board of Trustees Papers, ASC. Some of the duties of the faculty development coordinator were: publication of the *Faculty Forum* newsletter, publication of an in-house journal to provide a medium for writing, expansion of faculty seminar series, encouragement of luncheon discussions between faculty and students, and organization of workshops devoted to teaching skills.

46. Ibid.

47. Faculty Assembly Meeting Minutes, March 3, 1972, Faculty Assembly Papers; Ernest Bartell to Herbert Wessling, May 15, 1973, Bartell Papers, ASC. Promotion in rank was the only means of faculty salary increase besides COLA.

48. Some educators suggested that tenure impeded the need for renewal in colleges and universities. Others suggested it had an adverse effect on the possibilities of women and other minorities in the pursuit of teaching positions. See "Academic Tenure at Harvard University," *AAUP Bulletin* 58 (Spring 1972): 62–68.

49. Faculty Assembly Meeting Minutes, October 25, 1972 and November 8, 1972, Faculty Assembly Papers; College Council Meeting Minutes, November 28, 1972 and December 12, 1972, College Council Papers, ASC. Complacency in faculty ranks gave ammunition to those who sought quotas. Several suggestions were made to encourage creativity and stimulate faculty growth, including an early retirement plan, more frequent and planned sabbaticals and leaves of absence, faculty exchange programs, and a viable program of faculty development.

50. Board of Trustees to Members of the Faculty (Memo), May 5, 1973, Board of Trustees Papers; Herb Wessling to Colleagues (memo), November 19, 1973, Faculty Assembly Papers, ASC. AAUP guidelines stated, "Assuming they [faculty members] have fully earned an entitlement to tenure, there can be no justification for continuing them in a less favorable and more vulnerable status than their tenured colleagues."

51. At the time tenured members comprised 69 percent of the faculty. In the immediate future six professors would become eligible for tenure, with no prospects for retirement amongst the 77 full-time faculty members. Thus, the board believed the situation warranted special handling.

52. Board of Trustees Meeting Minutes, September 28, 1974 and October 9, 1976, Board of Trustees Papers, ASC.

53. Recall that when Stonehill was founded in 1948, the Brockton *Enterprise* proudly proclaimed that Holy Cross was opening a "Notre Dame of the East." Bartell was aware that his decision to bring with him from Notre Dame a few staff personnel (John Gerber, CSC, Edward [Ned] Reidy, CSC, F. James Burbank, CSC, and Sr. Suzanne Kelly) led some to perceive a "take-over" by Notre Dame. He was not aware, however, of the comment by the *Enterprise*. In one letter Bartell wrote,

"I returned to campus to find a vocal group of faculty and students threatening to impeach me for attempting to turn Stonehill into a 'Notre Dame of the East.' " See Bartell to Jaroslav Pelikan, April 20, 1973, Bartell Papers, ASC.

54. Ernest Bartell to Louis C. Stamatakos, June 9, 1972; Bartell to George Shuster, November 15, 1972, Bartell Papers, ASC.

55. "Report on the Committee on Governance," October 1, 1970, Corr Papers, ASC. Concerning the College Council the report stated, "The Council would have policymaking authority over all important issues within the college" and "The Committee is not attempting to define the meaning of 'important.' " The lack of specificity in the council's jurisdiction proved highly problematic.

56. The composition of the council of 12 members was divided into 5 faculty, 3 students, and 4 administrators. The administration could thus be overridden by a combined vote of faculty and students.

57. Vincent P. Wright, "Report to President's Quarter Century Conference," November 5, 1971; Ernest Bartell to Wright, February 26, 1973, Bartell Papers; Paul Gastonguay to College Council, April 24, 1973, College Council Papers, ASC.

58. Joint Session of the Governance Committee, the Board of Trustees, and the College Council on May 16, 1973, College Council Papers; *The Summit* (April 26, 1973, May 3, 1973, February 28, 1974), ASC.

59. Edmund Haughey to Ernest Bartell, September 19, 1973, Haughey Papers, ASC.

60. John Collins, memorandum, n.d. [February 1975], Horn Papers, ASC. The three members of the special committee were John Collins (chair), William Ribando, CSC, and Dr. Robert Binswanger.

61. Edward Casieri, C. James Cleary, John Gallagher, and Walter Mullen to Joseph Kauffman, March 14, 1975, Horn Papers; Ernest Bartell to Kauffman, March 6, 1975, Bartell Papers, ASC. Bartell believed the College Council was superfluous because two other tripartite committees, Academic and Student Affairs, already possessed jurisdiction over all matters he could envision.

62. Joseph Kauffman to Special Committee of the Board of Trustees, Stonehill College, April 28, 1975, Horn Papers, ASC.

63. David Arthur, "Report of Instructional Program," October 1974, Cleary–Dean Papers, ASC. Between the fall of 1970 and the spring of 1975 the number of student courses rose by 12.3 percent, but losses were significant in the languages: French down 63.3 percent, German down 50.8 percent, Spanish down 32.2 percent. Between 1969 and 1974 the number of students per teacher in languages dropped from 72.1 to 48. These losses translated into a rise of faculty salary cost per student in languages from $62.13 to $137.11 between 1969 and 1974. This rise of $74.98 can be measured against the closest discipline, English, which rose $27.13. The College average during the same period rose $9.31.

64. C. James Cleary to Ernest Bartell, Biweekly Reports (November 1, 1974 and December 2, 1974), Cleary–Dean Papers; W.C.H. Prentice to Ernest Bartell, December 20, 1974; Bartell to Prentice, January 2, 1975, Presidents Papers, ASC.

65. Edward MacLeod, "Transcript of Meeting with C. James Cleary," January 8,

1975, Language Department Papers; Cleary to Ernest Bartell, January 10, 1975, Cleary–Dean Papers, ASC.

66. Wheaton was a member of SACHEM.

67. Paul Foucré, Mario Giangrande, and Edward MacLeod to College Council, January 16, 1975, Cleary–Dean Papers, ASC.

68. College Council Meeting Minutes, January 16, 1975, College Council Papers, ASC. At the time, the College Council's governance jurisdiction was in debate, with both sides defining in different ways the word "important" in matters of College policy.

69. Academic Committee Meeting Minutes, January 20, 1975, Academic Committee Papers; "Statement on Discontinuance of French and German Programs," January 20, 1975, Cleary–Dean Papers, ASC.

70. C. James Cleary to Mario Giangrande, January 20, 1975; Cleary to Edward MacLeod, January 20, 1975; Cleary to Paul Foucré, January 20, 1975, Cleary–Dean Papers, ASC.

71. Memorandum of Faculty Affairs Committee, January 21, 1975, Cleary–Dean Papers; College Council Meeting Minutes, January 22, 1975, College Council Papers, ASC. In 1958 the AAUP published a "Statement on Procedural Standards in Faculty Dismissal Proceedings" as a supplement to its 1940 "Statement of Principles on Academic Freedom and Tenure." The 1958 statement gave precise directions to be followed in the removal of a tenured professor. Committee A of the AAUP in 1974 published more directions on the subject. Two sections of the 1974 statement were considered applicable by the faculty: (1) "The decision to discontinue formally a program or department of instruction will be based solely upon educational considerations, as determined primarily by the faculty as a whole or an appropriate committee thereof." (2) "Before the administration issues notice to a faculty member of its intention to terminate an appointment because of formal discontinuance of a program or department of instruction, the institution will make every effort to place the faculty member concerned in another suitable position." See "Termination of Faculty Appointments Because of Financial Exigency, Discontinuance of a Program or Department or Medical Reasons," AAUP Committee A, October 31 and November 1, 1974. For a more complete discussion of these guidelines, see Louis Joughin, ed., *Academic Freedom and Tenure* (Madison: University of Wisconsin Press, 1967): 36–45.

72. "On Institutional Problems Resulting from Financial Exigency: Some Operating Guidelines." *AAUP Bulletin* (Summer 1974): 267. The applicable section of the AAUP guidelines read: "The service of a tenured professor should not be terminated in favor of retaining someone without tenure who may at a particular time seem to be more productive."

73. Academic Committee Meeting Minutes, January 22, 1975, Cleary–Dean Papers; College Council Meeting Minutes, January 22, 1975, College Council Papers, ASC.

74. Paul Gastonguay to Ernest Bartell and C. James Cleary, January 23, 1975, Cleary–Dean Papers, ASC.

75. Faculty Assembly Meeting Minutes, January 29, 1975, Faculty Assembly Papers, ASC. At the same time, the Student Government Association met and voted no confidence in the President. SGA President George Hagerty delivered the message to the president.

76. William Ribando to Richard Finnegan, February 4, 1975, Language Department Papers; Finnegan "Report of the Ad Hoc Subcommittee of the Academic Committee," n.d. [September 1975], Academic Committee Papers, ASC.

77. Constance Schick, "Preliminary Report on the Revitalization of the Language Department," July 16, 1975, Cleary–Dean Papers, ASC.

78. Sol Gittleman and Paolo Cucchi, "Report on the Department of Foreign Languages at Stonehill College," October 27, 1975, Horn Papers, ASC.

CHAPTER II

A Progressive Expansion

Stonehill College, like all institutions of higher learning, exists for the benefit of its students. During its first 25 years, the College made great progress in the development of programs for student activities that provided an education in the social as well as the academic facets of life. In the early years service organizations, men's basketball, and regular theater productions were the lifeblood of student activity on campus. As the College expanded its physical plant, enrollment, and academic offerings, a similar development was experienced by athletics, clubs, and student activities that expressed the pulse of the day. The formation of the Communiversity (in the spring of 1970), initiation of a coeducational living experiment, discontinuance of the dress code, and establishment of Brother Mike's in the basement of O'Hara Hall signaled the end of *in loco parentis* and served as the harbinger of a movement toward a more liberal and free campus, in harmony with prevailing American attitudes toward daily life. Students at Stonehill College in the 1970s exhibited the progressive ideas of the day while experimenting with and expanding those concepts that had been the backbone of student life since the beginning.

The Progressive Campus Life

THE DECADE of the 1970s was ushered in under a cloud of protest and dissent that had dominated American life in the sixties. America's policy of involvement in Vietnam met continued resistance from a coalition of political liberals, veterans, and pacifists who captured the attention of the nation

Rev. Victor Caliri, CSC.

and led the country toward military withdrawal from Southeast Asia in 1973. The end of the Vietnam era, however, did not end discontent with America's military policy; the movement only changed in nature. Peace organizations such as the Fellowship of Reconciliation (FOR) and the Committee for a Sane Nuclear Policy (SANE) were joined by denominational fellowships such as *Pax Christi* in efforts to secure a nuclear testing freeze and a more pragmatic definition of deterrence. The signing of the Nuclear Non-Proliferation Treaty (1968) and the successful Strategic Arms Limitations Talks (SALT—1972) raised the hopes of American advocates for peace.[1]

Dissent in the new decade was muted; disputes, protests, and demonstrable public anger were experienced in less virulent ways. The violence and force demonstrated in the student protests, civil rights marches, and urban riots of the 1960s dissipated and were replaced by national outrage over the Watergate affair. The June 1972 break-in at Democratic headquarters at the Watergate apartments in Washington, D.C., initiated a two-year investiga-

Students on campus in the 1970s.

tion, including nationally telecast Congressional hearings, followed by the indictment and conviction of several conspirators and the unprecedented resignation of the president of the United States, Richard Nixon, in August 1974. The affair hit at the heart of the American political system and shattered the nation's confidence in public officials, a condition generally assumed by the majority of the nation's citizens.

Unlike earlier periods during which Stonehill acted as if in a time warp, the events of the seventies in American culture directly influenced the College's faculty and students. Need for a new direction in the relationship between the College and its students was perceived by the administration in the wake of the tension and change of the sixties and the demise of *in loco parentis.* Dean of Students Victor Caliri, CSC, like David Arthur, Paul Duff, and other administrators earlier, recognized the need for students to take responsibility for their lives and to grow as individuals, with the appropriate guidance, challenge, and example provided by faculty, administration, and staff. The College needed to revise its role as mentor in order to build a circle of trust within the Stonehill community. Caliri warned that a new day for student affairs had arrived: "Students in general cannot accept an institution of higher learning that attempts to control through rules and regulations their appearance, their dating habits and their private lives."[2]

Student response to contemporary events and the signs of the times was more evident on the Stonehill campus in the 1970s than any previous period. The proliferation of illegal drugs, so much a sign of the 1960s counterculture, led to the generation of a drug policy and its publication in the Student Handbook. Society's call for greater freedom in personal relationships was answered by an extension of the coed living experiment started in the fall of 1971. Bartell was encouraged by the success of the trial and the "uniformly supportive reaction" he received from parents. Former rules on parietals were rescinded so that by February 1976, a policy of 24-hour parietals in O'Hara Hall on weekends was extended to the entire week.[3]

National events and their ramifications became a major source of student activism on campus. The war in Vietnam continued to be a significant catalyst to student leaders who, in the wake of the Communiversity, sought solidarity with peace advocates throughout the nation. Almost every issue of *The Summit* carried editorials critical of the war and America's involvement. On November 3, 1971, Stonehill observed a national day of protest and strike against the war. Class attendance was optional, with special activities provided in lieu of regularly scheduled events. Six months later, in support of the April 22, 1972, national protest held in Washington, D. C., many Stonehill students gathered on the quadrangle the afternoon before and heard talks by Father Bartell and Professor Richard Finnegan about the war. In May 1972 over 250 Stonehill students marched six miles from campus to downtown Brockton to protest the war's escalation. The College Council voted to support the student march "as a means of expressing [its] feeling on the recent turn of events in the Vietnamese struggle."[4] Watergate also captured the attention of the campus. One *Summit* editorial expressed the prevailing sentiment: "Richard Nixon must resign. Impeachment cannot cure the ills inflicted by the Watergate scandals; indeed impeachment proceedings could add salt to the wound."[5]

Professor Ronald Fraser and his drama students.

Campus Sports and Activities

❦

BETTER UNDERSTANDING by students of contemporary national and international issues and their more active participation in extracollege affairs did not hinder or detract from traditional campus activities, which continued to flourish. Stonehill's theater arts society, a source of pride and student involvement since 1949, continued to provide quality productions and service as it expanded operations. Professor Ronald Fraser organized and guided the fortunes of the Stonehill Theater Company. Some of the many outstanding productions of the College theater were *The Crucible, Troilus and Cressida, One Flew Over the Cuckoo's Nest, Play It Again Sam, and A Doll's House.* The Greasepaint Players also produced several successes, such as *Fiddler on the Roof, Barefoot in the Park, Hello Dolly, The Sunshine Boys,* and *South Pacific.* In 1973 the Greasepaint Players inaugurated the first of three seasons of a highly successful summer theater program. During the first year 2,700 people attended a busy six-play schedule.[6]

Stonehill's theater arts program received a special boost in the fall of 1973 when it was announced that Hemingway Auditorium would be reno-

Greasepaint Players summer 1973 announcement.

vated into a 267-seat theater. The improvement was made possible by a generous grant from Mack Truck, Inc. The renovation was designed by the architectural firm of Rich, Lang and Cote. The Hemingway Theater was opened as part of the College's twenty-fifth anniversary celebration on April 26, 1974, with a production of *Hello Dolly* performed by the Greasepaint Players.[7]

Campus radio station WSTO, another branch of theater arts, provided news, music, and information on campus events on a daily basis. Greater professionalism of personnel and higher quality of programming were two significant improvements during this period. In September 1972 the 640 KHz AM site for the channel was changed to 91.3 MHz FM. The station name was changed to WSHL in February 1974 as part of the requirement to receive a license from the Federal Communications Commission. The station began to broadcast from the College Center (described later in this chapter), and a new antenna was erected atop Donahue Hall. Greater broadcast time allowed for expanded and varied programming.[8]

Stonehill continued to welcome many national figures to campus for presentations of all kinds. Clay Shaw, linked to a conspiracy in the assassination of John F. Kennedy, spoke in September 1971. That same semester Fr. James Harney, one of "the Milwaukee Fourteen" who burned draft records, and Madlyn Murray O'Hare, the well-known advocate for the removal of prayer from the classroom, came to Stonehill. The College also welcomed Rollo May, the existentialist psychotherapist, Michael Dukakis, Sargent Shriver, and Eammon Kennedy, Irish Ambassador to the United States. In June 1972 Stonehill initiated a lecture series, "Stonehill World Forum," to educate the College community more fully on the needs of the world; Secretary of Agriculture Earl Butz, was the inaugural speaker. Commencement speakers included Theodore Hesburgh, CSC, in 1972, Stonehill's own Herbert Wessling and Vincent Wright in 1974 and 1975 respectively, and John Collins, former Mayor of Boston, in 1977.[9]

Clubs and organizations played an integral role in campus life and served as the primary source of student involvement. The 1971–1972 College catalog listed 30 clubs and societies plus numerous student activities such as debate, student government, Confraternity of Christian Doctrine, and student honor societies. The dynamic environment of the period led to the creation of new groups and the dissociation of others. The Ames Society and Reachout were two service organizations born in the wake of the loss of the Donataire Society and Purple Key. Clubs and organizations expanded their efforts as students began to look beyond Stonehill and become more conscious of the general needs of society. Three honor societies, Phi Alpha Theta (history), Sigma Theta (science and math), and Delta Mu Delta (business) recognized student academic achievement.[10]

College publications provided a forum for personal student expression and the reporting of campus news and events. The *Cairn* published original essays, poems, and short articles by students. *The Summit* became more than a campus newspaper reporting sports, club activities, and plans for new academic programs and buildings. In the 1970s, student editors, under the watchful eye of faculty advisor Harry Eichorn, CSC, expanded its focus to cover significant national and international issues and events. Editorials explored this wider range while not neglecting important issues that touched the daily lives of the Stonehill community. The paper also presented in-depth reporting of the controversial events causing division on campus, especially the tenure quota debate and confrontations in governance and foreign languages. The paper became more free-form, allowing it to diverge at times from its normal format. Certain *Summit* issues were dedicated to contemporary topics such as human ecology, women's issues, and world hunger. In 1972 it began to publish supplements, beginning with a *Cairn* monthly addendum of photos, poems, and literary works. The seventies also featured regular faculty columns in the paper. Bartley MacPháidín, CSC, was a regular member of *The Summit* staff and wrote "A Foreign View"; James Chichetto, CSC, also made regular contributions in a column titled "At Random." Beginning in October 1973, Professor Chet Raymo combined his expertise as a scientist and writer in a regular column, "Under a Skeptical Star." The seventies also saw the genesis of the *Slummit*, a three-page satire of campus personalities and events.[11]

Sports programs continued to play a significant role in the evolution of campus life at Stonehill. As in other areas of the College, the sports program was viewed as a means to assist students in their personal development. James Dougher, director of athletics and men's basketball coach, reported to the President's Quarter Century Conference that all levels of athletics—intramurals, intercollegiate and club sports—were relevant to the College because they planted seeds of responsibility through team play that would germinate and grow in future life. Dougher believed that the intramural program was of the greatest significance, because students of all athletic levels could compete there for the pleasure of participation without the pressure of performance.[12]

While basketball, soccer, and baseball continued as the most popular men's sports, the seventies brought some changes and significant program additions. Started in the fall of 1970 and competing in the Eastern Collegiate Football Conference, the football team achieved a winning record (4–2) in its sophomore season. Football games became important fall sports events, filling a social need present since the founding of the College. During this period, intercollegiate athletic programs remained constant, but club sports grew with the addition of rugby and wrestling in the spring of 1976.[13]

Unquestionably the most significant growth in Stonehill's sports program in the 1970s was the introduction of new sports for women. This expansion was made possible when, in the fall of 1970, women's sports were placed under the sanction of the NCAA. In the spring of 1975 women's varsity softball came to campus. One year later club volleyball was introduced, with varsity and junior varsity teams in action by the fall of 1977.[14]

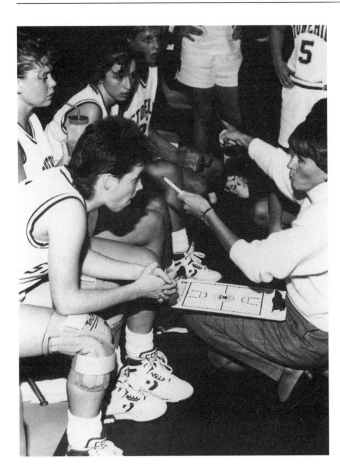

Coach Paula Sullivan instructs her players.

Women's basketball was reintroduced in the fall of 1971. An informal poll taken on campus showed great interest in resurrecting the women's program that had been started in 1959 under the direction of Virginia Yosgandes, dean of women, but was dropped in 1963. The favorable response led organizers of the effort to gather information from neighboring colleges about pitfalls and obstacles to avoid in reinstituting the program. An organizational meeting held in October drew 35 aspirants, from whom a team was chosen. When the Athletic Department informed the organizers that a new intercollegiate program could not be supported financially, a club team was started. Funds for operation were raised through raffles, a beer mixer, and donations. Enthusiasm was high as club officers and faculty worked together to schedule contests for the first season. Games were scheduled with Emerson, Boston College, Emmanuel, Jackson College, and Barrington. The team's first game was a victory over Brandeis on December 7, 1971. Dean of Students, John Heslin, coached the team for its first seven games. Paula Sullivan, former standout at Bridgewater State, guided the team the remainder of the season to an impressive 14–0 record.[15]

Expansion of Facilities

❧   STONEHILL'S EXPANSION of extracurricular programs and the aging of existing buildings necessitated the construction of new facilities on campus. Bartell's vision that Stonehill must become more attractive to commuters dictated the direction of the College's physical expansion in the seventies. With enrollment having reached a fairly constant level,[16] Bartell turned his attention away from dormitories to facilities that enhanced other aspects of student life.

The original student union and cafeteria was constructed in 1959 under the watchful eyes of Presidents James Sheehan and Richard Sullivan. From the time of construction, the facility was plagued by the College's penchant for underbuilding. Thus, in 1963 the facility was expanded to meet the need of a burgeoning enrollment. In the spring of 1971 the planning committee of the Board of Advisors suggested the need for a second expansion of the dining hall in anticipation of an additional 1000 students in the near future. The project received necessary approvals, and construction began in October 1971. The addition was completed the following February.[17]

Stonehill's usual tendency to underbuild was most obvious in its meager athletic facilities. When the College opened in 1948, the indoor pool and tennis court adjacent to the Ames mansion (now Donahue Hall) doubled as a classroom and, after some modifications, a basketball court. For more than 20 years the basketball team played its home games at local gymnasiums, principally the Brockton Armory, Oliver Ames High School in Easton, and West Junior High School in Brockton. As the College entered its second quarter century, the need for a modern athletic facility was readily apparent.

Plans for the construction of a physical education building were first entertained by John Corr. The president engaged W. Chester Browne, architect for Boland Hall, to sketch preliminary drawings for a building dedicated to intramural, club, and intercollegiate sports. The original plan was expanded in a contract signed with the Robert A. Green architectural firm that called for the design of a building to double as a gymnasium and dining facility. By November 1969 the plan called for a three-floor building housing a dining commons, full gymnasium with bleachers for 1200, and a recre-

College Center.

ational sports facility consisting of two auxiliary gymnasiums and two hand-ball courts.[18]

The proposed College Center became the centerpiece of Phase I of the Development for the Seventies campaign. Bartell was aware of his predecessor's earlier design investigation, and he decided that the time had come for a general recreational facility "even if it requires me to get out there with a pick and shovel." The ongoing development drive advertised the College Center in brochures and flyers seeking $2.5 million for its construction. Although this sum had not been raised at the time, Walter Mullen, director of development, suggested that construction begin before the target amount was raised, arguing that the building, once it began to take shape, would spur more contributions. The College Center's function required clear definition before construction could begin. The dining commons component of the facility was omitted when it was decided to expand the existing cafeteria. Additionally, the Board of Advisors recommended that the structure be capable of meeting long-range needs and that its design be consistent with the existing layout of the campus.[19]

Stonehill College twenty-fifth anniversary program.

THE PRESIDENT'S DINNER

honoring
STONEHILL COLLEGE
and its
TWENTY-FIFTH ANNIVERSARY

THURSDAY
MAY 31, 1973
7 O'CLOCK
THE LOWER CAMPUS

Ground-breaking for the College Center was held on June 14, 1972. Construction of the building, designed by the firm of Rich, Lang, and Cote, proceeded smoothly. The $1.3-million facility was dedicated on October 12, 1973, as part of Stonehill's twenty-fifth anniversary celebration. Michael Novak, the distinguished writer and analyst of the American Catholic Church and a 1956 graduate of Stonehill, delivered a speech, and Daniel Cronin, Bishop of Fall River, blessed the building.[20]

Campus ministry at Stonehill College was refashioned with the arrival of John McCarthy, CSC, in 1964 as the first priest assigned full time to this apostolate. McCarthy energetically expanded religious offerings to meet the needs of students in the post-Vatican II era. Programs such as a pre-Cana marriage preparation and Confirmation classes were initiated. Together with John Gerber, CSC, McCarthy offered a series of regularly scheduled (once or twice per month) conversations and discussions with faculty members called "The Knowledge and Experience of God." The campus ministry program also sponsored off-campus retreats, days and evenings of recollection, a lecture series, and campus-wide activities such as the observation of a one-day fast in support of Oxfam International.[21]

In the summer of 1975 McCarthy called for greater recognition of the work of campus ministry and more prominent status within the hierarchy of the College community. He suggested that the director of campus ministry be so placed in the governance structure as to be of assistance in all sectors of campus life. Echoing the traditional twofold understanding of Catholic education, he commented: "We feel that the nature of the academic enterprise and the apostolate of campus ministry requires that campus ministry be a central and integral element of Stonehill's Catholic character."[22] In December 1975 McCarthy invited a team of consultants to visit campus and review the campus ministry program. A report of the visit listed strengths and weaknesses and recommended that a team concept be brought to the program. This suggestion was implemented the ensuing summer when the provincial, William Ribando, CSC, assigned Ken Silvia, CSC, as the new director of campus ministry, with McCarthy and Richard Segreve, CSC, as assistant chaplains.[23]

Growth of the campus ministry program and the need to provide a permanent place of worship on campus led to the call for construction of a College chapel. The inadequacy of the Duffy basement chapel and office of campus ministry was recognized by the College Council in the spring of 1967. Nothing was done, however, until McCarthy approached Bartell and other members of the Holy Cross Community about the need to construct a chapel. McCarthy petitioned Walter Mullen, director of development, and the College treasurer, Edward Casieri, to make a new chapel a top priority in future fundraising and budget plans:[24]

> With the increased resident population of the College and the on-going effort to provide more adequately for the personal and communitarian needs of students, it would seem appropriate for us at this time to consider the construction of a visible, attractive and adequate chapel and religious center.

McCarthy argued that a chapel was needed to provide a religious presence on campus and to make religious exercises and spiritual counseling more

Rev. Thomas Feeley, CSC.

available.[25] The drive to build a chapel was boosted greatly with the reception of two generous donations of $100,000, each in the fall of 1974.[26]

At the direction of Bartell, a committee was formed in the fall of 1974 to investigate the feasibility of constructing a chapel on campus. The committee, chaired by Robert Kruse, CSC, first met in October to discuss three issues: housing diverse interests under one roof, chapel location, and building size. While campus ministry renewed its call for the facility, objections were raised on several fronts. The College Council was disappointed that planning had proceeded with little or no input from the various College governance committees. A student survey was generally negative in its reaction to the proposal. The Stonehill Alumni Association also objected on the grounds that needs such as faculty salaries, better science facilities, and improved student publications were higher priorities.[27]

After a year of meetings to investigate options, the committee in the fall of 1975 began preparation of a firm proposal for review by the College's administration. Citing too many commitments, Kruse resigned as chair, and the reins of the committee were given to Thomas Feeley, CSC. That fall a preliminary design offered by Willoughby Marshall, who had been retained for the project, was rejected by the committee, citing impractical plans, misleading cost estimates, careless drawings, and poor communication with

Chapel of Mary.

Stonehill officials. The committee also unanimously voted to rescind the contract to Marshall. The Austin Company of Whitman, Massachusetts, was then retained and immediately began to develop a new design.[28]

The chapel planning committee's final report recommended the construction of a chapel and human resources center. The addition of the human resources center, a major addition to the original plan, was promoted by Bartell, who believed that the joining of counseling services with campus ministry "will add a strong moral dimension to the full program [of] student services and will provide a Catholic environment for counseling, career planning and the like."[29] The committee agreed that the facility should serve as a place for the relief of soul, mind, and body. The report recommended that the chapel be built to accommodate 200, be located at the south end of the quadrangle, and provide private offices, common space, and living quarters for chaplains. Offices for counseling, career planning, and placement services, as well as space for an infirmary, were also designated.[30]

Institute of Justice and Peace bulletin.

Dorothy Day speaks on campus.

The chapel and human resources complex was constructed as part of Phase II of the Development for the Seventies drive for a complete cost of $660,000. Ground-breaking took place on May 20, 1977, and the building was completed 17 months later. The Chapel of Mary was blessed by Bishop Cronin on September 29, 1978.

Special Programs for Students

ERNEST BARTELL was appointed president of Stonehill on the eve of the College's twenty-fifth anniversary. The Quarter Century Conference of November 1971 provided an updated picture of all facets of the College as its first milestone of longevity approached. The formal celebration of Stonehill's silver anniversary began in the fall of 1973. The Founder's Day dedication of the College Center on October 12 was the first event. That same month Bartell announced the establishment of the Arnold B. Tofias Industrial Archives "to collect, maintain, and exhibit materials related to the economic and industrial history of the region." An extensive collection of shovels manufactured by the Ames Shovel Works in Easton was the central attraction of the new archives.[31] Additional celebratory events included lectures by Drs. Rachel Dunne and Rollo May, the aforementioned dedication of Hemingway Theater with a production of *Hello Dolly,* a faculty panel discussion on Catholic higher education, and performances of chamber music as part of the College Center Series.[32]

In the fall of 1973 the Institute of Justice and Peace, under the auspices of the Department of Religious Studies, was established at Stonehill "to provide an agency on campus to do as much as this College can do to further the concepts behind this intensely developing global yearning." Intended as a permanent forum for discussing the religious implications of justice and peace, the institute was founded and directed by Bartley MacPháidín, CSC, who relinquished control to Thomas Feeley, CSC, after one year. Under the institute's sponsorship, many well-known social reform advocates spoke at Stonehill, including Robert Coles, M.D., from Harvard; Frances Lee McGillicuddy, who asked the question, "How can you be Christian without being a feminist?"; and Dorothy Day, the avowed pacifist and founder of the Catholic Worker Movement.[33] Discussions and symposia on bioethics, the responsibility of science, and liturgy and life were additional highlights of the institute's offerings.

The absence of minority students and minority programs was addressed by Stonehill's administration during this period. In November 1971 black students and several members of the administration met to discuss student issues. The students called for more aggressive recruitment of blacks to the College, a student union for blacks, and the opportunity to establish an all-black townehouse. *The Summit* called for full consideration of the students' demands. Bartell agreed with the need to increase recruiting efforts by offering qualified minority students financial assistance. The scholarship program developed in 1968 by David Arthur to aid black students was implemented in the fall of 1972.[34]

Affirmative action came to Stonehill in March 1976, when Bartell committed the College "to a policy of non-discrimination in the educational programs and activities which it operates, and of equal opportunity for employment therein." David Arthur, appointed affirmative action officer, was charged to assure the College's compliance with civil rights and equal employment opportunities for all, act as an advocate for women and minorities, and review the College's adherence to government directives and policies with respect to discrimination.

The program of continuing education, in place at Stonehill since 1951, was reorganized and greatly expanded during the decade of the 1970s. Despite the insistence of John Weihrer, CSC, that continuing education must serve the broader needs of individuals, special groups, and the general community,[35] the credit Evening Division (which served only one need in the community) began to dominate the attention of Stonehill's administrators.

Disagreement over the direction of continuing education, coupled with personality conflicts, led to Weihrer's resignation as director of continuing education in April 1972. C. James Cleary was appointed as his replacement.[36]

The leadership change in continuing education was the catalyst for reorganization of the program. The academic dean, Edmund Haughey, appointed Robert Hardina of the Department of Religious Studies as director of the Program of Summer Institutes, thus dividing responsibilities in the continuing education program. Haughey gave the new director the mandate to "find and develop new ways to make the facilities of the College available to new clientele during the summer."[37] Two years later, however, the responsibilities of summer institutes and continuing education were again reunited under the new title, Conference and Institutes Division, with Hardina as director. Programs in five major categories were offered: residential summer recreational and academic programs, professionally oriented noncredit courses, government-funded programs, community service, and graduate workshops.[38]

The academic dean's concern over the administration of Evening Division, Continuing Education, and the Conferences and Institutes Division brought another reorganization to these programs. Horn's belief that more centralized control was necessary led, in the spring of 1977, to creation of the Division of Continuing Education as an umbrella for the three separate programs.[39] Leo O'Hara was appointed assistant dean for continuing education. The objectives of the new division were to extend higher educational opportunities to those not being served by the day program, to link the College and the outside community, to create a learning environment conducive to the needs of part-time students, and to integrate continuing education's goals and activities with the overall mission of the College.[40]

Holy Cross Seminary, built in stages to house a burgeoning seminarian population in the 1950s, had become a white elephant for the Holy Cross Community by the late 1960s, when vocations to religious life plummeted. In 1969 John Corr began discussions with Provincial Richard Sullivan on possible use of the facility as a College dormitory. The Holy Cross Community offered rooms to students as a form of assistance to the College and as a source of money to help pay the existing seminary debt. Corr decided, however, not to accept the offer, because Stonehill students would be forced to accept the rules of the house and thus sacrifice parietals.[41] At the 1970 Eastern Provincial Chapter, two proposals for the use of Holy Cross Seminary were examined. One plan suggested the building be used to house all Holy Cross religious, the Stonehill Community, the mission band, and retired and semi-retired religious as well as local chaplains. A second proposal,

Rev. William Braun, CSC.

calling for a committee to study the feasibility of converting the seminary into a "Center of Christian Community" was adopted by the chapter.[42]

The Chapter decree set in motion the establishment of an experimental Christian community at the seminary. William Braun, CSC, who had served as rector of the seminary since 1968, invited interested students to Holy Cross Center "in an attempt to create a more adequate community-life experience than is normally found in the dorms or the towne houses."[43] The arrangement was to be a coeducational community consisting of seminarians, students, priests, and laity not affiliated with Stonehill but interested in the concept of Christian community. The proposal was based on the beliefs that education is an affective as well as cognitive process, that learning is most effective when concepts have experimental as well as cognitive aspects, and that a learning community is society in microcosm.[44] A refashioned Holy Cross Center welcomed 18 women and 20 men to join 30 seminarians in the fall.

The Holy Cross Center experiment in Christian living grew out of Braun's vision that a new approach to community and seminary life was necessary. The program at the center consisted of three principal means of alternative learning. All participants were members of an L (for learning) group, a cadre of 10 to 12 people who met each week with 2 members of the center's staff. The purpose of the L group was twofold: to gain better self-understanding and knowledge of others and to increase the ease and skill in communicating one's feelings. Confrontation in these sessions was promoted, both to encourage creative behavior and to discourage destructive behavior. The second element of the program was house meetings, held approximately every three weeks. Patterned after early American town meetings, they afforded a platform for anyone to express opinions, present plans, clarify goals, or resolve conflicts without the fear of authoritarian reprisal. Work teams to prepare breakfast, clean the building, and wash dishes were the final feature of the program. Liturgical celebration, recognizing the ordinary as well as the spectacular in our lives, was an overarching element of this experimental community.[45]

Braun sought greater acceptance for the community experiment and more student participants by promoting the center as an alternative learning site. In February 1972 he petitioned the Academic Committee that six credits per semester be given students who successfully completed the program.[46] Although Braun argued that academic credit was justified by the time and energy the students had to expend in the alternative living framework, some committee members objected that the depth and quality of the center experience compared unfavorably with a classroom environment.[47] The lack of a decision at the time led Braun and Sr. Suzanne Kelly, in the fall, to propose an even greater program involving a hundred students who would receive nine credits each semester for participation in a program of classroom presentations, seminars, and L-groups.[48] The center program was never, however, granted academic credit.

The center's initial success and a continuing decline in religious vocations led to a formalized agreement between the College and Holy Cross on the use of the old seminary. In February 1973 Bartell suggested that the seminary serve the dual function of housing Stonehill students and providing a place for Braun's community-living experiment. This idea was accepted, with a one-year lease negotiated for the College's use of the facility; the following summer an extended lease was approved.[49] But the formal lease agreement could not halt the slow deterioration of Braun's experimental Christian community. The introduction of many students to the center as residents, but not participants, in the experiment led to apathy on the part of those who had committed themselves to the experiment a few years earlier. Disappointed that more than half of the community no longer attended meetings or L-group sessions, Braun continued to resist vertical structures of governance, offering instead an environment where "the freedom of the individual is tempered by the rights of others and where human and Christian values are examined and practiced."[50] The changed environment at the center, coupled with Braun's exodus from Holy Cross, spelled the end of Stonehill's experiment in Christian living. Despite the program's demise, one student of the period proclaimed, "Bill Braun raised the consciousness level of all students."[51]

ENDNOTES

1. Two good summaries of peace movements in this period are: Charles Chatfield, *The American Peace Movement: Ideals and Activism* (New York: Twayne Publishers, 1992): 135–64 and Lawrence S. Wittner, *Rebels Against War: The American Peace Movement, 1933–1983* (Philadelphia: Temple University Press, 1984): 276–300.

2. Victor Caliri, CSC, "Report to the President's Quarter Century Conference," November 5, 1971, Bartell Papers, ASC.

3. Meeting Minutes of Division Heads, November 17, 1970, Haughey Papers; College Council Meeting Minutes, May 19, 1972 and February 18, 1976, College Council Papers; Ernest Bartell to Mary Alico, December 6, 1971, Bartell Papers, ASC. "Parietals" was the term applied to visitation hours by men to women's dormitories and vice-versa.

4. *The Summit* (November 11, 1971, April 27, 1972, May 18, 1972); College Council "Resolution," n.d. [Spring 1972], College Council Papers, ASC.

5. *The Summit* (February 21, 1974).

6. Kevin Spicer, CSC, "The History of the Theater at Stonehill College" (April 21, 1986), Stonehill College Papers; *Stonehill College News* (July 1974), College Relations Papers, ASC.

7. Ernest Bartell to John J. McDevitt, November 7, 1973; Bartell to Zenon C.R. Hanson, April 5, 1974, Bartell Papers; *The Summit* (April 5, 1973, April 17, 1974), ASC. Originally Mack gave the College a truck that could be leased and then eventually sold, but in July 1973 a donation of $125,000 was received. The total cost of the project was $201,633. See Walter Mullen to Bartell, July 3, 1973, Bartell Papers; Development Brochure, College Relations Papers, ASC.

8. Chris Saunders and Tom Mulvey, "From Off-White to Orange and Blue: WSHL-FM" (May 18, 1977), Student Organizations Papers; *The Summit* (February 14, 1974), ASC. A more recent summary history of WSHL is found in *Stonehill* 7(1) (Winter/Spring 1988): 12.

9. *The Summit*, various issues; Commencement Programs, 1972 through 1978, ASC.

10. Stonehill College Catalogs, 1972–1978, ASC.

11. *The Summit*, numerous issues (Fall 1971 to Spring 1978). The first issue of the *Slummit*, similar to the *Plummit* of the 1960s, was published on May 18, 1972.

12. James Dougher, "Report to the President's Quarter Century Conference," November 5, 1971, Bartell Papers, ASC.

13. *The Summit* (February 10, 1976 and May 13, 1976), ASC.

14. Meeting Minutes, Division Heads, November 3, 1970, Haughey Papers; *The Summit* (April 30, 1975, October 28, 1976, and September 5, 1977 [*sic*] October 2, 1977).

15. *The Summit* (October 7, 1971 and November 18, 1971); "Brief History of Women's Basketball," Athletic Department Papers, n.d. [1971], ASC.

16. Between 1971 and 1977 enrollment gradually rose from 1591 to 1690.

17. Meeting Minutes for the Planning Committee of the Board of Advisors, March 11, 1971, Board of Advisors Papers; *The Summit* (October 28, 1971), ASC. John Corr had first looked at the feasibility of expanding the cafeteria in August 1969. Some members of the Board of Advisors suggested that a whole new facility be built, but the idea never won approval. The large student increase anticipated by the Planning Committee did not occur.

18. W. Chester Browne to John Corr, December 8, 1966; Robert A. Green, Jr., to Bernard Currier, December 28, 1967, College Center Papers; *The Summit* (November 20, 1968), ASC.

19. Ernest Bartell to Edward M. Donovan, March 28, 1972, Bartell Papers; Meeting Minutes of Division Heads, February 2, 1971, Presidents Papers; Planning Committee of the Board of Advisors, March 11, 1971, Board of Advisors Papers, ASC.

20. *The Summit* (February 24, 1972); "The Stonehill Letter," n.d. [1972]; *Stonehill College News* (September 27, 1973), Public Affairs Papers; Ernest Bartell to Michael Novak, August 16, 1973, College Center Papers, ASC. In attendance at the dedication was Mrs. Maurice Charles, daughter-in-law to Frederick Lothrup Ames. Her presence laid the groundwork for her future donation of money, leading to the construction of the Sally Blair Ames Sports Complex. See Chapter 14 for a complete discussion of Mrs. Charles' contribution to Stonehill.

21. John McCarthy, CSC, interview with the author, July 22, 1996, Stonehill College History Project Papers; John McCarthy and John Gerber, "Campus Ministry Report," December 5, 1973, "Report of Campus Ministry," January 1977, Campus Ministry Papers; *The Summit*, (October 14, 1973), ASC.

22. Memorandum from Campus Ministry, June 1, 1975, Campus Ministry Papers, ASC.

23. "Report of Campus Ministry," January 1977; "Campus Ministry—A Brief History Through 1980," n.d., Campus Ministry Papers, ASC; John McCarthy, Richard Segreve, and Ken Silvia to William Ribando, June 4, 1976, Stonehill College Papers, AHCFE. The consultant team was Laetitia Blain and Fathers F. Stephen Macher, C.M. and James W. Moran, C.S.P.

24. John McCarthy to Walter Mullen, September 13, 1973; McCarthy to Edward Casieri, December 11, 1973, Campus Ministry Papers, ASC.

25. "Campus Ministry" to Walter Mullen, January 27, 1974, Campus Ministry Papers, ASC.

26. Walter Mullen to Thomas Feeley, CSC, September 10, 1974, Bartell Papers, ASC. Bishop Daniel Cronin of Fall River and George Carney of Brockton made the contributions.

27. College Council Meeting Minutes, September 25, 1974, College Council Papers; Final Report, "Planning Committee for the Proposed Chapel and Human Resources Complex," n.d. [May 1976]; "A Statement by Campus Ministers," October 21, 1975, Joseph Murphy to Thomas Feeley, February 17, 1975, Campus Ministry Papers; group interview, 1970s, November 19, 1996, Stonehill History Project Papers, ASC. Some students objected to locating the chapel in the main quadrangle because it would occupy recreational athletic space. Additionally, it was believed that the College already possessed several places to attend Mass—Donahue Hall, O'Hara Hall, and the basement chapel in Duffy Academic Center.

28. Robert Kruse to Planning Committee for Chapel, September 11, 1975; "Report #1 of Planning Committee for Chapel," October 22, 1975; "Report #2 of Planning Committee for Chapel," November 14, 1975, Campus Ministry Papers; Edward Casieri to Ernest Bartell, February 15, 1977, Treasurer's Papers, ASC.

29. Quoted in News Release, May 8, 1977, Public Affairs Papers, ASC.

30. Final Report of Planning Committee for the Proposed Chapel and Human Resources Complex, n.d.; Robert A. Marcantonio to Ernest Bartell, November 19, 1975 and December 13, 1976, Campus Ministry Papers, ASC.

31. *Stonehill College News* (October 17, 1973), Public Affairs Papers; Ernest Bartell to Stanley VandenHeuvel, November 29, 1973, Bartell Papers, ASC.

32. Program for Twenty-Fifth Anniversary Observance, n.d., Bartell Papers, ASC. The College Center Series was initiated by F. James Burbank, CSC, the first director of the College Center. This was a cultural program which brought musicians and artists from the Boston area to Stonehill. Performers included the Wheaton Trio, Boston Symphony Orchestra Ensemble, Greater Boston Youth Symphony, and the New England Conservatory of Music.

33. Flyer, n.d. [1973], Justice and Peace Institute Papers.

34. *The Summit* (November 18, 1971); Minutes of Meeting Between Black Students and Administration, November 10, 1971; Edmund Haughey to John Corr, March 2, 1971, Haughey Papers, ASC. In the fall of 1971 there were 14 African-American students at Stonehill. In October 1976 Bartell reported that Stonehill's minority student enrollment continued to be less than 1 percent. He was hopeful that the new association with Hyde Park High School might stimulate recruitment of black students. See "President's Board Report," October 1976, Bartell Papers, ASC.

35. John Weihrer, CSC, "Report to President's Quarter Century Conference," November 5, 1971, Bartell Papers, ASC.

36. Chapter 7 describes the formation of the Evening Division and the appoint-

ment of Peter Donahue, CSC, as dean. A disagreement between Weihrer and Dona-hue on priorities in the multiple evening programs led Bartell to remove Weihrer, who accepted a position with Family Theater. See Ernest Bartell to John Weihrer, November 18, 1971, Presidents Papers; Weihrer to Bartell, April 15, 1972, Bartell Papers, ASC. Weihrer eventually left Holy Cross and was ordained a priest in the diocese of Houston, Texas.

37. Robert Hardina to Robert Horn, November 18, 1975, Horn Papers, ASC.

38. Stonehill College News (April 19, 1974), College Relations Papers; "Institu-tional Self-Study, Division of Continuing Education, n.d. [1978–1979], Continuing Education Papers, ASC. Examples of programs offered were: residential summer program—credit summer school sessions, conferences, senior citizen programs, high school enrichment and remedial programs; government programs—English as a sec-ond language and special programs for elementary and high school teachers; com-munity service—hosting conferences for Rotary International and liturgical conferences.

39. Robert Horn to Ernest Bartell, January 28, 1976. He wrote, "My suggestion is that the best solution would be to hire a Director of Continuing Education who would be accountable for the further development of the Evening College, Confer-ences and Institutes, Summer Session and the like. My feeling is that a professional would more than pay his way through an orchestrated and carefully planned devel-opment of Continuing Education at Stonehill."

40. Leo O'Hara to Robert Horn, March 2, 1977, Horn Papers; "Institutional Self-Study of the Division of Continuing Education," n.d. [1978–1979], Continuing Education Papers, ASC.

41. Richard Sullivan to John Corr, March 3, 1969, Provincial Papers–Sullivan; Provincial Council Meeting Minutes, October 17 and 18, 1969, Provincial Council Papers, AHCFE.

42. Thomas Feeley, CSC, "A Proposal for a Holy Cross Community Center," n.d., Hogan-Provincial Papers; Provincial Chapter Decrees, June 18–July 3, 1970, Provincial Chapter Papers, AHCFE.

43. William Braun, CSC, to "Invited Students," July 1970, Holy Cross Center Papers, AHCFE.

44. "Holy Cross Center Proposal," n.d., Holy Cross Center Papers, AHCFE.

45. *The Summit* (December 6, 1972), ASC. *The Summit* ran a four-page insert in this issue which discussed Holy Cross Center exclusively. Robert Kruse, CSC, a resi-dent in the center, commented about the experiment: "The program did not always work. . . . It was unwieldy in many ways [and] very taxing. One had to have a high tolerance for disorganization, uncleanliness, for dishes undone." Robert Kruse CSC interview with the author, July 11, 1996, Stonehill History Project Papers, ASC.

46. Braun measured success as pass or fail. This was the "grading" system used in evaluating participation.

47. Academic Committee Meeting Minutes, February 23, 1972, Academic Com-mittee Papers, ASC.

48. Ibid., October 25, 1972.

49. Ernest Bartell to William Hogan, February 7, 1973, Provincial Council Papers; Contract Between Stonehill College and the Holy Cross Fathers, March 3, 1973, Holy Cross Center Papers, AHCFE. The initial agreement provided that the College pay the Provincial Administration $10,000 and an additional $10,000 to Braun as Program Director. Negotiations between Holy Cross and College for the lease of the Center were protracted when disagreements occurred. A formal lease agreement was signed on October 4, 1974. See Edward Casieri to Ernest Bartell, February 12, 1974, Holy Cross Center Papers, AHCFE.

50. William Braun to "Students Living at the Center," August 1, 1974, Holy Cross Center Papers, AHCFE.

51. Group interview 1970s, November 19, 1996, Stonehill History Project Papers, ASC.

CHAPTER 12

Charting a New Academic Direction

Academic excellence, the life blood that courses through the veins of any successful educational institution, provides colleges and universities with the sustenance necessary for students to make contributions to society. Catholic higher education in America has always promoted its twofold function of providing the best scholarship in an environment promoting Christian values. The move toward separation of colleges and universities from their parent religious communities in the late 1960s and early 1970s provided more and fuller opportunities for the achievement of this goal through the application of increased resources and greater expertise. Catholic higher education in 1970 stood ready to open a new chapter in its long history of excellence.

Any cursory review of the history of Stonehill reveals that the College's hasty and poorly planned founding directly limited the institution's initial ability to offer a wide range of academic programs and majors. Despite this weakness, the commitment and service of many Holy Cross religious and dedicated laity allowed Stonehill to offer a core curriculum in liberal arts that provided a good general education for those who immediately searched for work and sufficient background for any who sought graduate degrees. Still, until the stewardship of John Corr and the direction of David Arthur in the latter half of the 1960s, Stonehill had not achieved any significant recognition within the academic community. The 1964 through 1966 self-study, conducted in the wake of full accreditation in 1962, developed many ideas for the College's academic programs that were implemented by Arthur. Progress was made in course offerings, more and better qualified teachers were hired, and innovative programs were initiated. The late 1960s provided the base upon which the Stonehill of future decades would be built. A progressive attitude toward academic excellence became the quest of the administrators and faculty who led Stonehill into the next decade.

An Academic Bonanza

FROM STONEHILL'S EARLIEST DAYS, the academic dean had been given the task of directing the College's academic life. During the administrations of George Benaglia and Francis Boland, however, the position became almost honorary, with the president making all academic decisions and leaving the dean little responsibility and less authority. This pattern began to change in the working relationship between Stonehill's fourth president, Richard Sullivan, and Aloysius Cussen, who served as academic dean from 1960 to 1966. It was David Arthur, however, who professionalized the office when Corr's less directive leadership style gave the dean a freer hand to operate.

Arthur's resignation in 1970 brought instability to the dean's office for the next five years. Edmund Haughey was appointed interim and then permanent dean. Having served during the transition of presidents, in the fall of 1973 he announced his resignation, effective the following spring. The following February Haughey left the College, citing an attractive position at Bridgewater State College as the reason for his premature departure. Bartell quickly appointed C. James Cleary as interim dean and formed a search committee to make recommendations for Haughey's permanent successor.[1] The committee, headed by Professor Dolores Shelley of the English Department, recommended Jacquelyn Mattfeld, associate provost and dean of academic affairs at Brown University. Mattfeld initially accepted, then promptly backed out, explaining that her resignation from Brown might cause a crisis "from which a good institution might never be able to recover."[2]

Mattfeld's vacillation kept the office of dean in flux. Bartell asked Cleary to stay on as interim dean and appointed Professor Frank Ryan of the English Department as his assistant. The College Council suggested to Bartell that Shelley's committee reopen its search for a permanent dean, but both the president and the committee demurred. Shelley offered her committee's resignation, which was accepted, and Bartell announced that the candidates for the position of dean would be screened and interviewed by him and the council and that he would make the selection.[3]

The appointment of Robert Horn as academic dean in July 1975 and the resolution of the governance and foreign languages conflicts stabilized the position of dean and the College's academic affairs. Horn, like Bartell, was a seasoned professional in higher education. Educated at Notre Dame and the University of Wisconsin, where he earned a doctorate in English, Horn—on sabbatical leave as president of St. Francis College in Biddeford, Maine—shared the president's vision of moving Stonehill's academic affairs in a progressive direction. This common understanding from the College's two top administrators intensified the direction of Stonehill's academic life forged in the sixties.[4]

Horn's philosophy of education was rooted in the Catholic tradition of higher learning that began to evolve in the wake of the Second Vatican Council. In an address to the faculty evaluating Stonehill's curriculum, he stated that the elusive blend of intelligence and conscience "should be the highest aim of a Stonehill education and its most enduring outcome for our students." Horn emphasized student self-discovery, the need to learn how to learn, and the development of the whole person. He challenged faculty members to raise their efforts to new heights:[5]

> Whatever we do now, whatever we may choose to do in the future, we should do very well. Our students have a right to expect that. We should not tolerate mediocrity in any component of our educational offerings. Both the level of what is being taught and the caliber and effectiveness of those teaching it should be the source of our pride as an educational community and the solid foundations upon which our reputation is built.

Horn dared Stonehill's students to accept necessary risks of growth and change that come along the educational road.[6]

Horn believed that Stonehill had the potential to do what it wanted on the academic front. With fears of financial difficulty, confrontation, and instability having dissipated, the time was right for the College to move aggressively forward as an institution of higher learning. He called for an *ad hoc* committee of the Academic Committee to review and possibly redesign the College's General Studies Program. The dean also suggested new programs, including studio and communication arts, health services, environmental studies, special needs education, international business and language study, government service and public administration, and paralegal studies.[7]

Stonehill's faculty also became more academically progressive at this time. As mentioned earlier, a rudimentary faculty development program had been started by Professors Chet Raymo and Anne T. Carrigg. Raymo noted the need for academic innovation:

> Stonehill, at this point in its history, has no unique character. Its strengths are the strengths of the typical liberal arts college, its weaknesses the weaknesses of the typical liberal arts college. Its history and the history of its curriculum

have the appearance of an accident. Stonehill is undistinguished today because of the caution of the past.

He called for the College to break out from its "boxed" curriculum of the past by placing greater emphasis on scholarship in research and classes.[8]

The call for a new direction in the College's academic life received its first tangible response in the fall of 1971. In a decision that mirrored a national trend, the Board of Trustees voted to end the first semester before the Christmas break. This decision was followed by an upper-level curriculum revision that increased students' latitude in selecting courses. The new program required 10 courses, 8 in a major field and 2 in general studies, and 10 electives in the upper biennium.[9]

Under the direction of Bartell, Haughey, and his successors in the dean's office, Stonehill's majors program expanded greatly in the 1970s. The 1971–1972 College catalog listed 18 majors, 3 each in science and business and 12 in liberal arts. While majors in child psychology and physical science were discontinued, new majors in Asian studies, international affairs, psychology (upgraded from a program), religious studies, and physics were added. Later, American studies and finance were added; law enforcement was changed to criminal justice. The arrival of Robert Horn and his new ideas on the curriculum led to the adoption of majors in health care administration and public administration.[10]

In the spring of 1975 Bartell and Horn began discussing the possibility of a nursing program at Stonehill. The new dean was hopeful that Stonehill could move into the allied health professions of nursing home management, nuclear medicine technology, and physician assistant, but he was most enthusiastic about nursing, which he declared would be "one of the most desirable career fields we could enter."[11] A nursing program, however, would require extensive and expensive additions to both facilities and faculty. So although a health care administration major was added in the fall,[12] the only move toward a nursing program was the addition of several new courses for the benefit of Brockton Hospital's nursing students.[13]

The need for additional major programs of study was recognized by Stonehill's academic administration and instituted, but the initiation of a minors program was the move necessary to redirect the curriculum in a progressive direction.[14] Horn supported the idea of a minor area of academic concentration and recommended it to the Academic Committee for its review. The committee acted favorably on the proposal, which called for 6 courses or 18 credits. The College Council, supported by the president, adopted the initiative and it was implemented in the fall of 1976.[15]

Although Horn left the adoption of minors to the discretion of individual departments, Stonehill's academic community enthusiastically responded to this new opportunity. Twelve departments offered 17 minor programs that resurrected some areas of study and recast others. Two former majors, Asian studies and public administration, were recast as minor programs; in the wake of the 1975 language controversy, German, French, and Spanish were placed under the umbrella of a new major in modern languages. One innovative minor took the form of interdisciplinary study in communication, international studies, and Irish studies.[16]

A tradition of evaluating academic programs at Stonehill had been begun by the self-study in the wake of the 1962 accreditation report, and it was continued by the governance and foreign language evaluations in 1975. Horn's review of the College's curriculum upon assumption of his office revealed the need for a similar study in the Department of Business. The dean sought someone who could review the department's records and recommend changes and direction.[17] His search brought Dr. Ossian Mackenzie of Rutgers University to campus in February 1976 to analyze the College's business programs. Mackenzie's report noted certain problems, offered recommendations, and concluded, "The Department definitely needs assistance in a curriculum revision. A knowledgeable consultant should work with the faculty on curriculum improvement."[18]

Mackenzie's report led to a visit by Dr. Richard Weeks of the University of Rhode Island in August to meet with the faculties of business and economics, the dean, and the president. Weeks' review and interviews revealed misdirection in the department, most visibly in an overemphasis on accounting to the detriment of management. He recommended extensive revisions in majors programs, more faculty development, and improvement in computer technology, including a mandatory computer course for students majoring or minoring in business.[19] The report prompted the dean to hire Dr. Ronald Webb of Penn State University to transform the Business Department as its new chair.[20]

Stonehill's education program made notable advances during the seventies. Special student teaching programs were begun with Brockton High School and Catholic "mission" schools in Clarksdale, Mississippi, and an Indian reservation in South Dakota. Both programs were successful and candidate teachers well received. The need in Massachusetts for qualified instructors for gifted and handicapped children led Stonehill, in cooperation with Boston's District IV public schools, to recommend a master's program in special education at the College. Although Bartell was not enthusiastic about initiating a full-blown master program, he was sensitive to the state's need for teachers. The program, however, was not implemented because of its cost and outside competition for students.[21] The highlight of the period was the March 1977 visit of the team representing the National Council for Accreditating Teacher Education (NCATE). In recommending accreditation of Stonehill's education program, the team remarked, "There is [at Stonehill] an exceptionally high level of institutional pride and a warm, responsive atmosphere conducive to learning."[22]

In contrast to the 1960s, when student unrest saw the suppression of many general education[23] requirements in colleges and universities, the seventies brought calmer seas and renewed interest in general studies from both practical and philosophical perspectives. A rationale for general education called for students to receive well-rounded educations as a means to become free and responsible men and women, aware of their own dignity and worth and able to accept responsibility for the world in which they live. Review of recent graduates had found them skilled but culturally and philosophically inept. The Carnegie Foundation for the Advancement of Teaching in its 1977 report, "The Missions of the College Curriculum," described general education as "a disaster area" that "was on the defensive and losing ground." General education was perceived to be "a hodge-podge of courses, permitting students to dip into one area or another like someone attending a wine tasting festival." The report called for more direction and underscored the need "to assert the value of undergraduate education. . . ."[24]

National interest in general education, following upon David Arthur's 1968 review of Stonehill's freshman grading policy, led to a general investigation of the College's freshman academic program, which would feature the proposed general studies courses. The Academic Committee appointed three subcommittees to (1) gather information on freshman courses, including their objectives, contents, methods, and impact on students, (2) investigate high school programs to determine the preparation students receive, and (3) research freshman programs at other colleges and universities.[25] The review of freshman studies was continued by Haughey, who supported a prescribed curriculum that would maintain Stonehill's status as a Catholic institution in the liberal arts tradition.[26]

In the fall of 1971 a program of general studies was introduced at Stonehill, with requirements in five academic areas: (1) philosophy and religious studies, (2) mathematics and natural science, (3) social science, (4) literature, and (5) language, creative arts, and behavioral science. Almost immediately the program was criticized for—among other things—giving students confusing options, putting first-year students in classes with upperclassmen, and not providing survey courses. A freshmen curriculum subcommittee, formed on April 9, 1972 to review the complaints, recommended that an academic advisement program be created to head off future problems.[27]

The establishment of general studies requirements initiated the formation of a core freshmen program at Stonehill College. The initial review led to cosmetic adjustments in specific requirements that changed almost year to year. The subcommittee's recommendation of a freshmen advisement program was enacted. Horn attacked the issue of general studies from the perspective of definition. He asked all departments involved with general studies to prepare concise statements of their purpose and goals and to define classes for majors and those for freshmen. He voiced caution on interdisciplinary approaches, leaving decisions in these areas to departments and faculty.[28] The difficulty of establishing general norms was further complicated by a concurrent review of the lower biennium program as a whole.[29] Still further complications came about when some faculty members suggested that general studies courses be distributed over four years rather than concentrated in the first two years.[30]

A second attempt to develop a concrete proposal for general studies was made in the spring of 1977. The College Council suggested "that within one year's time the Academic Committee and dean formulate a concrete definition of what constitutes a General Studies Curriculum."[31] The council's directive and the lower biennium study prompted Horn to establish a task force in March once again to review general studies and make a recommendation. The task force's report, delivered in October, stressed the teaching of ideas and provided specifics on disciplines to be studied in a three-year program.[32]

Faculty reaction to the recommendation was generally negative. A poll showed more support for plans proposed by individual faculty members than the task force's recommendation.[33] In the fall of 1977, after discussions critical of the task force's plan, the Academic Committee set up its own subcommittee to seek "a common methodology, if and to the extent that such can be found, for the General Studies program." This group's report was presented in May 1978, but no agreement was reached.[34] The only aspect of the freshmen program that led to consensus was the College Council's vote in October 1975 to restore freshman grades to the cumulative grade average.[35]

Stonehill College had never offered graduate degrees or courses, even though its liberal charter allowed the granting of all degrees save medical. Graduate credit was first investigated by Robert Hardina, director of conferences and institutes, for select summer programs designed for elementary and high school teachers. Courses would be evaluated by the dean, associate dean, director of summer institutes, and department chairs to assure that standards were met. "Guidelines for Graduate Credit in Education" was published in the fall of 1975, at which time the Academic Committee approved the plan.[36]

Stonehill's academic offerings also expanded through the introduction of the Stonehill College Abroad Program (SCAP). In the fall of 1973 a junior year-abroad program was started by the French Department in Nice, France. The city was chosen because of its location, temperate climate, and access to universities. Students could attend courses given by the director in residence, staff members of the Centre Universitaire Mediterranean, or the Université de Nice. That fall 13 Stonehill juniors and their resident director, Professor Mario Giangrande, inaugurated the program, which was "designed to integrate American students into the mainstream of French language and civilization."[37] This first venture into international study lasted only one year.[38] Another short-lived effort at study abroad was Stonehill's participation in the fall of 1975 in a program offered by Notre Dame for study at the National Taiwan University. Lack of student participation caused the programs to be dropped.[39]

A successful international program, however, was started in the fall of 1978, when Stonehill entered into an agreement with University College Dublin (UCD). In the spring of 1977 Bartell, responding to a mandate from the Board of Trustees to initiate a viable, well-managed, and on-going international program, began to negotiate with officials at University College. A pilot program, "Semester in Ireland," was offered that spring. A great success, it attracted 26 Stonehill students to study Irish history, politics, and related subjects.[40] In July 1977 officials of UCD traveled to Stonehill to work out a formal agreement. The program was approved by UCD in the fall. The next year 36 students (19 from Stonehill) inaugurated the new cooperative between Stonehill and University College Dublin. Students lived with local Irish families and attended classes in Irish society, history, literature, politics, and language.[41]

In the fall of 1975 the College initiated a special cooperative with the University of Notre Dame that allowed students to study engineering. In this "3–2 plan," as it was known, a student took liberal arts and pre-engineering courses at Stonehill for three years, then transferred to Notre Dame for two years of engineering courses. The student received two degrees, a Bachelor of Arts from Stonehill and a Bachelor of Science in one of several engineering disciplines from Notre Dame.[42]

A program of nontraditional learning, seeking to personalize education,

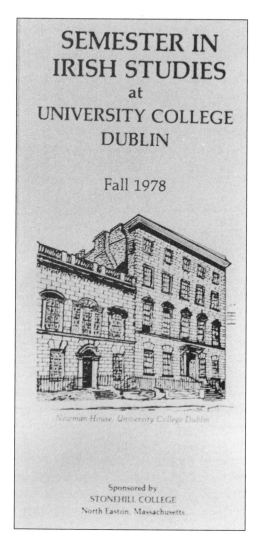

Pamphlet announcing University College Dublin, the overseas study program.

began to take form in 1972. The Academic Committee generated a future-oriented policy:[43]

> We seek to create a flexible framework geared to serve students that do not fit the traditional mold, who seek more independence, are willing to accept the responsibility for self-motivation, and wish to experiment in areas where the College does not, at present, provide legitimate academic programs.

The College recognized two general areas of nontraditional learning: work study, such as internships related to one's major, and living and learning experiences, such as the Peace Corps or VISTA. Student proposals for non-traditional credit were reviewed each semester and programs were tailored on an individual basis.[44] Academic Dean C. James Cleary was pleased with the program's first-year results: "This is an area of our general program which, if properly cultivated, holds much promise for the future."[45]

Establishment of a Reserve Officer Training Corps (ROTC) program had been part of the Stonehill dream almost from the outset. Francis Boland, a World War II Navy Chaplain, first investigated the possibility of ROTC in 1951, but the College's lack of accreditation and meager facilities doomed the effort at that time. In 1974 Bartell made overtures to the Navy to start an NROTC program, but was told that Stonehill's facilities were still inadequate. In April 1976, at the request of Bartell, Colonel John Peters, professor of military science at Northeastern University, visited Stonehill to discuss with College officials the initiation of ROTC on campus. The College Council supported the move and, in the fall of 1976, Army ROTC was first offered to freshmen and sophomores.[46]

The decade of the 1970s was one of growth and prosperity for the Evening Division. Peter Donahue, CSC, director of the Evening Division, followed the day college program as much as was practicable. He encouraged professors who taught in both divisions to teach the same courses in day and night classes. Donahue demanded that the quality of education must not suffer merely because students were mostly working adults. Rather, he aggressively promoted his "constant concern" that the Evening Division must maintain "a first-class status."[47] Concurrent with the day college, Evening Division expanded its academic programs so that, by the fall of 1978, three degrees—Bachelor of Arts, Bachelor of Science, and an Associate of Arts—and seven major fields were offered. Vigorous marketing and innovative programs kept student interest high, and by 1975 a record 591 students were enrolled.[48] Two significant program milestones in the decade were the attainment of economic self-sufficiency in its second year and the graduation of its first eight students in June 1973.[49]

Supporting the Academic Endeavor

❧   THE CUSHING-MARTIN LIBRARY was constructed to meet the College's immediate needs; future planning was not a realistic option because of economic constraints. When he assumed the office of president, it was painfully clear to Ernest Bartell that the library needed more space.[50] In January 1974 he formed a committee of faculty, students, and administrators, chaired by

Carol Fraser, director of the library 1966–1987.

the library director, Carol Fraser, to determine the College's needs and review alternative plans for expansion with architects. David Arthur, a member of the committee and former library director, outlined four specific needs: book stack area for 50,000 more volumes, reader space, staff work area, and space for user flow.[51]

The library expansion effort was launched on March 28 with a testimonial dinner at New York's Waldorf-Astoria Hotel in honor of Anthony Cascino, Chicago corporate executive and member of the Stonehill Board of Advisors, for whom the new wing was to be named.[52] Once initial design problems were corrected, construction of the Cascino wing proceeded smoothly. The project was awarded to Willoughby Marshall in March 1975. Marshall's original plan was rejected by the expansion committee because it was not sufficiently cost-effective and because library services would be severely curtailed during construction.[53] A revised plan was subsequently accepted by the committee, and construction began in August 1975. The new wing was dedicated on October 1, 1976, with Cascino and Bishop Daniel Cronin in attendance.[54]

The numerous advances in Stonehill's academic offerings during the seventies created a need for expanded support facilities. While technology had been long in evidence in business and education, Stonehill lagged in its efforts to provide the state-of-the-art equipment necessary to keep pace with

The Cushing-Martin Library after expansion.

the contemporary explosion of knowledge. Bartell reported the problem to the Board of Trustees: "Stonehill must make a greater commitment soon to computer learning if its students in many fields are not to be deprived of skills that will be considered basic to achievement in their future careers."[55] An effort to remedy this deficiency was made early in 1976 when the College made application to CAUSE (Comprehensive Assistance to Undergraduate Science Education) to secure computers and computer education for math and science laboratories.[56] Although the grant request was denied, Horn asked those who worked on the proposal to prepare a plan for a new computer facility for the College. In September 1977 the Thomas Lockary, CSC, Computer Laboratory, consisting of eight terminals, opened in Duffy Academic Center under the direction of Professor Raymond A. Pepin.[57]

Resignation and Transition

❧   IN JUNE 1977 Ernest Bartell unexpectedly resigned as president of Stonehill to become director of the Fund for the Improvement of Post Secondary Education (FIPSE), an agency of the Department of Health, Education, and Welfare. In announcing his resignation to the Board of Trustees he wrote, "I leave Stonehill with great reluctance."[58] Bartell's announcement brought

Bust of Cardinal Richard Cushing in the library.

forth plaudits from many fronts. In praising his fiscal expertise and restructuring of College governance, the board called him a "champion for the standard of excellence." C. James Cleary thanked him for instilling new confidence and pride in the College.[59] Bartell's presidency raised conflict with individuals and groups in the Stonehill community, but his vision of Catholic higher education in the post-Vatican II era placed Stonehill on a path and in a direction from which it has not deviated. One faculty member summarized his contribution:[60]

> President Bartell changed the role of the president of Stonehill from that of a person focusing inward on Stonehill to that of a person focusing outward toward the world. The worlds of government, business and higher education were the arenas that Ernie could engage and engaged well. To the degree that he was a recognized professional in higher education he was a symbol of Stonehill and thus Stonehill was recognized in fora much broader than in the past.

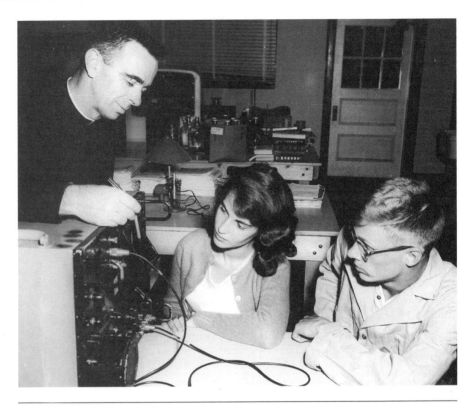

Rev. Thomas Lockary, CSC, with students in the laboratory.

Upon Bartell's resignation, C. James Cleary was named interim president, and the Board of Trustees swiftly set up a presidential search committee, chaired by the Provincial William Ribando, CSC.[61] Cleary felt that during this period of transition, his role was to hold things together until Bartell's permanent replacement was chosen.[62] The committee selected Bartley MacPháidín to be the eighth president of Stonehill College, effective February 1, 1978.[63]

*   *   *

The renewed spirit in American Catholic higher education in the 1970s was directed at Stonehill by a president who possessed new ideas and an energetic attitude. Ernest Bartell brought enthusiasm and expertise as a professional educator to his work, but his ideas and methods at times conflicted greatly with established policies, personnel, and the recent history of a less directive style in the office of president. Internal disagreements between Bar-

C. *James Cleary, interim president*
1977 and academic dean 1973–1975.

tell and members of the faculty on governance, tenure quotas, and foreign languages overshadowed his significant accomplishments in fostering Stonehill's academic programs and enhancing the College's reputation in Southeastern Massachusetts and beyond. Vision was necessary to lead the College as it entered a new era in its history following canonical alienation from the Congregation of Holy Cross. Ernest Bartell provided the vision and the leadership. As one man who lived the history stated, "I think Ernie Bartell's era was absolutely indispensable to the success story which is Stonehill today."[64] The foundations of that success story were in place; its construction was imminent.

ENDNOTES

1. *The Summit* (November 1, 1973, February 7, 1974), ASC.

2. "Campus Intercom," Stonehill College, May 24, 1974; Jacquelyn Mattfeld to Ernest Bartell, August 2, 1974, Bartell Papers, ASC. Stonehill officials in late May 1974 announced Mattfeld's appointment as dean, but by early August she had backed out. She remained at Brown with the title of dean of faculty and academic affairs. See Providence Sunday *Journal* (September 15, 1974).

3. Ernest Bartell to "Members of the Stonehill Faculty," n.d [August 1974]; Dolo-

res Shelley to Paul Gastonguay, September 18, 1974; College Council to Shelley, September 13, 1974; Gastonguay to Bartell, September 27, 1974, Bartell Papers, ASC.

4. *Stonehill College News* (March 10, 1975), Horn Papers, ASC.

5. Robert Horn, "Reexamining the Stonehill Curriculum," September 10, 1975, Faculty Assembly Papers, ASC.

6. *The Summit* (September 16, 1975), ASC.

7. Robert Horn, "Reexamining the Stonehill Curriculum," September 10, 1975, Faculty Assembly Papers, ASC.

8. Chet Raymo, "Notes on the Curriculum," n.d., Bartell Papers, ASC. No faculty reaction to Raymo's statement could be located. Related to faculty development was the initiation of a short-lived AAUP chapter. Raymo, James Kenneally, and C. James Cleary had helped organize and lead this organization between 1967 and 1969. The organization was not popular with faculty and thus died away in short order.

9. *Stonehill College News*, n.d [Fall 1971], Public Affairs Papers; Edmund Haughey, "Report of Academic Dean," Fall 1972, Haughey Papers, ASC.

10. Stonehill College Catalogs, 1971 to 1977, ASC.

11. Robert Horn to Ernest Bartell, May 19, 1975, Horn Papers, ASC.

12. Ibid., March 22, 1976. Horn believed that adoption of a health care administration major would demonstrate Stonehill's "commitment to a value-conscious liberal arts education."

13. Paul Gastonguay, "Summary Statement—Brockton Hospital and Stonehill College," February 24, 1977, Horn Papers, ASC. The College negotiated with Brockton Hospital officials on the feasibility of granting undergraduate credit for classes taken at Stonehill for the hospital's School of Nursing students. The program was to be implemented between the fall of 1977 and the fall of 1978. No formal agreement was reached at that time.

14. Robert Horn, "Annual Report," June 30, 1976, Horn Papers, ASC. The dean reported that the idea to start a minors program came from student representatives on the Academic Committee.

15. Robert Horn, "Something to Bear in Mind in Considering a Minor," n.d.; Horn to Ernest Bartell, March 1, 1976, Horn Papers; College Council Meeting Minutes, March 3, 1976, College Council Papers, ASC.

16. Stonehill College Catalogs, 1975–1978, ASC.

17. Robert Horn to William K. Laidlaw, Jr., December 31, 1975, Horn Papers, ASC.

18. "The Business Administration Program at Stonehill College," n.d. [spring 1976], Horn Papers, ASC. Mackenzie noted two problems: (1) not a single Ph.D or D.BA. in the department and (2) need for three additional faculty members to reduce present student/teacher ratio in the department of 135 to 1.

19. Richard Weeks, Consultation Report, Business Administration Curriculum, Stonehill College, n.d. [August 1976], Horn Papers, ASC.

20. Robert Horn to John Collins, "The New Business Chairman," n.d. [Fall 1976], Horn Papers, ASC.

21. Albert C. Ciri to Ernest Bartell, March 21, 1973; Bartell to Sr. Joan McVeigh, O.P., February 24, 1975; Ruth K. Connaughton to Ciri, September 30, 1975; Bartell to Ciri, October 8, 1975, Bartell Papers, ASC.

22. Robert Horn to Rolf W. Larson, April 20, 1977, Dean's Papers; Horn, "Annual Report," n.d. [June 1977], Horn Papers, ASC.

23. Edward B. Fiske, "Concept of a 'General Education' Is Reversed on College Campuses," *New York Times* (October 26, 1976). The concept of general education developed in the 1940s under such figures as Robert Maynard Hutchins at the University of Chicago, who maintained that a certain "core" of knowledge should be mastered for one to become an educated person. In the 1950s this idea was practiced by exposure to a variety of academic disciplines. The student revolution of the 1960s made many of these requirements no longer tenable.

24. "The Missions of the College Curriculum," n.d. [Fall 1977], Carnegie Foundation for the Advancement of Teaching. Several timely essays reported the demise of general education and the need in the 1970s for reinstitution of many requirements lost in the shuffle of the tumultuous 1960s. See Malcolm G. Scully, "General Education: 'A Disaster Area,' " *The Chronicle of Higher Education* (December 19, 1977); Gene I. Maeroff. "General Studies Under Scrutiny as Students Seek Relevant Courses," *New York Times* (December 14, 1977).

25. David Arthur to "Faculty," October 21, 1969, Arthur Papers, ASC.

26. Edmund Haughey to "Stonehill Community," March 2, 1971, Haughey Papers, ASC. In practice, the maintenance of a Catholic liberal arts tradition meant courses in theology, philosophy, literature, math or science, Western civilization, and a creative course in writing, speech, art or drama. Lastly, a course in social or behavioral science was integral.

27. "Report of Freshmen Curriculum Subcommittee," December 1974, Horn Papers, ASC.

28. "Report of *Ad Hoc* Subcommittee on General Studies," November 17, 1975, Horn Papers; C. James Cleary, "Annual Report of Acting Academic Dean," June 1975, Cleary–Dean Papers, ASC. Cleary had recommended that certain freshmen, with the consent of their academic advisor and the dean, be allowed to tailor programs for a particular chosen career. These students would be granted an exemption from general studies requirements. This policy was opposed by Horn.

29. Robert Horn to Ernest Bartell, January 24, 1977, Horn Papers; College Council Meeting Minutes, February 2, 1977, College Council Papers, ASC. Horn was working with the Academic Committee on requirements for the lower biennium, but no plan seemed satisfactory to all. This complicated the general studies debate.

30. Academic Committee Meeting Minutes, November 17, 1976, Academic Committee Papers, ASC. Robert Kruse, chairman of religious studies, was one who suggested that general studies should be spread over four years.

31. "The General Studies Program—Rationale," n.d. [1977], Horn Papers; College Council Meeting Minutes, February 9, 1977, College Council Papers, ASC.

32. Robert Horn, Memorandum, February 28, 1977; Horn to Ernest Bartell, April 7, 1977; Horn to "Faculty Member," October 4, 1977, Horn Papers; Academic Committee Meeting Minutes, October 19, 1977, Academic Committee Papers, ASC. The task force consisted of 12 faculty members, 3 students, and 3 administrators.

33. Robert Reordan, memorandum, October 28, 1977, Horn Papers, ASC. Reordan and Ronald Webb each submitted plans for general studies. Reordan's informal poll put his plan and that of Webb ahead of the task force proposal.

34. Academic Committee Meeting Minutes, November 3, 1977, November 9, 1977, November 16, 1977, April 26, 1978, and May 5, 1978, Academic Committee Papers, ASC.

35. David Arthur had eliminated freshmen grades from the cumulative average in 1968 because he believed that pressures of beginning college ill-effected performance and lowered grade averages. He felt this was not a true picture of a student's overall efforts. The decision to return freshmen grades to the cumulative average was out of concern for grade inflation. It was hoped that addition of freshmen marks would lower cumulative averages which were, in the opinion of the Board of Trustees, artificially high. See C. James Cleary, "Annual Report of Acting Academic Dean," June 1975, Cleary–Dean Papers; Cleary to Ernest Bartell, September 22, 1975, Bartell Papers; College Council Meeting Minutes, October 15, 1975, College Council Papers, ASC.

36. Robert Hardina, "A Proposal to Allow the Granting of Graduate Credit for Select Summer Institutes," n.d., Academic Committee Papers, ASC. A few graduate courses were started in the summer of 1974. Among the guidelines given were: (1) all courses would be designated for education and be primarily for elementary and secondary school teachers, (2) courses should not be research-oriented, (3) instructors should have terminal degrees, (4) emphasis should be on pedagogy, (5) local institutions with graduate programs should be asked if the course would be accepted by them, (6) each course should be evaluated by a graduate credit committee to assure quality and standards are kept. See also "Institutional Self-Study, Division of Continuing Education," n.d. [1978–1979], Continuing Education Papers, ASC.

37. "A Proposal to Establish a Stonehill College Junior-Year-Abroad Program," n.d. [Fall 1972]; Academic Committee Meeting Minutes, December 7, 1972, Academic Committee Papers; Stonehill College News, August 9, 1973, Public Affairs Papers, ASC.

38. Edward Casieri to Ernest Bartell, February 8, 1974, and April 26, 1974, Treasurer's Papers, ASC. The Nice program was not administered well from Stonehill. One student wrote to Bartell in disgust, "A number of us are very disappointed that the College has abandoned us." See David Franklin to Ernest Bartell, January 6, 1974, Uncatalogued Bartell Papers, ASC.

39. Charles Parnell to Robert Horn, October 1, 1975, Horn Papers, ASC. Carol D'Amato was the one Stonehill student who participated in the Taiwan program.

40. Ernest Bartell to Vincent Doyle and Joseph Malone, May 5, 1977, Deans' Papers; Robert Horn, "Annual Report," n.d. [June 1977], Horn Papers, ASC.

41. Robert Horn to Donal McCartney, August 19, 1977; Horn to Thomas Murphy, August 17, 1977; Robert Kruse to Sally Edwards, October 12, 1978, Deans' Papers; *The Summit* (December 14, 1977), ASC.

42. C. James Cleary to Joseph Hogan, September 25, 1974; Cleary to E.A. Perutti, October 7, 1974; Maryalice Moore to Cleary, n.d. [September 1974], Cleary–Dean Papers; *Stonehill College News* (January 8, 1975), Public Affairs Papers, ASC. Moore assured Cleary that the initiation of the 3–2 program would require no new courses.

43. "Stonehill College Policy on Non-Traditional Learning," n.d., Bartell Uncatalogued Material, ASC.

44. Proposals were evaluated on the basis of four questions: (1) What does the student propose to do? (2) What are the student's goals in this learning experience?, (3) How is the program to be evaluated for academic credit? (4) What faculty member will guide the project?

45. C. James Cleary, "Annual Report of Acting Academic Dean," June 1975, Cleary–Dean Papers, ASC.

46. Edward Casieri to Ernest Bartell, December 14, 1974, Treasurer's Papers; College Council Meeting Minutes, April 14, 1976, College Council Papers; John W. Peters, Memorandum, n.d. [summer 1976], Dean–Kruse Papers, ASC. Richard Lally was the first Stonehill student (fall 1977) to receive a ROTC scholarship. Lally made the military a career and returned in 1993 as Commander of the Charles River Battalion, based at Boston University, the overseer of Stonehill's ROTC program.

47. Peter Donahue, "Report to the President's Quarter Century Conference," November 5, 1971, Bartell Papers, ASC.

48. "Institutional Self-Study, Division of Continuing Education," n.d. [1978–1979], Continuing Education Papers, ASC. Some concern was present over the distribution of students in Evening Division with 82 percent enrolled in law enforcement and business administration and 18 percent in behavioral and social sciences. See "Stonehill Evening College Assessments and Recommendations," March 15, 1976, Evening College Papers, ASC.

49. "Stonehill Evening College Assessment and Recommendations," March 15, 1976, Evening College Papers, ASC.

50. Ernest Bartell to Thomas J. Bowler, December 19, 1974, Bartell Papers, ASC. He wrote, "Expanding the library is an urgent need for the College."

51. *Stonehill College News* (January 14, 1974), College Relations Papers; David Arthur to "Members of the Library Expansion Committee," n.d. [1974], Library Papers, ASC.

52. *The Summit* (February 7, 1974).

53. David Arthur, interview with the author, July 18, 1996, Stonehill History Project Papers, ASC. Willoughby's original design did not provide space for an additional 50,000 volumes. The committee wanted as little interruption as possible of

services. The first plan, which called for the removal of an exterior wall and enlargement of all windows, would curtail library services severely during construction.

54. *Stonehill College News*, n.d. [fall 1976], Public Affairs Papers, ASC. The Cascino wing added approximately 10,000 square feet of space to the building at a cost of $735,000, some $200,000 more than the original building's cost.

55. Stonehill College President's Board Report, October 1976, Bartell Papers, ASC.

56. Walter Gillespie to Maryalice Moore, June 15, 1976, Horn Papers, ASC. CAUSE was sponsored by the National Science Foundation. Stonehill asked for a $297,970 grant.

57. Ernest Bartell to Thomas Lockary, February 18, 1977, Bartell Papers; Annual Report "Thomas Lockary Computer Center," July 6, 1978, Kruse–Dean Papers, ASC.

58. Ernest Bartell to John Collins, June 7, 1977, Bartell Papers, ASC.

59. Board of Trustees Meeting Minutes, July 7, 1977, Board of Trustees Papers; C. James Cleary to Ernest Bartell, September 16, 1977, Bartell Papers, ASC.

60. Richard Finnegan to William Ribando, June 21, 1977, Provincial–Ribando Papers, AHCFE.

61. The committee was composed of representatives of students, faculty, the Board of Trustees, the Board of Advisors, and alumni.

62. C. James Cleary, interview with the author, July 16, 1996, Stonehill History Project Papers, ASC.

63. Board of Trustees Meeting Minutes, December 1, 1977, Board of Trustees Papers, ASC.

64. F. James Burbank, CSC, interview with the author, July 30, 1996, Stonehill History Project Papers, ASC.

CHAPTER 13

1978–1990

֍

Structure With Innovation—Academic Progressivism

The decade of the 1980s provided Stonehill College with many challenges, but these were turned into opportunities for advancement. Having rebounded from its internal struggles over governance and foreign languages, by 1978 the College stood poised to move forward on the academic front with a pedagogical program that combined a structured General Studies Program with innovative programs, including an expansion of international study, internships, new majors, and experimental projects. Progress and the wider outside recognition of the College, initiated through the leadership of Ernest Bartell, brought challenges in the need for new facilities, more and better-trained faculty, and expanded student programs in academics, sports, and activities. In order to support this expansion, the College required a larger and more stable economic base—one including an endowment.

As in all previous periods in Stonehill's history, the College's path was set and colored by the personalities and educational philosophies of its leaders. Bartley MacPháidín, CSC, who originally came to Stonehill in 1954 as an Irish-immigrant seminary student, returned to the faculty in 1966 and assumed the presidency in 1978. MacPháidín became, in many ways, a symbol of the College to the outside world. One graduate of the period accurately described the phenomenon: "Father MacPháidín was 'out there,' a man with the public. He told others that Stonehill was Harvard. People didn't know Stonehill, but they knew him and thus they believed the College was Harvard."[1] MacPháidín led a dedicated team of administrators and faculty who propelled the College beyond regional recognition to national renown as an undergraduate liberal arts institution.

American Catholic Higher Education in the 1980s

❧ HISTORIAN PHILIP GLEASON contends that the twentieth-century evolution of American Catholic higher education in concept and practice[2] did not change the fact that the institutional Church in the 1980s continued to voice the traditional twofold understanding of academic preparation and moral development. Pope John Paul II echoed Cardinal John Henry Newman's 1873 call[3] in promoting Catholic theological instruction and in his conviction that the institutional Church, represented by the bishops, was an active participant in the mission of higher education. In a 1979 address to presidents of Catholic colleges and universities, the Pope stated:[4]

> A Catholic university or college must make a specific contribution to the Church and to society through high quality research, in depth study of problems, and a just sense of history . . . . The goals of Catholic higher education go beyond education for production, professional competence, technological and scientific competence; they aim at the ultimate destiny of the human person, at the full justice and holiness born of truth.

In 1987 the Pope addressed leaders in American Catholic colleges and universities, emphasizing the bishops' role: "The Bishops of the Church," he proclaimed, "should be seen not as external agents but as participants in the life of the Catholic university in its role as protagonist in the encounter between faith and science and between revealed truth and culture."[5]

The United States Catholic bishops in 1976 outlined the role of Catholic colleges and universities as part of the Church's general mission to educate. Along rather traditional lines, the bishops described a threefold purpose of Catholic education: (1) to teach doctrine as the message of hope contained in the Gospels, (2) to build Christian community, and (3) to provide service to all humans. The episcopal leaders applied the post-Vatican II emphasis on social justice to education:[6]

> The success of the Church's educational mission will also be judged by how well it helps the Catholic community to see the dignity of human life with the vision of Jesus and to involve itself in the search for solutions to the pressing problems of society.

In addition to the hierarchy, American Catholic educators addressed pressing issues with higher education. The National Catholic Education Association (NCEA) listed five characteristics of American Catholic institutions of higher learning in the new era of canonical alienation:[7]

1. They are chartered as public trusts.
2. They are privately supported.
3. They sustain Catholic commitment through their institutional profession of Catholic identity.
4. They maintain a Catholic presence through departments of religion and philosophy and through Catholic administrators and faculty.
5. Their ultimate goal is to form persons who are capable of effectively undertaking their responsibilities in the Church and the world.

The association believed government support to be the most pressing need and infringement on institutional autonomy to be the greatest fear. In a 1976 position paper, the College and University Division of the NCEA declared that government "has an obligation to help," for "financial assistance of some sort is necessary [for Catholic colleges and universities] to survive." On the other hand, these educators championed institutional autonomy as imperative for survival:[8]

> Infringement on the freedom of college and university faculty to teach the results of their study and research would destroy the opportunity for the college to make its contribution to the Church. Freedom from outside constraints is the very breath of life for a college and university. An authentic Catholic institution of higher learning must be free to be Catholic.

University educators independently confronted the issue of the relationship of the Church and higher education. William Byron, SJ, president of The Catholic University of America, noted that rising costs, diminishing numbers of religious and priest educators, and changing values in American family life created new apostolic challenges for Catholic institutions of higher learning. He suggested that this new environment, coupled with greater national acceptance for Catholics and the Church's new recognition of cultural pluralism, called colleges and universities to a new role marked by openness and ecumenism, yet one that safeguarded the tradition. Father Richard McBrien, chairman of the Theology Department at the University of Notre Dame, referenced the famous book by Avery Dulles, SJ, *Models of the Church*,[9] in an essay arguing that the only way for the Church and higher education to be fully integrated was for colleges and universities to be vehicles of sacrament, service, and collegiality to the world. Contemporary challenges, according to McBrien, could best be met by allowing the university to serve uninhibited as a place of intellectual research and dialogue.[10] Another educator placed a heavy responsibility upon faculty at Catholic institutions for the future welfare of the Church: "Only Catholic educators possess the skills and professional competence to address this major problem of reclaiming and refurbishing the spiritual authority of the faith."[11]

Church educators also debated the role of Catholic institutions of higher learning in American society. More progressive-minded educators expressed the need for Catholic higher education to redefine itself in the environment created in the wake of Vatican II, canonical alienation, and the less-traditional outlook held by many members of the Faith. Educators promoted the idea that the main issue was not the Catholic university's abstract identity but, rather, understanding the identity of a pluralistic world and the relationship of Catholic education to contemporary society. As one educator put it, "The task of the university is the mediation of culture to the Church and the Church to culture."[12]

While the progressive view was most popular, conservative voices proclaimed their fears that Catholic higher education was going in the wrong direction. Traditional educators believed that progressive thinkers were misguided in their belief that the tradition of the Church in some way impeded intellectual dialogue. Absolute autonomy from the institutional Church and the demand of academic freedom only alienated colleges and universities from their parent body. One writer lamented, "How can any legitimate child of the Church . . . be separated from her embrace, be it an individual believer or a body of believers, even an institution of higher learning?" Traditionalists were also concerned about "specialization against universal knowledge, [a] preference for technology over culture, for freedom and discovery over transmission of acquired wisdom and the eternal verities."[13] The theologian James Burtchaell, CSC, feared that the direction of Catholic education was toward secularization.[14]

The specific issue of academic freedom was also widely debated in the eighties. Pope John Paul II held that academic freedom was contingent on truth:

> In the academic context, the respect for persons which pluralism rightly envisions does not justify the view that ultimate questions about human life and destiny have no final answers or that all beliefs are of equal value, provided that none is asserted as absolutely true and normative. Truth is not served in this way.

For the Pope, the truth of the faith is maintained by adherence to "the ecclesial context of Catholic theology," which provides "a special character" to higher education.[15] The National Conference of Catholic Bishops (NCCB) was more open in its position but concluded, "Commitment to the Gospel and the teachings and heritage of the Church provide the inspiration and enrichment that make a college fully Catholic."[16]

The position of the Pope on academic freedom was supported by only a minority of educators. One such writer believed that academic freedom was best expressed by a teacher's ability to develop in students "an enlightened and responsible sense of freedom." The Jesuit historian Edward Berbusse argued that certain limits to academic freedom were necessary:[17]

> Since the Church must have a guiding role in relation to all matters of faith taught and practiced in Catholic colleges, the college has a right to require of its professors—in the areas where faith is involved—a loyalty to the college's reason for existence.

However, the preponderance of opinion on this issue supported a more progressive stance. Theodore Hesburgh, CSC, claimed "that a Christian university is worthless in our day unless it conveys to all who study within it a deep sense of the dignity of the human person." However, such a belief did not change his conviction that academic freedom is "essential to the whole [Catholic higher education] enterprise." Other educators voiced the need for "a personal synthesis of faith and culture."[18] Thomas Oddo, CSC, president of the University of Portland, expressed a balanced conviction held by many Catholic educators:[19]

> We can, and must, do both—stand for a Catholic tradition, teach and promote a way of life and Christian values within our Catholic university communities, and yet assure that every idea can be pursued, every perspective considered with the care and the sensitivity that lets education flourish.

A New College Administration

WITHIN THE FRAMEWORK of Catholic higher education's struggle for self-definition and its continuing debates on institutional autonomy and academic freedom, Stonehill welcomed a new president and dean, whose collective influence would color the College's next twenty years. The resignation of Ernest Bartell in the summer of 1977 prompted William Ribando, CSC, provincial of the Eastern Province of Holy Cross, to form a presidential search committee consisting of trustees, advisors, faculty, one alumnus, and a student. Referencing the College's progress in the seventies, Professor Richard Finnegan recommended to Ribando, the committee chair: "Stonehill, I think, would be better served in the long run if the new president were to be in the same 'model' as Ernie Bartell."[20] The search committee selected three finalists, and the trustees selected Bartley MacPháidín, CSC.

MacPháidín was the first Stonehill graduate to assume the post of president. Returning to the College in 1966 as a member of the Theology Department, MacPháidín's expertise, enlightened pedagogy, and personality made him influential in College affairs from the outset. He was a popular teacher, founded the Institute of Justice and Peace, and was a regular columnist for *The Summit*. A gifted linguist, MacPháidín was a student of the existential philosophy of Sören Kierkegaard; he received his doctorate in theology from the Gregorian University in Rome. On May 21, 1978, he was formally inaugurated as Stonehill's eighth president by the Honorable John F. Collins, former mayor of Boston and chairman of the Board of Trustees.

From the outset MacPháidín set a course for the College that sought to balance the tradition of the Church and the need for academic excellence in all fields. He emphasized the imperative for Catholic colleges and universities to seek "cohesion and consistency between the vision of faith and the events that complete or make concrete that vision [of higher education]." Speaking of Stonehill, he insisted that the College must remain true to its religious heritage and educational mission through emphasis on philosophical and theological study, "because it is there that fundamental questions of meaning, of values, [and] of society are explicitly raised."[21]

MacPháidín outlined several significant issues faced by the College. In general he felt the challenge of delivering quality education and encouraging expansion at a time when many private colleges were in danger of closing their doors. More specifically, the new president realized the need to increase the College's endowment, maintain enrollment (while the pool of 18-year-olds was dropping), and make Stonehill better known. He further believed that a viable student aid program was necessary so that the College would appeal to middle and working class families who needed financial support for education. In an editorial, *The Summit* praised MacPháidín's openness and "concern for realistic considerations of each policy."[22]

The president almost immediately set in motion the process to review and establish new goals for the College. *The Summit* reported that "Stonehill would profit from a reexamination of its goals and mission, for the single reason that the external forces will force the College to reassess itself." A May 1979 "Statement on Goals," written by members of the College Council, outlined Stonehill's goals, with primacy remaining on the instruction of undergraduates in a four-year baccalaureate program. The statement emphasized Stonehill's commitment to quality education but also encouraged faculty "to engage in such research and scholarship as will aid their own

(Left) Rev. Bartley MacPháidín, CSC, president 1978–present.
(Right) Rev. Robert Kruse, CSC, academic dean 1978–1987

professional advancement and contribute to the quality of their teaching."
A belief in wholeness characterized the College's pedagogy:[23]

> The philosophy of education at Stonehill, while respecting the primacy of its
> educational mission, also seeks to aid the development of the student in other
> ways that complement intellectual growth. By the various supportive services
> that form part of the Student Life Division, the student is offered assistance in
> personal and social, religious and moral development.

One perceived problem immediately addressed by MacPháidín was
grade inflation.[24] *The Summit* in December 1978 reported that some graduate schools believed Stonehill's grading policy to be too lenient. The Academic Committee formed an *ad hoc* subcommittee to research the issue and
make recommendations. Guidelines for grade distribution were published
and departments were charged to "ensure that grade distributions of their
member faculty are not significantly higher than the College-wide distribution." Departments were also to implement specific strategies to correct or
adjust serious violations of the new grading policy. MacPháidín, as chair of
the College Council, adopted the new policy in May 1979.[25] Some immediate relief was experienced, but the problem persisted into the next decade.

After three years as academic dean, Robert Horn tendered his resignation and left the College in May 1978. Horn's years had been fruitful, with the establishment of the Lockary Computer Center, initiation of a faculty development program, expansion in continuing education, and assistance with the development of the University College Dublin foreign study program. A search committee formed in the fall of 1977 was unsuccessful in securing Horn's replacement. MacPháidín, after reviewing the committee's report, appointed Robert Kruse, CSC, then chair of the Department of Religious Studies, to an initial two-year term. The trustees unanimously confirmed the selection.[26]

Educated as a systematic theologian at the Gregorian University in Rome, Kruse was a progressive thinker,[27] yet one who believed in the need for balance between the academic and moral realms in Catholic education. He viewed Catholic higher education as the vehicle to foster conversation between the Church and the modern world. He promoted the idea that colleges and universities were "places where faculty and students come together to think, to examine, to reflect, to explore, and to judge." He passionately held that a liberal arts education was an attempt to satisfy a vital need for understanding the human condition, and that the Catholic college or university specifically was responsible for "locat[ing] the teaching of the Gospel at the heart of its thinking." He summarized the challenge: "The Catholic college, then, faces a demanding agenda: to prepare students for a responsible life in modern society and to do this in light of the wisdom of an ancient tradition."[28]

Kruse fearlessly proclaimed the need for Stonehill to profess and manifest its Catholic identity as an institution. He encouraged the faculty to reflect on what Catholic identity implied for the College's educational mission. On another occasion he boldly challenged the Faculty Assembly:[29]

> There seems no ready and simple answer to the question of our Catholic identity. Nevertheless, the lack of a convenient answer does not diminish the urgency and importance of the question. It is a far more weighty question for Stonehill than whether or not to introduce this or that major, whether or not to construct this or that facility. And yet, for the most part, we tend to treat the question with benign neglect.

Kruse argued that the maintenance of the College's Catholic heritage would require more dialogue between the intellectual community and the institutional Church than had occurred in the past. He contended that the development on campus of a Catholic consciousness to foster exchange between these parties should be a long-term goal of the institution.[30]

Academic Innovation and Development

WITH ITS GOALS STATEMENT in place and committed to an educational philosophy balanced between academic and moral realms, Stonehill entered into a reaccreditation review in 1979. Between October 28 and 31, a team of six educators, headed by Dr. Marie McHugh, assistant dean of the College of Arts and Sciences at Boston College, visited Stonehill. The team was generally impressed with the College's progress, citing specifically academic development and the school's concern for the personal welfare of its students. In recommending reaccreditation the evaluation report concluded: "Stonehill is a well-managed, fiscally sound college, where in every area those concerned have a good sense of the nature of the College as well as their own accomplishments and limitations."[31]

With reaccreditation completed, Kruse was free to renew previous efforts to initiate a general studies program. Although Stonehill officials had begun to discuss the concept of general studies in 1971, no agreement on the details of a program or its implementation had been reached by May 1978. In the fall of 1979, Kruse began to campaign vigorously for a curriculum of general studies, calling it "the principal task facing the Academic Division."[32] Kruse recognized that many Stonehill graduates were deficient in knowledge traditionally considered the mark of a liberal arts education because of insufficient departmental offerings. A general studies program, unified through the use of historical consciousness, methodology, and values in the construction of courses, would fill the lacunae perceived in the College's academic program. He concluded that general studies would be "the most coherent exercise in a liberal education shared by all Stonehill students."[33]

In March 1979 a program of general studies was approved by the Academic Committee and the College Council for implementation in the fall semester 1980. The "Western Heritage core," consisting of courses in religious studies, philosophy, social institutions, literature and fine arts, and a writing component was started in 1980. General studies courses in scientific inquiry and foreign culture were introduced in 1981; the quantitative techniques element followed in 1982.

The initial general studies program offerings underwent review by the Academic Committee, beginning in 1982.[34] Widespread satisfaction with the aims and elements of the policy was expressed, but problems were present with implementation. Areas of concern included the need to adjust course offerings to be more consistent with the specified goals of the program, an overabundance of courses in certain areas, and a lack of historical consciousness in pedagogy. Serious reservations were expressed with overspecialization in the area of social institutions and writing courses, where there was no means to measure a student's improvement.[35] Kruse defended the program, arguing that its effectiveness must be measured not so much on individual courses and student performance but rather on "how enduring a commitment to learning they conceive."[36]

The introduction of general studies was accompanied by the institution of a program of academic advisement. In the fall of 1978 Professor Sandra McAlister of the Biology Department was appointed to a newly created post, dean of freshmen. In her position, McAlister served as coordinator of student advisement, overseeing the orientation and evaluation of freshmen, needs of transfer students, and supervision of a learning assistance program. Maintenance of student interest and lowering freshmen attrition were the chief reasons for instituting the advisement policy. The program sought to inform students concerning academic policies and procedures, assist them in discovering their own strengths and weaknesses, help them identify specific goals, and coordinate the various resources available at Stonehill in order to satisfy their needs and aspirations. McAlister gathered volunteers among the faculty and administrators to serve as student advisors and developed an elaborate record-keeping system to ensure that students and faculty had the best information to achieve academic goals. McAlister saw the program through its formative years before returning to the classroom full time in the fall of 1985.[37]

Academic innovation at Stonehill in this decade was not limited to general education but was also present in specialized programs. In the spring of 1978 the College inaugurated domestic internships affiliated with The Washington Center for Learning Alternatives. Under the direction of Professor James Millikan, the program placed students in work-study programs with such groups as the Washington, D.C. Consumer Agency, Common Cause, the Department of Housing and Urban Development, and various Congressional offices. Interns worked 35 hours per week, kept a journal of their experiences, attended a weekly two-hour seminar, and submitted a major term paper on their experience upon returning to campus.[38]

International study, as exemplified by the University College Dublin (UCD) Program, was another example of academic innovation in the eighties. Initiated in 1978, the program was a great success. The first year 19 Stonehill students went to Ireland, taking courses in Irish history, Anglo-Irish literature, Irish politics, and contemporary Irish sociology. That fall Bartley MacPháidín led a Stonehill contingent that visited Ireland "to determine how the program is presently working out and to make plans for next year's program." The visitation team members were pleased with their observations and expressed confidence that the program would expand.[39]

(Left) Professor Sandra McAlister.
(Right) Professor Richard Finnegan.

The initial allure of the program, however, could not be sustained. By 1982 only four Stonehill students participated, raising fears for the future viability of the program. The UCD director, Richard Finnegan, advised the academic dean that student evaluations revealed that the integration of Irish and American students was poor, leaving Stonehill's participants with a feeling of alienation. However, the program rebounded in 1983 with 10 students and eventually stabilized with between 6 and 10 students annually by the end of the decade.[40] In the fall of 1996 Professor Edward McCarron became director of the UCD Program.

Stonehill's foreign study programs in general expanded and became formalized after 1982. That year, Professor Benjamin Mariante, appointed coordinator of foreign studies, declared, "There is great potential for study abroad. . . . The opportunities are virtually limitless and almost every student in every discipline is free to plan his own type of program."[41] Also in 1982, the College joined the New England/Quebec Student Exchange, a program that enabled Stonehill students to enroll in any of 10 Quebec province institutions on a full-time basis. Three years later, in 1985, the College joined in a cooperative with the American Institute for Foreign Study (AIFS), which provided Stonehill students with academic opportunities at several European institutions and professors with teaching assignments at Richmond College in London. This same year, Stonehill's International Internship Program, under the energetic direction of Associate Academic Dean, Paul Gastonguay, began with placements available in London, Dublin, Paris, Madrid, and Montreal.[42]

The introduction and demise of several academic programs during the 1980s reflected the desires of students and the need to remain competitive with local institutions of higher learning. Majors in mathematics/computer science and communication, plus a 3–2 engineering cooperative program with the University of Hartford (similar to that started with Notre Dame in 1974) were started in this decade.[43] The minors program was extremely volatile. Additions in computer information systems, theater arts, business administration, and labor relations were offset by the removal of international studies, adolescent studies, child development, and environmental studies. The Health Care Administration program was raised to department status in 1982. Technology advances were significant, including the purchase of a new College computer system and the initiation of a program to provide interest-free loans up to $4000 to faculty members for the purchase of personal computers and related software.[44]

The eighties also produced a pilot program to help meet the needs of women students. In the fall of 1981, special courses in women's studies were introduced into the newly created General Studies Program. Under the direction of Professors Barbara Estrin, Dolores Shelley, Rosemary Twomey, and Anne T. Carrigg, the program consisted of class discussions, guest lectures, and films directed toward career choices for women. The program aimed to make the educational process nonsexist by including the experience of women and connecting the classroom with the work environment. The program's rationale stated its ultimate goal as the creation of an independent Women's General Studies Program,[45] but this pilot program was never adopted.

The Learning to Learn Program, directed toward students needing assistance in developing the requisite skills for college-level academic pursuit, was started in 1985. The previous October Professor George Carey, while on sabbatical at Boston College, was introduced to Dr. Marcia Heiman, who had developed the program there. In November 1984 Heiman gave a two-day workshop at Stonehill to introduce interested faculty to her pedagogical method. In the spring of 1985 a class of 24 students, all of whom had experienced academic difficulties, enrolled in "Applications of Learning Theory." The class was favorably received by the students, who on the average raised their grade average 0.6 points in only one semester.[46]

Besides the pilot program for women's studies, the new General Studies Program was the impetus for the establishment of the Writing Center. In the fall of 1981 Father Eugene Green established the center in Duffy Academic Center as a place for students to receive assistance in their writing assignments. Green originally staffed the facility with a dozen students from his

"Pedagogy in Writing" course. In November Mary Carrigg became coordinator of the center, with faculty from the writing program as consultants. In the fall of 1988 the Writing Center moved to Stanger Hall and Patricia Fanning, a historical writer, was hired to staff the facility.[47]

Academic innovation at Stonehill College in the 1980s was also present in the Evening Division. Summer school, a branch of continuing education since its inception in 1950, increased its enrollment by 45 percent during the summer of 1978 with the addition of a second six-week session.[48] The Evening Division followed the day college in implementing the new General Studies Program in the fall of 1980. Leo O'Hara, associate academic dean for continuing education, agreed with the principles, goals, and purposes of the program, but he was concerned about its implementation because of the often nontraditional academic background of many evening students. He told Robert Kruse that requiring rigid conformity to the program might be harmful to transfer students. Additionally, he suggested that many evening students required additional support in the areas of written expression and quantitative techniques. He also informed the dean that local schools with evening divisions did not require foreign language. If Stonehill insisted on such a requirement, he believed, student recruiting might be jeopardized.[49] It was decided to maintain the same degree requirements but make admission standards more flexible.

The 1980s brought a change in leadership and an in-College review of the Evening Division. George Rogers, coordinator of the College's Hyde Park Program, was appointed director of the Evening College in September 1979, replacing Peter Donahue, CSC, who was suffering from ill health. In October 1981 an *ad hoc* committee was created by the College Academic Committee to review the Evening Division. The assessment was to be broad-based, including degree programs, governance, admissions policies, recruitment of faculty, and availability and adequacy of support services. The committee, which discovered inconsistencies between the day college and the evening college in programs and requirements, recommended the development of a strategic plan for continuing education and credit evening college consistent with that of the day school.[50]

In October 1981 MacPháidín acted on the *ad hoc* committee recommendations by creating a select committee on the Evening Division, chaired by Professor James Millikan. The committee's report in May 1982 suggested several revisions in policy and governance.[51] The recommendations, reviewed by the president and implemented by the dean, included readjustment of admission requirements for evening students, more complete integration of continuing education with the existing governance structure by adding Evening Division representatives to five different College committees[52] and to the College Council, and continuation of the same degree requirements for day and evening students.[53]

The specialized needs of Evening Division students led to the addition of degree programs during the eighties. In the fall of 1977 baccalaureate degree programs in law enforcement, business administration, health care administration, psychology, public administration, social studies, and sociology were offered. While major programs remained relatively fixed, four new minors (business administration, communications, psychology, and sociology) were added. One loss was the associate of arts degree in criminal justice, which, through the LEEP program, had been a mainstay of the Evening Division since its inception in 1970 but ceased to attract students when the government ended LEEP payments to those enrolled.

Rising from death by neglect in the mid-seventies, a baccalaureate program in nursing received significant attention in the decade of the eighties. In the spring of 1980 George Rogers recommended to Leo O'Hara that Evening Division begin a part-time bachelor's degree program in nursing to allow registered nurses the opportunity to continue their formal education, obtain a degree, and increase their career opportunities.[54] In the fall of 1982 65 students enrolled in the program. Problems with the enterprise arose almost immediately because of insufficient courses, lab space, and personnel. In 1983 Monica Adams was hired to administer the program, but problems grew and the number of students—although rising—was insufficient to make the plan viable.[55] Despite its problems, the nursing endeavor continued, and in 1986 it was raised to department status. That same fall Stonehill and Brockton Hospital entered a collaborative agreement in which the College agreed to provide science and liberal arts courses for the hospital's nursing students.[56]

The new program came to an end, however, when it was denied accreditation in October 1987. The report from the National League for Nursing concluded "that there was insufficient evidence that the established criteria [for accreditation] are being met." MacPháidín went to New York in February 1988 to attend an appeal hearing, but the earlier decision was upheld. Rather than operate an unaccredited program, it was decided in the spring of 1988 to phase out nursing over a two-year period.[57]

The noncredit wing of the Evening Division, which had provided multiple opportunities for working people since 1951, eliminated offerings that did not directly serve the goals of professional continuing education. However, new programs to meet the rapidly changing business climate were introduced. In the fall of 1981 O'Hara discontinued seven financially marginal programs but retained certificate programs in management, computer information systems, real estate, insurance, and small business.[58] A new name, "The Center for Community and Professional Education," indicated a different direction for continuing education. In the fall of 1978 the Center for Small Business was established "to offer a variety of non-credit programs designed to furnish existing and potential small businesses with essential survival and expansion skills."[59] The Conferences and Institutes Department offered new courses in effective speaking. In April 1982 the Stonehill Center for Women was begun to provide resources for the intellectual, professional, and personal growth of women, but it was short-lived, closing in September. New certificate programs in religious education, gerontology, paralegal studies, health care management, accounting, substance abuse, and management were created.[60]

Administrative Changes and Academic Continuity

ACADEMIC INNOVATION at Stonehill in the 1980s was marked by the College's first achievement of national recognition. On November 25, 1985, *U.S News & World Report*'s annual ranking of colleges and universities placed Stonehill fifth among the larger, comprehensive colleges and universities in the East. Of those so ranked, only Stonehill was founded in the twentieth century. MacPháidín used the opportunity to express his thanks to faculty, staff, students, and alumni for the efforts and support that had allowed the College to gain national recognition.[61]

Academic innovation and progress were not interrupted as the College experienced another transition in administrative leadership in 1987. The previous May Bartley MacPháidín was granted a six-month sabbatical by the Board of Trustees "for personal reasons and to study."[62] While the president visited several countries, including China, the Philippines, Italy, and his native Ireland, C. James Cleary served as interim president, a position he had held after the sudden resignation of Ernest Bartell in the summer of 1977. Six months after MacPháidín's return in the summer of 1987, Cleary retired after 39 years of dedicated service at Stonehill. One of the pioneers of Stonehill, Cleary illustrated the spirit of dedication that built the College and allowed it to gain acceptance in the academy. His legacy in the classroom and the boardroom served to inspire others to raise their own efforts to higher plateaus.

Cleary's decision to retire led to significant shifts in the College's administration. MacPháidín appointed Robert Kruse as executive vice president to fill Cleary's position. Fred Petti, professor of philosophy, agreed to serve as

Stonehill College receives first national ranking recognition. U.S. News & World Report *cover page, November 25, 1985.*

academic dean while a search committee, headed by Louis Manzo, CSC, of the Religious Studies Department, looked for a new person to head the academic division. The trustees unanimously approved these appointments.

During Petti's one-year term as dean, the College's fine arts interests—described in a 1987 report to the Board of Trustees "as a vast wasteland"—gained considerable ground. Dr. John Bishop of the State University of New York (SUNY) in Buffalo was engaged to give a two-semester course called The History of Western Art.[63] At this same time the Nakamichi Foundation Series, which brought musical concerts to campus, was started.[64]

The fall of 1987 also saw the beginnings of the Washington Education Project. In the summer of 1987 Senator Edward Kennedy (Democrat from

Professor Fred Petti, academic dean 1987–1988.

Massachusetts) called for a National Literacy Corps. Kennedy's plan was to obtain $20 million from the federal government to fund each of 800 colleges with $25,000 to establish programs for improving literacy in their region. In the Boston area four institutions—Endicott College, Boston College, Bunker Hill Community College, and Stonehill—responded to Kennedy's call. Funded privately by the Bank of Boston, Stonehill received a two-year, $25,000 grant, to be administered by the Washington Education Project, a nonprofit foundation.[65] Under the guidance of project directors Father Eugene Green and George Hagerty, six Stonehill students were sent as tutors to three Taunton elementary schools. In the spring of 1988 27 students participated in the program. The Washington Education Project lasted two years, then was replaced by the Stonehill Literacy Corps, a program in which students registered for a one-credit academic course focused on literacy and agreed to volunteer approximately 60 hours in the semester as literacy tutors for a local community agency. The Literacy Corps disbanded in 1993.[66]

The Stonehill Education Project was also launched in the fall of 1987. The program stated its purpose:[67]

> The fundamental goal of the Stonehill Education Project is to contribute to establishing a sense of educational wholeness through collaborative initiatives which link the resources of the College, area public schools, higher education, the business and political communities and others committed to improving the quality of education by making it more responsive to the developing needs of society.

Professor Rita Smith, Stonehill class of 1962 and *Time* magazine's teacher of the year in 1984, was asked to supervise the program, which provided professional and personal development for area educators. The project also investigated ways to make a teaching career more attractive to promising secondary and undergraduate students. Expanding its offerings in the next decade, the Education Project sponsored the Superintendent Center, Middle School Alliance, Catholic Educators Collaborative, North River Collaborative, and New Dimensions.[68]

Petti's one-year term ended on July 1, 1988, with the appointment of Sr. Jo-Ann Flora, SND, as academic dean. Between 1974 and 1983 Flora had served as an associate professor of linguistics at Trinity College in Washington, D.C. She then held the position of vice president and academic dean at the University of Albuquerque in New Mexico (1983–1985) and at Villa Maria College in Pennsylvania (1985–1988).[69]

Flora wasted no time in making her influence felt in the academic division. In September she ordered "a comprehensive review of the General Studies Program," citing as reasons its eight-year life to date and the forthcoming reaccreditation visit. Her goal was to examine the content, processes, and outcome of General Studies. This review led to a call for change, which continues today, in the definition and scope of the western core heritage.[70]

Flora was also the catalyst behind the Capstone project for gifted students. In May 1989 Dr. Martha Crunkleton, director of special studies at The College of the Holy Cross, met with faculty interested in developing a pilot program for seniors. Fourteen Stonehill professors attended the information session. A cadre of five faculty members developed an interdisciplinary and cross-cultural course, "Senior Seminar: Reflections of Freedom and Authority," which was offered in the spring of 1990.[71] Although the program was well received by students and faculty, it was discontinued after only one semester because of its cost.

A conflict between Flora and members of the Education Department arose shortly after she became dean. In the spring of 1989 Flora informed the department that she had decided to appoint a new chair from outside the present faculty. Although the education faculty "filed a formal grievance against the administration," President MacPháidín backed the decision of his academic dean. He appointed Fred Petti to oversee the department temporarily and encouraged the faculty to "continue to place the good of students above all else and . . . [to] carry out [their] academic obligations with the same high level of commitment [they] have consistently displayed in the past." The matter was settled in January 1990 when Robert Olivier was appointed chair of the Education Department.[72]

In 1989 Stonehill once again prepared for reaccreditation. In 1984 a five-year preliminary review had praised the College:[73]

> Stonehill seems to be firmly following its stated goals while flexibly responding to societal needs and institutional necessities. At the same time the College is fiscally stable while managing its long-term debt load. The combination of institutional stability and a firm sense of purpose should support the College as it faces the problems of the future.

Robert Kruse, appointed by MacPháidín to coordinate the reaccreditation effort, initiated a self-study, chaired by the associate academic dean, Paul Gastonguay. A number of subcommittees submitted reports, which were edited by George Hagerty and combined as the College's report to the New England Association. In October 1989 an eight-member accreditation team, headed by Dr. Paul J. Reiss, president of St. Michael's College, visited Stonehill. The team's report, which raised a few concerns, was generally favorable and recommended continuation of Stonehill's accreditation for another 10 years.[74]

Faculty Affairs

THE TENURE QUOTA battle contested in 1973 was resumed in the eighties, but in a subdued and nonconfrontational manner. In the spring of 1979 a report written by C. James Cleary, which examined the tenure quota system at Stonehill, had recommended that an adjustment upward to 75 percent (from the established 65 percent) be considered. The trustees' refusal to consider any increase in the quota[75] sparked a strong response from Academic Dean Robert Kruse:[76]

> If the Trustees are determined to do something decisive about the tenure question, then in my judgment they are wasting their time pussy-footing with the quota. Their better course of action would be to abolish tenure entirely. All the

Professor Chet Raymo (right) receives the first Louise Hegarty Award for teaching excellence from Dean Jo-Ann Flora, SND.

quota does is eliminate promising younger faculty while leaving several less productive tenured faculty firmly intrenched in their positions. If morale is going to be adversely affected, I would prefer doing so in a way that serves the academic best interests of the College.

Kruse recommended incentives for early retirement, selective training of faculty, and judicious filling of faculty positions as openings occurred. The 65 percent tenure quota continues today.

The 1980s was generally a period of quiet development for Stonehill's faculty. The initial faculty development efforts of Chet Raymo and Anne T. Carrigg in 1975 were expanded in the eighties. In 1978 a faculty grants office had been opened and charged with collection and dissemination of grant-relevant material to stimulate interest in filing for grants and to provide technical support in grant application. In 1985 the Office of Academic Development, evolving from the grants office, was created to reflect the desire of the College's administration and faculty to pursue external resources for the professional development of the College. George Hagerty was appointed the first director; Nan Mulford was selected to head the office in 1989.[77]

Stonehill continued its association with SACHEM in the 1980s. In the fall of 1981 a faculty lecture series was initiated in which Thomas Clarke, CSC, Richard Trudeau, and Barbara Estrin participated in consecutive years. SACHEM in general, however, appeared to be in a "malaise," with student activity in the academic exchange quite low.[78] In 1989 a management consultant, Carol Dorris, reviewed the consortium and concluded that the body suffered from an identity crisis. She recommended that SACHEM be reorganized for a mutually agreeable mission.[79] This reorganization did little, however, to give life to the consortium. Shifting interests and diverse attitudes led to the discontinuance of many SACHEM programs. While the consortium exists today, its place is not significant in the member institutions.[80]

Faculty achievement in the classroom was first formally recognized through the creation of The Louise F. Hegarty Award for Excellence in Teaching in 1989. (An effort in 1986 to initiate an excellence-in-teaching award had not gained the support of the academic dean, Robert Kruse, although he believed "the intent of the proposal was good.") The death in January 1988 of Louise Hegarty, professor of mathematics, was the impetus to again push for a teaching award. Promoted by Professors James Millikan and Anthony Celano, the Academic Committee recommended the establishment of an excellence-in-teaching award. Upon approval by the president, Bartley MacPháidín, criteria were set and a method for selection was adopted.[81] At commencement exercises on May 21, 1989, Professor Chet Raymo became the first recipient of the Hegarty Award.

ENDNOTES

1. Group interview, 1980s, February 4, 1997, Stonehill History Project Papers, ASC.

2. Philip Gleason, *Contending With Modernity: Catholic Higher Education in the Twentieth Century* (New York: Oxford University Press, 1995). Gleason's monograph is the best and most recent history of American Catholic higher education in this century.

3. In his treatise *Idea of a University*, Newman wrote: "If the Catholic Faith is true, a university cannot exist externally to the Catholic pale, for it cannot teach Universal Knowledge if it does not teach Catholic theology. . . . A direct and active jurisdiction of the Church over it [the Catholic university] and in it is necessary, lest it should become the rival of the Church with the community at large in those theological matters which to the Church are exclusively committed." See Discourse ix.

4. Pope John Paul II, "Address to Presidents of Catholic Colleges and Universities," in Alice Gallin, OSU. *American Catholic Higher Education: Essential Documents, 1967–1990* (Notre Dame, Indiana: University of Notre Dame Press, 1992): 130, 132.

5. Pope John Paul II, "Address to Leaders of Catholic Higher Education," in Gallin, *Essential Documents*, 287.

6. National Conference of Catholic Bishops, "To Teach as Jesus Did" (Washington, D.C., 1976): paragraph 10.

7. See "Relations of American Catholic Colleges and Universities With the Church," *Catholic Mind* 74 (October 1976): 52.

8. *Ibid.*, 62.

9. In two books, *Models of the Church* and *A Church to Believe In*, Dulles outlined several "models" of how the Church was operative in the modern world. These models were: institution, mystical communion, sacrament, herald, servant, and community of disciples.

10. Richard McBrien, "Catholic Universities: The Church's Mission," *Origins* 10 (February 19, 1981): 569–72.

11. Eugene Kennedy, "Reclaiming Our Spiritual Authority [Mission of Catholic Higher Education and the Role of Faculty Members]," *Current Issues in Catholic Higher Education* 13 (Summer 1992): 31.

12. William M. Shea, "Tradition and Pluralism: Opportunities for Catholic Universities," *Current Issues in Higher Education* 16(1) (Summer 1995): 38.

13. George Anthony Kelly, "The Church in Higher Education," *Social Justice Review* 78 (May–June 1987): 93–95; Timothy S. Healy, "The Contrary Model," *Daedalus* 117 (Spring 1988): 161–62.

14. Robert Thomas Reilly, "Have Catholic Colleges Kept the Faith?" *US Catholic* 52 (October 1987): 35; James T. Burtchaell, CSC, "The Decline and Fall of the Christian College," Parts I and II, *First Things* I (April and May 1991): 16–29 and 30–38. Burtchaell is presently completing a monograph describing the secularization of Christian higher education in the United States.

15. Pope John Paul II, "Address to Presidents of Catholic Colleges and Universities,"in Gallin, *Essential Documents*, 132; "Address to Leaders of Catholic Higher Education," in Gallin, *Essential Documents*, 287.

16. "Catholic Higher Education and the Pastoral Mission of the Church," NCCB Statement 1981, in Gallin, *Essential Documents*, 138.

17. J. Donald Monan, SJ, "Forming the Whole Person," *Catholic International* 2(21) (December 1–14, 1991): 1025; Edward J. Berbusse, SJ, "The Catholic College

vs. Academic Freedom," *Homiletic and Pastoral Review* 86 (August/September 1986): 17.

18. Quoted in Reilly, "Have Catholic Colleges Kept the Faith?" 36; David Burrell, CSC, "The Ideal of the Catholic University," *The Furrow* 31 (September 1980): 560.

19. Quoted in Reilly, "Have Catholic Colleges Kept the Faith?" 36. Father Oddo taught at Stonehill in the Religious Studies Department from 1974 to 1982, when he was appointed president of the University of Portland. He died tragically in October 1989 in a traffic accident.

20. Richard Finnegan to William Ribando, June 21, 1977, Ribando Papers, AHCFE.

21. Bartley MacPháidín, "Inauguration Speech for Brother Raphael Wilson, CSC," March 11, 1979; "President's Dinner Speech, May 30, 1979, MacPháidín Papers, ASC.

22. Brockton *Enterprise* (December 7, 1977), MacPháidín Papers; *The Summit* (May 10, 1978), September 26, 1978, ASC.

23. "Statement on Goals," May 9, 1979, College Council Papers, ASC.

24. Between 1968 and 1980, grade averages rose College-wide:

	FRESHMEN	SOPHOMORE	JUNIOR	SENIOR	MEAN
1968	2.41	2.57	2.73	2.73	2.62
1980	2.70	2.87	2.94	3.10	2.90

25. *The Summit* (April 25, 1979); *Ad Hoc* Subcommittee of Grading Report to Academic Committee, May 16, 1979, College Council Papers; Bartley MacPháidín to Robert Kruse, May 18, 1979, Kruse–Dean Papers, ASC. The grade distribution guidelines were: A and A−, 10%; B+, 10%; B, 25%; C and C−, 20% each; D+, D, F, 15%.

26. Two of the search committee's three finalists turned down the College's proposal and the third was not given a formal offer.

27. Recall that Kruse led the drive in 1971 to change the Department of Theology to Religious Studies, a move based on an educational and theological philosophy, generated in the wake of canonical alienation, that was very popular in the 1970s.

28. Robert Kruse, "The Liberal Arts in Career Programs," n.d. Kruse–Dean Papers, ASC. Referring to a liberal arts education he wrote: "Thus liberal education is an exercise in understanding the human condition, in examining the idea and the imagination, the experiment and the art, the passion and the prejudice, that have made us what we are. To enter into this exercise requires versatility and discipline of mind. It also requires at least some passion for the human condition. For liberal studies falters as often as not for want of feeling as for want of reason. A liberal education nurtures reason and feeling alike, for at the heart of liberal education is inquiry that is impassioned as well as critical."

29. "News Bureau," September 8, 1983, Public Affairs Papers; Robert Kruse, "Speech to Faculty Assembly," September 5, 1986, Kruse–Dean Papers, ASC.

30. Robert Kruse, "Annual Report," August 1, 1986, Kruse–Dean Papers; *The Summit* (November 15, 1988), ASC. In November 1988, in response to Kruse's essay, "In the Catholic Tradition," published in the winter 1988 issue of the *Stonehill Alumni Magazine*, a faculty forum, led by Professors Frank Ryan and Celia Wolf-Devine, discussed the question, "What Makes a Catholic College Catholic?"

31. Bartley MacPháidín to Mr. and Mrs. Ernest Charles, November 6, 1979, MacPháidín Papers; "Evaluation Report New England Association of Colleges and Secondary Schools, Standing Committee of Institutions of Higher Education, October 28–31, 1979; Vincent W. Duman to Bartley MacPháidín, May 9, 1980, Reaccreditation Papers, ASC.

32. Robert Kruse, "Speech to Faculty Assembly," September 1979; Kruse, "Recent Developments," n.d., Kruse-Dean Papers, ASC. Kruse stated, "It is for General Studies that I feel a particular responsibility as Academic Dean of the College, recognizing that the major and minor concentrations are rightly the concern of Department Chairpersons and Program Directors."

33. Robert Kruse, "Speech to Faculty," September 1979; "Speech to Faculty Assembly," September 1981, Kruse–Dean Papers, ASC. Kruse expressed his hopes for the program: "The new General Studies program is important for Stonehill College. With the institution of this program, the goals which the College has always sought to achieve may be realized with a distinction that surpasses past achievements. We may hope to graduate students who possess both greater sophistication of mind and a keener sense of responsibility for the human condition. We may hope to graduate students possessed by a passion to understand the world in which they live and an equal passion to make that world a better place."

34. Evaluations were conducted and changes made to the General Studies Program in the fall of 1984 and fall of 1987.

35. "Report of the Summer Subcommittee of the Academic Committee on General Studies," October 21, 1982, Kruse–Dean Papers, ASC. The subcommittee recommended that all freshmen be assigned to a writing course, either (1) basic writing (remedial), (2) college composition, or (3) free elective of other writing courses offered by the College. Those assigned to basic writing were to complete college composition in a subsequent semester.

36. Robert Kruse, "The Place of General Studies in the Stonehill Curriculum," July 20, 1983, Kruse–Dean Papers, ASC.

37. *The Summit* (September 19, 1978); Academic Advisement Manual, n.d. [1980], Dean's Papers, ASC. Prior to 1978, only students with declared majors were assigned advisors. Thus, until McAlister's appointment all undeclared students, generally freshmen and sophomores, had only the counseling center as a source for campus advice. McAlister continued to teach part time while serving as dean of freshmen.

38. *The Summit* (March 15, 1978), ASC.

39. *Ibid.*, October 25, 1978.

40. Robert Kruse, Annual Report, July 15, 1983; Richard Finnegan to Robert Kruse, February 12, 1986, Kruse–Dean's Papers, ASC.

41. *The Stonehill Review* 6(3) (Winter 1982), Public Affairs Papers, ASC.

42. Randy LeGrant to Ben Marianti [*sic*], November 7, 1985; Mariante to Le-Grant, December 16, 1985, Deans' Papers, ASC; pamphlet "International Internships," n.d., Stonehill College Papers, AHCFE. The AIFS signed an agreement with Stonehill, Merrimack, Assumption, St. John Fisher, St. Anselm, and St. Michael that gave these institutions foreign study opportunities for students and teaching assignments for faculty. Stonehill faculty participants were: Patricia Sankus, Virginia Polanski, and Marlene Benjamin.

43. As in the Notre Dame program, Stonehill students desirous of engineering degrees took three years of classes at the College and two in specialized engineering courses at Hartford.

44. Raymond A. Pepin to Stonehill Faculty, December 9, 1983, September 25, 1984, Deans' Papers, ASC.

45. Barbara Estrin, Dolores Shelley, and Rosemary Twomey to All Faculty, April 7, 1982; "Rationale for a Women's General Studies Program," n.d. [1981], Kruse–Dean Papers, ASC. The Rationale stated, "The women of Stonehill College seek a place in the Stonehill General Studies Curriculum and the historically-oriented General Studies faculty to promote, in a consistent and regular way, the goal of a Women's General Studies Program: the making of the self-determined woman."

46. George Carey, "Learning to Learn Program," October 5, 1984; announcement for "Learning to Learn" Workshop, October 25, 1984; Carey, "Evaluation of the Learning to Learn Program at Stonehill," December 1985, Kruse–Dean Papers, ASC.

47. *The Summit* (September 30, 1981, November 18, 1981, November 15, 1988), ASC.

48. Bartley MacPháidín, "Report to the Board," September 1978, MacPháidín Papers, ASC.

49. Leo J. O'Hara to Robert Kruse, August 16, 1978, Kruse–Dean Papers, ASC.

50. "Report of the *Ad Hoc* Committee, Evaluation of Evening Division, April 29, 1981. The Committee also recommended that all degree candidates, without exception, who have no prior college must possess the high school preparation requirements of the catalog. Numerous recommendations on admission requirements, preregistration, and academic standards were also made.

51. "Report Select Committee on the Evening Division," September 13, 1983, Kruse–Dean Papers, ASC. The committee's recommendations included: (1) eliminate the Academic Policy Committee of the Evening Division and replace it with an Evening Division Advisory Committee, (2) adopt a standard admissions policy, (3) ensure that the Associate Academic Dean for Continuing Education stresses the importance of maintaining academic quality in every course, and (4) ensure that department chairs evaluate adjunct faculty in a manner similar to that used in the day school.

52. The committees were: enrollment, planning, academic, career opportunities, and library.

53. Robert Kruse, Annual Report, July 1, 1984, Kruse–Dean Papers, ASC.

54. George Rogers to Leo O'Hara, March 3, 1980, Kruse–Dean Papers, ASC.

55. Leo J. O'Hara, Annual Report, Division of Continuing Education, 1983–84, Kruse–Dean Papers, ASC.

56. Agreement Between Stonehill College and Brockton Hospital's School of Nursing, September 1, 1986 to August 31, 1987, MacPháidín Papers, ASC. The College planned to provide science, psychology, and sociology courses in the school year and college composition during the summer.

57. Judith Allen to Bartley MacPháidín, October 27, 1987; MacPháidín to Allen, November 12, 1987; Allen to MacPháidín, February 12, 1988, MacPháidín Papers, ASC. The cooperative agreement with Brockton Hospital also ended in the spring of 1988.

58. Leo J. O'Hara, Annual Report, Division of Continuing Education, 1981–82, Kruse–Dean Papers, ASC.

59. *News Bureau* January 14, 1981, Public Affairs Papers, ASC.

60. Emilie Greeley to Faculty and Staff of Stonehill College, September 1982, Evening Division Papers, *News Bureau* (March 3, 1980, February 27, 1980), ASC.

61. Bartley MacPháidín to Alumnus, January 1986, MacPháidín Papers, ASC. *The Summit* reported that Stonehill was one of 129 schools evaluated in its category.

62. Board of Trustees Meeting Minutes, May 9, 1986, Board of Trustees Papers, ASC.

63. Robert Kruse to Faculty and Student Affairs Administrators, September 30, 1986, Deans' Papers, ASC.

64. See Chapter 15 for details on the initiation of the Nakamichi Series.

65. "Literacy Program Taps College Students as Tutors," n.d. *Christian Science Monitor* clipping, Petti Papers, ASC. Norman Manasa, at the University of Miami, developed the Washington Education Project. St. John's University in New York City was the first school to respond to Manasa's call.

66. Brockton *Enterprise* (August 10, 1987); Report of Results, The Washington Education Project, Inc., Fall Semester 1987, Flora Paper, ASC; Nan D. Mulford, "Quietly Making a Difference," n.d. Office of Academic Development, Stonehill College.

67. Stonehill Education Project, Annual Report, 1987–88, June 15, 1988, Petti Papers, ASC.

68. *Ibid*; Rita Smith, interview with the author (March 20, 1997). The Superintendent Center involved 46 school districts, the Middle School Alliance assisted 15 area towns, the Catholic Educators Collaborative involved 11 schools, and the North River Collaborative included 7 schools. New Dimensions was a program geared to expose intellectually gifted high school seniors to Stonehill and college life in general.

69. Bartley MacPháidín to Colleagues, March 2, 1988, MacPháidín Papers; Brockton *Enterprise* (April 13, 1989); *The Summit* (March 22, 1988), ASC.

70. Jo-Ann Flora, speech to College Assembly, September 9, 1988, Flora Papers, ASC. Although much discussion has taken place, there has been no change to the General Studies Program or its implementation.

71. Jo-Ann Flora to Peter Beishein, *et al.*, May 4, 1989; Flora, Annual Report, August 1, 1988; Flora, Annual Report, August 31, 1990. The team of professors was Richard Capobianco, Susan Mooney, Virginia Polanski, Gregory Shaw, and Richard Velkley.

72. Allan Leitman to Richard Shankar, May 31, 1989, Flora Papers; Bartley MacPháidín to Members of the Education Department, July 17, 1989, MacPháidín Papers; Fred Petti to Jo-Ann Flora, November 20, 1989, MacPháidín to Flora, January 22, 1990, Flora Papers, ASC. Allan Leitman was the original choice of the Education Department to serve as chair. In November 1989 Petti recommended Olivier to Flora in order that the Department not be ill-affected in its forthcoming NCATE accreditation inspection. Olivier had taught at Stonehill previously; he returned to the College from a position in the North Attleboro, Massachusetts school district.

73. Gordon S. Bigelow to Bartley MacPháidín, November 27, 1984, MacPháidín Papers, ASC.

74. Robert Kruse to All Faculty and Administrators, November 16, 1987, MacPháidín Papers; "Report of the New England Association of Colleges and Secondary Schools, January 19, 1990, Reaccreditation Papers, ASC. The visitation team, while writing a very positive report, noted five areas of concern: (1) need to establish an effective strategic planning process, (2) question of the adequacy of the number of full-time faculty for handling the responsibilities of teaching, in numbers of students and breadth of program, (3) need to establish a more effective pattern of communication and shared responsibilities, (4) need to establish a more diverse student body and staff, (5) need to bring about a more effective integration of the commuter student into the life of the College.

75. C. James Cleary to Bartley MacPháidín, April 19, 1979, "Report of the Planning Committee on Tenure and Promotion," Executive Vice President–Cleary Papers; MacPháidín to Faculty Members, September 21, 1979, MacPháidín Papers, ASC. In the fall of 1979, 68 percent of the faculty was tenured, and twenty others were on tenure track. Thus, 72 of 77 full-time faculty were tenured or in tenure-track positions.

76. Robert Kruse, Annual Report, July 15, 1983, Kruse–Dean Papers, ASC.

77. Jo-Ann Flora to Full-Time Faculty, March 10, 1989; Flora to Members of Search Committee for Faculty Development Director, May 5, 1989, Flora Papers, ASC.

78. In the 1982–83 academic year, four Sachem students attended Stonehill and ten Stonehill students attended classes at schools in the consortium.

79. Carol A. Dorris, "Mission Assessment, Mission Reformulation, and Strategic Planning Report," SACHEM, March 23, 1989, MacPháidín Papers, ASC.

80. As one example of how SACHEM continues, in 1996 the consortium offered intercultural and foreign language summer seminar programs for faculty.

81. College Council Meeting Minutes, May 12, 1986, College Council Papers; memorandum, n.d., Deans' Papers, ASC. Criteria for the Hegarty Award were: (1) Teacher's course objectives are clearly defined and ultimately achieved, (2) teacher stimulates further interest in the subject and imparts skills and demonstrates methods necessary to solve related problems independently, (3) teacher encourages questions and discussions on the material, (4) teacher communicates his/her knowledge effectively.

CHAPTER 14

A Resurgence in Growth

From its earliest days Stonehill College was limited in its ability to expand its physical plant. During its first quarter century, the College's growth was inhibited by governance and finances. Before canonical alienation in 1972, all decisions on construction required the consent of the Holy Cross Community, with permission at times required by the Superior General in Rome. Additionally, the early years were extremely lean financially. These two factors were responsible for Stonehill's penchant for underbuilding—that is, meeting the immediate need with little consideration for the future. Additions to Duffy Academic Center, the cafeteria, and the library were made as need arose. Although the College planners should be commended for their forethought in erecting buildings that allowed additions, the overall inability to build for anticipated growth slowed Stonehill's development.

During the 1970s Stonehill continued to experience little physical development because of the policy followed by the College's administration. However, achievements of the period—especially in academics and outside recognition of the College by leading educators—did not require expansion of the College's housing and classroom facilities. The major building projects (the College Center, expansion of the library, and the Chapel of Mary), were long overdue. A relatively slight rise in student enrollment (most of whom were commuters) and no need for new equipment to support the ongoing major programs allowed the College to operate successfully and grow without significant expansion of its facilities.

The period of the 1980s, however, saw massive development on the

Stonehill campus. Consistent with the rise of enrollment, expanded academic programs, greater financial stability, and better recognition within the academy, Stonehill experienced an explosion in construction that would have been thought impossible a generation earlier. Classroom and laboratory facilities, a recreational sports complex, and a new group of student dormitories greatly changed the College's landscape.

Renovations and Additions

❧

IN MAY 1982 the Board of Trustees suggested that an internal review be conducted to determine space and facility needs for the rest of the decade. The board's planning committee anticipated that new academic programs and rising enrollment would require more classroom space and possibly a new dorm. The 1982 report, referencing past accreditation and self-study reports that had noted the inadequacy of indoor athletic facilities, recommended that no new academic or athletic buildings be constructed, but suggested renovation of the Merkert (College Center) Gymnasium and recognized the Education Department's need for additional space. The review also suggested that the Board of Trustees establish a building fund distinct from the Fund for Endowment.[1]

David Ames, nephew of Frederick Lothrup Ames, announced in the fall of 1978 that he would donate 50 percent of his farm, situated directly across Route 138 at the auxiliary entrance to Stonehill. The other half of the farm, which earlier had been the home of the Ames family's prize Guernsey herd, was purchased by the College in April 1979.[2] The facility was renovated at a cost of $322,000 to serve as the new headquarters for the Buildings and Grounds Department of the College. The David Ames Clock Farm was dedicated on October 16, 1980.[3]

Stonehill's historical penchant for underbuilding became evident again in the need for an addition to the science building. In the fall of 1977, plans were drawn by Austin Company of New York for a three-level addition at an estimated cost of $1.5 to $1.7 million. But Stonehill's treasurer, Edward Casieri, expressed reservations about Austin's design and work practices and suggested that another architect be hired for the job.[4] A search led to the selection of Holmes and Edwards, Inc. of Boston in May 1978.

The new architect presented three proposals for the project: (1) renovation of the present building, (2) construction of a new building and conversion of the present building into a service facility, or (3) erection of completely new science and service buildings. Initially it was believed that the original structure should be leveled because of its age and hasty construction, but an inspection revealed that the building was perfectly sound. Thus,

David Ames speaks at the dedication of the David Ames Clock Farm.

the decision was made to build a new wing adjacent to the present building, which itself would be renovated.[5]

Construction of the new science building wing, under the direction of the Auburn Company of Whitman, took 15 months and cost $2,165,000. It featured classrooms, new labs, offices, and an observatory with two domes for telescopes. Classes were first held in the addition during spring semester 1980. On May 9, 1980, the new wing was dedicated as the James Merkert Science Center.[6] At the ceremony, Bartley MacPháidín underscored the College's pride but misread the future: "We are honored to be able to dedicate this building to James A. Merkert. It represents the last major building project for the College in the foreseeable future."[7]

Donahue Hall had served the College from the outset as home to every

(Above) Evans House residence for Holy Cross religious.
(Below) The "Barn" residence for Holy Cross religious.

College need save a gymnasium, including being home to the many Holy Cross religious who worked at Stonehill. Housing needs for the displaced religious had been met with two separate projects in the late 1970s. In the fall of 1977 the hay and horse barns of the old Ames estate had been renovated, making room for eleven religious.[8] Nevertheless, as late as 1980 some religious were still residing in Donahue. As the College grew, the need for administrative office space in Donahue became acute. Rooms used as living quarters for members of Holy Cross had to be evacuated immediately in order to provide space in what was becoming exclusively the College's administration building. MacPháidín wrote to William Ribando, CSC, provincial of the Eastern Province, offering to build a home on Community property at a location of its choice for those residing in Donahue. In the summer of 1981 a new residence named for Fr. Bill Evans, CSC, was constructed near the renovated "Barn."[9]

The removal of all residents from Donahue allowed a general renovation of the building. The Board of Trustees approved the project at an estimated cost of $500,000. The most significant aspect of the renovation was the establishment of the Mary Joan Glynn Library for Irish Studies. Glynn, a member of the Board of Trustees and vice president of marketing at Bloomingdale's, was honored at a testimonial dinner at the New York Hilton on October 29, 1981, at a fundraiser for the library project. The renovated library space, which held 2000 volumes dedicated to Anglo-Irish literature, was dedicated on May 7, 1982. Louise Kenneally was appointed Irish Studies librarian.[10]

Two additional renovation projects in the period significantly contributed to the College's mission to form the student in mind, body, and soul. Merkert Gymnasium, a portion of the College Center that had opened in 1973, was renovated between March and September 1983 at a cost of over $400,000. The floor space of the gym was doubled and locker room, shower, and staff facilities were added. In the summer of 1983 the building that formerly housed the Buildings and Grounds Department was redesigned and renovated as a new home for the Education Department.[11]

Campus beautification projects were also part of the 1980s building phenomenon. In August 1984 the access road to campus from Route 123 was rerouted to go west around the library and connect with the road leading from Route 138 into the campus. In the summer of 1986 Auburn Construction Company remodeled the central campus. A red-brick pathway was constructed in an east-west direction along the central artery of the lower campus; a similar pathway in the east-west direction of the central campus was added in 1988. A student and staff parking lot for 500 cars was enlarged between the rerouted campus road and the library.[12] In the fall of 1990 the

Main entrance (Route 123) to Stonehill College.

main entrance to campus at Route 123 was redesigned and beautified. At the same time Stonehill received word that traffic lights would be erected at the main and Route 138 entrances.[13]

New Facilities on Campus

✿   FROM THE ESTABLISHMENT of the College, the president had always resided with the Holy Cross Community, either in Donahue or in rented facilities in the local area. In 1980, however, Stonehill acquired the Hafstrom-Swanson House, a large duplex on Route 138 just north of the main part of campus and across from Moreau Hall, formerly the Holy Cross brothers' scholasticate. President MacPháidín moved to his new lodging in the summer of 1979.[14]

A shortage of student housing was a persistent problem in the 1980s. Throughout the decade *The Summit* commented on the situation, raising the issues of overcrowding and security. An annual event that always raised the ire of students and drew fire from all sides was the housing lottery. Each spring semester, all residents' names were entered into a computer-generated lottery that assigned numbers to students for the purpose of determining the

Hafstrom-Swanson House.

order in which they would choose their dorm for the next academic year. Beginning with the student who was assigned number one, residents chose the dorm and the specific room they desired. In the process, students bartered and made deals to secure a better place in the draw and their desired lodging. With incoming resident freshmen guaranteed rooms, many students were unable to keep friends or even roommates together. The lack of sufficient rooms often led to tripling of students at the outset of a semester. Upperclassmen were especially frustrated, believing that seniority should have its reward. One graduate of the period put it succinctly: "The director of housing was not the most popular person on campus." A cartoon in *The Summit* was equally critical of the lottery and its results: A college-age "hobo" stood with "bug eyes" of disbelief before a sign that read: "Stonehill—No Vacancy College."[15]

Attempts to rectify the housing crunch were initiated by MacPháidín and the residence life staff. Holy Cross Center, which had been the scene of an experimental living project in the seventies, now became a regular College dorm. Many freshmen (who would not have participated in the lottery) were assigned to this old seminary. The center's former status as a place for residents dedicated to noninstitutional living was lost in the process. Wilfred J. Raymond, CSC, who became the resident director of the center in 1980, explained the new direction:[16]

> A lot of the philosophy of the old "sem" was Bill Braun [,who] considered the sem as an experiment in Christian living. The new emphasis is to make the sem more a part of the College, to tie it in with the whole academic life on campus, while at the same time maintaining that it is a very special place to live.

MacPháidín realized that, in addition to opening Holy Cross Center for general student use, new dormitory facilities would be necessary. In January 1981 he secured permission from the trustees for the construction of a new dorm to house 50 students. A design by Holmes and Edwards proposed a building that was a hybrid of types of residence facilities already present on campus. Smaller than the institutional design of O'Hara and Boland, the plan called for suites, somewhat like those in the townhouses, to be constructed with common recreational facilities. Sullivan Hall, named for Stonehill's fourth president, Richard Sullivan, CSC, was completed at a cost of $565,000 and welcomed students in September 1981. This building became the first of five residences in an area that became known as Pilgrim Heights in September 1987.[17]

The construction of Sullivan Hall brought only a temporary respite from the persistent problem with student housing. Between 1978 and 1990 full-time student enrollment in the day college rose from 1700 to 1964, a 13.4 percent rise; resident population during the same period rose from 61 to 70 percent. The Board of Trustees considered the problem severe enough that offers of student admissions had to be altered for the class of 1988.[18] A special committee report analyzing the problem stated, "There are undesirable aspects to this problem. The Dean [of Admissions] is being denied the opportunity to select more qualified candidates from the residential category while being forced to accept a much greater number from among the commuter group." The report concluded:[19]

> It is evident to the Study Committee that there is a clear and pressing need for additional dormitory space. It is recommended that one Towne house be constructed to accommodate 51 students. It is also recommended that the facility be constructed for occupancy in January of 1985.

Pilgrim Heights student residences.

The severity of the housing shortage, which was now recognized by all parties, led to the construction of four more dormitories in the Pilgrim Heights complex. Even though Cascino Hall was completed in January 1985 and dedicated on October 23, a January 1987 internal report on the immediate facility priorities of the College indicated "student housing to be the highest priority area for Stonehill campus development." It recommended the construction of two additional dorms for 55 students each, one to be ready in the fall of 1988 and the second in the fall of 1990.[20] Flynn Hall, a residence for 81 students, was designed by Holmes and Edwards and built by Auburn Construction; it was dedicated on May 1, 1989. Benaglia Hall, a twin of Flynn, was dedicated on June 7, 1989.[21] In January 1993 the trustees authorized a new dormitory for 80 students in Pilgrim Heights. Sheehan Hall was ready for students in September 1993.[22]

Rising student enrollment and demands for resident living forced Stonehill to evaluate its technological facilities, especially in the realm of computers. The swift pace of technological advancement in higher education had outdistanced the facilities of Lockary Computer Center, established in Duffy in September 1977. In February 1980 Duncan MacQueen, a consultant from

Stanger Hall and Lockary Computer Center.

the MITRE Corporation, evaluated Stonehill's existing computer facilities and future needs. While MacQueen's report was very positive,[23] it did recommend that the College's central computer be replaced by a system built by Digital Equipment Corporation (DEC) that could meet Stonehill's computing needs for a minimum of five years in the future.[24]

The favorable report from the consultant and new upgraded hardware did not mask the reality that the College needed a building dedicated to academic computing. The academic dean, Robert Kruse, echoing the thoughts of Raymond A. Pepin, director of academic computing, appraised the situation: "Our principal need in the academic area is for a suitable computer building."[25] In February 1985 the trustees approved a proposal "to develop, construct, and equip" an academic computer center and to borrow $1.9 million to finance the project. The team of Holmes and Edwards as architects and Auburn Construction as contractor was secured for the building of Stanger Hall.[26] The $2.3 million facility, housing 100 computer work stations, office space, seminar rooms, and classrooms, was dedicated on May 1, 1987.

The construction of Stanger Hall helped fill the pressing need to bring the College on a technological par with its peer institutions in the academy, but the need for an indoor athletic facility was also acute. The College's inadequate sports facilities had been noted as early as the second attempt at accreditation in 1959. The construction of the College Center and its renovation had provided a needed facility for varsity basketball, but a recreational sports complex for the use of all students was still lacking. Construction of an indoor sports compound had been a goal of long-range plans,[27] but cost and needs in other areas had always been obstacles to the fulfillment of any such ambition.

Stonehill's receipt of a large endowment from the estate of Mrs. Maurice Charles, daughter-in-law of Frederick Lothrup Ames, was the catalyst in generating plans for a new sports complex. In 1954 Sally Blair Ames Langmuir (who died in 1965) established a trust in the name of her mother, Mrs. Maurice Charles, who was given power to exercise its terms. Mrs. Charles chose Stonehill as the beneficiary of the residue of her estate, including the trust. Ames' death in December 1985 eventually brought Stonehill an unrestricted gift of $3.85 million.[28]

With the need long identified and significant financial assistance secured, Stonehill began to plan a new sports complex. The College's 1987 internal review of facility needs and priorities reported:[29]

> In the next year, plans will be prepared for an addition to or new structure near the College Center that will have an indoor track, tennis courts, racketball courts, weight/exercise equipment, exercise game room, [and] locker rooms. . . . The goal is to have this facility available in the fall of 1988.

In January 1987 the trustees appropriated funds for a recreational center. Designed by Holmes and Edwards and built by Auburn Construction at a cost of $6.69 million, the Sally Blair Ames Sports Complex opened on January 30, 1989, and was dedicated on May 12.[30]

The construction of the Ames Sports Complex provided the opportunity to renovate the old recreational gym for other purposes. The 1987 facilities' review had suggested that the building could be transformed into a meeting facility for alumni and friends of the College, but concluded:[31]

> Nonetheless, in comparison with the needs at the cafeteria and the library, this project would have to receive a low priority status for at least the next five years, and only if an unusually favorable opportunity presented itself to the school could this project be seriously considered for implementation in the foreseeable future.

Sally Blair Ames Sports Complex.

Alumni Hall.

99TH CONGRESS
2D SESSION
H. R. 4244

To authorize funds to preser the official papers of Joseph W. Martin. Jr.

IN THE HOUSE OF REPRESENTATIVES

FEBRUARY 26, 1986

Mr. CONTE (for himself and Mr. MOAKLEY) introduced the following bill; which was referred to the Committee on Education and Labor

---

A BILL

To authorize funds to preserve the official papers of Joseph W. Martin, Jr.

1   *Be it enacted by the Senate and House of Representa-*
2   *tives of the United States of America in Congress assembled,*
3   SECTION 1. ASSISTANCE AUTHORIZED.
4   In recognition of the public service of the former Speak-
5   er of the United States House of Representatives, Joseph W.
6   Martin, Jr., and of the need for preserving the official papers
7   of Speaker Martin, the Secretary is authorized to provide
8   funds in accordance with the provisions of this Act to assist
9   in the construction of the Joseph W. Martin Institute for Law
10   and Society at Stonehill College, North Easton, Massachu-
11   setts.

House of Representatives bill 4244, allocating funds for the housing of Speaker Joseph Martin's papers.

Despite the lack of recommendation, favorable opportunity allowed plans for the renovation of the old gym to move forward. An original design by Ganteaume and McMullen, Inc., estimated at $1.9 million, was rejected in favor of the firm-fixed-price of $1.24 million offered by Holmes and Edwards, Inc.[32] Renovation of the facility into a conference and meeting center was completed in the spring of 1990, and in October the building was renamed Alumni Hall. The renewed facility was dedicated on May 8, 1992.[33]

Stonehill's national recognition by *U.S. News & World Report* in November 1985 plus its new autonomy, which had been gained through canonical alienation in 1972, brought many opportunities to the College.[34] In September 1985 George Hagerty, director of academic development, met

President Ronald Reagan signs legislation for the Martin Institute. Congressman Silvio Conte and Bartley MacPháidín flank the president.

with President MacPháidín to discuss the possibility of establishing an institute for law and society to serve the region of southeastern Massachusetts. As the repository for the papers of Congressman Joseph Martin,[35] the College could, it was thought, obtain a federal grant for the construction and maintenance of such a facility.

MacPháidín was impressed with the proposal and decided to pursue it fully. He immediately sought Congressional support for the plan, meeting with Congressman Joseph Moakley (Ninth District) in September 1986 and in the ensuing February with Congressman Silvio Conte (First District), a protégé of Joseph Martin. Cosponsored by Moakley and Conte, a bill, H.R. 4244, for the preservation and housing of the Martin papers, was introduced to Congress in September 1986 and was passed in October. MacPháidín traveled to Washington, D.C., to witness President Ronald Reagan's signing of the legislation into law on November 6.[36]

Public Law 99–608 established the Joseph Martin Institute for Law and Society. The measure authorized Congress to award Stonehill College $6 million for purposes of (1) preserving of the official papers and effects of Martin, (2) establishing a regional and national academic center of scholarly

The Joseph W. Martin Institute for Law and Society.

and applied research and public service, and (3) providing for the construction of an appropriate multipurpose facility to house the Martin Institute.[37] Congress authorized $4 million in fiscal year 1987 and $2 million in 1988 for the Martin Institute project.[38]

Construction of the Martin Institute began with a special groundbreaking ceremony on November 6, 1987, at which Professors James Kenneally and Richard Finnegan and Edward Martin, brother of the late Congressman, were the principal speakers.[39] The building was designed by Ganteaume and McMullen and built by Jackson Construction Company. The original plan had called for an expenditure of $3.5 to $4 million on construction and a "minimum of $2–$2.5 million be placed in a restricted, permanent Martin Endowment to support the on-going [*sic*] administration of proposed Institute programming." The proposal, which had recommended safeguards to keep construction and endowment monies separate, assumed that the institute could operate its programs on the interest generated from the endowment. Construction costs, however, vastly exceeded estimates, leaving no money for the suggested operational endowment.[40] It

Professor James Kenneally.

was thought that since construction costs were immediate, the government grant should be used to cover these expenses. Endowment funds for the institute's programming could be raised later as needed.

The Martin Institute was opened to classes and offices in the spring semester 1990. The College Archives, under the direction of Louise Kenneally, moved from Donahue Hall to the Martin building that spring.[41] The new building was formally dedicated on April 27, with Congressman Joseph Moakley as the featured speaker.

Concurrent with the planning and physical construction of the Martin building was development of the institute's future programming. A planning committee, chaired by George Hagerty, was charged with a threefold mission: (1) review existing materials prepared by College staff or available through Congressional sources, (2) identify program priorities that might be addressed by the institute, and (3) offer the College president and division heads recommendations and options for development of the institute.[42] Professor James Kenneally was named director of the Martin Institute, with Professor Robert Carver serving as his assistant.[43]

Programs sponsored by the Martin Institute were divided into three categories: education and research, public policy, and regional and policy analysis.[44] The Education and Research Division presented symposia and lectures, including a program on the Jewish Holocaust, Black History month lectures and associated events, a Pearl Harbor fifty-year retrospective, and a workshop to celebrate the centenary (1991) of Pope Leo XIII's social encyclical *Rerum Novarum*. Initiation of a program of Jewish-Catholic dialogue was another significant contribution of the Education and Research Division.[45] The Public Policy Division sponsored the Joseph Martin and Political Leadership Lecture Series and a faculty colloquium series. The Regional and Policy Analysis Division supported studies on property tax overrides, a United Way environmental task force, drug use and alcohol prevention, a mature worker program, a drop-out prevention program, and workplace education.[46]

ENDNOTES

1. "A Review of Space Requirements, 1983–1988," n.d. [September 1982], Board of Trustees Papers, ASC.

2. Jeffrey Friedman to Edward Casieri, April 5, 1979, Treasurer's Office, Stonehill College. Ames gave 25 percent of the farm to Milton Academy and 25 percent to Unity Church in Easton. Stonehill purchased these two parcels in one payment.

3. Board of Trustees Meeting Minutes, September 29, 1978, Board of Trustees Papers; President's Report, January 25, 1980, MacPháidín Papers, ASC.

4. Edward Casieri to C. James Cleary, September 10, 1977; Casieri to Bartley MacPháidín, March 28, 1978, Treasurer's Papers, ASC.

5. Edward Casieri to Bartley MacPháidín, March 28, 1978, Treasurer's papers; Casieri to members of the Site Plan Committee, May 2, 1978, Board of Trustees Papers, ASC.

6. James A. Merkert (1953–1978), son of Mr. and Mrs. Eugene F. Merkert, was a Stonehill Evening Division student at the time of his death.

7. *News Bureau*, Stonehill College, May 30, 1980, Public Affairs Papers, ASC.

8. William Ribando to CSCs Living in North Easton Area, April 6, 1977, Ribando Papers, AHCFE.

9. Bartley MacPháidín to William Ribando, December 4, 1980, Ribando Papers, AHCFE; *The Summit* (September 23, 1981), ASC. MacPháidín told Ribando that he was under great pressure to move religious out of Donahue to make space for administrative offices. The Board of Trustees agreed to transfer $200,000 from the Fund for Endowment to the Holy Cross Fathers for construction of a residence. Evans House was named in honor of Fr. Bill Evans, murdered in Bangladesh on November 13, 1971.

10. Bartley MacPháidín, speech to President's Dinner, June 2, 1982, MacPháidín

Papers; *News Bureau*, Stonehill College, October 20, 1981; *The Stonehill Review* 6(2) (Summer 1982), Public Affairs Papers; *The Summit* (February 24, 1982), ASC.

11. Bartley MacPháidín, Report to Board of Trustees, May 14, 1982; MacPháidín to Colleagues, January 26, 1983, MacPháidín Papers; *The Stonehill Review* 7(2) (Fall 1983), Public Affairs Papers; Board of Trustees Meeting Minutes, May 6, 1983, Board of Trustees Papers, ASC.

12. Edward Casieri to Charles Altieri, June 27, 1986, Flynn Hall Papers at Buildings and Grounds Department, Stonehill College.

13. *The Summit* (November 20, 1990); Bartley MacPháidín to J.T. Cronin, November 27, 1990, MacPháidín Papers, ASC.

14. In the fall of 1982 the house was named after the former owners, two sisters, Bertha Swanson and Anna Lunde (maiden name of Hafstrom).

15. Group interview 1980s, February 4, 1997, Stonehill History Project Papers; *The Summit* (April 11, 1989), ASC.

16. *The Summit* (December 10, 1980), ASC.

17. Special Study Committee on Housing to Executive Committee of the Board of Trustees, August 10, 1984, Student Residence Papers; Bartley MacPháidín to Richard Sullivan, March 6, 1981, MacPháidín Papers; *The Summit* (September 16, 1981), ASC.

18. In the class of 1988 resident applications were 86 percent and commuter applications 14 percent. The lack of student housing forced the dean of admissions to accept only 49.5 percent of the resident applicants, while being compelled to accept in excess of 70 percent of the commuter applicants.

19. Special Study Committee on Housing to Executive Committee of the Board of Trustees, August 10, 1984, Student Residence Papers, ASC.

20. Institutional Report to the Stonehill College Board of Trustees: A Profile of Immediate Facility Priorities and Future Planning Considerations, January 15, 1987, Board of Trustees Papers, ASC.

21. Charles M. Alteri to City of Brockton Department of Public Works, November 27, 1987, Benaglia Hall Papers, Buildings and Grounds Department, Stonehill College; Dedication Programs, Flynn Hall, May 1, 1989, Benaglia Hall, June 7, 1989, Buildings and Grounds Papers, ASC.

22. Bartley MacPháidín to Colleagues, January 26, 1993, MacPháidín Papers, ASC.

23. Duncan MacQueen to Robert Kruse, March 5, 1980, Kruse–Dean Papers, ASC. MacQueen wrote, "I would like to emphasize once more my strong feeling that academic computing at Stonehill is in very good shape indeed."

24. Summary—Computer Consultation with Duncan MacQueen, n.d., Kruse–Dean Papers. ASC.

25. Robert Kruse, Annual Report, July 1, 1984, Kruse–Dean Papers; *The Summit* (September 26, 1984), ASC.

26. Businessman John W. Stanger, after a distinguished career at General Electric Credit Corporation, became chairman of Signal Capital Corporation and chairman of Stanger Craig Associates, Inc.

27. *The Summit* (February 13, 1984 and October 24, 1984); Bartley MacPháidín to Colleagues, February 14, 1985, MacPháidín Papers; Edward F. Cassidy, Jr., to Edward Casieri, September 25, 1986, Presidents' Papers, ASC. In early 1984 Dr. Charles Ratto, dean of student affairs, and Raymond P. Pepin, director of athletics, proposed a recreational sports facility that would consist of four areas: (1) multipurpose facility for basketball, volleyball, and tennis that would be enclosed by a running track, (2) locker rooms, (3) health club with nautilus, free weights, and racquetball courts, and (4) a lounge and offices. At their winter 1985 meeting, the Board of Trustees heard arguments on the construction of an intramural athletic facility. There were diverse opinions on the size, scope, and means of funding for such a project. In September 1987 the LEA Group (Engineers, Architects, and Planners) submitted in their "Stonehill College 2000" Report a complete description of a student recreation facility, including location and general requirements.

28. Max Factor III, "Statement of Interest in Connection with Petition for Instructions for the Determination of Entitlement to Distribution of Termination of Trust," January 27, 1987, MacPháidín Papers; Board of Trustees Meeting Minutes, September 26, 1986, Board of Trustees Papers, ASC. Because of legal complications, Stonehill did not receive Charles' gift until the summer of 1987.

29. Institutional Report to the Stonehill College Board of Trustees: A Profile of Immediate Facility Priorities and Future Planning Considerations, January 15, 1987, Board of Trustees Papers, ASC.

30. *The Summit* (January 31, 1989), ASC; Karen O'Malley to Faculty, Staff and Administrators, April 17, 1989, Flynn Hall Papers, Department of Buildings and Grounds, Stonehill College.

31. Institutional Report to the Stonehill College Board of Trustees: A Profile of Immediate Facility Priorities and Future Planning Considerations, January 15, 1987, Board of Trustees Papers, ASC.

32. James S. Thomas to Robert Kruse, April 28, 1988; James P. Edwards to Robert Kruse, October 17, 1988, Executive Vice President–Kruse Papers; Contract Between Stonehill College and Holmes and Edwards, Inc., n.d. [1989], Physical Plant Papers, ASC.

33. Robert Kruse to All Faculty, Staff, Administrators, Students, October 30, 1991, Executive Vice President–Kruse Papers; Program for Dedication of Alumni Hall, May 8, 1992, Physical Plant Papers, ASC.

34. Canonical alienation, besides appointing lay men and women to the Board of Trustees and separating control policy decisions from the Congregation of Holy Cross, gave Stonehill (and Catholic colleges and universities) greater chances to obtain Federal education money. Since Catholic institutions were more ecumenical in perspective and less "controlled" by the Church, Federal money in support of building projects would not be perceived as support for any church and, thus, would avoid constitutional arguments on the separation of church and state.

35. Martin's papers had been deposited at Stonehill in two sections, in 1969 and 1975. See "A Proposal in Support of the Joseph W. Martin Institute for Law and Society," n.d., Executive Vice President Papers–Kruse, ASC.

36. Press Release, November 18, 1986, Public Affairs Papers, ASC.

37. Martin Institute Planning Committee to C. James Cleary, November 15, 1986, MacPháidín Papers, ASC.

38. Board of Trustees Meeting Minutes, January 30, 1987, Board of Trustees Papers, ASC.

39. *The Summit* (November 17, 1987), ASC.

40. "A Proposal in Support of the Joseph W. Martin Institute for Law and Society," n.d., Executive Vice President–Kruse Papers, ASC.

41. The College archives was started by the History Club in the spring of 1966. Father Augustine Peverada, CSC, was the first archivist, from 1967 to 1974. From 1974 to 1978 Professor J. Laurence Phalan was archivist, with Kenneally succeeding him. The archives, originally located in the lower floor of the library, were moved to Donahue Hall in 1983 and then to the Martin Institute in January 1990.

42. Martin Institute Planning Committee to C. James Cleary, December 1, 1986, Physical Plant Papers, ASC.

43. Jo-Ann Flora, Annual Report, August 1, 1989, Flora Papers, ASC.

44. The divisions were directed by: Education and Research, James Kenneally; Public Policy, Rob Carver; Regional and Policy Analysis, Robert Rosenthal.

45. On February 20, 1969, Stonehill initiated a Jewish-Catholic dialogue forum. John Corr served as honorary chair. Coordinators were: Frederick Andelman, American Jewish Committee; Colonel Paul McPherran, director of public affairs, Stonehill College; and Brother John Weihrer, CSC, Division of Continuing Education.

46. James Kenneally, Annual Report 1994–95, Joseph Martin Institute, n.d. [Summer 1995], Manzo Papers; Robert Carver, Annual Report, Public Policy Division, Martin Institute, n.d. [Summer 1992], Flora Papers; Robert A. Rosenthal, Annual Report, Center for Regional and Policy Analysis, Martin Institute, n.d. [Summer 1992], Flora Papers, ASC.

CHAPTER 15

The Student Perspective

Academic programs and physical facilities expanded in direct proportion to an increased, better-prepared, and more socially minded student body. In the 1980s Stonehill students could no longer be stereotyped as being New England-born, working-class, and first-generation college attendees. Whereas the sixties had transformed the nation and the seventies had healed divisions and regained prosperity, the eighties brought new frontiers to conquer. In this decade, Stonehill students were provided more opportunities than ever before. Through the leadership, vision, and example of a charismatic president and dedicated faculty and staff, Stonehill students were inspired to ever greater heights.

Times change and with time people, but the spirit that had made Stonehill a special place for thousands of students remained. The students of the eighties were more mobile, more financially sound, and better prepared academically for the rigors of higher education. In addition they found the campus a place where an intangible community spirit was built and bonds of friendship forged. Although different people in a new decade experienced greater opportunities in an atmosphere of innovation and progress, the perennial spirit and pride that had always characterized Stonehill remained.

Campus Events and Activities

AMERICAN SOCIETY of the 1980s was very different from that of the previous two decades. The end of America's involvement in Vietnam, a national swing toward conservatism, as illustrated by the two-term presidency of Ronald Reagan, and general economic progress made activism in all realms of society less popular. The atmosphere present in the country and on college and university campuses was more subdued. In other words, the time of student protest and radicalism had ended, and it was time to return to a more traditional, nonconfrontational educational pattern.[1]

A changed environment on the Stonehill campus in the 1980s, created by innovative and broader opportunities in the academic realm, an explosion of new buildings, and a new administrative leadership, was responsible for changing attitudes. While Stonehill students in the 1960s and early 1970s questioned authority and actively sought answers to significant contemporary issues facing society, those attending the College in the 1980s were more respectful of basic institutions and less likely to participate in groups, movements, or agencies that worked for solutions to public ills. Students described their experience in this decade as "comfortable," "secure," and "sheltered." Stonehill was a place where students could get as involved as they wished, but they exhibited no strong sense of voluntarism or commitment to outside activities. Students were generally content to do what was required, utilizing their time for study and personal commitments to work, family, and friends.[2]

The most significant common denominator for Stonehill students of the 1980s was their experience of community. Whether it was in a social connection at Brother Mike's, a casual meeting on a Boston street corner, or a coincidental sharing of adjacent seats on a plane, bus, or train, the bonds of friendship secured at Stonehill were unique. Most assuredly without any specific intention, Stonehill's student body bonded as a community that continues to sustain alumni to the present day.[3]

Although Stonehill in the eighties was generally a peaceful environment that produced little conflict between students, faculty, and administrators, the decade began with problems in the dorms linked to student apathy, disinterest, and abuse of alcohol. In the fall of 1978 a rash of vandalism in the dorms, linked to student drinking, raised concern in the Office of Student Affairs.[4] Dean Jack Gallagher, in response to the vandalism and in order to conform with a new Massachusetts law that raised the legal drinking age to 20, published new rules for alcohol use on campus. Initially a moratorium was placed on kegs of beer at all student- or College-sponsored functions on campus. When this move did not curtail vandalism, Gallagher established a more stringent policy that banned alcohol at all student functions, prohibited anyone under 20 years of age in a public place where alcohol was served, and restricted access to Brother Mike's to those of legal age, except when functions at the facility were alcohol-free.[5]

The vandalism generated by alcoholic abuse led to action by Student

Government Association (SGA) representatives, who believed the situation to be detrimental to the College's progress. In early December 1978, a campus-wide meeting sponsored by the SGA was held to address the issue of vandalism and an increasing "I don't care attitude on campus." SGA President Doug McIntyre told between 700 and 800 students, "Let's cut it [vandalism] out and start the growth process so that at the end of the year we can look with pride on what we did." Eighteen months later, in February 1980, SGA President Patrick Monahan targeted student disinterest:

> I do not intend to blame any student or student group for the lack of enthusiasm over campus issues in particular—the fact is, it exists. . . . Apathy, noncaring, disinterest—it exists elsewhere. What I am saying is this, let's be a leader among schools[;] let us begin to revive some of [the] energy tht [*sic*] exists in every one of us.

The principal problem of alcohol abuse was not eased until 1985, when Massachusetts raised its legal drinking age to 21, leading Stonehill to ban alcohol from all underclass (non-senior) dorms.[6]

The Summit, which candidly reported the news about vandalism and efforts to curb it, continued to serve the Stonehill community as the principal organ for the dissemination of news and comment concerning campus events and an ever-increasing interest in national and world affairs.[7] As the eighties dawned, the paper expanded to (generally) eight pages and began to publish almost weekly. Regular columns and features in the paper included "Ask the Authority," an essay that featured an interview with some person on campus who possessed a special expertise; "Campus Ministry Corner," which provided news on activities sponsored through the Chapel of Mary; and "Your Thoughts," a student opinion section. In the eighties the paper expanded its coverage of intramural sports, a regular feature in its early days. In the fall of 1989 "*The Summit* Personals," a series of short notes between students similar to the personals section of a daily newspaper were created. In the spring of 1990 the paper published articles in consecutive issues on topics of local importance, including an eye-opening series on "Violence on Campus."[8]

Problems with student apathy and abuse of alcohol were concerns of the eighties, but the beginning of the MacPháidín presidency will be remembered for how Mother Nature greeted the era. Few in southeastern Massachusetts, including students at Stonehill College, will soon forget their whereabouts on February 6, 1978, the day a blizzard struck, dumping thirty inches of snow and paralyzing the region. The College canceled classes for the week of February 7 through 13, but campus activity did not cease. While

(Above) Students take a break on the main quad.
(Below) Coeds walk through campus.

some students ventured out to local markets and liquor stores to dampen the effects of "cabin fever," others assisted in the emergency by staffing the College switchboard round the clock and assisting buildings and grounds personnel with snow removal. The students, fortunate that a large delivery of food had been made to the cafeteria just prior to the storm's arrival, were able to eat, with milk being the only rationed item. A special permit was obtained to burn refuse behind the cafeteria, as garbage pick-up was impossible. The situation became even more problematic when a flu epidemic spread rapidly among the students. Through it all, the Stonehill spirit of community survived. One student summarized her experience, "It was crazy, but fun."[9]

The 1980s also began with a wholesale change in the administration of student affairs. In January 1979 four prominent members of the student life staff, Jack Gallagher, dean of student life, his assistant, Bill Braun, CSC, Fr. Bob Marcantonio, director of counseling, and Bill Rose, housing director, resigned effective June 30, 1979.[10] Called the "midnight coup" by some students of the period,[11] the move was poorly received because of the popularity of those involved. The unexpected resignations prompted a cover-page cartoon in *The Summit* showing a help wanted sign at Stonehill College, with the caption, "Applications to be sent to B. MacPháidín, Pres." In the fall the new student affairs staff of Dr. Charles Ratto, dean of student life, Dr. Peter Scanlon, director of counseling, and Jim Doherty, CSC, director of student housing, was in place.[12]

Changed student attitudes and student life administrative shifts did not, however, in any way hinder the growth of student activities, which flourished in the eighties. Many new events, several of which were annual in nature, were started at Stonehill. Beginning in the fall of 1977 the College hosted the New England Association of College Admissions Counselors' College Fair. This program was a follow-on to similar fairs of the Catholic College Coordinating Council that Stonehill had hosted in the sixties. The event grew annually, so that by the end of the decade over 175 colleges and universities sent representatives who serviced some 7000 students from the surrounding region. Campus celebrations of various natures were scheduled throughout the academic year. A two-day "Renaissance Festival" in the spring of 1979, combining the efforts of Student Life and the Academic Division, offered lectures on Renaissance music and culture and a performance of "Romeo and Juliet" by Boston's Shakespeare Company. The Fall Carnival, sponsored by the Orientation Committee, the Ames Society, the Student Activities Office, and the SGA was initiated in 1988 to welcome the new academic year. Students were entertained by musicians and street performers and experienced the artistry of caricaturists, tattoo specialists, and personalized button makers; an obstacle course provided a challenge for the athletically inclined. Oktoberfest, sponsored by the Cultural Committee and held at Brother Mike's, brought a lively response from students in the fall semester.[13]

Activities initiated and operated exclusively by the social committee for students were also popular in the eighties. In December 1979 a campus-wide "College Bowl" competition was started. Teams of four members competed in a tournament-like playoff that generated a champion and four "all stars" who represented Stonehill in a regional College Bowl contest. In 1980 Stonehill's team placed sixth among schools competing in New England. In the mid-eighties, the College Center Spa was the site of "Air Band," a program of various musical and variety acts conducted by students. A contest for individual and group performers, graded by faculty and administrators, was the highlight of the evening. Las Vegas style "All Niters," also held at the College Center, made their appearance in the spring of 1987. Casino gambling, music and dancing, palm readers, and movies were some of the activities offered.[14]

While some students described the eighties as a period of apathy, Stonehill did experience in this decade manifestations of social awareness through activities sponsored by the Institute of Justice and Peace and the Campus Ministry. A day of fast, where monies saved from not eating were collected to benefit Oxfam International and the Holy Cross Fathers' mission in Bangladesh, became an annual event. It was always scheduled near Thanksgiving to allow deeper personal reflection on world hunger. Central America Awareness Week in the spring of 1985 featured a debate on American aid to the "Contra" guerrillas fighting government forces in Nicaragua. An Earth Day celebration in the spring of 1990 echoed the efforts of Tom Feeley, CSC, Sandy McAlister, and the Stonehill Ecology Association in the early 1970s.[15]

War and peace issues were raised in several campus events. "Disarmament Awareness Week," March 17–23, 1980, was held as Soviet troops occupied Afghanistan and Americans were held captive in Tehran. The Institute of Justice and Peace sought to dampen America's "war mentality" by offering a peace alternative. Representatives of the American Friends Service Committee (AFSC)[16] spoke on campus, videos were shown, and a Mass for peace celebrated. One year later "Peace Week," featuring panel discussions, movies, and featured speakers, aimed to explore the issue of nuclear war. Publication in May 1983 of the United States Catholic Bishops' Pastoral Letter, "The Challenge of Peace: God's Promise and Our Response," generated a panel discussion on campus the ensuing fall. Professor Bruce M. Russett of Yale University, a principal consultant to the bishops on the letter, and Michael Novak of the American Enterprise Institute for Public Policy

Research addressed the pros and cons of nuclear weapons and deterrence. Professors Louis Manzo, CSC, Richard Finnegan, and Una O'Connor, CP, participated in a panel discussion following the main presentations.[17]

Minor in scope and intensity compared with that of the late 1960s, student activism nevertheless was present on campus in the 1980s. In the spring of 1978 Professor James Kenneally had directed a boycott of textile manufacturer J.P. Stevens for allegedly unfair labor practices. In the mid-eighties some students and faculty questioned the College's investments in South Africa, which practiced apartheid. A faculty petition recommended that the trustees take the necessary steps to divest Stonehill's assets from companies operating in South Africa.[18]

Stonehill marked its fortieth anniversary with a series of events throughout 1988. The festive year began in January with a campus-wide winterfest. In March the Stonehill community gathered at Christo's II restaurant in Brockton for a lavish dinner, followed by a concert by Irish singers Liam Clancy and Tommy Makem. In the fall a seminar featuring David Farrell, CSC, provincial of the Eastern Province, and alumnus Michael Novak discussed the question, "What Makes a Catholic College Catholic?"[19] The celebration culminated with the anniversary Mass on October 12, with Bishop Daniel Cronin of Fall River presiding and Richard Sullivan, CSC, as homilist.[20]

College Clubs and Organizations

THEATER ARTS, one of the oldest and most respected student activities, 🖙 continued to provide high-quality entertainment for Stonehill students, faculty, staff, and administrators. In the fall of 1978 the Greasepaint Players merged with the Stonehill Theater. It was believed that combining the talent and resources of both groups would create productions of higher quality. The move led to the presentation of two plays per year, one in the fall and the second in the spring. In the fall of 1980 Patricia Sankus took charge of theater arts on campus, replacing Alan Jorgensen, who had died suddenly the previous spring. Under her guidance in 1981 theater arts became an academic minor and the Alpha Psi Omega honor society was reinstituted.[21]

Theater productions in the eighties offered some traditional favorites, but the accent was on the new and unusual. Before the merger, the Greasepaint Players had performed *South Pacific*, *Anything Goes*, and *You Can't Take It With You*. Under Sankus' direction, theater moved away from these traditional offerings and presented less familiar and many times cutting-edge plays. In the early eighties, audiences were treated to performances of *The Rimers of Eldrich*, *The Lady's Not for Burning*, *The Picture of Dorian Gray*, and *Shadow Box*. During the latter half of the decade, Sankus produced *Squaring the Clock*, *A Clearing in the Woods*, and *The Diviners*. *Equus* produced some controversy in November 1986, when acting president C. James Cleary ordered the nudity in a scene to be cut.[22]

In addition to productions by the Stonehill Theater Company, the College's theater enthusiasts were offered other plays. The Institute of Justice and Peace, commemorating 1979 as the year of the child, funded a production of *I Never Saw Another Butterfly*. *Fantasticks* was performed in the spring of 1980 by a traveling Broadway troupe. Four faculty plays, *Waiting for Godot*, *Young Man Luther*, *The Tempest*, and *The Caretaker* highlighted the acting ability of Professors Robert Goulet, Chet Raymo, George Branigan, and Albert Cullum, among others. In the fall of 1986 the cultural committee started dinner theater at the College Center Spa. For $5 a patron received dinner and a performance of *The Owl and the Pussycat*, performed by the Alpha Omega Players, a national touring company. The next year Stonehill Dinner Theater presented *Barefoot in the Park*.[23]

Throughout the eighties Campus radio WSHL–FM continued to broadcast news, sports events, and music from its studios in the College Center. In the winter of 1979 the station had petitioned the FCC to increase its power to 100 watts. Almost two years later approbation was received; increased power transmission was inaugurated in February 1982. The event was celebrated by honoring Professor Herbert Wessling for his dedicated service to Stonehill's pioneering radio efforts.[24]

WSHL experienced other significant milestones in the 1980s. Continuing a tradition started in the spring of 1974, the station conducted an annual marathon auction of seven consecutive days of nonstop broadcasting to raise money for station operations. In 1984 WSHL received a $100,000 grant from the estate of Joseph L. Sweeney "to help the station and enhance its potential." Station directors used a portion of the grant to purchase a UPI news machine and to remodel its production room in the College Center. In the fall of 1990, for the first time on a regular basis, the station expanded its programming to 24 hours per day.[25]

Student organizations such as the Stonehill Theater Company and WSHL-FM were complemented by many fine speakers who entertained and challenged the College community. In the spring semester 1978, the Institute for Justice and Peace and its director, Professor David O'Brien, had assembled a cadre of leading Catholic theologians and social scientists to deliver a series of 12 lectures under the general title, "The American Catholic Church and the Quest for Justice and Peace."[26] In the fall of 1989 the Business Department sponsored a series of five talks, "Becoming Adaptable to Managing in the Nineties" (titled the B.A.T.M.A.N. series). Furthermore, many

WSHL bumper sticker.

notable personalities sponsored by various College clubs spoke on campus, including the former American Ambassador to El Salvador, Robert White, "MASH" television star Larry Lindville, the former prime minister of Ireland, Charles Haughey, the noted philosopher and educator Ralph McInerny, the novelist Elizabeth Sewell, Boston *Globe* columnist Mike Barnicle, and the social activist, John C. Cort.[27]

Commencement in the eighties featured an impressive array of speakers from Church, state, and the press. Max Cleland, the youngest man to head the Veterans Administration (and elected to the United States Senate from Georgia in 1996), Bruce Ritter, O.F.M., founder of New York's Covenant House for the care of street children, Congressmen Tip O'Neill, Silvio Conte, and Dan Rostenkowski, writer George Plimpton, and television and radio journalist Charles Osgood addressed graduates during this decade.

Popular music concerts were not numerous, but several groups did perform on campus under the sponsorship of the social committee of the SGA. In October 1979 Livingston Taylor gave the first campus concert since 1974, entertaining 500 students in Merkert Gymnasium. Other performers on campus were Clannad, an Irish folk music group, and rock groups NRBQ, Beaver Brown, Southside Johnny, The Outfield, and Taylor Dayne.

Student service organizations, active at Stonehill from the outset, evolved to meet contemporary needs as they continued to offer assistance to the disadvantaged. The RFK Society, established in 1969 to provide sponsors for the Big Brothers and Big Sisters program in Brockton and Easton, became one of the most popular organizations on campus in the eighties. In the fall of 1980 the Father Allan Kraw Council (#7679) of the Knights of Columbus was founded on campus.[28] Fifty students were initiated on October 8, with Wilfred Raymond, CSC, a member of the Campus Ministry team, as organizer and chaplain.[29] The Stonehill Circle K Club, affiliated with Kiwanis International, was formed in the fall of 1989. The Tribe, a new club "to enhance student spirit and move out from apathy," was inaugurated at a fall 1990 pep rally to promote student interest in sports. The Organization for the Study of Gender Issues, which provided information on many student women issues, was started in March 1990.[30]

Besides serving as a comfortable environment for the sustenance and growth of many longstanding activities and clubs, the 1980s was a period of innovation in campus projects as well. In the spring of 1980 the first Mini University Series was offered. This collection of nonacademic courses for faculty and students was designed to be both educational and enjoyable. Courses ranged in length from two sessions to eight weeks and covered the gamut from macramé to aerobics to whale-watching.

Fine arts, which—with the exception of the Stonehill Theater Company—had received little attention at the College, began to blossom in the 1980s. Advancements in theater and academics were matched with cultural programs for students and the campus community. In the fall of 1982 the Stonehill Community Orchestra was formed under the direction of Douglas Anderson. It began with 15 members but within one year could boast of 35 musicians. The orchestra, which drew performers from Stonehill and the greater Easton area, performed four concerts annually in its first two years, playing such classical favorites as Camille Saint-Saëns' "Carnival of the Animals" and Jacques Offenbach's "Overture to Orpheus in the Underworld." The concerts, which at times featured outside soloists, were well received by students, faculty, and staff. In the fall of 1985, the orchestra, now conducted by Ann Davis, merged with the Wheaton College Orchestra because of the small numbers in both ensembles. By 1990 Stonehill's participation in the orchestra ended. The Wheaton orchestra is still active today.[31]

Stonehill's fine arts program received its greatest boost through participation in the E. Nakamichi Foundation, established and funded in 1985 to encourage the propagation and appreciation of baroque, classical, and other fine music forms.[32] In 1986 Stonehill received a grant of $55,121 from the foundation.[33] In September 1986 Richard Mazziotta, CSC, accepted appointment as the chairman of the Board of Trustees for the Stonehill College Nakamichi Endowment. Two years later a new board was appointed by Bartley MacPháidín, with Sr. Grace Donovan, SUSC, of Campus Ministry as chair. Beginning with classical guitarist Peter Clemente, who played the first concert on October 22, 1986, in the Chapel of Mary, the Nakamichi series brought to campus such talented artists as cellist Elsa Hilger, organist James David Christie, and the Boston Camerata.

Campus Ministry was the backbone of the College's mission to form the soul as well as the mind of students. From the time of its formal organization in 1964 by John McCarthy, CSC, students had been offered the sacraments, retreats, counseling, and marriage preparation. In April 1979 the director of Campus Ministry, Ken Silvia, CSC, asked for an official change in governance for his office. He suggested that Campus Ministry be placed organizationally under the executive vice president, removing it from the Student Life Division in order to emphasize that it served the entire College community, not merely the student body. His request was granted for a two-year trial period in 1981, and the new organization structure has continued ever since. Silvia also requested that the director be given ex-officio nonvoting status on the Academic Committee, the Student Affairs Committee, and the College Council.[34]

In July 1979 Richard Segreve, CSC, a member of the Campus Ministry team since 1976, was appointed director. Segreve immediately organized his office into five independent and active committees—spiritual development, educational training, social action, liturgy, and social—each headed by a member of the team. He also instituted a collection at the Sunday Masses, with offerings to be given to various worthy causes and groups in the local region. Under Segreve's tutelage, Stonehill's first lay Eucharistic ministers were installed by Bishop Daniel Cronin in March 1980.[35]

Through the eighties, Campus Ministry provided many of the ingredients of the intangible Stonehill spirit of community. Students built personal and spiritual relationships with many members of Holy Cross and others of the Campus Ministry team. The personal touch, through which a priest became a concerned and trusted friend, made a deep impression on many students. Sunday night Masses, called "Sunday-Nite Live," were well attended. Students willingly gathered at the Chapel of Mary out of desire for spiritual nourishment and as a support to the community. What happened in the chapel on Sunday evening became for many the principal subject of conversation on Monday morning.[36]

Student Sports

LIKE THEATER ARTS, debate, and campus radio, sports had been popular with students from the outset, but criticism of existing programs by people inside and outside the College raised concerns about the direction of Stonehill athletics. Aware of the criticism, MacPháidín in April 1978 appointed a 13-member special task force, chaired by C. James Cleary, "to undertake a review of the entire athletic program at the College." A report submitted in June spoke of "the value of athletics, as part of its commitment to the development of a 'total person.' " The task force suggested that the College make a greater commitment of funds and personnel to the development of athletic programs. Promotion of intramurals and varsity women's athletics, including more scholarships for female athletes, were specific recommendations.[37] The report also recommended that club sports, men's hockey and women's soccer, cross country, and volleyball, be raised to varsity status. The task force remained in place for two years after its initial report "to point out problem areas that may still exist and make recommendations for their correction to the President."[38]

Organizational changes in the Athletic Department were frequent in the 1980s. When Harry Hart, athletic director and men's basketball coach since 1975, left the College in the spring of 1978,[39] Tom Folliard, athletic director and men's basketball coach at Bryant College, was hired to replace Hart. Folliard served until the summer of 1984, when he was replaced by Raymond P. Pepin.[40] Paula Sullivan, women's basketball coach from the outset, was appointed assistant athletic director and coordinator of women's sports in September 1981.[41]

In addition to making personnel changes, the Athletic Department moved into a larger and more competitive league. In June 1980 Stonehill joined the Northeast Seven (NE-7) Conference. The league expanded in 1983 to eight members and eventually became the NE-10 in July 1987. Bartley MacPháidín presided over the conference, run by the college presidents, from 1986 to 1988.[42] His duties included calling meetings of the conference members, reviewing applications of colleges that wanted to join, and promoting a linkage between superior athletics and academic achievement.

Stonehill's intramural program expanded in response to the recommendations of the task force, which suggested more sports and coed participation. In the fall of 1978, men's intramurals included football, basketball, soccer, and softball; women participated in flag football, basketball, soccer, volleyball, and softball.[43] Sports added in the fall of 1978 were coed flag football and softball and men's street hockey. The ensuing spring, men's and women's badminton and coed tennis, racketball, and volleyball were added to the intramural offerings.

Men's sports at Stonehill in the 1980s garnered many achievements for teams and individuals. The hockey team posted its best season record ever, 14–8–1, in only its second year on the varsity circuit. Cross country, led by Craig Binney, competed for the first time in the National Catholic Cross-Country Invitational, held at Notre Dame in the fall of 1981. The tennis team had posted a College-best record of 13–2 in 1978. Soccer, under Coach Ernie Branco, won the NE-8 regular season title in 1985 and won consecutive NE-10 championships in 1990 and 1991. Baseball, coached by Lou Colitti and led by pitchers Ron Peterson and Richard Stuart and shortstop

1980 baseball team.

Bob Wooster, was ECAC cochampion in 1980. The team won the NE-10 conference crown in 1984 and 1985.

Stonehill's football squad took a prominent place in campus life during the decade of the eighties. Under Coach Cliff Sherman, the team competed on the club level until 1989. Midway through the 1985 season the team was rated number one in the nation for club programs. In the early eighties interior lineman Mike Tosone achieved All Conference and All American recognition.[44] In its first year in Division III varsity play (1989), the team won the ECAC championship with a 24–12 triumph over archrival Bentley College. Coach Sherman was selected coach of the year and nine players were selected for the All-Conference squad.[45]

The tradition of basketball as the premier sport on campus continued in the decade of the eighties. A change in philosophy led to scheduling occasional games with NCAA Division I opponents. In January 1977 the squad traveled to South Bend, Indiana, to take on Notre Dame. Although the score was lopsided against the Chieftains, 98–70, the Brockton *Enterprise* reported that the team held its own. A special student event for basketball opened the 1979–1980 season: A spirited pep rally in Merkert Gymnasium

Stonehill basketball in action against Providence College.

prepared students for the big game to be played the next day against the Providence College Friars. After a late afternoon roast beef dinner in the cafeteria, students boarded buses to travel to the game. Although Stonehill lost the contest 83–62, a good time was experienced by all.[46]

Stonehill's basketball program grew in the eighties through significant achievements by the team and individual players and rescheduling. The team won the conference championship three consecutive years (1980 through 1982). Bill Zolga, whom coach Tom Folliard called "the best all-around ballplayer I've ever coached," was the team leader in these years, earning

Men's basketball team celebrates 1988–1989 NE-10 championship.

the designation of All-American in 1979 and 1980.[47] The 1980 squad played in the North Central region of the NCAA Division II tournament, held at South Dakota State University, losing in the first round but winning the consolation game.[48] Bob Rietz was the team leader in the 1982 and 1983 seasons, being named to the All-American team both years and breaking the 2000-point barrier (2218), second only to Mike Allocco (2399) as the all-time Stonehill scoring leader. The 1982 team was undefeated in conference play and rated #15 in the NCAA Division II poll. Conference championships in 1987 and 1989 under Coach Raymond Pepin rounded out a highly successful period for Stonehill basketball. Zolga, Reitz, and Brian Cronin joined Mike Allocco as the four players honored to have their numbers retired.[49]

Women's athletics, which came into its own in the 1980s through the recommendations of the 1978 task force, kept pace with men's sports in

Mary Naughton scores 798th point and establishes a NCAA record.

Bartley MacPháidín, CSC, and Edward E. Martin.

excellence and achievement. Although the soccer team did not capture a conference championship in the eighties, it did post impressive records in four consecutive seasons, 1981 through 1984, winning 13 contests in both 1982 and 1983 under Coach Jim Jackson. Softball, coached by Fred Petti, achieved great success between 1979 and 1985, winning the State Division III title in 1980 and posting its best winning record, 25–8, in 1985. In tennis, Diane Anastasio won the Massachusetts state single's championship in October 1980.[50]

Women's basketball, under the guidance of Coach Paula Sullivan, achieved excellence and received recognition equal to the men's program. Conference championships were won in 1983, 1985, and 1987. The 1986–1987 squad, which achieved its best record to date, 27–5, was led by Lesli Laychak and Mary Naughton. The next season was special to team and coaches: The squad received a NCAA bid and Coach Sullivan was selected by the Women's Basketball Coaches Association as New England district coach of the year. This year also saw a first for the Stonehill women's basketball program—its first All-American selectee in Mary Naughton. The junior standout was selected ECAC player of the year, set an NCAA Division II national single-season scoring record with 799 points, and was honored as the Northeast Collegiate Athlete of the Year (Division II). Naughton went on to become the first Lady Chieftain to score more than 2000 points (2144) in her career. In addition to Laychak and Naughton, Nancy Smith, Ann Mallory, and Mary Anne Walsh were honored with the retirement of their numbers.[51]

Three new athletic awards to honor present and past athletic accom-

First Stonehill Athletic Hall of Fame inductees:
Nancy Smith, Paula Sullivan, Donald Prohovich, Bartley MacPháidín (president), Lou
Gorman, Michael Allocco, and Armond Colombo.

plishments at Stonehill were established in the 1980s. In 1982 the Edward
E. Martin Award[52] was introduced. One woman and one man from the
senior class were selected for their achievements on the athletic field and in
the classroom. The first recipients were Theresa Tardiff (volleyball and softball) and Mark Morrison (football). In the spring of 1989 the Stonehill College Athletic Hall of Fame was instituted. Athletic Director Ray Pepin
chaired a committee of nine, representing all areas of the College, to set
criteria for induction.[53] At a dinner held at Easton's Four Hundred Restaurant on May 5, eight people became the initial inductees: Bill Gartland, CSC,
athletic director from 1959 to 1963 was posthumously inducted. Known to
many as "Mr. Stonehill" because of his gregarious personality and almost
photographic memory for names, Gartland was remembered as a great pro-
moter of the College in his support for alumni throughout the years. The

other first-year inductees were Armond Colombo, Paula Sullivan, Lou Gorman, Nancy Smith, Mike Allocco, Don Prohovich, and Angelo Caranfa, Jr.[54] Also in the spring of 1989, the Rev. William F. Gartland Award for excellence in athletic achievement, to be awarded to one man and one woman annually, was first presented. The initial winners were Jon Cronin (basketball) and Kim Dunn (soccer).

ENDNOTES

1. Group interview 1970s, November 19, 1996, Stonehill History Project Papers, ASC. Students of the late seventies stated that the trends of the eighties began after 1975 at Stonehill.

2. Group interview, 1980s, February 4, 1997, Stonehill College History Project Papers, ASC.

3. *Ibid.*

4. *The Summit* ran many articles in its issues in 1978 and 1979 against the abuse of alcohol by students. Several letters to the editors, written by residents of the townehouses where the damage occurred, expressed anger at the paper's "bias" and "one-sided" analysis of the situation.

5. *The Summit* (March 14, 1979 and May 9, 1979), ASC.

6. Ibid., December 13, 1978, February 27, 1980, September 18, 1985, ASC.

7. Although *The Summit* was the official campus paper, *The Free Voice*, an underground bimonthly publication, was started to correct "the lack of quality in the content of the Summit." As with *Atman* and *Super Sheet* in the 1960s, this alternative voice was short-lived. In the spring of 1986 *The Summit* ran out of funds budgeted for the academic year. A request to the Student Activities Committee for additional money was denied. Thus, the paper was forced to cease publication after March 26. See Summit Editorial Board to Stonehill Community, April 8, 1986, Student Government Papers, ASC.

8. *The Summit* produced candid and pragmatic essays in this series, investigating violence and alcohol, sex and dating, and substance abuse. Reporters integrated the local experience into the national dilemma in provocative ways.

9. *The Stonehill Review* 2(2) (April 1978); *News Bureau*, February 16, 1978 and March 15, 1978, Public Affairs Papers, ASC. After the emergency was over, Stonehill students, faculty, and staff collected sixty boxes of clothing, canned goods, and dried food stuffs to be distributed to victims of the blizzard. The effort was coordinated by Professor Richard Shankar.

10. The resignation of Housing Director Bill Rose was immediate.

11. Group interview, 1980s, February 4, 1997, Stonehill College History Project Papers, ASC.

12. *The Summit* (February 7, 1979 and September 19, 1979), ASC. The position of Bill Braun, CSC, was eliminated, thus no replacement was needed.

13. *Ibid.*, September 12, 1989, October 10, 1989, March 1, 1978; Robert Kruse to Faculty, Staff, and Administrators, April 19, 1979, Kruse–Dean Papers, ASC.

14. *The Summit* (November 3, 1987, April 1, 1987, and April 11, 1989), ASC.

15. *Ibid.*, November 15, 1978, April 3, 1985, and April 24, 1990.

16. The American Friends Service Committee, founded in April 1917 by Quaker pacifists, was one of the leading peace organizations in twentieth-century American history.

17. *The Summit* (March 4, 1980, November 11, 1981, October 19, 1983); Schedule of Events, March 17–23, 1980, Justice and Peace Papers; *News Bureau*, November 13, 1981 and September 26, 1983, Public Affairs Papers, ASC.

18. *The Summit* (April 26, 1978); Group interview, 1980s, February 4, 1997, Stonehill History Project Papers; Stonehill Faculty to Board of Trustees, May 9, 1986, Board of Trustees Papers, ASC.

19. The panel was originally to include Catherine T. McNamee, CSJ, president of the National Catholic Education Association (NCEA), but she was unable to attend.

20. *The Summit* (February 9, 1988); Flyer "Makem and Clancy" College Relations Papers, ASC; Flyer "Stonehill 40th Anniversary," September 27, 1988; Program "40th Anniversary Mass," October 12, 1988, Stonehill College Papers, AHCFE.

21. *The Stonehill Review* 7(4) (Fall 1984), Public Affairs Papers, ASC; Kevin Spicer, "The History of Theater at Stonehill College," April 21, 1986, Stonehill College Papers, AHCFE.

22. *The Summit* (December 10, 1986), ASC.

23. *Ibid.*, April 25, 1979, March 15, 1978, March 27, 1980, October 29, 1986, November 3, 1987; *News Bureau*, February 28, 1980, Public Affairs, ASC.

24. *The Summit* (April 26, 1978, March 9, 1981, and February 10, 1982), ASC.

25. *Ibid.*, April 1, 1981, April 11, 1984, February 6, 1985, October 23, 1990.

26. David O'Brien, Loyola Professor of Roman Catholic Studies at the College of the Holy Cross in Worcester, Massachusetts and a leading historian of the American Church, served one year at Stonehill as director of the Institute of Justice and Peace. Through his influence, the 1978 spring series of speakers included Richard Clifford, SJ, and David Hollenbach, SJ, of Westin School of Theology; Philip Scharper of Orbis Books; Thomas Quigley of the Office of International Justice and Peace, United States Catholic Conference (USCC); and Gerald Mische of Global Education Associates.

27. *The Summit* (October 3, 1979, October 24, 1989); *News Bureau*, November 2, 1984, Public Affairs Papers, ASC.

28. Allan Kraw, CSC, class of 1968, was ordained a priest in February 1980. He died of cancer on May 7, 1980.

29. *The Summit* (October 22, 1980), ASC. The Knights of Columbus, a Roman Catholic fraternal order, was formed in New Haven under the direction of Father Michael McGivney in October 1881. Stonehill became the forty-first college campus to sponsor a Knights' council. A complete history of the Knights is found in Christo-

pher J. Kauffman, *Faith and Fraternalism: The History of the Knights of Columbus 1882–1982* (New York: Harper and Row, 1982) and its update, *Columbianism and the Knights of Columbus: A Quincentenary History* (New York: Simon and Schuster, 1992).

30. *The Summit* (April 3, 1990, October 16, 1990, May 1, 1990), ASC.

31. Ibid., October 6, 1982, September 28, 1983, February 27, 1985, September 25, 1985, December 11, 1985; Robert Kruse, Annual Report, July 1, 1984, Kruse-Dean Papers, ASC. Douglas Anderson tried to obtain academic credit for students in the orchestra, but the administration rejected the request. Lack of administrative support for the orchestra was one significant reason Stonehill's participation ended.

32. Nakamichi Foundation Bulletin I (1) (Fall 1988), Deans' Papers, ASC. In accordance with its goals, the Foundation awarded nearly fifty grants, totaling $3 million between 1986 and 1988.

33. In June 1986 Stonehill secured an award of 7000 shares of Nakamichi Corporation stock to establish a concert series. Sale of the stock in 1987 netted $55,121. See George Hagerty to Les Mitchnick, October 24, 1989, Deans' Papers, ASC.

34. Campus Ministry Council Meeting Minutes, April 11, 1979; Bartley Mac-Pháidín to C. James Cleary, September 10, 1981, MacPháidín Papers, ASC.

35. *The Summit* (October 21, 1979 and March 26, 1980), ASC.

36. Group interview, 1980s, February 4, 1997, Stonehill History Project Papers, ASC.

37. "Report of the Task Force on Athletics at Stonehill College," June 1, 1978, Athletic Department Papers, ASC. Originally the task force recommended increasing women's basketball scholarships from two to five between 1978 and 1983. However, by 1980 the recommendation was five scholarships by 1980 and a total of ten by 1983.

38. *Ibid.* Men's hockey and women's volleyball became varsity sports in 1978; women's soccer and cross country were raised in 1980. In December 1980 varsity sports teams at Stonehill were: Men—basketball, baseball, soccer, golf, tennis, and hockey (Division III); Women—basketball, softball, tennis, soccer, cross country, and volleyball. Sailing was a coed varsity sport.

39. Stonehill College News Release, April 28, 1978, Athletic Department Papers, ASC. Hart cited his reasons for leaving Stonehill: (1) a lack of sufficient time to devote to the basketball team, (2) lack of adequate staff, and (3) personal desire to move to a Division I basketball program.

40. The College had two men named Raymond Pepin: Raymond A. Pepin, professor of Economics and director of Lockary Computer Center, and Raymond P. Pepin, athletic director and men's basketball coach.

41. *News Bureau*, June 22, 1978, Public Affairs Papers; *The Summit* (September 16, 1981 and September 19, 1984); *Stonehill Alumni Magazine* I(1) (Fall/Winter 1985): 6, College Relations Papers, ASC.

42. Bartley MacPháidín, Report to Board of Trustees, October 3, 1980, MacPháidín Papers, ASC. The original NE-7 consisted of American International College, Assumption College, Bentley College, Bryant College, Springfield College,

Stonehill College, and the University of Hartford. The members of the NE-10 today are: Assumption, American International College, Bentley, Bryant, Quinnipiac, LeMoyne, Saint Anselm, Saint Michael, Merrimack, and Stonehill.

43. Report of Task Force on Athletics at Stonehill College," June 1, 1978, Athletic Department Papers, ASC. Task Force recommendations for fall intramurals were: Co-ed flag football and softball, men's football and street hockey, men's and women's ping pong, basketball, racketball, and tennis. Spring intramural offerings were women's flag football, men's and women's soccer, softball, volleyball, and badminton, and coed tennis, racketball, volleyball, and badminton.

44. *The Summit* (September 26, 1984 and October 23, 1985), ASC.

45. Ibid., December 12, 1989; "History of Stonehill Football," Sports Information Sheet, n.d [Fall 1991], Athletic Department Papers, ASC.

46. Brockton *Enterprise* clipping (January 19, 1977), in Athletic Department Papers; *The Summit* (November 28, 1979), ASC.

47. *The Summit* (February 7, 1979), ASC.

48. Ibid., February 26, 1980; Brockton *Enterprise* clipping (March 4, 1980), in Athletic Department Papers, ASC. Stonehill was honored to represent the conference in the NCAA Division II tournament, but a minor controversy arose as to why the team played in South Dakota and not the northeast regional as would be expected. Fred Petti, professor of philosophy and faculty NCAA representative, wrote to Ed Markey, chairman of the Northeast NCAA Selection Committee, complaining about the selection of Springfield College over Stonehill. Petti argued that Stonehill's squad was better in every aspect, concluding, "I consider the action of the committee to be blatantly self-serving and is a flagrant violation of the principle of equity and basic fairness."

49. *The Summit* (March 31, 1982, March 2, 1983, March 21, 1989), ASC; Athletic Records Summary, Sports Information Director, Stonehill College.

50. *The Summit* (May 7, 1980), ASC; Athletic Records, Sports Information Director, Stonehill College.

51. *The Summit* (February 11, 1987, March 22, 1988, September 20, 1988, February 14, 1989), ASC; Athletic Records, Sports Information Director, Stonehill College.

52. Edward E. Martin, the youngest brother of Congressman Joseph Martin, was an accomplished baseball player at Dartmouth College. He is a long-time benefactor of Stonehill College.

53. *Stonehill Alumni Magazine* 10(1) Summer 1989: 12, College Relations Papers, ASC. The committee sought alumni (at least five years after graduation) who had achieved milestones in the sports world and others who had contributed greatly to the Stonehill Athletic program.

54. In April 1997 the dining room in Donahue Hall was dedicated in Gartland's memory. Gorman (1953) was a major league baseball executive, Colombo (1955) was football coach at Brockton High School, Prohovich (1980) played baseball, Caranfa (1966) played soccer and was Stonehill's first All-American selectee, and Smith (1983) and Allocco (1972) played basketball.

CHAPTER 16

Toward the Millennium

The history of Stonehill College can be likened to a series of blocks, laid one atop another, that over fifty years have built an institution ready to meet the challenges of the twenty-first century. Established hastily to keep Franciscans from starting a college instead, Stonehill emerged as a nationally recognized institution of higher learning in the liberal arts tradition through the leadership and dedication of many Holy Cross religious and lay men and women who supported the founders' mission. Each succeeding decade brought new opportunities for the College to provide for the needs and desires of its students. Stonehill's presidents provided the leadership, vision, and perseverance that fashioned the foundation on which the College exists today.

The 1990s provided unique challenges to the College. The relationship between the Church and all institutions of higher education, a source of debate that had always been present in some degree, became center-stage in this decade. National recognition in 1985 placed the College in a position that created certain expectations. Financial, academic, and physical expansion became normative, and the College and its leaders felt the pressure of success and the new demands that it brings. Moving toward its fiftieth anniversary and the millennium, Stonehill, as a new member of an elite group in Catholic higher education, was forced to move forward, for stagnation would have been tantamount to failure. Led by Bartley MacPháidín, CSC, Stonehill College entered the nineties seeking to advance in service to Church and society.

The Catholic Church and Higher Education in the 1990s

IN 1980 THE Vatican Congregation for Catholic Education began the task of formulating a document that would define a Catholic university. A first draft, perceived by many educators as an attempt to "flesh out the precepts of Canons 807–814 in the new Code of Canon Law,[1] was sent to select *periti* for review. Following some revisions, a draft schema was forwarded to all bishops and college/university presidents throughout the world (650 schools) in 1985. The Association of Catholic Colleges and Universities (ACCU) also forwarded the draft to all 235 Catholic institutions of higher learning in the United States. Over one hundred respondents made criticisms of the schema, including a recommendation to recognize that various environments generate diverse opinions on education and a suggestion that maintenance of the Catholic character of an institution must be more than simply connection with the local bishop. More importantly, however, respondents suggested that autonomy of educational institutions was threatened by the schema.[2]

The ACCU suggested that the document's "judicial tone . . . is inappropriate to the relationship of the Church with the university." The critique argued that the schema must recognize two basic realities: (1) The university is a place for an intellectual journey toward truth and not a place where one receives "the truth" already known and packaged; (2) at the end of the twentieth century, we have a new understanding of and respect for genuine cultural pluralism and its impact on the ministry of education.[3]

In response to a request by Cardinal William Baum of the Sacred Congregation for Catholic Institutions,[4] Bartley MacPháidín organized a committee, chaired by Sr. Grace Donovan, to formulate a response to the draft schema. The committee, which met for two months, concluded in a noncontroversial report "that the time was not opportune for a wider circulation of the document in its present form." Stonehill's comments were sent to Superior General Thomas Barrosse, who presented them to Roman authorities, together with the responses of all five Holy Cross institutions under his jurisdiction in the United States.[5]

A third draft of the document, incorporating the recommendations of Catholic educators worldwide, was completed in 1988 for discussion at a Roman conference scheduled for April 1989. The Vatican session attracted 90 college and university rectors and presidents as well as 40 bishops. Seventy-five percent of the attendees signed a position paper supporting principles of academic freedom, autonomy of governing boards, and independence from direct ecclesiastical authority.[6]

Published on August 15, 1990, *Ex Corde Ecclesiae*, the final product of the protracted discussions on the relationship of the Church to Catholic universities and colleges, brought immediate challenges from American Catholic educators. Richard McBrien at Notre Dame claimed that the 1985 schema and, therefore, the final draft *Ex Corde*, was "unnecessary." He argued that all recently published documents pertaining to the Church and higher education—the 1972 International Federation of Catholic Universities Statement, the 1976 position paper of the College and University Division of the NCEA, and the 1980 United States Catholic bishops' pastoral, "Catholic Higher Education and the Pastoral Mission of the Church"—supported two major values: academic freedom and institutional autonomy. *Ex Corde Ecclesiae* challenged these ideas.[7] The theologian Catherine LaCugna, also from Notre Dame, contested the theological tenets of *Ex Corde*. Countering the document's assumption that the Church is the hierarchy, LaCugna offered the more contemporary view of the Church as the people of God. Also, she challenged *Ex Corde's* claim that the university is *in* the Church:[8]

> The search for truth and knowledge is not inconsistent with the mission of the Church; however, the autonomy of the university, to which the document [*Ex Corde*] adverts explicitly, requires freedom from ecclesiastical jurisdiction.

The threat to institutional autonomy, perceived by many in American Catholic higher education in the text of *Ex Corde Ecclesiae*, drew the strongest negative response.[9] Jesuit Father Ladislaus Orsy, suggesting that bishops and theologians have different roles in the activity of the Church, argued that the "mandate"—the requirement that professors of theological disciplines be recognized by ecclesiastical authority—will "aggravate the situation," and that in the United States such a mandate might open bishops and the Church to litigation and jeopardize accreditation because it removes a certain sense of freedom from the individual professor.[10] Bishop James Malone, retired Bishop of Youngstown, Ohio, expressed concern that the ordinances of *Ex Corde* could threaten the autonomy of the Catholic college or university.[11]

The question of autonomy in American Catholic higher education was highly significant from a legal point of view. Strict implementation of *Ex Corde* was perceived to be a threat to government funding for Catholic colleges and universities. Institutions that adopted in full the precepts of the document could be perceived as possessing a more exclusive religious orientation than that allowed in recent Supreme Court cases that had paved the way for Catholic colleges and universities to receive federal funds.[12] Educator Charles Wilson expressed the additional fear that accreditation could be jeopardized as two important accrediting criteria—institutional integrity and autonomy, as well as academic freedom—were challenged by *Ex Corde*. The ACCU asserted that in keeping with the 1976 *Roemer vs. Board of Public Works* case, Catholic colleges could lose all government aid if they ever were found to be "controlled" by the Catholic Church.[13] The moral theologian Father Charles Curran summarized the perceived problem:[14]

> If the existing and proposed legislation for Catholic higher education [*Ex Corde*] is enforced, then the courts could very well rule unconstitutional all aid to Catholic higher education since these institutions would no longer accept the autonomy of the university and academic freedom. Thus the very existence of Catholic higher education is in jeopardy.

Publication of *Ex Corde Ecclesiae* raised in earnest the more general issue of Catholic identity on college and university campuses. Pope John Paul II suggested that the "distinctive contribution to the wider field of higher education" made by Catholic colleges and universities was their maintenance of Catholic identity:[15]

> This identity depends on the explicit profession of Catholicity on the part of the university as an institution, and also upon the personal conviction and sense of mission on the part of its professors and administrators.

In *Ex Corde Ecclesiae* the Pope outlined in detail his understanding of Catholicity in an institution of higher learning. He listed the essential characteristics that "every Catholic university, as Catholic" must have.[16] Institutional autonomy must be measured in "adherence to the teaching authority of the Church in matters of faith and morals." The Pope argued that the role of the teacher was central to the maintenance of Catholic identity: "The identity of a Catholic university is essentially linked to the quality of its teachers and to respect for Catholic doctrine." Catholic members of the university community "are called to a personal fidelity to the Church with all that this implies." Freedom in research and teaching appropriate to each academic discipline is recognized "so long as the rights of the individual and the community are preserved within the confines of the truth and the common good." In order not to jeopardize Catholic identity, the Pope stated that the number of non-Catholic teachers should not be allowed to constitute a majority.[17]

Fear of professionalism and secularization that jeopardized Catholic identity was expressed by some educators in higher learning. One writer assumed that Catholic colleges and universities were more professional than before but wondered if technological and academic improvements had taken place at the expense of Catholic character and identity.[18] Martin Stamm, a consultant in higher education, claimed secularization had occurred, implying it was intentionally done to "buy" survival:[19]

> What is clear is that the laicization, begun with some skepticism in the 1960s, has been nearly completed within American Catholic higher education. It is also clear that institutional presidents/leaders perceive the process as having substantially benefitted their organizations, allowing their college/university to survive and thrive during the uncertain economic, social, and political times of the 1980s and 1990s.

Many Church educators echoed the progressive cry to remove traditional stereotypes from Catholic higher education, while insisting on the sovereignty of the university. Theodore Hesburgh, CSC, insisted that all qualifiers, such as public or private, Catholic, or American only detract from "the university [,which] must first and foremost be a university, or else the thing that the qualifiers qualify is something, but not a university."[20] David Burrell, CSC, Hesburgh Professor of Philosophy and Theology at Notre Dame, described as "insidious" the demand for a set of criteria by which anyone could recognize an institution as truly Catholic. However, in response to those who viewed the word *Catholic* in a university title as problematic, he wrote:[21]

> Far from introducing a contradiction the adjective [Catholic] can supply the healthy tension required to resist external pressure and internal inertia, so that institutions which try to be Catholic may also stand a better chance of becoming a university than those lacking such an incentive.

The historian David O'Brien, who served as the director of Stonehill's Institute of Justice and Peace from 1977 to 1978, emphasized the uniqueness of American Catholicism in the higher education debate. He presented a moderating message stressing that Church and university benefit from each other. O'Brien suggested that because the meaning of the terms "Catholic" and "American" change with time, those involved with the debate on Catholic higher education should temper any quick judgments that link secularization with the loss of Catholic identity. Additionally, he argued, "Building on these truths [of the intellectual life] will require us to go beyond the chronic contentiousness that so often surrounds the Catholic university." On the other hand he warned: "Too often the college or university has allowed a segregation of academic and religious matters that goes far beyond the authentic respect for the autonomy of the secular recognized by Vatican II."[22]

The debate over the ideas and implications of *Ex Corde Ecclesiae* and the general discussion on Catholic identity was followed by procedures to implement the precepts of the letter in American colleges and universities. In 1993 a committee of the NCCB, chaired by John Leibrecht,[23] bishop of Springfield–Cape Girardeau, drafted a set of eight ordinances to govern relations between local ordinaries and institutions of higher education in their dioceses. In order to maintain Catholic identity, the ordinances mandated that Catholic colleges undertake an internal review at least every ten years to assure congruence of their research and courses of instruction with *Ex Corde Ecclesiae*, that Catholic professors of theology request the mandate from competent ecclesiastical authority, and that institutional authorities and the diocesan bishop promote the teaching of Catholic theological disciplines in communion with the Church. These ordinances were adopted despite unanimous opposition from eight college and university presidents who served with the bishops on the drafting committee.[24]

In December 1994, after criticism of the draft ordinances had been received from many fronts, Bishop Leibrecht's committee agreed that more dialogue was necessary. Leibrecht called for comments from other bishops, college and university presidents, and others in the field for use in the generation of a draft to be distributed to the hierarchy in the summer of 1995 for review in the fall.[25] Discussion and debate on the American bishops' implementation of *Ex Corde* continued until the fall of 1996, when the hierarchy adopted "*Ex Corde Ecclesiae*: An Application to the United States."[26]

Stonehill College's initial response to *Ex Corde Ecclesiae* was found in the reaction of the president. Bartley MacPháidín saw the document as the culmination of the ongoing debate in American Catholic higher education that had begun in 1967 with the Land O'Lakes Statement. While respecting the official nature of the Apostolic Constitution, the president insisted that "it must first be adapted to our particular [American] circumstances." He sought to satisfy both sides in the debate, but demonstrated his progressive tone in a statement to the Stonehill community:[27]

> To abandon that which sets us apart as an educational institution, our religious character, would violate the trust passed on to us by our predecessors and by the founding religious community of the College. But violation of trust is minor to the most grievous lapse of all: the failure to make the unique and invaluable contribution to society that derives from the dialogue between reason and faith, and from the preservation of transcendence as a category which must have its place in all authentic learning.

In December 1991 MacPháidín formed a 10-member committee, chaired by James M. Duane, CSC, to plan Stonehill's formal response to *Ex*

Corde.[28] The committee discussed ways to engage the campus community in an ongoing reflection on the Catholic character of the College. It was decided that a symposium addressing Catholic higher education in the United States, the Holy Cross tradition in education, and the experience of Stonehill would provide a framework for continuing reflection and a context for discussion of how Catholicity affects issues of hiring, promotion, and campus culture.[29]

Early in the spring semester 1993, two events organized by the committee preceded the symposium planned for April. In January a "brown bag lunch" panel discussion titled "Catholic Identity in Daily Stonehill Lives," was held at the Martin Institute. One month later a second luncheon presentation, "Possible Paradigms of Catholicity at Stonehill," explored various models of Catholicity in American colleges.

The symposium was held on April 30, 1993, with James Lackenmier, CSC, president of King's College in Wilkes-Barre, Pennsylvania, as the featured speaker. In his address, "American Catholic Higher Education and the Holy Cross Tradition," Lackenmier made several important points. He spoke of "the obligations that an educated person has towards society" and the duty of Catholic educators to properly train students to meet these responsibilities. He described the Holy Cross charisma in education as "identifiable and real" and its adaptability as a principal strength.[30] Lackenmier stated that American Catholic colleges and universities should accept the norms of *Ex Corde Ecclesiae*, but that they should be implemented "in our particularly American context, which is characterized by pluralism, respect for individual rights, and—in our time at least—rapidly developing technology and questions about the creation and distribution of wealth in the context of a global economy."[31]

Faculty responses to Lackenmier's address strongly supported the precepts of institutional autonomy and academic freedom. Professor Richard Capobianco took issue with *Ex Corde*'s contention that the mysteries of humanity and the world are clarified in the light of divine revelation, claiming that "the Academy must tolerate *all* [Capobianco's emphasis] findings and allow the community of reasonable men and women in dialogue with one another to sort out what is genuine understanding and what is not."[32] Professor Katie Conboy echoed Capobianco's emphasis on academic freedom, but concentrated her comments on the need for Stonehill to promote adaptability in the future through diversity, governance structure, and the sense of community on campus.[33]

The symposium was not the final word in what would be an ongoing debate at Stonehill concerning Catholic identity. As the academic discipline most directly impacted by *Ex Corde*, the Religious Studies Department met

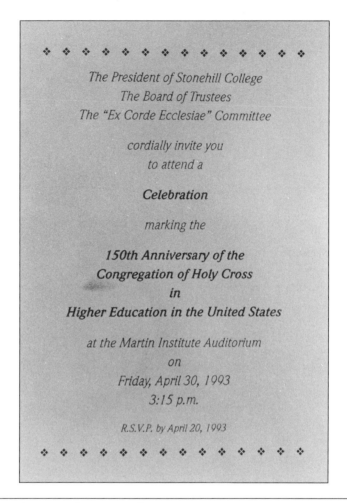

❖ ❖ ❖ ❖ ❖ ❖ ❖ ❖ ❖ ❖ ❖ ❖ ❖ ❖ ❖

The President of Stonehill College
The Board of Trustees
The "Ex Corde Ecclesiae" Committee

cordially invite you
to attend a

Celebration

marking the

150th Anniversary of the
Congregation of Holy Cross
in
Higher Education in the United States

at the Martin Institute Auditorium
on
Friday, April 30, 1993
3:15 p.m.

R.S.V.P. by April 20, 1993

❖ ❖ ❖ ❖ ❖ ❖ ❖ ❖ ❖ ❖ ❖ ❖ ❖ ❖ ❖

Ex Corde Ecclesiae *Conference, April 30, 1993.*

in December 1993 to discuss the proposed ordinances drafted by the eight-member bishops' committee of the NCCB earlier in the year. Faculty members "were disappointed and saddened . . . and not a little alarmed . . . both by the tone and content" of the ordinances.[34] In March 1995 Stonehill hosted a weekend seminar for presidents of Holy Cross institutions in the United States to discuss *Ex Corde*. Dr. Patricia Hayes, president of St. Edward's University, coordinated the conference. In April Bartley MacPháidín, CSC, Robert Kruse, CSC, Louis Manzo, CSC, and Professor James Kenneally discussed the document with Bishop Sean O'Malley in Fall River. O'Malley was pleased with the College's plans to implement *Ex Corde*.[35]

Commissions on Governance and Pluralism

CANONICAL ALIENATION in 1972 brought an end to the era of Holy Cross control of Stonehill by initiating shared governance, but the relationship between the College and the Congregation of Holy Cross remained unsettled. Efforts to formalize an agreement between the two led to an initial accord in 1983. A permanent pact, signed in June 1989, defined individual and mutual responsibilities, including the maintenance of a campus ministry program whose director would be a member of Holy Cross, the College's exclusive right to judge the qualifications of Holy Cross members presented for positions in faculty or administration, the College's agreement to pay and give benefits to religious in its employ, Holy Cross' commitment to make a monetary contribution each year, and finally the College's commitment to appoint a member of Holy Cross its president, if a suitable candidate could be found.[36]

With the relationship between the College and Holy Cross formalized, Stonehill was free to concentrate on other significant issues. College governance was once again in the spotlight when, in the fall of 1991, the Planning and Development Committee of the College recommended that MacPháidín establish presidential commissions to study pluralism and campus culture. The Commission on Campus Culture, chaired by Thomas Gariepy, CSC, was charged with assessing four areas: intellectual climate, Catholic character, governance, and the campus community. The commission met almost weekly between February and September 1992. Its report recommended that a consultant be engaged to conduct a campus-wide audit, to be followed by the formation of a presidential commission on governance that would address the concerns raised in the audit and develop a governance structure to meet these concerns.[37]

The commission's first recommendation brought Sr. Sally Furay, RSCJ, vice president and provost of the University of San Diego, to campus April 22–23, 1993. MacPháidín explained the necessity of a consultant: "Certain aspects of our governance are puzzling to visiting accreditation teams and are not meeting the needs of the times." During her stay, Furay spoke with administrators, faculty, and students, observed the operation of various committees, and reviewed the College's existing governance structure.

Furay's report presented her perceptions of Stonehill's governance structure and various attitudes toward it. She noted that faculty members were inactive, passive, and discontented because they perceived that their concerns and input would not be taken seriously.[38] Other observations of attitude were that the campus was unprepared for diversity, the faculty had difficulty getting its members to serve on committees, the faculty felt that its voice was not heard, the committee system was ineffective, the process of rank and tenure was obscure, and there was a lack of women in the administration. Structurally she noted the replacement of the College Council by division heads for decision making, lack of definition in top-level administrative roles, insufficient sharing in decision making, and decision making at times outside from established procedures. She concluded that Stonehill's governance structure was "basically flawed" and recommended that a simultaneous review of the governance structure and communication policies be conducted.[39]

The commission's report and the recommendations by Furay prompted MacPháidín to establish a commission on governance, the first effort to review governance internally since 1970. The commission, formed in October 1993 and chaired by the Honorable Judge Catherine Sabaitis, class of 1975, met for the first time in January 1994. After the addition of two elected members from the Faculty Assembly, the reconstituted commission met on March 25 and set its objectives.[40]

The commission's final report was submitted to the president on May 15, 1995. In general it recommended a reorganized committee structure, more emphasis on strategic planning, simplified lines of administrative authority, an increased faculty role in formulating academic policy, greater representation by staff on College committees, and an increased student presence in governance.[41] Some other major changes were also suggested in the report: elimination of the College Council, replacement of the Academic Committee with an academic council of three subcommittees—curriculum, general studies, and standards and evaluation—and retention of the Faculty Assembly as an information body only. It was also recommended that the responsibilities of the executive vice president be better defined to deal with the College's internal affairs. Finally the commission called for an *ad hoc* committee of the Board of Trustees to study its report and comment to the full board.[42]

Cultural diversity,[43] a problem at Stonehill noted by the Furay report, was an area of general concern throughout American Catholic higher education. Statistics showed that Catholic colleges and universities lagged behind American institutions in general in numbers of minority students.[44] In 1980 the NCCB had encouraged Catholic institutions to respond to the legitimate needs of minority groups, providing student aid and an education respecting various cultural heritages. One writer suggested this was the time for Catholic educators "to assume leadership in preparing for a more pluralistic national society."[45]

An environment supportive of diversity was considered essential to increase the number of minority students on campus. Colleges and universities had traditionally offered academic programs and student activities that gave little, if any, consideration to the needs of various ethnic groups. In other words, colleges had to overcome the general perception that they were not responsible for promoting multiculturalism. A conference on higher education held in Los Angeles in 1987 suggested, "To succeed, colleges must . . . create a seamless fabric of efforts, extending over the entire institution."[46]

Stonehill's lack of cultural diversity had been noted as early as 1986,[47] but a concerted effort to increase diversity did not begin until the nineties.[48] Fred Petti, vice president for administration, stated, "No school can be a mirror of society, but we must create a more accurate mix or students aren't being prepared to live in it." Robert Kruse referred to Stonehill's lack of diversity as "an institutional weakness."[49] The administration's recognition of need strengthened minority recruiting efforts on all fronts. Mailings were sent to minority students who were seen as potential matches with the school in Boston, Brockton, New Bedford, Springfield, and Providence. Other efforts included a high school visitation program, participation in the Student Training and Education Program (STEP—operating out of Brockton High School), establishment of a formal network with Holy Cross parishes having a significant minority population, and formation of an enrollment management committee in an effort to create an environment on campus that would accept pluralism.[50]

The 1990s drive to bring greater diversity found support among students as well. The November 4, 1991, issue of *The Summit* was dedicated to the subject of diversity. Articles on "How to Diversify" and "The Minority Experience" (an alumni response), editorials, and opinions on how to recruit minority athletes were offered in the paper. That same week Stonehill hosted the first of an annual "Fear No People Week," sponsored by the Committee Advocating Proactive Programming (CAPP). Other student projects to promote diversity were the sponsorship of individual community service, African Awareness Month, and Women's History Month.

In December 1991 a report of the Planning and Development Committee recommended that an internal Stonehill commission be appointed by the president to examine the issue of diversification, focusing on ways to increase the minority student population. In January MacPháidín formed a commission on pluralism, which was charged with setting "realistic goals for the recruitment, retention and graduation of a population diverse culturally, ethnically, economically and racially." The commission met from February to September 1993.[51]

After commending Campus Ministry and the Stonehill Education Project for their efforts to diversify programs and reach out to culturally and ethnically diverse groups, the commission's report made several major recommendations for increasing cultural diversity on campus: (1) that the president and the Board of Trustees take all necessary steps to achieve 8 percent minority enrollment by the year 2000, (2) that additional funding be sought and made available for programs to increase pluralism and diversity, (3) that a permanent advisory committee on pluralism and diversity be created, and (4) that a new administrative position, director of intercultural affairs, be created.[52]

MacPháidín established the permanent Advisory Committee on Intercultural Affairs in November, with Dean of Student Affairs Louis Saltrelli as chair. The committee set out to implement the recommendations of the presidential commission.[53] Committee members, who suggested that "the College needed to be more proactive in its commitment to diversity," were generally pleased with efforts on campus and in admissions to encourage diversification.[54] In the fall of 1992, Jean Hamler was appointed as the director of intercultural affairs. Hamler was generally impressed with Stonehill's efforts at diversity but, unlike Saltrelli, was critical of past admission practices: "Unless we can begin to admit a substantial number of students of color we *will not* [Hamler's emphasis] meet or come close to our stated goal of 8 percent by the year 2000."[55]

Stonehill's renewed efforts in cultural diversity included participation in novel programs to provide opportunities for minorities. On October 1, 1992, Project Challenge, a program of academic tutoring and counseling for area youth, was started. Students who entered the program in eighth grade and continued in it until graduation from high school would receive a full tuition scholarship to Stonehill or Massasoit Community College.[56] A successful effort in bringing foreign students to campus was also made in October 1992, when Stonehill signed a contract with Nippon Communications Network, a Japanese educational consulting firm, to admit at least five Japanese students to the College each year, beginning in the fall of 1993. In April 1993 the College received a $300,000 Balfour Foundation Grant for recruitment and support of minority students. This grant, along with $167,000 from the Congregation of Holy Cross, helped the College increase its minority financial aid budget by 66.4 percent in 1994.[57] In January 1994 Dwayne Sparks joined the Stonehill staff as director of the State Street Scholars in Business Program and coordinator of multicultural support services. The program was designed to attract candidates from inner-city schools to Stonehill and prepare them for careers in business and finance.[58]

THE 1990S WERE a period of academic innovation and progress at Stonehill, while the College's whole-person concept of education was worked out. Spiritual, moral, personal, and social development continued to be integral parts of the educative process. The academic program—the other half of a Stonehill education—prepared students for graduate schools and careers, for life-long learning, formally and informally throughout their lives, and for contributing enthusiastically to the world community.[59]

The College conducted a series of academic program reviews in the decade of the nineties.[60] An examination of the General Studies Program, initiated in 1989, investigated ways to revise the "Western Heritage Core" to make it more inclusive of other cultures. The assessment progressed slowly due to personnel changes on the Academic Committee, which conducted the evaluation of the proposed pilot program.[61] In 1992, after a thorough review, the College discontinued its 3–2 engineering cooperative programs with Notre Dame and the University of Hartford. A declining number of students, prohibitive costs, and frequent requests to add more prerequisites to Stonehill's program led to the decision.[62] A new Massachusetts law revamping the process of teacher preparation and licensing led the College to review its majors in elementary and early childhood education. Compliance with the new statutes required students who desired certification to major in one of the liberal arts or science disciplines and minor in elementary or early childhood education.[63]

Innovation in international programs[64] took a major step forward with the initiation of the Yaroslavl exchange. In the winter of 1987 Stanton Davis, a local philanthropist and former chief executive of Shaw's Supermarkets, approached Bartley MacPháidín with a proposal to further relations between the United States and the Soviet Union. Heartened by the summit between President Ronald Reagan and Soviet Leader Mikhail Gorbachev, Davis offered the College $200,000 to start a student and faculty exchange program between Stonehill and a college or university in the Soviet Union. In January 1989 a proposal from Stonehill for a cooperative program was circulated to the Soviet Union's State Committee of Public Education. At the same time a similar suggestion of collaboration with an American institution was made by Ian Kelly, counselor at the American Embassy, to Yaroslavl State University.[65] Yaroslavl officials became aware of the Stonehill proposal and were attracted because of compatibility with a liberal arts program and the College's orientation and size. In June MacPháidín sent a specific proposal to Yaroslavl that was accepted in September.[66]

Planning for a cooperative exchange between Stonehill and Yaroslavl began in January 1990. That month a team of representatives from Yaroslavl and the Russian ministry of higher education visited Stonehill and met with College officials. The visit ended with an initial two-year agreement[67] between the two schools that set up a student and faculty exchange. MacPháidín was elated about the cooperative:[68]

> This agreement launches a new stage in Stonehill's commitment to expanding foreign studies options for our students and to building greater diversity on campus. It represents a historic advance for the College, one that is large with potential.

In June 1990 the president, accompanied by Jo-Ann Flora, Fred Petti, and Professor George Gallant, who was appointed director of the new exchange, traveled to Yaroslavl to respond to the Russian visit six months earlier. The cooperative exchange became a reality in the fall when five Yaroslavl students enrolled at Stonehill. Nine Stonehill students spent the month of June 1991 in Russia attending classes at Yaroslavl and traveling.[69] The faculty exchange began in February 1991 when Valerie Tomashov offered a lecture course on the history of Russian art at Stonehill. George Gallant inaugurated Stonehill's professor exchange in the spring of 1993 with a series of lectures at Yaroslavl titled, "Decision Making in the Area of American Foreign Policy."[70]

In addition to the Yarolslavl cooperative, Stonehill's academic programs were enhanced by the establishment of new programs and facilities to assist students with the learning process. In 1988 a learning center, to be used for training and tutoring services, was started by Richard Grant and placed under the direction of Marilyn D'Andrea. In August 1991 Sr. Kathleen Gibney, SUSC, became the director of the center. In the fall of 1991 Stonehill started a cooperative with Curry College—the Program for Advancement in Learning (PAL)—to aid those with learning disabilities.[71]

Changes in the administration of the College's academic division accompanied the innovations of the nineties. In the fall of 1992 Jo-Ann Flora announced her resignation as dean, effective the next June. Bartley MacPháidín formed a 13-member search committee, headed by Chet Raymo, to recommend Flora's successor. After the committee narrowed the list to 125 candidates, three finalists were chosen, but none accepted the post when it was offered. In order to fill the dean's slot, MacPháidín appointed Louis Manzo, CSC, to a one-year term as interim dean.[72] A new search committee, chaired by Professor Hossein Kazemi, renewed the search for a permanent dean. In keeping with the committee's recommendation, in the spring of

Stonehill

Volume 12, Number 1   Summer 1990

AMERICAN 🏴 SOVIET EXCHANGE AT STONEHILL

Yaroslavl State University

АМЕРИКАНСКО-СОВЕТСКИЙ ОБМЕН В СТОУНХИЛЛ КОЛЛЕДЖЕ

ALUMNI MAGAZINE

Stonehill announces academic interchange with Yaroslavl State University.

1994 the interim dean, Louis Manzo, CSC, was appointed by the president and confirmed by the Board of Trustees as Stonehill's twelfth academic dean.[73]

Manzo wasted no time attacking perceived problems. Grade inflation, a national problem that had been first identified by Robert Kruse in 1983,[74] was the new dean's first order of business. Manzo cited statistics showing 66 percent of the class of 1993 and 43 percent of the entire student body on the Dean's List as indicative of a problem with grade inflation. He told the faculty, "Until we have clearer signs of student industry, I think it would be useful to examine our standards and grading practices."[75] In the fall of 1993 Manzo began implementing a plan to review all academic disciplines between 1993 and 2000, beginning with the departments of English and economics.[76]

Rev. Louis Manzo, CSC, academic dean 1993 to the present.

Academic computing services were enhanced and reviewed in this same period. In July 1991 the College adopted a versatile software package called SCAN, which promised to meet Stonehill's administrative computing needs into the next century. In October 1995 Brian Hawkins of Brown University reviewed the College's computer systems as they related to academic programs. Hawkins' report suggested that Stonehill needed a plan to improve academic and administrative infrastructure—hardware, software, and support personnel. He also recommended greater accountability for software, elimination of student computer laboratory fees, and improved faculty access to computers.[77] In the fall of 1996 Professor Raymond Pepin, after 19 years as head of Stonehill's computer services, returned to full-time teaching and was replaced by Paul Krueger.[78]

Army ROTC, started at Stonehill in 1976, continued its presence on campus, but its status was precarious in the decades of the eighties and nineties. The College's program, originally an extension center of Northeastern University, became affiliated with Boston University in August 1981.[79] Throughout this decade the Army repeatedly warned Stonehill that its participation (in numbers of cadets) was marginal. In the fall of 1986 the College's ROTC program was placed on Region Intensive Management status for failure "to produce 7 commissioned officers per year, as well as maintain a minimum of 9 students enrolled as MS III [junior] cadets."[80]

As the 1990s dawned, Stonehill's ROTC program was challenged on all fronts. The Center on Conscience and War recommended that ROTC students at Catholic colleges be required to attend lectures and workshops focusing on recent directives of Pope John Paul II, Vatican II, and the United States Catholic bishops on war.[81] In the fall of 1993 the program was placed on the Army's Effective Management Program (EMP) "as a result of our [the Army's] annual review and your unit weaknesses." The continued inability of Stonehill to attract students for ROTC led, in the summer of 1995, to the unit's removal as an extension center of Boston University.[82]

Changes in administration and program offerings were experienced in the Evening Division. Leo O'Hara, associate academic dean for continuing education, assumed a position at Providence College. George Rogers, who had served as director of Evening Division since 1979, was appointed to fill O'Hara's position, which was merged with that of director.[83] Rogers was responsible for instituting new certificate programs that satisfied public demand, including management, AIDS counseling, early childhood education, and public relations. Degree programs were also enhanced with a major in international studies and minors in religious studies, environmental studies, and gender studies.[84]

However, consistent decreases in enrollment in the continuing education and credit evening college courses in the nineties concerned the College's administration.[85] In the fall of 1996 Professor Raymond Pepin of the Economics Department reviewed the situation and concluded that "most or all of that decline [in enrollment] could have been avoided by employing a more aggressive pricing strategy."[86] Pepin's review prompted MacPháidín's appointment of a continuing education task force, chaired by George Rogers, charged with evaluating programs, marketing, and enrollment management in Evening Division. The task force submitted its report in May 1997, recommending expanded course offerings, greater faculty compensation, and improved marketing techniques.[87]

Amidst changes and reviews of dropping enrollment, Evening Division celebrated its silver anniversary. In March 1996 a banquet was held in the student commons for 250 people to mark the event. John Weihrer, the driving force behind the division's creation in 1970, was unable to attend, but revealed his pride in a statement read at the gala affair. Bartley MacPháidín also praised the accomplishments of Evening Division and its loyal faculty and administration for their commitment to individual attention, sacrifice, persistence, and hard work over the years.[88]

Evening Division concerns did not impede new and expanded academic programs implemented in the College's day school to give students greater opportunities to meet the challenge of increasing global needs. A bachelor of arts in chemistry, plus minor programs in Russian studies, history of art, and environmental studies, were added to the curriculum. In the spring of 1995 Stonehill's first formal master's program was approved.[89] (Massachusetts state certification requirements for accountants made the program a necessity.) A five-year master's program in accounting was made available to the class of 1999.[90] The first post-baccalaureate program was comple-mented by new undergraduate opportunities. Beginning with the class of 1996, students were given the opportunity to pursue a double major.[91] In the fall of 1994 the College began an honors program, headed by Professor Richard Capobianco.[92]

The decade of the nineties saw some proposals for additions to Stone-hill's academic offerings. Beginning in February 1992 the College began to actively pursue Congressional support for a $7.5 million reauthorization grant for the Martin Institute. The money was to be used to create the Theo-dore Hesburgh Community Service Compact, a central and permanent re-source for the 320 nonprofit organizations that provide services to the people of southeastern Massachusetts.[93] The initiative was shelved when federal funding was not secured. A task force to study the feasibility of a physician's assistant (PA) program recommended that the College engage a consultant from the Association of Physicians' Assistants. Wary of possible bias from a representative of the association, the academic dean, Louis Manzo, CSC, rejected the recommendation, and the program was eventually shelved.[94] In January 1997 MacPháidín established a cooperative 3–2 aca-demic program with Notre Dame in computer engineering, which com-menced in the fall semester. At this same time the president appointed a committee on graduate programs to generate ideas on two or three tracks for specialized masters' degrees.[95]

New Buildings and Facilities

❧ THE EXPLOSIVE NATURE of construction at Stonehill in the eighties con-tinued into the nineties. The College's long history of underbuilding was reversed in 1989, when plans for the construction of a new student dining facility to service a resident population of 1600 began to take form. Liviu Brill of Vitols Associates designed a multipurpose two-floor facility that would seat approximately 1000 students and 90 faculty for meals, plus pro-vide space for staff offices, student organizations, a large meeting room for 400, and student mail boxes and a post office.[96] Stonehill's sale of a $14-million bond allowed construction of "The Commons" to proceed. The $7-million facility, built by Jackson Construction of Dedham, opened in the spring semester 1992 to "rave reviews" by students.[97]

The persistent problem of insufficient student housing that had been met with the construction of Pilgrim Heights in the 1980s was given further attention in the nineties with the erection of two new dorms and renovation of the townhouses. The team of Vitols Associates and Jackson Construc-tion was used to build Villa Theresa[98] adjacent to the dining commons. The

The dining commons.

Villa Theresa.

Notre Dame du Lac Hall.

Colonial Court renovation.

residence, built for $3.2 million along the more institutional lines of Boland and O'Hara, yet with modern features of apartment living in the common spaces, welcomed 134 students in the fall of 1991. At the winter 1996 trustees' meeting, approval was given for the construction of another pod-style dormitory to house 100 to 125 juniors and seniors. Construction of Notre Dame du Lac Hall began in the fall of 1996, and students were welcomed in September 1997.[99] Colonial Court was renovated in the summer of 1997 by Auburn Construction at a cost of $1,944,581. Commonwealth Court is scheduled for renovation in the summer of 1998.[100]

Student and Campus Activities

STUDENT ACTIVITIES in the 1990s, guided by the new dean of student affairs, Louis Saltrelli, were characterized by continuity with the past and innovation for contemporary needs. Saltrelli used a holistic student development model as his philosophy in supervising his division. He believed that students needed programs to promote their identity and to further the community spirit that had always been significant on campus. As one of his first acts, he started the "Noon News Bulletin" "to enhance communication, provide information for reflection and thought, and thus help Stonehill become a more dynamic community."[101]

Emerging from the problems experienced on campus a decade earlier, the nineties was a period when numerous programs were started on campus to increase student awareness of alcohol abuse and to curtail drinking on campus. Although Saltrelli instituted a new alcohol policy for students in the spring of 1990,[102] Claudette Demers-Gendreau, coordinator of drug and alcohol prevention programs, believed that no significant reduction in alcohol consumption would occur without a change in attitude and commitment "from the top down."[103] Accordingly, programs to create a new attitude toward alcohol on campus were initiated. Alcohol Awareness Week (which became an annual event), October 22–27, 1990, brought speakers to campus and provided students with information on the problem of alcohol abuse and recommendations for encouraging alcohol-free activities. Greta Henglein, director of residence life, and Thomas Halkovic, CSC, director of student activities, combined their efforts in February 1991 to establish the Tomahawk Club in the College Center Spa. Open Thursday, Friday, and Saturday evenings, the club provided food, live music, and movies in an alcohol-free environment. The club operated, with varying schedules, until the fall of 1995, when the program was discontinued,[104] to be replaced by Thursday night all-ages events at Brother Mike's.

Claudette Demers-Gendreau promoted an alcohol-free policy in various

Dr. Louis Saltrelli, dean of student affairs 1989 to the present.

programs throughout the nineties. Under her direction, Active Concerned Educated Students (ACES), supported by a Fund for Improvement of Post Secondary Education (FIPSE) grant, was established at Stonehill in April 1991. Consistent with its two primary goals of counseling and program development, ACES sponsored the Tomahawk Club, the Chieftains Awareness of Responsible Drinking Program, and a chapter of Boosting Alcohol Consciousness Concerning Health of University Students (BACCHUS).[105] In the fall of 1992 Stonehill received a two-year $40,000 grant (also from FIPSE) to lead a consortium of eight local schools in generating alcohol prevention programs.[106] In February 1994 Stonehill and Demers-Gendreau were recognized in Washington, D.C., by FIPSE for "Recreating a Learning Community," a 17-step plan to decrease situations where alcohol is a factor.[107]

Specialized programs to curb problem behavior and adjust attitudes were complemented by probing essays in *The Summit*, which continued its movement toward professionalism. The paper explored contemporary issues with greater depth. Controversial topics such as sex on campus, abortion, homosexuality, the morality of war, sexual harassment, AIDS, alcohol abuse, smoking, and date rape were addressed in essays, editorials, and graphic pictorial advertisements.[108] In the nineties *The Summit*, under advi-

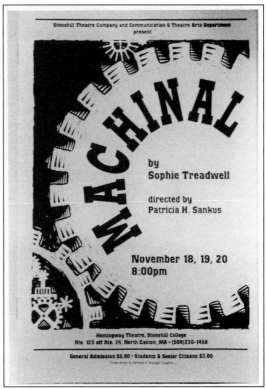

(Left) Playbill for A Bright Room Called Day.
(Right) Playbill for Machinal.

sor Bob Richards, earned awards for excellence from the Columbia Scholastic Press Association and the American Scholastic Association.[109]

Nontraditional plays, which were recognized for their excellence and achievement, continued to characterize the Stonehill Theater Company (STC) in the 1990s. The College community was treated to outstanding performances of *Money, Power, Murder, Lust, Revenge, and Marvelous Clothes, Unchanging Love, Heaven Bent, And They Dance Real Slow in Jackson, Landscape of the Body,* and *Holy Ghosts.* In January 1993 the STC was invited to perform its fall 1992 selection, *A Bright Room Called Day,* at Plymouth State College in New Hampshire as part of the New England Regionals of the Kennedy Center American College Theater Festival. In 1993 Stonehill was again invited to the same festival to perform *Machinal.*[110]

Stonehill continued to host outstanding speakers on campus through

Inaugural Eugene Green Lecture invitation.

You are Cordially Invited to Attend
The Inaugural Lecture
of
The Eugene Green Lecture Series
Tuesday, April 20, 1993
7:30 p.m.
at
The Joseph W. Martin Institute for Law and Society
Stonehill College
North Easton, Massachusetts
Guest Lecturer:
MICHAEL NOVAK
American Enterprise Institute for Public Policy Research

Stonehill College
(508) 230-1015

R.S.V.P.
by April 15

the creation of several new lecture series. In October 1990 Gerard O'Neill, Stonehill Class of 1964 and a Pulitzer Prize-winning investigative journalist with the Boston *Globe*, gave the first of four lectures, sponsored by the Martin Institute, titled "Restoring the Trust." In the fall of 1992 the W.B. Mason Forum on the Future of Southeastern Massachusetts was started, with Andrew Card, secretary of transportation under President George Bush. Marlin Fitzwater, White House press secretary under Presidents Reagan and Bush and former Senator Paul Tsongas of the Concord Coalition were among the speakers in the Mason Forum.[111] The Eugene Green Lecture Series, named for the popular professor and first director of the Writing Program, Father Eugene Green, was initiated in April 1993; Michael Novak was the first speaker. Others in this series included Brother Patrick Ellis, FSC, president of The Catholic University of America, and former Congressman Robert Drinan, SJ. In 1996 the Green Lecture Series merged with the Nakamichi Foundation program on campus.[112] The College community also welcomed to campus the civil rights leader James Farmer, special Watergate prosecutor Archibald Cox, and Representative Patricia Schroeder.

Stonehill hosted several significant events in the nineties that demonstrated the community's concern with national and international issues. The centenary of Pope Leo XIII's monumental 1891 social encyclical, *Rerum Novarum*, was commemorated by a day-long conference, cosponsored by Stonehill and the Diocese of Fall River and led by Fathers J. Bryan Hehir and James Hennesey, SJ. The onset of Operation Desert Storm in January 1991 generated a "teach-in," which was led by Professor James Kenneally.

In May 1993 the College welcomed the fifth spring conference of Women-Church, featuring feminist theologian Rosemary Radford Ruether. In October 1996 Stonehill was the site of a debate between Governor William Weld and Senator John Kerry, who were locked in a tight election battle for Kerry's seat in Congress.[113]

Stonehill also celebrated the accomplishments of its own community in the decade of the nineties. In the summer of 1994, the Maryalice Conley Moore Center was established. Named for the late professor of chemistry, the Moore Center aimed to increase campus awareness of such issues as sexual assault, sexual harassment, career options, age and gender bias, safety, and diversity.[114] On October 26, 1995, Stonehill hosted the United States premier of *Frankie Starlight,* a film based on the novel *The Dork of Cork,* by Professor Chet Raymo. Raymo joined Bartley MacPháidín and some 1500 students, faculty, staff, and administrators in the Sally Blair Ames Sports Complex for a gala evening. In September 1996 Stonehill held its first fall convocation honoring all seniors. The featured speaker, George Hagerty, class of 1975 and president of Franklin Pierce College, was awarded the President's Medal.[115]

Campus Ministry in the 1990s expanded its programs to Stonehill students and the regions of Brockton and Easton. A member of the staff since the 1992 spring semester, Daniel Issing, CSC, was named director of Campus Ministry in March 1993. Issing, invoking a 1988 summary description of Campus Ministry,[116] emphasized the value of community and the fostering of the common good on campus in giving his office a fivefold charge: ministry of the word and sacrament, pastoral care, service beyond the campus, religious formation, and evangelization. Issing supervised the operation of ten direct service groups, including the Ames Society, Circle K, Habitat for Humanity, the Knights of Columbus, and the RFK Society, as well as five social justice groups, including Amnesty International, Students for Environmental Action, and "Into the Streets."[117] The latter program, which started in January 1992, sponsored students who volunteered in local social service agencies. Highly successful and popular, "Into the Streets" became part of the freshmen orientation the ensuing fall.

Discussions for a possible redesign of the Chapel of Mary began in the fall of 1986. Four years elapsed, however, before Adé Bethune, a liturgical consultant from Newport, Rhode Island, conducted a needs assessment and made a report.[118] Wilfred Raymond, CSC, acting director of Campus Ministry, implemented some of Bethune's ideas, including the construction of a three-seat presidential bench in the Augustinian style and a new altar.

In October 1991 Bartley MacPháidín, CSC, established a committee to review Campus Ministry and make recommendations for renovating the

Campus ministry team in the early 1990s:
John McCarthy, CSC, Richard Mazziotta, CSC, Grace Donovan, SUSC, and Wilfrid
Raymond, CSC.

chapel.[119] Written by committee chair Richard Mazziotta, CSC, an interim report in May 1992 stated that although the chapel might be used for multiple purposes, it should be designed primarily to serve as the place where the Stonehill community assembles for celebration of the Eucharist. To this end, the report suggested the placement of the tabernacle in a separate location to allow private Eucharistic adoration, the construction of an immersion baptismal font, and exterior changes, such as the addition of a bell tower to make the building appear more like a chapel.[120] Although the report's recommendations were considered too elaborate, some changes were made. The original carpeted floor was replaced with marble to improve acoustics, the presider's chair—so prominent in Bethune's recommendations—was de-emphasized, and the chairs of the congregation were reconfigured.[121]

Men's soccer in action.

Campus and Intercollegiate Sports

STONEHILL'S ATHLETIC PROGRAMS, which had been reviewed by the 1978 task force, underwent a second evaluation beginning in the fall of 1993. Changing demographics, problems with scheduling, financial need, and the College's commitment to increased ethnic and racial diversity were prominent issues for the new task force on athletics appointed by Bartley MacPháidín. The committee was charged "to take a broad-based look at our athletic program," but no formal report was submitted.[122] The Intercollegiate Athletic Committee, recommended by the governance report of 1995, was approved by the College Council and established in March 1996.[123]

While the economic commitment of the College and coverage by *The*

1991 football champions celebrate win over Bentley.

Summit strongly favored intercollegiate athletics in the nineties, students continued to participate actively in intramural and club sports. As in earlier years, students competed in men's, women's, and co-ed intramurals during the fall and spring semesters. Some of the more specialized intramural offerings included three-on-three basketball, indoor soccer, floor hockey, whiffle ball, and golf. Club sports offered rugby and volleyball for men and rugby for women. Lacrosse, formerly a club sport, was raised to varsity status for men and women in the fall of 1997.[124]

Men's soccer reached some important plateaus in the 1990s. The team won the NE-10 championship in 1990 and 1991, led by Andy McMahon, who in 1991 became the second soccer player in Stonehill history to be recognized as an All-American. In 1992 Coach Ernie Branco reached his milestone one hundredth victory.[125]

Football continued its winning ways on the varsity level. The 1991

Men's basketball in action.

team, led by conference player of the year Glen Lindstrom and coach of the year Dave Swanton, won the Eastern Collegiate Football Conference (ECFC). In 1993 Stonehill's gridiron team moved from Division III to Division II and posted a 7–2–1 record under the leadership of Kevin Broderick, who was honored as an Academic All-American by the GTE Corporation. The next season Mike McLucas and Tony Dello Iacono were Stonehill's first recipients of the weekly Gold Helmet Award, presented by the New England Football Writers for outstanding performance. The 1995 squad won the regular NE–10 Conference title with a thrilling 39–36 triumph over arch rival Bentley College, snapping the latter school's 30-game winning streak.[126]

Men's basketball remained a popular recreational event for students, but the teams of the nineties could not match the exceptional performances of a decade earlier. In 1994 Stonehill hosted its first basketball tournament, the Holiday Inn Classic, winning the Thanksgiving weekend affair over the University of Massachusetts at Dartmouth. Standout players in the nineties were Ed Grzembski and Jon Cronin, whose 2301 career points placed him second on the alltime Stonehill list.[127] The team posted outstanding seasons in 1991–92 (19–11) and 1995–95 (19–9).

Women's sports, recognized in the 1980s with their elevation to varsity status, posted impressive records and saw many personal triumphs in the nineties. The tennis team, led by Terry Capobianco and conference coach of the year Sandy Xenos, won the NE–10 crown in 1991. The team repeated as champions in 1992, posting a perfect 14–0 match record. Team captain Pam Kelly led the volleyball team to its best record ever, 27–8, in the 1996 campaign. In 1996 field hockey, after two years in club sport status, began to compete on the varsity level, posting a creditable record of 8–8. Andrea Gillespie set individual records in track and led the team to its first triumph in the Tri-State Championship meet in the spring of 1996.[128]

The equestrian team, begun in November 1967 as a riding club under instructor Captain Fred Marsman, rose to national prominence in the decade of the nineties under coach William Barber. The team received an invitation to compete in the December 1992 Tournament of Champions Invitational in Plainesville, Ohio. Competition in 1993 through 1996 brought the team to the national championships, where it placed seventh in 1993 and fourth in 1995. Rider K.C. Coleman was selected to represent the United States in the International Intercollegiate Equestrian Association Nation's Cup, held in Egypt in December 1993.[129]

Under the direction of Coach Paula Sullivan, the women's basketball program achieved its greatest recognition in the 1990s. Sullivan herself reached a milestone on December 12, 1993, when she coached her 400th

Women's soccer in the 1990s.

victory, a 79–51 drubbing of Keene State. The 1993–94 and 1994–95 teams were the best in Stonehill history. The 1994 squad, NE–10 co-champions, finished the regular season ranked fifth nationally in Division II. In the NCAA tournament, the team reached the elite eight at Fargo, North Dakota. California State University at San Bernardino defeated Stonehill in the first round of the tournament, but the Lady Chieftains rebounded to defeat rival St. Anselm in the consolation. The 1995 squad, after capturing the NE–10 crown, again traveled to North Dakota to compete in the elite eight, sporting a perfect 29–0 record and a number two national ranking. Despite disappointment in the tournament, the team finished the season at 30–3, the best record to date.[130]

Women's volleyball in action.

Equestrian team.

The nineties produced a cadre of outstanding players who led their teams to various championships. In the early nineties Paula Kohs became only the second player to surpass the magical 2000 point (2017) barrier. Michelle Doonan, arguably the best ever to wear a Lady Chieftain uniform, led the teams that played in the elite eight. She was twice named NE–10 player of the year and was selected to the Kodak Women's Basketball Coaches Association All-America Team in 1994 and 1995. Upon Doonan's graduation, Kim Trudel and Sue Patchett formed a scoring and rebounding combination that frustrated opponents. Patchett, who became the first Lady Chieftain to score over 2000 points (2140) and grab more than 1000 (1149) rebounds in her career, repeated Doonan's feat by twice being selected to the Kodak All-America Team.[131]

A combination of tragedy and vast experience led in 1996 to the appointment of Paula Sullivan as director of athletics. In October 1995 Raymond P. Pepin, who had served as athletic director and men's basketball coach since 1984, died suddenly of a heart attack. A search committee rec-

Paula Sullivan, athletic director 1996 to the present.

ommended Sullivan for the athletic director post. Bartley MacPháidín approved the appointment in the spring of 1996, following Sullivan's retirement from coaching after twenty-five years at the helm of the Lady Chieftain basketball program.[132]

Stonehill's athletic facilities were expanded by the construction of a new multipurpose field adjacent to the Sally Blair Ames Sports Complex in the summer of 1995. Named for James "Lou" Gorman, class of 1953, and former major league baseball executive, the field—built at a cost of $130,000—was dedicated in September 1996 when Stonehill's baseball team played Boston College in an exhibition. The women's field hockey team inaugurated play on the field that same fall.[133]

The Capital Campaign and a New Library

❧   IN OCTOBER 1990 *The Summit* reported that the Office of College Relations, headed by Fran Dillon,[134] was investigating the case for a capital campaign, the first such development endeavor at Stonehill.[135] The drive initially looked to raise $18 million for expansion of the College's scholarship fund, promotion of faculty development, and—most prominently—the construc-

Dedication of Lou Gorman Field:
Lou Gorman and Bartley MacPháidín, CSC.

tion of a new library.[136] In late winter 1991 Thompson and Pendel Associates was retained by Stonehill to conduct a feasibility study for a capital campaign. The study, which reviewed the College's communications, news information, alumni affairs, and development programs, concluded that a "willingness was present" on the part of Stonehill to conduct a $20 million capital campaign but that lack of experience in such an effort would make the drive difficult.[137]

Stonehill's first capital campaign, a five-year drive titled "Securing the Vision," was launched on July 1, 1992. The $20 million goal was divided into four areas: $11 million for the new library, $5 million to attract a talented and diverse student body, $2 million as a base fund for permanent faculty development, and $2 million for sustaining unrestricted support through the annual fund.[138] The public phase of "Securing the Vision" was announced by MacPháidín in November 1994 at the Founder's Day Dinner,

Fran Dillon.

with guest speaker Michael Novak. On November 21, 1997, Stonehill celebrated the successful completion of the capital campaign with a gala dinner at Boston's Four Seasons Hotel.[139]

The need for expanded or new library facilities had been recognized as early as 1988. Three separate studies, one by a consultant, Jay Lucker of MIT, a second by an *ad hoc* library expansion committee, and the third by library director Edward Hynes, concluded that the old cafeteria (available for conversion after construction of the Commons) was not suitable for renovation as library space.[140] The firm of Ganteaume and McMullen, Inc. was thus engaged to conduct a study for a 22,400-square-foot addition to the present library.[141]

While all parties agreed that something had to be done to expand the College's library facility, the direction of the project remained unclear for some time. The basic options were: (1) construct a new library (2) build an addition to Cushing-Martin and construct a new building on the site of the old cafeteria, which would be razed, or (3) construct a library addition and renovate the cafeteria for academic use.[142] Hynes initially favored an addition over a new library, but his main concern was that any library changes

Library director Edward Hynes and his staff celebrate at topping-off ceremony for new library in September 1997.

be accompanied by enhancement in the overall academic program.[143] The Library Committee and Executive Vice President Robert Kruse also expressed their opinions that an addition would make the best use of College resources.[144]

With the direction of the project still in doubt, the architectural firm of Shepley, Bulfinch, Richardson, and Abbott was hired to conduct a feasibility study for library expansion. One option looked at expansion of the present library and a second investigated the possibility of renovating O'Hara Hall for use as a library. Although the architects concluded that O'Hara could be transformed "with only minor difficulties," both options were ultimately dropped in favor of a new library. In October 1990 *The Summit* quoted Robert Kruse: "A new library is the absolute number one building priority. Fr. MacPháidín is committed to building a new library."[145] Shepley, Bulfinch, Richardson, and Abbott submitted a final design for a 60,000-square-foot structure at an estimated cost of $11.5 million. Construction of the new library, built by Jackson Construction on the site of the student parking lot immediately west of the Cushing-Martin Library, began in May 1997, with a projected completion date of late summer 1998.

An Era of Accomplishments

❦

THE PRESIDENCY OF Bartley MacPháidín vaulted Stonehill College into national recognition in virtually every facet of higher education. Combining administrative expertise, a charismatic personality, tireless effort, and the opportunity to build upon the work of his predecessors, MacPháidín transformed Stonehill from a regional Catholic liberal arts college into an institution recognized as one of the premier colleges within its geographic domain and academic areas of concentration. This status was achieved without compromising the school's original purpose or the ideals that had served as the College's bulwark from the outset.

Building on the efforts of Ernest Bartell, MacPháidín was primarily responsible for the creation of an endowment that ranks twenty-second among all (reporting) Catholic colleges and universities in the United States.[146] The Fund for Endowment, originally authorized by the Board of Trustees in September 1974, stood at $2.55 million in June 1978, five months after MacPháidín officially became president. A survey at the time placed Stonehill's endowment per full-time student at 9 percent of the national average. During the 1980s, Stonehill's average annual endowment increased 21 percent, so that by 1988 the College ranked above 23.7 percent of all colleges and universities reporting. An average annual rise of 13 percent in the nineties found the endowment in 1994 ranked above 47.6 percent of all colleges and 72 percent of all (reporting) institutions with an endowment between $25 million and $100 million. In December 1997 Stonehill's endowment stood at $68,575,274.[147]

Stonehill is being recognized in the 1990s on a national level for its academic and athletic achievements and its service to the community. In December 1990 *Barron's Magazine* cited the College as one of its "300 Best Buys in College Education." The 1985 accolade bestowed by *U.S. News & World Report*, was repeated in 1994, 1995, 1996, and 1997 with the College rated fourth, third, and second (2 years), respectively, among "Regional Liberal Arts Colleges" in the northern region. *Money Magazine* in 1995 recognized Stonehill as one of the top one hundred institutions in the country providing a quality education at an affordable cost.[148]

Stonehill College in 1998 is a dream fulfilled for the men of Holy Cross and hundreds of other dedicated people whose collaborative efforts have brought the institution to its fiftieth anniversary. The College's success has been created through maintenance of a vision that has guided decision makers throughout the years. Bartley MacPháidín held the vision in full view during his long tenure as president. He understood the contribution of those who had gone before him and the need for today's College to provide a model for future growth and development. Maintenance of the vision will allow Stonehill in the future to "emerge confident and mature in its identity as a prestigious Catholic liberal arts institution with a reputation for being at the center of contemporary discourse." Hopeful and confident, MacPháidín looked toward a milestone in the College's history:[149]

> As we approach our 50th anniversary, we are about to complete our first full cycle of maturity. . . . It is imperative that we reassess what we stand for—if we are to fully exploit the rich legacy that we have inherited, and if we are to respond to the demands of the 21st century as an age which promises to be permanently on the edge of social and economic transition.

MacPháidín's vision and accomplishments at Stonehill have been noted by people on many fronts. Within the Holy Cross Community he has been recognized for his "unique and widely recognized contribution" to Catholic higher education and Stonehill, in particular. Mary Robinson, president of Ireland, referred to his "distinguished contribution to the educational life of his adopted country." One commentator summarized his 20 years of service as president:[150]

> Today, Stonehill stands as a more comprehensive, richer, and nationally recognized institution of higher education. Importantly, Stonehill has become more academically rigorous, respected, and selective. Indeed, you and Bob [Kruse] have elevated Stonehill into a first tier college of choice among both public and private colleges and universities in Massachusetts and New England.

When the Congregation of Holy Cross came to North Easton in 1935, a dream was born. At the outset this dream of a nationally recognized liberal arts college that would stand in the tradition of American Catholic higher education was rather dim. A hasty and ill-conceived foundation, economic problems, and the consequent inability to expand facilities made life hard during the College's first 15 years. Hope rose in 1962 with unrestricted accreditation. *This* was the first of many large construction blocks, such as buildings, academic expansion, leadership, and opportunity that built Stonehill College which today celebrates its golden anniversary. Presidential leadership was instrumental in this building process, but the College's history could not have been successful without loyal faculty and staff, dedicated

Central quad of campus in 1998.

alumni and students, generous friends and benefactors, and an optimistic spirit that is unique to Stonehill. Personalities will change and programs will rise and fall, but the spirit of Stonehill will carry it into the twenty-first century.

ENDNOTES

1. The revised Code of Canon Law, mandated by Pope John XXIII during his historical January 25, 1959, speech when he initiated the call for the Second Vatican Council, was published in 1983. Canons 807–814 come under Book III, Title III, Chapter II, "Catholic Universities and Other Institutes of Higher Studies," of the Code. Several of these canons, especially Canon 812 which states, "It is necessary that those who teach theological disciplines in any institute of higher studies have a mandate from the competent ecclesiastical authority," were perceived by American Catholic educators as jeopardizing academic freedom and institutional autonomy.

2. Alice Gallin, *American Catholic Higher Education: Essential Documents, 1967–1990* (Notre Dame, Indiana: University of Notre Dame Press, 1992), 189–90; J. Donald Monan, SJ, "Forming the Whole Person," *Catholic International* 2(21) (December 1–14, 1991): 1021; *Chronicle of Higher Education*, March 26, 1986, 20–24.

3. *Chronicle of Higher Education*, March 26, 1986, 24.

4. William Cardinal Baum to "President," June 26, 1985, MacPháidín Papers, ASC. Baum wrote to all presidents of Catholic colleges and universities in the United States, requesting their aid in reviewing the draft schema.

5. Grace Donovan, "Stonehill Contributes Commentary on Schema Concerning Catholic Higher Education," *Stonehill Review* (Fall 1986): 14, College Relations Papers, ASC.

6. Janet Stobat, "Catholic Colleges' Meeting Urges Vatican to Endorse Academic Freedom [and] Autonomy," *Chronicle of Higher Education* 35 (May 3, 1989): A15.

7. Richard McBrien, "What Is a Catholic University?" in Hesburgh, *The Challenge and Promise of a Catholic University* (Notre Dame, Indiana: University of Notre Dame Press, 1994): 161.

8. Catherine LaCugna, "Some Theological Reflections on *Ex Corde Ecclesiae*," in Hesburgh, *Challenge and Promise*, 117–125.

9. Section II: General Norms, Article 4.3 of *Ex Corde Ecclesiae* reads: "In particular, Catholic theologians, aware that they fulfill a mandate received from the Church, are to be faithful to the magisterium of the Church as the authentic interpreter of sacred Scripture and sacred tradition." Article 5.2 reads: "Each bishop has a responsibility to promote the welfare of the Catholic universities in his diocese and has the right and duty to watch over the preservation and strengthening of their Catholic character. If problems should arise concerning this Catholic character, the local bishop is to take the initiatives necessary to resolve the matter, working with the competent university authorities in accordance with established procedures and, if necessary, with the help of the Holy See."

10. Ladislaus Orsy, SJ, "Bishops and Universities: Dominion or Communion," *America* 169 (November 20, 1993): 13–14.

11. James Malone, "Implementing *Ex Corde Ecclesiae*: The Task Ahead," *Origins* 23 (February 17, 1994): 608–09.

12. A number of significant Supreme Count decisions in the late 1960s and 1970s set criteria for federal funds to go to Catholic institutions of higher learning. In *Horace Mann League vs. Board of Public Works* (1966), a group of Maryland taxpayers filed a Bill of Complaint against the governor, comptroller, and treasurer of the state and against Western Maryland College, St. Joseph College, Hood College, and The College of Notre Dame of Maryland, challenging the constitutionality of four grants totaling $2.5 million by the General Assembly to these four institutions in the construction of college facilities. After several appeals, the court finally sided with the Catholic colleges. In *Tilton vs. Richardson* (1971), a suit challenged the constitutionality of Title I of the Higher Education Facilities Act of 1963. Four Catholic colleges in Connecticut (Fairfield University, Albertus Magnus College, Ann-

hurst College, and Sacred Heart University) received federal construction grants for academic facilities totaling nearly $2 million. The 5–4 decision sided with the Catholic colleges. In the 1971 *Lemon vs. Kurtzman* case, the Supreme Court laid down a three-part test for determining the constitutionality of statutes authorizing government aid to religiously affiliated schools: (1) The statute must have a secular legislative purpose. (2) Its principal or primary effect must be one that neither advances nor inhibits religion. (3) The statute must not foster "an excessive entanglement with religion." See Charles H. Wilson, "*Ex Corde Ecclesiae* and American Catholic Higher Education: A Quandary or an Opportunity," *Current Issues in Catholic Higher Education* 14 (Winter 1994): 5–15; K.D. Whitehead, *Catholic Colleges and Federal Funding* (San Francisco: Ignatius Press, 1988); Joseph R. Preville, "Catholic Colleges, the Courts, and the Constitution: A Tale of Two Cases," *Church History* 58 (June 1989): 197–210; Preville, "Catholic Colleges and the Supreme Court: The Case of Tilton vs. Richardson," *Journal of Church and State* 30 (Spring 1988): 291–307.

13. Whitehead, *Catholic Colleges and Federal Funding*, 74–75. The Supreme Court stated in the 1976 Roemer case: "Despite their formal affiliation with the Roman Catholic Church, the colleges are 'characterized by a high degree of institutional autonomy.' None of the four receives funds from or make reports to the Catholic Church. The Church is represented on their governing boards, but . . . 'no instance of Church considerations into college decisions was shown.'" The ACCU feared that implementation of *Ex Corde Ecclesiae* would make this statement no longer viable.

14. Charles Curran, *Catholic Higher Education: Theology and Academic Freedom* (South Bend: University of Notre Dame Press, 1990): 115.

15. Pope John Paul II, "Address to Leaders of Catholic Higher Education," in Gallin, *Essential Documents*, 286.

16. Pope John Paul II, *Ex Corde Ecclesiae*, August 15, 1990, Section I #13. Quoting the 1972 document, "The Catholic University in the Modern World," the Pope listed the essential characteristics of the Catholic university: (1) A Christian inspiration of individuals and the university community, (2) reflection in the light of the Catholic faith upon human knowledge through research, (3) fidelity to the Christian message as it comes through the Church, and (4) an institutional commitment to the service of God's people.

17. *Ibid.*, Section I #27, General Norms, Article 2, #4 and #5, Article 4, #1, #3, and #4. The Pope not only called for a majority of Catholics in the faculty but stated, "Non-Catholic members are *required* [emphasis mine] to respect the Catholic character of the university, while the university in turn respects their religious liberty."

18. J. Donald Monan, SJ, "Forming the Whole Person," *Catholic International* 2(21) (December 1–14, 1991): 1024.

19. Martin J. Stamm, "Report on the Governance of American Catholic Higher Education in 1992," *Current Issues in Catholic Higher Education* 14 (Summer 1993): 15.

20. Theodore Hesburgh, "The Challenge and Promise of a Catholic University," in Hesburgh, ed., *The Challenge and Promise of a Catholic University*, 4.

21. David Burrell, "The Ideal of a Catholic University," *The Furrow* 31 (September 1980): 555–56.

22. David J. O'Brien, *From the Heart of the American Church: Catholic Higher Education and American Culture* (Maryknoll, New York: Orbis Books, 1994): 26, 67, 195.

23. The cardinal and bishops on the committee were: Cardinal James Hickey, Archbishops Oscar Lipscomb, Adam Maida, and Francis Schulte, and Bishops James Malone, James Griffin, and John Leibrecht.

24. Charles Curran, *et al.*, "*Ex Corde Ecclesiae* and Its Ordinances: Is This Any Way to Run a University or a Church?" *Commonweal* 120 (November 19, 1993): 14–15. These ordinances were to be considered for adoption by the NCCB as a body at the fall 1994 meeting and then sent to Rome.

25. John J. Leibrecht, "Implementing *Ex Corde Ecclesiae*," *Origins* 24 (26) (December 8, 1994): 445–46.

26. John J. Leibrecht to Bishops, Presidents, Learned Societies and Sponsoring Religious Communities, August 2, 1996, Bartley MacPháidín Presidential Papers, Stonehill College; "*Ex Corde Ecclesiae*: An Application to the United States," *Origins* 26 (24) (November 28, 1996): 381, 383–84. Among the ideas in this less dogmatic (compared with the draft ordinances) statement were: (1) That Catholic identity be affirmed in the mission statement of institutions, (2) that every effort be made to hire faculty aware and respectful of the faith tradition of the school, (3) that theologians are expected to present authentic Catholic teaching, and (4) that bishops and faculty members follow the June 1989 NCCB document, "Doctrinal Responsibilities: Approaches to Promoting Cooperation and Resolving Misunderstandings Between Bishops and Theologians."

27. Bartley MacPháidín to Colleagues, December 7, 1992, MacPháidín Papers, ASC.

28. James Duane and James Kenneally to *Ex Corde Ecclesiae* Committee, December 3, 1991, MacPháidín Papers, ASC. The committee members were: James Duane, CSC (chair), Louis Saltrelli, Jean Aurelio, John Broderick, Richard Capobianco, James Kenneally, Robert Peabody, Judy Sughrue, Rob Carver, and Katie Conboy.

29. *Ex Corde Ecclesiae* Committee Meeting Minutes, November 5, 1992, MacPháidín Papers, ASC.

30. Lackenmier's specific charism of Holy Cross higher education was threefold: (1) commitment to excellence, (2) concern for the personal formation of students, and (3) experience of collaboration, equality, and mutuality among those who participate in the mission of a Holy Cross college or university.

31. James Lackenmier, "American Catholic Higher Education and the Holy Cross Tradition," address at Stonehill College, April 30, 1993. This same address was originally given in October 1992 at the University of Portland as part of the sesquicentennial of Holy Cross education in the United States.

32. Richard Capobianco, "Response to James Lackenmier, CSC," April 30,

1993, MacPháidín Papers, ASC. Capobianco attacked religious authority as often failing the Academy in trying "to decide by fiat what needs to be decided by the community of thoughtful seekers." He stated the purpose of the Academy was to seek: "Genuine seeking, then, is simply incompatible with any kind of dogmatism or ideology. And that is why there really is no place at the Academy for unquestioning or unquestionable allegiances to social, political, or religious causes or principles. Our calling at the Academy is to seek authentically; indeed, our human calling is to seek authentically."

33. Katie Conboy, "Response: 150 Years of Holy Cross Education," April 30, 1993, MacPháidín Papers, ASC.

34. Peter Beisheim to Bartley MacPháidín, December 16, 1993, Bartley Mac-Pháidín Presidential Papers, Stonehill College.

35. Patricia Hayes, Memorandum to Holy Cross College and University Presidents, February 22, 1995, Bartley MacPháidín Presidential Papers, Stonehill College; Diane Ferreira to Stephen Avila, April 12, 1995, Executive Vice President–Kruse Papers, ASC. The seminar was held March 24–26.

36. "Agreement" between Stonehill College and Holy Cross Fathers, February 9, 1983, Incorporators Papers, ASC; "Statement of Principles, " June 1, 1989, Executive Vice President–Kruse Papers, Stonehill College. Stonehill used as its model a similar agreement between the Congregation and the University of Notre Dame signed in November 1977.

37. Bartley MacPháidín to Faculty, Student Government, Staff and Administration, January 23, 1992; Thomas Gariepy to Bartley MacPháidín, September 1, 1992; "Report of the Commission on Campus Culture, September 1, 1992, MacPháidín Papers, ASC.

38. Sally M. Furay, "Report to the President, Bartley MacPháidín, CSC, May, 1993, Executive Vice President–Kruse Papers, ASC. The 1989 reaccreditation report of the New England Association of Schools and Colleges (NEASC) had noted, "Attention needs to be given to the manner in which faculty in existing committees and councils actually represent the faculty not only in reacting to proposals, but also in the initiation of such policies." The NEASC report also spoke of the "need for faculty both individually and collectively to take greater responsibility for the development of policies of significant impact on academic programs."

39. *Ibid.*

40. Basic Objectives of Governance Commission, n.d., Executive Vice President–Kruse Papers, ASC. The basic objectives of the Governance Commission were: (1) Create faculty responsibility and accountability for academic policy and curriculum, (2) address the lack of mechanism for strategic planning, (3) increase operational effectiveness of administration, and (4) redefine committee structures to clarify lines of authority, eliminate excessive informality and facilitate communication.

41. Bartley MacPháidín to Stonehill Community, September 29, 1995, MacPháidín Papers, ASC.

42. Report of the Governance Commission, Stonehill College, May, 1995, MacPháidín Papers, ASC.

43. Four principal notions of diversity were present in the literature of the day: (1) Representation—the need to bring more under represented populations to campus. (2) Support—sustaining new students who come to campus. (3) Integration—make new populations part of the existing campus community. (4) Multiculturalism—creating a shared community which maintains the integrity of the different groups. See Arthur Levine, "The Meaning of Diversity," *Change* 23(5) (September/October, 1991): 4–5.

44. P.J. Zingg, "Missions Fulfilled and Forfeited: American Catholic Education and the Challenges of Diversity," *Educational Record* 72 (Summer 1991): 42. Statistics in 1992 showed:

	WHITE (%)	MINORITY (%)
All US Colleges	78.9	21.1
All Private Colleges	80.3	19.7
All Catholic Colleges	85.4	14.6

45. "Catholic Higher Education and the Pastoral Mission of the Church," NCCB Statement, 1980 in Gallin, ed. *Essential Documents*, 143–44; Zingg, "Mission Fulfilled and Forfeited," 40.

46. Scott Jaschik, "Major Changes Seen Needed for Colleges to Attract Minorities," *Chronicle of Higher Education* 34(13) November 25, 1987: A31; Raechelle L. Pope, "Multicultural-Organization Development in Student Affairs: An Introduction," *Journal of College Student Development* 34 (May 1993): 201.

47. *The Summit* (March 26, 1986), ASC. The paper reported that dean of admissions, Brian Murphy, was making efforts to interest minority students in Stonehill, especially African-Americans. Murphy told the paper that black students "perceive our college as a small, Irish-Catholic, suburban area college in New England." Murphy suggested that minority students would be attracted when a visible percentage of minorities were already on campus. This would happen when the environment was made attractive to their wants.

48. New England colleges comparable to Stonehill in their percentage of minority populations in 1991 were: St. Anselm (0.8), Providence College (2.6), St. Michael's (3.7). Stonehill's enrollment was 2.0 percent minorities at this time. See Fred Petti to David Farrell and James Duane, January 17, 1991, Executive Vice President–Kruse Papers, ASC.

49. *The Summit* (November 4, 1991), ASC.

50. "Minority Recruitment Efforts," n.d. [1991], Executive Vice President Papers, ASC.

51. Sub-Committee on Diversification to Planning and Development Committee, December 10, 1991, Executive Vice President–Kruse Papers; Bartley MacPháidín to Faculty, Student Government, Staff, and Administration, January 23, 1992; Commission on Pluralism, Report to the President, September 1, 1992, MacPháidín Papers, ASC.

52. Commission on Pluralism Report to the President, September 1, 1992, MacPháidín Papers, ASC.

53. Bartley MacPháidín to College Community, November 13, 1992, Mac-

Pháidín Papers, ASC. The committee's specific responsibilities were: (1) To assist in achieving pluralism on campus and monitor progress, (2) to mediate conflict that may arise is pursuit of greater diversity, and (3) to receive from all departments annual reports on their efforts to diversify.

54. Louis F. Saltrelli to Bartley MacPháidín, August 30, 1994; Saltrelli to Robert Kruse, September 1993, MacPháidín Papers, ASC.

55. *The Summit* (September 21, 1992, October 5, 1992, October 6, 1994), ASC; Jean R. Hamler to Louis Saltrelli, May 19, 1993, Bartley MacPháidín Presidential Papers, Stonehill College. *The Summit* reported in October 1994 that the percentage of minority students had doubled from 2 to 4 percent in four years.

56. *The Summit* (October 5, 1992); Bartley MacPháidín, speech to President's Club Dinner, October 17, 1992, MacPháidín Papers, ASC. Project Challenge was the brain child of Priscilla Tebbetts, who provided substantial funding for the project. It was administered by Jean Hamler at Stonehill.

57. *The Summit* (April 30, 1993, March 30, 1992, April 14, 1994); Fleet Bank Press Release, April 8, 1993, College Relations Papers, ASC; Bradley Beaupre to Bartley MacPháidín, June 26, 1995, Bartley MacPháidín Presidential Papers, Stonehill College. Stonehill originally sought a $500,000 Balfour Grant. Holy Cross donated $75,000 in 1992. In 1995 a $100,000 gift to the College's Capital Campaign "Securing the Vision" was made by Holy Cross, with $92,000 earmarked for minority scholarships.

58. *The Summit* (January 27, 1994, October 29, 1992); Bartley MacPháidín, Comments to Faculty Assembly, September 3, 1992, MacPháidín Papers, ASC. The State Street Scholars in Business Program awarded Stonehill $196,000. Terms of the agreement with NCN stated that at least five full-time degree students would be sent from Japan. The College provided a part-time ESL instructor for those students who needed assistance with English.

59. Academic Purpose Statement, May 2, 1990, Deans' Papers, ASC.

60. In an effort to improve its student learning environment, Stonehill (beginning in 1989) participated in a series of assessment workshops with representatives from Merrimack, St. Anselm, St. Michael's, and Assumption Colleges. Stonehill's team of Jo-Ann Flora, Paul Gastonguay, and Louis Saltrelli participated in the assessment conferences through 1993, hosting the event this last year. The conferences helped colleges to "learn about the value of assessment in higher education." See "An Invitation From the Stonehill Assessment Team," September 20, 1991; Assessment Team to Faculty and Administrators of Academic and Student Life Divisions, March 16, 1993, Flora Papers, ASC.

61. Report of the Presidential Commission on Campus Culture, September 1, 1992, MacPháidín Papers; *The Summit* (May 19, 1991 and March 23, 1992), ASC.

62. Jo-Ann Flora, Annual Report, July 31, 1992, Flora Papers, ASC; Bartley MacPháidín to Humphrey Tonkin, January 24, 1992; MacPháidín to Edward Malloy, January 23, 1992, Bartley MacPháidín Presidential Papers, Stonehill College.

63. College Council Meeting Minutes, May 7, 1991, College Council Papers; Jo-

Ann Flora Annual Report, August 31, 1991, Flora Papers, ASC. The Massachusetts law became effective on October 1, 1994.

64. International internships, originally offered only in the fall semester, became available in the spring as well in 1991. See *The Summit* (February 27, 1990), ASC.

65. Yaroslavl, one of the old Russian cities that comprise the "Golden Ring," was founded in 1010 on the Upper Volga River, about 180 miles northeast of Moscow. The state university, founded in 1803, today has 3000 students and specializes in the humanities.

66. Karen O'Malley, "American-Soviet Exchange at Stonehill," *Stonehill Alumni Magazine* 12 (1) (Summer 1990): 16–17, College Relations Papers, ASC; V.T. Aniskov, ed., *In Demidov's Name: Yaroslavl University—Its Past and Present* (Yaroslavl, Russia: Yaroslavl Technical University Publishing House, 1995): 505–16.

67. The initial agreement ran from July 1, 1990 to July 1, 1992. A second agreement for three years followed, with the pact to be renewed each three years thereafter.

68. O'Malley, "American-Soviet Exchange," 16.

69. Due to problems with language, Stonehill students initially spent only one summer month at Yaroslavl. The full semester exchange began in the fall of 1992. Students took survey courses in Russian history, philosophy, politics, culture, art, and music. Upon their return to Stonehill, students presented a research report and journal to the academic dean. One semester's credit was awarded for the program.

70. Aniskov, *In Demidov's Name*, 505–516.

71. Agreement of Affiliation Between Stonehill College and Curry College, September 5, 1991, Bartley MacPháidín Presidential Papers, Stonehill College; *The Summit* (October 7, 1991), ASC. Curry College in Milton, Massachusetts, is nationally known for its programs to aid those with learning disabilities.

72. *The Summit* (September 21, 1992 and April 30, 1993); Bartley MacPháidín to Colleagues, October 20, 1992; MacPháidín to Colleagues, May 13, 1993, MacPháidín Papers, ASC; Bartley MacPháidín to Academic Administrators Reporting to the Office of the Academic Dean, April 8, 1993, Bartley MacPháidín Presidential Papers, Stonehill College. The position of dean was offered but rejected by two of the final candidates. The position was not tendered to the third person.

73. *The Summit* (January 27, 1994 and March 30, 1994); Bartley MacPháidín to Colleagues, March 28, 1994, MacPháidín Papers; Board of Trustees Meeting Minutes, April 29, 1994, Board of Trustees Papers, ASC.

74. As academic dean, Kruse was very concerned with grade inflation. In a presentation to the Faculty Assembly he stated, "Is it possible that we are shortchanging our students by evaluating merely satisfactory work as good, and good work as excellent? Are we encouraging them to set lower standards for themselves by assigning to average work higher than average grades." See *The Summit* (September 21, 1983), ASC.

75. Louis Manzo to All Faculty Members, September 3, 1993, Manzo Papers; *The Summit* (October 7, 1993), ASC.

76. Jo-Ann Flora to Department Chairs, January 20, 1993, Deans' Papers, ASC. Flora actually initiated the program reviews.

77. Brian L. Hawkins to Louis Manzo, October 24, 1995, Academic Dean's Papers, Stonehill College.

78. Louis Manzo to the College Community, May 8, 1996 and May 14, 1996, Manzo Papers, ASC.

79. Robert Kruse, Annual Report, July 1, 1984, Kruse–Dean Papers, ASC.

80. William K. Seago to Bartley McFaddin [*sic*], May 16, 1986; Paul Gastonguay to Peter W. Lash, June 19, 1987, Bartley MacPháidín Presidential Papers, Stonehill College.

81. "ROTC and Catholic Higher Education," January 31, 1989, Center on Conscience and War, Charlestown, Massachusetts, Deans' Papers, ASC. The recommended lectures were not part of Stonehill's ROTC program.

82. James M. Lyle to Bartley MacPháidín, July 7, 1994 and June 1, 1995; MacPháidín to Lyle, July 6, 1995, Bartley MacPháidín Presidential Papers, Stonehill College; Academic Division News, August 1995, Manzo Papers, ASC. MacPháidín asked the Army to reconsider its order to shut down Stonehill's ROTC program as an extension center, but his appeal was not granted. ROTC still functions at the College, but with no guarantee of resident staffing.

83. Jo-Ann Flora to Members of the College Community, July 20, 1990, Flora Papers, ASC. In 1982 Rogers' title was changed to assistant academic dean for continuing education. At this time Evening Division and Summer School were combined administratively.

84. Evening Division Catalogs, 1990–1996, Evening Division Papers, ASC.

85. The Evening Division reached its peak enrollment in the fall of 1991 at 1127 degree and nondegree students. By the fall of 1997 enrollment was 650, a drop of 42.3 percent.

86. Raymond Pepin to Bartley MacPháidín, November 12, 1996; Pepin to Louis Manzo, January 2, 1997, Bartley MacPháidín Presidential Papers, Stonehill College.

87. Bartley MacPháidín to George Rogers, January 29, 1997; "Task Force Mandate," n.d., "Report of the Continuing Education Task Force," May 16, 1997. Bartley MacPháidín Presidential Papers, Stonehill College.

88. John Weihrer to George Rogers, March 16, 1996; Bartley MacPháidín, Speech, March 9, 1996, Evening Division Papers, ASC.

89. Jo-Ann Flora, Annual Report, July 31, 1992, Flora Papers, ASC. Discussion on a master's in accounting program for Evening Division was initiated in 1988. It was believed that the move would provide educational opportunities to the local community and would be economically profitable for the College. See Leo F. O'Hara to Bartley MacPháidín, August 25, 1988, MacPháidín Papers, ASC.

90. Paul Gastonguay, Annual Report, n.d. [Summer 1995], Manzo Papers, ASC.

91. Changes in Massachusetts law on the preparation of teachers led the College in the spring of 1995 to offer a second major for those in education. This privilege was made college-wide for the class of 1996. Students exercising this new opportunity were given only one degree. If majors differed in the degree awarded (BS or BA)

then the student chose the degree to be conferred. See College Council Meeting Minutes, May 3, 1995, College Council Papers, ASC.

92. College Council Meeting Minutes, May 2, 1994; Richard Capobianco to Colleagues, August 1, 1994, College Council Papers, ASC. The Honors Program took five years to develop because of no history of a similar policy and the constraints of the General Studies Program. The program encompassed all four years of a Stonehill education, with honors classes or seminars in philosophy and religion, literature, social institutions or scientific inquiry, and an interdisciplinary senior seminar.

93. Bartley MacPháidín to Theodore Hesburgh, January 13, 1994, MacPháidín Papers, ASC; "Activities in Support of a Proposal for the Reauthorization of the Joseph Martin Institute Act," September 29, 1994, Bartley MacPháidín Presidential Papers, Stonehill College. The College plans to re-initiate efforts for federal funding in 1998.

94. Sandra McAlister, *et al.* to Louis Manzo, September 20, 1995, Manzo Papers, ASC.

95. Bartley MacPháidín to Edward Malloy, January 29, 1997; MacPháidín to John Broderick, January 29, 1997, Bartley MacPháidín Presidential Papers, Stonehill College.

96. Liviu Brill to Robert Kruse, September 21, 1989; Louis Saltrelli to Brill, March 3, 1990, Executive Vice President–Kruse Papers, ASC.

97. Paul Bordieri to Robert Kruse, May 4, 1990, Executive Vice President–Kruse Papers; *News Bureau*, February 21, 1991, Public Affairs Papers; *The Summit* (February 3, 1992), ASC. The Commons has many notable features, including a food court, coffee and muffin shop, conference and entertainment rooms, and two very large rooms that can double as student dining areas or banquet rooms.

98. When originally constructed, Villa Theresa was called "New Dorm." In November 1997 the new name was given to honor four outstanding Catholic women in history: St. Teresa of Avila, St. Theresa of Lisieux, Edith Stein, a Jewish convert to Catholicism who took the religious name of Theresa, and Mother Theresa of Calcutta.

99. *The Summit* (January 25, 1996), ASC; John King to Ad Hoc Committee on New Residence Hall Design, March 3, 1996; Liviu Brill to Richard Cavanagh, May 17, 1996, Notre Dame du Lac Hall Records, Department of Buildings and Grounds, Stonehill College; Brill to Bartley MacPháidín, April 17, 1996, Bartley MacPháidín Presidential Papers, Stonehill College. Notre Dame du Lac Hall was designed for upperclass students, to approximate an apartment-type living arrangement. The cost of the entire construction project was $3,843,670.

100. *The Summit* (February 15, 1996); "Cost Report," Fall 1997, Buildings and Grounds Department, Stonehill College.

101. *The Summit* (September 12, 1989, September 19, 1989), ASC. Saltrelli replaced Charles Ratto, who served as dean of student affairs from 1979 to 1988.

102. Saltrelli's alcohol abuse policy was: (1) First offense: $50 fine and participation in one general alcohol education program sponsored by residence life. (2) Sec-

ond offense: $100 fine, ten hours of community service, parents notified by letter or phone, and an additional alcohol education session. (3) Third offense: loss of residence privileges for at least two semesters. See College Council Meeting Minutes, April 23, 1990, College Council Papers, ASC.

103. *The Summit* (October 28, 1991), ASC.

104. Ibid., February 12, 1991, October 7, 1991, October 5, 1995, ASC. The decision to close the Tomahawk Club was made by the Office of Student Activities.

105. *Ibid.*, February March 19, 1991, February 3, 1992, June 26, 1992.

106. *Ibid.*, September 24, 1992. The goal of the consortium program was to assist local institutions in setting up alcohol-free alternatives like the Tomahawk Club and to develop a network of trained professionals who could share ideas about substance abuse.

107. *Ibid.*, February 17, 1994.

108. *The Summit* addressed the issue of alcohol abuse at great length. An anti-smoking advertisement that showed what a person's face would look like if it were afflicted like the lungs with smoke was commonly run in the paper.

109. *The Summit* (April 30, 1993, April 27, 1995, May 2, 1996). In 1993 The Columbia Scholastic Press Association awarded the paper two Gold Circle Awards for design and editorial writing. For six consecutive years *The Summit* garnered "First Place" or "First Place with Special Merit" from the American Scholastic Press Association (1991–1996).

110. *Ibid.*, February 8, 1993, February 3, 1994, and April 28, 1994. Stonehill was only the second school ever invited to perform a play in two consecutive years. "Machinal" won special awards: Nicola Mantzaris—honorable mention acting award, Golden Hammer Award for technical excellence, and the Jack Stein Make-Up and Special Effects Award.

111. *Stonehill Alumni Magazine* 17(1) (Winter 1993): 15; *News Bureau*, November 10, 1993, College Relations Papers, ASC. The Mason Company gave Stonehill $60,000, $12,000 annually to support the forum, which would invite two speakers per year to a business breakfast to speak on an issue of importance to the future of the region.

112. George Hagerty and Joseph Ricciardi to Robert Kruse, May 14, 1991, College Relations Papers; Prospectus for the Creation of an Annual Lecture Series and Award Program in Memory of Rev. Eugene Green, n.d. [1992], Executive Vice President–Kruse Papers. Father Green died in 1989. Originally the Green series was twofold, a lecture program and a student essay contest. The winning essay was to be published in *Prologue*, a new campus journal. When the Green Lecture was absorbed by the Nakamichi Foundation Series, the inaugural concert recital was given by Kimberly Hess, the College organist.

113. *Stonehill Alumni Magazine*, 14(1) (Summer 1991): 20, College Relations Papers, ASC; *The Summit* (February 5, 1991 and October 3, 1996); Kathryn to Bishop Sean O'Malley, May 5, 1993, MacPháidín Papers, ASC. The 1993 Women-Church conference generated letters of protest from its content, which was perceived by some to be incompatible with a Catholic college.

114. *The Summit* (September 22, 1994), ASC. The first chair of the center was Jean Hamler.

115. *Ibid.*, October 19, 1995; Program for Academic Convocation, September 5, 1996, Presidents' Papers; *Stonehill Alumni Magazine* 23(1) (Winter 1996): 14, College Relations Papers, ASC.

116. "Summary Description" Department of Campus Ministry, n.d. [1988], Executive Vice President Papers, ASC. The Description stated, "Campus ministry at Stonehill College embodies the Catholic tradition of Stonehill College, not in an exclusive but in a unique manner. Through public worship services, sacramental programs, justice and peace activity, and pastoral care, the department serves the institution of Stonehill College, those who teach and work at the College, the students, neighboring communities, the universal Church."

117. Daniel Issing to Robert Kruse, Enclosure, "Campus Ministry," March 15, 1993; Campus Ministry Annual Report, July 1, 1991 to June 30, 1992, Executive Vice President–Kruse Papers, ASC.

118. Adé Bethune, "First Among Equals," August 27, 1990, Office of Campus Ministry, Stonehill College.

119. Bartley MacPháidín to Richard Mazziotta, October 17, 1991, Presidential Papers of Bartley MacPháidín, Donahue Hall.

120. Chapel Renovation Committee: Interim Report, May 15, 1992, Presidential Papers of Bartley MacPháidín, Donahue Hall; Richard Mazziotta to Bartley MacPháidín, May 15, 1992, Kruse–Executive Vice President Papers, ASC.

121. Daniel Issing, CSC, interview with the author, March 20, 1997.

122. Fred Petti to Bartley MacPháidín, July 23, 1993, Bartley MacPháidín Presidential Papers, Stonehill College; *The Summit* (February 3, 1994), ASC.

123. College Council Meeting Minutes, March 6, 1996, College Council Papers, ASC.

124. The full intramural offerings were: Men and Women: 3-on-3 basketball, floor hockey, full-court basketball, golf, indoor soccer, racquetball, softball, tennis, touch football, and volleyball. Men only: wiffle ball. Coed sports: 3-on-3 basketball, full-court basketball, softball, tennis, volleyball, and wallyball.

125. *The Summit* (September 19, 1991 and October 19, 1992), ASC.

126. *Ibid.*, November 4, 1991, February 1, 1993, June 25, 1993, September 22, 1994, October 6, 1994, and November 16, 1995.

127. *Ibid.*, December 7, 1994; Athletic Records, Sports Information Director, Stonehill College.

128. *Ibid.*, October 7, 1991, November 18, 1991, October 19, 1992, October 25, 1996, September 9, 1996, April 14, 1994, April 25, 1996.

129. *Ibid.*, September 20, 1993, November 23, 1992, April 5, 1993, April 28, 1994, December 7, 1994, April 25, 1996, November 18, 1993.

130. *Ibid.*, February 17, 1994, March 24, 1994, February 16, 1995, March 9, 1995, March 30, 1995.

131. *Ibid.*, March 30, 1995, March 2, 1995, March 30, 1994, March 3, 1994,

November 21, 1996; Athletic Records, Sports Information Director, Stonehill College.

132. Ibid., October 5, 1995, April 25, 1996; Bartley MacPháidín to Colleagues, April 17, 1996, MacPháidín Papers, ASC. Sullivan became Stonehill's first women athletic director. Her accomplishments are noteworthy: NE-10 Coach of the year, six times, more than twenty team wins achieved thirteen times, ten NCAA Division II tournaments, twice qualified for the elite eight, and overall record 478–158. See Karen O'Malley, "Paula Sullivan: A Stonehill Legend," *Stonehill Alumni Magazine* 24(1) (Summer 1996): 2, College Relations Papers, ASC.

133. *News Bureau*, October 18, 1995, Public Affairs Papers; Florence Tripp to Stonehill Community, September 11, 1996, Athletic Department Papers, ASC.

134. Bartley MacPháidín, Report to Board of Trustees, May 4, 1984; MacPháidín to Colleagues, June 9, 1988, MacPháidín Papers, ASC. In May 1984 Walter Mullen, the first professional fundraiser at the College, retired as director of development after fourteen years of service. In June 1988, Francis Dillon was appointed vice president for college relations.

135. Edward Hynes to Robert Kruse, April 4, 1989, Executive Vice President–Kruse Papers, ASC. Some may argue that the Development for the Seventies program was a capital campaign.

136. *The Summit* (October 2, 1990, April 9, 1991); "The Preliminary Outline of a Capital Campaign Case Statement for Stonehill College," January 1991, Executive Vice President–Kruse Papers, ASC.

137. Audit of College Relations Program for Stonehill College, June 1991, Bartley MacPháidín Presidential Papers, Stonehill College; David Thompson and Mary Helene Pendel to Bartley MacPháidín and Board of Trustees, September 1991, College Relations Papers, ASC. The additional $2 million (to a total of $20 million) represented the annual drive campaign goal of $400,000 per year for the five years of the capital campaign.

138. Francis X. Dillon to Board of Trustees, September 23, 1994, Board of Trustees Papers, ASC.

139. *The Summit* (February 13, 1997). The campaign raised over $22.5 million.

140. Steven Keller to Robert Kruse, April 28, 1988, Executive Vice President–Kruse Papers, ASC.

141. George R. Mathey to Bartley MacPháidín, January 22, 1990, MacPháidín Papers, ASC. The study was conducted in May 1988.

142. Initial cost estimates for the possibilities were: (1) addition to Cushing-Martin with renovation of cafeteria—$7,944,750, (2) addition and cafeteria is razed—$6,047,250, (3) new library on cafeteria site—$13,431,000, (4) new library on new site—(with cafeteria renovation), $15,328,000 (without cafeteria renovation), $13,431,000. See "Preliminary Library Construction Costs," October 27, 1989, Library Papers, ASC.

143. Edward Hynes to Bartley MacPháidín, September 18, 1989, MacPháidín Papers, ASC. Hynes wrote, "In the light of these comparisons, I believe that Stonehill should consider a program to develop the library, possibly in conjunction with the

review and revision of the General Studies Program. I would suggest something like an Academic Excellence Campaign that would provide a substantial increase in our acquisitions funding and general library support, as well as developing other areas of the academic program. Without such a program, the new library, whatever its final form, will be a building without a purpose."

144. Edward Hynes *et al.* to Planning and Development Committee of the Board of Trustees, April 20, 1990, MacPháidín Papers; Robert Kruse to Bartley Mac-Pháidín, May 2, 1990, Executive Vice President–Kruse Papers, ASC.

145. Library Committee Meeting Minutes, April 9, 1990, MacPháidín Papers; George Mathey to Robert Kruse, June 26, 1992 and August 26, 1992, Executive Vice President–Kruse Papers; *The Summit* (October 2, 1990), ASC.

146. Office of College Relations, Stonehill College. Compiled from 1996 NACUBO College and University Endowment study.

147. Edward Casieri, Treasurer's Report, 1995, 1994, 1988, 1978, Treasurer's Papers, ASC. Stonehill's endowment and fund acting as endowment was $24,635,000 in 1988 and $45,304,000 in 1994.

148. Bartley MacPháidín, Century Club Comments, December 1, 1990; Mac-Pháidín, Faculty Assembly Remarks, September 6, 1995, MacPháidín Papers; *The Summit* (September 26, 1996), ASC; *U.S. News & World Report*, "College Surveys," September 26, 1994, 114 and September 7, 1995, 140.

149. Bartley MacPháidín, written statement, n.d. [1993], MacPháidín Papers, ASC.

150. David Farrell to Bartley MacPháidín, September 23, 1991; James E. Samels to MacPháidín, May 21, 1996, Bartley MacPháidín Presidential Papers, Stonehill College; Mary Robinson to MacPháidín, January 25, 1993, MacPháidín Papers, ASC.

EPILOGUE

When the Congregation of Holy Cross came to North Easton in 1935, a dream was born. At the outset, the hope of a nationally recognized liberal arts college that would stand in the highest tradition of American Catholic higher education was dim. Stonehill College's hasty and poorly planned foundation caused many hardships, especially financially, during the early years. Yet, the College's first fifty years have been a great success story through the combined efforts of the Holy Cross Community and hundreds of lay collaborators who believed in the school's mission and potential.

During the 1950s Stonehill sought stability and recognition within the academic community, while experiencing its first physical expansion. A debt of $200,000, which the College incurred in its first 18 months of operation, restricted growth and created years of conflict between President Francis Boland and James Connerton, provincial of Holy Cross in the East. Liquidation of the debt, however, allowed James Sheehan to construct the first two additions to the College: Holy Cross Hall (Duffy Academic Center) and the Student Union. The decade ended on a high note, with the College receiving conditional accreditation in 1959.

The leadership and influence of Richard Sullivan, Stonehill's third president, placed the College on the path that would bring national recognition. Sullivan's vision led to the construction of O'Hara and Boland Halls, providing the opportunity for Stonehill to welcome students from a broader geographic area. Sullivan's wisdom and sense of justice guided him to champion the cause of women at Stonehill in the face of opposition from religious superiors in Holy Cross. Full accreditation in 1962, the construction of the Cushing-Martin Library, and resident students brought stability to the College after many years of uncertainty about its future.

Stonehill during the sixties and seventies, while not isolated from the mainstream of American higher education, did not suffer in any great measure from the rebelliousness of the era. Academic development through improvement of majors programs, the shift away from the tradition of *in loco parentis*, and revised grading were the legacies of John Corr and David Arthur. In 1972 the College and the Congregation of Holy Cross finalized canonical alienation, resulting in the legal separation of the two institutions. Stonehill, along with most Catholic institutions of higher learning, thus moved more clearly into the mainstream of American higher education, providing the opportunity for government support, and, most especially, greater collaboration between the religious and lay members of the faculty and administration. While this decade was not without the controversy created in the Foreign Language Department and the issues of college governance and faculty tenure, Stonehill emerged from the seventies, under the leadership of President Ernest Bartell, as a fully recognized and accepted institution in New England and beyond.

During the past twenty years, the College has been guided by Bartley MacPháidín, who with administrative excellence and collaborative expertise, has brought national recognition to Stonehill. Nationally cited for the first time in 1985 by *U.S. News & World Report*, Stonehill over the past decade has been commended for its quality of education and its ability to provide this service at a fair and reasonable price. The MacPháidín years have seen the campus transformed through the construction of several dormitories, the Martin Institute, a new dining commons, and the initiation of a new library, built after the College's successful completion of its first capital campaign.

The first fifty years of Stonehill College have seen much change and growth in the fulfillment of a dream. The academic excellence, physical plant expansion, and national recognition achieved by Stonehill could not have been imagined in the dark days of the fifties. Yet, through the dedication, perseverance, and hard work of hundreds of men and women, Stonehill proudly stands today as a college rich in tradition and confident of its place in American Catholic higher education. As she celebrates her golden jubilee, Stonehill stands ready for the challenges of the twenty-first century in her mission of service to the Church and society.

Appendices

Holy Cross Religious Serving at Stonehill College

Rev. Donald H. Abbott	1969–71, 1974–75	Br. James Denning	1967–68
Rev. Robert Adams	1970–72	Rev. John Denning	1993–95
Rev. Genaro Aguilar	1997–98	Br. John Dietzler	1957–66, 1967–68
Rev. David J. Arthur	1954–56, 1957–65,	Rev. James Doherty	1976, 1980–85
	1966–70, 1973–98	Rev. Peter M. Donohue	1970–80
Rev. Ernest Bartell	1971–77	Rev. James Doyle	1953–60
Rev. R. Bradley Beaupre	1997–98	Rev. James M. Duane	1991–94
Rev. George P. Benaglia	1948–54	Rev. Paul J. Duff	1960–73
Rev. James Bonfetti	1988–90	Rev. Thomas C. Duffy	1953–58
Rev. William Braun	1969–80	Rev. Harry B. Eichorn	1968–75, 1976–98
Rev. F. James Burbank	1973–77, 1991–98	Br. Joseph Faul	1951–60
Rev. Mr. Kym Bulger	1973–74	Rev. Thomas M. Feeley	1962–69, 1970–76,
Br. Donald Burke	1954, 1958–60		1978–85, 1987–98
Rev. Francis T. Cafarelli	1990–91	Rev. Raymond Finan	1949–50
Rev. Victor P. Caliri	1967–73	Rev. Leo Flood	1949–50
Rev. Thomas Campbell	1950–56	Br. Philip Foley	1961–65
Rev. Rudolph V. Carchidi	1992–98	Rev. Thomas Gariepy	1973, 1986–98
Mr. Daniel Cebrick	1994–95	Rev. William F. Gartland	1955–74, 1977–89
Rev. James Chichetto	1973–76, 1983–98	Br. Rene Gaudreau	1968–96
Rev. Thomas J. Clarke	1969–94	Rev. John Gerber	1973–74
Rev. Gerald P. Cohen	1965–77	Br. Peter Goodman	1983–94
Rev. Patrick R. Collins	1965–66	Rev. Richard M. Gorman	1960–67
Rev. Gerald Conmy	1968–70	Rev. Richard Gribble	1995–98
Rev. John T. Corr	1961–72	Rev. Robert F. Griffin	1957–64
Br. Honorius Corrigan	1949–50	Rev. Francis E. Grogan	1955–61
Rev. Albert Croce	1974–77	Br. Francis Gurley	1963–67
Rev. Aloysius E. Cussen	1960–77	Rev. Thomas M. Halkovic	1990–98
Rev. John F. Daly	1968–72	Rev. Edmund Haughey	1965–73
Rev. Victor Dean	1948–52	Br. Jerome F. Healy	1954–55
Rev. Anthony DeConciliis	1993–97	Rev. Marc J. Hebert	1951–52, 1957–69
Br. Michael Delaney	1973–74	Rev. Edward J. Hennessy	1962–63, 1964–66

Rev. William F. Hogan	1956–57, 1960–66, 1968–70	Rev. George B. Mulligan	1993–94
		Rev. James Murphy	1973–74
Rev. Francis J. Hurley	1960–84, 1985–98	Br. Lew Newton	1958–60
Rev. Daniel J. Issing	1992–98	Rev. Thomas C. Oddo	1977–83
Rev. Clement Kazlauskas	1963–68	Rev. Frank O'Hara	1948–49
Rev. William F. Keegan	1956–61, 1962–63, 1964–66	Rev. Lawrence Olszewski	1974–76
		Rev. Augustine J. Peverada	1964–70
Rev. Joseph P. Keena	1952–53, 1958–71, 1972–78, 1979–80	Rev. Francis J. Phelan	1972–75
		Rev. Roger Quilty	1963–66
Br. Francis Kennedy	1958–60, 1965–69	Rev. Wilfred Raymond	1980–93
Rev. Robert J. Kruse	1965–70, 1971–98	Rev. Edward J. Reidy	1974–76
Rev. John I. Lahey	1970–71	Br. Sergius (Harold) Rogan	1949–53, 1955–57
Rev. John Lanci	1993–95	Rev. E. Peter Royal	1957–61, 1965–67, 1969–70
Rev. Thomas Lane	1949–52		
Rev. Thomas Lockary	1955–69, 1970–88	Br. Oswald Rumrill	1948–49
Rev. Joseph A. Lorusso	1953–56, 1957–60, 1965–66	Mr. John Santone	1996–97
		Br. Peter Scarpignato	1960–66
Rev. James V. Lowery	1956–73	Br. Josephus Schaub	1948–51
Rev. John P. Lucey	1951–54, 1958–61, 1964–71, 1972–74, 1975–87	Rev. G. Michael Scully	1966–71, 1973–76
		Rev. Richard J. Segreve	1973–75, 1976–84
		Rev. Edward S. Shea	1948–54
Rev. Philip V. Lucitt	1963–64	Rev. James Sheehan	1951–58
Rev. Bartley MacPháidín	1967–74, 1975–98	Rev. Kenneth J. Silvia	1976–80
Rev. Henry Malone	1949–52	Rev. Joseph Skaff	1969–74, 1975–90
Rev. James B. Mannis	1970–71	Br. Albertus Smith	1989–92
Rev. Louis Manzo	1974–98	Rev. Marc E. Smith	1982–83
Br. Michael Massaro	1969–75	Rev. Kevin Spicer	1993–94
Br. Jerome Matthews	1961–63, 1964–67, 1983–84	Rev. Richard H. Sullivan	1951–52, 1954–57, 1958–64
Rev. Richard Mazziota	1980–94	Rev. Thomas C. Sullivan	1966–67
Rev. James P. McBreen	1968–69	Br. Laetus Triolo	1973–74
Rev. John E. McCarthy	1964–98	Rev. Francis M. Walsh	1966–68, 1971–98
Rev. Francis McFarland	1960–61	Rev. Peter Walsh	1989–92
Rev. John T. McGee	1961–65	Br. John Weihrer	1960–72
Rev. Robert McMahon	1973–74	Rev. Joseph F. Wiseman	1949–50
Br. William Modlin	1958–65	Rev. Robert Woodward	1948–49
Rev. James Moran	1948–50	Br. Herman Zaccarelli	1955–56, 1962–65, 1973–74
Br. John Mullan	1960–63		

Significant Administrative Positions

PRESIDENTS

George Benaglia, CSC	1948–1949
Francis Boland, CSC	1949–1955
James Sheehan, CSC	1955–1958
Richard Sullivan, CSC	1958–1964
John T. Corr, CSC	1964–1971
Ernest Bartell, CSC	1971–1977
C. James Cleary (Interim)	1977–1978
Bartley MacPháidín, CSC	1978–present

ACADEMIC DEANS

James Moran, CSC	1948–1950
John Lucey, CSC	1950–1954
James Doyle,CSC	1954–1960
Aloysius Cussen, CSC	1960–1966
David Arthur, CSC	1966–1970
Edmund Haughey, CSC	1970–1973
C. James Cleary	1973–1975
Robert Horn	1975–1978
Robert Kruse, CSC	1978–1987
Fred Petti	1987–1988
Jo-Ann Flora, SND	1988–1993
Louis Manzo, CSC	1993–present

DEAN OF STUDENT LIFE/AFFAIRS

Paul Duff, CSC	1961–1970
Victor P. Caliri, CSC	1970–1973
Sr. Suzanne Kelly	1973–1974
John A. Gallagher	1974–1979
Charles Ratto	1979–1988
R. William Barber (Acting)	1988–1989
Louis Saltrelli	1989–present

DIRECTORS OF DEVELOPMENT/COLLEGE RELATIONS

Thomas C. Duffy, CSC	1957–1960
James Lowery, CSC	1960–1967
Leo E. Weisner	1967–1969
Walter A. Mullen	1970–1984
Francis X. Dillon	1984–present

ATHLETIC DIRECTORS

George Sullivan	1948–1951
Joseph Cheney	1951–1957
Robert V. Daley	1957–1959
William Gartland, CSC	1959–1963
Paul Duff, CSC	1963–1967
George R. Blaney	1967–1969
James D. Dougher	1969–1974
Francis McArdle	1974–1975
Harry Hart	1975–1978
Thomas J. Folliard	1978–1984
Raymond P. Pepin	1984–1996
Paula Sullivan	1996–present

DIRECTORS OF CAMPUS MINISTRY

John McCarthy, CSC	1964–1976
Kenneth Silvia, CSC	1976–1979
Richard Segreve, CSC	1979–1982
John McCarthy, CSC	1982–1991
Wilfred Raymond, CSC (Acting)	1991–1992
Daniel Issing, CSC	1992–present

APPENDIX 3

Honorary Degree Recipients

RECIPIENTS	DEGREE	RECIPIENTS	DEGREE
1952		Beatrice H. Mullaney	Doctor of Laws
Bishop James L. Connolly	Doctor of Laws	Cardinal Lawrence Shehan	Doctor of Laws
Msgr. Cornelius T.H. Sherlock	Doctor of Laws	William H. Bannon	Doctor of Laws
Paul A. Dever	Doctor of Laws	**1957**	
		Bishop Lawrence J. Riley	Doctor of Laws
1953		John J. Desmond, Jr.	Doctor of Laws
Archbishop Richard Cushing	Doctor of Laws	Francis Millet Rogers	Doctor of Laws
Rev. Edward J. Gorman	Doctor of Laws	John Joseph Haley	Doctor of Laws
Harry K. Stone	Doctor of Laws		
Jospeh C. Duggan	Doctor of Laws	**1958**	
		Foster J. Furcolo	Doctor of Laws
1954		Msgr. Francis J. Lally	Doctor of Laws
Bishop Russell J. McVinney	Doctor of Laws	Dewey D. Stone	Doctor of Laws
Msgr. Timothy P. Sweeney	Doctor of Laws		
Charles Gerald Lucey	Doctor of Laws	**1959**	
Joseph A. DeMambro	Doctor of Laws	Cardinal Francis Spellman	Doctor of Laws
		Rev. George Benaglia, CSC	Doctor of Laws
1955		Frank M. Folsom	Doctor of Laws
Bishop Matthew F. Brady	Doctor of Laws	John M. Curley	Doctor of Laws
Msgr. Timothy F. O'Leary	Doctor of Laws		
John W. McCormack	Doctor of Laws	**1960**	
Joseph W. Martin, Jr.	Doctor of Laws	Luke E. Hart	Doctor of Laws
Robert B. Porter	Doctor of Laws	Msgr. Raymond T. Considine	Doctor of Laws
		Br. Ephrem O'Dwyer, CSC	Doctor of Laws
1956		Philip Hemingway	Doctor of Laws
Annabelle McConnell Melville	Doctor of Laws	Martin H. Spellman	Doctor of Laws

RECIPIENTS	DEGREE	RECIPIENTS	DEGREE
1961		**1964 Father John Corr's Inauguration**	
Bishop Thomas J. Riley	Doctor of Laws	George N. Shuster	Doctor of Laws
John A. Volpe	Doctor of Laws		
Clement C. Maxwell	Doctor of Laws	**1965**	
Wayne E. Clark	Doctor of Laws	Owen B. Kiernan	Doctor of Literature
Ralph D. Tedeschi	Doctor of Laws	Rev. Vincent C. Dore, OP	Doctor of Laws
		Frank E. Smith	Doctor of Laws
1962		Mother M. Benedict Young, SCMM	Doctor of Science
Bishop Robert F. Joyce	Doctor of Laws	Rev. Frederick R. McManus	Doctor of Laws
Michael J. Mansfield	Doctor of Laws		
Rev. Patrick J. Peyton, CSC	Doctor of Laws	**1966**	
J. Peter Grace	Doctor of Laws	Leverett Saltonstall	Doctor of Laws
Francis D. Mone	Doctor of Laws	Msgr. Charles A. Finn	Doctor of Laws
Richard J. Potvin	Doctor of Laws	Asa Philip Randolph	Doctor of Laws
		Helen C. White	Doctor of Literature
1962 Dedication of Cushing-Martin Library		Robert B. Woodward	Doctor of Science
Joseph P. Lally	Doctor of Laws	**1967**	
Henry E. Massoletti	Doctor of Communication Science	Walter A.G. Gropius	Doctor of Arts
Joseph L. Sweeney	Doctor of Laws	Bishop Jeremiah F. Minihan	Doctor of Laws
Richard H. Wright	Doctor of Science	Pauli Murray	Doctor of Laws
		William C.H. Prentice	Doctor of Laws
1963			
Msgr. John Tracy Ellis	Doctor of Literature	**1968**	
Msgr. Humberto Sousa Medeiros	Doctor of Laws	Walter Brennan	Doctor of Laws
Mary Ingraham Bunting	Doctor of Science	Peter Muirhead	Doctor of Laws
John J. Drummey	Doctor of Laws	Mary Reed Newland	Doctor of Literature
Emery J. LaLiberte	Doctor of Arts	Thomas L. Phillips	Doctor of Communication Science
Charles J. Lewin	Doctor of Literature		
		1969	
1964		Rev. Timothy J. Harrington	Doctor of Laws
Joseph E. Fernandes	Doctor of Communication Science	Margaret M. Heckler	Doctor of Laws
Edward M. Kennedy	Doctor of Laws	**1970**	
Loretta Quinlan	Doctor of Literature	Frank J. Ayd, Jr.	Doctor of Science
Myer N. Sobiloff	Doctor of Communication Science	Michael Collins	Doctor of Science
Rev. Michael P. Walsh, SJ	Doctor of Science	Rev. James W. Connerton, CSC	Doctor of Humanities

RECIPIENTS	DEGREE	RECIPIENTS	DEGREE
J. John Fox	Doctor of Laws	**1975**	
Rev. Raymond J. Swords, SJ	Doctor of Humanities	Msgr. Geno Charles Baroni	Doctor of Laws
		Anthony E. Cascino	Doctor of Business Administration
1971		Dixy Lee Ray	Doctor of Arts
Bishop Daniel Cronin	Doctor of Laws	Pascal Vincent Doyle	Doctor of Business Administration
Eric Hoffer	Doctor of Laws		
		1976	
1972		John F. Collins	Doctor of Laws
Rev. Theodore Hesburgh, CSC	Doctor of Humanities	Rev. Gerald J. Whelan, CSC	Doctor of Humanities
Edward Everett Martin	Doctor of Laws	Arthur Fiedler	Doctor of Arts
Patrick Edward McCarthy	Doctor of Humanities	Ann Ida Gannon, BVM	Doctor of Arts
Frances Marie Burlingame	Doctor of Literature	**1977**	
		Michael Novak	Doctor of Humanities
1973			
Harry Austryn Wolfson	Doctor of Literature	Maurice Charles	Doctor of Arts
Elizabeth D. Koontz	Doctor of Literature	Bishop Marcos G. McGrath, CSC	Doctor of Laws
Zenon C.R. Hansen	Doctor of Business Administration	Robert Coles	Doctor of Humanities
Martin Myerson	Doctor of Laws	Eugene F. Merkert (Awarded in February)	Doctor of Business Administration

1973 Presidential Dinner, Twenty-Fifth Anniversary

Harold G. Kern	Doctor of Journalism	**1978**	
Malcolm Y. Mackinnon	Doctor of Business Administration	Rev. Richard H. Sullivan, CSC	Doctor of Laws
Thomas J. Bowler	Doctor of Business Administration	Paul A. Samuelson	Doctor of Literature
		David M. Tracy	Doctor of Humanities
1974		Joseph N. Malone	Doctor of Business Administration
Ammon Barness	Doctor of Business Administration	Paul A. Freund	Doctor of Humanities
Vincent P. Wright	Doctor of Humanities		
Rev. Clarence W. Friedman	Doctor of Humanities	**October 1978 Board of Advisors Dinner**	
Kevin B. Harrington	Doctor of Laws	David Ames	Doctor of Business Administration
Talcott Parsons	Doctor of Arts		

RECIPIENTS	DEGREE	RECIPIENTS	DEGREE
1979		**1982**	
C. James Cleary	Doctor of Literature	Marvin S. Traub	Doctor of Humanities
Edward S. Skillin	Doctor of Literature		
Martha Ware	Doctor of Humanities	Siobhan McKenna	Doctor of Letters
		George A. Plimpton	Doctor of Letters
Robert Wood	Doctor of Literature	Romuald Spasowski	Doctor of Humanities
Elma I. Lewis	Doctor of Humanities		
Max Cleland	Doctor of Humanities	**1982 December Convocation**	
		Carmel B. Heaney	Doctor of Humanities
1980		William V. Shannon	Doctor of Letters
Mary Martin	Doctor of Arts		
Thomas Murphy	Doctor of Humanities	**1983**	
Jane Hayward	Doctor of Arts	Rev. John T. Corr, CSC	Doctor of Laws
Joseph D. Early	Doctor of Laws	Robert J. Donovan	Doctor of Letters
Archbishop Iakovos	Doctor of Humanities	Bianca Macias Jagger	Doctor of Humanities
Henry Margenau	Doctor of Humanities	Muriel Sutherland Snowden	Doctor of Humanities
1981		**1984**	
Robert M. Bennett	Doctor of Arts	Corazon C. Aquina	Doctor of Humanities
Robert E. White	Doctor of Laws		
Maryalice C. Moore	Doctor of Humanities	Edward P. Boland	Doctor of Laws
		Edmond N. Moriarity, Jr.	Doctor of Business Administration
Roger A. Saunders	Doctor of Humanities		
		Thomas P. O'Neill, Jr.	Doctor of Laws
Rev. Bruce Ritter, OFM	Doctor of Humanities	Anna Polcino, SCMM, M.D.	Doctor of Arts
		John W. Stanger (Awarded September 24, 1984)	Doctor of Business Administration
1981 President's Dinner			
Charles A. Fuller	Doctor of Letters	**1985**	
David E. Crosby	Doctor of Laws		
George E. Carney, Jr.	Doctor of Humanities	Fritz Eichenberg	Doctor of Arts
		Barbara A. Rockett	Doctor of Humanities
Dorothy M. Trower	Doctor of Arts		
Stanton W. Davis	Doctor of Humanities	Dan Rostenkowski	Doctor of Laws
		Brunetta R. Wolfman	Doctor of Letters

RECIPIENTS	DEGREE
1986	
Cardinal Jaime L. Sin	Doctor of Humanities
Bob Keeshan	Doctor of Arts
Tony Schwartz	Doctor of Communications
Josephine L. Taylor	Doctor of Humanities
Barbara A. Whelan, CSJ	Doctor of Humanities
1987	
Lee Abraham (Awarded January 15, 1987)	Doctor of Business Administration
Silvio O. Conte	Doctor of Arts
David S. Nelson	Doctor of Laws
Catherine T. McNamee, CSJ	Doctor of Education
Eugene J. Dionne, Jr.	Doctor of Letters
1988	
Yi Jian Gu	Doctor of Science
Rev. Guy Couturier, CSC	Doctor of Letters
Elsa Hilger	Doctor of Fine Arts
Frank A. Tredinick, Jr.	Doctor of Letters
John Joseph Moakley	Doctor of Laws
Arnold "Red" Auerbach	Doctor of Arts
1989	
Charles Osgood	Doctor of Letters
Martin J. Dunn, D.M.D.	Doctor of Humanities
Anna J. Schwartz	Doctor of Arts
Brian J. Donnelly	Doctor of Laws
Valerie Goulding	Doctor of Humanities
1990	
Rev. Avery Dulles, SJ	Doctor of Letters
Adé Bethune	Doctor of Arts
Rev. Louis Hage, OLM	Doctor of Letters
Marjorie FitzGibbon	Doctor of Fine Arts

RECIPIENTS	DEGREE
Mike Barnicle	Doctor of Humanities
1991	
William M. Bulger	Doctor of Letters
Rev. William J. Byron, SJ	Doctor of Philosophy
Robert R. Davila	Doctor of Humanities
Michael J. Roarty	Doctor of Business Administration
Dorothy Shields	Doctor of Arts
1992	
Rev. Ernest Bartell, CSC	Doctor of Laws
Mary Higgins Clark	Doctor of Letters
Donald Francis Flynn	Doctor of Business Administration
Patricia Jane Hakim	Doctor of Fine Arts
Rev. Richard W. Timm, CSC	Doctor of Humanities
1993	
Francis Joseph Mullin	Doctor of Business Administration
German Sevirovich Mironov	Doctor of Sciences
Dorothy James Orr	Doctor of Humanities
Raymond Leo Flynn	Doctor of Humanities
September 1973	
Albert Reynolds	Doctor of Laws
1994	
Bishop Sean O'Malley, OFM Cap.	Doctor of Humanities
Thomas F. Shields	Doctor of Humanities
Noel Pearson	Doctor of Arts

RECIPIENTS	DEGREE	RECIPIENTS	DEGREE
1995		Daniel F. Roche	Doctor of Humanities
Mary Elizabeth Cunningham Agee	Doctor of Humanities	Eileen S. Roche	Doctor of Arts
Leonard Florence	Doctor of Laws	Raymond Zimmerman	Doctor of Laws
Cathy Elizabeth Minnehan	Doctor of Humane Letters		
John Marks Templeton	Doctor of Philosophy	**1997**	
		Ellen M. Zane	Doctor of Business Administration
1996		Thomas A. Constantine	Doctor of Laws
Grace G. Corrigan	Doctor of Education	Richard D. Lehan	Doctor of Letters
Sol Gittleman	Doctor of Letters	Marguerite Anne McKenna Luksik	Doctor of Humanities

Enrollment

 ❧

Day College

YEAR	STUDENTS	YEAR	STUDENTS	YEAR	STUDENTS	YEAR	STUDENTS
1948	134	1961	829	1974	1649	1987	1922
1949	231	1962	942	1975	1673	1988	1964
1950	251	1963	1036	1976	1686	1989	1913
1951	293	1964	1156	1977	1690	1990	1964
1952	297	1965	1213	1978	1700	1991	1986
1953	262	1966	1224	1979	1714	1992	1955
1954	287	1967	1243	1980	1751	1993	2023
1955	351	1968	1350	1981	1755	1994	1943
1956	380	1969	1423	1982	1723	1995	2005
1957	415	1970	1480	1983	1741	1996	2059
1958	509	1971	1591	1984	1804	1997	2065
1959	538	1972	1605	1985	1849		
1960	651	1973	1631	1986	1834		

Evening Division (Fall)

YEAR	STUDENTS	YEAR	STUDENTS	YEAR	STUDENTS	YEAR	STUDENTS
1970	181	1977	689	1984	982	1991	1127
1971	314	1978	836	1985	990	1992	1084
1972	385	1979	929	1986	1016	1993	926
1973	512	1980	1006	1987	1022	1994	876
1974	573	1981	891	1988	1090	1995	827
1975	591	1982	1023	1989	1019	1996	711
1976	515	1983	1008	1990	1061	1997	650

Athletic Awards

ATHLETIC HALL OF FAME

1989

Rev. William Gartland, CSC — Athletic Director (Posthumously)

Armond Colombo (55) — Football Coach—Brockton High

Paula Sullivan — Women's Basketball Coach

Lou Gorman (53) — Baseball Executive
Nancy Smith (83) — Basketball
Mike Allocco (72) — Basketball
Don Prohovich (80) — Baseball
Angelo Caranfa, Jr. (66) — Soccer

1990

Rev. John McCarthy, CSC — Campus Ministry
Paul Sincero (53) — Basketball
William Zolga (80) — Basketball
Sharon Donovan (83) — Softball

1991

William Nixon (53) — Basketball
Ann Mallory (83) — Basketball
Robert Rietz (83) — Basketball
Robert Hegarty (58) — Baseball
1971 Men's Basketball Team

1992

Leo Denault (61) — Basketball

Daniel Neary (78) — Golf
Robert Percuso (78) — Baseball
Mary Anne Walsh (85) — Basketball
1980 Baseball Team

1993

Tom Dean (82) — Football
Lesli Laychak-Rendall (87) — Basketball
Sally Scully (81) — Softball
Mike Tosone (85) — Football

1994

Brian Cronin (89) — Basketball
Donald Edmonston (57) — Basketball
William Herlihy (52) — Basketball
Julie McGivern Walsh (85) — Softball
1982 Men's Basketball Team

1995

Mary Naughton (89) — Basketball
Henry Jackson (73) — Basketball
John Burke (80) — Baseball
George Zahringher (75) — Golf
George Peterson (64) — Basketball (Posthumously)
Women's 1983 Basketball Team

1996

Frank Strachan (90)	Football
Christine Pecevich (88)	Soccer
Christine Donovan (87)	Basketball
Ron Richard (68)	Basketball
Donna Fruci-Rigdon (85)	Softball
Edward Martin	Benefactor

1997

Michael R. Aubin (86)	Cross Country
Gerald J. Cunniff (66)	Baseball and Basketball
Kathryn S. Delaney (90)	Basketball
Teresa Duggan LaMonica (91)	Softball and Volleyball

EDWARD E. MARTIN AWARD

1982

Theresa Tardiff	Volleyball and Softball
Mark Morrison	Football

1983

Nancy Smith	Basketball
Michael Kennedy and Tom Reid (Tie)	Football and Athletic Committee

1984

Carlene Casciano	Volleyball
Joseph Gomes	Baseball

1985

Michael Tosone	Football
Julie McGivern	Softball

1986

Helen Phillips	Basketball and Softball
Michael Aubin	Cross Country
Andrew McKenna	Soccer

1987

David Skelly	Baseball
Christine Aubin	Cross Country

1988

Jennifer Twomey	Basketball
Gerard Roy	Football

1989

James McHugh	Soccer
Nicole Champagne	Softball

1990

Katy Delaney	Basketball
Anthony Lodovico	Soccer

1991

Bob Taylor	Soccer
Robin Ricci	Cross Country

1992

Andy McMahon	Soccer
Paula Kohs	Basketball

1993

Karen Beaulieu	Tennis
Kevin Broderick	Football

1994

Cindy Padden	Soccer
Mike Nelson	Football

1995

Chris Butler	Basketball
Morgan Surdyk	Equestrian

1996

Joe Maher	Tennis
Rebecca Bartlett	Soccer

1997

Kim Trudel	Basketball
Greg Ranieri	Football

REV. WILLIAM GARTLAND, CSC, AWARD

1991

Ed Grzembski	Basketball
Virginia Duggan	Basketball and Volleyball

1992

John Cronin	Basketball
Kim Dunn	Soccer

1993

Glen Lindstrom	Football
Jen Cazeault	Basketball

1994

Karen Patterson	Soccer
Kristen Morast	Basketball
P.J. Fernandes	Football

1995

Dan Gamache	Football
Jon Bruno	Soccer
Michelle Doonan	Basketball

1996

Dan Cahill	Football
Leo Bush	Baseball
Esther King	Basketball

1997

Sue Patchett	Basketball
Matthew Ramah	Soccer

Outstanding Alumnus Award

❦

1973

Gerard M. O'Neill (64)

In recognition of his achievements in the field of journalism and investigative reporting as head of the Boston *Globe's* Pulitzer Prize-winning Spotlight Team.

1974

Michael J. Novak (56)

In recognition of his achievements in the fields of philosophy and journalism. He is a nationally known author and Catholic intellectual in the post-Vatican Council II Church.

1975

Richard P. Flavin (58)

In recognition of his professional attainments in the field of broadcasting as a political satirist. He is renowned for his sharp wit, concise reporting, and political sensitivity.

1976

Lawrence J. Finnegan (52)

In recognition of his distinguished career as president and chairman of the board of Boston Mutual Life Insurance Company and for the high esteem in which he is held by his colleagues and by the Stonehill alumni.

1977

William T. Herlihy (52)

In recognition of his high ideals, which governed his every action as a successful businessman, a civic-minded citizen, and an outstanding parent.

1979

James L. "Lou" Gorman (53)

In recognition of his outstanding success in his distinguished career in baseball, which included management associations with the New York Mets, Kansas City Royals, Seattle Mariners, Baltimore Orioles, and Boston Red Sox.

1982
David I. Finnegan (64)   In recognition of his exceptional leadership talents and outstanding achievements in the careers of law, politics, and talk show host on WBZ radio.

1983
Ann L. Hagan (65)   In recognition of her achievements as vice president, Municipal Utilities Department at Merrill Lynch White Held Capital Markets Group in New York. The highest-ranking woman on Wall Street in municipal utilities, she subsequently developed a reputation as a superior investment banker with Smith Barney.

1984
Paul B. Flynn (57)   In recognition of his brilliant and exciting careers in the communications industry from reporter to editor, publicist to manager, publisher to president. He is presently executive vice president with *USA Today*.

1985
Rita E. Smith (62)   In recognition of a life devoted to education as an innovative, resourceful, and dynamic representative of the best in the teaching profession. She was awarded *Time* Magazine's "1984 Teacher of the Year."

1986
Richard D. Lehan (52)   In recognition of his distinguished career as a scholar, teacher, and literary figure. His research, publications, and lectures are widely acclaimed and respected.

1987
John E. Drew (65)   In recognition of his entrepeneurial abilities as developer of Boston's World Trade Center and Merchandise Mart, Horticultural Hall, Great Woods Center for the Performing Arts, and Constitution Plaza in Charlestown.

1989
Martin J. Kelly (64)   In recognition of his exceptional leadership talents and entrepreneurial vision in business as president of Northwest Administrators, Inc., which he founded in 1963 and led to greatness.

1990
William C. O'Malley (66)   In recognition of his integrity and professionalism in public service as Plymouth County district attorney since 1979.

1991
A. Michael DeSisto (62)   In recognition of his dedication to helping youth and their families. He has been an outstanding educator, a compassionate counselor, a popular author,

a skilled communicator, and founder of The DeSisto School, a therapeutic-educational community for troubled teenagers.

1992

Arthur "Bud" Colgan, CSC (68)

In recognition of his devotion to the life of the Catholic Church in the poor communities of Peru as a member of the Congregation of Holy Cross.

1993

Patricia Hanley-McCurdy (75)

In recognition of her professional achievements and dedication to community service as an educator, lawyer, and children's rights advocate and for the improvement of the foster care system.

1994

William P. Driscoll (68)

In recognition of his courage, skill, and exemplary service as a naval flight officer and highly decorated Vietnam veteran of over 200 combat missions.

1996

Robert E. Budge, M.D. (61)

In recognition of his distinguished accomplishments as an exceptional orthopedic surgeon and as a teacher, an administrative leader, an author, and a researcher at Saint Louis University.

1997

Jeanmarie Gribaudo, CSJ (87)

In recognition of her work as youth advisor to Boston Mayor Thomas Menino, especially her service with disadvantaged children and teenagers who exhibit destructive behavior. Her compassion, energy, and dedication were noted by *Boston Magazine* in her inclusion in its list of "the 50 most intriguing women in Boston."

Achievement Awards

REV. GEORGE P. BENAGLIA, CSC, AWARD

1972	Francis G. Lee
1973	Rev. John Lucey, CSC
1974	James J. Kenneally
1981	Rev. Aloysius Cussen, CSC
1982	Carol E. Fraser and Herbert A. Wessling
1983	Rev. John E. McCarthy, CSC
1985	Rev. Thomas Lockary, CSC
1988	Rev. William Gartland, CSC

LOUISE HEGARTY EXCELLENCE IN TEACHING AWARD

1989	Chet Raymo
1990	Warren F. Dahlin, Jr.
1991	Maura Geens Tyrrell
1992	Robert Carver
1993	Ralph Bravaco
1994	Debra Salvucci-Imbriani
1995	José Pérez
1996	John R. Lanci
1997	Rev. Rudolph Carchidi, CSC

EDWARD E. MARTIN PUBLIC SERVICE AWARD

1993 Donna Morse
Director, Literary Center, Attleboro, Massachusetts

1994 Brenda Rodrigues
Founder, Brockton Library Association

1995 Thomas F. Frizzell
Baseball Coach, Massasoit Community College

1996 Joanne M. Hoops
Executive Director, Boys and Girls Club, Brockton, Massachusetts

1997 Stephen M. Shephard
Police Officer, DARE Program, Attleboro, Massachusetts

PRESIDENT'S AWARD (COMMENCEMENT)

1989	Catherine Johnson
1990	Vasco Amorim
1994	Linda Sullivan
1997	Grace Donovan, SUSC

PRESIDENT'S CUP AWARD

1991	Donna Bain
1992	Ed Crisci, Kerry Foley, John Pestana
1993	Christopher Canning
1994	Christine Bridges, Susan Werstak
1995	Brian Foley, Chris Peraro
1996	Shelley Mundie
1997	Kevin Minoli

BIBLIOGRAPHY

Archives

Archives Stonehill College (ASC), North Easton, Massachusetts

Archives of the Holy Cross Fathers (Eastern Province) (AHCFE), North Easton, Massachusetts

Archives of the Holy Cross Fathers (Indiana Province) (AHCFI), Notre Dame, Indiana

Archives of the Holy Cross Fathers Generalate (AHCFG), Rome, Italy

Archives Holy Cross Brothers (Eastern Province) (AHCBE), Valatie, New York

Archives University of Notre Dame (AUND), Notre Dame, Indiana

Archives Franciscan Friars, Holy Name Province (AFFHN), New York, New York

Archives King's College (AKC), Wilkes-Barre, Pennsylvania

Oral Interviews

Rev. David Arthur, CSC—November 7, 1995 and July 18, 1996

Rev. Ernest Bartell, CSC—July 25, 1996

Rev. F. James Burbank, CSC—July 30, 1996

Rev. Thomas Campbell, CSC—September 15, 1995

Mr. C. James Cleary—July 16, 1996

Rev. Peter Donahue, CSC—June 19, 1996

Professor Paul Gastonguay—April 16, 1997

Rev. Daniel Issing, CSC—March 20, 1997

Rev. Robert Kruse, CSC—July 11, 1996

Rev. John Lucey, CSC—August 31, 1995

Rev. Bartley MacPháidín, CSC—April 3, 1997

Rev. John McCarthy, CSC—July 22, 1996

Mr. James Mullen—August 11, 1995

Brother Harold Rogan, CSC—August 6, 1995

Professor Rita Smith—March 20, 1997

Rev. Richard Sullivan, CSC—October 31, 1995

Group Interview, Stonehill Alumni of the 1950s—November 14, 1995

Group Interview, Stonehill Alumni of the 1960s—March 26, 1996

Group Interview, Stonehill Alumni of the 1970s—November 19, 1996

Group Interview, Stonehill Alumni of the 1980s—February 4, 1997

Secondary Sources, Books and Articles

"Academic Tenure at Harvard University." *AAUP Bulletin* 58 (Spring 1972): 62–68.

Allitt, Patrick. *Catholic Intellectuals and Conservative Politics in America, 1950–1985.* Ithaca, New York: Cornell University Press, 1993.

Aniskov, V.T., ed. *In Demidov's Name: Yaroslavl University—Its Past and Present.* Yaroslavl, Russia: Yaroslavl Technical University Publishing House, 1995.

Annarelli, James John. *Academic Freedom and Catholic Higher Education.* New York: Greenwood Press, 1987.

Astin, Alexander, Helen Astin, Alan Boyer, and Ann Bisconti. *The Power of Protest.* Washington, D.C.: Jossey-Bass Publishers, 1975.

Baehr, George B. *Chronicles of Fairfield University 1942–1992: Book Two: An Era of Steady Growth and Change.* Fairfield, Connecticut: Fairfield University Press, 1992.

Bartell, CSC, Ernest, "The Climate of an Academic Institution." *NCEA College Newsletter* 36(1) (September 1973): 1–6.

———. "The Enduring Non-Crisis in Higher Education." *Daedalus* 104(1) (Winter 1975): 16–24.

———. "Good News and Bad for Catholic Schools." *America* 126(13) (April 1, 1972): 343–45.

———. "On Trying to Define a Catholic College." *NCEA College Newsletter* 35(2) (December 1972): 1, 3.

———. "Pros and Cons of Public Funding for Catholic Schools." *Current History* (63) (August 1972): 62–67, 87–92.

———. "A Reaction." *Notre Dame Journal of Education.* 3(1) (Spring 1972): 66–68.

Beirne, CSC, Kilian. *From Sea to Shining Sea: The Holy Cross Brothers in the United States.* Valatie, New York: Holy Cross Press, 1966.

Bell, Daniel, and Irving Kristol, eds. *Confrontation: The Student Rebellion and the Universities.* New York: Basic Books, Inc., Publishers, 1969.

Berbusse, SJ, Edward J. "The Catholic College vs. Academic Freedom." *Homiletic and Pastoral Review* 86 (August/September 1986): 11–20.

Blaney, J.J. "How Christian Is the Catholic College?" *Catholic World* 184 (January 1957): 276–82.

Bonachea, Rolando E., ed. *Jesuit Higher Education: Essays on an American Tradition of Excellence.* Pittsburgh: Duquesne University Press, 1989.

Borkowski, F.T. "The University President's Role in Establishing an Institutional Climate to Encourage Minority Participation in Higher Education." *Peabody Journal of Education* 66 (Fall 1988): 32–45.

Brosnan, John F. "Catholic Higher Education: A View From Outside the Institution." *NCEA Bulletin* 56 (August 1959): 116–20.

Brown, SJ, Stephen. "Catholic Universities in America Today." *Irish Educational Record* 69 (January 1947): 20–28.

Browne, Henry J. "Catholics and the AAUP." *Commonweal* 65 (October 5, 1956): 7–14.

Brubacher, John S., and Willis Rudy. *Higher Education in Transition: A History of American Colleges and Universities, 1636–1968.* New York: Harper & Row, 1968.

Buckley, SJ, Michael. "The Catholic University as Pluralistic Forum." *Thought* 46 (Summer 1971): 200–12.

———. "The Catholic University and Its Inherent Promise." *America* 168 (May 29, 1993): 14–16.

———. "The Function of a Catholic University." *U.S. Catholic* 34 (September 1969): 47.

Buetow, Harold A. *A History of United States Catholic Schools.* Washington, D.C.: National Catholic Educational Association, 1985.

Bullard, Pamela. "Stonehill College: A Success Story." *Sunday Herald Advertiser* (May 13, 1973): "Pictorial Living" Section, 29, 31.

Burrell, CSC, David. "The Ideal of a Catholic University." *The Furrow* 31 (September 1980): 555–60.

Burtchaell, CSC, James T. "The Decline and Fall of the Christian College: Part I." *First Things* I (April 1991): 16–29.

———. "The Decline and Fall of the Christian College: Part II." *First Things* I (May 1991): 30–38.

Byron, SJ, William J. "Between Church and Culture: A Role for Catholic Higher Education." *Thought* 66 (September 1991): 310–16.

———. "Catholic Education in a Pluralistic Society." *Origins* 19 (March 15, 1990): 669–75.

Campion, SJ, Donald R. "Catholic Colleges Face Up to Change." *America* 121 (December 13, 1969): 590–92.

Carlin, David. "What Future for Catholic Higher Education?" *America* 174 (February 24, 1996): 15–17.

Casey, Kenneth J., and Gerald L. Hallworth. "Catholic Universities: Tomorrow Not Yesterday." *Catholic Educational Review* 67 (October 1969): 47–54.

"Catholic Higher Education in the 1970s." *America* 130 (January 26, 1973): 45.

"The Catholic University of Today." *America* 117 (August 12, 1967): 154–56.

Connelly, CSC, James T., ed. *The Chronicles of Notre Dame du Lac*. Notre Dame, Indiana: University of Notre Dame Press, 1992.

———. "An Eastern Province in 1938." Paper presented at the Conference on the History of the Congregations of Holy Cross, June 17, 1989, North Easton, Massachusetts.

———. "Educators in the Faith: The Holy Cross Congregations and Their Schools in the United States, 1865–1900." Paper presented at the Conference of the History of the Congregations of Holy Cross in the United States, June 15, 1990, New Orleans, Louisiana.

———. "Holy Cross in the United States: 150 Years." *CSC Internazionale* VI (1) (Fall 1991): 2–7.

Connors, Joseph B. *Journey Toward Fulfillment: A History of The College of St. Thomas*. St. Paul, Minnesota: The College of St. Thomas Press, 1986.

Contosta, David R. *Villanova University: American—Catholic—Augustinian*. University Park, Pennsylvania: Penn State University Press, 1995.

"Control of Catholic Universities." *Ave Maria* 105 (January 28, 1967): 4–5.

Corazzini, Arthur, *et al. Higher Education in the Boston Metropolitan Area*. Boston: Board of Higher Education, 1969.

———. *Higher Education in the Boston Metropolitan Area—Follow Up Study*. Boston: Board of Higher Education, 1971.

Corson, John. *Governance of Colleges and Universities*. New York: McGraw-Hill Book Company, Inc., 1960.

Cox, Harvey. *The Secular City: Secularization and Urbanization in Theologiocal Perspective*, Revised Edition. Toronto: The Macmillan Company, 1966.

Cramer, Jerome. "Academic Freedom and the Catholic Church." *Educational Record* 67 (Spring/Summer 1986): 30–32.

Cunneen, Joseph E. "Catholics and Education." *Commonweal* 58 (August 7–14, 1953): 437–41 and 461–64.

Cunningham, Lawrence. *The Catholic Experience*. New York: Crossroad, 1986.

Curran, Charles E. "Academic Freedom and Catholic Institutions of Higher Learning." *Journal of the American Academy of Religion* 55(1) (1987): 107–124.

———. *Catholic Higher Education, Theology and Academic Freedom*. Notre Dame, Indiana: University of Notre Dame Press, 1990.

———, *et al.* "*Ex Corde Ecclesiae* and Its Ordinances: Is This Any Way to Run a University or a Church?" *Commonweal* 120 (November 19, 1993): 14–26.

Dalcourt, Gerard J. "Lay Control of Catholic Colleges." *America* 117 (October 14, 1967): 412–14.

Davis, Paul I. *Chronicles of Fairfield University. Book Three: Turmoil and Triumph: The McInnes Years*. Fairfield, Connecticut: Fairfield University Press, 1992.

Davis, Thurston N. "Should Catholic Lambs Eat Ivy?" *America* 93 (May 21, 1955): 205–08.

Dodge, Donna Marie. "Beyond the Mission Statement: What Makes a Catholic College Catholic?" Ph.D diss., Columbia University, 1991.

Deferrari, Roy J. "Challenge to Catholic Colleges and Their Graduates." *Journal of Religious Education* 17 (October 1946): 162–71.

———. *Essays on Catholic Education in the United States*. Washington, D.C.: The Catholic University of America Press, 1942.

———, ed. *The Philosophy of Catholic Higher Education*. Washington, D.C.: The Catholic University of America Press, 1948.

———. *Some Problems of Catholic Higher Education in the United States*. Boston: St. Paul Publications, 1963.

Degnan, SJ, Daniel A. "Secularizing Catholic Colleges." *America* 118 (May 25, 1968): 696–99.

Dennett, Tyler. "Future of the Small College: Its Vocation in American Life." *Commonweal* 41 (April 6, 1945): 606–09.

Dineia, J.A. "Communion and Magisterium: Teaching Authority and the Culture of Grace." *Modern Theology* 9(4) (October 1993): 403–18.

Donahue, Francis, J. "Night Degree Programs in Catholic Colleges." *America* 77 (April 12, 1947): Supplement viii–ix.

Donahue, John W. "Catholic Universities Define Themselves: A Progress Report." *America* 128 (April 21, 1973): 354–58.

Donovan, John D. *The Academic Man in the Catholic College*. New York: Sheed and Ward, 1964.

Dressel, Paul L. *College and University Curriculum*. Berkeley, California: McCutchan Publishing Corporation, 1971.

Duffy, SJ, Charles F. *Chronicles of Fairfield University, 1942–1992 Book One: The Founding Years*. Fairfield, Connecticut: Fairfield University Press, 1992.

Dunn, CSC, William. "The Finest Country in the World." Notre Dame, Indiana: Indiana Province Archives Center, 1985.

———. *Saint Edward's University: A Centennial History*. Austin, Texas: Saint Edward's University Press, 1986.

Eble, Kenneth E. *Professors as Teachers*. San Francisco: Jossey-Bass, Inc., Publishers, 1972.

Ellis, John Tracy. "American Catholics and the Intellectual Life." *Thought* XXX (Autumn 1955): 351–88.

———. "Contemporary American Catholicism in the Light of History." *The Critic* 24 (June/July 1966): 8–19.

———. *Perspectives in American Catholicism*. Baltimore: Helicon, 1963.

———. "The Role of the Catholic University: Homily at the University of San Francisco." *The Catholic Mind* 74 (January 1976): 27–32.

———. "A Tradition of Autonomy." In *The Catholic University: A Modern Appraisal*, ed. Neil G. McCluskey, SJ, 206–70. Notre Dame, Indiana: University of Notre Dame Press, 1970.

Emil, IHM, Mary. "Is Tomorrow Expendable?" *Apostolic Perspectives* 4 (July 1959): 16–21.

"End of Living Endowment." *America* 116 (February 25, 1967): 269.

"*Ex Corde Ecclesiae*: An Application to the United States." *Origins* 26 (November 28, 1996): 381, 383–84.

Falise, Michel. "The Catholic University: A Project for the Faculty." *Catholic International* 2(21) (December 1–14, 1991): 1014–20.

Farrell, Allan P. "National Enrollment Statistics for 1947–48." *America* 78 (December 13, 1947): 285.

———. "Enrollment in Catholic Universities and Men's Colleges. 1947–1948." *America* 78 (January 31, 1948): 485–86.

Finnegan, Darrell F.X. *The Function of the Academic Dean in American Catholic Higher Education*. Washington, D.C.: The Catholic University of America Press, 1951.

Fitzgerald, Paul A. *The Governance of Jesuit Colleges in the United States, 1920–1970*. Notre Dame, Indiana: University of Notre Dame Press, 1984.

Fitzpatrick, Edward A. "Are We Ready to Face the New Problems of College or Adult Education?" *Catholic School Journal* 47 (February 1947): 42–43.

———. "Catholic College of the Future." *Catholic School Journal* 55(8) (October 1955): 255–58.

———. *The Catholic University and the World Today*. Milwaukee: Bruce Publishing Company, 1954.

Fitzsimmons, M.A. "The Catholic University: Problems and Prospects." *Notre Dame Journal of Education* 4(3) (Fall 1973): 250–57.

Fleege, Urban H. "Challenges Confronting Catholic Higher Education." *Homiletic & Pastoral Review* 57 (July 1957): 914–18.

———. "Challenges Confronting Catholic Higher Education: Raising Standards Amidst Rising Enrollments." *Homiletic & Pastoral Review* 57 (August 1957): 1002–07.

Foote, Caleb, Henry Mayer, *et al*. *The Culture of*

the University: Governance and Education. San Francisco: Jossey-Bass, Inc., Publishers, 1968.

Frankel, Charles. "An Academy Enshrouded." *Change* 9 (December 1977): 24–29, 64.

Gaffney, J. Patrick. "Contemporary Perspectives on the Church and Catholic Higher Education." *Horizons* 3 (September 1976): 87–90.

Gallin, OSU, Alice, ed. *American Catholic Higher Education: Essential Documents, 1967–1990.* Notre Dame, Indiana: University of Notre Dame Press, 1992.

———. "Catholic Education and the Liberal Arts." In *The Future of the Catholic Church in America,* ed. John Roach, 97–111. Collegeville, Minnesota: Liturgical Press, 1988.

———. "Catholic Higher Education Today—the Challenge of Ambiguity." *Cross Currents* 43 (Winter 1993/94): 484–87.

———. "Catholic Universities Facing New Cultures." *Seminarium* 25 (April–September 1985): 304–14.

———. *Independence and a New Partnership.* Notre Dame, Indiana: University of Notre Dame Press, 1996.

———, ed. "Synthesis of Responses to Vatican Statement from 110 U.S. Catholic Colleges." *Chronicle of Higher Education* 32 (March 26, 1986): 20–24.

Gleason, Philip. "Changing and Remaining the Same: A Look at Higher Education." In *Perspectives on the American Catholic Church, 1789–1989,* eds. Stephen J. Vicchio and Virginia Geiger, SSND, 223–30. Westminster, Maryland: Christian Classics, Inc., 1989.

———. "Catholic Intellectualism Again." *America* 112 (January 23, 1965): 112–19.

———. *Contending With Modernity: Catholic Higher Education in the Twentieth Century.* New York: Oxford University Press, 1995.

———. "The Crises in Catholic Universities: An Historical Perspective." *Catholic Mind* 64 (September 1966): 43–55.

———. "Freedom and the Catholic University." *NCEA Bulletin* 65 (November 1968): 21–29.

———. *Keeping the Faith: American Catholicism Past and Present.* Notre Dame, Indiana: University of Notre Dame Press, 1987.

Goldstein, Israel. *Brandeis University: Chapter of Its Founding.* New York: Bloch Publishing Company, 1951.

Grant, Mary A., and Thomas C. Hunt. *Catholic School Education in the United States: Development and Current Trends.* New York: Garland Publishing Inc., 1992.

Greeley, Andrew. "The Catholic Campus." *The Critic* 25 (October/November 1966): 84–89.

———. *The Changing Catholic College.* Chicago: Aldine Publishing, Company, 1967.

———. *From Backwater to Mainstream: A Profile of Catholic Higher Education.* New York: McGraw-Hill, 1969.

———. "A New Breed." *America* 110 (May 23, 1964): 206–09.

Greenstein, J. "Must American Catholic Colleges and Universities Remain Mediocre?" *Duquesne Review* 9 (September–Fall 1964): 155–65.

Gribble, CSC, Richard. "The Infamous Debt: Stonehill College, 1948–1954." Paper presented at the Conference on the History of the Congregations of Holy Cross, June 14–16, 1996, Wilkes-Barre, Pennsylvania.

Grimes, CSC, Donald J. "Vision and Fulfillment: Bishop William J. Hafey, the Congregation of Holy Cross and the Founding of King's College, 1943–1946." Paper delivered at the Conference on the History of the Congregations of Holy Cross, June 14–16, 1996, Wilkes-Barre, Pennsylvania.

Grollmes, SJ, Eugene E., ed. *Catholic Colleges and the Secular Mystique.* St. Louis: B. Herder, 1970.

Hallinan, Paul J. "The Responsibility of Catholic Higher Education." *NCEA Bulletin* 60 (August 1963): 145–52.

Hanley, Philip. *The Catholic Junior College in the United States as a Community College.* Notre Dame, Indiana: University of Notre Dame Press, 1949.

Hassenger, Robert, ed. *The Shape of Catholic Higher Education.* Chicago: University of Chicago Press, 1967.

———. "Student Freedom on the Catholic College Campus." *Ave Maria* 109 (February 8, 1969): 7–12.

Healy, Timothy S. "The Contrary Model." *Daedalus* 117 (Spring 1988): 61–62.

Helmreich, Paul C. *Wheaton College 1834–1912: The Seminary Years.* Norton, Massachusetts: Wheaton College, 1985.

Henle, SJ, Robert J. "Future Challenge to Catholic Education." *NCEA Proceedings* 45 (1948): 275–86.

"Hesburgh's Law; Notre Dame University." *Commonweal* 89 (March 14, 1969): 719–20.

Hesburgh, CSC, Theodore. "Action in the Face of Student Violence." *Catholic Mind* 67 (April 1969): 13–19.

———. "Catholic Education in America." *America* 155 (October 4, 1986): 160–63.

———. "The Catholic University in Modern Context." *Catholic Mind* 78 (October 1980): 18–25.

———. "The Catholic University in Today's World." *Origins* 9 (April 3, 1980): 681–84.

———, ed. *The Challenge and Promise of a Catholic University.* Notre Dame, Indiana: University of Notre Dame Press, 1994.

———. "The Changing Face of Catholic Higher Education." *NCEA Bulletin* 65 (August 1969): 54–60.

———. "Looking Back at Newman: The Catholic University Today." *America* 106 (March 3, 1962): 720–21.

———. "Preparing for the Millennium." *Origins* 12 (November 4, 1982): 337–42.

———. "The Vision of a Great Catholic University." *Catholic Mind* 66 (February 1968): 42–54.

———. "The Vision of a Great Catholic University in the World of Today." *Notre Dame Journal of Education* 4 (Fall 1973): 228–38.

Hitchcock, James. "How Is a Catholic College or University Catholic in Practice?" *Catholic Mind* 74 (January 1976): 7–21.

Howells, Dorothy Elia. *A Century to Celebrate: Radcliffe College, 1879–1979.* Cambridge, Massachusetts: Radcliffe College, 1978.

Hope, Arthur J. *Notre Dame: One Hundred Years,* Revised Edition. South Bend, Indiana: Icarus Press, 1978.

Horchler, Richard. "Time Bomb in Catholic Education." *Look* 30 (April 5, 1966): 23–25.

Horrigan, Alfred F. "Can the Small College Survive?" *Commonweal* 61 (January 28, 1955): 452–54.

Hunt, Michael. *College Catholics.* Mahwah, New Jersey: Paulist Press, 1993.

———. "All Is Not Lost: An Early Look at the Class of '96." *Commonweal* 120 (April 9, 1993): 18–21.

Jacob, OSU, Martha A. "Catholic Colleges: An Idea Lives." *America* 144 (January 3–10, 1981): 8–10.

Jaschik, Scott. "Major Changes Seen Needed for Colleges to Attract Minorities." *Chronicle of Higher Education* 34(13) (1987): A1, A31–A32.

Josephina, CSJ, Sr. "Are Catholic Colleges Producing Moral Morons?" *Spiritual Life* 1 (June 1955): 113–21.

Jencks, Christopher, and David Riesman. *The Academic Revolution.* New York: Doubleday & Company, Inc., 1968.

Joughin, Louis, ed. *Academic Freedom and Tenure.* Madison: University of Wisconsin Press, 1967.

Kayal, P. "The Final Solution of College Unrest." *Commonweal* 92 (March 27, 1970): 53–54.

Kehoe, CSC, Joseph A. "Holy Cross in Oregon, 1902–1980." Notre Dame, Indiana: Indiana Province Archives Center, 1982.

Kelly, George Anthony. "The Church in Higher Education." *Social Justice Review* 78 (May/June 1987): 89–95.

———, ed. *Why Should the Catholic University Survive? A Study of the Character and Commitments of Catholic Higher Education.* New York: St. John's University Press, 1973.

Kennedy, Eugene. "Reclaiming Our Spiritual Authority [Mission of Catholic Higher Education and the Role of Faculty Members]." *Current Is-*

sues in *Catholic Higher Education* 13 (Summer 1992): 26–31.

Knille, Robert. "Catholic Action in a Catholic College." *Integrity* 3 (September 1949): 35–43.

Kreyche, Gerald F. "American Catholic Higher Learning and Academic Freedom." *NCEA Bulletin* 62 (1965): 211–21.

Krolikowski, Walter. "The Protean Catholic University." *Thought* 48 (Winter 1973): 465–73.

Kruse, CSC, Robert. "In the Catholic Tradition." *Stonehill* 7(1) (Winter 1988): 2–4.

LaForest, CSC, Laurian. "Moreau Hall, North Easton, Massachusetts: A Brief History." Unpublished paper, 1990.

Langan, SJ, John P. *Catholic Universities in Church and Society: A Dialogue on Ex Corde Ecclesiae.* Washington, D.C.: Georgetown University Press, 1993.

Lawler, Justus George. *The Catholic Dimension in Higher Education.* Westminster, Maryland: The Newman Press, 1959.

Leahy, SJ, William P. *Adapting to America: Catholics, Jesuits, and Higher Education in the Twentieth Century.* Washington, D.C.: Georgetown University Press, 1991.

———. "The Rise of the Laity in American Catholic Higher Education." *Records of the American Catholic Historical Society of Philadelphia* 101(3–4) (1990): 17–32.

Leary, John P. "The Bishops and the Catholic College." *Ave Maria* 107 (February 10, 1968): 6–9.

Leibrecht, John. "The Bishops, the University and *Ex Corde Ecclesiae*." *Origins* 23 (February 17, 1994): 605, 607–08.

———. "Implementing *Ex Corde Ecclesiae*." *Origins* 24 (December 8, 1994): 445–46.

Levine, Arthur. "The Meaning of Diversity." *Change* 23(5) (September/October 1991): 4–5.

Lipset, Seymour M., and S.S. Wolin, eds. *The Berkeley Student Revolt.* New York: Doubleday Anchor, 1965.

MacDonnell, SJ, Joseph F. *Chronicles of Fairfield University 1942–1992, Book Six: Ignatian Character.* Fairfield, Connecticut: Fairfield University Press, 1992.

Magner, J.A. "Concept of a Catholic University." *The Catholic University of America Bulletin* 20 (October 1952): 1–4.

Maher, John. "Catholic Colleges Say They Don't Want Vatican to Increase Control, Supervision Over Them." *Our Sunday Visitor* 64 (April 25, 1976): 3.

Malloy, CSC, Edward A. *Culture and Commitment: The Challenge of Today's University.* Notre Dame, Indiana: University of Notre Dame Press, 1992.

———. "The Religious Impact of Catholic Higher Education: Is There a Gap Between What Catholic Universities Proclaim and What They Practice?" In *American Catholic Identity: Essays in an Age of Change*, ed. Francis Butler, 1–19. Kansas City, Missouri, Sheed & Ward, 1994.

Malone, James. "The Catholic University and the Catholic Community." *Origins* 16 (June 19, 1986): 116–18.

———. "Implementing *Ex Corde Ecclesiae*: The Task Ahead." *Origins* 23 (February 17, 1994): 608–09.

Manier, Edward, and John Houck, eds., *Academic Freedom and the Catholic University.* Notre Dame, Indiana: Fides Publishers, 1967.

Mayhew, Lewis B. *The Smaller Liberal Arts College.* New York: The Center for Applied Research in Education, Inc., 1962.

McAvoy, CSC, Thomas T. "The Catholic Liberal College and American Studies." *Catholic Educational Review* 54 (May 1956): 295–311.

McBrien, Richard. "Academic Freedom in Catholic Universities: The Emergence of a Party Line." *America* 159 (December 3, 1988): 454–58.

———. "Catholic Universities: The Church's Mission." *Origins* 10 (February 19, 1981): 569–72.

McCluskey, SJ, Neil G. *Catholic Education Faces Its Future.* Garden City, New York: Doubleday & Company, Inc., 1968.

———, ed. *The Catholic University: A Modern Appraisal.* Notre Dame: University of Notre Dame Press, 1970.

———, ed. *Catholic Education in America: A Documentary History.* New York: Bureau of Publications: Teachers College, Columbia University, 1964.

———. "The New Catholic College." *America* 116 (March 25, 1967): 414–17.

McGrath, John J. *Catholic Institutions in the United States: Canonical and Civil Law Status.* Washington, D.C.: The Catholic University of America Press, 1968.

McKeon, Valerie Ann. "History of St. Anselm College." Ph.D. diss., Boston College, 1985.

McLaughlin, SJ, L.W., John Courtney Murray, SJ, and Pedro Arrupe, SJ. *The University in the American Experience.* New York: Fordham University Press, 1966.

McMullen, L. "Pope Calls on America's Catholic Colleges to Strengthen Their Religious Identity." *Chronicle of Higher Education* 34 (September 23, 1987): A16–A17.

McKevitt, SJ, Gerald. *The University of Santa Clara: A History, 1851–1977.* Stanford, California: Stanford University Press, 1979.

McManus, W.E. "G.I. Crisis in the College." *Catholic Educational Review* 44 (February 1946): 73–77.

Meyer, Cyril F. "Financing Catholic Higher Education." *America* 78 Supplement (April 3, 1948): xiv–xvi.

———. "Forming the Whole Person." *Catholic International* 2(21) (December 1–14, 1991): 1021–25.

Mullaly, SND deN, Sr. Columba. *Trinity College, Washington, D.C.: The First Eighty Years, 1897–1977.* Westminster, Maryland: Christian Classics, Inc., 1987.

Murphy, Vincent M. *Chronicles of Fairfield University 1942–1992. Book Four: Building Years: Change and Development.* Fairfield, Connecticut: Fairfield University Press, 1992.

"New Catholic Colleges." *America* 73 (May 12, 1945): 106.

Newman, John Henry. *The Idea of a Catholic University.* (Reprint) New York: The America Press, 1941.

Niemeyer, Gerhart. "The Need for the Catholic University." *Review of Politics* 37 (October 1975): 479–89.

Noonan, John T. "Academic Freedom and Tenure: St. John's University (N.Y.)." *AAUP Bulletin* 52 (1966): 12–19.

North, Arthur A. "Why Is the American Catholic Graduate School Failing to Develop Catholic Intellectualism?" *NCEA Bulletin* 53 (August 1956): 179–89.

O'Brien, David J. "The Church and Catholic Higher Education." *Horizons* 17 (September 1990): 7–29.

———. *From the Heart of the American Church: Catholic Higher Education and American Culture.* Maryknoll, New York: Orbis Books, 1994.

———. "The Holy Cross Case: Crisis in Jesuit Education." *Commonweal* 103 (October 8, 1976): 647–53.

O'Malley, Karen. "American-Soviet Exchange." *Stonehill* 12(1) (Summer 1990): 16–18.

———. "Paula Sullivan: A Stonehill Legend." *Stonehill* 24(1) (Summer/Fall 1996): 2–3.

O'Malley, CSC, Maurus. "The First Permanent Foundations of the Holy Cross Fathers and Brothers in the Eastern States." Paper presented at the Conference on the History of the Congregations of Holy Cross, May 26, 1985, Wilkes-Barre, Pennsylvania.

Ong, SJ, Walter J. *American Catholic Crossroads.* New York: Collier Paperback, 1962.

Orsy, SJ, Ladislaus. "Bishops and Universities: Dominion or Communion." *America* 169 (November 20, 1993): 11–16.

———. "A Catholic Presence." *America* 120 (April 5, 1969): 396–97.

Parent, CSC, Louise. *The First Twenty-Five Years of Notre Dame College, Manchester, New Hampshire.* Manchester, New Hampshire: Notre Dame College, 1975.

Perlmutter, Oscar W. "The Lay Professor." *Commonweal* 68 (April 11, 1958): 31–34.

Pick, John. "Education and the Postwar World." *America* 72 (February 3, 1945): 347–48.

Plough, James Howard. "Catholic Colleges and the Catholic Educational Association." Ph.D. diss. University of Notre Dame, 1967.

Pope, Raechelle L. "Multicultural-Organization Development in Student Affairs: An Introduction." *Journal of College Student Development* 34 (May 1993): 201–205.

Poznar, Walter. "The Survival of the Humanities." *Liberal Education* 63(March 1977): 19–25.

Power, Edward J. *Catholic Higher Education in America, A History.* New York: Appleton-Century-Crofts, 1972.

———. *A History of Catholic Higher Education in the United States.* Milwaukee: Bruce Publishing Company, 1958.

———. "Is the Catholic College Academically Respectable?" *Homiletic & Pastoral Review* 56 (June 1956): 734–41.

"Prevailing Winds on the Catholic Campus, Symposium." *The Critic* 22 (December 1963–January 1964): 56–61.

Preville, Joseph R. "Catholic Colleges, the Courts, and the Constitution: A Tale of Two Cases." *Church History* 58 (June 1989): 197–210.

———. "Catholic Colleges and the Supreme Court: The Case of Tilton vs. Richardson." *Journal of Church and State* 30 (Spring 1988): 291–307.

Ratterman, SJ, P.H. *The Emerging Catholic University.* New York: Fordham University Press, 1968.

Reedy, CSC, John, and James E. Andrews. "Control of Catholic Universities; Holy Cross Rethinks Its Relationships to Notre Dame and Portland Universities." *Ave Maria* 105 (January 28, 1967): 16–19, 30–31.

Reilly, Robert Thomas. "Have Catholic Colleges Kept the Faith?" *US Catholic* 52 (October 1987): 34–40.

"Relations of American Catholic Colleges and Universities with the Church." *Catholic Mind* 74 (October 1976): 51–64.

Robbins, David L. *A History of Suffolk University, 1909–1996.* Boston: Suffolk University, 1966.

Roddy, Jr., E.G. *Merrimack College: Genesis and Growth 1947–1972.* North Andover, Massachusetts: Merrimack College Press, 1972.

Rolff, R.W. "Are Catholic Colleges So Bad?" *Catholic World* 185 (June 1957): 204–09.

Ryan, John J. *The Idea of a Catholic College.* New York: Sheed and Ward, 1945.

Sachar, Abram L. *Brandeis University: A Host at Last,* Revised Edition. Hanover, New Hampshire: Brandeis University Press, 1995.

Scherer, Jacqueline. "Ferment on the Campus." *Month* 40(6) (December 1968): 325–31.

Schiffrin, Andre, ed. *The Cold War & The University: Toward an Intellectual History of the Postwar Years.* New York: The New Press, 1997.

Schoder, SJ, Raymond. "What Catholic Colleges Are For." *American Ecclesiastical Review* 163 (September 1970): 154–65.

Schubert, Frank D. "From Theology to Religion: A Study in American Roman Catholic Secularization as Reflected in Selected American Roman Catholic College Religious Curricula, 1955–95." Ph.D. diss., Boston University, 1987.

Searle, John R. *The Campus War.* New York: The World Publishing Company, 1971.

Shea, George W. "Black Students at Catholic Colleges." *America* 131 (September 14, 1974): 108–10.

Shea, William M. "Tradition and Pluralism: Opportunities for Catholic Universities." *Current Issues in Higher Education* 16(1) (Summer 1995): 34–48.

Shelley, Thomas J. *Dunwoodie: The History of St. Joseph's Seminary.* Westminster, Maryland: Christian Classics, 1993.

Skillin, Edward. "Veterans on Campus." *Commonweal* 44 (April 26, 1946): 32–35.

Smith, Page. *Killing the Spirit: Higher Education in America.* New York: Viking Press, 1990.

Stamm, Martin J. "Report on the Governance of American Catholic Higher Education Institutions in 1992." *Current Issues in Catholic Higher Education* 14 (Summer 1993): 10–16.

———. "The New Guardians of American Catholic Higher Education: An Examination of Lay Participation on the Governing Boards of Roman Catholic-Affiliated Colleges and Universities." Ph.D. diss., University of Pennsylvania, 1979.

———. "The Laicization of Corporate Governance of Twentieth Century American Catholic Higher Education." *Records of the American Catholic Historical Society of Philadelphia* 94(1–4) (1983): 81–99.

Stobat, Janet. "Catholic Colleges' Meeting Urges Vatican to Endorse Academic Freedom Autonomy." *Chronicles of Higher Education* 35 (May 3, 1989): A15, A22.

Szablewicz, John W. *Fifty Years of Excellence: A History of Fairfield College Preparatory School.* Fairfield, Connecticut: Fairfield University Press, 1992.

"To Teach as Jesus Did." National Conference of Catholic Bishops. Washington, D.C.: United States Catholic Conference, 1973.

"Text of Pope John Paul II's Address to Leaders of U.S. Catholic Colleges." *Chronicle of Higher Education* 34 (September 23, 1987): A17–A19.

Vasoli, Robert H. "Catholicism on the Catholic Campus." *Thought* 47 (Fall 1972): 330–50.

Vererka, F.B. "Defining a Catholic Approach to Education in the United States, 1920–1950." *Religious Education* 88 (Fall 1993): 523–42.

Wade, SJ, Francis C. *The Catholic University and the Faith.* Milwaukee: Marquette University Press, 1978.

Walch, Timothy. *The Diverse Origins of American Catholic Education: Chicago, Milwaukee, and the Nation.* New York: Garland, 1988.

Walsh, Joseph L. "Law and Order on the Catholic Campus." *Commonweal* 90 (September 19, 1969): 562–63.

Walters, CSJ, Annette. "Why Is the American Catholic College Failing to Develop Catholic Intellectualism?" *NCEA Bulletin* 53 (August 1956): 172–78.

Wakin, Edward. "Can Catholic Colleges Afford to Stay Catholic?" *US Catholic* 43 (September 1978): 29–34.

Weaver, Gary R., and James H. Weaver, eds. *The University and Revolution.* Englewood Cliffs, New Jersey: Prentice-Hall, Inc., 1969.

Weigel, SJ, Gustav. "American Catholic Intellectualism—A Theologian's Reflection." *Review of Politics* 19 (July 1957): 275–307.

———. "Enriching the Intellectual Life of the Catholic College." *NCEA Bulletin* 52 (May 1956): 7–21.

Whelan, James F. *Catholic Colleges of the United States of America at the Middle of the Twentieth Century.* New Orleans: Loyola University Press, 1952.

Whitehead, K.D. *Catholic Colleges and Federal Funding.* San Francisco: Ignatius Press, 1988.

Wilson, Charles H. *"Ex Corde Ecclesiae* and American Higher Education: A Quandary or an Opportunity." *Current Issues in Catholic Higher Education* 14 (Winter 1994): 5–15.

Wolff, Robert Paul. *The Ideal of the University.* Boston: Beacon Press, 1970.

Wuthnow, Robert. "Restructuring of American Religion: Further Evidence." *Sociological Inquiry* 66(3) (August 1996): 303–29.

———. *The Restructuring of American Religion: Society and Faith Since World War II.* Princeton, New Jersey: Princeton University Press, 1988.

Zingg, P.J. "Missions Fulfilled and Forfeited: American Catholic Higher Education and the Challenges of Diversity." *Educational Record* 72 (Summer 1991): 39–44.

INDEX